OLD PEWTER
ITS MAKERS AND MARKS
IN ENGLAND, SCOTLAND AND IRELAND

" Through the days of scorching sun from August back to May, my mind went back to the goodly cheer of December, to blazing logs and bright, frosty nights, with black, diamond-studded skies, to close-drawn curtains and the dreamy play of firelight on pictures, pewter, walls and ceiling, to the companionship of books . . . a great content took hold on me."

(Source Unknown.)

AN "ATTENDANCE-SUMMONS" TO A LIVERYMAN OF THE PEWTERERS' COMPANY, TWO CENTURIES AGO.
(From a fine imperssion of this rare print, in the collection of Thomas Warburton, Esq., of Manchester, by whom the photograph was courteously supplied.)

OLD PEWTER
ITS MAKERS AND MARKS
IN ENGLAND, SCOTLAND AND IRELAND
AN ACCOUNT OF THE OLD PEWTERER & HIS CRAFT

By HOWARD HERSCHEL COTTERELL

*ILLUSTRATING ALL KNOWN MARKS AND
SECONDARY MARKS OF THE OLD PEWTERERS
WITH A SERIES OF PLATES SHOWING THE
CHIEF TYPES OF THEIR WARES*

CHARLES E. TUTTLE COMPANY
RUTLAND, VERMONT

Published by the Charles E. Tuttle Company, Inc.
of Rutland, Vermont & Tokyo, Japan
with editorial offices at
Suido 1-chome, 2-6, Bunkyo-ku, Tokyo, Japan

© 1963 by Charles E. Tuttle Co., Inc.

Library of Congress Catalog Card No. 29-22959

International Standard Book No. 0-8048-0443-5

First edition published 1929 by B. T. Batsford Ltd., London

First Tuttle edition published 1963
Eleventh printing, 1985

PRINTED IN JAPAN

"A · Flask · of · Wine, a · Book · of · Verse—and · Thou
Beside me singing in the Wilderness—
And Wilderness is Paradise enow."

OMAR KHAYYÁM.

TO
MY · HONOURED · FRIEND
FOR · FORTY · YEARS,

MY · WIFE
HELEN · GERTRUDE · COTTERELL

TO · WHOM · IT · HAS · MEANT
SO · MANY · HOURS · OF · LONELINESS,

IN DEEPEST AFFECTION
I DEDICATE
THIS WORK

———

" AMAVIMUS, AMAMUS, AMABIMUS."

PREFACE

The Times Literary Supplement in reviewing Mrs. Jerrold's *Story of Dorothy Jordan* some years ago said :—

> Any new writer may legitimately return to any old subject if he can either add to the stock of information or throw fresh light upon the existing stock by inspecting it from a new point of view.

It is claimed for the present work that it satisfies both these requirements, for not only does it add *very largely* to the stock of information but it throws fresh light on the existing stock some of which is based on insecure foundation.

First and foremost then, it is written in the hope of throwing new light on certain points which have, I believe, hitherto been wrongly interpreted and judged from a totally wrong point of view, but which are unfortunately, more or less generally accepted. Of these the most important is the question of the chronology of the touches on the existing touchplates at the Hall of the Worshipful Company of Pewterers of London and I here make bold to state my *entire* disagreement with nearly all that has hitherto been written under this heading, for with certain reservations in reference to the earlier part of the first existing plate and some few other touches, I have in Chapter III. endeavoured—I trust successfully—to prove that the marks thereon were *struck* in good chronological order.

In making a statement of this nature, I am fully aware that I make of myself a target for critics, but my conviction, backed by that of others best able to form an opinion in this matter, is so strong that I am prepared to stand by my statement.

In compiling this work, *no note* has been taken of Continental Pewter and no attempt made to give an exhaustive dissertation on the pewter *industry* in general, which desirable object has already received the attention of other writers in works which will be found mentioned on a later page in the Bibliographical list. Its object is rather to enable the Connoisseur to date, appreciate and understand his treasures and, by the illustrations, to train the eye and taste of the less experienced towards the acquisition of that alone which is beautiful and therefore desirable. It is the outcome of the great need I felt *as a collector*, of a single work to which I might turn at any time, with a reasonable hope of finding there at one opening, and without wading through touch-plates, lists of Freemen, appendices, etc., etc.—all that was known of the maker, locality and date of any marked piece of British Pewter.

Commenced early in the year 1905, in its embryo stages, it was seen by fellow-collectors and antiquaries who urged upon me the desirability of extending it and putting it into more permanent form to fill the hiatus long felt by others in common with myself.

These friendly representations led me into a field of research much larger and wider than was my original intention, and one of which had I realised the extent at the outset, would almost certainly have resulted in this humble contribution to the literature on the subject remaining, as was my first intention, my personal notebook.

However, such as it is, with the assurance that no effort has been spared, no labour deemed too great to ensure its accuracy, and with no desire other than that it may be of service to my readers, it now goes forth to take its meed of praise or criticism.

Of the marks illustrated, little need be said save that each one was *most carefully* drawn in pencil by myself, from the actual marks themselves or from careful rubbings.

In making these sketches, I have tried to bear in mind the fact that strict and slavish fidelity to the original was of vastly greater importance than beauty of line or anatomical or geometrical perfection.

Where my sketches are incomplete, they represent all that it was possible to decipher, accurately, of marks badly struck or worn down by use. No guess-work or conjecture has been allowed to enter into the details of such incomplete sketches, which occur at intervals throughout the work, though in many cases such a course would have seemed easy and safe. Many of the sketches have been built up piecemeal from as many as ten or a dozen or more different rubbings of the same mark. It will also be noted, that several of the touches, which are almost indecipherable on the touchplates themselves, are here illustrated with all their details clear and distinct. This because clear impressions have come under my observation which enabled me to fill in the lacunae; *e.g.* Samuel Seaton, No. 4173 (Touch 387, L.T.P.); Richard Webb, No. 5007 (Touch 458, L.T.P.); Robert Parr, No. 3526 (Touch 352, L.T.P.); Nicholas Okeford, No. 3429 (Touch 596, L.T.P.), etc., etc., etc.

Whilst speaking of these sketches I must record my grateful thanks to my kinsman, Arthur N. Cotterell of Bristol, for his yeoman service in inking over many of my pencilled sketches for the blockmakers.

The names of no members of the Worshipful Company of Pewterers of London have been included of a date later than c. 1850, without special reason. The late Mr. Englefield, a Past Master of the Company, informed me that he had been, for something like half a century, the only member actually engaged in the craft.

As it is only by co-operation between collector and author that anything approaching a *complete* collection of marks will ever be attained, and while claiming that the present volume goes *much* further towards this desirable end than any work on the subject which has preceded it, one knows that there must exist marks not recorded here. I appeal therefore to their owners or custodians, to send to me to the address given below, good rubbings, photographs or *accurate* sketches of any such marks, in order that, step by step, a list complete as possible may be built up, if not for our own use, for that of succeeding generations of collectors and antiquaries.

One cannot without justly meriting the accusation of ingratitude, omit one's thanks, shared by all collectors and lovers of Old Pewter, to Mr. H. J. L. J. Massé for all his wonderful pioneer work in connexion with the subject. To him must ever belong the credit for having first directed into the channels of intelligibility, many streams of information which to-day are at the service of collectors the world over.

In fairness also to myself, may I say, that not one word or illustration of the present work is pirated from his.

On the eve of sending this work to press, my friend Mr. Bertrand Johnson, C.C., a Past-Master of the Worshipful Company of Pewterers of London, sends me the result of a prolonged study of the records of his Company, and one has little hesitation in saying that it is *one of the most important contributions* to our knowledge of the subject which has ever been made, for he has succeeded in elucidating no fewer than some one hundred and sixty of those touches which bore the *initial letters only* of the makers' names and the ownership of which has—up to now—been a total enigma.

His method of procedure has been, a systematic search through the Accounts, Minute Books and lists of "Openings," *i.e.* leave granted to members to strike their touches and open shop, and the result is one for which all lovers of old pewter will for ever stand heavily indebted to him.

Space forbids that I enlarge at length upon his discoveries, but to take an example :

> Touch 992 L.T.P., which has for its device a slipped rose and thistle with the bothering four initials "W. M. E. G.," suggestive of continental influence ; but under Mr. Johnson's careful scrutiny this becomes William Munden, 1757. Y., and Edmund Grove, 1753. Y.

Over and above all this, his note that they were granted "Mr. Charlsley's Touch," also enables us to identify Touch 842, L.T.P., with same device and W.C., as that of William Charlsley, and Mr. Johnson himself confirms this by an entry of the latter having struck Touch 842 L.T.P.

And so one might go on, but the inference is obvious. Moreover as Mr. Johnson has covered practically the whole of the touchplates—confirming my theories as to correct chronology, expounded at length in Chapter III—I have been almost tempted to change the title of that Chapter, renaming it—in the well-known words of Disraeli—" Illustrating the Obvious."

The results of Mr. Johnson's labours are incorporated in the present work and my readers will share my gratitude to him and the satisfaction I feel, *that they did not arrive too late for inclusion.*

Little now is left to me but to record my gratitude to those whose co-operation has been instrumental in making this work possible. The courtesy and helpfulness of so many collectors and others, demands, even at the expense of a somewhat lengthy list of names, that my indebtedness to many of them be recorded individually, lest I lay myself open to a charge of discourtesy, by "lumping" them together into a meaningless "omnium gatherum." I therefore place on record, my sincerest thanks to the Master, Wardens and Court of the Worshipful Company of Pewterers of London for affording me access to their Yeomanry and Livery Lists, etc., and for the privilege of giving facsimile illustrations of their five existing Touchplates ; the Society of Antiquaries of Scotland for a similar courtesy, and the Authorities of the following institutions : The British Museum for plaster casts of Tokens and photographs of Trade-cards ; The Victoria and Albert Museum, S. Kensington ; The Guildhall Museum ; The National Museum, Dublin ; The Kelvingrove Museum, Glasgow ; The Committee of the Bristol Museum and Art Gallery ; The Somerset County Museum, Taunton Castle ; The Countess of Mayo (Trade-Cards) ; Mrs. Carvick-Webster ; Miss Chichester and Messrs. John S. Amery ; A. H. Baldwin (Tokens) ; Frank Bevan ; Herbert Bolton, D.Sc., F.R.S.E. ; Frederick Bradbury ; Francis Buckley ; Frederick Cattle (Trade-Cards) ; T. Charbonnier ; Walter G. Churcher ; Luther Clements (Tokens) ; Herbert M. Cooke ; Lewis Clapperton, M.A., C.A. (for invaluable help in obtaining for me many of the illustrations of Scottish Church pewter, and in many other ways) ; F. Ellis ; the late W. J. Englefield ; W. J. Faulkner, F.R.N.S. (Tokens) ; W. J. Fieldhouse, C.B.E., F.S.A. ; Lionel J. Fletcher (Tokens) ; Reginald Flint ; Ambrose Heal ; E. Hollis, F.Z.S. (Tokens) ; A. H. Isher ;

Capt. A. Sutherland-Graeme, A.R.I.B.A.; C. Reginald Grundy, Editor "The Connoisseur"; Capt. Nelson G. Harries, C.A.; Gilbert L. D. Hole, W.S.; Rev. A. G. Kealy, R.N. (Retired); A. E. Kimbell; The late Col. G. B. Croft-Lyons, V.P.S.A.; J. O. Manton (Tokens); Capt. H. E. May; T. S. Milligan; Antonio F. de Navarro, F.S.A.; Fra. H. Newbery; Jno. Palmer of Ludlow, for his invaluable help in connection with the Ludlow Guild of Hammermen; Charles G. J. Port, F.S.A., for his carefully chosen series of spoons, with notes, etc., etc.; Major John Richardson, D.S.O.; H. Simonds, F.S.A.; H. Tapley-Soper, F.R.Hist.S.; W. D. Thomson; Harry Walker; Thomas Warburton, F.R.N.S.; Lloyd F. Ward, A.R.I.B.A.; J. R. Ward; the late Charles Welch, F.S.A., for leave, readily given, to make extracts from his *History of the Worshipful Company of Pewterers of London*; M. S. Dudley Westropp, M.R.I.A., my co-author of *Irish Pewterers*; Edward Williams; Francis Weston, F.S.A.; the late L. Ingleby Wood, whose masterly work, *Scottish Pewter Ware and Pewterers*, I have laid heavily under contribution; A. B. Yeates, F.R.I.B.A., F.S.A.; Dr. A. J. Young; also to Malcolm Bell, who many years ago, though accumulating materials for a work on similar lines, most generously handed over to me all his MSS., Notes, etc., etc., for me to incorporate with my own.

Finally, to my daughter, Gertrude Joan Cotterell, for much careful work in connection with the Index to Devices and " Hall-Marks," and typing much of the MSS., for Press; and to my Publishers, Messrs. B. T. Batsford Ltd.—or as I would prefer to put it—To Capt. Harry Batsford and Mr. W. H. Smith, Directors, for their exquisite care in the production of the book itself.

To these and to all others who have helped me, I can but inadequately express my sincerest thanks for invaluable help, so readily given at all times.

Those of my readers who would intelligently understand the pages which follow, and derive from them the assistance they have been designed to afford, are directed to a careful study of the short " Explanatory Note " immediately preceding Chapter I.

The Little House, Croxley Green, Herts.

CONTENTS

ARRANGEMENT OF THE ILLUSTRATIONS

EXPLANATORY NOTE

SOME explanation of the arrangement of this work, which I will make as brief as possible, will facilitate its usefulness to the reader.

I have thought it advisable, in order to save confusion when referring to other works on the subject, to adopt as far as possible the same abbreviations as are used therein. These are as shown at the beginning of Chapter VI.

Following the introductory matter, in Chapter I is given a short review of the History of the craft; Chapter II will be found to deal mainly with pewter marking with such references as appear in the records bearing on the point. Chapter III gives an account of the old Pewterers and their touches and touchplates and endeavours to correct one or two flagrant—but more or less generally accepted—errors. Chapter IV is devoted to those secondary marks some of which are complementary to, but to be distinguished from, the chief touches as struck upon the touchplates, and concludes with a few notes on collectors' difficulties, Pewterers' Tokens, Trade-Cards, etc. In Chapter V is given a series of illustrations of examples of purest type. These illustrations have been chosen mainly in the hope of fixing dates for varying types, for which purpose I have, *where possible*, selected pieces bearing known marks or dated inscriptions, in order that the periods ascribed to them may become standardised and entirely reliable.

The bulk of the volume, Chapter VI, comprises a list arranged in dictionary order, of Pewterers with their dates, locality and other information of interest concerning them, and with illustrations of their marks and secondary marks where possible; each mark appearing *in conjunction* with the information concerning its owner, thus avoiding all references to touchplates, lists of Freemen, appendices, etc., etc., etc. Each item is numbered in the left hand margin, for ease of reference in writing, the number alone covering all the particular details given of any pewterer or mark.

The professional critic may suggest that instead of jumbling up London, Scottish, Irish, York, Bristol and other pewterers into one huge alphabetical list, as in Chapter VI, they would have been of greater interest arranged in separate groups; or again, the chronological system may find its advocate, and there is much to be said for both methods, but my decision on this point has been arrived at after most careful thought, and in the interest of, and in consultation with, those to whom the volume is intended to be of the greatest service, as opposed to those of the local historian and topographer or the Literary Critic.

In giving the names of Pewterers, apprentices have been included for the reason that many of them subsequently took up their Freedom and became Masters although no special allusion to their having done so appears in the records. Examples of this are found in the cases of Adam Ramage, Robert Edgar and many York Pewterers.

On the other hand many who had been admitted to their Freedom never set up in business for themselves but were content to work as journeymen or " Covenant-men " to others, and so never had occasion to apply for " leave " to strike their touches, which would have been useless to them unless in business in their own names. *Hence so many entries without touches.*

The names of the Coppersmiths, Braziers and white-ironsmiths are also included amongst Scotch and Irish pewterers for the reason that many of them—especially during the second half of the eighteenth century and onwards—made pewter-ware as well (*e.g.* Patrick Bissett and many instances amongst Irish Pewterers), and in the Perth Incorporation of Hammermen all the apprentices until the year 1762 were bound to " The Coppersmith's and Pewterer's Art." [1] After this date no trade is specified.

Immediately following this list of pewterers will be found a list—Chapter VII—of those touches, also in dictionary order, in which nothing but the initial letters of the Maker's name, appears with the device. In connection with these little can be said or done beyond illustrating them. Opposite many are given, in italics, the names of *possible* owners. Where several are given it leaves us more baffled than ever. Where one alone appears, the temptation to jump to a conclusion must be resisted unless something in the device lends colour thereto by pun, rebus, similarity to other touches in the same family, or other valid reason, for if the touch is of a date earlier than say 1690, which in nine cases out of ten it *will* be, we must bear in mind the fact that the Yeomanry lists at Pewterers' Hall date back no further than 1687 and there *may* have been any number of pewterers eligible for the particular touch just prior to that date, but of whom unfortunately no record remains.

There is, however, cause for some satisfaction in the fact that the number of these Touches is *slowly* diminishing, *e.g.* Jonathan Ingles, John Cowsey (or Coursey), Ralph Hulls, Stephen Bridges, Henry Hammerton, James Hitchman, Richard Mastead, Samuel Seaton, etc., etc. In the first three cases *both* touches have been struck upon the Hall-plates for those to see who had the eyes to recognise and couple them together, and in the last five, rubbings have come to hand with the same device and the maker's name *in extenso*. Further, Mr. Bertrand Johnson's wonderful discoveries have enabled me to transfer some one hundred and sixty marks from this Chapter to Chapter VI.

Herein will be seen the desirability—which I urge again at the risk of repetition, on all collectors—of sending to me to my address given in the preface, rubbings of any marks of which they may have knowledge and which are not to be found illustrated in the pages which follow. It is the only way of clearing up these ambiguous touches.

In Chapter VIII are illustrated those Touches which bear neither name, initials nor other indications as to their ownership. They are classified as " Obscure " and must so remain until such time as they are found in conjunction with initials, or, more desirable still, the maker's name in full.

Chapter IX, the index to devices, will, I venture to hope, prove one of the most helpful features of the whole work, for in it are noted all the main component devices of every touch illustrated in Chapters VI, VII and VIII.

To give an example of the usefulness of this Index ; John Baskerville, whose touch is a rose and thistle dimidiated, beneath a crown, will be found mentioned under " Rose,"

---

[1] " *Scottish Pewter-ware and Pewterers.*"   L. Ingleby Wood.

" Thistle " and " Crown," so that, be the name and two of the main devices worn away—say the crown and the dimidiated rose—the remaining part—in this instance the thistle—will enable the touch to be identified and the piece dated and appreciated at its value, for broadly speaking (there are *very* few exceptions) no two touches, other than those of different members of the same family or firm, had devices *exactly* similar to one another.

Maker's address labels such as " Drury Lane," " Crooked Lane," " Fenchurch St.," etc., have been included in this index as also the labels bearing such words as " London Superfine," " Superfine Hard Metal," etc., but not the word " London " alone or the palm branches and pillars, one or other of which appear at the side of a large proportion of the touches as filling-in or containing ornament only. Their inclusion would have served no useful purpose and would have tended to make the index cumbersome and unwieldy.

The " Company " marks of the Rose crowned and X crowned have been omitted for a like reason.

By means of this index, a most indistinct mark, with no sign of the maker's name or initials, so long as some *definite* feature of the device remains, may be identified in a majority of cases with as great certainty as though the whole were visible. From years of experience in using it, this has been proved over and over again.

Chapter X is devoted to an index to those marks which, for want of a better name, one is forced to describe as " Hall-marks," a designation which though totally incorrect (for they had nothing to do with the Hall of the Company) is used throughout this work when referring to those four (more or less) small marks resembling the Hall Marks of the Goldsmiths. Where these contain initials they are arranged alphabetically, and where no initials appear they are grouped as well as may be at the end of the Chapter as " Unknown," unless the users of such uninitialled marks are known, in which case reference is made to their respective owners as in the case of those bearing initials.

Here we may pass on to those Chapters which it is hoped may throw some fresh ray of light on an industry which ranked so conspicuously in the environment of our ancestors, be one peer or peasant, schoolmaster or scullion.

Throughout the volume I use the letters " L.T.P.," or " E.T.P.," when referring to the position of a certain touch on a touchplate, thus " 31 L.T.P." means *touch* 31 *on the London Touchplate*, or " 102 E.T.P." means *Touch* 102 *on the Edinburgh Touchplate*, and so on.

If I am referring to the numbers which *I* have given to Pewterers or Marks *in left hand margin* in Chapters VI, VII and VIII, I merely give them so : No. 31, No. 2145 and so on.

FIRST LIST OF SUBSCRIBERS

FRANK ALLEN, Esq., Chicago, Ill., U.S.A.

R. S. W. ANDREWS, Esq., Broadway, Worcestershire.

Messrs. ANGUS & ROBERTSON, LTD., Sydney, N.S.W.

Mrs. WILLARD BARBOUR.

V. WILLOUGHBY BARRETT, Esq., Tarrytown-on-Hudson, N.Y., U.S.A.

J. H. BEAN, Esq., C.B.E., Dudley, Worcs.

GUY E. BEARDSLEY, Esq., Hartford, Connecticut, U.S.A.

R. BROUGHTON BERKELEY, Esq., Worcester.

Messrs. BICKERS & SON, LTD., London.

Messrs. B. H. BLACKWELL, LTD., Oxford.

FREDERICK BRADBURY, Esq., Sheffield.

J. N. BRAMWELL, Esq., Balboa, California, U.S.A.

Messrs. BRENTANOS, Paris.

Signor M. BRETSCHNEIDER, Rome.

HAROLD BRIGHT, Esq., B.A., London.

BRISTOL MUSEUM AND ART GALLERY, per H. Bolton, Esq., M.Sc., Director.

ERIC M. BROWETT, Esq., Birmingham.

Mr. CHAS. E. BRUMWELL, Hereford.

Mr. ALEX. BRUNTON, Edinburgh.

Messrs. J. & E. BUMPUS, LTD., London.

HENRY W. BUSH, Esq., F.R.G.S., Beckenham, Kent.

CARDIFF PUBLIC LIBRARY, per Harry Farr, Esq., Chief Librarian.

JAMES CAREW, Esq., London.

Dr. HERBERT CHARLES, London.

GEORGE VICTOR BELLASIS CHARLTON, Esq., Thrapston.

Miss CHICHESTER, Arlington Court, near Barnstaple.

WALTER G. CHURCHER, Esq., London.

LEWIS CLAPPERTON, Esq., C.A., Glasgow.

WILLIAM CONNAL, Esq., Glasgow.

HERBERT M. COOKE, Esq., Purley.

Mr. ERNEST COOPER, Bournemouth.

Messrs. J. E. CORNISH, LTD., Manchester.

ERNEST A. COTTERELL, Esq., Walsall.

The late JOHN N. COTTERELL, Esq., Walsall.

ROBERT COULTHARD, Esq., Ulverston, Lancs.

J. CRAWFORD, Esq., Tredegar, Mon.

Messrs. CRICHTON & CO., LTD., New York, U.S.A.

J. MITCHELL DAVIDSON, Esq., Ashtead.

M. J. C. DAVIS, Esq., Fenny Compton, Warwickshire.

Messrs. A. & F. DENNY, LTD., London.

Messrs. DOUGLAS & FOULIS, Edinburgh.

Messrs. EASON & SON, LTD., Dublin.

Alderman J. FULLER EBERLE, Clifton, Bristol.

EDINBURGH ROYAL SCOTTISH MUSEUM.

The late HUBERT H. EDMONDSON, Esq.

E. H. EGLINGTON, Esq., Hammerwich, Nr. Lichfield.

The late W. J. ENGLEFIELD, Esq., London.

EXETER UNIVERSITY COLLEGE AND CITY LIBRARY, per H. Tapley-Soper, Esq., Librarian.

WILLOUGHBY FARR, Esq., Edgewater, New Jersey, U.S.A.

Wm. Jas Faulkner, Esq., F.R.N.S., M.B.N.S., Sutton House, Endon, Stoke-on-Trent.

Mr. A. J. Featherstone, Birmingham.

James C. Fenton, Esq., Cleckheaton, Yorks.

The late W. J. Fieldhouse, Esq., C.B.E., Austy Manor, Warwickshire.

Messrs. W. & G. Foyle, Ltd., London.

George H. Frazier, Esq., Philadelphia, Pa., U.S.A.

William Danger Fripp, Esq., Clifton, Bristol.

John H. D. Frith, Esq., Chaddesden, near Derby.

A. Fynde, Esq., Regent's Park, N.W.

Messrs. Galignani's Library, Paris.

Messrs. Galloway & Porter, Cambridge.

John Gibbins, Jr., Esq., Birmingham.

H. Martin Gibbs, Esq., Barrow Court, Flax-Bourton, Somerset.

Burns Gillam, Esq., New York, U.S.A.

Mrs. Lawrence Glen, Glasgow.

Gloucester Public Library, per Roland Austin, Esq., Chief Librarian.

Cyril F. Goode, Esq., Park Langley, Beckenham, Kent.

Messrs. W. F. Greenwood & Sons, Ltd., York.

The Rev. G. A. M. Griffiths, London.

Captain Arthur Grimwood, Birmingham.

H. P. Hadfield, Esq., Maghull, Liverpool.

H. J. Halle, Esq., New York, U.S.A.

Edward R. H. Hancox, Esq., Nacton, Ipswich.

Capt. N. G. Harries, Wightwick, Nr. Wolverhampton.

Messrs. Hatchard, London.

Librairie Jules Hausdorff, Antwerp.

Sydney Hazeldine, Esq., Worthing.

Ambrose Heal, Esq., Beaconsfield, Bucks.

W. J. P. Hodgkins, Esq., Remuera, Auckland, N.Z.

Gilbert L. D. Hole, Esq., Edinburgh.

Capt. W. de L. Holmes, Weston-super-Mare.

Ernest Hunter, Esq., Chesham Bois, Bucks.

A. H. Isher, Esq., Cheltenham.

Messrs. William Jackson (Books), Ltd., London.

Harold Jenkins, Esq., Groombridge, Sussex.

Bertrand Johnson, Esq., London.

Mrs. Gerald Johnston, Kingsway, Slough.

Rev. F. Meyrick Jones, B.A., Woodlands Manor, Mere, Wilts.

F. R. Kelley, Esq., Cheadle Hulme, Lancs.

Alfred E. Kimbell, Esq., London.

A. Frederick Kinghorn, Esq., Glasgow.

Messrs. Kirkhope & Son, Glasgow.

J. F. Knowlson, Esq., Levenshulme, Manchester.

Messrs. Marshall Laird, Los Angeles, Cal., U.S.A.

Mrs. Jesse Lasky, New York, U.S.A.

Ledlie L. Laughlin, Esq., Princeton, N.J., U.S.A.

Mr. Le Vimo, Holywood, California, U.S.A.

Law Leyton, Esq., London.

Mrs. G. Lloyd, Hampton Court House, Hampton Court, Middlesex.

Luke Vincent Lockwood, Esq., New York, U.S.A.

Major J. L. Lovibond, Underwood, Hexham.

The late Lt.-Col. G. B. Croft Lyons, F.S.A.

Lee McCanliss, Esq., New York, U.S.A.

Major A. L. Mackinnon, Aberdeen.

Mr. David McMorran, Port Huron, Michigan, U.S.A.

Messrs. Macniven & Wallace, Edinburgh.

Messrs. Maggs Brothers, London, W.

H. S. G. Mair, Esq., St. Peter's-in-Thanet.

Lt.-Colonel E. W. Margesson, Worthing.

Messrs. Matthews & Brooke, Bradford.

Messrs. Mawson, Swan & Morgan, Ltd., Newcastle-upon-Tyne.

M. A. Louis de Meuleneere, Bruxelles.

Mrs. George M. Millard, Pasadena, California, U.S.A.

Moore's Book Shop, Sydney, N.S.W.

Major Morris, London.

The Rt. Hon. the Earl of Mount Edgcumbe.

Charles S. Murray, Esq., Ashtead, Surrey.

Antonio de Navarro, Esq., F.S.A., Broadway, Worcs.

Richard Neate, Esq., London.

Nebraska University, per Gilbert H. Doane, Esq., Librarian.

Northampton Central Museum, per Reginald W. Brown, Esq., Chief Librarian and Curator.

Mr. John Orr, Edinburgh.

Messrs. Osmond and Matthews, Ltd., London.

Messrs. Palmer, Howe & Co., Manchester.

Messrs. Parker & Son, Oxford.

Edgar A. Parr, Esq., Melbourne, Australia.

Cyril G. Parsons, Esq., Bristol.

James G. Paterson, Esq., London.

E. Richmond Paton, Esq., B.A., F.Z.S., M.B.O.U., Hareshawmuir, by Kilmarnock.

W. J. Pavyer, Esq., St. Albans.

The Worshipful Company of Pewterers London.

J. Curtis Platt, Esq., Scranton, Pa., U.S.A.

Charles G. J. Port, Esq., F.S.A., Worthing.

Dr. P. Seymour Price, London.

Messrs. Bernard Quaritch, Ltd., London.

Mr. John Read, Bolton.

Major John Richardson, D.S.O., Falmouth.

Frederick H. Rickwood, Esq., West Wickham, Kent.

Messrs. Robertson & Mullens, Ltd., London.

A. E. Robins, Esq., Beaconsfield, Bucks.

Charles Rose, Esq., Brussels.

Messrs. F. Sangorski & G. Sutcliffe, London, W.

Messrs. Chas. J. Sawyer, Ltd., London.

Mr. Henry B. Saxton, Nottingham.

Albert E. Seal, Esq., London.

Roland J. A. Shelley, Esq., F.R.Hist.S., London.

Messrs. Sherratt & Hughes, Manchester.

Messrs. S. W. Simms & Co., Bath.

Messrs. Simpkin, Marshall, Ltd., London.

ARCHIBALD SLOAN, Esq., Amersham Common, Bucks.

Messrs. W. H. SMITH & SON, LTD., Cheltenham.

Messrs. W. H. SMITH & SON, LTD., London.

Messrs. W. H. SMITH & SON, LTD., Newport, Mon.

Messrs. W. H. SMITH & SON, LTD., Paris.

Messrs. SOTHERAN & Co., LTD., London.

Messrs. G. E. STECHERT & Co., London.

Messrs. B. F. STEVENS & BROWN, LTD., London, W.C.

HENRY E. STILGOE, Esq., M.Inst.C.E., Putney, S.W.

Mrs. J. A. STIRLING, Ham Common, Surrey.

Herr F. STURM, Riedlingen, Germany.

Captain A. V. SUTHERLAND-GRAEME, A.R.I.B.A., Bedford Park, W.

FREDERICK J. H. SUTTON, Esq., New York, U.S.A.

SYDNEY PUBLIC LIBRARY, N.S.W., Australia.

Dr. GREVILLE B. TAIT, Archpool, Handcross, Sussex.

Mr. JAMES THIN, Edinburgh.

Major S. J. THOMPSON, D.S.O., Codsall, Staffs.

W. D. THOMSON, Esq., Moseley, Birmingham.

TIMES BOOK CLUB, London.

Major O. L. TRECHMANN, Westaway, Barnstaple.

Messrs. TRUSLOVE & HANSON, London.

O. G. N. TURNBULL, Esq., Putney, S.W.

E. W. TURNER, Esq., M.A., Herne Bay.

JOHN F. VAUGHAN, Esq., Tettenhall, Wolverhampton.

HARRY WALKER, Esq., Denton, Nr. Manchester.

THOMAS WARBURTON, Esq., Cheetham Hill, Manchester.

LLOYD F. WARD, Esq., A.R.I.B.A., Birmingham.

T. T. WARREN, Esq., Beith, Ayrshire.

Mrs. CARVICK WEBSTER, Orangefield, Monkton, Ayrshire.

FRANCIS WESTON, Esq., F.S.A., Croydon.

Messrs. WHITCOMBE & TOMBS, LTD., Auckland, N.Z.

EDWARD WILLIAMS, Esq., Hutton Rudby, Yorkshire.

HARRY WILLIS, Esq., Golders Green.

ALFRED B. YEATES, Esq., F.R.I.B.A., F.S.A., London.

ARCHIBALD JOHN YOUNG, Esq., Manchester.

R. P. YOUNG, Esq., Bourton Manor, Bourton-in-the-Water, Glos.

Messrs. H. YOUNG & SONS, LTD., Liverpool.

CHAPTER I

HISTORICAL INTRODUCTION

To those who would know the full story of the Craft or " Mystery " of the Pewterer in bygone years the fates have been more than usually kind, for we have in the late Charles Welch's monumental and fascinating *History of the Worshipful Company of Pewterers of London* a carefully chosen and extensive series of extracts from the records preserved at Pewterers' Hall, and it would be idle to attempt to give more than a very general epitome of his two volumes in a work of this nature. One's difficulty is not what to say, but what to leave out and still give a useful passing glance at the main points of interest.

Again one is confronted with a work of front-rank importance in the late lamented L. Ingleby Wood's *Scottish Pewterware and Pewterers*.

At the time of writing it would seem that these two publications will remain for very many years the standard works in so far as the historical side of the industry is concerned in England and Scotland, and to them in the future writers will have to turn for their main facts of history.

On pondering the facts one is staggered by the ignorance prevailing amongst the general public on the subject of pewter, the metal which at one time was used in place of all those modern innovations which have supplanted it—block-tin, electro-plate, china, glass, earthenware, galvanised iron, aluminium, etc., etc. Wipe out all the articles made in these materials from your home, and in their place substitute the same or similar articles made in pewter—basins and bowls, plates and dishes, flagons and ewers, tankards and mugs, cups and porringers, salts and mustards, peppers and spice-boxes, candlesticks, inkstands, snuff and tobacco boxes, spoons and even forks, church plate, coin of the realm and hundreds of other articles—one then begins to realise what an enormous industry pewter-making was, and yet within a hundred—nay, fifty or sixty—years of its decline the average person's first questions will be " What is pewter ? " " When was it used ? " —" Sic transit gloria mundi ! " It is difficult to think of *anything* which has bulked more largely in the lives of generation after generation, but even now, after so short a lapse of time there seems to be not one in a hundred who would know it if they saw it !

That pewter was made and used by the Romans is evidenced by the many pieces which have come down to us and which are still found from time to time in excavations in this country. In the British Museum we have preserved many interesting pieces discovered during excavations at Appleshaw, near Andover, Hants., in 1897, some of which would seem to be of the fourth century A.D., and by the courtesy of the Bristol Museum and Art Gallery Committee and the Director (Dr. Herbert Bolton) I am enabled to illustrate some pieces found in excavating the site of a Roman Villa at Brislington in 1901, also a dish from Major Thompson's collection, dating from the second or third century A.D., and found during excavations in Cambridgeshire. See Plate II, p. 3.

From this time onwards there is a long hiatus until the eleventh century, when we have in 1076 a further reference to pewter in this country at the Council of Winchester, by which it was ordered that pewter be allowed to be made into chalices for use in poor parishes in place of the wooden ones then in use, and which latter were forbidden in future at the same Council.

In 1175, at a Council at Westminster, this ruling, in so far as pewter is concerned, was reversed, which in its turn was also forbidden, the bishops being ordered not to consecrate pewter chalices.

From *Coroners' Jury Rolls* we have the following :—

> 14 Feb. 1326. Goods of Walter de ANNE, who fled from justice, were seized by the Sheriff: they included *a pot and salt-cellar of peautre* worth 4d., . . . *four pewter dishes* worth six pence.

And again, under date 25 March 1338 :—Cheapside, *William le Peautrer* is mentioned.

Turning from these early references to the actual fashioning of pewter wares, we find that the earliest records we have are the first Ordinances of the London Guild or Company, made in the year 1348 wherein the Guild is referred to as the " Craft of Pewterers."

The main object of these ordinances was to ensure a high standard of quality and workmanship.   The full text is given in Welch, *op. cit*. i. 2.

The first ordinances of the York guild are dated 1419, though one " Willelmus de Ordesale, peutrer," is mentioned in 1347/8, and those of the Bristol Guild, dated 1456, adopt the same assay as was laid down for use by their London confreres and their ordinances follow much the same general lines throughout.   The full text of the York ordinances appeared in the *Reliquary*, April 1891, and those of the Bristol pewterers are illustrated in facsimile at Plate III, p. 9, and transcribed at pages 7 and 8 of the present work, by the courteous permission of the Committee of the Bristol Museum and Art Gallery.

The earliest references I have found to pewterers' organisations of various towns are as follows :—

The Ordinances of the Pewterers' Guild of London - - - - - - in 1348
The Ordinances of the Pewterers' Guild of York - - - - - - in 1419
The Calendar of Freemen of King's Lynn - - - - - - in 1445/6
The St. Luke's Guild of Norwich - - - - - - - in 1449
The Ordinances of the Pewterers' Guild of Bristol - - - - - - in 1456
The Incorporation of Hammermen of Edinburgh - - - - - - in 1496
The Incorporation of Hammermen of Ludlow - - - - - - in 1511
The Company of Goldsmiths, Plumbers, Glaziers, Pewterers and Painters of Newcastle-upon-Tyne - - - - - - - - - - in 1536
The Incorporation of Hammermen of St. Andrews - - - - - in 1539
The Incorporation of Hammermen of The Cannongate, Edinburgh - - - in 1546
The Incorporation of Hammermen of Perth - - - - - - in 1546
The Guild of Smiths of Dublin - - - - - - - in 1556
The Incorporation of Hammermen of Aberdeen - - - - - in 1579
The Incorporation of Hammermen of Dundee - - - - - - in 1587
The Guild of Smiths of Kingston-upon-Hull - - - - - - in 1598
The Incorporation of Hammermen of Stirling - - - - - - in 1605
The Incorporation of Hammermen of Glasgow - - - - - - in 1648
The Guild of Smiths of Cork - - - - - - - in 1656
The Guild of Smiths of Youghal - - - - - - - in 1657

PLATE II

A ROMAN PEWTER EWER

C. 200 A.D. ; height 13¼″.

Discovered during excavations at Brislington, Bristol, and now in the Bristol Museum.

(Reproduced by permission of the Committee of the Bristol Museum and Art Gallery.)

ROMAN PEWTER DISH (obverse)

Probably 3rd century A.D. Diameter 15½″.

Found during excavations in Cambridgeshire.

Collection of Major S. John Thompson, D.S.O., Oaken

ROMAN PEWTER DISH
(reverse)

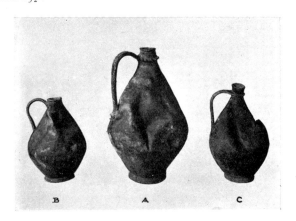

ROMAN PEWTER EWERS

C. 200 A.D. ; heights, B 7¾″, A 12½″, C 9″.

The inset line-drawing show the decorations on the handles. From the same excavations as the Roman Pewter Ewer above and now in the Bristol Museum.

(Reproduced by permission of the Committee of the Bristol Museum and Art Gallery.)

3

Mention of a " searcher for false wares " is made in the Exeter Acts Books for 1562, thus showing that some sort of organisation was in being there at that time.

The above are *not* in *all* cases the dates *of the foundation* of the Guilds ; but refer to the first mention I have discovered of the pewterer's Craft as being connected with them.

LONDON.

The London Ordinances of 1348 set up two standard alloys which are thus described in the original :—

> . . . All manner of pewter, as dishes saucers platters chargers pots square cruets square chris-matories and other things that they make square or cistils that they be made of fine pewter and the measure of Brass to the Tin as much as it will receive of his nature of the same and all other things of the said craft that be wrought as pots round that pertain to the craft to be wrought of Tin with an alloy of lead to a reasonable measure and the measure of an alloy of a C.tyn is XXVI. lb. of lead, and that is called vessels of Tin for ever.

That is to say that fine pewter was to be of pure tin with an admixture of as much brass as its own nature would permit, and second quality, or as it is called " vessels of tin," was to be a hundredweight of tin to twenty six pounds of lead.

Two years later, however, one finds, on 29th June, 1351, the Wardens of the Company stating to the Mayor and Aldermen of the City, who had before them one John de Hiltone for making false wares ; that "To one hundred weight of 112 pounds of tin, there ought to be added no more than 16 lbs. of lead." This places the amount of lead at ten pounds less than is permitted by the above mentioned ordinances.

The above will give some idea of the composition of pewter in its earlier days, but the amount varied from time to time. This work, however, is not intended for the scientist or metallurgist but for the Connoisseur and Collector, so I propose to pass on to those other points which demand a passing word in this Chapter.

In 1444 the Company obtained by an order of Common Council the right to purchase one fourth part of all the tin coming up to London for sale.

In 1475 the Company was so firmly established as to commence the building of its own Hall on a site in Lime Street which they had previously purchased, and on which to-day the present Hall stands. The first building was destroyed in the great fire of 1666, and with it many priceless records of the Company's earlier activities.

Records of the visitations of Plague in 1563 and 1665 show that the Company paid its full toll in victims to these dread visitations, and in the latter year it had three Masters within a few weeks. Mr. Seeling, who was present at a Court on the 5th September, died four days later ; his successor, Ralph Marsh, elected the 19th October, died and was buried on the 20th, Nicholas Kelk being elected later to the same office.

The Company had to be ready at short notice to provide a body of soldiers fully armed when called upon, and for this purpose an armoury was provided at the Hall. They also had to attend pageants, properly dressed and equipped ; to contribute at not infrequent intervals towards loans to the Sovereign ; in short they took their full part in the national and civic life of the times.

Side by side with the craft of the Guild was the religious organisation which found its outward expression in The Brotherhood of the Assumption of Our Lady. The Yeomanry (or Freemen) also was associated with the Fraternity of St. Michael the Archangel.

The former held their annual festival at the Grey Friars and the latter at All-Hallows, Lombard Street, to which also the former was transferred in 1495. In 1600 this election-day festival was again transferred from All-Hallows to St. Dionis, Backchurch, in which parish the Company's Hall was situated.

Numerous Charters were obtained by the Company, the first, and therefore the most important, being that of 13 Ed. IV. (1473), which amongst other things gave them the right of search throughout England for faulty wares. A second from the same king in 1478 confirmed the previous one as also did others granted by Henry VII in 1504, Henry VIII in 1512, Elizabeth in 1559 and James I in 1606.

In 1638 King Charles I confirmed the previous ones and again enforced the order that all wares should be marked by the maker. Charles II confirmed this in 1673 and slightly extended its privileges, which in turn were confirmed by the Charters of James II in 1685 and Queen Anne in 1702.

The marking of pewter was first made compulsory in the London Company in 1503/4 by Act of Parliament, but it was not until 1567 that it was enforced by Act of Parliament in Scotland.

The Company set up stringent regulations for the good government of the Craft. Members were not allowed to go to law with each other, but had to refer their differences to the Court of the Company. Standards of quality, both of workmanship and alloy, were set up and in earlier days rigidly enforced, hours and methods of work were strictly regulated, and any breach of the Company's rules was severely dealt with regardless of the position of the delinquent, and instances are on record of apprentices and even journey-men being brought to the Hall and whipped in open Court for failure in this respect.

All this tended towards the attainment and up-holding of that high reputation which English pewter had achieved, not only at home but on the Continent of Europe, and to those of us who are familiar with it the reason is not far to seek, for whereas English and Scottish pewter is usually of fine metal and well wrought, one looks in vain for these qualities in some of the metal which has reached these shores from certain countries across the Channel.

So long as the Company upheld their right of search for faulty wares and unflinchingly enforced their regulations all went well with the industry, but towards the middle of the eighteenth century their faith in their own powers began to wane. One sees their regulations modified one by one and disobeyed, the right to search neglected, and insubordination amongst its members beginning to manifest itself, until by the beginning of the nineteenth century it was but the shadow of its former self, and so, jostled from within, and having to face competition with its modern rivals externally, the industry gradually declined after a valiant record of many centuries of usefulness.

So much for the London pewterers, whose ordinances formed the chief basis for those of other Pewterers' Guilds, short notices of which provide the theme for the concluding part of the present Chapter, the towns and cities being arranged in alphabetical order.

BEWDLEY.

There was at one time a considerable amount of pewter ware manufactured at Bewdley, Worcs., or in that part of it which lies east of the River Severn and known as Wribbenhall, where there remains to this day, indicative of the fact that at one time the industry must have been of some importance, a narrow thoroughfare named " Pewterer's Alley." I have paid several visits to the town and district in the hope of gathering information concerning the local craftsmen, but all I have been able to glean is a few facts from the courteous Town Clerk, Mr. Stanley Hemmingway, and the venerable Parish Clerk, Mr. Clarke.

The trade seems to have been well founded there by the reign of King William III when the Bancks family were famous for their pewter wares and *possibly* some of the number of Bancks marks illustrated but unplaced in Chapter VI were used by this family. Other names associated with the industry there were, Ingram, Vickers, Cotterell, Timins, Wheeler—a spoon maker—Nest and lastly John Carruthers Crane who, retiring in 1838, sold his moulds to James Yates of Birmingham, an inventory of which with many of the original moulds I have been allowed to inspect through the courtesy of the present owners, Messrs. Gaskell & Chambers.

Further details of the above names are given in some cases, in Chapter VI, but one must regret that in proportion to the apparent extent of the industry there and the time spent in endeavouring to unearth the past, the information is decidedly meagre and disappointing.

BRISTOL.

The ordinances of the Guild of Pewterers of Bristol are preserved in the famous *Little Red Book of Bristol,* and are here illustrated in facsimile (Plate III, p. 9) by the courteous permission of the Museum and Art Gallery Committee of that City, having previously appeared in my *Bristol and West-Country Pewterers,* issued as one of the official handbooks of the Bristol Museum. Transcribed they read as follows :—

ORDINANCES MADE FOR THE MYSTERY OF PEWTERERS CRAFT.

Memorandum the 20th day of August the year reigning of King Henry the VIth after the conquest, XXXVth (1456-7). The right worthy and reverent Sirs, William Canyng, Mayor of Bristol and William Damme, Sheriff of the same and all the right wise and discreet Council of the said Town, for great, urgent and necessary causes them moving, and for the good governance and the great tranquility, prosperity and avail of the said Town of Bristol, to be had and kept in the Craft and Mystery of Pewterers, have ordained, set, enacted, established and (? caused to) be enrolled, the ordinances and acts that hereafter followeth.

First, it is ordained, enacted and established that from this day forward all men using (the) Pewterer's Craft within the said Town and Shire shall make all vessels, called pewter vessels and all pots called pewter pots, basins, ewers and all other things made of pewter, that it be made of good, lawful and sufficient metal after the rule and assay of London and that all manner of such vessels that ought to be beat after the rule of the Craft of old time used, that it have his sufficient beating and not to be sold otherwise upon pain of XXs. to be levied of any man of the said Craft that doth the contrary thereof, half to the said Craft and the other half to the Chamber.

Also, that the morrow upon All Halloweve day, that all men of the said Craft go together at the calling of the Master of the said Craft for the time being and choose them a Master of the said Craft for the year following and present him to the Mayor and there to take his oath by the Mayor's Ordinance truly and duly to search in the Craft, every week once and to arrest and present to the Mayor and Chamberlains all such defaulty as they can find contrary to any point of the ordinance before written upon the pain before rehearsed.

And what Master that doth not duly call the fellowship of the said Craft as is above written shall lose for every day that he so faileth after All Halloweve day, 12d., half to the said Craft and the other half to the Chamber. And every man of the said Craft that will not appear after due warning to the choosing of the Master in form aforesaid shall lose for every default, 12d., half to the said Craft and the other half to the said Chamber.

And so, what Master do not duly and truly make search and present all that defaulted that may be known and found in the said Craft contrary to the ordinance above said or any point thereof, shall lose for every default 6s. 8d. half to the said Craft and the other half to the said Chamber.

Also it shall be lawful to every Master for the time being that when he departeth out of the Town in his lawful business, to make a " debite " (deputy) for (the) time of his absence, a good man of the said Craft, giving him his whole power and oath in performing of all the articles above written, and what man of the Craft that will refuse to take upon him that said charge and to do therein as it is above written, shall lose at every time 40d., half to the said Craft and the other half to the said Chamber.

It is of course much to be regretted that these " Ordinances " make no reference to the marking of pewter. On the other hand it is a cause for rejoicing that this ancient document is preserved to us, since it establishes beyond question the fact that *there was* a Guild of Pewterers at Bristol, which fact so far as I am able to gather has not been recorded hitherto apart from my monograph already referred to, in any work on this subject. A further interesting point is that the assay used in the London Company was—as in the case of York—adopted as the standard at Bristol.

In addition to these ordinances the names of all Freemen Pewterers of Bristol from 1559-1318 and all apprentices bound to Bristol pewterers from 1600-1799 have been extracted from the Bristol Burgess Lists and Apprenticeship Registers respectively by the late Mr. W. T. Pountney, of that city, and by arrangement with him some years before his death, are incorporated in the Alphabetical List of Pewterers, Chapter VI.

These names, which total up to about six hundred, were *not* included in my *Bristol and West-Country Pewterers*, but are here published for the first time and are of the very highest importance and enable us to identify many marks which hitherto have remained enigmatic to collectors.

EXETER.

That some sort of Guild was in being at Exeter is obvious from the following, for the fact of the existence of a searcher implies that of the Guild which appointed him.

The extract is taken from " Illustrations of Municipal History from the Act Books of the Chamber of the City of Exeter," by Professor Walter J. Harte, M.A., and appeared in the *Transactions of the Devonshire Association*, 1912

> The **XXI** of September 1562, Gregorie Jane, pewterer, sercher appointed for the serche of the trew makinge of pewter vessel wth in this Citie of Exon, dyd bringe yn and make seasure of certeyn tynney pewter pottes that is to say, iiij quarte pottes & V lytle coops wch pottes beinge vewed as well by the said Gregorie, John Stephens & . . ., were founde defectyve and not made or wrought accordinge to the statutes, upon wch verdicte it was proved the pottes to be forfeyted and therfor thone halfe to remayne to the use of the Citie & thother to the use of the same seasures.

HULL.

In Rev. J. Malet Lambert's *Two Thousand Years of Guild Life* it is shown that there was formed in 1598 at Kingston-upon-Hull a Company including the Goldsmiths, Smiths, *Pewterers*, Plumbers, Glaziers, Painters, Cutlers, Musicians, Stationers, Bookbinders and

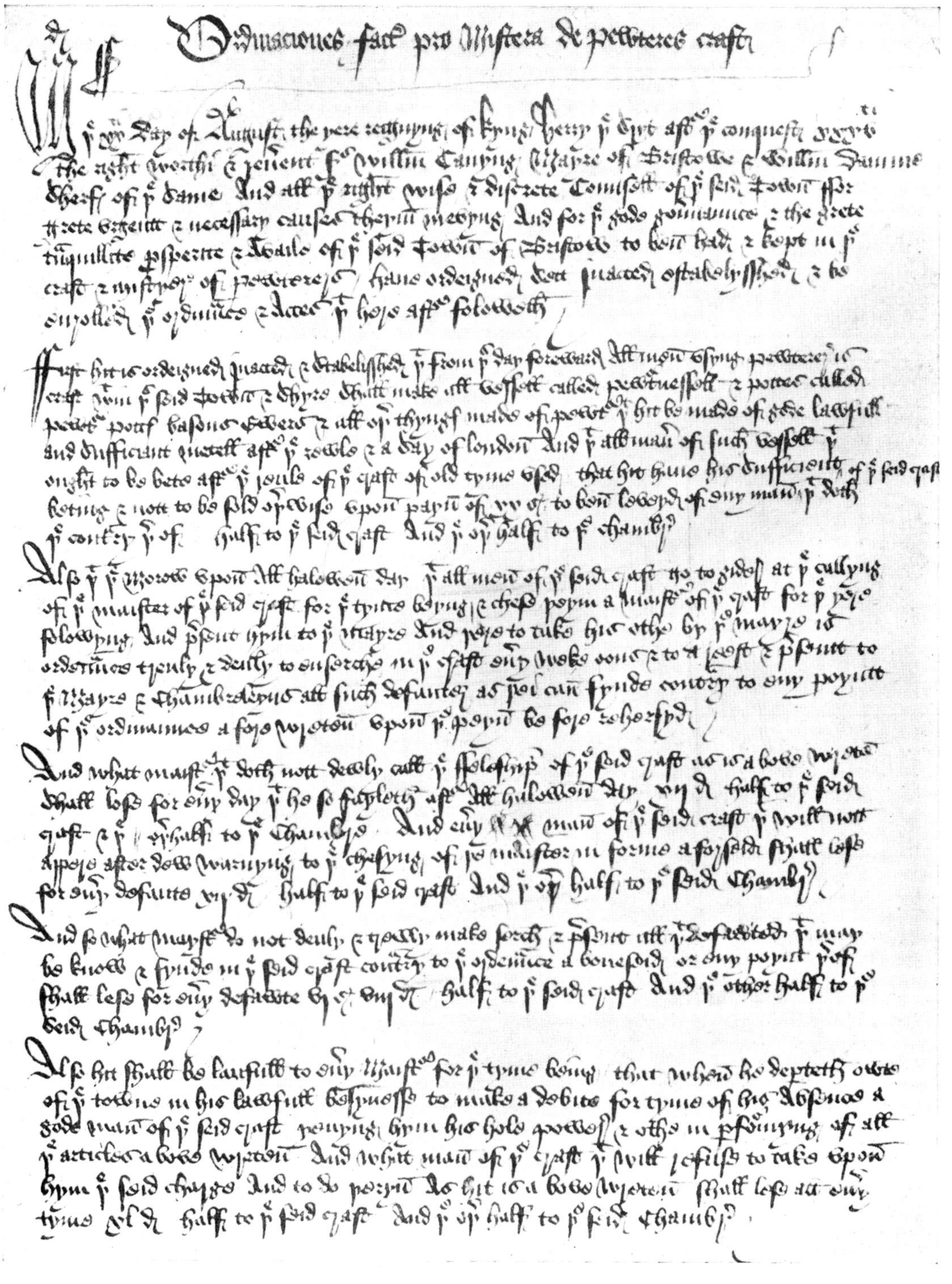

PLATE III

THE ORDINANCES OF THE PEWTERERS' GUILD OF BRISTOL
(*By permission of the Committee of the Bristol Museum and Art Gallery*)

PLATE IV

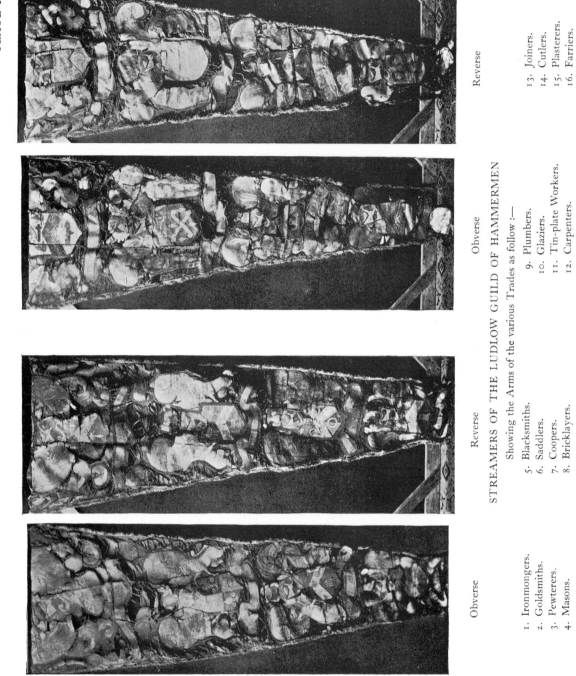

Reverse

Obverse

Reverse

Obverse

STREAMERS OF THE LUDLOW GUILD OF HAMMERMEN

Showing the Arms of the various Trades as follow :—

1. Ironmongers.
2. Goldsmiths.
3. Pewterers.
4. Masons.

5. Blacksmiths.
6. Saddlers.
7. Coopers.
8. Bricklayers.

9. Plumbers.
10. Glaziers.
11. Tin-plate Workers.
12. Carpenters.

13. Joiners.
14. Cutlers.
15. Plasterers.
16. Farriers.

Basket Makers, and Mr. Lambert remarks that "both for municipal purposes and for mutual protection, union was necessary, and the mere fact of the weakness of their independent position, irrespective of the natural connexion of their trades, seems to have drawn them together into one society."

Thomas Smith, Senr., *Smith*, and Thomas Scupholme, *Pewterer*, were elected the first searchers to the new Guild, and as Mr. Lambert rightly remarks

> The Searchers of this Company must have been handy men, and when the smith and pewterer went their rounds, the musicians, dancing masters, plumbers, painters, stationers and basket makers must have exercised creditable restraint in allowing their work to be judged by these worthy officials.

The ordinances, signed by thirty members, of whom George Marshall and Thomas Scupholme represented the pewterers, enact that all the above trades shall henceforth be one society ; to have one Warden and two Searchers chosen yearly who were to be sworn the day after the election. Bond was to be taken in the name of the Mayor and Burgesses of Kingston-upon-Hull for the performance of any account, debt, damage, demand, etc. . . . ; none but free Burgesses of the town of Kingston-upon-Hull were to be members of the Company or to sell wares within the town except on market and fair days ; they were to make their own laws, ordinances and orders for good rule, order and government, etc., and to fix fines for their breach, for the enforcement of which the Warden and Searchers had power to "distreyne the goodes or cattels of the offender ;" and none other than such as were born within the town were to be taken as apprentices without the consent of the Mayor and Aldermen.

A second set of ordinances, dated 1664, gives the Company or Guild as embracing the Goldsmiths, Smiths, Pewterers, Plumbers, Glaziers, Painters, Cutlers, Basket-makers, Spurriers, Plasterers, Stationers, Bookbinders, and Nailors.

LUDLOW.

At Ludlow, Shropshire, there was a very well organised Guild of Smiths, or Hammermen, many and most interesting details of which have been sent to me by Mr. Jno. Palmer, Curator of the Ludlow Museum and a well known Antiquary, and upon which the following notes are chiefly based.

Unfortunately there is no record of marks or touchplates at Ludlow, Salop, but there are most interesting Banners or "Streamers" as they are called, still remaining to bear witness to the trades comprised within the fraternity. These streamers, some fifteen feet long, one of which bears date 1734, are of silk, very much frayed, with fringes. On the obverse and reverse of these Banners are represented the arms of sixteen trades viz.:— Ironmongers, Plumbers, Goldsmiths, Pewterers, Masons, Blacksmiths, Saddlers, Coopers, Bricklayers, Glaziers, Tin-plate workers, Carpenters, Joiners, Cutlers, Plasterers, and Farriers. Each of the Arms are represented with helm, crest, mantling, supporters and motto, as will be seen by the accompanying illustrations (Plate IV, p. 10).

These streamers were carried on all state occasions and at the May-day celebrations by the youngest freemen of the Guild.

The smiths with some fifteen other trades would seem to have formed themselves into a trading fraternity under the title of "Smiths and others ;" some time prior to the reign of Richard I, for mutual protection and benefit.

In an ordinance of Richard, Duke of York, father of Edward IV, whilst Lord of the Castle of Ludlow, and confirmed by " the twelve and twenty-five," the then governing body of the town, it is laid down that :—

> No manner Craft make no foreign brother but it be a man of this same town, dwelling and occupying the same craft that he is made brother of under payne of X. li, so as it playnly apperth under the Dukes seale and the common seale of the town to be forfit as ought times as it may be proved.

King Edward IV, by his Charter dated 7th December, 1461, granted to the Burgesses of Ludlow, their heirs and successors for ever, that :—

> They have in their town or borough aforesaid, the merchants guild with a company and all other customs and liberties to the guild aforesaid pertaining, and that no one who is not of that guild shall use any merchandize in the aforesaid town or suburbs of the same unless by the licence and leave of the same burgesses, their heirs and successors.

The Guild, Company or Fraternity, as they are variously styled, held their meetings in the South Aisle of the Parish Church on the spot formerly occupied by the Warwick Chapel, beneath the Eastern window, where they held pews and where they transacted their business, adjourning when the business was done to one of the neighbouring Inns.

In 1511 a Charter was granted wherein the following trades appear as forming the Guild :—Smiths, Ironmongers, Saddlers, Braziers, Pewterers, Spurriers, Bucklemakers, Brygand iron makers, Armourers, Masons, Cardmakers, and Coopers. Under this Charter the Guilds were ordered to choose amongst themselves six of the " most honest and saddest men " to be called by the name of the six men, and two stewards to be called by the name of Stewards, the six men and the two Stewards to continue in office for two years from the date of election and the Stewards yearly to make an account before the six men of all such monies and goods as shall come to their hands.

In this Charter it was provided that any master summoned and not appearing at a meeting upon his summons, was to be fined by the Stewards in half a pound of wax, and every master who was apprenticed in the town of Ludlow to any of the occupations shall have his Freedom in the Guild on payment of 6s. 8d., and those not apprenticed there on payment of 13s. 4d. Any journeyman of any of the said occupations, rebuking his master, was to forfeit half a pound of wax as often as he offended. This wax of course was for candles to be used in the services of the Church.

The first record of proceedings of the Guild is in 1539, when certain alterations were made in the election of Stewards and the fees payable by masters on their admission to freedom.

Under these new rules the six men were to choose but one Steward and the whole body of the fellowship the other, and the fees for admission differed according to different trades, the list of which varied considerably from that of 1511 and included sixteen trades instead of twelve, the pewterers paying 10s. 8d. for admission if apprenticed in the town and 40s. 8d. if otherwise.

In 1575 a new " Composition " was drawn up under the seal of the Guild and that of the Borough, and approved on the 3rd April, 1576, by the Law Officers of the Crown at Bridgnorth.

This Composition is a long document the main items of which were similar to those already in force.

The Stewards were each required to give a bond with sureties for £40 on election.

Members were forbidden to bring actions against fellow-members without the consent of the six men under pain of forfeiting 3s. 4d.

Apprentices could not be bound for less than seven years which must end when they attained the age of 24. The apprentice to be made free of his occupation on payment of the customary fee.

A "Foreigner"—a term used to denote one who was not apprenticed in the town— had to produce testimonials showing where and with whom he served his apprenticeship, and that he had been of good name and fame during that time. Should he fail to comply but set up in business without being made free of the fraternity he was fined 3s. 4d. for every day he so offended.

The Bailiffs and Council were given power to correct, reform, amend or alter any ambiguity that might arise in any clause.

The charge to Masters on being made free provided for their attendance at meetings when summoned under pain of a fine of 3s. 4d., their payment of Hall money—1s. per year—and a fine of 3s. 4d. for using railing words or commencing a suit against a brother-member without leave, or procuring work out of another master's hands. It concludes :—

> No master of the fellowship shall suffer his servant or prentyce to come to the occupation's supper, only such as shall pay their IIIId, upon payne of forfeiture of IIIs. IVd., and lastly—You nor your wief (*sic*) or other in your behalf, shall not use to knele in the occupacon's pewes before you have been Steward.

About the year 1580 there are in the minutes and Steward's account books, many instances of money being spent on the furnishings of soldiers, the Stewards having the care of the small collection of arms belonging to the Guild.

Like other similar organisations, the Ludlow Guild spent much of its revenue from fines, etc., on feasts both annual and special, the Stewards at one time being allowed "a pottle of sack and a pottle of claret" for their Stewards' suppers.

The year 1600 saw the membership of the Guild totalling about sixty-five free masters. After the year 1694 the admission forms bear a shilling Inland Revenue stamp.

Amongst the meetings of the fraternity were, Election day, Stewards' Hall, Quarterly meetings (reduced in 1790 to two), with special and private meetings.

Members were summoned to the meetings by notice and by the ringing of a bell.

Election day was formerly held on a Sunday, afterwards altered to the Saturday next, after Holy Rood day and finally to a Tuesday early in May.

The fine for refusing to serve as Steward, which had been variously 13s. 4d. and 20s., was eventually fixed at £5.

The six men were chosen as a rule from the latest past Stewards; the four Key-keepers and the Box-keeper being chosen next.

"Stewards' Hall" was generally held on Whit Monday. In later years the Audit was transferred from Election day to this meeting.

Up to the year 1710 the clerk had been chosen from amongst their own members, but in this year Richard Perks, town clerk of Ludlow, was appointed to the office and had certain perquisites allotted to him in the way of fees.

About this time the silversmiths, clockmakers, cabinetmakers, etc., were admitted to the fraternity.

In 1792 a motion was set on foot for getting rid of the six men on the ground that they should have no more power than other members. Though this motion was apparently successful it was rescinded at the next meeting.

As in other Guilds trouble commenced early in the nineteenth century and from circa 1815-1835 it showed itself in the difficulty experienced in getting members to take up their freedom. The death blow came in 1835, in the shape of the Municipal Corporations Act, which enacted that any man might carry on any lawful trade in any borough whether free of any trade guild or not.

The fraternity drifted on for some years after this until one by one its old members passed away, its pews being removed from the Church in 1860.

The old Membership badge (or "ticket") of the fraternity is illustrated at p. 74, Plate XII, from a very rare example in the possession of Mr. Thomas Warburton of Manchester. It is of copper, one and a half inches in diameter, the edges are milled diagonally and the reverse is blank for the reception of the member's name or number—or both.

LYNN.

Amongst the several thousand names of Freemen admitted at Lynn there are not more than twenty-nine pewterers covering, at more or less regular intervals, the period 1445 to 1697. Their names appear in Chapter VI in the Alphabetical list of pewterers.

NEWCASTLE-UPON-TYNE.

The earliest reference to pewterers in this city which I have come across, and to which my attention was drawn by Mr. Thomas Warburton, is in Jackson's *English Goldsmiths*, where one finds it recorded that the Goldsmiths of Newcastle—who are mentioned as early as 1248—were incorporated in 1536 together with the freemen of certain other trades as a "COMPANY OF GOLDSMITHS, PLUMBERS, GLAZIERS, PEWTERERS and PAINTERS." This charter still exists among the Plumbers' archives.

The Company was governed by "Four Wardens, viz. a Goldsmith, a Plumber, a Glazier and a *Pewterer or* a Painter.

By Act of Parliament in 1702, the Goldsmiths of Newcastle were constituted an independent Corporation, but with the exception of an interval from 1707-1711 they continued in association with the Plumbers, Glaziers, *Pewterers* and Painters until 1716, when they finally separated themselves.

I am under a further debt to Mr. Warburton for the photograph which he made for me—reproduced at p. 74, Plate XII—of the Arms of the Plumbers, Pewterers and Glaziers, as given in *The Armorial Bearings of the several Incorporated Companies of Newcastle-upon-Tyne, with a brief Historical Account of each Company, together with notices of the Corpus Christi, or Miracle Plays, anciently performed by the Trading Societies of Newcastle-upon-Tyne*, by James Walker and M. A. Richardson, 1824.

Speaking of previous engravings of these Company Arms, John Brand, in his *History of Newcastle-upon-Tyne*, 1776, says :—

> They (The Arms, as used in Newcastle) are copies, but not exact ones, of the Societies of London in Stowe's "Survey of the City" and certain it is that, with the exception of the seals of the Societies of Merchants; Masters and Mariners; and Hoastmen, no special grant of Arms has ever been made to the Incorporated Companies of Newcastle-upon-Tyne.

The names and marks of such Newcastle craftsmen as I have been able to collect from various sources will be found throughout Chapter VI.

NORWICH.

To Mr. Arnold H. Miller, Town Clerk of Norwich, I am indebted for the following notes with regard to the Norwich pewterers

In regard to the Pewterers' Guild. Up to the fifteenth century the Guilds in Norwich were mostly of a religious character and the crafts were attached to these guilds. Apparently the crafts elected two masters save in the case of the worsted weavers, who chose six. It was ordained that each craft should freely and yearly choose of her craft within herself two masters for the year coming; which two masters should be presented by bill written to the Mayor and take oath to make good and true search of all defaults found in the same craft, and that all notable defaults found in the craft should be well and truly presented to the Mayor without concealment, etc.

Until 1450 the Pewterers were attached to the St. Luke's Guild and were expected to attend the procession of their craft on its festival day and also the civic processions. All the citizens of any craft who had the means, were to have a livery provided by the wardens, the cloth for which must be woven within the liberties, and renewed every year. But when a member of any particular craft was elected to an estate of an alderman of the city, he was not required to wear more than the hood of the livery of his craft. Further, no man might take the clothing of a craft unless he were a citizen enrolled under that craft, and held a house of tenement, or at least a chamber and resided in the city. To ensure all crafts should have a different clothing and distinct from that of the Mayor and aldermen, the colours selected by them must be passed by the Chamberlains, and the colours worn by the Mayor and Aldermen during two previous years might not be adopted.

St. Luke's Guild, composed of the pewterers, braziers, bell-founders, plumbers, glaziers and painters, was at first entirely responsible for the production of the pageants, although it is not known when it introduced them. In 1527 the guild is discovered petitioning the Mayor that, being unable any longer to bear the expenses entailed by the annual display on Whit Monday, it might be relieved by each craft producing one pageant on that day.

The order of the procession of the crafts on Corpus Christi day was laid down in 1449, and those responsible for the 9th Pageant were the " Dyers, Calaundrers, Goldsmythes, Goldbeters, and Sadelers, Pewtrers, Brasiers—the Birth of Christ with sheperdes and three Kynges off Colen."

After the Reformation considerable alteration took place in the Guilds and the occupations were divided into twelve grand companies and although the idea may have been taken from London, there was no similarity other than the name between the grand companies of London and Norwich. Each of the groups was assigned to one of the petty wards, the two Aldermen of which became the masters, and as the list is given in a socially descending scale and the wards taken in the usual order, the arrangement was by no means inappropriate.

In this grouping which was communicated at an assembly held on 19 August, 20 Jas. I (1623), the Pewterers were found in the sixth group, with the goldsmithes the ironmongers, smythes, sadlers, brasyers, glasyers, cutlers, plomers, clockmakers, and bell-founders.

SUNDERLAND.

It is understood that there was formerly a " Pewterers' Lane " in Sunderland, but I can find no evidence that the trade there assumed any considerable proportions, though we have evidence of its existence in the mark of William Alder, whose mark will be found illustrated in its proper place in Chapter VI.

YARMOUTH.

As at Lynn, amongst some thousands of Freemen admitted there is but little indication that the pewter industry assumed any definite standing, for I have discovered here but two pewterers—and of these one is doubtful in 1471, the other appearing in 1561.

YORK.

The ordinances of the York Pewterers' Guild designedly follow the same general lines as those of the London Company. They date from 1419, and a later ordinance of 1540 enjoined that every member should strike his touch upon all wares and that an impression of such touch was to be left at the Hall (or Common Chamber). This of course implies that a touchplate, or as it is called in the document, a " counterpayne " was in use, but it must be feared it has long since been destroyed, for no trace of it can be found.

OTHER ENGLISH CENTRES.

Barnstaple, Birmingham, Chester, Liverpool, Manchester, Wigan, all provide us with some evidence of pewter activity though no organised Societies would seem to have guided their destinies, and failing evidence to the contrary one must regard the appearance of pewterers there as more or less sporadic. In the case of Chester—one of our most ancient cities—one expresses some surprise that this should be so, and Birmingham supplies us with nothing until the late eighteenth century, as one would expect.

SCOTLAND.

At the end of this volume facsimiles of the two existing Edinburgh Touchplates are given and the names and marks of all known Scottish pewterers appear at frequent intervals throughout Chapter VI, with a mention—at the commencement of the present Chapter— of the earliest references to the Guilds in the various cities and towns ; but for that fuller information on the subject which one's readers may desire, access must be available to Mr. Ingleby Wood's volume, already quoted in these pages.

IRISH.

The early history of the Pewterers' Craft in Ireland is shrouded in almost impenetrable mystery. Whilst one sees the Pewterers' Guilds of London, Edinburgh, York and Bristol existing as flourishing institutions, governed by their own regulations and ordinances and each controlled by its own master and wardens, yet no such guild, so far as is at present known, existed *separately* for the *pewterers* of Dublin or Cork, or even of Ireland, for in Dublin they were one of the trades comprised within the Guild of Smiths, and that they were one of the units embraced in the Society of Goldsmiths in Cork, is shown by the following extract :—

On May 31st 1656 John Sharpe, goldsmith ; Robert Goble, brazier ; Edward Goble, brazier ; John Hawkins, sadler ; Thomas Holmes, sadler ; Robert Philipps, sadler ; were appointed trustees for the Society of goldsmiths, braziers, *Pewterers*, founders, plummers (*sic*), white-plate workers, glaziers, sadlers, upholsterers and the like, *then incorporated* by the name of The Master, wardens and Company of the Society of Goldsmiths for the City of Cork.

It seems but natural to suppose that the pewterers of other towns in Ireland, belonged to similar Corporations ; of this, however, we have no *direct* evidence, with the exception of Youghal, where according to the Charter of that city in the reign of King James I, the Mayor, Bailiffs and Burgesses of Youghal were empowered to divide themselves into divers Guilds according to their divers arts, trades and mysteries.   Each Guild to have a convenient place for assembly and every Guild may yearly choose one Master and two Wardens, who are to exercise the office for one year and no more.

In pursuance of this Charter we find that a Company of Hammermen comprising the goldsmiths, blacksmiths, *pewterers*, shipwrights, house carpenters, joiners, coopers, tilers, masons, cutlers, braziers and glaziers were incorporated in Youghal, September 15th, 1657.

The Council Book of the Corporation of Kinsale, under date the 19th March, 1687, records :—

> William Walsh, sworn Master of the Company of Blacksmiths, goldsmiths, cutlers, glaziers, braziers and *other* hammermen that work by fire, who are to take out a new Charter and to pay £8 for the same, March 25th instant.

These " other hammermen " in all probability included the pewterers.

An early reference to the use of pewter in Ireland is found in an Account Roll of Holy Trinity Priory, Dublin, where, in the Seneschal's accounts for the year 1344, it is stated that one dozen saucers of pewter or tin, one dozen dishes, one dozen of plates of pewter and two dozen chargers, were bought for the Prior's use for the sum of seven shillings, and that Walter the goldsmith was, by special agreement, paid 9d. for marking them.

In 1556 the Dublin Corporation Records give the following :—

> Ordained that no pewterer bringing pewter to be sold, out of England or elsewhere, being no freeman of this City, shall sell any of their pewter, till the same be brought into the Common Hall, there to be sold only in gross to Freemen of this City upon pain of forfeiture of all such wares as the *foreign pewterer* shall be found selling contrary to this order, the one half to the Spier and finder and the other half to the Treasury.

Of later references to the craft the following may be of interest :—

IRISH STATUTES, 9 WILL. III, c. XIV (1697).

An Act (of which the following is an epitome) for the redress of certain abuses in making pewter and brass.

> Whereas much pewter and brass is made, wrought and vended in this Kingdom which is not of such fine metal as ought to be, it is enacted—that Pewterers and Braziers are not to sell or change new or old pewter save in open fairs or markets or in their own public shops or houses.
> New pewter or brass vessels are to be of as good fine metal as those cast in London.
> No metal to be seized or forfeited except as is in possession of a person using the trade.
> Hollow-wares of lay metal are to be according to the assize of lay metal wrought in London.
> Makers are to have their own particular marks.
> None to use false beams or weights.
> Masters and Wardens of the Craft or expert persons appointed by magistrates of Cities, may search and seize suspected goods and apprehend the offenders.

This last paragraph, which speaks of " Masters and Wardens of the Craft," would seem rather to point to separate guilds of pewterers, but this is not supported by any of the evidence to hand and one must, it seems, rather interpret the words as referring to the

Masters and Wardens of those larger fraternities of which the pewterers and braziers were but units, as in the cases of Cork, Dublin and Youghal cited above.

The *Dublin Intelligence* of 24th January, 1713, gives the following :—

> Whereas several broakers (*sic.*), tinkers and hawkers go about from house to house in this City and Suburbs selling and exchanging new and old pewter and brass, whereby many are much imposed upon and cheated and many houses robbed of pewter and brass. This is to give notice that whosoever shall find any of the said persons either buying, selling or changing new or old brass or pewter, or any tinkers casting spoons, or giving notice to any of the pewterers that keep shops, so that the offenders may be brought to justice, shall not only have half the value of the unlawful pewter that shall be so found, but also 20s. and the poor of the parish 20s. more, for every dish, plate, porringer, tankard, quart, spoon or other piece of pewter or brass they can prove was bought, sold or changed by them as aforesaid contrary to an Act of Parliament entitled " An Act for the redress of certain abuses in making pewter and brass " (*see preceding extract*).

This Act is again referred to in *Lloyd's News Letter* for 9th, 20th and 23rd February, 1714 :—

> A warning to the Publick against counterfit Pewter which is made and sold in Cork, Limerick, Birr, Waterford, Killkenny, Galway, Lorganclinbrasil (*sic.*) and other places in this Kingdom contrary to an Act of Parliament in force in this realm since the year 1697, entitled, an Act for the redress of certain abuses in making Pewter and Brass, 9, Will III. Chap XIV.
>
> That since the commencement of the aforesaid Act, it is found by computation that there has been sold in this Kingdom as much coarse, adulterated pewter, as amounted to £20,000, which when sold again will not be worth or yield half that money, whereby it appears that the public is defrauded of more than £8,000 besides the workmanship of the said goods in so short a time, and Her Majesty has lost the sale of £20,000 worth of block-tin besides the duties inwards and outwards of the same, amounting to the sum of £2,800 at least and the said abuses are a loss to Her Majesty's revenue of at least £400 a year, and her subjects do lose about £1,000 a year by it, besides the inconveniency (*sic.*) of having ill-wrought, course (*sic.*) and unservicable goods put upon them. In regard therefore the said abuses are so prejudicial to Her Majesty and her subjects and that the same are also practised against the aforesaid Act of Parliament.
>
> This is therefore to caution all manner of persons from being for the future imposed upon ; viz :—that all pewter carried about the country from house to house, for sale by travellers, chapmen and others, may be deemed notoriously bad as aforesaid except what pewter that is sold by some persons as have or may give in good security to sell none of the said unlawful goods on any pretence whatever, contrary to the said Act ; that most of all the pewter sold by brokers and ill designing pewterers for 12d or 13d per lb., retail, is course base metal and is as great imposition on the public as it would be to sell so much counterfiet silver for sterling. That all good pewter, made of block-tin and other rich ingredients, pursuant to the Act, is sold for 14d per lb., and not under, by reason block-tin is a commodity peculiar to the Crown and a certain price fixed thereon so that no one soever can buy it under that fixed price.
>
> That all pewter which has not any sound and is soft metal without the pewterer's name stamped thereon, the same may be deemed bad pewter and seasable by the Act.
>
> That all new pewter sold by Seamen and other strangers under colour of English pewter, is suspicious and frequently seized upon for its badness.

The above extracts show that in Ireland—as in England and Scotland—much spurious alloy was used, but much of what little *known* Irish pewter has come down to our time is of very good quality, made from fine metal and possibly imported from England, for in 1744 the amount so imported-in-the-mass into Ireland was nearly *nine tons*, the actual amount paid for the same being £792 2s. 7d., at the rate of £4 10s. per hundredweight.

That this trouble concerning tinkers and spurious metal did not diminish as time went on is shown by the following extracts from the Irish *House of Commons Journal* under the dates given :—

July 27th, 1719.

> Petition of James Maculla, Edward Bloxham, James Johnston and William Hodgert, pewterers of Dublin, on the behalf of themselves and other pewterers of Ireland, to rectify abuses committed in making pewter and brass.

and November 1st, 1753.

> Petition of the manufacturers of block-tin in Ireland, stating that owing to the great importation of Rouen, Burgundy and Marseilles earthenware, the trade of the pewterers is at a standstill.

Having thus briefly reviewed the chief pewtering centres of the British Isles we pass on to a consideration, in the succeeding chapter, of Pewter-Marking.

CHAPTER II

THE HISTORY OF PEWTER-MARKING

AS TOLD IN THE RECORDS OF THE WORSHIPFUL COMPANY OF PEWTERERS OF LONDON.

THE late Mr. Charles Welch having very readily consented to my making the fullest use of his invaluable *History of the Worshipful Company of Pewterers of London* and, as any student of the subject of Pewter-marks *must* turn to these records as his starting point, I have gratefully taken him at his word and extracted therefrom, by again going carefully through the two volumes, such references as throw light on the subject of the present work.

These extracts, though extremely interesting, do not give us that full knowledge for which we seek. The earlier touchplates perished—it must be presumed—with Pewterers' Hall i₁ the great fire of 1666, for although reference is made in 1550 to a plate " with every man's mark therein " no trace of such plate is to be found, nor of the book referred to in 1663 in which every man's mark was to be registered.

In transcribing these extracts, while preserving the exact phraseology, I have, after careful thought, deemed it advisable—though robbing my readers thereby of the old-world charm which clusters around them in the original—to dispense with the early forms of spelling which would only add difficulty of reading to what must at best be a very dry chapter. The object of this book will be best served by accurately placing the facts on record in the simplest and most interesting way possible.

To those who would like to read them in their pristine quaintness I can do no better than direct them to the volumes referred to above. In one or two instances the temptation to preserve the original spelling has proved too strong to resist, but these are the exception rather than the rule.

The first mention one finds of *Official* Marks of the Company is in 1474/5 :—

Itm. Delivered a ponchon of iron with the broad arrowhead for the forfeit mark.

Here Mr. Welch very wisely remarks :—

As it was doubtless the fate of all vessels marked with this broad arrow to be forfeited and melted down without delay, it is not probable that any example so marked is now procurable as a treasured specimen by the Collector of old Pewter.

Instances are in existence which bear " a broad arrow-head," but only to earmark them as " for Government service."

The above marking iron is referred to in an inventory of the Company's possessions taken in 1489/90 as follows :—

A punchon of Iron with a broad arrowhead graven therein.

The next reference to what were probably Official marks is in 1492/3 :—

Paid for 4 new marking Irons for hollowware men 2s.

20

PLATE V

BROAD QUAY, BRISTOL, FROM A PAINTING IN BRISTOL ART GALLERY, BY PETER MONAMY (1670-1749)

Reproduced by permission of the Bristol Museum and Art Gallery Committee.

In the bottom right hand corner may be seen the shop of Richard Going, Pewterer, with his pewter-wares in the window.

No record can be discovered of the device on these irons.

In 1509/10 appears another Official mark of the Company of the use of which we have no certain knowledge (though Mr. Welch suggests it may have been used to denote fine quality as opposed to the forfeit mark of the broad arrowhead), " The strake of tin." This is one of the Charges in the Arms of the Company which are : Azure, a Chevron or between 3 strakes arg. ; upon the chevron 3 Roses gu. stalks, buds and leaves vert.

These Arms appear on the *touches* of several provincial pewterers though in no single instance on that of a London Craftsman, the granting of the use of which to individual members would have savoured of Official patronage unless accorded to all. John Townsend used these Arms in his " Silver-marks," but these silver marks had no official recognition. Presumably the country pewterers hoped to suggest by this pilfering of its Arms, some connexion with the London Company itself.

A further Official marking punch is referred to in 1548/9, and of this we are left in *no* doubt as to its intended use : —

> Paid for a marking Iron of the fleur-de-lys to mark stone pots (lids) with . . . 10d.

In an inventory of 1550 is the following :—

> Marking Irons with the badges or marks of the Craft . . . 2.

and in 1564/5 the following :—

> Paid for a hammer and chisel and mending the broad arrowhead to assay the tin 3s. 4d.

It will be remembered that in 1474/5 this same device was spoken of as " the forfeit mark."

The next mention of an Official marking Iron is in 1671/2 when, on 15 Aug. :—

> It was agreed and so ordered that from henceforth no person or persons whatsoever shall presume to strike the rose and crown with any additional flourish or the letters of his own or another's name whereby the mark which is only to be used for goods exported, may in time become as other touches and not distinguished.

Here it will perhaps not be without interest to note those regulations which refer to the using of these official marks.

At a Court held 8th June, 1552/3 :—

> It was agreed that all those that lid stone pots should set their own marks in the inside of the lid and to bring in all such stone pots into the Hall whereby they may be viewed if they be workmanly wrought and so be marked with the mark of the Hall on the outside of the lid. Also, everyone that maketh such stone pots shall make a new mark such mark as the Master and Wardens shall be pleased with, whereby they may be known from this day forward. . . .

(Here Mr. Welch notes that the Jury Book orders the maker's mark *as well as that of the craft* to be placed *outside* the lid.)

I know of no single example of a stone pot with pewter lid of English make, which has come down to our days, though continental specimens are of almost every day occurrence.

At a Court held 3rd September, 1553/4 :—

> The Master, Wardens and (court of) Assistants with the whole clothing, hath granted that John Curtys should have for marking of every dozen of stone pots, whosoever brought them to mark, one farthing.

On 14th August, 1556/7 :—

> It was agreed by the Master, Wardens and Assistants that Harry Tompson should have the view and marking of all stone pots and he should mark none but those that be substancially wrought and for his painstaking in the same he should have his house rent free until further orders were taken, beginning at Michaelmas next and so forward.

(Harry Tompson was deprived of this post on 27 November, 1558/9.)

It was ordered on 17th March, 1580/1 :—

> that none of the Company shall make any " Close stole pans " to sell to any upholsterer or any other man but that every one of the said " close stole (stool) pans " shall weigh 3 lb the piece and that the maker of the said pans shall bring every one of them before they put them to sale unto the Beadle of the Hall to have the mark of the Hall set on them and if in case any " stole pans " shall hereafter be found made and not marked with the touch of the House and of less weight than 3 lb the piece, then the maker shall pay for every pan so found . . . 12d.

It is doubtful what is referred to here as " the mark of the Hall." The " rose and crown " was in 1671, as will have been seen, the Company's mark for goods exported, there was further the " fleur-de-lys " for stone pot lids and the " Strake of tin and lilypot " of which we have no information. In all probability this mark of the Hall *was* the Tudor Rose crowned, for this seems to be regarded in the present day—certainly more by a general concensus of opinion than by any proof one can find—as *the* " Mark of the Hall."

Turning from the Official Marks of the Company ; the first reference to the private marks—or touches as they were technically called—of individuals is in 1487/8 :—

> 2 spoons of the gift of Walter Walsh and Katherine his wife *with his mark* and name on the one and on the other Saint Katherine, gilt, weighing 2½ oz.

The next reference is in an inventory of 1489/90 :—

> Of the gift of the said Robert Turnour a " stope pot " weighing 6 lbs *marked with his own mark.*

In the book of inventories under date 1550 is the following :—

> The names of them that gave napery to the Hall in the 3rd year of King Edward VIth, Jan. 1 :— First Mr. Curtys gave a plain tablecloth for the high table, a dozen of plain napkins *marked with his mark* and a towel of Cambric.

(This mark of Mr. Curtis will be found illustrated in its proper place in the present work.)

The practice of makers impressing marks upon their wares though in use many years previously is for the first time made compulsory by an Act of 19. Hen. VII, 1503/4, Cap. 6, wherein it is enacted, inter alia :—

> Also that it may by the same authority be enacted and established that no manner of person nor persons of what degree or condition soever he or they be of, shall from henceforth make no hollow-wares of pewter, that is to say Salts & Pots that is made of Pewter called lay-metal, but that it may be after the assize of pewter lay-metal wrought within the City of London ; and that the makers of such wares shall mark the same wares with the several marks of their own to the intent that the (makers) of such wares shall avow the same wares, by them as is abovesaid, to be wrought and that all and every of such wares not sufficiently made and wrought and not marked in form abovesaid, found in the possession of the same maker or seller to be forfeited.

In the year 1550 is found the first reference to a touchplate which consisted—or those now in existence do—of a plate *of pewter* some one eighth of an inch in thickness and varying somewhat in shape. Upon this plate every member of the Company after serving his apprenticeship and taking up his freedom was compelled, before setting up in business for himself, to strike the impression of that device which had been granted to him by the Court and which he was compelled, by the Act just cited, to impress upon all wares made by him in the future, " to y entent that the (makers) of such wares shall avowe the same wares by them as is above said to be wrought."

This, the earliest touchplate of which we have record, is mentioned in the inventory taken in 1550 as follows :—

A table of Pewter with every man's mark therein.

In 1667/8 was purchased the first of the existing touchplates :—

Paid for a plate to strike the touches on . . . 8s.

another was bought in 1673/4 :—

Paid for a new pewter plate to strike touches on . . . 6s. 6d.

and a further plate was acquired in 1703/4 :—

Paid John Frith for a plate to strike touches on . . . 8s. 9d.

The subject of the touchplates will be found fully dealt with in the next chapter, but these few notes therefrom seemed not entirely inappropriate here even at the risk of repetition.

The following extracts refer to those general orders of the Court concerning their control over the whole question of pewter-marking.

In the Ordinances of 1564, under the marginal note of " An order for marking of Wares and Touches " is the following :—

Also it is agreed that every one of the said fellowship that maketh any ware shall set his own mark thereon, and that no man shall give for his proper mark or touch the Rose and Crown with letters nor otherwise but only to him to whom it is given by the fellowship. Nor that no man of the said craft shall give one anothers mark neither with letters nor otherwise but everyone to give a sundry mark, such one as shall be allowed by the Master and Wardens for the time being, upon pain to forfeit and pay for every time offending to the Crafts box 13s. 4d.

On 13th December, 1574/5, it was

ordered that from henceforth for evermore none of the Company shall cast any metal into strakes whereby to utter or put them to sale, before and until such time as the workman or owner thereof hath caused them to be searched and seen as other wares usually are, and over that, for their better and true trial of workmanship, the owner or worker of such strakes to set and fix upon every strake so to be cast, his proper mark or else to forfeit and pay for every pound weight wrought or cast to the contrary, one penny.

On 20th March, 1592/3, it was

Ordered that all the Company shall set their touches upon a new plate and that they shall pay 2d. apiece and one penny to the Clerk and another to the beadle.

Owing to wares having been made deficient in weight from the standard, it was ordered on 7th March, 1612/3 :—

That everyman's old touch shall be presently brought to the Hall and new touches with difference thereto be struck to the purpose aforesaid, and which to be done before the 13th day of this month.

Several makers of " lay " were on 10th Nov. 1613/4 found guilty of adulterating their metal and were ordered to bring their touches to the Hall and there to strike a new touch marked with this year of 1614 that it may be known who were the offenders therein.

30th March, 1618 :—

Memorandum, that whereas the laymen have this day altered their touches. . . .

A further charter was obtained in 1637/8, among the new clauses in which is the following :—

3rdly. That all makers of pewter vessels of any kind shall set his peculiar mark or touch upon the same for the avoiding of abuses, as is used within the City of London.

At a general Court held 22nd February, 1648/9, the following head of a petition was—*inter alia*—submitted and adopted :—

That all measures for liquid commodities may be made of such metal or stuff as will take the fair impression of a seal.

On 11th December, 1661/2, it was

Ordered by the Court that all lay men do alter their touches within fourteen days with the date of 1663.

And on 17th December, 1662/3, it was

Ordered by a general Court that *all* touches be made with the date 1663 and that they be registered in a book at the Hall within a month.

(Mr. Welch says this book cannot be found.)

On 19th December, 1666/7, it was

Ordered that every spoon maker shall alter his touch immediately after Christmas next from which time all spoons shall be made exactly to the assay.

The Court on 19th March 1673/4 considered a complaint against divers persons of the Mystery for laying aside their old touches which the Company had Cognizance of and instead thereof use other new ones without leave from the Company. It was ordered that all new touches be struck on the plate at the Hall before the next Court.

On 13th December, 1676 :—

It was ordered that no one should put the word LONDON on his touch.

Upon reading the XVIIth Ordinance to the Court on 20th June 1688/9 Mr. Stone and others complained of the frequent breach of that ordinance in striking other touches on their ware than they struck upon the Company's plate and instanced in Mr. Hancock, Mr. Taylor Mr. Bridges, Mr. Nicholls.

(The variants of the touches of Mr. Nicholls and Mr. Taylor, complained of above, will be found illustrated in Chapter VI under their respective owners' names.)

On 19th December, 1688/9 :—

Thomas Taylor was admonished for striking on his ware the place of his abode, being so much more than he struck or registered upon the Hall Plate. (*See* Chap. VI).

It was ordered on 14th August, 1689/90 :—

That Mr. Sands alter his Rose and Crown stamp by taking out the place of his abode.

Complaint was made to the Court on 19th Nov. 1690/1 against Samuel Hancock for Striking his name at length upon his trencher plates and at each end thereof is struck his own touch and the Rose and Crown, and for striking the letter X upon *ordinary* ware, which is a mark generally used by the Mystery to distinguish *extraordinary* ware.

This seems to be the earliest reference which throws light on this mark so familiar to all lovers of pewter. It is passing strange that some more definite information should not be given to us.   On the European Continent it implied an alloy of tin and lead in the proportion of ten to one.

The next four extracts show such an unstable frame of mind on the part of the Officials of the Company as to foreshadow therein the seeds of that lack of control over its members so soon to make itself manifest and which eventually, coupled with the discontinuance of their country searches, robbed the Company of all its pristine usefulness.

On 17th December, 1690/1 :—

It was ordered that no member of the Mystery shall strike any other mark upon his ware than his touch or mark struck upon the plate at the Hall and the Rose and Crown stamp and also the letter X upon extraordinary ware.   Yet nevertheless that any member may add the word LONDON to the Rose and Crown stamp or in his touch.   The question being put whether any member may have liberty to strike his name at length upon hard metal or extraordinary ware, *it passed in the negative*.

On 12th October, 1692/3 :—

At a Court held this day it was resolved " Such as have not their names *within the compass of their touches were allowed to put them at length within the same.*

On 24th April, 1693/4 :—

The committee debating the matter of persons striking their names at length upon their wares within or besides their touches or mark struck on the Hall plate, are of opinion that the practice of striking the worker's or maker's name at length within or besides their touches registered or struck at the Hall is against the general good of the Company and that all such persons as have set their names at length within their touches now in use shall alter their several marks or touches by leaving out their name and register and strike at the Hall their respective new or altered touches *without any persons name* therein.

On 11th August, 1697/8 :—

It was ordered that none should strike any other mark upon ware than his own proper touch and the Rose and Crown stamp ;   that any man may strike his name at length *between* his touch and the Rose and Crown, also the word LONDON.   None may strike the letter X except upon extraordinary ware, commonly called hard metal ware.

Small wonder that from this time onward members began to act, each according to his own impulse !

On 11th March, 1702/3.   It was

ordered that from henceforth all candlemoulds shall be made of pewter perfectly fine, and that the maker thereof shall mark every such mould that he shall make with his own proper mark or touch.

Complaint was *again* made[1] on 10th Oct. 1705/6 " against country pewterers for striking LONDON on their wares."

On 21st March, 1733/4 :—

Resolved that all pewter wares *ought*[2] to be touched before they go out of the hammerman's hand.

24th September, 1740/1 :—

A committee reported that nothing could be done to prevent country pewterers from striking LONDON or MADE IN LONDON on their ware, without application to parliament.

[1] The italics are mine, I can find no trace of the previous complaint.
[2] Again the italics are mine.   Time ago the word would assuredly have been *shall* or *must*.

13th March, 1746/7.   A committee

reported upon touches and the following bye-law based upon their recommendation was passed on 25th June :—That all wares capable of a large touch shall be touched with a large touch with Christian name and surname either of the maker or vendor at full length in plain Roman letters, and small wares shall be touched with the small touch (with a penalty of one penny per pound for default).

The last general resolution concerning pewter-marking is on 15th March, 1759, when it was

Ordered that all candle-moulds shall be made of fine metal for the future and that all worse than plate (or fine) or shall want the initial letters of the maker's name on the head of the mould, shall be brought to the Hall to be defaced. (*See* the previous order above in 1702/3.)

That the Company in earlier years exercised a rigid control over its members is evident on almost every page of Mr. Welch's work, and those references which bear on the subject of the marking of pewter, including fines for untouched or faulty wares, alterations and additions to marks as marks of disgrace, the regulation of a choice of device by individual makers, etc., etc., form the subject of practically the whole of the remaining part of the present chapter.

FINES :—

1526/7.   Received for a fine for salts unmarked . . . 12d.
Received of William Aprise for a fine for delivering vessels unmarked with his touch according to the ordinance . . . 5s.
6 Dec. 1554/5.   Fines for naughty workmanship and not touching their ware
> William Readman 6 bow potts . . . 6d.
> Hugh Wadelow. 2 Collecks . . . 2d.
> (& sixteen others.)

1557/8.   Taken as a fine at Sturbridg fair (Cambs) of Harry Ractlyf (for) a 3lb platter not marked . . . 3d.
1565.   Received the 23rd Day of March for untouched ware . . . 2s.
Received the 17th day of June for untouched ware 3s. 3d.
1595/6.   Received of Thomas and Richard Steventon, a fine for selling 2 cwt 22 lbs of tavern pots unto Henry Cotton untouched, the same suspected to be less than measure . . . 20s.
1615/6.   At a search day the 12th Aug., among various fines was 4d. for two antique candlesticks untouched.
1629/30, 19 Aug.   Nicholas Wright for a cistern of fine (metal) being 54 lbs weight, untouched, was fined . . . 12d.
1653/4, 16 Feb.   Lawrence Dyer for untouched ware and making of false plate called silvorum, the which ware is seized and detained by the Company.
1660/1, 8th Aug.   Mr. Aileffe was ordered to pay 4s. for his worme (probably the worm of a still) not being touched.
1667/8.   John Skinn was fined 1s. (26th Sept.) for neglecting to put his touch on both parts of a pair of cranes.
1722/3, 8th Aug.   Six ordinary plates of Francis Whittle, on which he had impressed the words SUPERFINE HARD METAL were ordered to be defaced and broken.

MARKS OF DISGRACE ADDED TO TOUCHES :—

1556/7, 21st Oct.   At a Court held this day there was a new mark devised by the Master, Wardens & Assistants, for Robert West, which was a W.f. and he denied it and would not have it.

(Robert West had been " sent to the Warde " on the 5th May " for making of false measure pots " and later, on 14th June was " Quyte dismissed out from the occupying the Crafte and Mistery of Pewterers. . . .")

Apparently, however, he was forgiven, for on 31st March, 1558/9, he is

> ordered to bring in his wife upon Friday next to reconcile herself to Mr. Cacher and others for her naughty mysdemeanor of her tonge towards them.

> 1566/7, 14th May. James Taverner was called before the Court for that he hath falsely and deceitfully wrought the knops of 26 Stills and filled the same knops with lead contrary to the true order of making them. . . . And for the trespass that he now hath done his mark is taken from him which heretofore was admitted him and that he now shall have a mark with a double ff for that this is not the first time that he hath trespassed in the Company.

(This mark of " f " may have stood for " fined for falsehood [or faulty work]," and the double " ff " would seem from the above to be used for more than one offence.)

A further—and the only other recorded instance of its use is found on 15th July, 1595/6, when at a Court held this day :—

> Humfry Weetwood having been found in confederacy with Thomas Cowes to make ear-dishes, beakers and " godderdes of gobbetes " of false metal, 4 grains worse than lay, the which wares have been sold unto the country not only unto the discredit of us all, workmen in London, but also a great wrong and loss to those which shall hereafter melt those again. Touching forfeiture of those dishes we leave them to the Queen and the taker and Humfry Weetwood and Thomas Cowes to make satisfaction unto the pewterers in the country which bought them of either of them. And further, they being punished by imprisonment, we further order that Humfry Weetwood shall submit himself unto all the Company and confess his fault and to desire to think of him and to accept of him again as a brother of the Company which he did in the presence of the whole Company, being further enjoined to bring in his touch and that for knowledge hereafter of his falsehood he shall have for his touch a double ff, and also that he shall put in sureties for his true and honest dealing in his trade.

> 1655/6, 11th Sept. Mr. Cox to have such a touch as the Company shall order with R & C and a knot about it and 1656.

>> Mr. Welch remarks : " Some bad ware was seized from this maker for which he was ordered to take a new touch and was probably the Ralph Cox described as a prisoner in the call-list for this year."

> On the same day. Mr. Goudge to make his touch R.G. with a knot about it and 1656.

The following are instances of the enforced alteration of touches without any particular mark of disgrace being specified :—

> 1575/6, 27th June. Henry Langshawe is found faulty for that he hath made certain lay pots with false metal and thereupon should have been committed to ward. Nevertheless because of his humble submission they have ordered, if at any time he be found to do the like falsehood again to be banished the Company for ever. And also to new alter his touch which he now hath. To which agreement he hath put his hand.

> 1606/7, 6th July. Dudley, Keersey and Dawes, being partners, have made lay worse than assay 17 grains and they are fined to pay for it 40s. that is to say 13s. 4d. a piece and that they shall alter their touch and set the year of our Lord upon the touch.

The extracts which follow are indicative of the power wielded by the Company over the marks of its individual members :—

> 1565/6. At a court held on 8th May. For a matter in variance between Peter Kilborne and Richard Warde for the touch of the hammer and the crown which of them should use it, it shall be determined the next Court day.

At the next Court, 17th June. It was agreed that Richard Warde should give the touch of the hammer and the crown for that his wife sometime the wife of William Hartwell, did give the same before, and that the said Richard Warde shall give unto Peter Kilborne towards the graving of a new touch . . . 12d.

1569/70, 16th March. It was agreed that Hugh Colyer's Rose and Crown shall be made lesser as Mr. Haiselles is because none hath so great but the Queen's majesty.

1617/8, 19th March. Ordered that Mr. Brocklesby and Mr. Thomas Smithers shall forthwith amend and make perfect their marks.

(Both were members of the Court of Assistants.)

1617/8, 10th Dec. Mr. Peter Brocklesby was ordered forth-with to bring in one of his marks, no member of the Company being allowed to have more than one mark,

1622/3, 29th May. Walter Ricroft giving for his mark three ears of corn is now ordered to make the same one ear and letters.

1622/3, 3rd July. Thomas Hall maketh request to the Court that he may use or strike Mr. Sheppard's touch which was granted.

1622/3, 24th July. The same touch was this day granted to John Netherwood in regard that Thomas Hall hath left it off.

1655/6, 9th Oct. Clement Wastell desired the court that they would be pleased to let him strike a small touch with C.W. for his small salts. The Court gave him to answer, could not allow of but one touch but further did give consent that (he) should make his small touch in the same form as his other and the same to the Hall to be brought and there left.

1667/8, 18th June. Will Jones complained against Towden (Taudin) for making distinction between fine and double refine and that his customers as well as others may know his fine by his single touch and his double refine by his double touch. Mr. Towden replied that the reason why he made such distinction was for that he gave servants double wages for that which he called double refined. The Court acquainted him that the statute made no other distinction of Pewter than fine and lay and charged him to desist in his aforesaid practice.

1683/4, 20th March. John Skyn complained against Thos Porter for striking upon his ware part of his touch. Ordered by consent of parties that the said Porter shall strike the "Angel and glister serreng."

(*Note.* I am indebted to Mr. Malcolm Bell, author of *Old Pewter*, for elucidating this mysterious touch. It refers to the "Angel and Clyster syringe" (*see* No. 3730, Chap. VI.)

1687/8, 17th July. Theophilus Redding who formerly was admitted to strike a touch of three tulips, now desired to have liberty to strike a new touch which was allowed him upon his promise to take no advantage or make any complaint of any other man for striking the former touch. (*See* No. 3867, Chap. VI., where both touches are illustrated.)

1693/4. Among goods seized by the Clerk on 26th Sept. from Wm. Barton were one "Betty Pot" marked T.C. and two wine quarts deep lipped of Anthony Redhead's make and stamped on the lid with the sign of the swan.

1709/10, 12th Oct. Leave is granted to Thomas Peisley to strike a large touch notwithstanding he hath already struck upon the Hall plate a small touch with two letters only. (*See* No. 3598, Chap. VI.)

1712/3, 13th Aug. At a Court on this day, John Walmsley of Gainsborough asked permission to strike for his touch the Lion rampant with a crown over the head. Ordered—29th Oct.— that he may strike the hart and crown (*see* No. 4938, Chap. VI.) but not the word LONDON. This affords an interesting instance of the admission of country Members, *without* leave to use the word LONDON.

1725/6, Sept. John Blenman had leave to strike his touch the same as was used by Abraham Ford who has left off his trade and who consented thereto. (*See* Nos. 453 and 1714, Chap. VI.)

1747/8, 13th Oct. Ordered that Thomas Burford and James Green be at liberty to strike their touches together upon producing their copies of their Freedoms to the Master or the Clerk. (*See* No. 698, Chap. VI.)

1749/50, 13th Dec. Ordered that Charles Puckle Maxey be at Liberty to strike his touch of the pelican and globe instead of the touch late James King's. (*See* No. 3149, Chap. VI.)

The following three notes record all that one is able to glean on the much discussed subject of imitation " Hall-marks "

1635/6, 17th March. The order from the Lord Mayor and Court of Aldermen concerning the striking of the marks proper to the goldsmiths was read and ordered to be observed.

1681/2, 10th Aug. John Blackwell was charged with selling trencher plates without any other mark than the silver marks and was fined . . . 20s.

1754, 14th Nov. Ordered that Messrs. Bourchier and Richard Cleeve be permitted to dispose of twelve dozen of scalloped raised brim plates and dishes in proportion without any other touch than their silver touch.

There remains in the present chapter but to note those items which refer to " leave to open shop " :—

1576/7, 27th Feb. Received of William Steven for licence to open shop and for occupying another man's touch . . . 3s. 4d.
                    (Presumably the other man was dead or retired.)

1659/60, 9th July. Henry Pauling paid opening and struck his touch 3s. 4d. If complaint be made of his touch being the anchor and rose, he promiseth to alter it.

1666/7, 10th Oct. James Taylor, driving a trade of himself and using of his mother's touch, referred himself to the Court (and was leniently dealt with).

1685/6, 14th Jan. Ordered that every man before being admitted to his mark, do bring a piece of proof work.

1726/7, 10th Aug. Edward Bradstreet in Shugg Lane, Piccadilly, struck his touch . . . 6s. 8d. (*See* No. 551, Chap. VI.)

1758, 16th March. Ordered that William Fasson be admitted to strike his touch *so soon as he hath taken up his freedom of the City and not before.* (*See* No. 1639, Chap. VI.)

It cannot be said that the foregoing extracts in any way satisfy one's craving for knowledge, but read in conjunction with the succeeding chapter, I trust they will be found to throw interesting light and some fresh knowledge on the subject of pewter marks, which it seems almost unnecessary to add were *always* impressed, *never* engraved. There is *no* exception to this rule.

Before passing on it may be well to call attention here to the loose method of spelling which is met with in all old documents and which causes so much trouble to the student. It is by no means uncommon in the records of the Pewterers' Company to find the same man's name spelt differently in the Yeomanry and Livery lists, and again in his touch, but when one recalls the fact that everything was spelt, often by illiterate scribes, according to its sound, the marvel is that the result is no worse, and this note is inserted merely to enforce the fact that too much reliance cannot be placed on the actual spelling of a name. The safest guide is the spelling in the touch itself.

CHAPTER III

THE OLD PEWTERERS AND THEIR TOUCHPLATES

HAVING read in the previous chapter what the records have to tell us of the marks (or touches), as used by the pewterers, we now turn to some consideration of the users of such marks—the pewterers themselves—and the plates at the Hall on which the marks were impressed.

A correct understanding of the various grades in the Company is essential to a true interpretation of these touchplates, and the sweeping away of certain erroneous impressions which have obtained up to the present.

The chief of these, a clear definition of the term FREEMAN and the question of the chronological order of the touches on the touchplates are the objects aimed at in the present chapter.

Mr. Antonio de Navarro, F.S.A.—a name revered by all lovers of old pewter—in the Preface to his *Causeries on English Pewter*, says :

> On the subject itself, there is nothing new it would seem, to communicate, nothing new to discover, unless it be some Rosetta Stone that would establish the Chronology of the Pewterer's touches.

One cannot, of course, *ever* prove that touches dated 1642 and 1645 followed by one dated 1620 are *in* chronological order but if one can give a valid reason for such an irregular order of dates and prove that they were *struck* in chronological order, then I think it will be admitted that any suggestion that the touches were punched more or less where the owner wished to put them and the blank spaces filled up subsequently with other touches and of other years, apart from being a great reflection on those Officers of the Company who had the regulating of these matters, is so utterly improbable as to need but little contradiction, for one cannot believe that any Company, ranking so high among the City Companies as did the Pewterers', would have been lax enough to permit anything of so haphazard a nature.

The clearing up of the other point is necessary because one finds in other works on the subject, in giving the " List of Freemen," the names only of the Livery are included. Certainly the Livery were Freemen, but if the list is intended to be complete, *it certainly is not. No list of Freemen which excludes the Yeomanry can be so.*

More glaringly wrong than the above is the following :

" L. means took up his *Freedom, i.e.* joined the Livery."

That is precisely what it does *not* mean. Freedom and Livery are, and always were, two totally distinct and different grades.

We will consider this latter point first, for upon that hangs the question of chronology ; and here let it be said that these corrections are made in no carping spirit but in order

32

that *where so much is uncertain*, we may at least interpret rightly that of which there can be no possible doubt.

Let us try to follow the budding pewterer from the moment he or his parents decide that such shall be his occupation, until the time when he sets up in business for himself and rises to the Livery and then we can cast a passing glance towards those high offices in the Company which will open out before him.

Some contemporary light is thrown upon the apprentices' position in *A general description of all Trades*, London, 1747. Printed by T. Waller at the Crown and Mitre, opposite Fetter Lane, Fleet Street, where in speaking of Pewterers it gives the following :—

> Making of Pewter consists chiefly of two parts:—1. Melting, casting and turning which is one person's business, the harder work and not so healthy. 2. Hammering or planishing, which is another's, one workman but seldom doing all the operations.
>
> It is an ancient useful trade, most of them are large shop keepers and very considerable dealers which and the planishing part is reckoned a very pretty employ for a smart youth, with whom must be given as an apprentice not less than £20, whose working hours are from six to eight at which a journeyman can get 15, 18 or 20s. a week ; and it requires £500 to set one up handsomely . . .

Having made his decision to become a pewterer, the lad looks about for some master craftsman willing to take him as an apprentice. Such an one having been found he is duly bound for a period of seven or more years, indeed on the 27th September, 1555, an Act of Common Council provided :

> That no person should be admitted to the Freedom of the City before reaching the age of twenty four, nor were apprentices to be taken for fewer years than such as would bring them to that age on coming out of their time.

During his apprenticeship he lived with his master and was bound to accompany him to Church on Sunday and Holy Days both morning and afternoon and generally was subject to the strictest discipline.

Several instances are in the records of women becoming free and the following of a girl being bound apprentice.

> 1713/4, 13th April. A girl named Lucy Sellars was bound at the Hall in the ordinary course as an apprentice for seven years to Elizabeth Read, widow of Samuel Read.

His term of apprenticeship being duly completed and before he was permitted to set up in business for himself even if in a position to do so, he had to become a Freeman of the Company.

The Freeman's oath is given in Mr. Welch's *History*, i. 30 and 31, and " from an entry under date of 10th November, 1672/3, it appears that new Freemen on their admission were accustomed to take the Freeman's oath kneeling." *Ibid.*, ii. 145.

That Freedom does *not* mean " joined the Livery " is proved, if proof be needed, by the following :—

The names in the existing *Yeomanry* lists at the Hall of the Worshipful Company of Pewterers of London are entered as follows :—

" Ackland, Thomas, *Admitted to Freedom* 11th August, 1720," and so on right through its pages. This said Thomas Ackland did not take Livery until 5th July, 1728, some *eight years after his freedom.*

Also in 1456/7. The roll of the members of the Company in this year's account and that of the following year, contains three divisions :

1. The brethren that pay quarterage. *These are the Livery or Clothing.*
2. Them that be no brethren and pay quarterage. *These are the Freemen or Yeomanry* who had obtained licence to set up in business or open shop for themselves.
3. Covenantmen and Apprentices.

(Welch, i. 20.)

That these covenantmen or journeymen *were Freemen* is proved by the following :

1495/6. At this time they (the Yeomanry or Freemen) appear to have consisted of *all the members of the Company who were not brethren,* Liverymen, Masters or " of the clothing " as the senior members of the Craft were variously called. Between this class and that of the apprentices, the Yeomanry (who were also known as Freemen or Bachelors) occupied a middle place, they were members of the larger body and shared all the privileges which this involved, attended the annual election ceremonies and festival as well as the quarterly assemblies of the Company. They were probably also consulted with the rest of the Fellowship by the Master and Wardens on occasions of special emergency when matters affecting the interests of the trade were being considered. They included the smaller masters and journeymen and their ranks were constantly reinforced by the apprentices who completed the term of their indentures and were admitted to Freedom. On the other hand the Senior Freemen were from time to time summoned to the ranks of the Livery, so that the number of the Yeomanry or Freemen remained pretty constant. .... (Welch, i. 79 and 80.)

From the above it will be seen that the apprentice's next step on completing his indentures was " Freedom," and before attaining to the Livery he had to strike his touch and open shop, for *the Livery were elected only from among those freemen* who had shaken off the fetters of servitude and opened shop and become of some importance in the Company. If he was not immediately in a position to " open shop " for himself, still, he had to take his Freedom before he could even work as a journeyman to another shopkeeper for none but Freemen and apprentices were allowed to work at the trade (Welch, ii. 195), *see also* (Welch, ii. 124), when Towden was ordered to employ only Freemen as journeymen. He might go on working as a journeyman for years before being in a position to strike his touch and open shop, *hence the reason so many touches were struck long after the date when their owners took up their Freedom,* but it was incumbent on them to have done so before being elected to the Livery, except in the cases of public men whom the Company occasionally " delighted to honour," but who, beyond being members of the Company had no interest in the trade.

As evidence that a man was not even allowed to set up in business until the Company felt he had some means of keeping it up successfully, one may cite the following :—

1557/8, 30 Dec. At a Court held this day it was agreed by the Master Wardens and Assistants and the whole Livery that the Master and Wardens shall not licence any to open shop unto such time as the person that cometh out of his years do come before the Master, Wardens and Assistants and bring his Master with him to make report of his behaviour, substance and what workman he is, so that he may be known whether he be worthy to set up or not. (Welch, i. 198.)

Similar orders were passed in 1558/9 and 1564.

1567/8. Gabriel Spencer is licensed to open shop the 12th day of February 1567 and hath paid therefor 3s. 4d. His master Robert Hustwaith hath made report of his substance 20 Marks (£13 6s. 8d.).

So thirteen pounds, six shillings and eightpence was considered sufficient for a man to strike his touch and open shop, but to be on the Livery one had, according to an order of the Court of Aldermen of the City of London in 1698/9, to be worth £500, this being the amount fixed for the status of Liverymen of the smaller companies at that time. The amount had previously varied from £200 upwards.

I trust no further proof is necessary of the fact that a man must have struck his mark and set up in business and made money thereat before he could aspire to the honour of being " summoned to the Livery." THEREFORE THE QUESTION OF THE CHRONOLOGICAL ORDER OF THE TOUCHES DEPENDS ON THE FACT THAT A MAN MUST HAVE STRUCK HIS TOUCH BETWEEN THE TIME OF TAKING OF HIS FREEDOM AND THAT OF BEING ELECTED TO THE LIVERY AND MUST BE JUDGED FROM THIS VIEWPOINT ALONE.

Our apprentice then has completed his indentures and, as has been shown above, must have taken his Freedom as the next step before he could proceed further, either as a journeyman or start in business for himself. Let us presume that through financial disability to do otherwise he works for a period of ten years as a journeyman, meanwhile saving all he can towards that day when he hopes to open his own shop.

Such day having arrived he makes application to the Court for a touch and for leave to strike it on the Hall plate in order that thereon may remain for all time the impress of the mark whereby the goods which he is to make in his own name are to be known and identified.

Before this leave was granted, as will have been seen in the order of 1557/8, he had to appear before the Court with the master for whom he had but recently been working, and not only to satisfy them of his behaviour, substance and working ability, but as further proof of the last he had to produce for their satisfaction an " essay " or " test " piece so that they with their own eyes could judge of his workmanship.

On the 4th August, 1558/9 each applicant for leave to strike his touch and open shop had to bring

> a sample of his work and so to be seen, viewed and adjudged by the Master, Wardens and Assistance.

Again on the 16th March, 1619/20,

> It was ordered that no one should set up as a workman before submitting a proof piece of his own making to be examined by the Master Wardens and Assistance.

And on the 14th January, 1685/6, it was

> Ordered that every man before being admitted to his mark, do bring a piece of proof work.

A touch would of course have been quite useless to a journeyman because he would have to strike his master's touch on all wares made for his master in exactly the same way as workmen to-day have to use the trade devices and marks of the firm for whom they work. That this was so may be gathered from the following :—

On 20th December, 1602/3,

> It was found that John Frethrene, being a journeyman as the Company judged, yet he hath been a chapman in secret and *bought and sold as a householder* (or master man) *and that contrary to order hath not presented his touch nor asked leave to open shop*, the court judgeth that he shall pay for his quarterage and search money due, 8s. and 3s. 4d. for opening his shop and 5s. for his fine, the which money amounting unto (about) 17s. the said John Frethrene promiseth to pay before

Candlemas next, witnesseth his own hand. The Court considering his poverty receiveth 10s. in full payment of the whole.

Thus a man was *not allowed to have a touch as a Journeyman* and immediately the Company found the above mentioned John Frethrene, although outwardly a journeyman, was carrying on a trade as a master-man in secret, they arraigned him and forced him to enter that grade higher than a journeyman which he had endeavoured to occupy without its attendant expense and responsibilities.

This brings us to the lowest grade in the Company who were allowed to strike a touch, namely those pewterers who, after obtaining Freedom, felt that they could command sufficient capital and support to warrant them in applying for leave to strike their touches and so open shop for themselves.

There are very many names in the Yeomanry lists for whom no touches can be found upon the Hall plates. These it must be presumed are those of pewterers who from lack of means or the desire to do otherwise, *worked as Journeymen all their lives*, for there would be many more journeymen than masters.

On 13th October, 1747/8, it was

Ordered that Thomas Burford and James Green be at liberty to strike their touches upon producing their copies of their Freedoms to the Master or the Clerk.

And on 16th March, 1758, it was

Ordered that William Fasson be admitted to strike his touch so soon as he hath taken up his Freedom of the City *and not before.*

We will now assume that the applicant's essay piece has been found satisfactory and leave granted to select (subject to the Court's approval) a device for his mark and to strike the same on the touchplate and set up in business for himself as a fully fledged pewterer.

From this point he can but look ahead with longing eyes to the dignified positions of Livery, Stewardship, Court of Assistants, Renter-Warden, Upper-Warden and finally the Mastership of the Company as the highest honour the Company of itself could give, and even pass on, as several of its members had, to the Lord Mayoralty of the City and the Accolade. Here we may leave the erstwhile apprentice gazing on and resolving to achieve some if not all of these honourable positions.

In later years when the Company had but perhaps one fifth of its members who were actually following the trade—as for instance in 1792, in the printed list of the London Livery, when out of 77 members of the Company only 19 were described as pewterers—it was not uncommon for a man to be elected to the Yeomanry and the Livery on the same day, but this, generally speaking, applies to that decadent period which has little interest and is therefore irrelevant to the subject at issue.

One instance alone is in the records of a man being admitted to his touch before taking Freedom :—

On the 17th May 1654/5 William Pettiver, apprenticed to Oliver Roberts is not to be made free till next Court, but to have leave to strike Mr. Barnard's touch in the meantime. (Welch, ii. 119.)

This special permission proves it to have been an exception.

One can but imagine that the deferring of his Freedom was in the nature of a punishment.

The existing Yeomanry list at Pewterers' Hall dates back to c. 1687, and that of the Livery to c. 1451.

At this point and with the proven fact as our guide, that *touches had to be struck after Freedom and before Livery*, we turn to the consideration of the Touchplates and the marks struck upon them.

.   .   .   .

As will have been seen from the preceding chapter the practice of the marking of Pewter had obtained from very early times, and these marks occupy a position in regard thereto, almost as important as, and somewhat analogous to that occupied by the Hallmarks to the work of the silversmiths.   They are our principal means of identifying specimens and were, from the beginning of the sixteenth century, struck by the owner on commencing business, upon plates kept for the purpose at the Halls of the various guilds of Hammermen or Pewterers.

These plates, touchplates, counterpanes or counterpaynes as they were variously styled, provided a permanent record of each man's mark, whereby wares bearing a particular touch might be traced back to the maker in case of faulty workmanship or the use of inferior metal.   Their use was intended as a guarantee that the pieces were " workmanly wrought " and though this often proved not to be the case, it is no argument against the principle intended.

From time to time all members were—as will have been seen in Chapter II—ordered to strike a new touch upon their wares, but failing such order all members were to strike upon their wares the touch originally struck by them upon the plate at the Hall *and no other*.

There are fortunately preserved to this day five of the London touchplates and two of those used by the Hammermen Incorporation of Edinburgh.   That they were in use in York too is shown by the Ordinances of the Guild of Pewterers of that City wherein they were ordered in 1540 to stamp their marks upon a " counterpayne."   Of such York touchplates—as also the earlier ones of the London and Edinburgh Guilds—no trace is left to us beyond the record of their having existed.

The earliest mention of a London touchplate is in 1549 where the following appears :
" A table of Pewter with every man's mark therein "—but that there was at least one earlier seems certain for the striking of touches was made compulsory in 1503/4, which would of itself necessitate some record being kept.   A later one is mentioned in 1592, when it was ordered that " All the Company shall set their touches on a new plate."

As with the earlier touchplates, so with any written evidence which may have existed, all seem to have perished in the terrible fire of 1666 when Pewterers' Hall was destroyed.

Those still in existence date back beyond the time of this awful visitation for the reason that many of the old touches, some bearing earlier dates, were restruck on a new plate after the fire, as will presently be explained.   Their range covers partially the period from c. 1635-1666 and wholly the period 1666—c. 1823, at about which latter date the last touch was struck (prior to that of Mr. Englefield, which was struck in 1913), a silent witness to the gradual decay of what at one time was a most important industry.

Of the five existing London Touchplates the earliest was purchased after the fire in 1668.

Paid for a plate to strike the touches on . . . 8s. (Welch, ii. 137.)

This in all probability was not brought into use until circa 1670, when the Hall had been rebuilt and things began to resume their normal aspect again.

The second plate was purchased in 1674.

> Paid for a new pewter plate to strike touches on . . . 6s. 6d.   (Welch, ii. 150.)

This plate, which did not come into use until c. 1680, was certainly purchased in good time, perhaps in view of the rapid manner in which the earlier plate just mentioned was being filled up, owing to the older members restriking thereon their touches which had formerly been struck on the last of the missing plates.   Further comment on this point will be made later.

The third touchplate was bought in 1704.

> Paid John Frith for a plate to strike touches on . . . 8s. 9d.   (Welch, ii. 174.)

This plate, it would seem, came into use in the same year in which it was purchased.

Of the acquisition of the fourth and last plates we have nothing in the records to guide us.

The periods covered by the touches on these five plates, covering nearly three centuries may be put down roughly as follows :—

1st   from circa 1635 to circa 1680 (Touches   1- 351)
2nd   from circa 1680 to circa 1704 (Touches 352- 614)
3rd   from circa 1704 to circa 1734 (Touches 615- 849)
4th   from circa 1734 to circa 1800 (Touches 850-1069)
5th   from circa 1799 to circa 1823 (Touches 1070-1090, with that of the late W. J.
Englefield, struck in 1913)

First Mr. Welch in his *History* of the Company, then Mr. Massé in his *Pewter Plate* (First Edition), and finally Mr. Markham in his *Pewter Marks and old Pewter Ware*, reversed the order of the third and fourth touchplates, and perhaps herein may be divined the commencement of the theory of the bad chronological order of the touches.   Mr. Massé corrected this error in his Second Edition of *Pewter Plate*.

The two Edinburgh touchplates or counterpaynes, like those of the London Company, are of pewter ; all but the last two touches being stamped on the earlier one.

The first undated touches are evidently earlier than 1600 which is the year in the first *dated* mark.

The periods covered by these two plates are :

1. End of sixteenth century to circa 1749.
2. From circa 1749 to circa 1760.

So far as is at present known these and the five London ones are the only existing British Touchplates and all are illustrated in the present work ; in facsimile.

That others were used at York has been shown above and for all we know to the contrary there may have been some in connexion with the Bristol Guild of Pewterers and the various Guilds of Smiths and Goldsmiths in Ireland with which the pewterers were allied, as also with the Incorporation of Hammermen of the Cannongate, Glasgow, Perth, Aberdeen, Dundee, Stirling, St. Andrews, etc., etc.

The London makers combined every conceivable device and design in their touches and it is impossible to ascribe a definite date to any particular shape or design.   In the earlier ones, usually small, the mark was contained by a plain or beaded oval or circle, later, palm branches crept in at the sides as additional ornament or filling-in matter.

These in turn were to some extent supplanted by touches with pillars at the sides and straight or arched tops, while later still every conceivable shape came into use.

It is quite impossible to limit these varying designs to any stated period, but it is safe to say that the touches with pillars at the sides made their appearance in the first decade of the eighteenth century. Each of the other forms appears in bewildering variety throughout almost the whole period, although the palm branches dwindled to such diminutive proportions as to be hardly recognisable as such.

The variety of the devices exceeded that of the shapes containing them and can best be gauged by reference to the alphabetical index to the former contained in this work.

Among these devices is one type which has been of great assistance in giving the clue as to ownership, when only the initials of the maker were included. The type referred to is that where the maker's name is hinted at by a punning device or rebus.

Turning to known marks of this kind one realises how fond the pewterers were of adopting it, *e.g.* Henry Adams, who used for device " Adam and Eve in the garden "; the family of Bacon, who used " A pig "; James Bishop, whose touch represents " a Bishop with Mitre, etc "; John Belson, who used " a bell over a sun "; Robert Borman, who used " a boar's head "; George Rooke, who used a " rook "; Henry Napton, " Neptune "; Edward Trahern, " Three Herons "; John Trout, who used a " trout "; Thomas Buttery, who used a " Butterfly "; Thomas Gosling, a " gosling "; etc., etc.

The designs of the Edinburgh touches were far more uniform than those on the London touchplates, for from the end of the sixteenth to the middle of the eighteenth century they took for the most part the form of the triple-towered castle of Edinburgh with the maker's initials and sometimes the date, and it was not until the latter half of the eighteenth century that they seem to have adopted a type of touch more in accordance with those used by their London brethren, such as a rose and crown (*see* Fleming) and a bird on a globe (*see* Kinniburgh, Hunter, etc.).

And now I must endeavour to unburden myself of the task of throwing light on the chronology of the London touchplates.

First then let me state boldly at the outset that with the exception of the first 140 or 150 touches on Plate I—of which I will speak immediately—there are not twenty out of the remaining nine hundred and fifty touches which lend colour to any such theory that makers were allowed to strike their touches where they liked.

Turning to the first hundred and forty touches (or thereabout) on Plate I. It would seem unnecessary to reiterate the fact that the very existence of touchplates implied a desire to have a *permanent* record of *every* man's mark. This being so *what* is *more certain* than that those pewterers then living whose marks had been struck upon the last plate— so recently destroyed in the great fire—should be called upon to *restrike* such touches on the new plate? Looked at from this point of view not only does it throw a new light on the earlier touches on Plate I, but it strengthens the view set forth on an earlier page that far from being lax in such matters the Court *insisted* on the older members' touches being struck first and thus for all time re-established for us the record, on the new touchplate, of their seniority.

If further evidence be needed, let us consider the first few touches and see if with any show of reason we can allocate them and give a just reason for their present order.

First then is the mark R.L. with a star and rays of *light*. The Latin word for Light —lux, lucis—is not unlike Lucas ! Is there a Lucas about this time ? Yes, indeed there is ; Robert Lucas, R.L., too in the touch, and *Robert Lucas* was Master of the Company in 1667 and no doubt did endless work towards restoring the Hall after the fire. Is it in the *very least* surprising to find him taking the place of honour ?

Touch No. 2 (repeated), John Silk, there is *no* doubt about his name, it is " at length " in his touch. Who is he, and why so near the place of honour ? He is a doyen of the Company, was Master in 1658 and possibly the oldest past-master alive.

Touch No. 3, A.M., evidently that of Anthony Mayor, who was one of Robert Lucas's Wardens in 1667. Next comes N.K., another veteran, to wit Nicholas Kelk, who was master in 1665, the year preceding the fire ; next T.H., = Thomas Haward, Master in that year (1666) of desolation, next R.M. with a martin, = Robert Marten, who was Warden with Thomas Haward in 1666.

It might be possible to continue on these lines, but is there need for more ; is not the inference apparent ?

It may of course be said that all this is conjecture, but even if that be granted, did ever one see such a string of coincidences as the way in which the names of these " lions " of the Company dovetail with the initials in these early touches, could conjecture savour more of truth ? And as if to strengthen the case, one is left in no doubt in the case of John Silk.

After the places of honour had been safeguarded, then came the marks of those other members the record of whose touch marks had been lost with the old plate, interspersed with those of members who had obtained leave to open shop about this time.

It is interesting here to note the effect of two orders of the Court to which attention has been called on an earlier page. First the order of 17th December, 1662/3, " . . . . that all touches be made with the date 1663. . . ." Out of the batch under discussion, seventeen bear this date. The second is the order of 19th December, 1666/7. " Ordered that every spoonmaker shall alter his touch immediately after Christmas next from which time, etc., . . ." As the result we find in the ninth row, no less than twelve touches bearing the date 1668, all of them well known to those interested in old pewter spoons. Other dated touches in this one hundred and forty are as follows, one of 1640, one of 164 ?, one 1646, two 1655, one 1656, one 1657, two 1664, two 1665, four 1666, fifteen 1668 (in all), and one 1671.

The earliest *dated* touch—1640—(which is not the earliest on the plate—see below) is apparently that of Nathaniel Mills, Touch, 48 L.T.P., and this date would refer either to the date of his opening shop or of his Freedom. If this be so, as is generally believed, he is an instance of a prolonged stay in the ranks of the Yeomanry, for he was not called to the Livery until 1668, in which year he was also fined for not serving the office of Renter Warden, and in 1672 was fined again for not serving as Upper Warden. He never rose to be Master, and herein would seem to be the proof of the fact that from 1640 until his taking Livery in 1668, he was one of those poorer small masters who had a hard struggle to " make a go " of his business and had not the necessary monetary qualification to be a Liveryman until twenty eight years after setting up for himself. Additional circumstantial evidence, in support of this being his touch, may be found in the device of the *Mill* wheel punning with *Mills*.

Other instances of a prolonged stay in the Yeomanry may be found in the cases of John Kent, thirty-one years, Robert Peircy, twenty-seven years and Thomas Piggott, who took his Freedom in 1698, but was not on the Livery until 1725.

The next dated touch has the initial letter of the Surname, and the last figure of the date indecipherable.

The one dated 1646 is in all probability that of Anthony Rolls, 1658, L., for the hand in the device is certainly grasping a bundle of *rolls* or a *roll*.

Of the undated touches the earliest (and so far as one can say, the earliest on the plate) is that of John Silk who restruck second only to the " present " Master, Robert Lucas. In 1640, the time of the earliest *dated* touch, he was so far advanced in the Company as to pay the fine for not serving the Office of Steward, and in all probability his touch was struck in the late twenties or early thirties of the seventeenth century.

Two small touches in the fifth row—Nos. 39 and 40 L.T.P.—bear the same device, with the initials F.L. as in Francis Lea's touch No. 18 L.T.P., and may have been allowed him to stamp on his smaller wares. He was a toymaker and would therefore *need* a very small punch, *see* Welch, ii. 139. Mr. de Navarro has a piece by this maker which is probably a toy salt and very rare.

In the hope that enough has been said to account for the seeming irregularity of these early marks we may now turn our attention to the remaining nine hundred and forty.

A few moments reflection will suffice I think to show that the date in a touch is, of itself, not sufficient to go by, for it may mean any one of the several things which we will immediately proceed to consider, taking as examples what would seem to the casual observer to be, " glaring instances of misplacement."

The date may refer to :

1. The year of a man's taking his Freedom.
2. The year when the man struck his touch and set up in business.
3. The year when the firm was originally founded.

Let us examine some of the touches which come within the scope of *the above three broad general rules.*

1. Is instanced in the case of Charles Hulse, who obtained his Freedom in 1690, and his touch bears the date (16)90.
2. Is instanced in the case of George Canby, 1694, Y. Touch dated (16)95, which he had leave to strike on 16th April, 1695.
3. An instance of this may be found in the case of Jonathan Cotton, Junr., Touch No. 866 L.T.P., dated 1705, though he did not obtain his Freedom until 1735. Probably he was not born at the date given in his touch, but on referring back to Jonathan Cotton, Senr., we find *he* was made free in 1704 and had leave to strike his touch on 20th April, 1705, and his touch bears the same date, 1705, and embodies the same devices. Hence the date in the touch of J. Cotton, Junr., refers back to the foundation of the firm by J. Cotton, Senr., and is identical in meaning with the phrase one so often sees to-day on business note paper, " Established sixty years ago," etc.

A second and even more interesting instance is found in Touch No. 1000 L.T.P. Struck c. 1763, it bears the date 1732 with the device " the worm of a still beneath an imperial crown," and is the mark of Nathaniel Meakin, Junr., 1761, Y.

The date in this touch refers back to the foundation of the firm as Darling & Meakin (Thomas Darling, 1741, L., and Nathaniel Meakin,

1726, Y.   1741, L). See Old London Directories—and their touch may be found with same device and date (No. 843 L.T.P.) with initials T.D.—N.M. struck in its proper place.

In the London Directory for 1776 Nathaniel Meakin, Junr., is given as a " worm tub maker of Houndsditch."

Superficially judged, these dated touches may seem to lend a trace of colour to the theory that they are out of order but after such divergencies as have been seen under the third heading above, it may I think be assumed that the date, though helpful in many cases and in all authentic, in so far as it refers to *something*, is in no instance sufficient *of itself* to prove a mark is struck out of its proper place, and if, of those exceptions I shall shortly enumerate, one is able to explain away all but a few—less than half a dozen—it may safely be taken for granted that the remainder will eventually yield to similar fortunate inspirations.

The one and only safe guide in determining this question of chronology is that upon which I laid special stress earlier in this chapter, viz. : A touch *must* be struck, unless good reason to the contrary can be adduced, *before taking Livery and after Freedom*. The intervening period may be one or fifty one years, and here alone is scope for seeming lack of chronological order—*but, it must have been between those dates* unless covered by one of these two exceptions :

A.   A second touch being allowed.

B.   What one may term " patrimonial " cases, *i.e.* those cases where a son was working with his father or another senior partner and would have no need of a second touch until the father's or senior partner's death.

Instances of both cases are on record, a few of which may be cited as follows :

A.   Thomas Peisley, to whom a second touch was allowed by the Court (Welch, ii, 178). Both his touches appear on the touchplates, Nos. 635 and 670 L.T.P. (*See* No. 3598, Chap. VI.)

Thomas Swanson, who on succeeding to the business of S. Ellis was allowed to change his first touch of a talbot, No. 991 L.T.P., to one embodying Ellis's device of a golden fleece, No. 1008 L.T.P. Two plates by this maker, at one time in the writer's collection, bear the words " Successor to S. Ellis, London."

B.   Alex. Cleeve, Junr., Bourchier Cleeve, Joseph Donne, Thomas Giffen, Robert Jackson, John Jupe, Joseph Spackman and many others. Of these names one is able to speak with absolute proof to hand in the cases of Joseph Donne and John Jupe, for the dates of their predecessor's deaths are known and their own touches were struck almost immediately afterwards, maintaining the old devices, and merely substituting their own Christian names.

There are many touches which were never struck upon the Hall plates, *e.g.* James Spackman, Thomas Alderson, Fasson & Sons, etc., but they embody the devices used by predecessors and may be accepted as perfectly authentic because the names of many of their owners are in the Yeomanry and Livery lists, and apparently they were used as by right, their fathers or predecessors having struck and used them previously, only the names having been changed.

A further fact which has contributed to this theory of lack of chronology may be found in the ascribing of certain touches in former works to the wrong names, *e.g.*,

Touch 367 L.T.P., to Joseph Rooker, *instead of to* Joseph Brooker (See No. 611A., Chap. VI.); Touch 504 L.T.P., to William Ridgley, *instead of to* William Buckley (No. 672, Chap. VI.); Touch 365 L.T.P., to Edward Randall, *instead of to* Edward Burchall (No. 696A., Chap. VI.), etc., etc.

Let us now turn to those remaining exceptions which come under none of the various headings set out above.

Touchplate 1.

1. Ralph Hulls, 1668, f.S. His Touch, No. 208 L.T.P., is struck c. 1672, some considerable time after Livery, with his name in full and device, a grasshopper or locust.

     The explanation may be found on turning to Touch No. 47 L.T.P. which with the same device and initials, R.H., struck c. 1656, is undoubtedly his first mark and the date refers to his Freedom or his setting up in business.

2. W.H. (William Heaton), with a date ? (16)87. This touch has been struck four times in all, first, No. 335 L.T.P., indecipherable, and secondly No. 342 L.T.P., struck thrice, "all in a heap," so to speak, and the result is such a mix-up as to make it by no means certain whether the date should be 87 or 78, for on careful inspection of the original through a magnifying glass the date looks something like 787

Touchplate 2.

3. S. Lawrence, 1667, L. Touch, No. 357 L.T.P., struck c. 1681, fourteen years after Livery.

     Here again the same explanation may be found as in Exception 1, for his original mark, No. 123 L.T.P., bearing same device and his initials S.L., was struck in its proper place after the fire.

4. Thomas Smith, 1684, L. Touch, No. 428 L.T.P., struck c. 1687, after Livery and bearing date 1675, so it is apparently some twelve years out of place.

     The same explanation again applies for the date 1675 refers back to his previous touches, Nos. 258 and 258*b* L.T.P. The former bearing date 1674 and the latter 1675, and both of which bear the same device as in No. 428, and his initials T.S. The dates 1674 and 1675 doubtless refer to those of Freedom and his setting up in business.

5. John Cowsey, 1667, L. Touch, 430 L.T.P., struck and dated 1686, some twenty years after Livery.

     His first touch, No. 49 L.T.P., was struck in its proper place after the fire with the same device and initials I.C.

Most of the above afford instances of the granting of a second touch, with name in full.

6. Jonas Durand, 1695, L. Touch, No. 557 L.T.P., dated 1699, four years after Livery.

     The explanation of this may be found in Welch ii. 169, where in 1697 he was refused permission to *alter* his touch by adding the words, "nephew of Taudin," thus proving that *so early as 1697 he had another touch.* On 21st June, 1694, he was granted leave to strike this earlier touch and to be partner with his uncle, Mr. Taudin.

7. J.E. (John Emes, Junr.), with date (16)86. No. 578 L.T.P., struck c. 1700, some fourteen years after the date given in the touch itself.

The explanation is to be found on referring back to touch No. 244, L.T.P. (John Emes, Senr.), dated (16)75 and struck in its proper place with the same device and initials, in fact the same touch with the date altered.

John Emes, Senr., died during his Mastership in 1700, when his son, who *was apprenticed to him in* 1686, immediately took up his Freedom and struck his touch.

8. W.B. (William Browne), with date 1675. Touch, No. 629 L.T.P., struck c. 1706, some thirty-one years after the date given in the touch.

The date almost certainly refers to the Freedom or foundation of the firm by a predecessor. Touch, No. 82 L.T.P., bears the same device and initials T.B., and was struck c. 1670, but I can as yet offer no real explanation for this touch.

9. Thomas Piggott, 1725, L. His touch, No. 800, is struck c. 1729, some four years out of place.

I can give no definite explanation of this, but a possible reason is that his name in the Livery list at Pewterers' Hall *follows* that of John Piggott, 1738, L., and therefore the date 1725 is possibly a clerical error, a by no means infrequent occurrence.

That mistakes of this kind are not unknown in the records is shown in the cases of William Adams, Nathaniel Adams, William Hill, etc., whose dates respectively are given as follows :

W. Adams, 1668, L.; 1659, *f.S.*   1668, f.R.W., etc.
N. Adams, 1692, L.; 1672, *f.R.W.*, etc.
W. Hill, 1668, L.; 1660, *S.*; 1668, f.R.W., etc.

All of which are quite absurd and impossible, a man was *not* fined for declining to take the Renter-Wardenship *twenty years before being called to the Livery* !

Touchplate 4.

10. Wm. de Jersey, 1744, L. He had leave to strike touch, No. 970 L.T.P., on 19th June, 1755, eleven years later, *but on* 21*st March,* 1744, *he was also granted leave to strike a touch* which apparently he deferred until 1755 for no earlier touch appears on the touchplate.

11. W.H. (William Hitchins), with date 1709. Touch, 984 L.T.P., struck c. 1759, apparently fifty years out of date. He had leave to strike his touch on 19th June, 1755.

This date refers back to touch No. 663 L.T.P., which has the same device date and initials, and was that of the founder of the firm, William Hitchins, Senr., 1705, Y.

These then represent the sum total of those touches which superficially seem to warrant the assertion that they are struck out of order. Of the eleven there are but three (Nos. 2, 8 and 9) which can I think admit of any doubt.

Before venturing to put this chapter into print it was submitted to two or three well known authorities on the subject and their opinion supports the one here given in its entirety.

To be perfectly frank, and as if to refute all that has been said above, there *is* one touch so decidedly and so glaringly out of place that a cursory glance at once satisfies one that it was never—in the original scheme of arrangement—intended to be where it is.

The touch referred to is that of Theophilus Reading, struck *on* the line dividing the second and third rows on the first touchplate.

He was no " lion " of the Company, his name does not even appear in the Livery lists, and the Yeomanry lists are lost before c. 1687, so we may rest assured he did not rise even to the Livery. Why then does his touch appear in this place of honour—why indeed ?

Let us see what the records say of him. In Mr. Welch's *History of the Company*, ii. 158 is the following :—

> Theophilus Reading who formerly was admitted to strike a touch of the three tulips now (July 17th 1687-8) desired to have liberty to strike a new touch which was allowed him upon his promising to take no advantage or make any complaint against any other man for striking his former touch.

This " former touch " of the three tulips will be found, No. 263 L.T.P., with his initials T.R. and date (16)76, struck in its proper place in 1676 on the first touchplate. What argument then can be put forth in support of his later touch being struck, apparently twenty years earlier ? He may have been one of those vain creatures—by no means confined to the seventeenth century—who must be in the " front row " and who (the first touchplate being full some years previous to 1687) resented his second touch being on a later plate than his earlier one and so by hook or by crook, by bribery or stealth, eventually succeeded—to his satisfaction may be, but to our bewilderment—in impressing it where we find it to-day. It is from the very design itself, obviously of later date than those touches by which it is surrounded.

Thus then we have this touch and the three others—Nos. 2, 8 and 9 from the preceding group, four in all—for which we can give no absolute explanation. Can any reader *still* be misled into thinking that these four (out of 1100)—and for a few of these four *some* explanation is given—are sufficient to justify the opinion that touches were struck haphazard in accordance with the whims of individual pewterers ?

Apart from proof, can one imagine any of these craftsmen *desiring* to sacrifice his proper place, for would not each one recognise that in the striking of these touches he was creating a silent witness to the order of precedence of the various members of the Company ?

One can but imagine that the pewterer whose touch was due for impression at the top of the plate and who struck it in the centre or at the bottom would have been referred back for attention by a mental specialist forthwith. The whole idea is so quixotic that were it not equally mischievous and important, it would have been unworthy the trouble entailed in refuting it.

Mr. Bertrand Johnson's researches—referred to in the Preface—do but add confirmation to my contention of correct chronological sequence, for, with the exception of the first one hundred and fifty marks on the first touchplate—which, as we have seen (and is generally admitted), are the re-struck touches of pre-Fire pewterers, interspersed with some few new ones—he has " unearthed " the dates when leave was granted for the striking of *all but some two hundred* of the remaining touches on all the five touchplates. The matter is too obvious to admit of further labouring the point.

Here then I propose to leave the question of chronology to the individual judgments of my readers and to turn—after a few passing remarks on the decline of the industry—to those secondary marks, some of which usually accompany the maker's proper touch.

     .   .   .   .

One of the first symptoms that all was not well with the Pewter industry is found in an entry on the 16th March, 1675/6, when " The Court ordered that the quarterage paid by journeymen should be reduced to 3d. quarterly on account of their want of employment through the deadness of trade," and in this connexion—A Special Court was held on the 22nd January, 1710/11, " to consider measures for the improvement of the trade which is now reduced to a very deplorable condition both in this Kingdom and in foreign parts."

Further evidence is to be found in the great number of insolvencies recorded in the *London Gazette* throughout the eighteenth century.

Nor was lack of trade the only spectre the Company had to combat, for in the middle of the eighteenth century a mild form of unrest was making itself manifest as is shown in this order of 18th March, 1756 : " At a General Court the Master charged the members not to employ persons that had not taken up their Freedom. Several offences of this kind had occurred lately, showing a tendency of the trade to break away from the Company's control."

Here indeed was a novel experience for the Court after the almost lamb-like way in which its members had been wont to carry out its behests ! After this shock one is almost prepared for the next item, wherein the germ of trades-unionism begins to develop as is seen in the following, on the 19th June, 1759. " Upon the representation of the Livery that there was a combination carrying on by the journeymen, to raise their wages and to work only when they pleased, the Court promised to take it into their consideration in what manner to remedy the evil complained of."

We are not in possession of the Court's conclusions, but it matters not, the end is already in sight.

Harrassed by its members from within, who perforce sought higher wages for what little work there was, and pressed from without by the ever growing popularity, cleanliness and usefulness of china and pottery, the industry had gradually to give place until by the beginning of the nineteenth century another of the glories of earlier times, another of those institutions which one has come to look upon as so purely English, so reminiscent of Bluff King Hal and " the good old days," had dwindled into the veriest shadow of its former self. The Company still goes on but there is no great industry to govern. Instead it turns its resources and energy to charity, education and fellowship, a by no means ignoble end to a glorious past.

CHAPTER IV

SECONDARY MARKS, COLLECTORS' DIFFICULTIES, PEWTERERS' TOKENS AND TRADE-CARDS, ETC., ETC.

By the term " Secondary Marks " is implied all those marks which may from time to time be found in conjunction with, but differing entirely from, " The Maker's Proper Touch as struck upon the Touchplates at Pewterers' Hall."

We will consider them in the following order :

THE CROWNED TUDOR ROSE.
THE CROWNED "X."
LABELS. ("LONDON," "MADE IN LONDON," QUALITY LABELS, MAKERS' ADDRESS LABELS, ETC.)
"HALL-MARKS," (SO CALLED).
SCOTTISH AND IRISH SECONDARY MARKS.
OWNERS' INITIALS.
BOARD-OF-TRADE, or "EXCISE MARKS."

.   .   .   .   .   .

THE TUDOR ROSE, CROWNED.

This, as will have been seen in Chapter II, has been referred to as denoting various things :

a. "The Mark for goods exported."
b. Probably the one referred to as " The Mark of the Hall."
c. A maker's Proper Touch.

In 1564 its use was entirely forbidden as a maker's proper touch, except by special permission—which was very rarely granted. As is the case with the Arms of the Pewterers' Company, so it will I think be found, that one will search in vain for either as the device in the *Touch* of a London Pewterer, without some such addition as the Maker's initials or " Sunbeams," an example of which latter is given in fig. 1. I know of no single instance to disprove this statement, though their use by provincial pewterers was frequent, as will be seen on reference to the Index to Devices in this volume.

Its use with initials at sides is shown in fig. 2, and this is how one generally finds it on London pieces, in those few instances where it was permitted.

FIG. 1.

FIG. 2.

None of these, however, need occupy our minds for long, for it is in its wider use as *a complementary mark* to the touch-mark of the maker, upon which it is our desire to throw light, for the most cursory glance over the marks in Chap. VI will show that it was used by hundreds of pewterers *as a secondary mark*, and it is in this sense we have to give it consideration, and of which figs. 3 and 4 are typical examples.

From the middle, or latter quarter of the seventeenth century onwards, it appears on almost every plate and dish one sees and yet—the records are silent.

In 1690/1, as has been seen in a previous chapter, it was ordered that " No member of the Mystery shall strike any other mark upon his wares than his touch or mark as struck upon the hall-plate *and the Rose and Crown stamp and also* the letter " X " upon extraordinary wares, and it is this combination we usually find.

FIG. 3.   FIG. 4.   FIG. 5.   FIG. 6.   FIG. 7.

But this order becomes the more inexplicable in view of the regulation passed but twenty years earlier (1671/2), when it was ordered to be used *only " for goods exported."*

Strangely enough, the most illuminating evidence as to its meaning, is derived from an Act of Parliament, passed in the reign of Charles I (1641), for regulating the makers of pewterwares in *Scotland*, wherein it states :—

> . . . it is ordained that the pewterer or founder of tin, shall put the mark of the Thistle and the Deacon's Mark with his own name upon every piece that he shall happen to cast and that the same shall be *of the finest pewter marked with the Rose in England.* . . .

and again in 1663 a further Act ordains :—

> . . . pewter to be of the same quality *as that marked with the Rose in England.*

Here then we have it referred to *definitely* in two Acts of Parliament as *a Quality Mark*, and in this sense it must of course be regarded. . . . " The Quality Mark " or " Mark of the Hall."

That it was, from the middle of the seventeenth century, used on pieces for home use, as well as for those exported, is proved by almost every London plate one comes across to-day. We have no explanation given as to why the *two* quality marks, The Rose and the " X," were to be stamped on the same piece.

Before proceeding further it may be well to illustrate the types of Rose and Crown as used on the continent of Europe, and of which therefore the collector of British pewter exclusively must beware. Fig. 5 shows a small initial letter of the maker's name appearing in the heart of the Rose ; figs. 6 and 7 illustrate the maker's initials as appearing either within the arches or upon the circlet of the Crown. All these features, as well as the diminutive size of the one in fig 6, are practically unfailing tests for continental pewter ; I know of no single instance of their occurrence on British pieces.

Turning our thoughts to the varieties of form taken by this Rose and Crown mark, we find that in many cases its containing lines took a shape the same as, or very similar to, those of the maker's touch with which it appeared. Instances of this may be noted as follows, in Chap. VI :

Straight sides and domed tops - -	Nos. 962, 963, 1861, 2750, 5233, etc.
Oval - - - - -	Nos. 1466, 4693, 5136, etc.
Oblong - - - -	Nos. 1909, etc.
Circular - - - -	Nos. 1586, 2773, etc.
Ornamental - - - -	Nos. 37, 1343, 1416, 2693, 2694, etc.
Square - - - - -	Nos. 2894, 4379, etc.

Other examples will present themselves to any one caring to prosecute the subject further in the same chapter.

On the other hand, many Rose and Crown marks differ entirely in form from those of the accompanying maker's touch, but this in no way detracts from their usefulness as a means of identification, for in almost every case they differ from each other, and it would be a difficult matter to find two Crowned Rose marks exactly alike. In the first place *they were made to differ*, moreover, they were cut by hand, not turned out by machinery in those days. They are a means of identification to which hitherto all too little attention has been paid.

The use of this device in Scotland dates back only to the mid-eighteenth century. It had no meaning as a quality mark, but bore either the name of the city or the maker, *e.g.* Nos. 1154, 1694, 2529, 3054, 218, 1288, 2473, etc., see Chap. VI.

I know of *no single instance* of its use in Ireland, either as a quality mark or as the device in a maker's touch.

.   .   .   .

THE " X," CROWNED.

From the Company's point of view—but not from that of the connoisseur—the next in importance of the secondary marks is this " X " crowned, fig. 8.

In early days it was reserved exclusively to denote extraordinary quality of metal, but it is found to-day in many more or less reputable public-house measures and tankards of the Victorian period of whatsoever quality they be. On the continent this mark represented an alloy of tin and lead in the proportions

FIG. 8.

of ten to one, and such may have been the original intention in this country, but there is nothing more definite to guide us than the above reservation, for extraordinary or Hard Metal ware.

These two then—the Rose Crowned and the " X " Crowned—were marks over which the Company exercised *absolute* control, and the wrong use of which was punishable by fines and other dire penalties.

The marks which follow, though certainly under the control of the Company—as indeed everything was in the days of its full power—are in a different category from the above, which were Official Marks of the Company, and, as distinct from these latter, we come to a series over the use of which the pewterer himself would seem to have been allowed a considerable amount of latitude and freedom.

LABELS (of various kinds).

The first of this series refers to the use of such words as " London," " Made in London," etc., see figs. 9-13.

FIG. 9.   FIG. 10.   FIG. 11.   FIG. 12.   FIG. 13.

At the first blush the presence of any of these upon a piece of old pewter would seem to afford convincing proof of London manufacture, but in reality this was very far from being the case, for the Company were constantly trying to restrain the provincial pewterers from striking " LONDON " on their wares.   One has only to turn up—*inter alia*—such well known Bristol makers as Robert Bush, Thomas Page, Burgum & Catcott, etc., and the Duncombs of Birmingham, to realise what the London Company was " up against " in this problem.   The case of John Duncomb of Birmingham is a particularly flagrant one, for he not only used a Label bearing the word " London " but, in and around the Duncomb Arms he put the words " John Duncomb Freeman of," and this *in spite of the fact* that he had, in 1706, been expressly refused such freedom by the London Pewterers' Company.

From the above it will be seen then that these words are totally unreliable as a guide to provenance, unless accompanied by the touch of a known London pewterer, or are known to have been used by one.

FIG. 14

A more honourable form of this Label is shown in fig. 14, wherein, whilst the use of the word " London " is still retained, the addition of the words " made of pewter from " imply, either that it was made out of London, or of London pewter bought in bulk and fashioned in the country.   This last type is found on many North-country marks.

The form of such Labels was legion and the ones shown are culled at random from Chap. VI.   They give us an additional clue to origin when everything else fails.

A further type of Label is that which purports to convey some special information as to the alloy of which the piece is fashioned, some examples of which are shown in figs. 15-19,

FIG. 15.   FIG. 16.   FIG. 17.

and apart from saying that fig. 17 is found only on Irish pewter, they seem to call for little further comment.   An explanation of the term " French Metal " as used in fig. 19, will be found on several of the Trade-cards illustrated on a later page in the present chapter.

Towards the end of the seventeenth century, when the Company's strict ideas about advertising had been somewhat modified, we find Labels appearing with the makers'

Fig. 18.

Fig. 19.

Fig. 20.

Fig. 21.

names in full. Sometimes these bore the name alone, at others the address, and again, others show both name and address together. Their use as a means of identification is too obvious to require stressing. Examples of each type are shown in figs. 20-25.

Fig. 22.

Fig. 23.

Fig. 24.

Fig. 25.

" HALL-MARKS."

The last type of mark which the maker impressed *as referring to himself*, and one of the utmost importance from the connoisseur's point of view, is that of the three, four or more—usually four—devices contained in small shields or cartouches, struck in a row and resembling the Hall-mark of the Goldsmiths.

For want of a better designation one must it seems follow the general acceptance of the term and call them " Hall-Marks," though nothing was ever more certain than that *they were nothing of the kind*, for neither had they connexion with, nor were they in any way recognised by, the Authorities at Pewterers' Hall. On the contrary, the Company was in constant trouble with the Goldsmiths over them, which in 1635 culminated in the Court of Aldermen *forbidding* their use by the Pewterers. This order may have been observed temporarily, but Chap. VI is full of instances of its being flagrantly disobeyed later in the same century. Figs. 26-28 show typical examples of these marks.

Fig. 26.

Fig. 27.

Fig. 28.

One of the earliest instances of their use is that of Nicholas Kelk (No. 2704, *q.v.*), who was a Freeman of the Company as early as 1641 (probably earlier). He would therefore have full knowledge of this ruling of the Court of Aldermen in 1635. The fact however remains that, from c. 1675 onwards, the Pewterers used these " Hall-marks " quite freely, without let or hindrance, so long as they were accompanied by their proper touches.

On early examples the " Hall-Mark " is found on the front of a plate or dish, generally on the rim but occasionally in the well, with the maker's touch on the back, and this method would seem to have obtained until the second quarter of the eighteenth century, but from this period onwards it was the custom to stamp all these marks on the back, in the centre.

It is a most unusual thing to find a piece, of later date than about 1735, with the " Hall-Marks " on the front.

Turning to the speculative side of these " Hall-Marks." So long as the initials in them are the same as in the maker's touch, all is easily understandable, but this does not by any means always happen ; *e.g.* John Home, No. 2393, who used a " Hall-Mark " wherein the initials " S.S." appear. This " Hall-Mark " is known to be that of Samuel Smith, No. 4379. The question we have to answer is—Which of the two made the piece ?

In the remarks which follow reference must be understood to London pewterers only, for if we turn to country craftsmen, we find " confusion worse confounded," and in such cases as those of the Duncombs ; Birch & Villers ; Yates & Birch ; Yates, Birch & Spooner ; James Yates, etc., the intermingling of such marks leaves but little hope of an ultimate unravelling.

To return to the London makers. Let us first see what solid groundwork of fact there is upon which we may erect a sound construction, and here surely—as in all difficulties —one fact stands out, viz. Since no one but the maker was allowed to stamp his touch on a piece, the touch shows the maker ! So much will be granted, and this I believe to be the crux of the whole matter, for however many sets of " Hall-Marks " one may find, *with the same touch*, the touch proclaims the maker in no faltering tone, for no one else *dare* strike it. There was however no regulation to say what " Hall-Mark " a maker should or should not strike, indeed the regulation was that he should strike none at all ! Hence, since defiance was the order of the day, there was nothing to prevent a maker striking his own, or those of a dozen or more of his best customers, for let it be understood that some of the larger makers supplied their goods to factors in country places, which in addition to the maker's touch (which *had* to appear) would also bear the special " Hall-Marks " adopted by such factor. An instance of this may be found in my *Bristol and West Country Pewterers*, p. 14, where it will be seen that in *Felix Farley's Journal* for certain dates in 1765, Robert Bush had such a working arrangement with Joseph Spackman of London, Robert Bush being the only man in Bristol licensed to sell his specialities.

The same thing is apparent in the goods one buys every day in this twentieth century. If you buy a penknife it will bear the name of the cutler who made it in Sheffield, but—in addition—if the retailer be of any account, it will bear his name as well ; you are, however, in no doubt as to which was the maker.

Let us then consider the question of " Hall-Marks " with this analogy in mind, and in its various combinations. These are as follow :

1. Two or more different touches, using the same " Hall-Marks."
2. One touch appearing on different pieces, with differing " Hall-Marks."
3. One touch with a " Hall-Mark " bearing differing initials from those in the touch.

As instances of No. 1 we may take the following :

Samuel Smith (No. 4379), 1727, Y., used touch No. 796 L.T.P., and a Label " Made on Snowhill, London," in conjunction with his own " Hall-Mark " (S.S., etc.). *John Home* (No. 2393), 1749, Y., used touch No. 965 L.T.P., and a Label " Snowhill, London," with Samuel Smith's " Hall-Marks " as above. *Nathaniel Barber* (No. 250), 1777, Y., used touch No. 1037 L.T.P., and the same Label and " Hall-Marks " as John Home !

Here then we have three men using the same " Hall-Marks " and address and two of them with the same device in their touches ; how can it be explained ? In 1754 John Home *was given* " *consent* to strike Mr. Warden Smith's Touch," but on the 19th June,

1755, he was ordered a new touch " as Smith still uses the old one."   This at any rate will account for the finding of Smith's " Hall-Marks " with Home's touch !   Smith was a well known maker and the adoption of any marks which would show a connexion with him would be a tremendous help to a beginner, as Home then was.   The use of the same marks by Barber was probably due to a business succession, for by the time he took out his Freedom in 1777, Home had been free nearly thirty years and probably retired then and sold his connexion to Barber.   Home was Warden in 1771, and as we find him taking no further office after that, the inference most certainly is that he either retired or died shortly after.

Samuel Smith had previously been in partnership with Edward Leapidge, from which connexion he derived the right to the use of the Leapidge device of the Hare and Wheat-sheaf.

A further instance of combination No. 1 is found in the case of Thomas Swanson (No. 4593), 1753, Y., and Samuel Ellis (No. 1547), 1721, Y., the latter, who died in 1773, having used touch No. 746 L.T.P., and " Hall-Marks " with his initials " S.E."

Swanson, who had originally struck touch No. 991 L.T.P., with the device of a Talbot, was in 1765 given leave to strike Mr. Ellis's touch of the golden fleece, which he did, see touch No. 1008 L.T.P., at the same time retaining Ellis's " Hall-Marks " as those of a well known maker—and adding a Label with the words " Successor to S. Ellis, London."

These two instances throw a wonderful light—and that the light of *actual fact*—on these pieces with the " Hall-Marks " of a different pewterer.

The same line of argument may be applied to the second and third combinations, in fact it may be taken for granted that, when the initials of the " Hall-Marks " differ from those in the touch, one of two things may be assumed : either they are the " Hall-Marks " of a predecessor in the same firm, or the " Hall-Marks " of some large factor, stamped either by himself or for him, by the maker.

.   .   .   .

SCOTTISH AND IRISH SECONDARY MARKS.

The quality mark, and apparently the only one, recognised in Scotland during the sixteenth century was the Hammer Crowned, and during the seventeenth century and onwards, the Thistle which, as has already been shown, was to be used on metal of the same quality as that marked with the Rose in England.

"Hall-Marks " came into use both in Scotland and Ireland in the mid-eighteenth century, in which, in Scotland, a Thistle and a small Rose frequently appear, and in Ireland a Harp and the figure of Hibernia.   The Label " English Block Tin " would seem to be confined to Ireland and the Rose Crowned is entirely unknown there.   The Crowned " X " though in general use in both countries had no official meaning as it had in England.

.   .   .   .

OWNERS' INITIALS.

And now the story of secondary marks, *as peculiar to the maker*, is told, and there remains but to draw attention to those other marks appearing on specimens, which are neither the maker's marks nor the mark of any guild or Company of Craftsmen.

First there are the initials of the owners, usually two or three, and less frequently four or more appear. When three are used (fig. 29) the upper one is the initial letter of the surname and the lower ones of the Christian names of the husband and wife, thus the one here illustrated might be that of Howard and Gertrude Cotterell.

C
HG
FIG. 29.

I am indebted to Mr. John S. Amery of Ashburton for a definite instance of this for he has in his possession plates made by Benjamin Parham, bearing the initials I.M.S., which were those of his ancestors James and Margery Sparke, who were married in 1767, also others by the same maker bearing the initials of other ancestors, W.F.F.—William and Francis Fabyan who were married in 1774.

Again these sometimes appear with each letter crowned, as in the X crowned, and frequently one has been asked " if they are specimens from some Royal Household ! " No, if they were, such pieces would be far less numerous than they are to-day. The old pewterers in all probability had sets of these punches, containing one for each letter of the alphabet. Some had their sets plain as shown in the first illustration, others were in small shield shapes, as in the Hall-Marks while others again had them with these little crowns. This surely is the explanation of these " Royal " pieces !

Another theory put forward is that they were thus marked in the days " When pewter was taxed ! "

However . . . the full name of W. R. Locke which appears on a piece in Mr. Edward Williams' collection, fig. 30, is quite evidently that of some quite ordinary mortal, who probably could not " sport a crest " and so had his pewter stamped with his name, but I do not find his name amongst the Kings of England ! This example should assuredly give the *quietus* to this canard for all time.

FIG. 30.

FIG. 31.

An example with the initials struck triangularly, in the most familiar way, is shown in fig. 31.

.   .   .   .

CRESTS AND COATS OF ARMS AND INSCRIPTIONS.

Coats of Arms and Crests which are true to the laws of Heraldry may also serve roughly to date pieces to those versed in the intricacies of that abstruse science, but what a difference in point of time may be occasioned by the omission even of a mark of cadency ! They certainly add to the interest and value of specimens.

Authentic inscriptions, with dates, may be generally assumed to refer to the time when the piece *was fashioned*, for broadly speaking it was not the custom to engrave second hand pieces, either for presentation or otherwise, though this of course occasionally happened.

EXCISE MARKS.

The only remaining marks to be mentioned are those which appear on mugs, tankards, flagons and other vessels for holding liquids ; the verification stamps of the Weights and Measures Department of the Board of Trade, otherwise known as " Excise Marks."

These are by many mistaken for makers' touches, but with which of course they have no connexion whatever.

Until about the year 1877 each Borough and County had its own stamp, usually consisting of the Town or County Arms or some other well known local badge or emblem, accompanied at times by letters or numerals of varying type to denote the year, somewhat after the manner of the date letters in silvermarks.

Since that time however these have, with few exceptions, been discarded in favour of the uniform type of stamp which consists of a crown over the initials of the reigning sovereign (V.R., E.R., or G.R.), beneath which is a number representing the Town or County and beneath this again the date letter or figure often appears.

These marks are of little interest beyond the fact that one often finds pieces bearing those of several reigns, showing that they have been in use over a fairly extensive period and failing other marks one can at least be certain they are as old as the oldest appearing on them.

FIG. 32.

FIG. 33.

Before we pass to those chapters which will it is hoped, coupled with this and the preceding ones, enable the student rightly to interpret the bulk of the marked pieces which may come under his notice, it may not be out of place to say a word or two concerning a few of the questions one is constantly being asked by collectors, and perhaps the most frequent is—How to distinguish between Pewter and Britannia Metal.

BRITANNIA METAL.

This is the greatest nightmare to some collectors and one which requires care in answering. It is no use saying that Britannia Metal contains no lead, whereas Pewter contains as much as twenty five per cent., with its other constituent parts. That is all quite simple to the metallurgist and scientist, but every collector is not an analytical chemist, nor is he anxious to chop pieces off his treasures for the purpose of analysis ! Then again, it has been said that pewter drawn across a piece of paper will leave a blackish mark, darker or lighter according to the proportion of lead present in the alloy and that Britannia will leave none. I have this moment tested three pieces of known Britannia metal, and they *do* leave a blackish grey mark. All these things seem to me to bewilder collectors however, and are off the track of helpfulness, whereas there are some *really helpful* axioms to bear in mind. First, avoid *anything* bearing the names Dixon, Wolstenholme, I. Vickers, Broadhead and Atkin, Ashberry or " Colsman's Improved Compost," also, anything bearing the word SHEFFIELD, for the pewter industry was not one of Sheffield's staple trades. Messrs. James Dixon and Sons of that city laid one of the chief ghosts by their letter to *The Connoisseur*, March 1918, page 156, wherein they say that :—

Pewter has most certainly never been made here within the memory of our oldest employee, who has been with us sixty-four years. In the description of our firm in the *Sheffield Directory* for 1825, we are described as manufacturers of Britannia Metal goods, etc.—*no mention being made of pewter*. Also we have in our possession, old labels which were certainly prior to 1825, and *these contain no mention of pewter*. We have several instances of work people whose families have been here from three to four generations and none of these remember hearing their fathers or grandfathers mention pewter at any time. Furthermore, we have no tools or remains of tools for

making pewter. *We have often come across pieces of our own Britannia Metal which have been erroneously included amongst well-known collections of pewter . . .*
The conclusion to be drawn from the above evidence is obvious.

In July 1920 I wrote Messrs. Dixon saying that the above was not in accordance with a statement published in their *Centenary Souvenir*, wherein (c. 1906) it was set down that the firm was " amongst the foremost of the manufacturers of PEWTER, Britannia Metal and the Celebrated Old Sheffield Plate."

To this they courteously replied as follows, under date 26th July, 1920 :—

We have referred to our " Centenary Souvenir " and also to the letter of ours which appeared in the *Connoisseur* of March 1918, which we hereby confirm *in all its details*. The fact that the word PEWTER appears in the former document *must be considered an error*.

In the *Connoisseur* for March 1921 I went fully—and dare I hope finally ?—into this much debated point.

Another point to guide one is—*never* buy anything with a small catalogue number impressed into it, the pewter which collectors seek is pre-catalogue-times ; and again, the design of most Britannia Metal wares, and the " feel " of all of it, is different from that of pewter, but it is only experience which guides one in this latter respect.

Finally Britannia Metal was not made until the very end of the eighteenth century, so should cause little trouble, for the very reason that collectors do not as a rule include pieces of so late a type, unless for some special reason, even if the question of the metal is assured.

" SILVER-PEWTER ! "

Close your ears and your purse-strings when dealers talk of " Silver-pewter." There was no such thing permitted by the ordinances of any known guild. Some may have been made from an alloy which by chance had lead of a slightly argentiferous nature, *but that is all*.

PEWTER REPLICAS OF SILVER " GIVEN " TO STUART KINGS ?

This is a theme whereof the lives are even as numerous as those of the domestic Tabby ! The story takes various forms, according to the teller's frame of mind. Its period is the seventeenth century ; the King's name is given variously as Charles I, James II, or Charles II—I think William III has escaped so far ! It runs on these lines . . . During the wars (which wars are not stated) loyal subjects gave up their silver (either voluntarily *or by confiscation*) to replenish the King's depleted exchequer, for use in " the wars " or for his personal requirements, and that in return, and as a pledge of repayment " when the said King came into his own " (which never happened), EXACT REPLICAS IN PEWTER, MARKS AND ALL, WERE GIVEN IN EXCHANGE ! A variant says that the silver marks of the particular year were put upon such pieces.

The high-water mark of absurdity was reached in the Christmas number of a magazine which after recapitulating *a* version of the above said " They are probably the only instance of the Hall-mark upon any article *not* made in silver." To prove his case and to show that proof of this *Stuart* loyalty was still in being, " this knowing fellow " proceeds to illustrate as an example . . . A hot-water plate with loose top, whereon appears the mark of Samuel Cocks, *who did not obtain his leave to set up in business until the end of George III's long reign* —1819 to be precise !

It would seem unnecessary to say more but . . . Does it seem likely that in those stirring times *opportunity* could be found for making exact replicas in pewter of the thousands and thousands of pieces of silver so given (or confiscated) ?   The answer seems obvious.

DATE LETTERS ON PEWTER ?

Another point one has been called upon many times to discuss is—have the Old English letters which one finds from time to time in pewterers' " Hall-Marks " any bearing on the date when pieces were made, after the manner of the date letters of the silversmiths ?

One can but presume that the old pewterers had *some* idea in their minds when adopting these Black Letters, *most probably* the imitation of silvermarks, but the suggestion of their being used as date letters is not supported by known examples.

First one finds them used as the initials of the maker's name, see Baldwin, Baskerville, Elderton, Fryer, Hulls, Laffar, Tubb, etc., in Chap. VI.

Secondly one finds others as follows :—

Bourchier Cleeve, 1736, Y. and L., used old English " F " which is the date letter for 1761 ; John Pettit, c. 1685, used old English " E," which is the date letter for 1662/3 ; William Buckley, 1689, Y., used old English " D," the date letter for 1661/2, and John Silk, 1693, Y., used old English " R," the date letter for 1674/5.

From these few examples one can but draw the inference that they are not to be depended upon for the purpose of dating pieces, but the deciding factor is found in the fact that *the letters were not altered from year to year by the pewterers*, for one has come across examples of differing types and periods by the same maker, but the " Hall-Mark "—as also the date, if any, in his chief touch—remained always the same, whereas one of the main ideas of the silversmiths' Hall-marks is of course *the change annually of the date letter*.

LOZENGE-SHAPED TOUCHES.

A further point which proves a difficulty to some, is found in the lozenge-shaped touches which occur from time to time and the question is put—are they the touches of women ?—This of course is a confusion with the laws of Heraldry, which enjoin that the Arms of a lady shall be borne on a lozenge instead of upon a shield, but it does *not* apply to the marks of pewterers, in witness whereof the following instances of touches within a lozenge are given, the registration of the striking of each one *by a man* being evidence enough for our present purpose :—

Touch, 247 L.T.P., struck by Christopher Thorn ; touch, 282 L.T.P., struck by John Jackson ; 289 by William Waters ; 331 by Nathaniel Rider ; 544 by Anthony Warford ; 545 by John Thomas ; and 719 by William Warkman. *See* Nos. 4731A ; 2557A ; 4977A ; 3945A ; 4962A ; 4709 ; and 4967, in Chap. VI, respectively.

The above are some of the questions asked by those collectors who seek to limp along on the crutch of exact information.

ASSAYING INSTRUMENTS AT PEWTERERS' HALL.

Before considering the care of Old Pewter let me say a word concerning the interesting picture at the top of p. 59, Plate VI, which I am permitted to illustrate here through the kindness of the Master, Wardens and Court of the Worshipful Company of Pewterers of London, and of Mr. Walter Churcher who took the photograph specially for these notes.

The instruments shown are the ones used by the Company's officials for " assaying the tin," that is, in testing the alloy of various grades of metal. The late Mr. Englefield gave me the following explanation of their use :—

> The two front instruments, the one lying on and the other against the wood-block, are assay moulds for casting discs of exact size, one side of this mould being deeply concave and the other almost flat, both bearing surfaces being very accurately faced. The long arms act as levers for keeping the two edges together, tightly pressed, and are secured by a locking bar at the end, by which means discs of the same size are ensured.

> First a disc of *pure tin* would be cast, as the lighter metal in the pewter alloy, any admixture of lead or other metal making the resulting disc heavier, and in weighing the disc of mixed metal it was designated as so many grains heavier than that of pure tin, hence the various qualities of metal used in the trade became known as so many " grain " metal.

> The Company rigorously insisted on certain goods being made from a particular standard of alloy, and the inspectors in visiting the various shops, would test the metal used by these discs.

> The nippers set upon the wooden block, were used for removing the projecting piece—or " Tadge " as it is technically called—from the edge of the disc and which was caused by the metal which remained in the aperture through which, in its molten state, it was poured into the mould.

The inscriptions on these moulds are interesting. The more ornate one in front is engraved " F. Mathews, Master, 1728 ; J. Elderton, L. Dyer, Wardens." The one lying *on* the block is engraved " J. Allen, Master, 1767 ; J. Wingod, R. Pitt, Wardens."

.   .   .   .   .   .

THE CARE OF OLD PEWTER.

The question whether pewter should be cleaned or not must finally be one for individual taste to decide, but one cannot imagine the issue being long in doubt to anyone who has seen and studied the results of both methods.

Oxide left on pewter is, so far as my experience goes, not as quiescent as it may appear, for my belief is that if kept in too cold an atmosphere it increases in thickness and gradually will " pit " into the metal and corrode it away, and the more intense the cold the quicker the process. This theory would seem to be supported by the views of Professor Cohen in his lecture on " Allotropy and the Tin-pest," some notes from which are given on the concluding pages of the present chapter.

Apart, however, from the question of advisability, the aesthetic side clamours for consideration. In its days of constant use our ancestors would vie with one another in their endeavours to " outshine " each other. We must not emulate that spirit to the extreme point, but to first remove, by as gentle a process as may be, all the scale one can without damage to the piece, and afterwards to maintain and improve it by an occasional polish, is surely to get the fullest pleasure out of one's treasures, while preserving them at the same time.

Many years ago I happened upon the beautiful passage which appears on the Half-Title of this volume. The author's name was not given—I think it was in a morning paper—so I am unable to give it over his name, as one would have liked to do. However, it has a very appropriate message for us here, for " The dreamy play of firelight " on the

PLATE VI

INSTRUMENTS AT PEWTERERS' HALL FOR "ASSAYING THE TIN"

EXAMPLES OF UNCLEANED AND CLEANED PEWTER PLATES

pieces in those collections where cleaning is tabooed must be productive of anything but the " great content " experienced by those of us who know it in its brighter state !

I know of nothing which can give greater repose to the soul than the picture conjured up in the above morsel, a picture which, through the habit of cleaning my pieces, coupled with a contented nature, I long since transformed into a daily environment.

To others I can but say . . . Try it ! The picture of a cleaned and an uncleaned plate, side by side, on p. 59, Plate VI, from another photograph taken specially by my friend Walter Churcher, may assist you in arriving at a decision on the point.

METHODS OF CLEANING.

Each collector has his own particular method of cleaning his pieces, and the following have all been tried and found good. In putting them to the test it will be well, when adopting the more drastic treatments, to use old gloves, or better still rubber ones, and not to try them at all with open cuts on the hands *or in new clothes !*

For heavily corroded pieces :—

  a. Dissolve a pound of caustic potash thoroughly in 4 gallons of boiling water, place the pewter in this solution and boil for two or three hours, taking care that something (old cloths will do) is between the pewter and the bottom and sides of the vessel, to save the pieces coming into too close contact with the heat. Clean with finest Calais Sand or Monkey Soap and give a final polish with powdered rotten stone, whitening or any other plate powder or polish.

  b. Wash in soap and soda and then paint all over the surface with a 50% solution of Hydrochloric Acid (Spirits of Salts). Leave this on for a few minutes and clean off with the finest emery powder and water. Give a good wash in hot soapy (Hudson's) water and repeat the process if necessary, then polish as in *a.*

  c. In 3 quarts of boiling water dissolve 2 oz. Caustic Soda, 2 oz. Rocklime, 6 oz. common salt and 8 oz. common soda. When dissolved and cold add 2 gallons of cold water and place the pewter in it and allow to remain until the scale softens and comes away, then scour with fine Calais Sand or Monkey Soap and finish as in *a.* Mr. Rowed gives this method in his *Collecting as a Pastime*, and says he never had the surface of the pewter injured in any way by the strong solution and that the liquor may be used over and over again until it has lost its nature.

  d. One of Mr. Churcher's methods is to soak in paraffin for say two days, then as corrosion softens, rub with finest emery powder and more paraffin. It takes time and patience but is effective. Clean and polish as in *a.*

Many collectors will not hear of drastic methods but the process by other means is " funereally " slow. The first plate I ever bought, by Henry Little, was *heavily* corroded and I removed every trace with a cork-end dipped in Shinio and finest emery *flour* (*not* powder), but I had no fingertips left and cramp in every finger, and am bound to admit that there was *no* advantage over the more rapid methods.

If polishing liquids such as " Shinio," " Bluebell " or similar kinds be used, a far better and more lasting result will be obtained by seeing that all the " polish " *is rubbed off ;* this is of far greater import than the amount you rub on, for the more one's pieces are rubbed with the final chamois leather, the more enduring will be the polish, and tarnish will be slower in making itself manifest.

For merely dirty pieces, but not corroded :—

Place them in boiling, or very hot water in which a good lump of common washing soda has been thoroughly dissolved. Do *not* boil, but allow them to soak for a few hours if necessary, repeating the process if once does not suffice. Polish as before.

For an occasional polish after one's treasures have once been thoroughly cleaned, powdered rotten stone or whitening applied on a damp soft rag and finished with a dry leather, is all that will be necessary.

A method of cleaning highly favoured on the continent of Europe is the " Pewter-Grass, Ash-lye " process, the chief ingredients of which are, a lye made of wood ashes and some whisps of Pewter-grass, scouring-grass, or Horse-tail (*Equisetum Hiemale*).

Mr. Robert M. Vetter of Amsterdam, my collaborator in *European Continental Pewter*, who swears by it, sends me the following details of the process :—

Make an infusion of wood ashes—any wood will do but no coal or other ash—about four handfuls to a gallon of boiling water. Let this stand for a day. Reheat and place in it the objects to be cleaned, allowing them to stay there for about two hours. Take care that they are completely immersed and that no air-pockets are left, otherwise they will cause ugly streaks on the surface and the process will have to be repeated. Choose Pewter grass which grows by the side of a rivulet or a boggy place, and not from railway embankments, as this latter will be found too oily and sooty. See that all grit and sand is shaken from the roots, which latter should be removed. Take a good handful of this grass and remove one object from the ash-lye, put a smear of soft soap on it (not necessary but helpful) and rub it vigorously with the grass, which from time to time should be dipped in the lye, meanwhile let the object you are cleaning, rest on a heap of wet pewter grass which will save scratching.

This rubbing will quickly produce a bright polish if the piece is not too dirty, though in obstinate pieces it may take a long time to polish evenly all crevices and corners.

Rinse in cold water from time to time, to see how the cleaning progresses, and when the polish is even all over, rinse again in cold water and *let the object dry naturally by draining and evaporation*. DO NOT DRY BY WIPING OR BY WARMTH, which would leave streaky smudges of scale.

Pewter once so cleaned, will remain dry and bright for a very long time and will not need cleaning again for at least a year, and then it will need very little rubbing if the first cleaning has been a thorough one.

If kept in cupboards, behind glass doors, and away from the fumes of coal, gas and tobacco, it will last practically indefinitely.

The polish obtained is not of a bright silvery description but of a subdued and thoroughly pewtery nature.

The ash-lye should be kept as warm as possible during the cleaning and the pewter not allowed to stay in it too long otherwise it will become dulled and require further rubbing.

This method should not be used for heavily scaled pieces for it will brighten the better parts but make the others blacker. No more harm will happen to the hands than in doing ordinary laundry work, for which in former days ash-lye was used, and it does not matter whether the grass be old or young, except that—as with human beings and cats—the old has a tendency to be more scratchy !

.   .   .   .

PEWTERERS' TOKENS.

It would seem almost unnecessary to say anything in regard to the history of, or the causes which gave rise to the use of Tokens in this country, but for the information of those who do not know, it may be well to state that they were the outcome of the urgent need for small change, a fact which is borne out by the Commonwealth *pattern* farthing, illustrated—though not a token—(see No. 1), and which bears the words " For necessary Change " on the reverse.

It is true that there were in use from early times, silver pennies, half-pennies and even farthings, but their diminutive size and the consequent ease with which they were lost, each militated against their popularity and there was undoubted need of a more convenient small coinage, but there was also—especially in the official mind—a great prejudice against the use of a base metal.

In the year 1613 King James I sold the Patent rights of striking copper farthings to one of his subjects, an arrangement confirmed later by Charles I, but in private hands it led to such abuses that it was foredoomed to failure, the issuers adopting the suicidal attitude of refusing to re-change the quantities which from time to time accumulated in the tradesmens' hands.

However, time went on and the need became so urgent that these latter conceived the plan of issuing what have now become known as tokens, which indeed they were, tokens of the fact that they would be accepted back in part payment of future purchases by the individual tradesman who issued them, thus Samuel Ogden of Haworth says on his token, " I will exchange my (1670) 1d." (*See* No. 34.)

The lists which I am able to give comprise :—

a. Tokens which it is known were used by pewterers.

b. Tokens which, though no trade, or a trade other than that of the pewterer is mentioned, bear as their chief device, either the Arms of the Pewterers' Company or other emblem alluding to the metal or to articles fashioned from it, and which therefore *may* have been those of pewterers too, or have other connexion with the craft.

Immediately following *my* numbers, is given the reference to each in Williamson's edition of Boyne's *Trade Tokens of the Seventeenth Century*, the abbreviations " Obv." and " Rev." meaning *Obverse* and *Reverse* respectively.   I should be grateful for photographs, good rubbings or plaster casts of those few which are not illustrated.

1. *This is not a token proper* but a Commonwealth *pattern* farthing in pewter. It is not referred to in Boyne or Williamson and is included here, first—because it *is* of pewter—and secondly, to enforce the point that there was at this time a need for such change, as indeed is plainly stated upon it.   The details of it are as follows : *Obv.*, $\frac{1}{4}$OZ·OF·FINE·PEWTER = In a garland of roses, the initials T.K., and on a shield, a cross. *Rev.*, FOR·NECESSARY·CHANGE· = In a shield, a harp over a sun radiated.

The following from *Several Proceedings of State Affairs*—a weekly newspaper—will not be without interest :—

27 April 1654. . . . This night (April 26th) are come out new farthings weighing a quarter of an ounce of fine pewter : that so the people may never hereafter fear to lose much by them : the harp on one side and a cross on the other, with a T.K., above it.

The following Tokens were used by pewterers :—

2. (London, p. 656, No. 1708.) *Obv.*, s·m·a·in·littl·brittain· pewterer·1667. (In five lines.) *Rev.*, The Pewterers' Arms (no legend). (Large ¼d.) This is the token of Samuel Attley (No. 142, Chap. VI).

3. (Not in Williamson or Boyne.) *Obv.*, iohn·baker·of·king-ston· = An arm holding a hammer. I.B. *Rev.*, vpon·hvll· pewterer· = A·1665. (½d.) *See* No. 202A, Chap. VI.

4. (Yorkshire, p. 1320, No. 132.) *Obv.*, iohn·baker· = An arm holding a hammer. *Rev.*, of·hvll·1665· = i·b· (¼d.) *See* No. 202A, Chap. VI.

5. (Ireland, p. 1388, No. 453.) *Obv.*, francis·banckes·of = A pot of lilies. *Rev.*, gallway·pewterer· = F.B. 1d. (Undated 1d.) *See* No. 225, Chap. VI.

6. (London, p. 656, No. 1706.) *Obv.*, iohn·bird·1668· = A bird with a branch in its mouth, lime·street. *Rev.*, at· pewterers·hall· = his·half·penny. (½d.) *See* No. 428, Chap. VI.

7. (Ireland, p. 1377, No. 287.) *Obv.*, ignativs·browne·in· = i·i·b· 1d. *Rev.*, high·stret·dvblin·pevtr· = A flagon· 1671. (1d.) *See* No. 626, Chap. VI.

8. A variant, a separate die from the above. Not given in Williamson or Boyne. A third die variety is known.

9. A die variety of No. 10, *q.v.*, . . . not given in Boyne or Williamson. The date in this is (16)57, instead of (16)63.

10. (Ireland, p. 1377, No. 290.) *Obv.*, ionathan·bvtterton· pewter· = A dog with a bird in its mouth. *Rev.*, er·high· streete·dvblin·63· = I.B. 1d. *See* No. 756, Chap. VI.

11. (Gloucestershire, p. 251, No. 176.) *Obv.*, samvell·canner· in· = A tankard. *Rev.*, tewkesbvry·pewterer· = s·c· (Undated ¼d.) *See* No. 795, Chap. VI.

12. (Ireland, p. 1370, No. 178.) *Obv.*, iohn·fryers·in·1668· = A ship. *Rev.*, of·clonmel·pevterer· = 1d. *See* No. 1790, Chap. VI.

12a. (London, p. 694, No. 2176.) This *is* in Williamson's edition of Boyne's *Trade Tokens of the Seventeenth Century*, 1889-91, but *it is not indexed* : *Obv.*, robert·gisberne·in·the· =

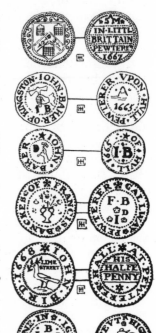

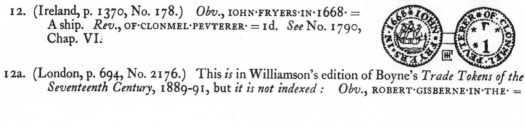

HIS·HALFE·PENNY. *Rev.*, OLD·PELLMELL·PEWTERER· = R·A·G·1667. (½d.) *See* No. 1883, Chap. VI.

13. (Warwickshire, p. 1215, No. 182.) *Obv.*, THOMAS·HEATH· 1666· = A melting pot between T·L·H· *Rev.*, IN·WARWICK· PEWTERER· = HIS·HALF·PENY· (½d.) *See* No. 2255, Chap. VI.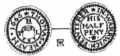

14. (Sussex, p. 1175, No. 113.) *Obv.*, IOHN·HENTY·OF· = I·H· A fleur-de-lys. (Undated ¼d.) *See* No. 2269, Chap. VI. *Rev.*, LEWES·PEWTERER· =

15. (Kent, p. 350, No. 59.) *Obv.*, THOMAS·HVTTEN·PEVTERER· = The Pewterers' Arms. *Rev.*, IN·CANTERBERY·1669· = A griffin. 1d. *See* No. 2494, Chap. VI.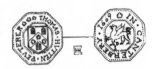

16. (London, p. 548, No. 434.) *Obv.*, STEPHEN·MABBERLY·AT· = The Pewterers' Arms. *Rev.*, BROAD·STREET·EAND· = S·E·M·67· (¼d.) *See* No. 3028, Chap. VI.

17. (London, p. 534, No. 246.) *Obv.*, HENRY·NAPTON·IN· = The Pewterers' Arms. *Rev.*, BISHOPSGATE·STREET· = HIS·HALF·PENY·1670. (¼d.) *See* No. 3346, Chap. VI.

18. (Derbyshire, p. 118, No. 13.) *Obv.*, IOSEPH·SHERWINN·OF· = 1666. *Rev.*, ASHBOVRN·PEWTERER· = HIS·HALF·PENY. (½d.) *See* No. 4245, Chap. VI.

19. (Illustrated in Dalton's *Eighteenth Century Tokens*.) *Obv.*, ROBT·WHYTE·PEWTERER = NO·40·COWGATE·HEAD. *Rev.*, LAMPS·OILS·COTTONS·&C. (In four lines.) (¼d. in pewter, Edinburgh, c. 1806.) *See* No. 5130, Chap. VI.

The following Tokens bear the Pewterers' Arms :—

20. (Not in Williamson, but its position there will be, Yorkshire, No. 103*a*.) *Obv.*, IOHN·BENSON· = HALF·PENY· *Rev.*, IN· HOLLIFAX·1670· = The Pewterers' Arms. (½d.)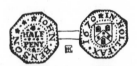

21. (London, p. 783, No. 3281.) *Obv.*, ROBT·BRISTOW·CHESE- MVNGER· = The Pewterers' Arms. *Rev.*, AT·WAPING·WALL· = R·M·B. (Undated ¼d.)

22. (Oxfordshire, p. 925, No. 38.) *Obv.*, THOMAS·BVRGES· = The Pewterers' Arms. *Rev.*, OF·BISTER·1665· = T·M·B. (¼d.)

23. (London, p. 647, No. 1599.) *Obv.*, IOHN·FVRNIS·IN·KING· STREETE·IN·WESTMINSTER. (In six lines.) *Rev.*, The Pewterers' Arms. (No·text.) Williamson gives this incorrectly as the Bowyers' Arms.

24. (Kent, p. 377, No. 422.) *Obv.*, WILLIAM·READE·IN·MILTON· = The Pewterers' Arms. *Rev.*, NEERE·GRAVESEND·1666· = HIS·HALF·PENY· (½d.)

25. (Kent, p. 377, No. 423.) *Obv.*, WIL·READ·IN·MILTON· = The Pewterers' Arms. *Rev.*, NEAR·GRAVES·END· = W·M·R. (Undated ¼d.)

26. (Warwickshire, p. 1208, No. 91.) *Obv.*, IOHN·SMITH·IN· = The Pewterers' Arms. *Rev.*, COVENTRY·1651· = I·L·S· (¼d.)

27. (Devonshire, p. 137, No. 25.) *Obv.*, RICHARD·WEBER·IN. = The Pewterers' Arms. *Rev.*, BARNESTABLE·1667· = A flower between R.W. (¼d.) (The Webbers were well known as pewterers of Barnstaple, *see* also No. 36 below.)

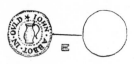

28. (Kent, p. 356, No. 128.) *Obv.*, MARY·WILLIS·1669· = The Pewterers' Arms. *Rev.*, OF·CRANBROOCK· = HER·HALF· PENY. I.M.W. (½d.) (*Note.* Mary Merriam of Goudhurst, Kent, and John Willis of the same, clothier, were married by the minister of Cranbrook on September 16th, 1661. Mary Willis, widow, was buried there on Aug. 13th, 1678.)

The following bear emblems which may refer to pewter, such as " The Pewter Pot," " The Pewter Platter," &c. :—

29. (London, p. 615, No. 1215.) *Obv.*, IOHN·ABBOT·IN·OVLD· = A baluster measure. *Rev.*, GRAFELD·LANE·IN·WAPING· = I·E·A· (Undated ¼d.) (*Note.* . . . This device is described by Williamson as a " Black-jack," but I share the opinion expressed by Oliver Baker in his *Black-jacks and Leather Bottells* that it is distinctly a pewter measure. H.H.C.)

30. (London, p. 651, No. 1646.). *Obv.*, YE·PEWTER·POT·IN· = An alehouse pot. *Rev.*, LEADENHALL·STREE· = I·E·B.

31. (Staffordshire, p. 1059, No. 95.) *Obv.*, IOH·COMBERLADG·HIS· HALF· = A bell, 1664. *Rev.*, PENY·IN·WOLVERHAMPTON· = A tankard.

32. (London, p. 585, No. 872.). *Obv*, IOSEPH·INMAN·AT·THE· = A tankard. *Rev.*, TANKERD·HOVSE·IN·DREWRY·LANE·1668. (In five lines.) (½d.)

33. (Yorkshire, p. 1326, No. 193.) *Obv.*, WILLIAM·GOO . . . ER·HIS·PENY· = A tankard (?). *Rev.*, THE . . . TE·OF·LEEDS·1669· = A jug (?). (1d.)

34. (Yorkshire, p. 1318, No. 119.) *Obv.*, SAMVELL·OGDEN·OF·HAWWORTH· = A tankard. *Rev.*, I·WILL·EXCHANGE·MY·1670· = 1d.

35. (Worcestershire, p. 1277, No. 70.) *Obv.*, WILLIAM·MOUNT-FORD· = A tankard. W.M. *Rev.*, IN·KIDDERMINSTER·1666· = HIS·HALF·PENY. (½d.)

36. (Devonshire, p. 137, No. 23.) *Obv.*, IOHN·WEBBER·OF· = A flagon. *Rev.*, BARNESTABLE·1666· = I·W·conjoined, large, filling the field. (*See* No. 5016, Chap. VI.)

37. (London, p. 711, No. 2389.) *Obv.*, RED· + ·STREETE·1657· = THO·WHITLE. *Rev.*, CORNER·BEECH·LANE· = A baluster measure. (*Note.* . . . The same comments apply to this device as to that in No. 29 above.)

38. (Buckinghamshire, p. 53, No. 124.)   *Obv.*, CHRISTOPH·CLIFTON. = A pot of lilies.   *Rev.*, IN·STONEYSTRATFORD· = C·I·C. (¼d.) (*Note.* . . . The owner of this token, apart from the fact that the Lily-pot was a badge of the pewterers, may well have been a pewterer for I have a record of a pewterer of this name of unknown provenance, *see* No. 987, Chap. VI.)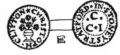

39. (London, p. 725, No. 2573.)   *Obv.*, THE·PEWTER·PLA· = A plate.   *Rev.*, ST·JOHN·STREETE = I·E·M. (¼d.)

40. (London, p. 614, No. 1208.)   *Obv.*, YE·PEWTER·PLATTER· = T·M·W.   *Rev.*, IN·GRACIOVS·STREETE· = A platter.

. . . .

PEWTERERS' TRADE-CARDS.

Here we must give a passing word to another interesting side issue of the Pewterers' Craft ; their so-called " Trade-Cards."

Mr. Ambrose Heal—than whom we have no higher authority on the subject—in his *London Tradesmen's Cards of the Eighteenth Century*, remarks that the term " Trade-Cards," though the one finding most general acceptance, is not altogether satisfactory, for not only were they " not confined to tradesmen, but they were not of pasteboard," as the name " Card " would seem to imply.

Tradesmen's Bills or *Shopkeepers' Bills*, the alternative titles, are not so good, for although they were frequently used for Bills (or accounts), this was not their main purpose, for they were used by tradesmen who *also* used ordinary invoice headings.

Thus Mr. Heal reasons that these cards—in reality, sheets of paper—were for making an announcement to their patrons, in much the same way as business cards are used to-day.

In other words they served the double purpose of advertisement and possibly a trade " visiting card ! "

Up to the period of the restoration any such attempt at advertisement, or at taking away the trade of a fellow craftsman was most sternly put down and the offender subjected to fines and other forms of punishment, which acted as a sufficient deterrent, until the latter part of the seventeenth century, when the hold of the Company upon its members began to slacken through lack of faith in its own powers.   From about this time—as will have been seen in Chapter II, p. 27, when the question whether members be allowed to strike their names within their touches, led to such vacillating decisions—members began to pay less respect to the authority of the Company and to act more in accordance with their own desires until, by the middle of the eighteenth century, anything approaching the discipline of former years had ceased to exist.

A careful inspection of the " Cards " which are illustrated here, will reveal many points of interest.   The term " French pewter," as used in a Label by John Jupe, is explained.   The ostrich device, as found in the touches of the KING family, assumes a fresh meaning ; a human touch is seen in the child admiring the toys in Robert Peircy's Card ; Old Pewterers in the acts of hammering and pouring the molten metal, appear on the King and Kenrick Cards ; The Bill from E. & H. Carpenter to — Howard Esquire (afterwards Duke of Norfolk), is a *true* Bill, as opposed to a Trade-Card ; details of the location and designation of the various pewtering establishments are revealed here as in no other place.   These and a hundred other interesting points will repay careful study.

AN INTERESTING PEWTER MEDAL.

Lord Mayor's Day, 9th Nov., 1885.
Lord Mayor—Alderman Sir John Staples,
A Past Master of the Worshipful Company of Pewterers.

One of the Cars in the 1885 Procession, represented a Pewterer's Shop, wherein the processes of casting, turning, hammering, soldering and finishing, were actually shown in operation by Mr. W. J. Englefield (and assistants), of the firm of Brown & Englefield of London.

The Pewterers were dressed in the costume of Edward IV's day, and during the Procession medals—of which both obverse and reverse are illustrated in Plate xii were struck and thrown to the people along the route, the recipients throwing silver coins into the car, in return.   Many of the tools and appliances used on the car had been in use by the firm's predecessors for nearly two centuries.

The description of the medal is as follows :—

Obv.   ALDERMAN·STAPLES·P·M·, LORD·MAYOR·1885-86 = The Arms of the Pewterers' Company.
Rev.   CAST·IN·THE·PROCESSION·9TH·NOV^r   ·1885·BY·BROWN·&·ENGLEFIELD·PEWTERERS·112·&· 113·G^t·SAFFRON·HILL·   (In eight lines.)

Diameter, $1\frac{23}{32}$ ins. (From an example in the Author's collection.)

Mrs. Englefield, with her son and daughter, have recently presented examples of this medal to a few of his friends, as a souvenir of her husband's memory.

THE LONDON MARK !

This is a phrase used glibly by many smaller dealers, and by others desiring to give an "atmosphere" to quite ordinary pieces when offering them for sale ; also by many budding collectors who have been beguiled by such blandishments ; but of course there is no such thing as *The* London Mark !

There are hundreds of London marks but no individual one which may be so singled out as to lay claim to so unique a designation.

If any one seems more entitled to it than another, assuredly it is the word London, but it is far more often used in conjunction with the Rose crowned, and at times even with the crowned " X."   That the Rose crowned, the crowned " X " and the word London *are* London marks, there is of course no gainsaying, but so also are all those eleven hundred touches struck upon the London Touchplates !

It is quite wrong therefore to refer to *any* single one as *The* London mark, to which the correct (if perplexing) rejoinder should always be . . . Which one ?

In concluding the present chapter one cannot do better than give the gist of a most important lecture, delivered by Professor Cohen of Utrecht on 13th June, 1911, before the Faraday Society, with whose consent the following notes are made.

PLATE VII

PEWTERERS' TRADE CARDS

1. JOHN ALDERSON. (No. 39 q.v.)
(Engraved by Barak Longmate, Noel St., Soho.)

2. JAMES BULLOCK (No. 685 q.v.)

3. E. & H. CARPENTER (No. 805A q.v.)

4. E. CARPENTER (No. 805B q.v.)

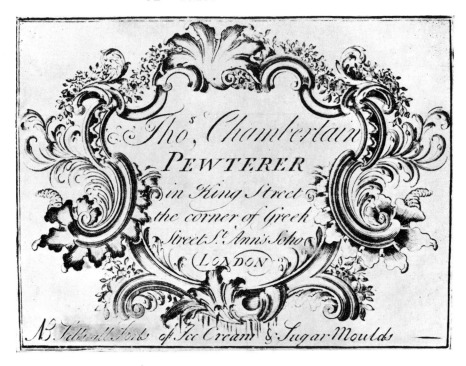

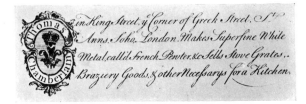

5, 6, and 7. THOMAS CHAMBERLAIN (No. 873 *q.v.*)

8. ROBERT PEIRCY HODGE (No. 2355 *q.v.*)

9. GEORGE HOLMES (No. 2383 *q.v.*)   10. JOHN JUPE (No. 2693 *q.v.*)
                                                      (*Engraved by* J. Warburton)

11. JOHN KENRICK (No. 2712 *q.v.*)

12 and 13. RICHARD KING (No. 2749 q.v.)

14. RICHARD KING (No. 2750 q.v.)
(*Engraved by* T. Wigley)

15. JOHN LANGFORD (No. 2823 q.v.)

16. WILLIAM LIFE (No. 2933A q.v.)

72

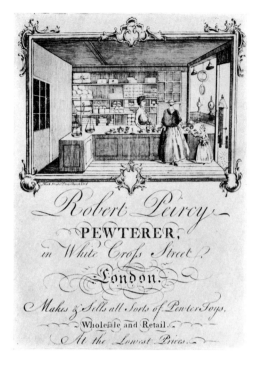

17 ROBERT PEIRCY (No. 3596 q.v.)
(*Engraved by* J. Kirk, St. Paul's Churchyard)

18. FRANCIS PIGGOTT (No. 3683 q.v.)

19. WILLIAM SANDYS (No. 4110 q.v.)
(*Engraved by* I. Sturt ; *Designed by* T. Baston)

73

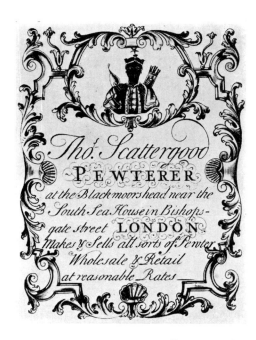

21. JOHN WATTS (No. 4992 q.v.)

20. THOMAS SCATTERGOOD (No. 4139 q.v.)

22. RICHARD YATES (No. 5344 q.v.)

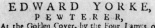

23. EDWARD YORKE (No. 5358 q.v.)

24. MEMBERSHIP BADGE OF THE LUDLOW GUILD OF HAMMERMEN. *See* p. 14.

25. ARMS OF THE PEWTERERS-PLUMBERS AND GLAZIERS OF NEW-CASTLE-UPON-TYNE. *See* p. 14.

25A AND 25B SHOW THE OBVERSE AND REVERSE RE-SPECTIVELY, OF THE MEDAL REFERRED TO ON P. 68, AS STRUCK IN THE LORD MAY-OR'S PROCESSION OF 1885.

25A.

25B.

ALLOTROPY, OR THE TIN-PEST.

Professor Cohen reports on this phenomenon as follows :—

The main facts about the decay of tin were first recognised by O. L. Erdmann in 1851, on some organ pipes in the Castle Church of Zeitz, Prussian Saxony. He attributed the decay to the repeated concussions (? vibrations) to which these pipes were subject, causing a mechanical disintegration.

In the winter of 1868, Fritzsche was consulted on the decay of some Banca tin blocks, which had been kept in a Petersburg custom-house during the winter, and had changed into a dull grey, crumbling powder. Fritzsche first suspected cold as the cause of the decay and subsequently proved this by experiment. He also found that popular belief had long since attributed the appearance of tin-pest to *cold*.

When Fritzsche heated the grains of decayed tin in hot water, they became bright again, *whilst contracting*. Whether the heat was dry or wet did not matter. White tin cooled artificially, became brittle and grey and *expanded* at the same time.

When grey tin was fused, it changed into ordinary white tin again and the transformation could be repeated.

Fritzsche thus proved that decayed tin is not *bad* tin, yet after the organ pipes of a church in Ohlau, Silesia, which had been restored in 1837, were found badly decayed and full of holes in 1884, organ builders did not consider tin a suitable material for new pipes, a prejudice shared by manufacturers of Art objects.

Professor Cohen's attention was first drawn to the matter when a badly corroded ·35 Kilogramme block of tin was returned by a Moscow firm to Rotterdam because an adulteration was suspected. The tin was found however to be very pure, containing not more than ·05% of impurities.

Experimenting with it, Cohen confirmed and extended the observations of Fritzsche and he demonstrated that the case of grey and white tin was entirely analogous to that of ice and undercooled water.

Below its normal freezing point water can exist in two modifications, viz. the stable modification, or ice, and the metastable condition of carefully undercooled water.

When a small crystal of ice, *i.e.* of the solid phase of water, is introduced into undercooled water, the whole bulk will freeze in an instant. The temperature of 0° Centigrade (33° Fahrenheit) is called transformation or transition point.

Professor Cohen then shows how he proved that a similar transition point exists for tin at 18° C., (64·4° Fahrenheit) below which it is metastable, *i.e.* may exist in either the white or grey state, and he further describes the experimental arrangement by which he measured the expansion of 30% taking place during the transformation.

This enormous increase in volume leads to the disintegration of the white tin when passing into the grey modification (water also expands when freezing), warts begin to appear on the surface of the diseased metal, the tin swells and the warts afterwards crumble into a grey powder.

Since the transition temperature of 18° C. (64·4° F.) is *so low*, it might be objected that white tin should practically be unknown, but the change is very slow and we know from the analogy of water that undercooling is possible. Yet, if the theory be correct, all tin should turn grey as soon as the temperature falls below 64·4° F., and Professor Cohen found that this was so. He examined the tin coins and Art objects of Museums and made enquiries of dealers in tin-ware, and was able to show photographs of some very badly corroded objects—coins, coffee-pots, organ-pipes, etc.—which were covered with warts and holes. At ordinary temperatures, as just stated, the change proceeds very slowly, at lower temperatures more rapidly.

When a block of good Banca tin was brought into contact with grey tin at 5° Cent., (23° F.), the change was very marked in a few weeks, whilst a block kept at +15° C. (59° F.) was not badly corroded after eight years.

The decay or transformation starts from a particle of grey tin, as a small crystal of ice—a germ—dropped into the undercooled water becomes a centre for the formation of other crystals.

In a precisely similar way every particle of grey tin becomes a centre for the formation of more grey tin.

The transformation advances very slowly in the dense metal, the particles of grey tin acting like the germs of a disease, and in this sense it may be said that the tin is infected and that all tin is liable to infection with the tin-disease or tin-pest.

In the cold galleries of Museums, the danger of tin-infection is particularly great and the Museum disease is very prevalent but *it can be prevented* by keeping the temperature above 18° C. (64·4° F.).

Alloys may have a retarding effect, but their action is not yet fully understood; it is in pure metal that the tin-pest is most pronounced. That the grey tin always contains some oxide, does not disprove Professor Cohen's assumption, the fine grey powder would naturally oxidise far more readily than the compact metal.

This oxidisation may prevent the ready reconversion by heat. Refusion with some carbon, to reduce the oxide, is recommended.

Similar phenomena are mentioned with regard to lead and antimony as well as the fact that it is known that tin plates are unsuitable as receptacles for ice, a lead tin alloy being used instead.

Professor Cohen refers to a *pewter* dish found at Appleshaw, Hants., now in the British Museum, as *tin*, so that one is forced to conclude that he uses the terms pewter and tin as synonymous. Further, a coffee pot which he exhibited was of pewter.

PLATE XIII

THREE CENTURIES OF BALUSTER MEASURES

The names by which these are known to collectors, are :—

ENGLISH.   SCOTTISH.

" Wedge "   " Hammerhead "   " Bud "   " Double-Volute "   " Embryo-Shell "   " Ball "

Found only in pewter, and nowhere outside the British Isles, the Baluster, with various modifications of detail, was our great national measure for more than three centuries, and occurs from quarter Gill to Gallon capacity. Covering the whole period, Hen. VIII-Victoria (left to right), *the same six measures*, each of the half pint size, appear above *in the same order in each row*, arranged to show : 1. Profile, 2. Front, and 3. The Lid attachments of a matchless series in the collection of Harry Walker, Esq., of Manchester.

CHAPTER V

ILLUSTRATIONS OF EXAMPLES OF PEWTER-WARE

In response to the wishes of many collectors and friends, an attempt is made in this chapter to give a really reliable and representative series of illustrations of examples of purest type.

In selecting the pieces for illustration one of my chief aims has been to secure specimens bearing *known* marks or dated inscriptions, as being the *only sure* means of attributing dates to them. *Type* is *not* an infallible guide, for though it may be taken for granted that, broadly speaking, the pewterers more or less closely followed the silversmiths, it must not be overlooked that they evolved many designs *of which no silver examples are known*, and further, any maker desirous of so doing, could give rein to his desire and reproduce the types of any preceding period.

In America there are many instances of the Stuart-type of flat lidded tankard being made well into the *latter half* of the eighteenth century, and which might quite easily be accepted in this country as genuine examples of the Stuart period by many a collector who esteems himself well versed in Pewter lore !

A further well known example of this is seen in Mr. Antonio de Navarro's " Sandwich " Chalice and cover, which, but for the mark of John Shorey—who was an eighteenth century craftsman—would almost certainly have been considered of the same period (1510) as its prototype in silver at Sandwich, Kent.

In many early examples the marks alone offer but little assistance, for the reason that they give us nothing beyond the makers' initials in a lozenge, shield, or other small device, and in some instances one has been forced—when supported by due evidence of age, etc.—to resort to the " type " test.

A further aim has been to draw upon collections which have not hitherto been illustrated over and over again, as so many have been—until one has come to look for them in each succeeding volume as one does for the perennials in one's garden !

In this connexion, however, it is quite impossible to give anything like a representative series without frequent mental migrations to the pewter rooms of one's friends, Mrs. Carvick Webster, Messrs. Lewis Clapperton, W. J. Fieldhouse, Antonio de Navarro, Charles G. J. Port, Major John Richardson, Alfred B. Yeates, Dr. Young and many others. There is nothing in the world of British Pewter—so far as my knowledge goes— to compare with some of their early treasures, and did one refrain from illustrating the many fine pieces to be found there and in other well known collections, one would have but a sorry representation of the earlier types.

Nothing therefore of a freakish or unusual nature has been allowed to creep in for obvious reasons, but just those pieces alone are illustrated which were the daily companions of generations of our ancestors, in church, and home, and which—perhaps on that account alone—make such a call upon our affections to-day.

In compiling this chapter one's chief difficulty has been, not so much " What *to* include " as " what *not* to include," and many collections have been laid under contribution in assembling the series of illustrations which follows, wherein the ownership of each piece, with dimensions, etc., is indicated wherever possible, and to the various owners of which my sincere thanks are now tendered for their ready permission to illustrate them here.

Difficulties of course beset the path of anyone essaying correctly to describe some of the pieces which have come down to our time.

To indicate a few of these one may mention the difficulty of distinguishing between Jugs and Flagons ; small Flagons and large Tankards ; Tankards and Measures ; (many of which of course served the dual purpose) ; Chalices and Domestic drinking-cups ; Patens and Plates ; Alms dishes and Domestic dishes ; etc., etc.

There is far too great a tendency amongst collectors to elevate their " every-day " pieces into the sublime light of ecclesiastical association, to connect them with historical happenings, with baronial feastings and revellings, and so ordinary pie or porridge dishes become baptismal basins or bleeding bowls ; cups and bowls are mentally transformed into christening cups or punch bowls ; plates into patens ; and so on. One longs to associate pewter with punch or toddy, and large dishes or chargers with boar's head and venison, but it is better to err on the side of truth and give to them—failing *undoubted* evidence to the contrary—their simple titles, dish, bowl, or basin, than to surround them with a fictitious halo created in one's own imagination.

No other metal lends itself so readily to these soarings into the realms of romance, and though one *does* hope that " that dear little piece upon one's dresser " was once a baptismal basin, *far* more probably was it the medium whereby the cotter's steaming evening meal was transferred from kitchen hob to supper table.

One would like entirely to eliminate the use of the word " Jug " as applied to pewter, for it strikes one as just as inapposite as does the word " Flagon " when applied to earthenware ; *ewer* is a more appropriate term, for it does not jar the senses in any degree.

In conclusion one can but say, that the same care has been exercised in classifying and describing the pieces illustrated, as one has endeavoured to use in all the other details of this work. The illustrations speak for themselves and, coupled with the usually brief notes accompanying each piece, should be of inestimable value to the Connoisseur.

The first three illustrations are given merely to show the decorative qualities of old pewter when properly displayed against old oak or whitened walls, both of which played a predominant part in its environment in earlier days in the homes of your ancestors and my own.

.   .   .   .

The illustrations in this chapter are grouped into sections thus : in the BOWL section will be found illustrated—Baptismal, Barbers', Domestic, Punch and other Bowls ; in the CUP section will be found—Caudle, Communion, Domestic, Loving, Posset and other Cups ; and so on, but on reference to the index on the following page, any required item may be turned up immediately.

To save redundancy, beneath the first piece illustrated from any collection, the owner's name and provenance are given in extenso, thus : " In the collection of Thomas Green, Esq., B.A., of Greytown," second and subsequent illustrations from the same collection appear as follows : " In the Green Collection."

INDEX TO THE ILLUSTRATIONS ON THE FOLLOWING PAGES

NOTE.—The *Mark numbers* referred to beneath the illustrations in this chapter refer to *my* numbers in the left hand margins throughout Chapters VI, VII and VIII. This will also indicate whether their provenance is England, Scotland or Ireland.

THE FOLLOWING ABBREVIATIONS occasionally occur

" S.E."= Exhibited at the *Scottish Exhibition of National History, Art and Industry*, Glasgow (1911).

" P.L."= Exhibited at the *Loan Exhibition of Old Pewter held in Provand's Lordship*, Glasgow (1909).

PLATE XIV

THE DISPLAY OF OLD PEWTER

PEWTER IDEALLY DISPLAYED

Fine pieces in the Collection of T. S. Milligan, Esq., Edinburgh.

In the " Old Oak Room."

PLATE XV

THE DISPLAY OF OLD PEWTER

PEWTER AGAINST WHITENED WALLS
Collection of Dr. A. J. Young, Manchester.

b

PEWTER AGAINST OLD OAK
In a former home of the Author's.

a

83

a

Engraved " Bow Meeting, 1724 " (Exeter).
Diameter, 15½ ins., Rim, 2¾ ins.   Mark No. 944 (Samuel Clarke).
Collection of Major John Richardson, D.S.O., Falmouth.

b

Engraved " Chapel of Banff, 1811 " (S.E. & P.L.).
Diameter, about 12½ ins. Mark No. 4161 (Wm. Scott).
By courtesy of the Rector and Vestry of St. Andrew's
Church, Banff.

c

Engraved " St. Peter's Church, Walworth, Surry
(*sic*), 1827."   Diameter, 10⅜ ins.   Mark No. 1063
(Compton).   One of a set of six in the collection of Mrs.
Carvick-Webster, Monkton.

b

BAPTISMAL BASIN in original wrought-iron Bracket. C. 1800 (P.L.). Mark No. 994 (Arch'd. & William Coats). By courtesy of the Kirk Session of Kilbirnie Parish.

ENGLISH BEAKER. Probably Tudor. Height, 4⅝ ins. Touch illegible. One of the few existing examples of genuine early English Beakers. Collection of A. B. Yeates, Esq., F.S.A., F.R.I.B.A., London.

c

BAPTISMAL BASIN in original wrought-iron Bracket (S.E. & P.L.). C. 1780. By courtesy of the Kirk Session of Lochwinnoch Parish.

d

Engraved, "FOR THE USE OF THE CHURCH OF DRUMELZIER, 1781" (*See* its Companion Ewer, Plate XLIII, *c*). (S.E.). Diameter, about 14 ins. No Marks. By courtesy of the Minister and Kirk Session of Drumelzier Parish Church.

e

Engraved, "RICHARD BELL, CHURCH WARDEN, 1824." Width, 6 ins.; height, 3⅜ ins. Possibly a Piscina. No marks. Collection of Antonio F. de Navarro, Esq., F.S.A., Broadway, Worcester

g

Engraved, "THE GIFT OF ROBERT TENNENT, 1746." (S.E.). Mark No. 1475 (Jonas Durand). For some time in the collection of Charles R. Cowie, Esq., this piece was given back by him in 1923, to its former home, Glasgow Cathedral, and is reproduced here by courtesy of the Cathedral Authorities.

f

BASIN AND EWER (S.E.). Engraved, "KIRK OF BALFRON, AUGᵗ. 16, 1742." By courtesy of the Kirk Session of Balfron Parish.

a

BARBERS' BOWL

with depression for (?) Soap and with wriggle-work decoration. C. 1690. Diameter, 12½ ins.; Depth, 2½ ins. Mark No. 5977 (I.T.).

In the de Navarro Collection.

b

C. 1730. Length, 16 ins. Mark No. 3611 (Hilary Perchard). In the Yeates Collection.

c

C. 1760. Diameter, 10½ ins.; base, 3¼ ins.; width of rim, 1¾ ins.; height, 3 ins. Mark No. 118 (Ash & Hutton). Collection of A. H. Isher, Esq., Cheltenham.

d

BARBER'S "REMINDER" BASIN

Engraved, "SIR; YOUR QUARTER IS UP." C. 1780. Diameter, 5 ins.; height, 3 ins. No marks. Similar bowls were presented before his clients by the barber, to remind them that another quarter's payment was due. Collection of Walter G. Churcher, Esq., London.

a

COLANDER. C. 1790. Diameter, 11½ ins.; height, 5⅛ ins. Marked, LONDON in curved label with X and Crown. Formerly in the Author's Collection.

b

PUNCH BOWL. Engraved, "THE LONDON PUNCH HOUSE." C. 1750. Height, 3¾ ins. "MADE IN LONDON" Rose and Crown Mark. In the Yeates Collection.

c

BROTH BOWL. Inscribed, "LINCOLN'S INN, 1704." Height, 3 ins.; diameter, 5½ ins. No marks. Collection of Chas. G. J. Port, Esq., F.S.A., Worthing.

d

DOMESTIC EWER AND BOWL. Probably c. 1790, but no details available. Photograph courteously supplied by Messrs. J. Kyrle Fletcher, Ltd., Newport, Mon.

e

PUNCH BOWL. Monteith type. C. 1800. Diameter, 10 ins.; height, 5½ ins. Mark No. 40 (Thomas Alderson). In the de Navarro Collection.

Decorated in relief, the maker's name : Wil(l)iam Gra(i)ng(e)r, forms a feature of
the design around the base, as also the date, 1616. Height, 9½ ins. Resembling
the Nuremberg " Edelzinn " and the French " Orfèvrevie d'Étain," this glorious
piece is in the Victoria and Albert Museum, S. Kensington, and is reproduced
here by courtesy of the Authorities of that Institution.

a

Probably sixteenth century. *Pricket* type. Height, 6 ins. No marks. Formerly in the Hilton-Price Collection, where it was described as " Fifteenth century, dug up in Thames Street." Collection of Lewis Clapperton, C.A., Glasgow.

b

Probably c. 1660. Height, 6⅝ ins. *Trumpet-based* type. Very rare. Mark No. 5848 (R.P.). Clapperton Collection.

c

Square-based type, round pillar. C. 1670. Height, 10 ins. No marks. In the Carvick-Webster Collection.

d

Square-based type, square pillar. C. 1670. Height, 8 ins. No marks. One of a pair in the Carvick-Webster Collection.

a

Round-based type, with knopped stem. Latter
half of seventeenth century. Height, 6½ ins.
No marks. In the Port Collection.

b

Octagonal-based type, with knopped stem.
Possibly of the late Cromwellian period.
Height, 6 ins.; across base, 4¾ ins. Mark No.
5452 (R.B.). In the de Navarro Collection.

c

Octagonal-based type, with octagonal
shield and band of relief decoration around
the upper flat collar of base. C. 1675.
Height, 8⅛ ins. No marks. In the
de Navarro Collection.

d

Octagonal-based type, with octagonal
shield, and undecorated foot. C. 1675.
Height, 7⅜ ins.; width of base, 5¼ ins.
No marks. Richardson Collection.

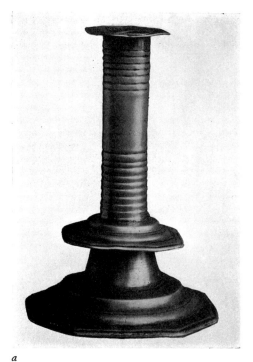

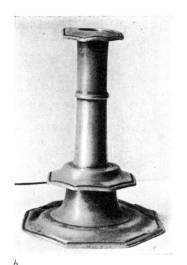

a

Octagonal-based type, c. 1675, with octagonal shield and pillar partially covered with horizontal reedings. Height, 7⅝ ins. ; base, 5¼ ins. Mark illegible. Churcher Collection.

b

C. 1680. As *a*, but with pillar almost plain. One of a pair in the Collection of W. J. Fieldhouse, Esq., C.B.E., F.S.A., of Wootten-Wawen.

c

C. 1675. As *a*, but pillar entirely covered with reedings. Yeates Collection.

d

Scalloped-based type, with scalloped shield. C. 1680. Height, 6½ ins. ; base, 4⅞ ins. Mark unknown. Collection of W. Danger Fripp, Esq., Bristol.

e

C. 1690. *Round-based* type, with round shield. Height, 10⅜ ins. ; diameter of base, 7⅞ ins. Mark No. 5862A (T.P.). Collection of H. H. Edmondson, Esq., Preston.

a

Twelve-sided type, without shield. C. 1690. Height, 7¼ ins. ; across base, 5⁵⁄₁₆ ins. Mark No. 1101 (Benjamin Cooper, dated 1680). One of an extremely fine pair, generously restored by their owner, H. C. Moffatt, Esq., of Salisbury, to their original home at New College, Oxford, the Arms of which appear on their bases.

b

Octagonal-based type, with round shield and relief ornament around collar. Bulbous baluster stem. C. 1690. Height, 7⅜ ins. ; base, 5½ ins. No marks. In the de Navarro Collection.

c

Taper-Stick. *Octagonal-based* type, with octagonal shield and band of relief decoration on collar. C. 1690. Height, 3⅝ ins. ; base, 3⅝ ins. No marks. In the de Navarro Collection.

d

The base of this candlestick, indeed all but the upper half of knop and candle socket are identical in design with the taper-holder in *c*. C. 1690. This is one of Mr de Navarro's recent finds, but as he is abroad I can give no details.

a

Octagonal-based type, with round shield, bulbous baluster stem and plain foot. C. 1695. Height, 8½ ins. No marks. Recently donated from his collection by Captain Nelson G. Harries to the Worshipful Company of Pewterers of London.

b

Round-based type, with ovoid-knopped baluster stem and cup-shaped shield below socket. C. 1700. Height, 7 ins.; diameter, 6 ins. No marks. Port Collection.

c

Octangular-based type, with baluster stem. C. 1690. Height, 8¼ ins.; base 5¾ ins. Mark unknown. Very rare type. Collection of Gilbert L. D. Hole, Esq., W.S., Edinburgh.

d

Octangular-based type, with octagonal shield and plain pillar stem and gadroon decoration. C. 1695. Height, 8½ ins.; base, 6 ins. Mark No. 5511 (I.C.). Collection of Mrs. Black.

b

Square-based type, with plain pillar. First quarter eighteenth century. 5½ ins. high; 3¼ ins. base. No mark. Recently donated from his collection by Captain Nelson G. Harries, to the Worshipful Company of Pewterers of London.

a

Adam type, square base and engraved pillar. C. 1780. Some 10 ins. high. No marks. Collection of Captain W. de L. Holmes, of Weston-super-Mare.

c   *d*

C. 1770-1820.   C. 1800-1840.
Formerly in the Author's Collection.

e

Square-based, Corinthian pillar type. C. 1800. 9¾ ins. high. Mark, LONDON, with X and Crown. Property of the Glasgow Corporation, by whose kind permission I am able to illustrate it here.

f

Varying forms of *Baluster-stemmed* Candlesticks. C. 1775-1820 or later. Heights, left to right: 6⅞ ins., 6⅛ ins., 9⅝ ins., 4⅛ ins. (Not British) and 7¾ ins. Photographed specially for this work from examples formerly in the Collection of W. D. Thomson, Esq., of Birmingham.

a

Pair of very rare " Coasters," or wine-slides. C. 1800. In the de Navarro Collection. No marks. Diameter about 5½ ins.

b   Obverse.   *c*   Reverse.

Dated 1690. ⅞ in. diameter, edge engrailed. A brass plug is inserted through centre. Collection of Henry Symonds, Esq., F.S.A., Taunton.

d   Obverse.   *e*   Reverse.

Pewter Crown Piece, struck at Oxford in 1644. 1⅝ in. diameter. In the de Navarro Collection.

PEWTER FARTHINGS

(⅞ in. diameter)   (1 5/32 in. diameter)   (⅞ in. diameter)
CHARLES II   JAMES II   WM. AND MARY

Obverse   Reverse

f   *g*   *h*   *i*

De Navarro Collection   Carvick-Webster Collection.   Churcher Collection
(*Presented by* the Author)   (*Presented by* the Author)

A copper plug is usually inserted in the centre.

PLATE XXVIII

SEPULCHRAL AND OTHER CHALICES

a

Sᴇᴘᴜʟᴄʜʀᴀʟ Cʜᴀʟɪᴄᴇ ᴀɴᴅ Pᴀᴛᴇɴ. Found in the tomb of an Ecclesiastic. 13th century. Height of Chalice, 3¾″. Diameter of Paten, 4¼″. Navarro Collection.

b

Cʜᴀʟɪᴄᴇ, with Cᴏᴠᴇʀ Pᴀᴛᴇɴ, late 16th century type. Height 7¼″. Mark No. 6113. Navarro Collection.

c

Cʜᴀʟɪᴄᴇ with relief decoration. Early 17th century, no details available. Navarro Collection.

d

Sᴇᴘᴜʟᴄʜʀᴀʟ Cʜᴀʟɪᴄᴇ, from the grave of a Priest at Witham-on-the-Hill, near Careby, Lincs. Probably 13th-14th century. Height 6″. Clapperton Collection.

a

CHALICE. Mid-17th century type. Height 7″.
No marks. Navarro Collection.

b

CHALICE. Mid-17th century type.
Height 7½″.   Mark No. 6001
(I.W.).   Yeates Collection.

c

IRISH CHALICE, from Comber, Co. Down.
Latter half of 17th century.   Height 8″.
No marks. Port Collection. (The fellow
Chalice is in the Yeates Collection.)

d

(*See also* Plate L. *g*.)

CHALICE.   Mid-17th century.
Height 7¾″. Mark No. 5917 (C.S.).
Navarro Collection. (Fellow
Chalices are in the Young Collec-
tion and the Mason Collection.)

e

IRISH CHALICE, 1690-1700.   Height 6½″.   No
marks.   Port Collection.   (A similar example is
in the National Museum, Dublin.)

f

CHALICE, with knopped Stem,
c. 1680.   Height 8″.   No marks.
Yeates Collection.

g

BEAKER CHALICE (S.E.), c. 1670.   En-
graved "CUP H.E. for BREISS. M. E. KEITH
MINR."   Height 7¾″; diameter at top 3⅞″.
Mark No. 5882 (G.R.).   (Mr. Keith was
Minister at Birse, 1666-84.)   By courtesy
of Rev. Alexander Waters, The Manse,
Birse, Aboyne.

a

SCOTTISH CHALICE (S.E.). Engraved "BELONGING TO THE ASOCIATE (*sic*) CONGREGATION IN EAST OF FIFE, 1743." Height 9″. No mark, but an Alms Bowl, similarly inscribed, bears Mark No. 5292 (Alex. Wright). In the Collection of Francis Weston, Esq., F.S.A. (formerly the Robert McVitie Collection).

b

ENGLISH CHALICE, c. 1765. Height 8″. No marks. One of a pair in the S. J. Thompson Collection.

c

ENGLISH CHALICE. Engraved "Meeting House, Maidenhead, 1784." Height 7⅜″. No marks. Port Collection. One of a pair, the fellow being in the Richardson Collection.

d

SCOTTISH CHALICE (S.E.). Engraved "BELONGING TO THE ASOCIATE (*sic*) CONGREGATION AT LESLEY, A.D. 1762." Height 8½″. One of a pair in the Weston Collection.

98

a

SCOTTISH CHALICE (P.L.). Height 9¼″, c. 1785. Mark No. 1943. (Graham & Wardrop). One of a set of four. Clapperton Collection

c

SCOTTISH CHALICE (S.E.). One of a pair, engraved " By the Minister & Kirk Session of the Parish of Calander in Monteith, for the use of the said Parish. August 3d, 1765." By courtesy of Rev. T. Burnett Peter, B.D., Minister of the Parish of Callander, Perthshire.

b

SCOTTISH CHALICE (P.L.), c. 1790. Height 9⅛″. Mark No. 5323 (John Wylie). Clapperton Collection.

d

SCOTTISH CHALICE AND COVER. Engraved with the Sacred Monogram within a Glory, c. 1790. Height 8″. By courtesy of the Rector and Vestry of Old St. Paul's Episcopal Church, Edinburgh.

e

SCOTTISH CHALICE, c. 1800. Height 8½″. No marks. Clapperton Collection.

PLATE XXXII

CHALICES AND DOMESTIC CUPS

a

SCOTTISH CHALICE (S.E. & P.L.). Engraved, "RELIEFF (*sic*) CONGREGATION, COLINSBURGH, 1801." Height 8⅛". Weston Collection.

b

ENGLISH CHALICE, c. 1800. Height 7". No mark. Navarro Collection.

c

SCOTTISH CHALICE (S.E.). Engraved, "SECOND RELIEF CHURCH, PROVOST WYND, CUPAR, 1831." Height 8⅞". No mark, but an Alms Bowl, similarly engraved, bears the *eagle* mark of Robert Kinnibrough. Weston Collection.

d

SCOTTISH CHALICE (?) (S.E. and P.L.). One of two, not *exactly* alike. These are regarded by their owners—St. Andrew's Church, Banff—as Chalices, and they were so described at the Scottish and Provand's Lordship Exhibitions, but it would be hard to conceive anything less suited to the purpose. ? Late 17th century. By courtesy of the Rector and Vestry of St. Andrew's Church, Banff.

e

DOMESTIC CUP, c. 1650. Height 3⅝". Mark No. 5836 (I.P.). Navarro Collection.

f

ENGLISH FOOTED CUPS, domestic, c. 1800-1825. Illustrated to show the varying types. Churcher Collection.

a

CAUDLE or POSSET CUP, c. 1690.   Height about $2\frac{1}{2}''$.
No marks.   Yeates Collection.

b

POSSET CUP, c. 1690.   Height about $5\frac{1}{2}''$.
No marks.   Navarro Collection.

c

CAUDLE CUP, c. 1725.   Height $1\frac{7}{8}''$; diameter
$2\frac{1}{4}''$; length of handle $3\frac{1}{4}''$.   Mark No. 6140.
Navarro Collection.

d

POSSET CUP, c. 1650.   Height about $2\frac{1}{2}''$.   Mark illegible.
Yeates Collection.

e

POSSET CUP, c. 1690.   Height about $5\frac{1}{4}''$.   Mark
detrited.   Yeates Collection.

f

COVERED POSSET CUP, c. 1705.   Height $5\frac{1}{2}''$ to lip.
Mark No. 3807 (John Quick).   Navarro Collection.

a

LOVING CUP. Dated 1690. Height 5½". No mark. The initials are those of Andrew Butcher and Helen Palmer, and it was—until the end of last century—in the family of the original owners. Collection of A. W. Cox, Esq.

b

LOVING CUP, c. 1720. Height 6"; diameter at lip 6½". No marks. Young Collection.

c

TWO-HANDLED CUP, c. 1820. 4½" high. Mark No. 2037 (Grove). Thomson Collection.

d

LOVING CUP, c. 1820. Height 7½". Mark No. 810 or 812 (Carpenter). In the Young Collection.

e

CHILD'S FEEDING BOTTLE, 6" high, c. 1800. No marks. Port Collection.

f

INVALIDS' FEEDING CUPS, or PAP-BOATS, c. 1800. Lengths vary from 3½"-4¼". It is unusual to find these with marks other than the " X " and Crown as seen in the centre example. Harry Walker Collection.

102

a

ENGLISH FLAGON, c. 1615. Height to lip, 9⅛″. No mark is visible (early Flagons usually had the mark—if any—on the handle). W. D. Thomson Collection.

b

SHOWS LID, engraved "SAYNT POVLES, 1616," and thumbpiece of the type illustrated in *a* above. From a fine example in the Young Collection.

c

ENGLISH FLAGON, engraved "THOMS. HYETT CHURCH WARDEN, 1722." This flagon, a century out of date for this type, shows a debased attempt by an English pewterer, to revert to a former type. The pleasing little porringer-shaped Chalice is also interesting. By courtesy of the Rector and Churchwardens of Snowshill Church, near Broadway, Worcs.

PLATE XXXVI

FLAGONS

a

ENGLISH FLAGONS. A magnificent pair, engraved " 1634, Sct Marye Northgate. THOMAS
GILBERT & WILLIAM WOOTTON CHURCH WARDENS. DECEMB 13TH." Extreme height 14″. Mark
No. 5614A (E.G.). Collection of E. W. Turner, Esq., M.A., Herne Bay.

b

ENGLISH FLAGON. The only one I
have seen of this type. Early 17th
century. Fieldhouse Collection.

c

ENGLISH FLAGON. Same type as in *a*,
above, but showing details of thumb piece—
with its heart-shaped piercing, etc. A very
fine piece, some 10¼″ extreme height, in the
Richardson Collection.

d

ENGLISH FLAGON. Same type as
in *a* and *c*, above, but with un-
knopped lid. A fine example,
some 13″ in height, in the Young
Collection.

104

a

ENGLISH FLAGON, c. 1650. Height to lip, 9½″. Mark No 3092 (Robert Marten). Photo courteously supplied by A. Fynde, Esq., London.

b

ENGLISH FLAGON, c. 1675. An extremely fine and rare type, 13″ high to top of knop, 9⅜″ to lip. Mark No. 5748 (G.K.). Richardson Collection.

c

PAIR OF SCOTTISH FLAGONS, engraved " For the use of the Holy Sacrament of our Lord's Supper, in the South East Parioch of Edinburgh, Anno 1688." (S.E. & P.L.). Height 11½″. By courtesy of the Kirk Session of Tron Church, Edinburgh.

PLATE XXXVIII

FLAGONS

a

ENGLISH FLAGON of the unlidded type. Engraved "Richard Coleman in Breed, 1687." Height 6½". No marks. Fieldhouse Collection.

b

ENGLISH FLAGON, c. 1690. Height to lip, 7¼". Mark No. 5975 (I.T.). Navarro Collection.

d

c

ENGLISH FLAGON of the unlidded type. Engraved: "EDWARD HILL AT YE RED LYON IN YE POULTERY 1670." Height about 7". Found under the floor of the "Red Lion" when it was pulled down to make room for a Bank near the Mansion House. Yeates Collection.

SCOTTISH FLAGON of the type known as "Pot-Bellied" (S.E.). One of a pair which, though differently inscribed, are the gifts of the same donor—Walter Jamieson—and bear the same date, 1680. They are of *Scots* quart size = ¾ gallon English. This fine pair, one of which is reproduced by courtesy of "Country-Life," are in Brechin Cathedral where the records of the Kirk Session give us the following :

"1680. Walter Jamieson, Bailye & Kirk Master "gave two tinne (*i.e.* Pewter) Quart Stoops for the "Communion Tables."

a

b

SCOTTISH FLAGON with dated Latin inscription which translates " This flagon was bought by the Kirk Session of Kilmadock, for the use of the Lord's Supper, 1702." No marks. Height 13″. Port Collection.

ENGLISH FLAGON, engraved " JACOB HALLAM, JOHN LEESON, CHURCHWARDENS, 1729." From St. Stephen's Church, Sneinton, Notts. Height 9½″. Mark No. 6031 (W.W.), same as *c* below. Port Collection.

c

d

e

ENGLISH FLAGON, engraved, " FETHER-STONE PARRISH, 1702." 10¼″ high. Mark No. 6031 (W.W.). Same maker as *b* above. Yeates Collection.

A PEWTER " REHOBOAM "! (P.L.), c. 1700. Capacity 2 Gallons. No marks. Engraved with the Crests of Shaw-Stewart, Bart., and the Badge of Nova Scotia. A fine piece in the Clapperton Collection.

ENGLISH FLAGON, c. 1720. Height about 10½″. Mark No. 6002 (I.W.). Yeates Collection.

a

ENGLISH FLAGON, made for a Scottish Church (P.L.), c. 1720. Extreme height 15½″. Mark No. 1475 (Jonas Durand). By courtesy of the Rector and Vestry of Old St. Paul's (Episcopal) Church, Edinburgh.

b

SCOTTISH FLAGON (or LAVER), c. 1720. Height 6¾″. No mark. Clapperton Collection.

c

YORK FLAGON. One of the rarest types in pewter, c. 1725. No marks. Carvick-Webster Collection.

d

ENGLISH FLAGON, c. 1725. Height about 11″ to lip. Marks illegible. Yeates Collection.

e

AN EXTREMELY FINE YORK FLAGON. Engraved with date 1725 and the names of four Church wardens in a decorated Cartouche. Height 12″. Mark No. 2185 (Edmund Harvey). Carvick-Webster Collection.

a

ENGLISH FLAGON, c. 1725. Extreme height
12½". Mark No. 3372 (John Newham).
Sutherland-Graeme Collection.

b

ENGLISH FLAGON. Engraved with Arms and " THOS
CULLYER, HEADSMAN; DAVID WORTLEY, SAMUEL SMITH,
SUPERVISORS, 1745/6." From a Woollen Manufac-
turers' Guild at Norwich. English Guild flagons in
Pewter are very rare. Height 13". No marks. Port
Collection.

c

ENGLISH FLAGON. Engraved " THE GIFT OF
WILLIAM CHICHESTER & JOHN RICHARD
CHURCHWARDENS, 1748." Height about 13".
No marks. Fieldhouse Collection.

d

ENGLISH FLAGON. Engraved " RICHARD COCK CHURCH-
WARDEN, 1734." Height about 7". Mark No. 1503
(W. Eden). Port Collection.

PLATE XLII

FLAGONS

a

IRISH FLAGON. Engraved "FOR THE PARISH
CHURCH OF ENNIS MCSAINT, 1758." Height 11".
No marks. National Museum, Dublin, by whom
the photograph was courteously supplied.

b

IRISH FLAGON (S.E.), c. 1745. One of a pair from
Lurgan, Co. Armagh. Unlidded type. Height 9¾".
Mark No. 1719 (Roger Ford). Weston Collection.

c

ENGLISH FLAGON, c. 1765. Height to
lip 8½". No marks. A fine and well-
balanced piece. S. John Thompson
Collection.

d

ENGLISH FLAGON. A most grace-
ful and dignified piece about 12"
high, c. 1745. No marks. Fieldhouse Collection.

e

ENGLISH FLAGON of fine proportions,
c. 1765. Extreme height 12¾". Mark
No. 3330A (Munden & Grove). W. D.
Thomson Collection.

a

ENGLISH (or possibly SCOTTISH) FLAGON, c. 1770. Height about 9″. Collection unknown. *Peccavi!*

b

ENGLISH FLAGON, c. 1780. Height 14¾″. No marks. Richardson Collection.

c

(*See also* Plate xvii, *d*.)

SCOTTISH FLAGON. Engraved "FOR THE USE OF THE CHURCH OF DRUMELZIER, 1781" (S.E.). Height 7½″. No marks. By courtesy of the Minister and Kirk Session of Drumelzier Parish Church.

d

SCOTTISH FLAGON. Inscribed "ST. JOHN'S CHURCH," c. 1790. Height 12″. Mark No. 1943 (Graham & Wardrop). Weston Collection.

e

SCOTTISH FLAGON, c. 1790. A fine and dignified type, worthy of the best period. Height 13″. Mark No. 1943 (Graham & Wardrop). Richardson Collection. An identical pair are in the Clapperton Collection.

f

ENGLISH FLAGONS, c. 1790. The two outside examples are the typical Ale Flagons of the period, with perforated "gratings" at the base of the spout to keep back the hops from pouring into Tankards. Height of centre flagon, 9″. Carvick-Webster Collection.

g

SCOTTISH FLAGON. A decadent 19th century example, engraved "GRAHAM STREET CHURCH, AIRDRIE, 1833." Height 8½″. Mark No. 4959 (G. & H. Wardrop). Weston Collection.

a

FOOD BOTTLE. Used for carrying a reserve supply of milk for suckling newly born lambs, which were fed from feeding bottles similar to the one in Plate xxxiv. *e*, but with a longer nipple. Probably c. 1760. Height 8½″. Mark No. 5747A (H.J.). Turner Collection.

b

INKSTAND—or STANDISH. Engraved "FOR THE GOVERNOUR AND COMPANY OF COPPER MINERS IN ENGLAND. By I.H., 1744." Length about 9″. No marks. Edmondson Collection.

c

INKSTAND WITH PEN DRAWER, c. 1790. Length about 7″. No marks. Young Collection.

d

IRISH DOUBLE-FLAPPED INKSTAND, with sand sprinkler, wafer space and ink-well under one flap and a full length compartment for pens under the other. c. 1775. Length 7⅛″. Mark No. 2242 (John Heaney). In the National Museum, Dublin, by whom the photograph is courteously supplied.

e

INKSTAND, with two drawers and two ink-wells, c. 1800. About 4½″ long. No marks. Collection of Frederick Bradbury, Esq., of Sheffield.

f

IRISH CUBE-SHAPED INKSTAND, with two drawers and removable top with four pen-holes, c. 1800. Size 3″ × 3″ × 3″, exclusive of Cap. Mark No. 4125 (Silvester Savage). Carvick-Webster Collection.

a

LID OF A MEDIÆVAL BALUSTER MEASURE. English
"Hammer-head" type. With Merchant's mark and
head of an early English King. Probably 16th century. Collection of R. Garraway-Rice, Esq., F.S.A.,
etc., London.

b

ENGLISH BALUSTER. "Wedge"
Type. 16th century. Height 6½".
No marks. The unusually "waisted"
body should be noted. Collection
of M. J. C. Davis, Esq., of Fenny
Compton.

c

THE LID OF THE EXTREMELY FINE ENGLISH
BALUSTER MEASURE, illustrated in "*d*." The
mark, as will be seen, is struck four times, the
whole being in practically perfect state.

d

ENGLISH BALUSTER. "Wedge" Type.
One of the finest examples I have seen.
16th century. Height 4½". Mark No.
5554B (S.D.). Harry Walker Collection.
(*See also* Plate XIII.)

a

ENGLISH BALUSTERS. "Hammer-head" type. Heights to lip: left to right, 6¾", 5½", 4⅞", and 6¾". Marks Nos. 5759 (A.M.) and Crowned H.R.; 5560 (W.D.); none, but same owner's initials as last; and 3092 (R.M.). A magnificent series in the Harry Walker Collection.

c

ENGLISH BALUSTERS. "Bud" type, *Quart* to ½ Gill. Left to right these are marked: W.R., beneath a Crown; I.B. on lip; and the third and fourth bear Mark No. 5560 (W.D.) dated 1670. Another finely marked series in the Harry Walker Collection.

b

ENGLISH BALUSTER. "Bud" Type, c. 1720. Height to lip, about 3½". No mark. A most interesting and unique piece, in that, around the handle are fitted several loose flat bands, sealed with Government Inspectors' verification mark of a Crown and G.R. Richardson Collection.

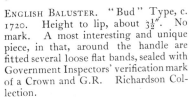

d

ENGLISH BALUSTERS. "Double-volute" type, Gallon to ½ Gill, the first type upon which the bulbous terminal to the handle appears. A further fine set in the Harry Walker Collection. Mr. Walker is very wisely specialising in British Measures and has got together an unique series of Balusters.

a

ENGLISH BALUSTER. Unlidded type of the "Bud" period, c. 1700. Height 3⅜". No mark. Carvick-Webster Collection.

b

ENGLISH BALUSTERS, unlidded type of the "Double-volute" period, c. 1750-1800. Left to right, Quart to Gill and on the extreme right, a Gill size converted—by the added lip band—from Old English Wine Standard to Imperial Standard. No marks. Carvick-Webster Collection.

c

EXTREMELY RARE MEASURE, dated in mark (16)68. Height 2⅜". Mark No. 5724A (I.I.). Richardson Collection.

d

THE ENGLISH BALUSTER COMPARED WITH AN OLD LEATHER "BLACK-JACK", to show the analogous outline and handle sweep. From a photograph made for me by Mr. Walter Churcher from examples in his own collection.

e

To ensure that the contents of their barrels contain full measure (the capacities of the barrels being subject to slight variations) the Imperial Service Wine Association, of Mark Lane, London, invariably fill them, as shown in the picture, from Government Stamped Measures of the type shown in *g*. Photo courteously supplied by H. T. Anderson, Esq.

g

WEST COUNTRY TYPE. Quart to ½ Gill. Late 18th century. No marks. Heights 6½" to 2⅞". A very rare set in the Richardson Collection.

f

DOUBLE MEASURE (¼ Gill and ½ Gill), c. 1800. Frequently erroneously described as a "Duck & Hen's Egg-Cup" for which however it answers admirably. No marks. Author's Collection.

i

A SET OF 19TH CENTURY ENGLISH PEAR-SHAPED TAVERN MEASURES from "Half-a-Quartern" to Gallon. The use of these measures is continued to the present day. In the collection of F. N. Miller, Esq., of London.

h

A VERY PLEASING VARIANT OF WEST-COUNTRY MEASURE, c. 1790. Mark unknown. Height about 3". Young Collection.

a

STANDARD MEASURE, c. 1710. Height 7¼″; weight 9¾ lbs. No marks, but on the front is a circular disc bearing in relief, the Arms of Stirling—A lamb upon a Rock—surrounded by the legend "STIRLINI OPIDVM." Clapperton Collection. Similar examples are in the Young and the Carvick-Webster Collections.

b

SCOTTISH "POT-BELLIED" MEASURES. Lidless type, c. 1690-1710. Extremely rare. Marks not recorded. Carvick-Webster Collection.

c

SCOTTISH "POT-BELLIED" MEASURES, extremely rare, c. 1690-1710. From left to right they are *Scots Pint*, 9½″, mark 5745 (W.I.); *Chopin*, 7⅝″, same mark; *Mutchkin*, 6″, mark 1289 (Lachlan Dallas); *Scots Gill*, 3¾″, no mark; *Scots Pint*, 9½″, no mark. Measurements are to the lip. Young Collection.

d

UNIQUE SERIES OF UNCRESTED TAPPIT-HEN SHAPED MEASURES (Scottish). 18th to early 19th centuries. They range in height from 3¾″ to 11¾″. The capacities being, left to right, *Scots Gill*, 3¾″; *English Gill*, 4⅝″; *Scots Two Gills*, 5″; *English Half Pint*, 5¼″; *Mutchkin*, 6½″; *English Pint*, 7½″; *Chopin*, 8½″; *Scots Pint*, THE *Tappit-hen* = 3 English Pints, 10″; *English 14 Gills*, 10¾″; and *English Half Gallon*, 11¾″ (Tappit Hens are seldom found with makers' marks, though one or two of this series are, as also others in the Port, Richardson and Young Collections). Clapperton Collection.

e

THE CRESTED TAPPIT-HEN AND THE ABERDEEN TYPE without lids, but with hinge lug—unslotted for hinge—on the handle. Sizes, 12″ to 6½″, 18th century. No marks. Clapperton Collection.

a

RARE SCOTTISH MEASURE, probably c. 1760, with Aberdeen mark. A similar piece is in the Smith Institute Museum, Stirling. Height about 3½″. Young Collection.

b

SCOTTISH BALUSTERS, "Ball" type, c. 1750-1830. Heights to lip, 6″ to 3″ (Quart to ½ Gill). Marks not known. Carvick-Webster Collection.

c

SCOTTISH BALUSTER. "Embryo-Shell" type. Dated 1826. Height to lip 4 1/16″ (½ Pint). Mark No. 2766 (Kinniburgh & Son). Author's Collection.

d

PEAR-SHAPED SCOTTISH MEASURES. Glasgow, double domed type, Quart to ½ Gill. Early 19th century. Carvick-Webster Collection.

e

"ABERDEEN" TYPE OF LIDLESS SCOTTISH BALUSTER, with hinge section unslotted (*see also* Plate xlviii, *e*. Mark No. 5865 (W.P.), dated 1663. Engraved "PHILLIP BLACKWELL." Height 5¼″. A fine piece, in the Richardson Collection.

f

PEAR-SHAPED SCOTTISH MEASURES. Upper row, Glasgow single domed type; lower row, Edinburgh type. Early 19th century. Carvick-Webster Collection.

g

SCOTTISH THISTLE-SHAPED MEASURES, c. 1800. One of the rarest of types. Sizes: Pint, 6½″; Gill, 4¼″; ½ Gill, 3½″; ¼ Gill, 2½″. All but the latter bear the Glasgow City Arms mark. The Pint is in the possession of M. T. Young, Esq., and the three smaller sizes J. R. Warren, Esq.

h

SCOTTISH PEAR-SHAPED MEASURE, unlidded type, c. 1840. Height 4 3/16″. Mark No. 1802 (R. Galbraith). Author's Collection.

PLATE L

IRISH MEASURES. PEPPERS, PATENS

a

IRISH MEASURES. Lidless and handleless type, of Baluster form. Early 19th century, $\frac{1}{4}$ Gill to $\frac{1}{2}$ Pint. In the Young Collection.

b

IRISH " HAYSTACK " or " HARVESTER'S " MEASURES. Early 19th century. An extremely fine set of seven, all bearing Mark No. 153 (Austen & Son). Gallon to $\frac{1}{2}$ Noggin. In the Harry Walker Collection.

c

PEPPERS AND SPRINKLERS formerly in the collection of the late Alban L. G. Distin, of London, showing many of the forms in which this necessary article was fashioned. c. 1750-1850. Heights, $3\frac{1}{2}''$ to $5\frac{1}{2}''$.

d

PATEN with the name " LITLE (*sic*) BARTON " stamped on rim. c. 1670. Diameter, $9\frac{1}{2}''$; rim, $1\frac{15}{16}''$. No mark. A very interesting piece in the de Navarro Collection.

e

f

(S.E. & P.L.). FOOTED PATEN, made by an English Pewterer for a Scottish Church. The centre is engraved with a sacred Monogram in a Glory, as in *f*, with the words " ACCIPITE COMEDITE." Mark No. 2393 (John Home). In St. Andrew's Church, Banff. Photographs courteously supplied by the Rector and Vestry of the Church.

g

See also Plate xxix, *d.*

MID 17TH CENTURY. Diameter $7\frac{1}{8}''$; rim $1\frac{1}{2}''$. Mark No. 5917 (C.S.). The Chalice is by the same maker. Probably the finest Chalice and Paten existing in private hands by a known London maker. In the Young Collection.

a

POSSIBLY A PATEN, 16th or early 17th century. Diameter $5\frac{3}{8}''$; rim $\frac{9}{16}''$; Depth $\frac{7}{8}''$. No marks. Found in excavations North of Holborn. In the de Navarro Collection.

b

16TH CENTURY PLATE. Diameter $8\frac{1}{4}''$; rim $1\frac{1}{2}''$. No marks, but Gothic style letters are stamped on rim. This and *c* were dug up in Walbrook. In the de Navarro Collection.

c

POSSIBLY 15TH OR 16TH CENTURY PATEN. Diameter $5\frac{1}{4}''$; rim $1\frac{7}{16}''$. No marks. The device of a Pewterer's Hammer is on the rim. Dug up in Walbrook and now in the de Navarro Collection.

d

THREE FINE EARLY PLATES, probably 16th century. Diameter of largest, $12\frac{1}{4}''$. All found at Witham on the Hill, Lincs. No marks. In the Yeates Collection.

e

"HAMMERMARKS." My good friend Mr. Churcher—at my request—searched through his stock of Plates which—apart from his collection, he keeps for his famous Pewter Suppers—for the one with most distinct hammer marks around the bouge and this he photographed for me as a well-defined example.

f

PROBABLY 16TH CENTURY. Diameter $13\frac{1}{4}''$; rim $1\frac{3}{4}''$. Touch 6098 (*q.v.*). Dug up when excavating on the site of extensions to Guy's Hospital in 1899. The badge on the rim—a feather beneath a Tudor Crown—may be that of Henry VII's eldest son. Formerly in the Hilton-Price Collection and now in the de Navarro Collection.

Maker's Touch.

g

16TH CENTURY. Probably a Paten. Diameter $6\frac{3}{8}''$; rim $1\frac{3}{8}''$. The mark, very indistinct—which may be a Wyvern—is illustrated with the piece. It bears the Arms of New College, Oxford, four times, on the rim, and it was restored to that College, with the pair of Candlesticks in Plate xxiv. *a*, by H. C. Moffatt, Esq.

PLATE LII

PLATES AND DISHES

a

b

16TH CENTURY. 8½″ diameter; 1″ rim. No marks. Recovered from the Spanish Armada Galleon "FLORENTIA" sunk in Tobermory Bay. In the de Navarro Collection.

DATED 1621. Diameter 8⅝″; rim 1¼″. Mark No. 5701 (*q.v.*). In the Carvick-Webster Collection.

c

d

A FINE "ROSE-WATER" DISH, with central Boss, c. 1620. Diameter 17¼″. Mark unknown. Collection of E. H. Eglington, Esq., of Hammerwich.

ONE OF TWO WITH DIFFERING DESIGNS. Dated 1661. Possibly "Marriage Plates." Extremely fine. Diameter 9½″; rim 1 17/32″. Mark No. 2474. In the Collection of Mrs. A. E. Lennox, of Bristol.

e

PAIR OF VERY RARE PLATES, almost flat, but the edges are *slightly* raised. Dated 1677. Diameter 9⅝″. Mark No. 5694 (W.H.). In the Richardson Collection.

b

MID 17TH CENTURY PLATE. 8½″ diameter. Mark unknown. Another fine example in the Carvick-Webster Collection.

c

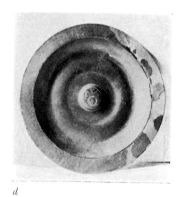

d

a

A COMPOSITE PLATE. Made from photographs taken by Mr. Walter Churcher and from which I have taken triangular sections to form this picture, which shows—with the exception of the broad rimmed—the ordinary types in use from c. 1600 until the decline of the industry, thus: *Type 1*, early 17th century; *Type 2*, c. 1650-c. 1695; *Type 3*, c. 1660-c. 1705; *Type 4*, c. 1660-c. 1705; *Type 5*, c. 1700-c. 1750; and *Type 6*, c. 1735 to the end.

A CHARLES II. "ROSEWATER" DISH, with enamelled centre Boss bearing the Royal Arms and initials, shown on larger scale in *c*. Very fine. Diameter about 18″. In the Fieldhouse Collection.

e

20″ CHARGER with Arms, Crest, Helm, Mantling and Supporters of Charles II. Engraved with foliage around rim and in the bouge, the inscription "VIVAT REX CAROLUS SECUNDUS BEATI PACIFICI. 1662." Mark No. 5972B. A magnificent piece. In the Yeates Collection.

f

A VERY BEAUTIFULLY ENGRAVED PLATE. 8½″ diameter. Mid 17th century. Mark No. 5668. In the Clapperton Collection.

PLATE LIV

PLATES AND DISHES

a

FOUR FINE BROAD-RIMMED STUART DISHES as follows : *Left*, Diameter 15″ ; Rim 3½. Mark No. 5468 (T.B.). *Centre (back)*, Diameter 20″ ; Rim 3⅞″. Mark not known. *Centre (front)*, Diameter 12″ ; Rim 2¼″. Mark No. 5694 (W.H.). *Right*, Diameter 15″ ; Rim 2⅝″. Mark No. 5073 (W. Wetter). In the W. D. Thomson Collection.

b

AN EXTREMELY FINE SERIES OF LATE 17TH CENTURY NARROW-RIMMED PLATES. *Left and Right* (Engraved), marks unknown. *Inside left*, Mark unknown. *Centre back*, Mark No. 279 (Wm. Bartlett). *Centre*, Mark No. 1992 (Greenbanck). *Inside right*, Mark No. 5549 (I.D.). *On Mirror* (below), Mark No. 6069. Diameters from 7″ to 9″. In the W. D. Thomson Collection.

a

ONE OF SEVERAL FINE STUART DISHES now in the Guild House at Henley-in-Arden. Engraved " HenLey (*sic*) 1677," on a shield with Stuart Mantling. This old Guild House has been entirely restored by the genial Lord of the Manor, William J. Fieldhouse, Esq., C.B.E., F.S.A., J.P., by whom this fine photograph was courteously supplied.

b

AN EXTREMELY FINE WEST-COUNTRY (? ALMS) DISH, or PLATE, c. 1690. Diameter 8⅞"; rim 1⅜"; depth about 2". Mark No. 989 (Robert Clothyer). In the Collection of Capt. Alan Sutherland-Graeme, A.R.I.B.A., of London.

c

BROAD-RIMMED PLATE, c. 1670. *Plates* of this type are very rare, though in the *Dish* sizes they are frequently met with. Diameter 9¾", rim 1⅝". Mark No. 5694 (W.H.). In the Sutherland-Graeme Collection.

d

THE " REEDED-EDGE " TYPE, c. 1690. Diameter 9" to 9½". From a photograph courteously supplied by A. E. Kimbell, Esq., of London. The one on right is in the Sutherland-Graeme Collection.

e

THE "SINGLE-REEDED" TYPE. Dated 1717. This is one of the plates from Old Staple Inn and bears their badge—" The Woolsack." It is inscribed " EX DONO. I. K. PR.", *i.e.* by John Kock, Principal in 1716/8. In the Churcher Collection.

f

PART OF A SET OF " MERRY MAN " PLATES, c. 1750. Diameter 9½". The set, of which Nos. 3, 4 and 5 are shown, read: 1, " What is a Merry Man ? "; 2, " Let him do what he can "; 3, " To entertain his Guests "; 4, " With wine and Merry Jests "; 5, " But if his wife does frown "; 6, " All merriment goes down." In the Fieldhouse Collection.

a

DECAGONAL PLATE AND DISH, a very rare type. Mid 18th century. The Plate is 9¼″ between parallels and bears the mark of Robt. Nicholson (No. 3400), and the Dish, 15″, that of Richard King (No. 2750). In the W. D. Thomson Collection.

b

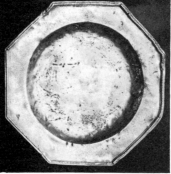

c

d

OCTAGONAL PLATE with Decorated Edge, c. 1780. Diameter 9″. Mark No. 1466 (S. Duncumb). One of a set of six in the M. J. C. Davis Collection.

OCTAGONAL PLATE with beaded and reeded edge, c. 1755. Diameter 9″. Mark No. 3697 (Richard Pitt). In the Carvick-Webster Collection.

OCTAGONAL PLATE with lenticular-beaded edge, c. 1755. Diameter 9″. Mark No. 4139 (Thomas Scattergood). One of a set of twelve in the de Navarro Collection.

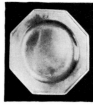

e

f

g

OCTAGONAL PLATE, with double reeded edge, c. 1755, by George Bacon (Mark No. 180). 9″ diameter. In the Yeates Collection.

OCTANGULAR-OVAL DISH, double reeded edge, c. 1755. Length 12⅜″; breadth 9⅛″. Mark No. 873 (Thomas Chamberlain). Engraved with the Arms of David Garrick. In the de Navarro Collection.

OCTAGONAL PLATE with gadroon edge, c. 1780. Diameter 9″. Mark No. 4801 (Townsend & Giffin). In the Yeates Collection.

PLATE LVII

PLATES AND DISHES (Oval, Hot Water, etc.)

a

OVAL DISHES, 14″-24″ in length. Late 18th century. They mostly bear Mark No. 1466 (S. Duncumb). In the W. D. Thomson Collection.

b

c

DATED 1839, and 12″ diameter, this piece is engraved : "LINCOLNS INN, 1839, Sir C. F. W., T.," *i.e.* it was acquired during the Treasurership of Sir C. F. Williams, Recorder of Ipswich. In the W. D. Thomson Collection.

OVAL HOT-WATER DISH, c. 1800. 33″ long, 21½″ wide, weight 38 lbs. Mark not known. The handles seem very small for a dish of such proportions. In the Collection of Frank Creassey, Esq., of Nottingham.

d

e

ONE OF THE PIECES recently donated by Capt. Nelson G. Harries to the Worshipful Company of Pewterers of London. An 8″ Hot-water Plate, c. 1820. Engraved, "Senr. Masters Table, Ch. Ch.", *i.e.* Christ Church College, Oxon. Mark No. 1004 (Samuel Cocks).

OBLONG, WAVY-EDGED SALVER, engraved in centre with the Arms of the Earls of Wilton, c. 1820. 12″ long, 10″ wide. No marks. In the Richardson Collection.

a

WAVY-EDGED PLATES. Latter half of 18th century. About 9″ diameter. Left to right : *Five lobed*, doubled reeded edge ; *Eight lobed*, plain edge ; *Five lobed*, reed and gadroon edge ; *Eight lobed*, single reeded edge. In the Churcher Collection.

b

FIVE LOBED, WAVY-EDGE PLATE with Scroll and Shell decoration, c. 1760. 9½″ diameter. Mark No. 4755 (James Tisoe). Formerly in the Pesman Matthews Collection.

c

GADROON-EDGED PLATE. One of a set of six, c. 1770. Marked X and crown. In the Carvick-Webster Collection. The absence of knife-cuts and the small indentations suggest their having been used as Alms-plates.

d

15″ FOOTED PLATTER, the platter being quite flat, with moulded edge and the foot some 6″ in diameter, c. 1700. Mark No. 672 (William Buckley). In the Yeates Collection.

e

g

f

A VERY FINE FOOTED PLATE, c. 1680. Upper and under sides shown. Diameter 10″ ; Height 2½″. Mark No. 4569 (John Stribblehill). A beautifully engraved achievement of Arms adorns the centre of the plate. In the Carvick-Webster Collection.

AN EXTREMELY FINE LATE 17TH CENTURY FOOTED-PLATE, the foot being identical with that of the Candlestick in Plate xxiv. *b*. Diameter 8½″ ; Height 3″. Marks not known. One of the pieces recently donated by Capt. Nelson G. Harries, to the Worshipful Company of Pewterers of London.

PLATE LIX

FOOTED PLATES AND SCALE PLATE

a

c

b

UPPER AND UNDER SIDES OF A FINE GAD-
ROONED FOOTED PLATE, dated 1708 inside
the foot, *q.v.* Diameter 9″. Mark No.
1723 (Thomas Forde). In the Isher
Collection.

d

UPPER AND UNDER SIDES OF A FOOTED PLATE, c. 1710. Diameter
11″; height 3⅜″. Mark No. 4453 (Thomas Spencer). In the
Port Collection.

e

f

UPPER AND UNDER SIDES OF A FOOTED
PLATE from Newcastle-upon-Tyne, c.
1750. Diameter 9″; height 3″. Mark
No. 3001 (George Lowes). In the Young
Collection.

g

SCALE-PLATE, c. 1820. Diameter 10″. Mark No. 1004 (Samuel
Cocks). Collection of Edward Hancox, Esq., of Ipswich. (*Note.—*
Many questions have been asked and much thought given as to the
use of these flat platters, but in an old Catalogue which is before me
as I write they are illustrated and described as " Scale-Plates."—
H.H.C.)

127

PLATE LX

PIERCED STRAINING DISHES, QUAIGH, PORRINGERS

a

PIERCED STRAINING DISH, c. 1695. Diameter 13⅝".
Mark No. 2720 (John Kenton). In the Collection
of R. Percy Garbett, Esq., of Paignton.

b

OVAL STRAINING DISH, c. 1755. Length 15¼"; width 11".
Mark No. 873 (Thomas Chamberlain). A Coat of Arms is
on the rim. In the Carvick-Webster Collection.

c

ENGLISH PORRINGER, c. 1715. Diameter about 4⅛".
Mark No. 2105 (Henry Hammerton). In the W.
D. Thomson Collection.

d

This picture illustrates that *Rara Avis*, a genuine SCOTTISH PEWTER QUAIGH,
c. 1670. Diameter of Bowl 5"; length over all 8". There may be the remaining traces of a mark on one ear, but it is by no means clear. In the
Clapperton Collection.

The Quaigh is peculiar to Scotland where it has obtained for centuries. They
are usually of wood or Silver and pewter specimens—of which but two or
three are known—are the rarest of all.

e

FINE ENGLISH PORRINGERS, marked as follows : left to right and top to bottom : No. 2105 (Henry Hammerton), c. 1715 ; No. 5617
(I.G.), c. 1720 ; 5476 (T.B.), c. 1690 ; 118 (Ash & Hutton), c. 1760 ; and 2843 (T. Lanyon), c. 1725. The Bowls are 4" to 4½"
in diameter. In the W. D. Thomson Collection.

a

THE COMPLETE PORRINGER.

d

THE COMPLETE PORRINGER.

b

THE LID.

e

THE LID.

c

INSIDE THE BOWL.

THREE ASPECTS (*a, b,* and *c*) OF A VERY FINE RELIEF-DECORATED PORRINGER, with Cover, c. 1725. Possibly by Henry Smith, No. 4353, 1724 Y., who made porringers of this identical pattern. Diameter of bowl 6″; height of bowl 2¼″. The three Lions seated upon the cover convert it into a tray when reversed, for holding the bowl and raising it from the polished surface of the table. In the Yeates Collection.

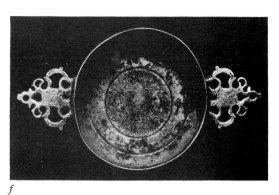

f

INSIDE THE BOWL.

THREE ASPECTS (*d, e* and *f*) OF A SIMILAR BUT EARLIER PORRINGER. Diameter of bowl 6″; height of bowl 2⅜″. c. 1690. Mark No. 4903A (John Waite). Another extremely fine piece in the Yeates Collection.

a

TRIANGULAR SALT, c. 1650. One of a pair $1\frac{5}{16}''$ high with $2''$ depression. Mark of an unknown maker. In the de Navarro Collection.

b

SPOOL-SHAPED SALT with curved arms for dust shield. Probably c. 1650. Height about $5\frac{1}{4}''$. Mark unknown. In the Carvick-Webster Collection.

c

OCTAGONAL SALT, c. 1675. Height $2\frac{1}{4}''$; diameter of base $4\frac{3}{4}''$. Mark No. 5591 (I.F.). In the de Navarro Collection.

e

OCTAGONAL SALT, c. 1675. One of a pair, some $2\frac{1}{4}''$ in height. In the de Navarro Collection.

d

TOY SALT, c. 1670. Diameter $2''$; height $1''$. Mark No. 2882 (Francis Lea, who was a toy-maker). In the de Navarro Collection.

g

CAPSTAN-SHAPED SALT. Probably c. 1680. Height $2\frac{3}{8}''$; Diameter at base $3\frac{1}{2}''$. Mark not known. In the W D. Thomson Collection.

h

CAPSTAN-SHAPED SALT, c. 1680. Height $2\frac{3}{4}''$. One of the pieces recently donated by Capt. Nelson G. Harries to the Worshipful Company of Pewterers of London. No mark.

f

c. 1680. Height $2\frac{1}{4}''$. In the Yeates Collection.

i

CAPSTAN-SHAPED SALT, c. 1685. Height $2\frac{7}{8}''$; base $3\frac{1}{2}''$. Mark indecipherable. In the Clapperton Collection.

k

CAPSTAN-SHAPED SALT, with lenticular beading, c. 1695. Height $2\frac{7}{8}''$; base $2\frac{7}{8}''$. In the de Navarro Collection. Mark No. 5869 (E.T.).

l

CAPSTAN-SHAPED SALT with lenticular beading, c. 1695. Height $2\frac{3}{4}''$. Mark indecipherable. In the Clapperton Collection.

a

c. 1710. Diameter 2⅜″; height 1¹⁰⁄₁₆″. Mark not known. In the de Navarro Collection.

b

c. 1710. Height 2⅛″; diameter at base 2⅝″. No marks. In the Churcher Collection.

c

c. 1710. About 2″ in diameter. One of a pair in the Young Collection.

d

c. 1710. Diameter 3³⁄₁₆″; height ⅝″. Mark No. 5515 (I.C.). One of a pair in the de Navarro Collection.

e

c. 1715. OCTANGULAR TRENCHER SALT. In the de Navarro Collection. No details available.

f

c. 1720. Height 1⁹⁄₁₆″; length 3⅜″. No marks. One of a pair in the de Navarro Collection.

g

c. 1715-1720. 1⅛″ high; 2¾″ base. Mark unknown. In the de Navarro Collection.

h

CUP SALT, c. 1740. Height 3¼″; diameter at base 4½″. No marks. In the Hole Collection. The base of this Salt may well have been cast from the same mould as the lids of contemporary tankards.

i

c. 1710. Height 1¾″; diameter at base 3⅜″. Mark No. 5408A. A very rare type. In the Churcher Collection.

k

c. 1775. SMALL CUP SALT with beaded edge. Height 1″; diameter 2″. In the de Navarro Collection. No marks.

l

c. 1750. CUP SALT, about 3″ high and 3″ diameter. Typical of the mid-18th century. In the Young Collection.

m

c. 1760. Height 1½″; diameter 3″. In the de Navarro Collection. No marks.

a

b

c

d

SNUFF BOXES c. 1800. These interesting minutiæ, of which a representative series is shown, were made in great variety of form and design from about 1¼″ to 4″ long. In the Harry Walker Collection.

PLATE LXV

HORN SNUFF-MULLS, CHIMNEY ORNAMENTS, SPICE CANISTER

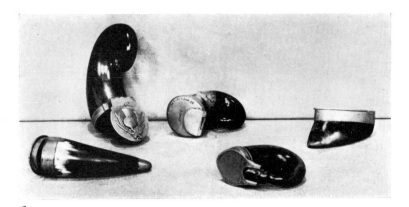

a

HORN SNUFFS, mounted in Pewter, c. 1800. In the Harry Walker Collection.

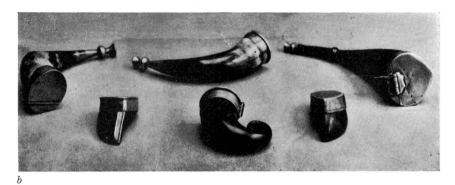

b

HORN SNUFFS, mounted in Pewter, the one on the left, the one in the centre of back row, and the one in centre of front row bear Mark No. 1477 (Durie). In the Harry Walker Collection.

c

CHIMNEY ORNAMENTS, c. 1800. No marks. Height 4″.
Navarro Collection

d

SPICE CANISTER, c. 1790. Height 3½″ over all. No marks. Presented to the Author by Capt. Nelson G. Harries, in whose Collection its fellow remains.

a

PEWTER SPOONS. No. 1, " Ball Knop," 13th-14th centuries. 2, " Acorn Knop," 14th-16th centuries. 3, " Horned Head-dress Knop," early 15th century. 4, " Maidenhead Knop," 15th and 16th centuries. 5, " Monk's Head Knop," 16th century. 6, " Chanticleer Knop," 16th century. 7, " Hexagonal Knop," 16th century. From examples in Mr. Port's unrivalled Collection.

b

PEWTER SPOONS. No. 8, " Lion Séjant Knop," 16th century. 9, " Melon Knop," 16th century. 10, " Apostle Knop," 16th-17th centuries. 11, " Baluster Knop," 16th century. 12, " Horsehoof Knop," 16th-17th centuries. 13, " Seal top," 16th-17th centuries. 14, " Slip-top," or " Slipped-in-the-stalk," 16th-17th centuries. From examples in the Port Collection.

PLATE LXVII

SPOONS

15   16   17   18   19   20   21

a

PEWTER SPOONS. No. 15, " Puritan," latter half of 17th century. 16, " Early Rounded-End " (evolution type), late 17th century. 17, Small, turned-up, Rounded-end, late 17th century. 18, " Pied de Biche," " Split-End," or " Trifid " (as this type is variously designated), late 17th century. 19, Ditto, Chocolate Spoon. 20, Ditto, early type. 21, Ditto, variant. From examples in the Port Collection.

22   23   24   25   26   27

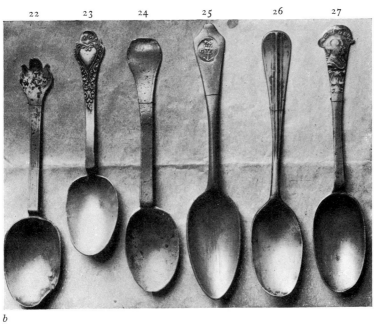

b

PEWTER SPOONS. No. 22, " Pied-de-Biche," fully developed, late 17th century. 23, Ditto, decorated. 24, " Rounded-end," early 18th century. 25, Wavy-end, c. 1700. 26, " Ribbed-Stem, rounded-end," early 18th century. 27, " Rounded-end," variant, mid 18th century. From examples in the Port Collection.

a

CASTING-MOULD FOR " PIED-DE-BICHE "
TYPE OF SPOON, c. 1690. Length 9″. In
the Warburton Collection.

b

EIGHTEENTH CENTURY SPOON RACK WITH MOULD,
c. 1700, for casting " wavy-end " spoons. In the
Port Collection.

c

EIGHTEENTH CENTURY SPOON RACK with
"slip-top" spoons. In the Carvick-Webster
Collection.

d

PART OF A PEWTER STILL, or ALEMBIC. Dated
1766. Height 24″ ; diameter 12″. No marks. In
the Port Collection.

An Extremely Rare Tankard of the Stuart Period, made probably c. 1650, to commemorate the execution of King Charles I., of whom a small relief portrait is inside the cover. This fine example is of typically early, squat shape, the dimensions being: $3\frac{7}{8}''$ diameter at base; height to lip $3\frac{3}{8}''$; extreme height $4\frac{1}{2}''$. It is marked on the inside with an hour-glass in beaded circle (and may be either No. 5552 or 5904). The thumb-piece too is typical of the mid 17th century. This unique piece is a recent addition to the Carvick-Webster Collection.

a

SOME EXCEPTIONALLY FINE LATE STUART TANKARDS, with interesting engraving, in the
Carvick-Webster Collection. Latter half of 17th century.

b

THE UNIQUE SEQUENCE OF SIZES OF LATE STUART TANKARDS in Mr. de Navarro's Collection,
ranging from $3\frac{3}{8}''$ to $6''$ (to lip). Latter half of 17th century.

c

A FINE SERIES OF LATE STUART TANKARDS in the Young Collection, effectively arranged to
show details of thumb pieces, lip serrations etc. Latter half of 17th century.

138

a

FINE WILLIAM AND MARY TANKARD, dated 1694. No marks. With punched Acanthus leaf decoration. Photographed by Mr. Walter Churcher and reproduced by special permission of the Master, Wardens and Court of the Worshipful Company of Pewterers of London, from a Tankard in their Collections.

b

AN EVOLUTIONARY TYPE, showing the advent of the fillet around the drum. A rare example, c. 1695. Height $5\frac{1}{2}''$ to top of lid. Mark No. 5748 (G.K.). In the W. D. Thomson Collection.

c

SOME STUART TANKARDS, latter half of 17th century in the Clapperton Collection. Height 4″ to 6″.

d

A VERY RARE AND BEAUTIFUL MUG, some 5″ in height, c. 1710. Mark No. 2498 (Wm. Hux). In the Yeates Collection.

e

ANOTHER FINE QUEEN ANNE MUG. In the de Navarro Collection.

f

A VERY RARE LIDLESS TANKARD of the Queen Anne period, c. 1705. Mark No. 3762 (I. Pratt). In the Yeates Collection. Lidless Tankards of this earlier period are much harder to find than the lidded types.

PLATE LXXII

TANKARDS

a

TANKARDS, showing the arrival of the double-domed lid with retention of the plain drum.   c. 1695-1715.
In the Carvick-Webster Collection.

b

THE COMPLETED TRANSFORMATION FROM STUART TO GEORGIAN, with the double-domed lid, fillet around
drum and the more developed handle and handle finial, c. 1710-1740.   In the Carvick-Webster Collection.

c

From c. 1715-1780, the example on the right evincing the decadence of the later period : the terminal of
handle set flat against the body and general lack of character.   In the Carvick-Webster Collection.   The
centre one is the earliest of the three (c. 1715), the one on left, c. 1740.

PLATE LXXIII

a

PEAR-SHAPED LIDDED ENGLISH TANKARDS, c. 1755-1790. Five of these bear the marks of well-known Bristol Pewterers, the other two are unmarked. In the Churcher Collection. Nos. 1, 3, 4 and 7 are by members of the Bush family and 6 is by Burgum & Catcott.)

b

c. 1800. A VERY BEAUTIFUL AND DIGNIFIED—IF LATE— TANKARD. Quart size. By John Carruthers Crane of Bewdley (No. 1197). In the Churcher Collection.

c

EARLY 19TH CENTURY TANKARDS. Heights *left* 3⅛″ to lip ; *right* 5⅛″ to lip. In the W. D. Thomson Collection.

d

c. 1800. Height 6⅝″ to lip. Marks none. Formerly in the Charbonnier Collection.

e

"PEWTERS." As awarded from the mid 19th century for Rowing Prizes, etc. They have Glass bottoms and are of little interest to collectors.

f

A FINE UNLIDDED TANKARD, c. 1720. Height about 4½″. Mark No. 6107. In the Carvick-Webster Collection.

b

c. 1780.   Quart size.   No marks.
English.

a

An Interesting Lidless Tankard, c. 1720. Engraved,
"stanion town pinte."   Height 4½".   Mark No. 1503
(W. Eden).   Stanion is a village near Kettering, and this
may have been used there as a Standard Measure.   In the
Collection of G. V. Charlton, Esq., of Thrapston.

c

A very fine and rare Lidless Tankard of wonderfully
squat proportions.   Probably c. 1675.   No marks.   Height
4⅝", diameter at base 4¾".   In the Young Collection.

d

Scottish Unlidded Tankard, c. 1800.   A
fine purposeful type, some 6" in height.
Capacity ⅘ths Standard Quart.   In the Young
Collection.

e

19th Century Domestic and Tavern Pots
of varying forms.

142

PLATE LXXV

TEA CADDIES AND POTS, BED-WARMER, TUREEN

a

BLUE ENAMEL ON PEWTER, the chasing being done right through the enamel to show the pewter beneath. c. 1780. Height 4½″. Mark No. 3697 (Richard Pitt). In the de Navarro Collection.

b

A VERY FINELY ENGRAVED TEA CADDY with steel lining, lock and key and small brass handle on top, c. 1790. Height 5″; length 6½″. No marks. In the Carvick-Webster Collection.

c

TEA POT, c. 1760. Height 4½″. Mark No. 3697 (Richard Pitt). In the Port Collection. (Genuine Pewter Teapots are very rare, nine hundred and ninety-nine out of every thousand so called " Pewter " tea and coffee pots are Britannia Metal.)

d

BED-WARMING PAN, for Hot Water, very rare in Pewter, c. 1775. 12″ diameter; 3″ deep. Mark No. 39 (John Alderson). Filled by unscrewing the handle from neck. Length over all 46″. Collection of Rev. A. G. Kealy, R.N., of Maltby.

e

TEAPOT, c. 1785, by Pitt & Dadley (No. 3694). 4½″ high. In the Port Collection.

f

SOUP TUREEN, c. 1820. Length 14½″. Mark No. 1063 (Thomas Compton). In the Port Collection.

a

TOBACCO BOX, finely engraved, c. 1760. Height 6″.
Mark No. 3697 (Richard Pitt). In the Port Collection.

b

WINE-FUNNEL OR TUNDISH, c. 1750. Height 7″.
Mark of A. Hincham (No. 2329). In the Port
Collection. These funnels are very rarely marked.

c

d

(*c* and *d*) show the side and end respectively of a very
fine WINE-COOLER, some 23½″ in length and 18½″
broad, bearing Mark No. 1475 (Jonas Durand). Early
18th century. In the de Navarro Collection.

e

WATER KARAFE, c. 1820. Height 7¾″. No marks.
Navarro Collection.

CHAPTER VI

ALPHABETICAL LIST OF PEWTERERS, WITH ILLUSTRATIONS OF THEIR MARKS WHERE KNOWN

THE following abbreviations are used throughout this chapter:

M. - following a date signifies year of election to the Office of Master.

U.W. - following a date signifies year of election to the Office of Upper Warden.

R.W. - following a date signifies year of election to the Office of Renter Warden.

S. - following a date signifies year of election to the Office of Steward.

f. - preceding any of the above signifies that the pewterer paid the stipulated fine to be excused from serving in the Office specified.

S. - followed by " of " = Son of.

L. - following a date signifies year of election to the Livery or Clothing.

Y. - following a date signifies year of election to the Freedom or Yeomanry of the London Company.

F. - following a date signifies year of election to the Freedom in other than the London Company.

L.T.P. signifies that his mark appears on the London Touchplates.

E.T.P. signifies that his mark appears on the Edinburgh Touchplates.

BENNETT Book signifies that the information is to be found in a book at Pewterer's Hall, which is inscribed—"The Guift of Mr. John Bennett, Master of the Company of Pewterers London, Anno Dñi 1679, for Regestering the names of the Members of the said Company, both of the Clothing and Yeomanry in Order as they have borne Office and are sett up."

This book gives details of the owners of *many* touches who are *not mentioned* in the Yeomanry or Livery Lists, and is a most valuable record.

The numbers which appear at the left-hand margin are those referred to in the " Index to Devices," Chapter VII., and have been given to each pewterer or mark to facilitate reference in writing, and to achieve conciseness in writing out Museum Labels, etc., etc.; *e.g.* No. 2425 will carry all that is known of William Howard.

A

1. ABBOTT, JOHN, London : 13 May 1693, L.
2. ABBOTT, THOMAS, London : 19 June 1712, Y.
3. ABBOTT, THOMAS, London : 16 Aug. 1792, Y.; 16 Aug. 1792, L.; 1796, f.S.; 1803, f.R.W.; 1810, U.W.; 1811, M. Died 17 Mar. 1852, age 83.
4. ABDYE, WILLIAM, London : 1556, mentioned (Welch i. 192) as being in trouble with a brother craftsman.

5. ABERNETHIE, JAMES, Edinburgh : 1640, F. Touch, 42 E.T.P.

6. ABERNETHIE, JAMES, Edinburgh : 1660, F. Touch, 66 E.T.P.

145

7. ABERNETHIE, JAMES, Edinburgh : 1669, F. Touch
? 70 E.T.P.

8. ABERNETHIE, JOHN, Edinburgh : 1647, mentioned.
9. ABERNETHIE, JOHN, Edinburgh : 1678, mentioned.
10. ABERNETHIE, WILLIAM, Edinburgh : 1649, F.
Touch, 49 E.T.P.

11. ABRAHAM, HENRY (his Christian name is given as
Harry in Y Lists and Henry in L Lists), London :
7 Sept. 1550, Y.; 1561, S.; 1571, R.W. (In
the Yeomanry Lists his name, though in the same
handwriting as other names, is written in pencil.)
12. ACKLAND, THOMAS, London : 11 Aug. 1720, Y.;
5 July 1728, L.; 1739, f.S.; 1743, R.W.
13. ACTON, SAMUEL ETHEE, London : 1755, Y.
14. ADAM, JOHN, Cannongate, Edinburgh : 1793, F.,
White-ironsmith.
14A. ADAM, JOHN, Lynn : mentioned from 1454 to 1478.
15. ADAMS, HENRY, London (Piccadilly) : 14 July 1692,
L.; 1699, f.S.; 1713, R.W.; 1721, U.W.;
1724, M. Touch, 431 L.T.P., which he had
leave to strike in 1686/7. He was married on
2 June 1692, at St. Mary's, Savoy, to Anne
Wheeler.

16. ADAMS, NATHANIEL, London : 14 July 1692, L.
[sic]; 1672, f.R.W., f.U.W., and f.M. In this
latter year he paid the fines for these various
offices in order to be allowed to transfer to the
Glass-sellers' Company. The date shown as his
date of taking Livery is evidently an error in the
records for 1672, L.
17. ADAMS, ROBERT, London : 19 Dec. 1667, L.;
1669, f.S.; 1678, R.W.; 1683, U.W.
18. ADAMS, WILLIAM, London : Touch, 280 L.T.P.,
which he had leave to strike in 1677.

19. ADAMS, WILLIAM, London : 10 Aug. 1668, L.;
(? 1658) 1659, f.S. [sic]; 1668, f.R.W.; 1671,

U.W.; 1677, f.M. Touch, 59 L.T.P. Restruck
after the great fire c. 1670. Died 1681.

20. ADAMSON, ANDREW, Edinburgh : 1711, apprenticed
to Walter Patterson.
21. ADAMTHWATE, THOMAS, York : 1581, F.
22. ADDAMSON, Walsall : 1587, buried at Walsall.
23. ADDYS, JOHN, Bristol : 6 Aug. 1608, F. Apprenticed
to Miles Hobson.
24. ADENBROOK, WILLIAM, London : 1756, Y.
25. ADES, JOHN, Bristol : 3 Mar. 1562, F., and is
mentioned in 1572/3 and 1587. Son-in-law of
John Northall (q.v.). Lived in High Street.
26. ADEY, GEORGE, Bristol : S. of David Adey. Apprenticed
to Robert Bush, 11 Sept. 1784.
27. ADKINSON, WILLIAM, London : Touch, No. 205
L.T.P., which he had leave to strike in 1671/2.

28. ADLAM, AMBROSE, Bristol : 12 Jan. 1638, F.
Married the widow of Thomas Gwinnell,
Pewterer, of Bristol.
29. ADYSON, JOHN, Bristol : 14 Oct. 1650, F. Apprenticed
to Humphrey Coup (? Cox).
AFFERTON, see ASSERTON.
30. AFFLECK, EBENEZER, Edinburgh : 1719, apprenticed
to Alexander Coulthard.
31. AINSWORTH, JEREMIAH, London : 11 March 1702,
Y.
32. AKAM, CHRISTOPHER, York : 1718. Apprenticed
to Leonard Terry 15 Aug. 1718. Son of John
Akam.
33. ALCOCK, CORNELIUS B., Dublin : 1808, mentioned.
33A. ALDER, THOMAS, Sunderland : 1754. Dead in
1764.
34. ALDER, THOMAS, London : 28 Nov. 1667, L.
35. ALDER, WILLIAM, Sunderland : c. 1700.

36. ALDERMAN, THOMAS, London : 1637, Y.

37. ALDERSON, GEORGE, London : 20 June 1728, Y. Touch, 887 L.T.P.

38. ALDERSON, SIR GEORGE, London : July 1817, Y.; 21 Aug. 1817, L.; 1817, f.S.; 1817, f.R.W.; 1821, U.W.; 1823, M. Sheriff of London 1817. Died 1826. Touch, 1084 L.T.P.

39. ALDERSON, JOHN, London : 21 June 1764, Y.; 20 June 1771, L.; 1777, f.S.; 1782, R.W Touch, 1010 L.T.P. In 1792 was in business at 33 Carnaby Market. *See* his Trade Card.

39A. ALDERSON, MARY, London : In 1817 was at 15 Great Marlborough Street.
39B. ALDERSON, M——, London : In 1801 was at 33 Carnaby Street, Carnaby Market.
40. ALDERSON, THOMAS, London : c. 1790-1825. He made the pewterware for the Coronation Banquet of George IV., much of which is at Pewterers' Hall and some in private collections. (*See* Sketch below.)

41. ALDERWICK, RICHARD, London : 16 June 1748, Y. Touch, 959 L.T.P. Was given leave to strike his Touch in 1752.

42. ALDERWICK, RICHARD, London : 17 October 1776, Y. Touch, 1035 L.T.P.

43. ALEXANDER, JOHN, Edinburgh : 1804, apprenticed to Adam Anderson.
44. ALEXANDER, PAUL, London : 1511, R.W.; 1516, U.W. (His name is spelt Alyxander in the records.)
45. ALEXANDER, ROBERT, Glasgow : 1664, Freeman White-ironsmith.
46. ALEXAUNDER, THOMAS, London : 1457, apprenticed to Thomas Dounton; 1479 and 1484, R.W.; 1488, 89, 95 and 99, M. (Spelt Alyssanndre in records.)
46A. ALKIN, FRANCIS, London : Died in 1681 (" Bennett " Book).
47. ALLAN, JAMES, ? Edinburgh : 1656, mentioned. (Ingleby Wood, p. 50.)
48. ALLAN, WILLIAM, Edinburgh : 1677, apprenticed to Alexander Weir.
49. ALLAN, WILLIAM, Cannongate, Edinburgh : 1749, Freeman White-ironsmith.
50. ALLANSON, EDWARD, London : 2 Oct. 1702, L.
51. ALLEN, GEORGE, London : 18 March 1790, Y.
52. ALLEN, GEORGE, London : 19 March 1829, Y.
53. ALLEN, HENRY, York : 1574/5, F.
54. ALLEN, JAMES, London : 17 March 1725, Y.; 19 June 1740, L.; 1752, f.S.; 1756, R.W.; 1765, U.W.; 1766, M.; 1767, died.
55. ALLEN, JOHN, London : 21 Aug. 1679, L.; 1685 f.S.; 1693, f.R.W; 1697, U.W. Touch, 197 L.T.P., dated 1671, and which he had leave to strike in 1671/2.

56. ALLEN, JOSHUA, London : 10 Oct. 1689, Y.
57. ALLEN, RICHARD, London : 6 Aug. 1668, L.; 1668, f.R.W.
58. ALLEN, THOMAS, London : 1553, S.; 1563, R.W.; 1565 and 66, U.W.; 1572, 75, 81 and 82, M. (Spelt Allyn in records.)

59. ALLEN, THOMAS, London: mentioned as working in a metal called " Silvorum " with Major Purling in 1652. Died in 1681. (" Bennett " Book.)
60. ALLEN, WILLIAM, London: 16 Dec. 1736, Y.
61. ALLEN, WILLIAM, London: 1675. Was admonished for faulty ware. Mentioned, 1679-86 in the " Bennett " Book. Touch, 240 L.T.P., which he had leave to strike in 1674/5.

62. ALLEN, WILLIAM, York: 1667-74, apprenticed to John Busfield. 1693, 94, Searcher to the Company.
63. ALLEN, WILLIAM, York: 1711/12, mentioned as a pewterer.
64. ALLET, WILLIAM, London: 1581 and 1592, mentioned. (Welch, i. 290 and ii. 15.)
65. ALLINE, JOHN, Edinburgh: In 1671 was apprenticed to Thomas Alline.
66. ALLINE, THOMAS, Edinburgh: Mentioned in 1671 as master of the last named.
66A. ALLISON, JOHN, Norwich: 1586/7, F.
66B. ALLMOND, JOHN, Manchester: Partner in Ford & Allmond in 1791.
67. ALLOM, PETER, London: 9 Oct. 1707, Y.
68. ALLON, WILLIAM, York: 1686-7, F.
69. ALLUM, RICHARD, of ?: c. 1670-1710.

ALLYN, see ALLEN.
ALYSSANNDRE, see ALEXANDER, THOMAS.
ALYXANDER, see ALEXANDER, PAUL.
70. AMBROSE, WILLIAM, London: 13 Oct. 1763, Y.
71. AMERSON, MICHAEL, London: 22 Sept. 1774, Y.
72. AMISS, JOSIAH, London: 14 Dec. 1727, Y.
73. ANABLE, JOHN, Bury St. Edmunds: 1533, Tenant of the Haberden.
74. ANAYSON, JOHN (? MAGSON, q.v.), Bury St. Edmunds: 1523, M.
75. ANDERSON, ADAM, Edinburgh: 1734. ? Touch, 134 E.T.P.

76. ANDERSON, ADAM, Edinburgh: 1749, Freeman Tinsmith. Shop in 1793 was at 51 South Bridge.
77. ANDERSON, ADAM, Edinburgh: 1794, Freeman.
78. ANDERSON, ADAM, Glasgow: 1777, Freeman White-ironsmith.
79. ANDERSON, JOHN, Edinburgh: 1692, apprenticed to James Herrin.
80. ANDERSON, JOHN, Dublin: 1798-1829, mentioned.
81. ANDERSON, WILLIAM, Edinburgh: 1632, apprenticed to Cornelious Tayleour.
82. ANDERSON, WILLIAM, Edinburgh: 1647, apprenticed to Andro Borthwick. ? Touch, 58 E.T.P.

83. ANDERSON, WILLIAM, Edinburgh: 1719, apprenticed to John Cuthbertsone.
84. ANDERSON, WILLIAM, Edinburgh: 1749, apprenticed to Adam Tait.
85. ANDERSON, WILLIAM, London: 1583, was a master pewterer at this date.
86. ANDERSONE, GEORGE, Edinburgh: 1714, apprenticed to Walter Pattersone.
87. ANDERSONE, JOHN, Edinburgh: 1693, F. Touch, 94 E.T.P.

88. ANDERSONE, ROBERT, Edinburgh: 1697, F. Touch, 98 E.T.P.

89. ANDERTON, JAMES, of ?: c. 1700.

90. ANDERTON, THURSTON, Dublin: Disfranchised for irregularities in 1575.
91. ANDREWS, RICHARD, London: 1553, was a member of the Company chosen to serve as a soldier for the defence of London Bridge against Sir Thomas Wyatt in this year.
92. ANDREWS, ROBERT, London: 17 June 1703, Y.
92A. ANDREWS, WILLIAM, London: Mentioned as a voter in 1724.
93. ANGEL (L), JOHN (see also ANSELL), London: 1677, f.R.W., f.U.W. and f.M.

94. ANGEL, PHILEMON, London: 1 May 1691, L. Touch, 414 L.T.P., which he had leave to strike in 1683/4.

95. ANNISON, WILLIAM GLOVER, London: 11 Oct. 1742, Y., of Crooked Lane. Touches, 933 and 947 L.T.P. He was given leave to use the same device as John Jones. *See* 2661.

96. ANNSELL, STEPHEN, London: 1451, R.W.; 1455, U.W.

97. ANSELL, JOHN, London: 16 Dec. 1714, Y. Touch, 708 L.T.P., which he had leave to strike on 4 April 1717.

98. APPLETON, HENRY, London: 19 Oct. 1749, Y.; 13 June 1751, L.; 1762, f.S.; 1769, f.R.W.; 1782, f.U.W.; 1784, f.M. Was granted leave to use his Coat of Arms in his Touch in 1750. Touch, 943 L.T.P. In 1792 was in business at 108 Fenchurch Street.

99. APPLETON, JOHN, London: 17 March 1768, Y.; 12 Aug. 1779, L.; 1785, S.; 1795, f.R.W.; 1799, U.W.; 1800, M. 1819 died. Touch, 1032 L.T.P.

100. APPLETON, JOHN, London: 13 Oct. 1803, Y.
101. APPS, JOHN, London: 15 Dec. 1785, Y. Died 1831.
102. APPS, PHILIP, London: 20 June 1754, Y.

103. APRISE, WILLIAM, London: 1526, fined in this year for selling wares untouched with his mark.
104. ARCHER, CAPTN. WILLIAM, London: 1632, f.S.; 1646, R.W.; 1649, U.W.; 1653, M. Assay Master in 1654, in which year he was fined for keeping shop in Bow Fair, contrary to order.
105. ARDEN, JOSEPH, London: 23 Aug. 1821, Y.; 23 Aug. 1821, L.; 1832, f.S.; 1844, f.R.W.; 1847, U.W.; 1848, M.
106. ARDEN, RICHARD EDWARD, London: 19 Mar. 1829, Y.; 19 Mar. 1829, L.; 1839, f.S.; 1849, R.W.; 1851, U.W.; 1852, M.
ARLICHESEYE, *see* DE ARLICHESEYE.
ARMERER, *see* ARMURER.
ARMESTRONGE, *see* ARMSTRONG.
107. ARM(ING)ER, THOMAS, of ?: c. 1750.

108. ARMISTON, HENRY, Cork: 1753, mentioned.
109. ARMORER, JOHN, London: 1457, apprenticed to Thomas Dounton.
110. ARMSTRONG, THOMAS, London: 1557, expelled from the Company for refusing to pay the Company's charges and to bear office.
111. ARMURER, JOHN, London: 1457, apprenticed to Piers Bishop. 1477, Beadle to the Company.
112. ARNOTT, GEORGE, London: 9 Oct. 1735, Y.
113. ARNOTT, THOMAS, London: 11 Mar. 1702, Y. Touch, No. 633 L.T.P.

114. ARRETTE, London: 1569, Dead. His wife is mentioned at this date as having her apprentice " sold " to pay a debt.
115. ARTHUR, JOHN, London: 24 Mar. 1803, Y.
116. ASHBERRY, ——, probably of Sheffield: serious collectors would not include pieces bearing this name.
117. ASH, GREGORY, Bristol: 4 Mar. 1741, F. Son of Richard Ash, apprenticed to Ann, widow of Edward Gregory, 7 Jan. 1733. Mentioned in 1761. Mentioned in the 1754 Bristol Poll Book as of St. Mary-le-Port. Partner in the firm Ash & Hutton (*q.v.*).

118. Ash & Hutton, Bristol: c. 1760. Partners, Gregory Ash (above) and William Hutton.

119. Ashenhurst, Peter, Cork: 1759, mentioned.
120. Ashley, James, London: 15 June 1820, Y.; 18 Oct. 1821, L.; 1833, f.S.; 31 Mar. 1851, died, age 77. Shop at 131 Minories. Touch, 1083 L.T.P.

121. Ashley, James, London: 19 Dec. 1850, Y.; 19 Dec. 1850, L.; 1857, f.S.; 1869, R.W.; 1872, U.W.; 1873 and 1874, M. Shop at 131 Minories.
122. Ashley, Thomas James Thurston, London: 15 Mar. 1821, Y.; 9 Dec. 1824, L.; 2 Sept. 1852, died, age 60. Touch, 1090 L.T.P. A note in the records says that the name was first entered as Thomas Thurston Ashley, the additional name of James being added 18 Oct. 1821 by order of the Court.

123. Ashley, Thomas, London: 24 Oct. 1822, Y. Died 1838.
124. Ashlyn, Lawrence (see also Astlyn), London: 1559, S.; 1563, f.R.W.
124A. Ashman, Joseph, London: Mentioned as a voter in 1724.
124B. Ashton, James, Wigan: Mentioned in 1793.
125. Ashton, John, London: 1589. Fined in this year for going to law with a fellow member—Raffe Cowley—instead of submitting his case to the Court.
126. Aspline, William, London: 1615. Was a master at this date.
127. Asserton, John, London: 1495, R.W.; 1500, 1501 and 1506, U.W.

128. Assh, William, London: 1457, apprenticed to William Laye and mentioned again in 1476.
129. Astlyn, John (see also Ashlyn), London: 1504, L.; 1514, R.W. He gave a spoon on being admitted to the Livery.
130. Astlyn, Lawrance, London: 1487 and 1491, R.W.; 1494, U.W.; 1497, 1504, 1505, 1508, 1509, 1515, 1516, 1521, 1522 and 1527, M.
131. Astlyn, Sir Robert, London: 1505-15, mentioned in Mr. Welch's History of the Company (i. 98).
132. Astlyn, Walter, London: 1518, R.W.; 1525 and 1531, U.W.; 1534, M.
133. Atkeys, Jo., London: 1567. Was ordered to put away an apprentice.
134. Atkinson, Joseph, London: 15 Dec. 1763, Y.
135. Atkinson, William, London: 14 Aug. 1718, Y.
136. Atkinson, William, London: 16 Nov. 1672, he was married at St. Mary Magdalene, Old Fish Street Hill, to Martha Hartwell. He is described as a pewterer of St. Paul's, Covent Garden. ? Touch, 205, q.v. under W. Adkinson.
137. Atlee, William, London: 13 Aug. 1696, Y. Touch, 533 L.T.P., which he had leave to strike on 13 Aug. 1696.

138. Atmeyer, William, London: In 1586 obtained a loan from the Company under the will of a certain Mr. Lotton. He was appointed in 1592, one of a committee of eight to treat with a Mr. Gyffard anent the exportation of tin. In the same year he was fined for being absent from a burial.
139. Attersley, Robert, London: 20 Mar. 1788, Y.
140. Attersley, Sarah, London: 20 April 1854, Y.
141. Atterton, Robert, London: 12 Oct. 1693, Y. Touch, 501 L.T.P., which he had leave to strike on 12 Oct. 1693.

142. Attley, Samuel, London: 19 Dec. 1667, L. In Little Britain. See his token.
143. Attwood, William, London: 19 June 1718, Y.; 20 May 1736, L.

143A. ATTWOOD, WILLIAM, London: c. 1680. ("Bennett" Book.) Touch, 377 L.T.P., which he had leave to strike on 22 Mar. 1683.

144. AUCHINLECK, GILBERT, Dundee: 1759. Freeman White-ironsmith.

145. AUCHINLECK, JAMES, Dundee: 1749, Freeman White-ironsmith.

146. AUCHINLECK, ROBERT, Dundee: 1742, Freeman White-ironsmith.

147. AUDOUIT, JAMES, Dublin: 1682, F. A French refugee.

148. AUERY, JOHN, London: was a master workman in 1629, when he is mentioned as having had an apprentice.

149. AUGHTON, JOHN, of ?: c. 1730.

150. AUGUSTONE, JOHN, London: 15 Dec. 1692, Y.

150A. AULGER, ROBERT, London: c. 1680. ("Bennett" Book.)

AUNSELL, see ANNSELL.

151. AUSTEN, JOHN S., Cork: mentioned in 1852 as of 10 Adelaide Street.

152. AUSTEN, JOSEPH, Cork: mentioned in 1795 and again in 1817, when he was at North Main Street. He died in 1845.

153. AUSTEN, JOSEPH & SON, Cork: Were at 54 North Main Street, 1828-33.

154. AUSTEN & SON (cf. the Munster Iron Co.), Cork: Were at 97 Patrick Street in 1844.

155. AUSTEN, ROBERT, Cork: mentioned in 1812 and in 1817 as of Patrick Street. He died in 1817.

156. AUSTEN, ROBERT, London: In 1619 was fined for making bad spoons. 1639, S.; 1651, R.W.; 1657, U.W.; 1659, M.

157. AUSTEN, THOMAS, London: In 1623 was of Fleet Lane, when he was ordered to be brought before the Court by an officer, evidently for some breach of rule. 1639, S.

158. AUSTIN, JAMES, London: 11 Oct. 1764, Y.

159. AUSTIN, JOHN, London: 18 June 1719, Y.

160. AUSTIN, RALPH JOHN, London: 15 Dec. 1796, Y.; 23 Oct. 1806, L. Died 9 Dec. 1856, aged 82 years.

161. AUSTIN, SAMUEL, London: 13 May 1693, L.; 9 Oct. 1701, S.

162. AUSTIN, WILLIAM, London: In 1666 was arraigned for accusing a fellow member of falsely mixing his metal. 28 Nov. 1667, L.

AVERY, see AUERY.

163. AWGER, THOMAS, London: Fined in 1552 for making bad salts.

164. AWMOND, THOMAS, York: 1604/5, F.

165. AXFORD, DANIEL, Bristol: Apprenticed to John Baldwin, Bristol, 28 Aug. 1674. Turned over to John Batchelor, 1677.

166. AXFORD, JACOB, Bath: Mentioned in Bristol Poll Books for 1774 and 1781 as a pewterer and country Voter.

167. AXFORD, JONATHAN, Bristol: 17 July 1675, F. Had an apprentice bound to him in 1686.

168. AXFORD, JOSEPH, Bristol: 20 Oct. 1774, F. Apprenticed to Allen Bright.

168A. AYERS, WILLIAM, London: c. 1680. ("Bennett" Book.)

169. AYLIFE, WILLIAM, London: In 1661 was fined for "his worm not being touched." 28 Nov. 1667, L.

169A. AYMOS, JNO., London: c. 1680. ("Bennett" Book.)

B

170. BABB, BERNARD, London : 15 Aug. 1700, Y. Touch, 577 L.T.P., which he had leave to strike on 2 Dec. 1700.

171. BABBICUM, PHILIP, Bristol : Son of Jacob Babbicum. Apprenticed to Richard Gibson, 29 Jan. 1621.
172. BABY, JESSE, London : 17 Oct. 1805, Y.
173. BACCHAWE, RICHARD, London : 1457. He is mentioned at this date as having been an apprentice to Mr. Coldham.
174. BACHE, RICHARD, London : 16 Dec. 1779, Y. ; 23 Aug. 1804, L. Touch, No. 1049 L.T.P. In 1801 his shop was at St. Catherine's.

BACHELER, *see* BACHELOR.

175. BACHILER, THOMAS, London : 1457. Was apprenticed to John Veysy.
176. BACKESTER, RICHARD, Bristol : 18 Aug. 1651, F. Apprenticed to William Haile.
177. BACKHOWSE, ROBERT (*see* also BAKEHOWSE), London : Fined in 1561 for bad wares.
178. BACKHOWSE, JOHN, London : In 1578 he worked with a certain Thomas Poole and made spoons. In 1591 he was fined for hawking pewter.
179. BACON, BENJAMIN, London : 22 June 1749, Y. Touch, 979 L.T.P. Was granted leave to strike his Touch in 1758.

180. BACON, GEORGE, London : 19 June 1746, Y. ; 18 Dec. 1746, L. ; 1758, S. ; 1762, R.W. Died 1771. Was in business in The Strand. Touch, 921 L.T.P. Was given leave to strike his Touch on 20 June 1746.

180A. BACON, GEORGE, London : Was given leave to strike his Touch in 1758.
181. BACON, THOMAS, London : No mention of his name in the Y. or L. Lists, but Touch, 768 L.T.P., he had leave to strike on 22 April 1724.

182. BADCOCK(E), JOHN, London : 15 Mar. 1764, Y.
183. BADCOCK(E), THOMAS, London : 4 Oct. 1688, Y.
184. BADCOCK(E), THOMAS, London : 13 Feb. 1787, Y.
185. BAGGS, JOHN, London : In 1672 was Beadle to the Company and permitted to take an apprentice.
185A. BAGNEY, JAMES, London : On a voting list in 1724.
186. BAGSHAW, GEORGE, London : 13 Oct. 1808, Y. ; 15 Mar. 1810, L. ; 1817, f.S. ; 1848, Beadle. Died 12 Jan. 1864.
187. BAGSHAW, RICHARD, London : 17 Dec. 1772, Y. ; 16 Mar. 1809, L. ; 1814, f.S. Touch, No. 1058 L.T.P. (Compare his Touch with that of Benjamin Townsend, No. 967.)

188. BAGSHAW, RICHARD, London : 13 Dec. 1827, Y. ; 13 Dec. 1827, L. ; 1838, f.S. ; 1848, R.W. Died 7 Oct. 1849.
189. BAGSHAW, THOMAS, London : 19 June 1800, Y. ; 15 Mar. 1810, L. ; 1816, f.S. Died 1827.
190. BAILEY, JOHN (*see* also BAYLEY), London : 14 June 1750, Y. ; 11 April 1764, L. ; 1770, f.S. ; 1778, f.R.W. ; 1788, U.W. ; 1789, M. Dead 1809.
191. BAILEY, SOPHIA, London : 15 June 1809, Y.
192. BAILY(E), ANDREW, Glasgow : 1658, was a Freeman White-ironsmith.
193. BAILY(E), EDWIN, Bristol : Apprenticed to his father, Thomas Baily, 9 Nov. 1704.
194. BAILY(E), THOMAS, Bristol : Mentioned with his wife Avice in 1680. Dead in 1706.
195. BAIN, ADAM (? BANE), Edinburgh : In 1719 was apprenticed to Thomas Inglis.

196. BAIN, ALEXANDER, Edinburgh : No date given, but from his mark and the pieces whereon it appears he would be early nineteenth century.

197. BAIN, WILLIAM, Edinburgh : In 1804 was apprenticed to Robert Kinnieburgh.
198. BAINTON, JEREMIAH, London : 14 Aug. 1718, Y.
199. BAKEHOWSE, WILFRED, London : 1558, Y. Was in business in Blasing Lane.
200. BAKER, CHARLES, London : 30 June 1783, Y.
201. BAKER, CHRISTOPHER, Blagdon, Somerset : Apprenticed to John Batcheler, Bristol, 31 Aug. 1681.
202. BAKER, HUMPHREY, London : In 1577 was fined for faulty wares and in 1598 was in trouble with his workman George Miller.
202A. BAKER, JOHN, Hull : 5 June 1662, F. His shop was in High Street. *See* illustrations of his tokens. He died in 1710.
203. BAKER, JOHN, London : In 1457 was evidently a Freeman of the Company, for he is given as a covenant servant to John Gugge the younger.
204. BAKER, RICHARD, Bristol : Mentioned c. 1665.
205. BAKER, SAMUEL, London : 1678, S.
206. BAKER, WILLIAM, London : 1553, R.W. ; 1558, U.W.
207. BAKER, WILLIAM, London : In 1457 was apprenticed to Thomas Dounton.
208. BAKER, WILLIAM, London : 1450, M.
209. BAKER, WILLIAM, London : In 1457 was apprenticed to Piers Bisshop.
210. BALDWIN, CHRISTOPHER, of Wigan. Will proved at Chester, in 1725 : c. 1690-1725.

210A. BALDWIN, HENRY, Liverpool : In 1793 was a Pewterer, Brazier and Tinman, at 50 Pool Lane.
211. BALDWIN, JOHN, Bristol : 17 Mar. 1654, F. Apprenticed to Peter Lodge. Dead in 1677. Mentioned in 1674.
211A. BALDWIN, RALPH, Wigan. Letters of Administration at Chester in 1744.
211B. BALDWIN, ROBERT, Wigan. Will proved at Chester in 1695.
212. BALDWIN, ROBERT, Wigan. Letters of Administration granted at Chester, in 1726 : c. 1690-1726, judging by types on which his marks appear.

213. BALDWIN, W., of ? : Early eighteenth century.

214. BALL, JOHN (*see also* BULL), London : 4 May 1826, Y. and L. Died 1830.
214A. BALL, ROBERT, London : c. 1680. (" Bennett " Book.)
215. BALLANTINE, JOHN, Glasgow : In 1775 was a White-ironsmith.
216. BALLANTYNE, JOHN, Edinburgh : 1755, F.
217. BALLANTYNE, WILLIAM, Edinburgh : 1742, F. Died c. 1748. Touch, 137 E.T.P.

218. BALLANTYNE, WILLIAM, Edinburgh : 1749, F. Touch, 139 E.T.P. In 1773 his shop was in Cowgate Head.

219. BALLANTYNE, MRS. WILLIAM, Edinburgh : From 1780 to 1786 continued the business of the last named.
220. BALLARD, WILLIAM, London : 18 Mar. 1741, Y.
221. BAMPTON, THOMAS, London : 23 Mar. 1775, Y.
222. BAMPTON, WILLIAM, London : 7 Mar. 1742, Y. ; 16 Dec. 1756, L. ; 1765, S. ; 1774, R.W. ; 1783, U.W. ; 1785, M. and was dead in 1799.

In 1776 and 1792 his shop was in Bishopgate Street. Touch, 937 L.T.P. Was given leave to strike his Touch on 14 Dec. 1749.

222A. BANCK(E)s, ADAM, of Milngate (? Chester). Will proved at Chester in 1716; c. 1690/1716.

223. BANCK(E)s, ANDREW, Dublin: 1624, F. Later mention of him is found in 1647.
224. BANCK(E)s, CHRISTOPHER, Bewdley: died c. 1870.
224A. BANCK(E)s, CHRISTOPHER, Bewdley: Mentioned in a directory in 1790.
225. BANCK(E)s, FRANCIS, Galway: Died in 1687. *See* illustration of his token.
226. BANCK(E)s, GEORGE, Edinburgh: In 1804 was apprenticed to John Sibbald.
227. BANCK(E)s, I. & Co., ? Bewdley: The set of " Hallmarks " which accompany this maker's Touch *may* be those of Christopher Bancks above. c. 1800-1820.

228. BANCK(E)s, JAMES, of Wigan. Will proved at Chester in 1755. He probably succeeded Ralph Wilson of Chester whose name appears with his own.

229. BANCK(E)s, NICHOLAS, Dublin: 1648, F. Later mention of him is found in 1660.
230. BANCK(E)s, PETER, Kilkenny: Mentioned in 1713.
231. BANCK(E)s, RALPH, Dublin: 1610, F.

232. BANCK(E)s, ROBERT, ? Galway: c. 1675. Note the similar device, the pot of flowers, to that on Francis Banckes' token above.

232A. BANCK(E)s, ROBERT, Wigan. Will proved at Chester in 1692.
233. BANCK(E)s, ROGER, Dublin: 1627, F.
234. BANCK(E)s, R——, of ?: Appears with the mark of Thomas Banckes.

235. BANCK(E)s, THOMAS, of ?: c. 1690. *See* last mark.
236. BANCK(E)s, WILLIAM, of ?: c. 1700. Probably William Bancks of Kilkenny (*q.v.*).

237. BANCK(E)s, WILLIAM, Dublin: 1583, F.
238. BANCK(E)s, WILLIAM, Kilkenny: Mentioned in 1687.
238A. BANCK(E)s, WILLIAM, Bewdley: Mentioned in a directory in 1790.

239. BANCK(E)s, WILLIAM, Bewdley: Died c. 1847.
240. BANCK(E)s, WILLIAM, of ?: c. 1690.

(Note the three different spellings)

BANE, *see* BAIN.
241. BANFIELD, JOHN, Dublin: Is mentioned in 1732 and died 1771.
242. BANGHAM, WILLIAM, London: 21 Mar. 1805, Y.
243. BANKS, GEORGE, Edinburgh: Apprenticed in 1804 to John Sibbald.
244. BANKS, JOHN, London: In 1620 was brought up before the Company for a debt to one Daniel Smith.
245. BANNISTER, THOMAS, London: 25 Sept. 1701. Y.

246. BARBER, HENRY, Ludlow: 9 June 1634, F. Pewterer and Brazier.

247. BARBER, JAMES, London: 17 Mar. 1831, Y.

248. BARBER, JOHN, London: In 1457 was apprenticed to Richard Kyrke.

249. BARBER, JOSEPH, London: 18 Mar. 1773, Y.; 16 Oct. 1777, L.; 1783, S.; 1792, R.W.; 1796, U.W.; 1797, M. Died 26 April 1834, aged 86.

250. BARBER, NATHANIEL, London: 16 Sept. 1777, Y.; 20 June 1782, L.; 1787, S. The *London Gazette* records his Bankruptcy on 22 Mar. 1788. Touch, 1037 L.T.P. Was in business in Snowhill. (Compare the Touch of John Home, whom he probably succeeded.) *See* note pp. 52 and 53.

251. BARBER, SAMUEL, London: 29 Aug. 1782, Y.; 22 June 1786, L.; 1792, f.S. Died 1823.

252. BARBER, WILLIAM, Evesham, Worcs.: Mentioned in 1701.

253. BARCLAY, ROBERT, London: 21 Oct. 1756, Y.

253A. BARFORD, RICHARD, London: c. 1680. ("Bennett" Book.) Touch, 229 L.T.P., which he had leave to strike in 1674/5.

254. BARKER, JOHN, London: In 1553 was one of a body of soldiers raised from the Company to defend London Bridge against Sir Thomas Wyatt. 1567, S.; 1577, R.W.; 1585, U.W.

255. BARLAND, GEORGE, Perth: In 1750 was an apprentice to David Young.

256. BARLOW, JOHN, London: 20 Mar. 1698, Y. Touch, 554 L.T.P., which he had leave to strike on 7 April 1699. Compare his mark with those of Johnson & George Smith.

257. BARNADYNE —— (? CARNADYNE, *q.v.*), London: Mentioned in 1591.

258. BARNARD, ——, London: In 1655 his Touch was granted to William Pettiver (*q.v.*), who was about to be made a Freeman. One must assume that Barnard was either dead or retired, or his Touch would not have been granted to another man.

259. BARNARD, JAMES, Bristol: Apprenticed to Humphrey Beale, 5 Feb. 1654.

260. BARNES, JOHN, London: 20 June 1717, Y. Of St. Bennet's, Paul's Wharf. Insolvent in 1729.

261. BARNES, THOMAS, London: 4 Aug. 1726, Y.; 3 Aug. 1738, L. Touch, 835 L.T.P., which he had leave to strike in 1728.

262. BARNES, WILLIAM, London: 20 Dec. 1770, Y. Touch, 1034 L.T.P. (*cf.* Touches of Robert Patience and Thomas Wheeler.)

263. BARNET, JOHN, London: In 1475 was apprenticed to Thomas Dounton.

264. BARNETT, ROBERT, London: 16 Oct. 1783, Y.; 23 June 1803, L.; 1807. f.S.; 1815, f.R.W. Died 1829. Touch, 1059 L.T.P. (*Cf.* Touch of Robert Jupe.)

265. BARNSDALE, NICHOLAS, London: In 1574 was fined for frequent absence from Hall and rudeness to the Master of the Company.

265A. BARNWELL, ROBERT, London: Of the Temple. Mentioned in a voters' list of 1722.

266. BARON, JOHN, London: In 1457 was a journeyman to John Gugge the elder.

267. BARO(WE), STEPHEN, London: In 1553 was one of a body of soldiers raised from the Company to defend London Bridge against Sir Thomas Wyatt. In 1559 he was fined for selling wares below the standard price.

268. BARRETT, HENRY, London: Mentioned as being dead in 1574.

269. BARRETT, MRS. HENRY, London: Mentioned as endeavouring to carry on the business of her late husband, the last named.

270. BARRETT, LANCELOT, London : 17 Mar. 1763, Y.
271. BARRINGTON, WILLIAM, Dublin : Mention is found of him in 1824 and again in 1839.

BARRO, *see* BARO.

272. BARRON, ROBERT, London : 14 Dec. 1786, Y. and L. Died May 1793.
273. BARRON, SAMUEL, Bristol : S. of Wm. B., Bristol. Apprenticed to his father, 25 Nov. 1697.
274. BARRON, SAMUEL, Wells : S. of Saml. B., Wells, decd. Apprenticed to Wm. Barron, Bristol, 21 Oct. 1693.
275. BARRON, WILLIAM, senr., Bristol : Mentioned in 1697. Apprenticed to Richard Clifford, 4 Oct. 1671, F.
276. BARRON, WILLIAM, junr., Bristol : 13 July 1702, F. Son of Wm. Barron, senr., Bristol. Apprenticed to his parents, 31 July 1693.
276A. BARROW, PETER, Stockport : In 1805 was at Underbank.
277. BARROW, RICHARD (*see* also BARO), London : 28 Nov. 1667, L.
277A. BARROW, THOMAS, Shrewsbury : Mentioned as of Pride Hill, Shrewsbury, in *Salopian Journal*, 9 Dec. 1795.
278. BARTLETT, WALTER, Northampton : In 1623 had faulty wares seized at Rowell Fair.
279. BARTLETT, WILLIAM, of ? : c. 1740-1770.

280. BARTON, DANIEL, London : His smaller Touch, *q.v*, bears the date 1670 and is found on slip-top spoons. 20 Aug. 1678, L.; 1684, S.; 1692, R.W.; 1699, U.W. Touches, 181 and 298 L.T.P.

281. BARTON, DANIEL, London : 24 May 1700, Y. Touch, 573 L.T.P., which he had leave to strike on 24 May 1700.

281A. BARTON, JOHN, Manchester : In 1791 was a partner in Barton & Fishwick.
282. BARTON, JOSEPH, London : 18 Dec. 1718, Y.
283. BARTON, RICHARD, London : 22 Jan. 1718, Y.
284. BARTON, THOMAS, London : In 1457 was a journeyman to William Crowde and in 1463 was in such low water as to receive alms from the Company.
285. BARTON, WILLIAM, London : In 1693 he had bad wares seized.
285A. BARTON & FISHWICK, Manchester : John Barton and Robert Fishwick opened shop in 1791. Formerly with Thomas Radford.
286. BARTRAM, JAMES, York : 1568, F.
287. BARWYCK, RICHARD, London : In 1588 was in trouble with the Company for going away from London and returning to work there without leave.
288. BARWYCKE, THOMAS, London : In 1591 was in Breed Street, where he had bad wares seized.
289. BASKER, GEORGE, London : In 1557 was before the Company for debt.
290. BASKERVILLE, JOHN, London : 20 June 1695, L. He was buried 24 Aug. 1702 at St. Vedast, Foster Lane. Touch, 474 L.T.P., which he had leave to strike on 14 Dec. 1691.

291. BASKERVILLE, THOMAS, London : 14 Oct. 1731, Y.
292. BASNETT, JAMES, London : 15 Mar. 1821, Y. and L.
293. BASNETT, NATHANIEL, London : 19 Mar. 1767, Y.; 19 June 1777, L.; 1782, f.S.; 1791, f.R.W.; 1796, f.U.W.; 1797, f.M.
294. BASSETT, ISAAC, London : 11 Oct. 1722, Y.
295. BATCHELER, JOHN, Bristol : His name is spelt variously Batcheler, Batchelor, Bacheler, &c. in the records. 10 Feb. 1676, F. Apprenticed to Thomas Lodge. Died c. 1713. His business was carried on by his widow, Honor, until about 1727.

296. BATCHELOR, JOHN, London : 17 Oct. 1762, Y.

297. BATE, JOHN, Dublin: Mentioned in 1746 and 1768, and died 1780.
298. BATE, GEORGE, Aylesbury: In 1557 was found in possession of false wares which were seized.
299. BATES, GEORGE, Bristol: 14 Feb. 1756, F. Apprenticed to Thomas Page, Bristol, 16 Dec. 1747.
300. BATEMAN, AARON, senr., London: 15 Mar. 1721, Y.
301. BATEMAN, AARON, junr., London: 13 June 1734, Y.
302. BATEMAN, AARON, London: 11 Oct. 1744, Y.
303. BATEMAN, BENJAMIN, London: 18 June 1719, Y.
303A. BATEMAN, DANIEL, London: c. 1680. ("Bennett" Book.)
304. BATEMAN, FRANCIS, London: 23 Sept. 1708, Y.
305. BATEMAN, JOHN, London: 1653, S.; 1663, R.W.; 1668, U.W.; 1670, M.
306. BATEMAN, MOSES, London: 20 Mar. 1700, Y.
307. BATEMAN, THOMAS, London: 9 Aug. 1733, Y.
308. BATEMAN, THOMAS, London: 16 Dec. 1742, Y.
309. BATEMAN, THOMAS, London: 9 June 1774, Y.
310. BATES, GEORGE, Bristol: Mentioned as of St. Michael's, Bristol, in the Bristol Poll Books of 1774, 1781 and 1784.
311. BATHURST, JOHN, London: 20 Dec. 1705, Y.; 19 May 1715, L.
312. BATHUS, WILLIAM, London: 22 June 1797, Y. Touch, 1070 L.T.P.

313. BATIE, ANDRO, Edinburgh: In 1617 was apprenticed to George Gledstane.
314. BATTE, JOHN, London: In 1457 was a journeyman to John Kendale.
315. BATTE, THOMAS, London: Was fined in 1671 for non-payment of quarterage to the Company.
316. BATTESON, ABRAHAM (? BATTISON), York: Apprenticed on 24 Dec. 1675 for seven years to Robert Smith. Obtained his Freedom in 1698/9. Was searcher to the York Guild in 1701, 1702 and 1703, and is last mentioned in 1729.
317. BATTESON, JOHN, York: 1684, F.
318. BATTESON, JOHN, York: Apprentice from 21 Dec. 1707 for seven years to Abraham Batteson. 20 June 1733, F. 1725 and 1726, Searcher to the Company.
319. BATTESON, THOMAS, London: 28 Nov. 1667, L. Touch, 86 L.T.P.

320. BATTESON, WILLIAM, London: Pewterer of St. Helen's, married Mary Bennett at all Hallows-in-the-Wall, 12 Mar. 1673.
321. BAWDYN, FRANCIS, London: Was in 1568 whipped before the Company for robbing his master John Collier.
322. BAXTER, JOHN, London: 1505, L.; 1513, R.W.; 1517 and 1528, U.W.; 1531, M. He presented a spoon to the Company on his election to the Livery.
323. BAYLEY, ZACHARY, London: Dead before the 3 Aug. 1625.
324. BAYNE, JAMES, London: Mentioned in 1556.
325. BAYSBROWN, CHRISTOPHER, York: 1493/4, F.
326. BAYTE, RICHARD, London: Mentioned in 1566.
327. BE, JOHN (? BEE), York: 1530/31, F. Was one of the City Chamberlains in 1553, and the last mention one finds of him is in 1566.
328. BEAKER, RICHARD, Bristol: Apprenticed to Robert Read, Bristol, 17 Nov. 1649.
329. BEALE, HUMPHREY, Bristol and Othere, Somerset: 6 Mar. 1647, F. Apprenticed to William Pascall, Bristol, 4 Sept. 1639. Died in 1655.
330. BEAMONT, WILLIAM, London: 20 June 1706, Y. Touch, 683 L.T.P.

331. BEARD, EDMUND, Banwell, Somerset: Apprenticed to William Lansdown, Bristol, 5 April 1755.
332. BEARD, SAMPSON, London: 1 May 1691, L.
333. BEARD, THOMAS, London: 21 June 1688, Y.
334. BEAR(D)SLEY, ALLISON, London: 22 Mar. 1704, Y.; 21 June 1711, L.; 1717, f.S.; 1728, f.R.W., f.U.W. and f.M.
335. BEAR(D)SLEY, EDWARD, London: 19 June 1735, Y. and L.; 1744, S.; 1749, R.W.
336. BEAR(D)SLEY, JOB, London: 22 Aug. 1678, L.
337. BEAR(D)SLEY, JOB, London: 22 Mar. 1704, Y.; 21 June 1711, L.
337A. BEART, FRANCIS, Norwich: 1622, F.
337B. BEART, FRANCIS, Norwich: 1655, F.
337C. BEART, JOHN, Norwich: 1661, F.
337D. BEART, SAMUEL, Norwich: 1668, F.
338. BEASLEY, ——, London: In 1714/5 was accused of using poor metal in his goods.
339. BEATH, ——, London: Was contemporary with Peter Lekeux, early nineteenth century, and was in business in Princes Street, Soho. This mark

appears in conjunction with that of Lekeux, whose pieces he probably factored.

340. BEATHIE, GEORGE, Perth: In 1759 was apprenticed to David Young.
341. BEAUCHAMP, ROBERT, Bristol; Mentioned in 1763.
342. BEAUMONT, JOHN, London: 19 Aug. 1830, Y. and L.
343. BEAVINS, ARNOLD, Haverfordwest: Apprenticed to John Knowles, Bristol, 30 Dec. 1657.
344. BEAVOR, JOSEPH, Bristol and Swansea: 9 July 1727, F. Apprenticed to Edward Gregory, Bristol, 26 Sept. 1713.
345. BECK, WILLIAM, London: 7 Oct. 1725, Y.
346. BECKETT, THOMAS, London: 17 Dec. 1702, Y.; 19 May 1715, L.; 1721, S.; 1731, R.W. Died 1731. Touch, 611 L.T.P., which he had leave to strike on 23 April 1703.

347. BEDDOW, NATHAN, London: 6 Aug. 1730, Y.
348. BEDEL, JOHN (? BIDDLE), London: 1698, f.L.
349. BEDYLL, WILLIAM, London: In 1457 was apprenticed to William Crowde.
   BEE, see BE.
350. BEECRAFT, RICHARD, London: 10 June 1736, Y.
351. BEEHOE, JOSIAS, London: 23 Mar. 1720, Y.
352. BEESLEE, FRANCIS, London: 14 Dec. 1693, Y.
353. BEESTON, GEORGE, London: 13 Oct. 1743, Y.; 16 Dec. 1756, L.; 1765, S. Touch, 939 L.T.P. (Cf. John Hayton.) Was given leave to strike his Touch in 1749.

354. BEESTON, JAMES, London: 17 June 1756, Y.
355. BEITH, ROBERT, Glasgow: 1794, F. White-ironsmith.
356. BEKER, RICHARD, Bristol: 30 Sept. 1659, F. Apprenticed to Robert Reed.
357. BEKWITH, ROBERT, York: 1499, F., by patrimony.
358. BEKWITH, THOMAS, York: 1589, F., by patrimony.
359. BEKYRSTAFF, RICHARD, London: Apprenticed in 1457 to John Parys.

360. BELL, DAVID, Perth: Was an essay-master in 1712.
361. BELL, JAMES, Edinburgh: 1794, F.
362. BELL, JOHN, London: 17 Dec. 1724, Y.
363. BELL, JOHNE, Perth: 1628, F.
364. BELL, LAURENS, Aberdeen: Mentioned in 1581.
365. BELL, RICHARD, York: 1536, F.
366. BELL, ROBERT, York: 1569, F.
367. BELL, ROBERT, London: 18 Oct. 1748, Y.
368. BELL, WILLIAM, London: 23 Mar. 1703, Y.
369. BELL (? s), HENRY, of ?: c. 1740.

369A. BELSHER, RICHARD, London: c. 1680. ("Bennett" Book.) Touch, 225 L.T.P., which he had leave to strike in 1673/4.

370. BELSHER, WILLIAM, London: Mentioned in 1716.
371. BELSON, JOHN, London: 10 Oct. 1734, Y.; 25 Aug. 1748, L. Dead in 1783. Touch, 890 L.T.P. Was in business in Fish Street Hill and Worcester Street in the Park, Southwark. He had leave to strike his Touch on 20 Sept. 1738.

372. BELSON, RICHARD, London: 13 Aug. 1724, Y.
373. BELTON, ROBERT, Bristol: 9 Feb. 1671, F. Married Jane, daughter of Robert Langford. Dead in 1695, when his widow was carrying on the business.
374. BELTON, ROBERT, Bristol: Apprenticed to his father, Robert Belton, 28 Oct. 1686, and is mentioned in 1706.
375. BELTON, THOMAS, Bristol: 12 Aug. 1706, F. Apprenticed to his father, Robert B., 16 Sept. 1690.

375A. BENHAM, J., London : c. 1840. In Wigmore St.

376. BENNET(T), EDWARD, Bandon : Died in 1773.
378. BENNET(T) & CHAPMAN, London : c. 1761. Their Touch was struck No. 994 L.T.P. The Partners were William Bennett, 1758, Y., and Oxton Chapman, 1760, Y. They were given leave to strike their Touch on 19 Mar. 1761.

379. BENNET(T), JOHN, London : 1656, f.L.; 1661, f.S.; 1669, R.W.; 1674, U.W.; 1679, M.
380. BENNET(T), JOHN, London : 1653, R.W.
381. BENNET(T), PATRICK, Perth : 1726, F.
382. BENNET(T), PHILIP, London : 1542, R.W.
383. BENNET(T), THOMAS, London : 11 Nov. 1700, Y. Touch, 580 L.T.P., which he had leave to strike on 2 Dec. 1700.

383A. BENNET(T), THOMAS, London : c. 1680 (" Bennett " Book). His name does not appear after 1684.
384. BENNET(T), THOMAS, Scilly, Glamorgan : Mentioned in the Bristol Poll Book of 1781 as a Country Voter of Scilly.
385. BENNET(T), THOMAS, Bristol and English Bicknor, Glocs. : 19 Mar. 1761, F. Apprenticed to Wm. Calder, Bristol, 5 Nov. 1749, and turned over to James Reid, Bristol, 5 Feb. 1752. Mentioned in the Bristol Poll Book of 1774 as of St. Augustine's, Bristol.

386. BENNET(T), T——, Bristol : c. 1720. His mark appears in conjunction with the " Hall Marks " of Joseph Giddings, suggesting a possible business partnership or succession.

387. BENNET(T), THOMAS, London : 18 June 1807, Y.
388. BENNET(T), WILLIAM, London : 1662, Y.; 1672 S.; 1673, f.R.W., f.U.W. and f.M.
389. BENNET(T), WILLIAM, London : 19 Oct. 1758, Y. Touch, 998 L.T.P. Was a partner in Bennett & Chapman ; see their Touch above, wherein the same Arms appear impaling those of (?) Chapman.

390. BENNET(T), WILLIAM, London : Died in 1524. Had his shop on Tower Hill.
391. BENNET(T), WILLIAM, London : In 1457 was an apprentice to Richard Lawton.
392. BENNTLE, JOHN, Wotton-under-Edge, Glocs. : Apprenticed to Stephen Cox, Bristol, 12 Oct. 1736.
393. BENSON, ARTHUR, Hawkshead, Lancs. : S. of Brian Benson. Apprenticed to John Benson, Bristol, 2 Aug. 1605, for seven years.
394. BENSON, ARTHUR, Langdale, Westmorland : S. of Solomon Benson. Apprenticed to Bernard Benson, Bristol, for nine years from 4 Feb. 1626.
395. BENSON, BERNARD, Hawkshead, Lancs. : S. of Brian Benson. Apprenticed to Richard Hollenbrock, Bristol, 4 May 1601. Mentioned in 1637.
396. BENSON, BERNARD, Hawkshead, Lancs. : S. of Brian Benson. Apprenticed to John Knowles, Bristol, 22 June 1655.
397. BENSON, EDWARD, London : In 1611 was fined for faulty wares.
398. BENSON, GEORGE, Bristol : Mentioned, with his wife Frances, from 1601 to 1625.
399. BENSON, GEORGE, Bristol and Scelwith, Somerset : 26 June 1646, F. Son of Wm. Benson. Apprenticed to Bernard Benson, Bristol, pewterer, and Marie his wife, for eight years from 7 Feb. 1637.
400. BENSON, JOHN, Bristol : Mentioned, with his wife Matilde, from 1605 to 1617.

401. BENSON, JOHN, London : 9 Oct. 1740, Y. Touch, 904 L.T.P.

402. BENSON, JOHN, London : 9 Mar. 1740, L.; 1752, S.
403. BENSON, ROBERT, York : 1449/50, F.
404. BENSTON, JOHN, London : Was in 1556 a subscriber to a testimonial to Sir Thomas Curtis, a former Master of the Company, on his election to the Lord Mayoralty of the City.
405. BENSTON, JOHN, Bristol : Son of Richard. Apprenticed to Thomas Gwinnell, Bristol, and Alice his wife, 14 Mar. 1621.
406. BENTON, RALPH, London : 11 Aug. 1681, L. Touch, 274 L.T.P. Omitted from Y. List after 1684. ("Bennett" Book.)

407. BENTLEY, C., London : c. 1840. Of Woodstock Street.

408. BERNARD, ONESIPHORUS, London : 15 Mar. 1722, Y. A partner in the firm of White & Bernard. Touch, 743 L.T.P. (q.v.).
409. BERNARD, PETER, Bristol : 8 Dec. 1736, F.
410. BERNERS, THOMAS, London : 14 Dec. 1699, Y.
411. BERROW, JOHN, junr., Bristol and Brecon : 17 April 1711, F. · Apprenticed to John Bacheler, Bristol, 30 Dec. 1703. Mentioned in the Bristol Poll Books of 1734 and 1739 as of St. James's, Bristol.
412. BERROW, JOHN, senr., Bristol and Brecon : Mentioned in 1703.
413. BESOUTH, JOSEPH, London : 15 Mar. 1759, Y.
414. BESSANT, NATHANIEL, London : 17 Dec. 1702, Y. Touch, 603 L.T.P.

415. BESWICK, THOMAS (? URSWYCKE), London : 1505, L.; 1515 and 1516, R.W.; 1530, U.W.; 1533 and 1540, M. Presented a spoon to the Company on admission to the Livery.
416. BETTE, JOHN, Bristol : Dead in 1590.
417. BETTS, THOMAS, London : His Touch, No. 341 L.T.P., was struck c. 1680. Mentioned in the "Bennett" Book, 1679-1686.

418. BETTY, EDWARD, Bristol and Woolley, Somerset : 8 Sept. 1691, F. S. of Robert. Apprenticed to John Bacheler, pewterer, Bristol, 11 May 1682.
419. BEVERIDGE, DAVID, Perth : Apprenticed to David Young, 1772.
420. BEWLAY, THOMAS, York : Apprenticed on 6 Jan. 1726 for seven years to John Battison. Son of Isabell Bewlay.
420A. BEXHILL, SAMUEL, London : Was on the voting list in 1724.
421. BIDDLE, JOHN (? BEDEL), London : 1700, L. He was summoned to accept the Livery on 7 Aug. 1700.
422. BHYTYNG, JOHN, London : 1480, R.W.
423. BIDMEAD, JONATHAN, London : 17 Oct. 1728, Y.
424. BIGG, RICHARD, London : In 1557 was servant to Thomas Fisher and William Jones.
425. BIL(L)ING, SAMUEL, Coventry : c. 1675-1707. Mayor of Coventry 1704/5; Died 19 March 1707, aged 57.

426. BILLS, WILLIAM, London : 11 Dec. 1701, Y.
427. BINFIELD, JOHN, London : 22 Mar. 1710, Y.
428. BIRD, JOHN, London : Died in 1667, having been Beadle to the Company. *See* his token, whereon his address is Pewterers' Hall, Lime Street.
429. BIRCH, ROBERT, Mangotsfield : S. of Robert. Apprenticed to James Powell, Bristol, and Mary his wife, 27 June 1771.
430. BIRCH & VILLERS (*see* also YATES & BIRCH), Birmingham : c. 1775-1820. *See* note under "Duncumb."

430A. BIRKENHEAD, JNO., London : c. 1680. ("Bennett" Book.)

431. BISHOP, JAMES (*see* also BYSSHOP), London : 18 Mar. 1724, Y. Touch, 781 L.T.P., which he had leave to strike in 1724.

432. BISSHOP, GEORGE, Bristol : 8 Aug. 1642, F. S. of John. Apprenticed to Thomas Hobson and Elizabeth his wife for eight years from 20 Dec. 1634.

433. BISSET, DAVID, Perth : Was a Master in 1773.

434. BISSET, PATRICK, Perth : In 1771 was Freeman pewterer, White-ironsmith and Coppersmith.

435. BLACK, CHARLES, Aberdeen : In 1731 was apprenticed to William Johnston.

435A. BLACKER, JOHN, London : c. 1680. ("Bennett" Book.)

436. BLACKMAN, JOHN, London : 17 June 1703, Y.

437. BLACKWELL, BENJAMIN, London : c. 1679. Touch, 320 L.T.P., struck c. 1679. Mentioned in the "Bennett" Book from 1679-1686. In 1696 and 1712 he was at the South End, East Side, of London Bridge.

437A. BLACKWELL, BENJAMIN, of ? : Appears with date 1741 at Pishill Church, Oxon.

438. BLACKWELL, JOHN, London : Was fined in 1681 for "untouched" ware.

439. BLACKWELL, THOMAS, London : 20 Mar. 1706, Y.

440. BLACKWELL, THOMAS, London : 1547, R.W.

440A. BLACKWELL, TIMOTHY, London : In 1675 he was on the South End, East Side, of London Bridge.

441. BLA(Y)DES, RALPH, York : Apprenticed to Ralph Symson. 1517/8, F. Was one of the City Chamberlains, 1544/5 and last mention found of him is in 1549/50.

442. BLAGRAVE, WILLIAM, London : 11 Aug. 1664, L. ; 1668, f.S.

443. BLAIKIE, JOHN, Perth : Was in 1771 an apprentice to Patrick Bisset.

444. BLAK, THOMAS, London : In 1457 was apprenticed to Walter Warde.

445. BLAKE, JOHN, London : 10 Aug. 1699, Y.

446. BLAKE, JOHN, London : 22 Aug. 1786, Y. ; 20 June 1793, L. ; 1797, f.S. ; 1804-06, R.W. Died 1809.

447. BLAKE, JOHN, London : 15 Mar. 1810, Y. ; 15 Mar. 1810, L. ; 1816, f.S. ; 1827, R.W. ; 1830, U.W. ; 1832, M.

448. BLAKENEY, JOHN, London : In 1457 was a covenant man to Robert Chamberleyn.

449. BLAND, HENRY, London : 14 Dec. 1732, Y.

450. BLAND, JOHN, London : 18 June 1730, Y. ; 20 Mar. 1734, L.

451. BLAND, WILLIAM, London : 17 June 1703, Y.

452. BLAND, WILLIAM, London : 23 June 1726, Y.

BLAYDES, *see* BLADES.

453. BLENMAN, JOHN, London : In Sept. 1726 he was granted leave to have Abraham Ford's Touch (*q.v.*) on account of the latter having given up business, 20 Sept. 1726, Y. Touch, 797 L.T.P. He was apprenticed to Wm. Ellwood.

454. BLEWETT, JOHN, London : 18 Dec. 1707, Y. Touch, 652 L.T.P.

455. BLEWETT, ROBERT, London : 22 Mar. 1738, Y.

456. BLEWETT, THOMAS, London :· 16 June 1736, Y.

457. BLINMAN, JOHN, Bristol : ⎱

458. BLINMAN, JOSEPH, Bristol : ⎰ c. 1846, these two brothers were in partnership with J. W. James at 81 Temple Street. A Mr. Emerson was also a partner, and the firm was eventually succeeded by Peter Llewellin (*q.v.*), a nephew of Blinmans'.

459. BLISS, JOHN, London : 12 Aug. 1708, Y.

460. BLISS, ROBERT, London : 18 Mar. 1735, Y.

461. BLISSETT, WILLIAM, London : 14 Oct. 1697, Y.

462. BLOWFELDE, WYLLM, London : 1457, mentioned as being " of the Brethern " (or free) at this date.

463. BLOXHAM, EDWARD, Dublin : Mentioned in 1719, when he was one of four petitioners to the Irish House of Commons for the rectification of certain abuses in the pewter and brass industries.

464. BLUNT, JOHN, London : 11 Aug. 1681, L. Touch, 323. L.T.P., which he had leave to strike in 1678/9.

465. BLUNT, OSWELL, London : In 1596 was appointed a collector of levies from the yeomanry of the Company. In 1603 he was in Bread Street.

466. BLUNT, THOMAS, London : 18 Dec. 1746, Y.

467. BLYTE, ARCHIBALD, Edinburgh : In 1633 was an apprentice to Robert Somervell.

468. BLYTHE, EDMUND, Oxford : Mentioned in 1630.

469. BLYTHE, JOHN, York : 1427/8, F.

469A. BLYTHE, ROBERT, Norwich : 1451/2, F.

470. BOARDMAN, THOMAS (see also BORDMAN), London : 20 Mar. 1728, Y. ; 28 Nov. 1746, L. ; 1756, S. ; and was dead in 1773. Touch, 899 L.T.P. Was given leave to strike his Touch on 13 Aug. 1741.

471. BOARDMAN, THOMAS, junr., London : 17 Mar. 1763, Y.

473. BODAM, NICHOLAS, London : Was Beadle to the Company in 1564 and 1573.

474. BODE, PHILIP, London : 18 June 1761, Y.

475. BOGG, JOHN, York : 1620/1, F. Had an apprentice bound to him in 1642.

476. BOLT, RICHARD, London : In 1476 contributed towards the cost of some feast vessels.

BOLTON, see BOULTON.

477. BOND, JOHN, London : 22 June 1775, Y.

478. BONE, ANNE, London : 18 Dec. 1755, Y.

479. BONKIN, JONATHAN, London : 21 Mar. 1699, Y. Touch, 722 L.T.P., which he had leave to strike on 31 Jan. 1717.

480. BONKIN, JONAT, London : Touch, No. 307 L.T.P., which he had leave to strike in 1678, but there

is no mention of his name in the Y. or L. Lists. Died 1681. ("Bennett" Book.)

481. BONOUR, ALEXANDER, York : 1413, F.

482. BONVILE, JOHN, London : His Touch, No. 366 L.T.P., which he had leave to strike on 7 April 1682. His name does not appear in the records, but is in the "Bennett" Book from 1679-1686.

483. BOOST, JAMES, London : 21 Mar. 1744, Y. ; 19 Oct. 1758, L. ; 1767, S. Touch, 956 L.T.P. Was given leave to strike his Touch in 1751.

484. BOOTH, EDWARD, York : 1671/2, F. Son of Richard Booth, below, and brother of Samuel.

485. BOOTH, JOHN SMALE, London : 23 Oct. 1755, Y.

486. BOOTH, RICHARD, York : Father of Edward and Samuel. Was a Freeman in or before 1661/2, and is mentioned later in 1671/2.

487. BOOTH, SAMUEL, York : Son of Richard and brother of Edward, above. 1661/2, F.

488. BOR(D)MAN, ROBERT, London : 12 Dec. 1700, Y. Touch, 594 L.T.P., which he had leave to strike on 4 Feb. 1701. His name is spelt with the "D" in the records and without it in his Touch.

489. BORINGTON, WILLIAM, Bredon, Worcs. : S. of Thomas. Apprenticed to Robert Bush, junr., Bristol, 5 Sept. 1796.

490. BORNE, RICHARD, London : Was one of a body of soldiers raised from the Company in 1553 to defend London Bridge against Sir Thomas Wyatt.

491. BORNE, ROBART, London : Was one of a body of soldiers raised from the Company in 1553 to defend London Bridge against Sir Thomas Wyatt. In 1563 he was receiving Charity from the Company as a poor brother.

492. BORRON, WILLIAM, Bristol: Mentioned in the Bristol Poll Book of 1721 as of Redcliff, Bristol.

493. BORTHWICK, ANDRO, Edinburgh: 1620, F. Touch, 25 E.T.P.

494. BORTHWICK, GEORGE, Edinburgh: Apprenticed in 1657 to John Syde.

495. BORTHWICK, WILLIAM, Edinburgh: Apprenticed in 1719 to Walter Waddel.

496. BORTHWICK, WILLIAM, Edinburgh: Mentioned as dead in 1654. ? Touch, 53 E.T.P.

497. BOSHER, RICHARD, Bristol: Mentioned in the Bristol Poll Book for 1754 as of St. Michael's, Bristol.

498. BOSS(E), SAMUEL, London: 19 Dec. 1695, Y.; 19 May 1715, L. Touch, 589 L.T.P., which he had leave to strike on 29 Aug. 1701.

498A. BOSTON, BEZA, London: c. 1680. ("Bennett" Book.)

498B. BOSTON, JABEZ, London: c. 1680. ("Bennett" Book.) Touch, 190 L.T.P., which he had leave to strike in 1670/1.

499. BOSWORTH, THOMAS, London: 17 Aug. 1699, Y. Touch, 564 L.T.P., which he had leave to strike on 17 Nov. 1699.

500. BOTELER, JOHN, London: 15 Mar. 1743, Y.; 25 Aug. 1748, L. Touch, 910 L.T.P. Was given leave to strike his Touch in 1743.

501. BOUCHIERE, FRANCIS, Bristol: Mentioned in the Bristol Poll Books of 1721 and 1734 as of S.S. Philip and Jacob, Bristol.

502. BOUER, JOHN, London: Was a Journeyman in 1457 to John Gugge the elder.

503. BOULTINGE, JOHN, London: In 1556 was fined for bad wares. 1564, S.; 1575, R.W.

503A. BOULTON, GEORGE, Wigan: Partner in William Burgoine & Co. The partnership was dissolved in 1824, Boulton continuing the business.

503B. BOULTON, JAMES, Wigan: His partnership with Thomas Boulton was dissolved on 29 Nov. 1798, and is recorded in the *London Gazette*.

504. BOULTON, RICHARD, London: Was a Master man in 1614.

504A. BOULTON, THOMAS, Wigan. Letters of Administration at Chester, in 1750.

505. BOULTON, THOMAS, Wigan: c. 1760 to 1798, in which year he died. *Cf.* Fairbrother. His partnership with James Boulton was dissolved on 29 Nov. 1798, and is recorded in the *London Gazette*.

506. BOURMAN, JOHN, London: Served in place of John Shawe in a body of soldiers raised by the Company in 1584.

507. BOUSFIELD, JAMES (? BUSFIELD and BOWFIELD), York: 1567, F. He is mentioned later in 1603/4 and 1608/9.

508. BOUSFIELD, JOHN, York: 1590/91, F.

509. BOUSFIELD, JOHN, York: Is mentioned 1634/5, and again in 1640/41.

510. BOUSFIELD, JOHN, York: Son of Thomas Bousfield, to whom he was apprenticed, 1 May 1656 for seven years. 1663/4, F., by patrimony, was searcher to the Company in 1667, in which year he is further mentioned as having an apprentice bound to him.

511. BOUSFIELD, MARMADUKE, York: Son of William Bousfield. 1633/4, F., by patrimony.

512. BOUSFIELD, ROBERT, York: 1603/4, F., by patrimony.

513. BOUSFIELD, THOMAS, York: Son of John Bousfield. 1640/1, F., by patrimony. Searcher in 1671, and is also mentioned in 1663/4 and 1678/9.

514. BOUSFIELD, THOMAS, York: 1689, F.

515. BOUSFIELD, WILLIAM, York: 1605/6, F. Was one of the City Chamberlains in 1631/2, and is mentioned again in 1633/4.

516. Bowal, Robert, Edinburgh : 1621, F.
517. Bowcher, Francis, Bristol and Marlborough, Wilts. : 29 Oct. 1689, F. Apprenticed to John Stevens (or Sheppard), Bristol, and Elizabeth his wife, 12 Sept. 1681. Mentioned again in 1714.
518. Bowcher, Francis, Bristol : 8 Aug. 1713, F. S. of Francis.
519. Bowcher, Phillippe, Bristol : S. of Francis B., senr. Apprenticed to his father and mother (Martha), 2 Aug. 1714.
520. Bowcher, Richard, Bristol : S. of Francis B., senr. Apprenticed to his father and mother, 22 Mar. 1706.
521. Bowcher, Richard, Bristol : 30 June 1747, F. Married Sarah Gill.
522. Bowcher, Richard, London : 10 Aug. 1727, Y. Touch, 805 L.T.P., which he had leave to strike in 1728.

523. Bowden, John, London : 12 Mar. 1701, Y.
524. Bowden, Joseph, London : 22 Mar. 1687, Y. Touch, 542 L.T.P., which he had leave to strike on 9 Mar. 1697. Bankruptcy recorded 18 Mar. 1721.

525. Bowden, William, London : In 1679 was the Company's Beadle. Was brought before the Company at this time on a charge of encouraging illicit trading, but was acquitted.
526. Bowen, ——, ? Bristol : His name appears on public-house pots, c. 1860.

BOWEN

527. Bowen, Hopkin, Ludlow : Apprenticed to Richard Johnson, 30 Sept. 1720, F.
527A. Bower, Michael, Gloucester : Mentioned in 1662 in Marriage Licence.
528. Bowie, Charles, Perth : In 1760 was apprenticed to David Young.
529. Bowler, Henry, London : 24 Mar. 1757, Y. Touch, 974 L.T.P. Was granted leave to strike his Touch in 1757.

530. Bowler, John, London : 16 Oct. 1760, Y.

531. Bowler, Richard, London : 23 Oct. 1755, Y. Was given leave to strike his Touch in 1762. Touch, 1001 L.T.P.

532. Bowler, Samuel Salter, London : 18 Mar. 1779, Y. Touch 1038 L.T.P.

Bowlting, see Boulting.
533. Bowring, Charles, London : 19 Oct. 1820, Y. and L. Died 14 July 1864.
534. Bowyar, Andrew, London : Was a Freeman before 1584. In 1588 he was fined for employing a stranger woman to engrave on his pewter instead of a brother member, and again in 1590.
535. Bowyar, John, London : Is mentioned in 1587 as a maker of spoons, and in 1594 apparently he purchased an annuity from the Company.
536. Bowyar, William (see also Cowyer), London : 1620, S. ; 1628, f.R.W. ; 1638, f.U.W. ; 1642, f.M. Mr. Welch gives this man as William Grainger, but his name is plainly Bowyer in the Livery List at the Hall of the Company.
537. Bowyar, Richard, London : Married to Joan Underwood on 3 June 1661 at St. Botolph's, Aldersgate.
538. Box, Edward, of ? : c. 1720-1740.

539. Boyden, Benjamin, London : 22 June 1693, Y. Touch, 511 L.T.P., which he had leave to strike on 5 Dec. 1694.

539A. BOYDEN, RICHARD, of ? : c. 1700. Date (16)99 in Touch. *Cf.* Elizabeth Royden.

539B. BOYDEN, RICHARD, Cambridge : Advertised to sell his moulds in the *London Gazette*, 20 Jan. 1690.

540. BOYDEN, THOMAS, London : 19 Dec. 1706, Y.

541. BOYDEN, THOMAS, London : 18 Mar. 1735, Y.

543. BOYLSON, EDWARD, London : Was a Master in 1611.

544. BOYNE, GEORGE, York : Was an apprentice in 1484.

545. BOYS, NICHOLAS, London : 17 Oct. 1728, Y.

546. BRADFORD, RICHARD, London : 11 Oct. 1705, Y.

546A. BRADFORD, WILLIAM, London : c. 1680. (" Bennett " Book.)

546B. BRADLEY, HENRY, London : Had leave to strike his Touch, 268 L.T.P., in 1675/6.

547. BRADLEY, JOHN, York : 1613/4, F. Was one of the City Chamberlains in 1628/9, and had an apprentice bound to him in 1651.

548. BRADSHAW, SYMOND, London : In 1553, contrary to rule, he left London for the country, and on his return was employed by Richard Williamson, for which the latter was fined.

549. BRADSHAW, WILLIAM, of ? : c. 1750.

550. BRADSHAW, WILLIAM, Ludlow : 1542, F.; 1544, M. 1566, died ; buried at Ludlow.

551. BRADSTREET, EDWARD (? BREADSTREET), London : 23 Mar. 1720, Y. Of Shugg Lane, Piccadilly. His Touch, No. 785 L.T.P., was struck on the

10 Aug. 1726/7 (*vide* Welch, ii. 186). Spelt Breadstreet in records.

552. BRADSTREET, RICHARD, London : 14 Dec. 1727, Y. Touch, 818 L.T.P. (*Cf.* the Touch of Arthur Smalman), which he had leave to strike in 1730.

553. BRAEDWOOD, EBENEZER, Edinburgh : Apprenticed in 1798 with James Sibbald.

553A. BRAFIELD, RICHARD, London : c. 1680. (" Bennett " Book.) Touch, 408 L.T.P., which he had leave to strike in 1684/5.

554. BRAILESFORD, PETER, London : 28 Nov. 1667, L. Touch, 63 L.T.P.

555. BRAINE, JOHN, of ? : c. 1725.

LONDON

555A. BRAINE, WILLIAM, London : c. 1680. (" Bennett " Book.) Touch 356 L.T.P., which he had leave to strike on 29 Oct. 1681.

556. BRANT, JOHN, London : 10 Dec. 1818, Y.

557. BRASTED, HENRY, London: 1 Oct. 1692, Y. Touch, 534 L.T.P., which he had leave to strike on 13 Aug. 1696.

558. BRAVELL, MARY, London: 25 Sept. 1712, Y.
559. BRAVELL, WILLIAM, London: Touch, No. 483 L.T.P., which he had leave to strike on 16 June 1692, but his name does not appear in the Y. or L. Lists.

560. BRAY, THOMAS, London: His name appears without date in the records, but in such a place as to indicate c. 1730.
560A. BRAYLY, ROBERT, Taunton: Signed an inventory in 1690.
561. BRAYNE, WILLIAM, London: 20 Dec. 1705, Y. BREADSTREET, see BRADSTREET.
562. BRERETON, GEORGE, Dublin: Mentioned in 1749.
562A. BRETT, EDWARD, London: Had leave to strike his Touch in 1727.
563. BRETT, THOMAS HERVEY, London: 17 June 1773, Y.
564. BRETTELL, JAMES, London: 21 Mar. 1688, Y. His Touch, dated 1690, is No. 477 L.T.P.

565. BREVYLL, THOMAS, London: Was in 1457 an apprentice with John Turnour.
566. BREWERTON, JOHN, London: Mentioned as having, contrary to its rules, gone to law in 1608 with a fellow member of the Company.
567. BRICHE, JOHN, London: Was in 1457 an apprentice with John Lambard.
568. BRIDBROKE, THOMAS, London: Was in 1457 an apprentice with Thomas Smyth.
569. BRIDGEHAMPTON, WILLIAM, Bristol: S. of Thomas. Apprenticed to William Whibby and Anne his wife, eight years from 1 Sept. 1618.
570. BRIDGER, JOSEPH, London: 19 Dec. 1723, Y.
571. BRIDGES, ——, London: Was accused in 1688 of using a Touch other than that he struck upon the touchplate.

572. BRIDGES, STEPHEN, London: 15 Dec. 1692, Y. Touch, 527 L.T.P., which he had leave to strike on 7 April 1696.

573. BRIGGE, WILLIAM, York: 1472/3, F.
574. BRIGHT, ALLEN, Bristol and Colwell, Herefordshire: 2 Nov. 1742, F. S. of Henry. Apprenticed to William Watkins, Bristol, and Mary his wife. 1 Nov. 1735. Premium, £45. Died in 1763.

575. BRIGHT, ANN & CO., Bristol: Successors of Allen Bright, Ann being his widow. Advertised in *Felix Farley's Journal* (Bristol) in Aug. 1765, when their address was The Back, Bristol.
576. BRIGHT, ROBERT. Bristol: Son of William. Apprenticed to Allen Bright and Ann his wife, 16 Feb. 1756.
577. BRIGSTOCK, JOSEPH, LONDON: 13 Dec. 1733, Y.
578. BRIMSDON, CHRISTOPHER, Wotton Bassett, Wilts.: S. of John. Apprenticed to Robert Showard, Bristol, 16 Mar. 1642.
579. BRISTOWE, JOHN, London: Was of the Livery in 1457.
579A. BRISTYMER, THOMAS, Norwich: 1522/3. Son of Henry.
579B. BRISTYMER, WILLIAM, Norwich: 1539/40.
580. BRITTAIN, THOMAS, Clapton, Somerset: S. of Arthur. Apprenticed to Thomas Hale, Bristol, and Martha his wife, 3 Nov. 1796.
581. BRITTON, SAMUEL, Bristol: Advertised in the Bristol *Oracle* of 6 June 1759, when his business address is given as " at the sign of the Dog's Head in the Porridge Pot, Castle Street."

582. BROAD, JOHN, London : 22 Mar. 1704, Y.

582A. BROADBANK, THOMAS, London : On the voting list for 1724.

583. BROCKLESBY, PETER, London : In 1600 was appointed an assessor for the Livery, 1616, U.W. ; 1623, f.U.W. (*sic!*) ; 1629, M.

584. BROCKLESBY, PETER, London : 1627, f.S. ; 1636, U.W. ; 1638, sued for arrears of money due from him under his wardenship.

585. BROCKLESBY, PETER, London : 28 Nov. 1667, L.

585A. BROCK, RICHARD, Chester : Dead in 1762, when he is referred to in the *London Gazette.* In 1751 he had an apprentice.

586. BROCKS, DAVID, London : 22 Oct. 1702, Y. Touch, 604 L.T.P., which he had leave to strike on 4 Jan. 1702.

587. BRO(A)DHURST, JOHN(ATHAN), London : 17 Dec. 1719, Y. Touch, 735 L.T.P., which he had leave to strike in 1720.

588. BRO(A)DHURST, JONATHAN, London : 16 Dec. 1731, Y.

589. BRO(A)DHURST, SAUL, London : 15 Dec. 1748, Y.

590. BRODIE, JAMES, Edinburgh : In 1697 was an apprentice with William Harvie.

591. BRODIE, JOHN, Perth : In 1780 was a Freeman.

592. BRODIE, JOHN, Perth : In 1780 was an apprentice with Patrick Bissett.

593. BRODRYG, RICHARD, York : 1524/5, F.

594. BRODSHOE, ROBERT, Dublin : 1589, F.

595. BROKE, JOHN, London : In 1463 was in receipt of alms from the Company.

596. BROKYLSBY, WILLIAM, Lynn : 1497/8, F.

597. BROKYNG, JOHN, London and Braynford : In 1475 was a country member of the Company.

598. BROME, WILLIAM, London : Was Clerk to the Company and resigned in 1614.

599. BROMFIELD, JOHN (? BRUMFIELD), London : 13 Mar. 1745, Y. Touch, 919 L.T.P. Was given leave to strike his Touch on 14 Mar. 1745. His name, spelt with an *o* in the Yeomanry list, is Br*u*mfield in his Touch.

600. BROMFIELD, WILLIAM, London : 16 Oct. 1777.

601. BROMLEY, JOSEPH, London : In 1601 was one of a deputation from the Company to the Queen.

602. BROMLEY, WILLIAM, London : In 1583 he received a grant from the Company during an illness.

603. BROOK, EDWARD, Bristol : Mentioned in the Bristol Poll Book for 1739 as at St. Mary Redcliff.

604. BROOK, PHILIP, Bristol : Mentioned in the Bristol Poll Books of 1722, 1734 and 1739 as of St. Thomas's, Bristol.

605. BROOKE, PETER, London : 13 Dec. 1764, Y.

606. BROOKE, WILLIAM, London : Was fined in 1598 for making false wares.

607. BROOKS, EDWARD, Bristol : 10 Oct. 1739, F. Apprenticed to his father, Philip, and mother, Marie, 18 May 1722.

608. BROOKS, JOHN, London : 1627, f.S. ; 1637, R.W. ; 1644, f.U.W.

609. BROOKS, JOHN, London : 11 Aug. 1698, Y.

610. BROOKS, PHILIP, Bristol and Evesham, Worcs. : 17 July 1708, F. S. of Edward. Apprenticed to Thomas Salmon, Bristol, and Marie his wife, 25 Oct. 1693. Mentioned in 1737

611. BROOKS, RICE, London : 28 Nov. 1667, L.

611A. BROOKER, JOSEPH, London : c. 1680. (" Bennett " Book.) Touch, 367 L.T.P., which he had leave to strike on 7 April 1682.

611B. BROUGH, CUTHBERT, Newcastle : Dead in 1752.

611C. BROUGH, JANE, Newcastle : Mentioned in 1752.

612. BROUGHS, BENJAMIN (*Cf.* BURROUGHS), Somerton, Somerset : Mentioned as a Country Voter in the Bristol Poll Book for 1774.

613. BROWARS, EDMOND, London : Had a standing at Gravesend Fair in 1541.

614. BROWN(E), ALEXANDER, Edinburgh : 1717, F. Touch, 103 E.T.P.

615. BROWN(E), ALEXANDER, Edinburgh : In 1688 was an apprentice with Samuel Walker.

616. BROWN(E), BENJAMIN, London : 4 Aug. 1726, Y. Touch, 814 L.T.P., which he had leave to strike in 1727.

617. BROWN(E), CONEY JOHN, London : 14 Dec. 1786,
Y. Died 1836. Touch, 1063 L.T.P.

618. BROWN(E), DAVID, Perth : 1777, F. Founder and
Brazier.
619. BROWN(E), DAVID, Edinburgh : 1794, F.
620. BROWN(E), EDMUND, London : Was Clerk to the
Company from 1551-1569, in which latter year
he died.
621. BROWN(E), EDWARD, Newport, Mon. : S. of
Maurice. Apprenticed to Thomas Hobson,
Bristol, 1643.
622. BROWN(E), GEORGE, Perth : Mentioned in 1709.
623. BROWN(E), GEORGE, Edinburgh : 1711, F. Died
1715.
624. BROWN(E), GEORGE, York : 1526/7, mentioned.
Father of the next named.
625. BROWN(E), GEORGE, York : 1526/7, F. Son of the
last named.
626. BROWN(E), IGNATIUS, Dublin : Mentioned in 1671.
See illustration of his tokens.
627. BROWN(E), JAMES, Perth : In 1775 was an apprentice with William Richardson.
628. BROWN(E), JOHN, Edinburgh : 1761, F. Touch,
142 E.T.P. In 1773 his shop was in Grassmarket.

629. BROWN(E), MRS. JOHN, Edinburgh : Widow of the
last named. She carried on his business from
1780 to 1793.
630. BROWN(E), JOHN, Dublin : Mentioned in 1744.
631. BROWN(E), JOHN, London : 20 Oct. 1757, Y.
Touch, 1002 L.T.P. Was in partnership with
John Lewis 1761, Y. ; and Joseph Brown, 1762,
Y. They were given leave to strike their Touch
on 15 Mar. 1764.

632. BROWN(E), JOHN, London : 19 June 1712, Y.
633. BROWN(E), JOHN, London : 16 Dec. 1756, Y.
634. BROWN(E), JOHN, London : 16 Oct. 1777, Y.
Died 1839.
635. BROWN(E), JOHN, London : In 1457 was an apprentice with Nicholas Walker, and in 1494 he presented a form to the Company.

635A. BROWN(E), JOHN, Gloucester : Was recorded a
Bankrupt in 1720. The mark under No. 639
may be his.
636. BROWN(E), JOHN, London : Was fined in 1558 for
bad language to a brother member.
637. BROWN(E), JOHN, Bristol and Bedminster : 13 Oct.
1732, F. S. of Samuel. Apprenticed to John
Lovell, junr., Bristol, 25 Aug. 1725.
638. BROWN(E), JOSEPH, London : 16 Dec. 1762, Y.
Touch, 1002 L.T.P. *See* under John Brown,
with whom and John Lewis he was in partnership.
639. BROWN(E), J——, of ? : Early eighteenth century.
? John Brown, No. 635A.

640. BROWN(E) MARTIN, London : Touch, 517 L.T.P.,
struck c. 1695, but his name is not found in the
records.

641. BROWN(E) NICHOLAS, London : In 1556 he served
in the war with France as a gunner for the
Company.
642. BROWN(E), PHILIP, London : 20 Oct. 1757, Y.
642A. BROWN(E), RALPH, London : c. 1680. ("Bennett"
Book.) Touch, 160 L.T.P., which he had leave
to strike in 1669/70.

643. BROWN(E), RICHARD, London : 19 Mar. 1729, Y.
Touch, 837 L.T.P., dated 1730, which he had
leave to strike on 5 Aug. 1731.

644. Brown(e), Richard, London : 23 June 1785, Y.
645. Brown(e), Richard, London : In 1476 was a subscriber to a set of Feast vessels for the Company.
646. Brown(e), Richard, Bristol and Wrington, Somerset : 13 Feb. 1680, F. Apprenticed to Wm. Pascall, Bristol, 22 Aug. 1657. Mentioned in 1705.
647. Brown(e), Robert, London : In 1614 and 1620 was fined for infringement of the rules of the Company.
648. Brown(e), Robert, Wells : Apprenticed to Thomas Munke, Bristol, 24 Mar. 1627.
649. Brown(e), Robert, Glasgow : 1681, F. Pewterer and White-ironsmith.
649A. Brown(e), Robert, Edinburgh : Touch, 132 E.T.P. Dead in 1745.

650. Brown(e), William, Edinburgh : Was dead in 1741. ? Touch, 128 E.T.P.

651. Brown(e), William, London : 20 Dec. 1705, Y. Touch, 629 L.T.P., which he had leave to strike on 11 Jan. 1705.

652. Brown(e), William, London : In 1543 was a soldier in the war with France.
Brown & Englefield, see Englefield.
653. Browne & Swanson, London : Touch, 991 L.T.P. struck c. 1760. Partners, Thomas Swanson (q.v.) and —— Browne.

654. Brownlee, James, Glasgow : 1648, F.
655. Broxup, Richard, London : 16 June 1757, Y.
656. Broxup, Richard, London : 20 June 1793, L. ; 1796, f.S.
657. Bruce, John, Edinburgh : In 1749 was an apprentice with Adam Anderson.
658. Bruce, Thomas, Edinburgh : In 1714 was an apprentice with William Herring.
659. Bruce, Thomas, Edinburgh : Mentioned as being dead in 1749.
Brumfield, see Bromfield.

660. Bryan, Egerton, London : Touch, 228 L.T.P., which he had leave to strike in 1674/5. Died 1681.

661. Bryan, John, Yarmouth : 1561, F.
662. Bryant, John, London : 19 Oct. 1749, Y.
663. Bryce, David, Edinburgh : 1660, F. Touch, 56 E.T.P.

664. Bryden, Alexander, Edinburgh : 1717, F. ? Touch, 105 E.T.P.

665. Brydfield, William, London : In 1457 was apprenticed with Thomas Dounton.
666. Bryers, John, London : 16 June 1715, Y.
667. Brykley, Richard, London : In 1457 was apprenticed with John Kendale.
668. Bryon, Thomas, Bury St. Edmunds : 1526.
Brystymer, see Bristymer.
669. Buchanan, James, Glasgow : 1791, F. White-ironsmith.
670. Buckby & Hamilton, London : c. 1720. Partners, Thomas Buckby and ? Alexander Hamilton.

671. Buckby, Thomas. London : 21 June 1716, L. Touch, 592 L.T.P., which he had leave to strike on 14 Nov. 1701.

671A. BUCKINGHAM, THOMAS, London. In 1817, was at 24 Swallow St.

672. BUCKLEY, WILLIAM, London: 20 Mar. 1689, Y. Touch, 504 L.T.P., which he had leave to strike on 3 July 1690.

673. BUCKMASTER, THOMAS, London: In 1631 he transferred into another Company.

674. BUCKYNNES, JOHN, Edinburgh: In 1719 was apprenticed with James Edgar.

675. BUCLENNAND, JAMES, Edinburgh: 1643, F. Touch, 43 E.T.P.

676. BUDDEN, DAVID, London: Touch, 163 L.T.P., which he had leave to strike in 1669/70.

677. BUDDEN, DAVID, London: 17 Dec. 1701, Y. Touch, 605 L.T.P., which he had leave to strike on 4 Jan. 1702.

678. BUDDING, HENRY, London: 20 Mar. 1739, Y.

679. BUGBY, THOMAS, London: 13 Dec. 1694, Y.

680. BULL, JOHN (see also BALL), London: 1676, S. Touch, 97 L.T.P.

681. BULL, THOMAS, London: 23 June 1726, Y.

682. BULLARDYNE, ROBERT, London: Fined in 1593 for absenting himself in the country for seventeen years.

683. BULLEVANT, JAMES, London: 28 Nov. 1667, L. Touch, No. 67 L.T.P. Mentioned in 1678.

684. BULLOCK, ANTHONY, Bristol: 17 July 1675, F. Apprenticed to Thomas Willoughby and turned over to Erasmus Dole. Mentioned in 1695.

684A. BULLOCK, BENJAMIN, Penzance: Bankrupt in 1793.

684B. BULLOCK, HENRY, London: c. 1680. ("Bennett" Book.)

685. BULLOCK, JAMES, London: 11 Oct. 1750, Y.; 17 June 1752, L. Touch, 946 L.T.P. He was struck off the membership of the Company in 1754. His business was in Jermyn Street. *See* his Trade-card. Was given leave to strike his touch in 1750.

686. BULLOCK, JAMES, London: 17 Mar. 1763, L.; 1770, S. Shop in Bond Street.

687. BULLOCK, OLIVER, Dublin: In 1711 was in Back Lane.

688. BUNKELL, EDWARD, Edinburgh: Was a Master in 1729 and died c. 1756. Touch ? 127 E.T.P.

689. BUNKELL, EDWARD, junr., Edinburgh: 1741, F.

690. BUNNERBELL, ROBERT, Edinburgh: 1633, F.

691. BUNTING, DANIEL, London: 24 June 1784, Y.

692. BUNTING, ROBERT, London: 1 Oct. 1691, Y.

693. BUNYNGE, RICHARD, London: Fined in 1575 for buying from an apprentice.

694. BURCH, EDWARD, London: 11 Aug. 1720, Y.

695. BURCH, SAMUEL, ? same as 696, below, London: 13 Oct. 1715, Y.

696. BURCH, SAMUEL, ? same as above, of ? This may be the mark of the last named, but it was never struck upon the Touch Plates, nor any other bearing his name.

696A. BURCHALL, EDWARD, London: c. 1680. ("Bennett" Book.) Touch, 365 L.T.P., which he had leave to strike on 12 May 1682.

697. BURD, GEORGE, Dundry, Somerset: S. of Wm. Apprenticed to Bernard Benson, Bristol, for nine years from 13 Feb. 1633.

698. BURFORD & GREEN, London: Touch, 929 L.T.P. They were given leave to strike their Touch on 13 Oct. 1748. Partners, Thomas Burford, 1746, Y., and James Green, 1750, L. Their business was in The Poultry. Partnership dissolved in 1780, when Green retired from the firm.

699. BURFORD, RICHARD, Bristol: 12 Dec. 1748, F. S. of Ralph. Apprenticed to Thomas Lissley, Bristol, 7 Nov. 1741. Premium £5 5s.

700. BURFORD, THOMAS, London: 19 June 1746, Y.; 11 Oct. 1750, L.; 1761, f.S.; 1766, f.R.W.; 1778, was U.W. during the latter part; 1779, M.; and was dead in 1783. A partner in Burford & Green, see their mark.

701. BURGE, ANTHONY, Bristol: Dead in 1695.

702. BURGES, EDWARD, London: Fined in 1638 for buying old metal contrary to regulations.

702A. BURGES, ROBERT, London: c. 1680. ("Bennett" Book.)

703. BURGES, THOMAS, Bicester, Oxon.: Issued a token bearing date 1665 and the device of the Pewterers, Arms. See list of tokens at end of Chap. IV.

704. BURGES, THOMAS, London: 25 April 1701, Y. Touch, 595 L.T.P., which he had leave to strike on 28 Jan. 1701.

705. BURGEYS, JOHN, London: Was in 1457 an apprentice with John Kendale.

705A. BURGOINE, WILLIAM & Co., Wigan: William Burgoine and George Bolton. Partnership dissolved 11 Dec. 1824. Bolton continuing the business.

706. BURGUM, HENRY, Bristol and Littledean, Glocs.: 27 Sept. 1760, F. S. of Henry. Apprenticed to Allen Bright, Bristol, and Ann his wife, 27 Sept. 1752. Mentioned as of St. Thomas's, Bristol, in the Bristol Poll Books of 1774 and 1784, and in that of 1781 as of St. Michael's. A member of the firm of Burgum & Catcott, see their mark.

707. BURGUM, HENRY, JUNR., Bristol and Littledean, Glocs.: 29 April 1784, F., by patrimony. S. of Henry Burgum Senr. Mentioned in the Bristol Poll Book of 1784.

708. BURGUM & CATCOTT, Bristol and Littledean, Glocs. Partners, Henry Burgum the elder, see above, and George Symes Catcott. Stanley Hutton, in his Bristol and its Famous Associations, says that in 1768 their business was at No. 2 Bristol Bridge. He also gives some interesting personal notes about the partners, and portraits of them. In Aug. 1765 the firm advertised in Felix Farley's Journal. Partnership was dissolved on 16 Feb. 1779. (London Gazette.)

709. BURLEY, WILLIAM, London: In 1594 was, as an apprentice, transferred from (? the late) John Crose to Thomas Smackergill.

710. BURNETT, EDWARD, London: 21 Mar. 1727, Y.

711. BURNAM, JOHN, London: Mentioned in 1551 and in 1556 his servant served for him during his absence from home as warden of the Yeomanry, and in the same year he was for some reason not stated "Banysshed the company for ever."

712. BURNS, ROBERT, Edinburgh: 1694, F. Touch, 96 E.T.P.

713. BURNS, MRS. RALPH, London: Was a Freeman in 1457.

714. BURRNS, RICHARD, Bristol: Mentioned with his wife Frances from 1605-1610.

715. BURROUGHS, BENJAMIN (cf. BROUGHS), Bristol and Somerton, Somerset: 9 Mar. 1768, F. S. of John. Apprenticed to Robert Bush, Bristol, and his wife Elizabeth, 30 Mar. 1757. Premium £10. Mentioned in the Bristol Poll Books for 1781 and 1784 as a country Voter.

716   BURROUGHS, EDMOND, Dublin: Is mentioned in 1752. His business, from which he retired in 1768, was in Capel Street. Died 1778. He was Warden of the Guild of Smiths in 1747. He was succeeded in business by his son William. See No. 718.

717.   BURROUGHS, THOMAS, Bristol: 2 Dec. 1678, F. Apprenticed to Thomas Pascall, Bristol, and Jane his wife, 24 Oct. 1671. S. of William.

718.   BURROUGHS, WILLIAM, Dublin: Son of Edmond, succeeded to his father's business in 1768 and died in 1771.

719.   BURROWES, JOHN, Bristol: Mentioned with his wife Rachel from 1572 to 1602.

720.   BURT, ANDREW, London: 7 Oct. 1802, Y. and L.; 1805, f.S.; 1813, R.W. Buried 8 Jan. 1851.

721.   BURT, THOMAS, London: 1607, Y.; 1612, f.S.; 1619, f.R.W.; 1630, U.W. Was apprenticed to a Mr. Cowes ten years before he claimed freedom.

722.   BURTON, GEORGE (see also ONTON), York: 1643/4, F., by patrimony. He is again mentioned in 1667/8 and 1684/5. Father of John, below.

723.   BURTON, JAMES, Dundee: 1737, F. White-ironsmith.

724.   BURTON, JOHN, York: 1667/8, F., by patrimony. Son of George, above.

725.   BURTON, JOHN, York: Mentioned in 1700/01 as a pewterer and Hollow-ware man and again in 1704/5 and 1738/9.

726.   BURTON, JOHN, London: His Touch, No. 142, was struck on the L.T.P., c. 1670, but no mention of him is found in the records.

727.   BURTON, JOHN, London: 20 Mar. 1689, Y.

728.   BURTON, MUNGO, Edinburgh: 1709, F. Touch, 112 E.T.P.

729.   BURTON, ROBERT (? BUXTON), London: Is mentioned in 1611 as a work-master. 1612, S.; 1619, R.W.

730.   BURTON, THOMAS, London: Was Warden of the Yeomanry in 1562. 1562, S.; 1569, R.W.; 1569, died.

731.   BURTON, THOMAS, York: Mentioned in 1711/2.

732.   BURTON, WILLIAM, London: 1668, f.S.; 1675, R.W.; 1680, U.W.; 1685, M. His Touch, No 38 L.T.P., was restruck after the great fire of London.

733.   BURTON, WILLIAM, London: His Touch, No. 354 L.T.P., was struck c. 1681, but no mention of his name appears in the records.

734.   BUSBY, ALEXANDER, Dublin: Mentioned in 1820. BUSFIELD, see BOUSFIELD.

735.   BUSH, JAMES, Bristol and Winford, Somerset: 6 Aug. 1660, F. S. of Wm. Bush. Apprenticed to Alice, widow of Edward Lovering, Bristol, 13 May 1652, for eight years.

736.   BUSH, JOSEPH, Bristol: 27 Nov. 1674, F. Apprenticed to Erasmus Dole.

737.   BUSH, ROBERT, SENR, Bristol and Bitton, Glocs.; 19 June 1755, F. S. of William. Apprenticed to Thomas Lanyon, Bristol, and Anne his wife, 2 June 1748. Premium £50. Advertised in *Felix Farley's Journal* in July and Aug. 1765: wherein he claims to be working in conjunction with Joseph Spackman, late of Fenchurch Street, but then of Cornhill, London. He is mentioned as of St. Mary-le-Port, Bristol, in the Bristol Poll Books for 1774 and 1781. In 1765 he is referred to as being in High Street.

738.   BUSH, ROBERT, JUNR., Bristol and Bitton, Glocs.; 7 Jan. 1796, F., by patrimony. S. of Robert B., Senr.

739. BUSH, ROBERT & CO., Bristol and Bilton, Glocs.: Mentioned in 1793 in Matthews' first *Bristol Directory* as pewterers, brass and coppersmiths, of 20 High Street, and St. Thomas Street. The partnership, which was composed of Robert Bush, James Curtis and Preston Edgar, appears in the *London Gazette* as dissolved on 30 July 1793.

740. BUSH & PERKINS, Bristol and Bitton, Glocs., c. 1775: Partners, Robert Bush, above, and Richard Perkins, *q.v.*

740A. BUSH, R. & W., Bristol and Bitton, Glocs.: In 1805 were in Thomas Street.
740B. Bush & Walter. Walter died in January 1779.

741. BUSH, WILLIAM, London: 15 Dec. 1709, Y.
742. BUSH, WILLIAM, Bristol: S. of William. Apprenticed to John Sands, 11 Aug. 1688.
743. BUSH, WILLIAM, Bristol: S. of Robert. Apprenticed to his father, 30 April 1792.
744. BUSHE, JOHN, London: Was in 1560 a carver at the Yeomanry Feast.
745. BUSHELL, JOHN, London: 17 Oct. 1728, Y.
746. BUTCHER, ABRAHAM, Bristol: S. of Langley Butcher. Apprenticed to Roger Willoughby and Sarah his wife, 15 Aug. 1673.
747. BUTCHER, JAMES, SENR., Bridgewater, Somerset: His will was proved at Taunton, 15 Sept. 1698.

In it he mentions his son James and John Johns, Bristol, Pewterers.
748. BUTCHER, JAMES, JUNR., Bridgewater, Somerset: His will was proved at Taunton, 24 Oct. 1720.

749. BUTCHER, GABRIEL, London: 1611, S.; 1627 and 1631, U.W.; 1633 and 1635, M. He was in 1612 one of the "seizers" of false wares for the Company.
750. BUTCHER, ROBERT, London: 1615, S.; 1625, R.W.; 1635, U.W.; 1639, M.
751. BUTCHER, THOMAS, London: 1635, S.; 1645, R.W.; 1652, U.W.
752. BUTCHER, WILLIAM, Bridgewater, Somerset: Mentioned in 1737.
753. BUTLER, JAMES, Bristol: 12 Oct. 1812, F. Apprenticed to Preston Edgar and his wife Rebecca, 24 July 1794. S. of Edward.
754. BUTLER, JOHN, London: 20 Dec. 1770, Y.
755. BUTLER, JOSEPH, London: 21 June 1739, Y.
756. BUTTERTON, JONATHAN, Dublin: Mentioned in 1663 and died 1683. *See* Illustrations of his tokens.
757. BUTTERY, JAMES, London: 17 Oct. 1765, Y.
758. BUTTERY, THOMAS, London: 16 Mar. 1692, Y. Touch, 496 L.T.P., which he had leave to strike on 16 Mar. 1692.

759. BUTTERY, THOMAS, London: 17 June 1756, Y. Touch, 973 L.T.P. Was given leave to strike his Touch on 16 June 1757.

760. BUTTERY, THOMAS, London: 16 Aug. 1730, Y.
760A. BUTTERY, WILLIAM, London: Touch, 434 L.T.P., which he had leave to strike in 1686/7.

761. BYCETER, JOHN, London: In 1457 was an apprentice with Robert Chamberleyn.
BUXTON, *see* BURTON.

762. Byllynge, Robert, London : Was a Freeman in 1457.

763. Byrd, John, London : 1633, f.S.; 1648, R.W.; 1650, U.W.; 1654, M.

764. Byrne, Gerald, Dublin : Mentioned in 1791.

764A. Byrne, Thomas, Dublin : Mentioned in 1820.

765. Bysshop, Piers, London : 1452, 1461, 1472 and 1479, M.

C

765A. Cabell, Joseph, London : c. 1680. ("Bennett" Book.) Touch, 383 L.T.P., which he had leave to strike on 4 Oct. 1682.

766. Cable, Joseph, London : 21 Mar. 1699, Y.

767. Cable, Peter, London : 8 Aug. 1717, Y.

768. Cable, Thomas, London : 10 Oct. 1706, Y.

769. Cade, Thomas, London : Was in 1457 an apprentice of Piers Bysshop.

770. Cade, Thomas, Bristol : Mentioned c. 1700.

771. Cadell, James, Senr. (? Cadle and Cudell), Bristol : Described in 1589 in Walter Davies's Will as of High Street, and mentioned in 1617.

772. Cadell, James, Junr., Bristol : S. of Jacob, Senr., to whom he was apprenticed, 16 Feb. 1600. Mentioned in 1620 with his wife Joan.

773. Cadell, John, Bristol : S. of James C., Senr., apprenticed to his father and mother, Bridgette, 4 Oct. 1609.

773A. Cadell, John, Bristol : 8 July 1569, F. Apprenticed to William Hayle.

774. Cadell, Tinobus, Bristol : Was apprenticed to Wm. Hayle, Pewterer, Bristol, 3 July 1569.

775. Cadogan, Joseph, Bristol and Lanvrechva, Mon. : 11 Feb. 1680, F. S. of William. Apprenticed to William James and his wife Ann, 6 Aug. 1673.

776. Ca(t)cher, Anthony, London : Mentioned in 1551.

777. Ca(t)cher, Edward, London : 1544 and 1546, U.W.; 1556, 1557 and 1561, M. He was an Alderman of the City of London.

778. Caffee, Francis, London : Was a Freeman in 1668.

779. Calcott, John, London : 14 Dec. 1699, Y. Touch, 590 L.T.P., which he had leave to strike on 14 Nov. 1701.

780. Calder, William, Bristol : Mentioned 30 April 1744. Died in 1752.

781. Calvin, Thomas, Bristol : Mentioned in the Bristol Poll Books of 1774, 1781 and 1784 as of S.S. Philip and Jacob, Bristol. Apprenticed to Allen Bright and his wife Ann, 20 Oct. 1753.

782. Calye, Stephen, London : Of Westminster. In 1552 it was ordered that no one of the Company should have any further dealings with him. His fault is not stated. He is again mentioned in 1559 and in 1562 he obtained redress from the Company against a fellow-member, Richard Harrison.

783. Callis, William, London : 1510, R.W.

784. Cam, John, Bristol : 16 July 1735, F. Married Mary Veal. Mentioned in 1738.

785. Cambridge, John, London : His Touch is No. 460 L.T.P., which he had leave to strike in 1686/7, but no mention of his name is found in the Y. or L. Lists.

786. Cambrigge, John, London : In 1457 was a journeyman to John Kendale.

787. Camdon, John, Bristol and Hereford : S. of David. Apprenticed to Abrahan Yeore, Bristol and his wife Joan for seven years from 19 Feb. 1620.

788. Campion, John, London : 19 Mar. 1662, L.; 1668, f.S.; 1676, R.W.; 1681, U.W.; 1686, f.M.

789. Campbell, James, Edinburgh : 1595, F.

790. Campbell, Patrick, Perth : 1733, F. Pewterer and Coppersmith.

791. Campbell & Co., Belfast : Mid nineteenth century.

792. Canby, George, London : 14 Mar. 1694, Y. Touch, 518 L.T.P., dated (16)95, and which he had leave to strike on 16 April 1695.

793. Caney, Joseph, Junr., London : 21 Mar. 1744, Y.; 16 June 1748, L.; 1758, f.S.

794. CANEY, JOSEPH, London : 11 Mar. 1707, Y.
795. CANNER, SAMUELL, Tewkesbury : c. 1670. Mentioned on his token (*q.v.*).
796. CANSON, WILLIAM, Bristol and Gloucester : 2 Dec. 1664, F. S. of Wm. Apprenticed to William Millard and Jane his wife, 4 Dec. 1657.
797. CARDWELL, JOHN (*see* also CORDWELL), London : 10 Oct. 1723, Y. Was given leave to strike his Touch in 1747.
798. CARDYNALL, JOHN, London : 1473, R.W.; 1480, U.W. Apprenticed with Robert Chamberleyn in 1456.
799. CARE, GEORGE, London : In 1585 was one of a number chosen from the Company to serve the Queen as " trayned soldyars."
800. CARLETON, WILLIAM, York : 1522/3, F.
801. CARLILL, JOHN, York : 1508/9, F., by patrimony.
802. CARLOSS, EDWARD, London : 19 June 1718, Y.
803. CARMAN, JOHN, London : 23 June 1803, Y.
804. CARMICHAEL, THOMAS, Cannongate, Edinburgh : 1763, F. White-ironsmith.
805. CARNADYNE, ALEXANDER, London : 1595, R.W.
805A. CARPENTER, E. & H., London : In 1769 were at Panton Street, Haymarket. Partners, Elizabeth and Henry Carpenter (1740, Y.).
805B. CARPENTER, ELIZABETH. London : Partner with Henry Carpenter in 1769. She is probably the widow of John C., who in 1738 was appointed in place of her husband as pewterer to The Royal Hospital, Chelsea. *See* her Trade-card and her receipted bill.
806. CARPENTER, HENRY, London : 24 Mar. 1708, Y.
807. CARPENTER, HENRY, London : 9 Oct. 1740, Y. Partner in E. & H. Carpenter, Panton Street, Haymarket.
808. CARPENTER, HENRY, London : 24 Mar. 1757, Y. and L.; 1767, f.S.; 1775, R.W.; 1784, U.W.; 1786, 1809 and 1816, M. 1819, died. In 1792 was in business at 25 Haymarket.
809. CARPENTER, JOHN, London : 19 June 1701, Y. Touch 587 L.T.P., which he had leave to strike. 18 July 1701.

810. CARPENTER, JOHN, London : 21 June 1711, Y.; 9 Aug. 1739, L. Touch, No. 718 L.T.P., which he obtained leave to strike on 16 July 1717. Pewterer

to Royal Hospital, Chelsea. Appointed 1738, died 1747, and his widow appointed in latter year.
811. CARPENTER, THOMAS, London : 17 Dec. 1713, Y.
812. CARPENTER & HAMBERGER, London : c. 1798. Touch, No. 1066 L.T.P. Partners, Henry Carpenter and John Hamberger, 1794, Y. (*q.v.*), who succeeded to the Carpenters' business.

CARPENTER

812A. CARPENTER & SON, London : In 1777 were at St. James's, Haymarket.
813. CARR, JOHN, Bristol : c. 1750.

814. CARR, JOHN, London : 1696, Y. Touch, 537 L.T.P., which he had leave to strike on 12 Mar. 1696.

815. CARR, JOHN, London : 13 Dec. 1722, Y. Touch, 752 L.T.P., which he obtained leave to strike in 1723.

816. CARR, JOHN, London : 21 Mar. 1744, Y.
817. CARR, JOHN, London : 19 June 1760, Y.
818. CARR, RICHARD, London : 23 Mar. 1737, Y.
819. CARR, ROBERT, London : 12 Aug. 1736, Y. Had leave to strike a Touch in 1736, but it is not on the Touchplates.
820. CARRON, DAVID, London : 21 June 1722, Y.
821. CARRYE, JOHN, London : 1526 and 1531, R.W.; 1537, U.W.; 1543, 1544 and 1552, M.
822. CARSE, JAMES, Glasgow, 1792, mentioned as a coppersmith.
823. CARSHILL, ARCHIBALD, Glasgow : 1700, F. Pewterer and White-ironsmith.
824. CARSTOUNE, ALEXANDER, Edinburgh : 1657, mentioned.

825. CARTER, A., London : c. 1750.

826. CARTER, JAMES, London : Touch, No. 392 L.T.P.
which he had leave to strike on 9 Nov. 1683. No,
mention of his name appears in the Y. or L. Lists,
but it is in the " Bennett " Book from 1683.

827. CARTER, JOHN, London : 27 Sept. 1688, Y.
828. CARTER, JOSEPH, London : Touch, 798 L.T.P.,
dated 1726. No mention of his name in the Y.
or L. Lists, but he had leave to strike this Touch
on 6 Oct. 1726.

829. CARTER, JOSPEH, London : 16 Dec. 1784, Y. ; 20
June 1793, L. ; 1797, f.S. ; 1804, f.R.W. ;
1811, U.W. ; 1812, M.
830. CARTER, PETER, London : 14 Dec. 1699, Y.
Touch, 567 L.T.P., dated 1699, which he had
leave to strike on 14 Dec. 1699.

831. CARTER, RAFFE, London : Was Clerk to the Company, 1570-75.
832. CARTER, RICHARD, London : 7 Oct. 1725, Y.
833. CARTER, SAMUEL, London : 17 Oct. 1771, Y. and L. ;
1778, S. ; 1784, R.W. ; 1793, U.W. ; 1794, M.
1827, died.   Of Blackman Street Livery Stables.
834. CARTER, THOMAS, London : In 1632 he was
chosen Steward on Lord Mayor's day ; was a
Master in 1615 ; 1644, R.W. ; 1648, U.W.
835. CARTER, THOMAS, London : c. 1700.

836. CARTON, JOSEPH, Dublin : 1659, F.
837. CARTWRIGHT, THOMAS, London : 19 Mar. 1712,
Y. ; 24 July 1719, L. ; 1726, f.S. ; 1733, f.R.W. ;
1742, U.W. ; 1743, M. Touch, No. 698
L.T.P., which he obtained leave to strike in
1715.

838. CARY, NICHOLAS, Bristol : S. of Richard. Apprenticed to Thomas Hobson and Elizabeth his wife,
17 Dec. 1632.
839. CARY, THOMAS, London c. 1687. Touch, No.
429 L.T.P. No mention of him in Y. or L.
Lists, but his name is in the " Bennett " Book
from 1686.

CARY, see also CARRYE.
840. CASIMER, BENJAMIN, London : 10 Aug. 1704, Y.
Touch, 617 L.T.P., which he had leave to strike
on 30 Sept. 1704.

841. CASSE, JAMES, Glasgow : 1791. Freeman white-
ironsmith and coppersmith.
841A. CASSER, FRANCIS, London : c. 1680. (" Bennett "
Book.)
842. CASTELL, ROBERT, London : 1452, Y.
842A. CASTLE, GEORGE, London : c. 1680. (" Bennett "
Book.)
843. CASTLE, JNO, London : Touch, No. 293 L.T.P.,
which he had leave to strike in 1677. Not
mentioned in Y. and L. Lists, but is in the
" Bennett " Book from 1678-1686.

844. CASTLE, THOMAS, London: Touch, No. 463 L.T.P., which he had leave to strike on 20 Mar. 1689.

845. CASTLE, JOHN, London: 14 Oct. 1703, Y.
846. CASTLE, LAWRANCE, London: Was a servant of Thomas Shackle. His death is registered on 27 Aug. 1686 at St. Dionis Backchurch.
847. CASTLE, WOODNUTT, London: 15 June 1732, Y.
847A. CASTON, JOHN, Bristol: S. of John. Apprenticed to Bridgett, widow of Philip Lane, 7 June 1627. Apprentice discharged Dec. 1628.

CATCHER, EDWARD, see CACHER.

848. CATCHER, JOHN, London: In 1564 was steward at a Shroving dinner. 1577, R.W.; 1581 and 1583, U.W.; 1585, M. Alderman of the City in 1588 and in 1598 was fined for false wares. Left legacies for the Company.
849. CATCHER, THOMAS, London: 1584, R.W.
850. CATCOTT, GEORGE SYME, Bristol: 30 Mar. 1754, F. S. of Rev. Alexander Stopford Catcott. Apprenticed to Stephen Cox and Susannah his wife for seven years from 12 Jan. 1744. Premium £52 10s. See Burgum & Catcott above. He is mentioned in the Bristol Poll Books of 1774 and 1781, and Boswell in his *Life of Johnson* speaks of their meeting with " George Catcott the Pewterer " at Bristol on 29 April 1776. Again Stanley Hutton in his *Bristol and its Famous Associations* gives a portrait of him (p. 60) after the painting by Edward Bird, R.A., and speaks of him as follows (p. 60):

" About this time (1768) Chatterton made the acquaintance of George Catcott and Henry Burgum, who were partners in a pewtering business at No. 2 Bristol Bridge.

" Catcott, who was a fussy self-important and eccentric man, sadly lacking common sense, but possessed of extraordinary credulity, greedily swallowed all that Chatterton told him respecting the Rowley Poems."

And on pp. 68 and 70 Chatterton in his curious last Will and Testament, gives and bequeaths :

" All my vigor and fire of youth to Mr. George Catcott, being sensible he is in most want of it." and then apostrophises him thus :

" Thy friendship never could be dear to me Since all I am is opposite to thee, etc., etc."

851. CATER, JOHN, London: 17 Mar. 1725, Y.; 26 Oct. 1752, L.; 1761, f.S. Touch, 792 L.T.P., struck c. 1728 (*cf.* Touch of A. Carter).

He was given leave to strike his Touch on 17 Mar. 1725.

852. CATLIN, JOHN, London : 12 Oct. 1693, Y.
853. CATTELL, JOHN, Bristol: 7 May 1650, F. S. of John Cattell, Senr.
854. CATTELL, JOHN, ? Bristol: Mentioned c. 1640-1660.
855. CAVANAGH, JOHN, Dublin: Mentioned in 1761 and died in 1772.
856. CAVE, JOHN, London: 1488, R.W.; 1492 and 1496, U.W.
857. CAVE, JOHN, Bristol : c. 1650-1690.

858. CAVE, JOHN, Bristol : S. of Thomas. Apprenticed to his father and mother Martha, 23 April 1705.
859. CAVE, THOMAS, SENR., Bristol and Chipping Norton : 18 Aug. 1684, F. S. of Thomas. Apprenticed to Roger Willoughby, 7 May 1677. Mentioned in the Bristol Poll Book of 1734 as of Redcliff, Bristol.

860. CAVE, THOMAS, JUNR., Bristol and Chipping Norton : S. of Thomas. Apprenticed to his father and mother Martha, 21 Dec. 1713. Mentioned in 1734.
861. CAVE, WILLIAM, London : 20 Mar. 1728, Y.
862. CAVERD, RICHARD, York : 1536, F.
863. CAY, JOHN, Edinburgh : In 1800 was in business at 22 Leith Street as a white-ironsmith.
864. CAYFORD, FRANCIS, London : 19 June 1707, Y.
865. CEAZCER, WILLIAM, London : 25 Sept. 1712, Y.
866. CERTAIN, JOHN, London : 15 Mar. 1743, Y.

CHABROLES, see SHABROLES.

867. CHALK, AGNES, London : Contributed towards a set of Feast vessels in 1475.
868. CHALK, WILLIAM, London : 1482, R.W.

869. CHALKE, THOMAS, London : Apprenticed in 1457 with Morys Panton.

870. CHALMERS, ROEDERICK, Edinburgh : In 1773 was in business at head of Libberton's Wynd.

871. CHALMERS, MRS. ROEDERICK, Edinburgh : Widow of the last named. Carried on the business from 1786-1793.

872. CHAMBERLAIN, JOHNSON, London : Touch, 853 L.T.P. Struck c. 1734, but no mention of his name is found in the records.

873. CHAMBERLAIN, THOMAS, London : In the lists of Openings and Touches, leave was given to Thomas Chamberlain to strike on 20 Mar. 1734. 3 Aug. 1732, Y.; 24 June 1739, L.; 1751, f.S.; 1754, R.W.; 1764, U.W.; 1765, M. His Trade-card, q.v., gives his address as King Street, corner of Greek Street, St. Ann's, Soho. He is mentioned until 1806. He was later a partner in Chamberlain & Hopkins.

874. CHAMBERLAIN & HOPKINS, London : In 1776 the partnership was dissolved on 13 Feb., Hopkins carrying on the business in Greek Street, Soho. Partners, Thomas Chamberlain and William Hopkins.

875. CHAMBERLAYN, THOMAS, London : 1500 and 1501, R.W.; 1507 and 1510, U.W.; 1517, 1518, 1526, 1532 and 1536, M.

876. CHAMBERLAYN, JOHN, London : Was in 1457 an apprentice with Stephen Tod.

877. CHAMBERLEYN, ROBERT, London : 1452 and 1456, U.W.; 1458 and 1466, M.

878. CHAMBERLEYN, WILLIAM, London : In 1457 was a Covenant man to Robert Chamberleyn and in 1474 was sent as a searcher for the Company to Chelmsford Fair.

879. CHAMBERS, RICHARD, York : In 1684 was a Freeman.

880. CHAMBERS, RICHARD, York : Was apprenticed 15 July 1691 for seven years to Janne Waid (a woman); is mentioned in 1718/9, and had apprentices bound to him from 1712-19, 1717-25, 1725-32 and 1731-38. He obtained his Freedom 1699-1700. Son of William Chambers. Searcher to the Company in 1706, 1712, 1713, 1716, 1717, 1722, 1723, 1729, 1731, 1736 and 1737.

881. CHAMBERS, WILLIAM, York : Was apprenticed to Richard Wroghan on 20 June 1665 for seven years. Obtained his Freedom by patrimony in 1672/3, was searcher to the Company in 1679, 1681 and 1685, and the last mention found of him is in 1699-1700.

882. CHANDLER, BENJAMIN, London : 15 June 1721, Y.

883. CHAPMAN, BENJAMIN, Bristol : 19 Mar. 1721, F. S. of John. Apprenticed to Honor, widow of John Bacheler, 2 Mar. 1713.

884. CHAPMAN, CATESBY, London : 15 June 1721, Y. Touch, 756 L.T.P., which he had leave to strike on 15 June 1721.

885. CHAPMAN, GEORGE, London : 19 Mar. 1772, Y.

886. CHAPMAN, OXTON, London : 18 Dec. 1760, Y. Partner with Wm. Bennett, 1758, Y., in Bennett & Chapman (q.v.). Touch, 994 L.T.P. Was given leave to strike this Touch on 19 Mar. 1761. See also BENNETT & CHAPMAN.

887. CHARLESLEY, JOHN THOMAS, London : 18 Mar. 1730, Y.

888. CHARLESLEY, WILLIAM, London : 19 June 1729, Y.; 3 Aug. 1738, L.; 1750, S.; 1754, f.R.W.; 1763, U.W.; 1764, M. Died in 1770. Touch, 842 L.T.P. Cf. note under William Munden. He was given leave to strike this Touch on 15 June 1732.

889. CHARLETON, GEORGE, London : 16 Mar. 1758, Y.

890. CHARLETON, NICHOLAS, London: 15 Mar. 1759, Y.
891. CHARSLEY, W——, of ? : c. 1800.

892. CHARTER, RICHARD, London: Is mentioned as having an apprentice in 1583.
893. CHASSEY, JOSEPH, London: 1650, S.; 1658, f.R.W.
894. CHAULKLEY, ARTHUR, London: 21 June 1722, Y.
895. CHAWNER, ROBERT, London: 1568, R.W.; 1573 and 1580, U.W.
896. CHAWNER, WILLIAM, London: 20 Oct. 1757, Y.; 29 June 1761, L.; 1768, f.S.; 1777, f.R.W. In business in New Bond Street.
896A. CHECKETT, JOSIAH (? CHEQUETT), London: c. 1680. ("Bennett" Book.)
897. CHEESE, CLEMENT, London: 12 June 1828, Y.
898. CHERRY, GEORGE, London: 11 Dec. 1729, Y.
899. CHESSLIN, RICHARD, London: 19 Mar. 1662, L.; 1668, f.S.; 1677, R.W.; 1682, U.W.; 1686, f.M.
900. CHESTER, GEORGE, London: 1615, R.W.; 1624, U.W.; 1628 and 1634, M.
901. CHESTER, JOHN, London: Fined in 1651 for appearing at the Guildhall without his Livery Gown.
902. CHESTON, RICHARD, York: 1439-40, F.
903. CHETWOOD, JAMES, London: 16 Dec. 1736, Y.
904. CHILD(E), EDWARD, Bristol: 15 July 1639, F., by patrimony. Dead in 1680.
905. CHILD(E), JOHN, London: 1534, R.W.
906. CHILD(E), JOHN, London: Was Warden of the Yeomanry in 1611; 1621, R.W.; 1632 and 1634, U.W.; 1636, f.M.; 1643, M.
907. CHILD(E), JOHN, London: 15 Aug. 1700, Y. Touch, 586 L.T.P., which he had leave to strike on 22 May 1701.

908. CHILD(E), LAWRENCE, London: 10 Aug. 1693, Y.; 2 Oct. 1702, L.; 1723, R.W. Touch, 526 L.T.P., which he had leave to strike on 19 April 1695.

909. CHILD(E), LAWRENCE, London: 14 Dec. 1727, Y.

910. CHILD(E), RICHARD, London: 16 Mar. 1758, Y.
911. CHILD(E), STEPHEN, JUNR., London: 13 Nov. 1758, Y.
912. CHITWELL, SAMUEL, London: 17 Mar. 1691, Y.
913. CHRICHTOUNE, GEORGE (see also CRICHTOUNE), Edinburgh: 1664, F. Touch, 67 E.T.P.

914. CHRISTIE, ROBERT, Edinburgh: Apprenticed in 1654 to Thomas Edgar.
915. CHRISTIE, WILLIAM, Edinburgh: 1652, F. Touch 52 E.T.P. Mentioned in 1665.

916. CHRYSTIE, ANDREW, Perth: Fined in 1665, with Thomas Thornebourne, pewterer, for being in possession of bad metal which they had purchased from William Christie, Edinburgh, and a Dundee pewterer.
917. CHURCHER, ADAM, Petersfield: Was apprenticed to Dorothy, widow of Lawrence Warren, on 8 Nov. 1683. His Touch, it will be noted, is dated 16-92. There is no record of his taking up his Freedom. Joseph King (1691, L.) had sent him rough pewter, but the Court ordered him not to do so again, since Churcher was not a Freeman.

918. CHYRCHE, RAYNALD, Bury: A country member (in 1475) of the London Company.
919. CLACK, RICHARD, London: 24 Mar. 1735, Y.; 20 June 1754, L.
920. CLARIDGE, BENJAMIN, London: 1672, f.R.W.
921. CLARIDGE, CHARLES, London: 18 Mar. 1756, Y.; 12 Dec. 1758, L.; 1790, Beadle. 1817, Died. Touch, 981 L.T.P. Was given leave to strike his Touch, 31 Oct. 1758. In 1792 was at 96 Ratcliffe Highway.

922. CLARIDGE, JOSEPH, London : 13 Aug. 1724, Y. ;
24 June 1739, L. ; 1751, f.S. ; 1754, f.R.W.
Touch, 810 L.T.P. (*cf.* Touch of Thomas Cooke),
which he had leave to strike in 1727.

923. CLARIDGE, THOMAS, London : 21 June 1616, Y.
Touch, 707 L.T.P., which he was granted leave
to strike on 27 Mar. 1717.

924. CLARK(E), CHARLES (*see* also CLERKE), London :
20 Oct. 1791, Y.

925. CLARK(E), CHARLES, Waterford : 1790-1810. In
1805 was at Baronstrand Street.

925A. CLARK(E), CHRISTOPHER, London : 1679-86.
("Bennett" Book.) Touch, 206 L.T.P., which
he had leave to strike in 1671/2.

926. CLARK(E), GEORGE, York : 1634-5, F. Mentioned
again in 1647.

927. CLARK(E), GEORGE, York : Mentioned in 1720-21 as
a pewterer and father of Samuel Clark (*see* below).

928. CLARK(E), HENRY, London : Fined in 1520 for
disobedience and for reviling a brother-member.
In 1532 he was fined again for being absent from
some function not stated. 1541, R.W. ; 1548
and 1552, U.W. : 1555, M.

929. CLARK(E), JAMES, London : 21 Oct. 1784, Y.
930. CLARK(E), JAMES, Edinburgh : 1722, F. Touch,
124 E.T.P.

931. CLARK(E), JAMES, London : 17 June 1731, Y.
932. CLARK(E), JAMES, London : 10 Oct. 1745, Y.
933. CLARK(E), JOHN, Perth : 1796, F. In 1801 he is
described as a Coppersmith and Brassfounder.
934. CLARK(E), JOHN, London : 28 Nov. 1667, L. ;
1670, f.S. ; 1683, f.R.W., f.U.W. and f.M. A
spoon maker.
935. CLARK(E), JOHN, London : 20 Oct. 1765, Y. ;
18 Mar. 1773, L. ; 1779, f.S. ; 1788, R.W.
Of Towman's Pond, Southwark. Partner in
Clarke & Greening. Was given leave to strike
his Touch, 14 Mar. 1765.
936. CLARK(E), JOHN, London : 15 Dec. 1814, Y. ; 4
Sept. 1869, died.
937. CLARK(E), JOHN, London : 21 Oct. 1756, Y.
938. CLARK(E), JOSIAH, London : 11 Dec. 1690, Y.
Touch, 514 L.T.P., which he had leave to strike
on 6 Jan. 1694.

939. CLARK(E), MARK, London : 21 Mar. 1699, Y.
940. CLARK(E), NATHANIEL, London : 6 Aug. 1730, Y.
941. CLARK(E), RICHARD, 24 Mar. 1736, Y.
942. CLARK(E), RICHARD, London : 13 Aug. 1696, Y.
Touch, 535 L.T.P., which he had leave to strike
on 25 Aug. 1696.

943. CLARK(E), SAMUEL, York : 1720-21, F., by patrimony. Son of George Clark, above.
944. CLARK(E), SAMUEL, Exeter : c. 1720.

945. CLARK(E), SAMUEL, London : 11 Aug. 1720, Y. ;
12 Oct. 1732, L. He is described in the records
as " a cork cutter ! "

946. CLARK(E), THOMAS, London: 1543, R.W. He is mentioned in 1549 as paying a fine for some misdemeanour with John Mathews at Fairs.

947. CLARK(E), THOMAS, London: 22 June 1671, Y.; 22 Sept. 1685, L.; 1699, R.W.; 1706, U.W.; 1711, M. Touch, 347 L.T.P., struck c. 1680.

948. CLARK(E), WILLIAM, London: 19 Dec. 1695, Y. Touch, 529 L.T.P., which he had leave to strike on 18 June 1696.

949. CLARK(E), WILLIAM, London: 6 April 1721, Y.

950. CLARK(E), WILLIAM, London: Touch, 484 L.T.P., which he had leave to strike on 17 Mar. 1691, but no mention of a Wm Clarke is found about this date in the Y. or L. Lists.

951. CLARK(E), WILLIAM, London: In 1583, being then an apprentice with Wm. Anderson, was transferred to Richard Charter.

952. CLARK(E), WILLIAM, London: 20 Jan. 1726, L.; 1733, S.; 1739, f.R.W.; 1749, f.U.W.; 1750, 1751 and 1755, M. Touch, 733 L.T.P., which he had leave to strike in 1721.

953. CLARK(E), WILLIAM HENRY, London: 19 Aug. 1819, Y. and L.; 1830, f.S.; 1840, R.W.; 1842, U.W.; 1843, M.

954. CLARK(E) & GREENING, London: Touch, 1007 L.T.P., struck c. 1765. The partners were John Clark, 1765, Y.; and Richard Greening, 1756, Y.

955. CLARKSONE, JAMES, Edinburgh: In 1710 was apprenticed to John Watson.

956. CLARKSONE, JOHN, Edinburgh: Was a Master in 1724.

957. CLAYTON, EDWARD, Bristol: S. of Edward. Apprenticed to Thomas Page and his wife Mary, 30 Oct. 1750.

958. CLAYTON, RICHARD, London: 18 Mar. 1741, Y.

959. CLAYTON, ROBERT, London: 22 Oct. 1772, Y.

960. CLEEVE, ALEXANDER, London: 4 Oct. 1688, Y.; 15 Aug. 1689, L.; 1696, S.; 1705, R.W.; 1715, U.W.; 1719 and 1728, M. Touch, 457 L.T.P., which he had leave to strike on 20 June 1689. He succeeded Nicholas Kelk, and at first retained his device and "Hall Marks," merely substituting his own name. His shop was next to Tom's Coffee House on the West Side of Cornhill.

961. CLEEVE, ALEXANDER, London: 22 Mar. 1715, Y.; 21 June 1716, L.; 1724, S.; 1735, f.R.W.; 1744, f.U.W.; 1745, f.M. Touch, 791 L.T.P. Struck c. 1728, when he succeeded to his father's business. He was given leave to strike a Touch in 1716, but did not do so at that time, for on 27 Sept. 1716 he was given leave to be partner with his father.

961A. CLEEVE, ANN & BOURCHIER, London: Were at Cornhill in 1740.

962. CLEEVE, BOU(R)CHIER, London : 16 Dec. 1736, Y. and L.; 1744, f.S. and f.R.W.; 1755, f.U.W.; 1757, f.M. Was given leave to strike his Touch on 22 June 1738. Was in partnership with Richard Cleeve, *vide* Welch, ii. 194. Lived at Foots-Cray Place, Kent.

962A. CLEEVE, BOU(R)CHIER, JUNR., London : Was given leave to strike his Touch on 20 Mar. 1750. Touch, 951 L.T.P.

963. CLEEVE, BOU(R)CHIER & RICHARD, London : c. 1754.

964. CLEEVE, EDWARD, London : 22 Mar. 1715, Y.; 21 June 1716, L.

965. CLEEVE, ELIZABETH, London : 15 Feb. 1742, Y. Daughter to Deputy Alexander Cleeve (1719, M.).

966. CLEEVE, GILES, London : 15 Aug. 1706, Y. Touch, 832 L.T.P., which he was given leave to strike on 19 Mar. 1729.

967. CLEEVE, GILES, London : 19 June 1740, Y.

968. CLEEVE, MARY, London : 15 Feb. 1742, Y. Daughter of Deputy Alexander Cleeve (1719, M.).

969. CLEEVE, RICHARD, London : 19 May 1743, Y.; 23 June 1743, L.; 1754, f.S.; 1760, f.R.W. In partnership with Bouchier Cleeve.

970. CLEGHORN, DAVID, Edinburgh : Was apprenticed in 1704 with David Symonds.

971. CLEMENT, CHRISTOPHER, Bristol and Coakley, Somerset : 20 July 1693, F. S. of Christopher. Apprenticed to Roger Willoughby, Senr., 3 June

1686, and turned over on the 8 Aug. 1687 to John Bacheler. Mentioned in 1738. In the Bristol Poll Book for 1734 he is entered as of St. Stephen's, Bristol, and in that of 1739 as of St. James's, Bristol.

972. CLEMENTS, CHRISTOPHER, Cork : Mentioned in 1697.

973. CLEMENTS, JOHN, London : 13 Mar. 1747, Y.; 13 June 1751, L.; 1761, f.S.; 1767, R.W.; 1781, f.U.W.; 1782, M. Of St. Paul's Church-yard.

974. CLEMMONS THOMAS, London : 18 June 1713, Y.

974A. CLENAGHAN, ——, Dublin : Mentioned in 1713.

975. CLENAGHAN, WILLIAM, Dublin : Mentioned 1740-1773.

976. CLENY, JOHN, London : In 1457 was an apprentice with William Eyer.

977. CLERK(E), GEORGE, (*see* also CLARK). York : 1471/2, F.

978. CLERK(E), JOHN, York : 1536-7, F.

979. CLERK(E), JOHN, London : In 1457 was a Journeyman to John Parys.

980. CLERK(E), NICHOLAS, London : His burial is mentioned in 1495/6.

981. CLIFFE, FRANCIS, London : 22 Mar. 1687, Y. Touch, 476 L.T.P., which he had leave to strike on 23 Mar. 1690.

982. CLIFFE, JOHN, London : 1588, R.W.; 1594 and 1597, U.W.; 1599, 1602 and 1607, M.

983. CLIFFE, JOHN, London : 1587, Y.

984. CLIFFE, THOMAS, London : 1630, R.W.; 1639, U.W.

985. CLIFFORD, RICHARD, Bristol and Arlingham, Glocs.: 6 Mar. 1644, F. S. of Richard. Apprenticed to Thomas Hobson, 27 Mar. 1638. Died 1677.

986. CLIFT, JOSEPH, London : 18 June 1696, Y.

987. CLIFTON, CHRISTOPHER, (?) York : c. 1730. *Cf.* Wm. Smith, No. 4402.

988. CLIFTON, ROGER DE, York: 1356/7, F. He is described as " a ledebeter " which probably means " a pewterer."

989. CLOTHYER, ROBERT, Chard, Somerset : Mentioned c. 1670-1710.

(Appears with date 1707)

(Appears with date 1695)

990. CLOTHYER, WILLIAM, Bristol and Chard : 30 July 1705, F. S. of Robert. Apprenticed to Thomas Salmon and Marie his wife, 20 April 1698.

991. CLOUDESLEY, NEHEMIAH, of ? : c. 1675-1710.

992. CLOUDESLEY, TIMOTHY, of ? : c. 1700-1730.

CLYFFE, see CLIFFE.

993. COATS, ANDREW, Glasgow : 1793, F. Brass-founder, etc.

994. COATS, ARCHIBALD & WILLIAM, Glasgow : Mentioned in 1799 as pewterers. Their Mark appears with " Hall-Marks " of Wm. Hunter, q.v.

995. COATS, WILLIAM, Edinburgh : In 1793 he had a shop in Calton and in 1800 in New Street, Canongate.

996. COATS, WILLIAM, Edinburgh : His mark appears with the Hall marks of Wm. Hunter (Cf. M.C.). See A. & W. Coats.

997. COBHAM, PERCHARD, London : 12 Oct. 1732, Y. COBNER, see COPNER.

998. COCK. HUMPHREY, London : 1670, f.R.W., f.U.W. and f.M.

999. COCKBURN, ANDREW, Edinburgh : 1741, F. In 1774 had a shop in Bowhead Well.

1000. COCKBURN, THOMAS, Edinburgh : 1711, F. Touch, 114 E.T.P.

1001. COCKEY, W——, Totnes : Married in 1741 to Hannah Reynolds. In 1767 he was a witness at the marriage of his sister Mary to Thomas Windeatt, Tavistock. A William Cockey was appointed in 1792 as a Trustee of a Charity for the Minister and Poor of the Town Meeting, Totnes.

1002. COCKINSKELL, EDWARD, London : 22 June 1693, Y.

1003. COCKLEY, ——, London : Supplied (or was accused of supplying) bad pewter in 1615 for a funeral.

1004. COCKS, SAMUEL (see also Cox), London : 11 Mar. 1819, Y. and L. Touch, 1080 L.T.P.

1005. CODDE, STEPHEN (? TODDE), London : 1458, R.W.; 1464 and 1467, U.W.

1006. COE, THOMAS, London : 19 Mar. 1807, Y.

1007. COGENS, JOHN, London : In 1457 was a Master.

1008. COGGS, JOHN, London : 9 Oct. 1712, Y.

1009. COHED, THOMAS, London : Died 1425.

1010. COK, WILLIAM, London : In 1457 was an apprentice with Thomas Grove.

1011. COKE, JOHN, London : In 1457 was an apprentice with John Whitehed. In 1475 he subscribed towards a fund for providing a set of feast vessels.

1012. COKE, JOHN, London: 11 Oct. 1694, Y. Touch,
512 L.T.P., which he had leave to strike on 19
Dec. 1694.

1013. COKE, ROBERT, York: 1476/7, F.
1014. COKONOW, JOHN, London: was a Liveryman in
1457.
1015. COKTON, ROBERT OF, London: In 1457 was an
apprentice with Stephen Auncell.
1016. COLDHAM, JOHN, London: 1456 and 1465, M.
1017. COLDHAM, JOHN, London: In 1457 he was apprenticed with Wm. Smallwood.
1018. COLDWELL, GEORGE, Cork: Mentioned in
1773.
1019. COLE, ANDREW, London: Of St. Martin's in the
Fields. Married at St. Gregory's, 25 Sept.
1662, to the daughter of Thomas Fountain, St.
Margaret's, Westminster.
1020. COLE, BENJAMIN, London: 1668, f.S.; 1672,
R.W.; 1678, f.U.W.; 1683, M.
1021. COLE, JEREMIAH, London: 14 July 1692, L.
Touch, 316 L.T.P., struck c. 1679.

1022. COLE, JOHN, London: c. 1727, his Touch was
struck, No. 765 L.T.P., but no mention of his
name is in the records.

1023. COLE, ROWLAND, London: See Rowland Poole.
1024. COLE, THOMAS, Bristol: S. of John. Apprenticed
to Edward Hackrigge and Anne his wife for
nine years from 30 April 1612.
1025. COLEBORNE, RICHARD, London: 13 Aug. 1724, Y.
1026. COLES, ALEXANDER, London: 22 Mar. 1693, Y.
1027. COLES, JOSEPH, Barnstaple: 1679. Mentioned
in Barnstaple Record, No. 1244.
COLEMAN, see COLMAN.
1028. COLIERSON, JOHN, York: 1499, F.
1028A. COLLER, JOHN, Norwich: 1613, F.
1028B. COLLER, JOSEPH, Norwich: 1622, F.
1028C. COLLER, ROBERT, Norwich: 1640, F.

1029. COLLET(T), EDWARD, London: 18 Mar.
1773, Y.
1030. COLLET(T), GEORGE, Youghal: Mentioned in
1787.
1031. COLLET(T), THOMAS, London: 9 Oct. 1735, Y.;
11 Aug. 1737, L. Touch, 862 L.T.P., which
he had leave to strike in 1735.

1032. COLLIER, BENJAMIN (see also COLYER), Bristol and
Flax-Bourton, Somerset: Mentioned with
Elizabeth his wife in 1745.
1033. COLLIER, EDWARD, Ludlow: Apprenticed to
Richard Plumer, 18 June 1754.
1034. COLLIER, HUGH, London: Used for his Touch
the Rose and Crown which he was required to
alter in 1570. He was free in 1565.
1035. COLLIER, JOHN, London: Was robbed by his
apprentice, Francis Bawdwyn, in 1569, and the
latter was " whipped in open Court there and
then for his offence."
1036. COLLIER, JOSEPH, London: Was married on 25
Aug. 1670 to Grace Multon, and is mentioned
in the " Bennett " Book from 1679-1686.
Touch, 172 L.T.P., which he had leave to
strike in 1669/70.

1037. COLLIER, NICHOLAS, London: In 1583 was chosen
one of a committee appointed to fix the selling
prices of pewter wares. 1600, R.W.; 1604,
U.W.
1038. COLLIER, PETER, London: 22 Aug. 1720, Y.
Touch, 730 L.T.P., which he was given leave to
strike 22 Aug. 1720.

1039. COLLIER, RICHARD, London: 19 Aug. 1669, L.
Touch, 131 L.T.P., restruck after the great fire
c. 1670.

1040. COLLIER RICHARD, London : 20 June 1706, Y.; 20 June 1728, L.; 1737, S.; 1742, R.W. Touch, 649 L.T.P., struck c. 1708.

1041. COLLIER, ROBERT, London : Fined in 1570 " for contemptuous words."
1042. COLLINGS, JOHN, London : 19 Mar. 1690, Y.
1043. COLLINS, CHARLES, Cork : Mentioned in 1734 and 1753.
1044. COLLINS, DANIEL, London : 17 Oct. 1776, Y.; 23 June 1785, L.; 1791, f.S.; 1799, f.R.W.; 1805, U.W.; 1806, f.M. 1809, died.
1045. COLLINS, DANIEL, London : 18 June 1833, Y. and L.; 1842, f.S.; 1852, R.W.; 1854, U.W.; 1855, M.
1046. COLLINS, DANIEL THOMAS, London : 13 Dec. 1804, Y.; 19 Mar. 1812, L.
1047. COLLINS, HENRY, London : 22 June 1704, Y.
1048. COLLINS, HENRY, JUNR., London : 12 Dec. 1751, Y.
1049. COLLINS, JAMES, London : 24 Mar. 1803, Y.; 17 Oct. 1811, L.
1050. COLLINS, JOHN, Bristol : 2 Oct. 1812, F. Apprenticed to Thomas Hale. In the Bristol Poll Book of 1812 he is mentioned as of Bedminster Road, and in a MS. Poll Book for 1820 as of Terrace, Bedminster.
1051. COLLINS, JOSEPH, Bristol and Mangotsfield : 19 Dec. 1792, F. S. of Benjamin. Apprenticed to Richard Hale, 24 May 1784.
1052. COLLINS, ROWLAND, Bristol and Gloucester : 23 Sept. 1665, F. S. of William. Apprenticed to Edward Lovering, Bristol, and Alice his wife for seven years from 8 Aug. 1636. Mentioned in 1674.
1053. COLLINS, SAMUEL, London : 12 Oct. 1732, Y.; 15 Dec. 1768, L. 1770, died.
1054. COLLINS, WILLIAM, Gloucester : Mentioned in 1636.
1055. COLMAN, JOHN, London : Journeyman to Robert Hacche, 1457.
1055A. COLMAN, WILLIAM, London : Touch, 502 L.T.P. which he had leave to strike on 31 Jan. 1694.

1056. COLSMAN, ——, (?) London : Early nineteenth century. This maker is of little interest to serious collectors.

1057. COLSON, JOSEPH, London : Mentioned in 1698. 24 June 1700, Y.
1057A. COLSON, JOSEPH, London : Mentioned in the " Bennett " Book from 1679-1686. Touch, 179 L.T.P., which he had leave to strike in 1670/1.

COLTON, see COULTON.

1058. COLYER, CHRISTOPHER, York : 1522/3, F., by patrimony. One of the City Chamberlains in 1539/40. Son of the next named.
1059. COLYER, HUGH, London : Was Free in 1565. In 1569 he was ordered to reduce the size of his Touch of " The Rose and Crown."
1060. COLYER, JOHN, York : Father of the last named. Mentioned in 1522/3, in which year he was one of the City Chamberlains.
1061. COMPERE, JOHN (or COMPERT), London : 10 Dec. 1696, Y. Touch, 563 L.T.P., which he had leave to strike on 17 Nov. 1699.

1062. COMPTON, GREGORY, London : Of St. Botolph, Aldgate, was a witness to the marriage of Thomas Court and Mary Stampes, 8 Mar. 1683 (or 1688).
1063. COMPTON, THOMAS, London : 5 Aug. 1802, Y.; 24 Sept. 1807, L. 1817, died. Succeeded to the business of his father-in-law John Townsend who died in 1801, to whom he was apprenticed in 1763 and whom he joined in partnership in 1780, vide " John Gray, Pewterer."

He was succeeded by his second son, Townsend Compton, in 1817. In 1793 his address was Osborn Place, Brick Lane.

1063A. COMPTON, T. & H., London : In 1817 were at 9 Booth Street. Spitalfields. This firm was Thomas Compton, and both he and his son Henry died about the same time, c. 1817.

1064. COMPTON, THOMAS & TOWNSEND, London : Father and son, c. 1801-17.

1065. COMPTON, TOWNSEND, London : Son of and partner with Thomas. He died in 1834, and was succeeded by Townsend & Henry Compton, q.v.

1065A. COMPTON, TOWNSEND & HENRY, London : 1834, c 1869.

1066. COMYN & ROWDEN, London : c. 1770. A specimen bearing their name is in the Guildhall Museum, London.

1067. CONDUIT, JOHN, Bristol and Bath : S. of George. Apprenticed to Preston Edgar and his wife Rebecca, 24 Oct. 1793.

1068. CONEY, JOHN, London : 20 Mar. 1755. Y.

1069. CONNEL, MATTHEW, Glasgow : In 1776 is mentioned as a pewterer, and in 1778 as a coppersmith.

1070. CONSTEIN, ALEXANDER, Edinburgh : Apprenticed in 1669 with Archibald Napier.

1071. CONSTINE, ALEXANDER, Edinburgh : Mentioned as being a Freeman in 1667.

1072. CONSTINE, WILLIAM, Edinburgh : Was a Freeman in 1664.

1073. CONSYTT, MATHEW, Bristol : 6 May, 1618, F. Married Alsys Browne.

1074. CONYNGHAME, WILLIAM, Edinburgh : 1764, F.

1075. COOCH, JOSHUA, London : 19 Mar. 1761, Y.

1076. COOCH, WILLIAM, London : 16 Dec. 1731, Y.; 17 June 1752, L. Touch, 844 L.T.P., which he obtained leave to strike on 11 Oct. 1733.

1077. COOCH, WILLIAM, London : 23 Mar. 1775, Y. Touch, 1029 L.T.P., struck c. 1775.

1078. COOK(E), EDMUND, London : 19 June 1701, L.

1079. COOK(E), EDWARD, London : 16 Mar. 1769, Y.

1080. COOK(E), HUGH, York : 1616/7, F., by patrimony Son of Thomas. Last mention found of him is in 1652/3.

1081. COOK(E), ISAAC, London : 11 Aug. 1692, Y. Touch, 487 L.T.P., which he had leave to strike on 11 Aug. 1692.

1082. COOK(E), JAMES, York : Son of Thomas. 1632/3, F., by patrimony.

1083. COOK(E), JAMES, Bristol : S. of Ambrose. Apprenticed to Thomas Hale and Martha his wife, 5 Sept. 1791.

1084. COOK(E), JOHN, London : Gave a spoon to the Company on being raised to the Livery in 1504.

1085. COOK(E), JOHN, London : 22 Mar. 1770, Y.

1086. COOK(E), JOHN, York : 1652-3, F., by patrimony. Son of Hugh.

1086A. COOK(E), JOHN, Manchester : In 1773 was a pewterer and brazier in Deansgate.

1087. COOK(E), NICHOLAS, London : In 1584 he received a loan from the Company under the terms of a certain Mr. Lotton's will.

1088. COOK(E), RALPH, Newcastle-on-Tyne : Mentioned in 1536.

1089. COOK(E), RICHARD, York : Was free in 1599.

1090. COOK(E), RICHARD, London : 21 Oct. 1756, Y. Of Old Fish Street. Was gazetted as insolvent on 2 June 1761.

1091. COOK(E), SAMUEL, London : 15 June 1727, Y. Touch, 813 L.T.P., which he had leave to strike on 31 May 1728.

1091A. COOK(E), SAMUEL, Derby : Father of White Cooke No. 1094.

1092. COOK(E), THOMAS, London: 14 Aug. 1690, Y. Touch, 565 L.T.P., which he had leave to strike on 14 Dec. 1699 (cf. Touch of Joseph Claridge).

1093. COOK(E), THOMAS, York: 1588/9, F., by patrimony. He is mentioned at intervals up to 1633.

1094. COOK(E), WHITE, London: 22 Mar. 1720, Y. On 19 June 1712 he was apprenticed to Samuel Jackson.

1095. COOK(E), WILLIAM, Bristol and Gloucester: 5 Dec. 1795, F. S. of Ambrose. Apprenticed to Richard Hale, 24 May 1784. Of the Dings, out-parish, Bristol, mentioned in the Bristol Poll Book of 1812.

1096. COOK(E), WILLIAM, London: 22 June 1704, Y.; 18 Aug. 1707, L.

1097. COOK(E), WILLIAM, York: In 1599 was refused his freedom until he produced a satisfactory essay piece.

1098. COOK(E), WILLIAM, York: Mentioned in 1588/9 as father of the next named

1099. COOK(E), WILLIAM, York: 1588/9, F., by patrimony. Son of last named.

1100. COOK(E) & FREEMAN, London: Touch, 824 L.T.P., struck c. 1731. The partners were William Freeman, 1728, Y.; and Samuel Cooke, 1727, Y.

1101. COOPER, BENJAMIN, London: 19 Mar. 1684, L.; 1697, f.R.W.; 1703, U.W. The following is

noted against his name in the records: "Fine returned 21 Mar. 1727." He had leave to strike Touch, 339 in 1679/80.

1102. COOPER, BENJAMIN, London: 12 Oct. 1727, Y.

1103. COOPER, CHARLES, London: 1810, Y. Died, 3 Feb. 1856, aged 67 years.

1104. COOPER, GEORGE, London: 24 Oct. 1822, Y.

1105. COOPER, GEORGE, London: 14 Oct. 1777, Y.

1106. COOPER, GEORGE, London: 5 Aug. 1802, L.; 1804, f.S.; 1811, R.W.; 1817, U.W.; 1819, M. 18 May 1833, died.

1106A. COOPER, JOHN, London: Touch, 378 L.T.P., which he had leave to strike on 22 Mar. 1684.

1107. COOPER, JOHN, London: 4 Oct. 1688, Y. Touch, 465 L.T.P., which he had leave to strike on 24 May 1690.

1108. COOPER, JOHN, Bristol and Sherborne, Dorset: 2 Aug. 1661, F. S. of Randall. Apprenticed to Peter Lodge, 21 April 1651.

1108A. COOPER, MATTHEW, Dorchester, Dorset: 1724.

1109. COOPER, RANDALL, Bristol and Sherborne, Dorset: Mentioned c. 1650.

1110. COOPER, RICHARD, London: 24 Sept. 1818, Y. and L.; 1828, f.S.; 1839, f.R.W.; 1841, U.W. 27 Dec. 1841, died, aged 51.

1111. COOPER, THOMAS, London: Touch, 31 L.T.P. Was brought up for making bad wares in 1668, but excused on his stating it was an accident.

1111A. COOPER, THOMAS, London: Is mentioned in the "Bennett" Book from 1679-86. Touch, 326 L.T.P., which he struck in 1678/9.

1112. COOPER, THOMAS, London: 19 June 1817, Y. and L.; 1824, f.S.; 1834, R.W.; 1836, U.W.; 1838, M. 19 Feb. 1844, died, age 69.

1113. COOPER, THOMAS, JUNR., London : 1 May 1834, Y. and L.; 1842, f.S.; 1853, f.R.W.; 1855, U.W.; 1856, M.

1114. COOPER, THOMAS, Aulton Priors : Mentioned in 1633 as a Bondman to a marriage licence.

1115. COOPER, WILLIAM, London : 1655, f.S.

1116. COOPER, WILLIAM, London : 12 Oct. 1727, Y.

1116A. COPNER, THOMAS, Barnstaple : Successor to Nicholas Shepherd, January 1792.

1117. CORBET, DAVID, Glasgow : In 1784 was an apprentice with Stephen Maxwell.

1118. CORBET, JAMES, Dundee : 1668, F.

1119. CORBET, JAMES JOSEPH, London : Of St. Martin's Lane. Is mentioned as a witness at a wedding in 1775.

1120. CORBYN, RICHARDE, London : Mentioned in 1569/70. He was fined for a misdemeanour in 1570/1.

1121. CORDELL, JOHN, London : 14 Mar. 1765, Y.

1122. CORDELL, JOHN, London : 19 Mar. 1729, Y.

1122A. CORDEN, THOMAS, London : c. 1680. (" Bennett " Book.)

1123. CORDWELL, WILLIAM (see also CARDWELL), London : 18 Mar. 1756, Y.

1124. CORDWELL, WILLIAM, London : 14 Oct. 1790, Y. Died 1834.

1125. CORMELL, JOHN (? CORNELL), London : Touch, 410 L.T.P., which he had leave to strike in 1684/5, struck c. 1685. No mention of his name is in the Y. or L. Lists, but it is in the " Bennett " Book from 1684-6.

1126. CORNEWELL, WILLIAM, London : Was a Master in 1614.

1126A. CORNHILL, GILBERT, London : Touch, 164 L.T.P., which he had leave to strike in 1669/70.

1127. CORNHYLL, WILLIAM, London : Was in 1593 an apprentice with Maurice Pellytory, but on account of his master's poverty was transferred to Thomas Steventon.

1128. CORNOCK, THOMAS, Bristol and Haverford West : S. of Daniel. Apprenticed to Gregory Ash, Bristol, and Mary his wife, 20 May, 1754. Premium £50.

1129. CORSE, THOMAS, London : 14 Mar. 1694, Y.

1130. CORTYNE, JOHN, Edinburgh : 1630, F.

1131. COTTERELL, HENRY, Bewdley : c. 1800.

1132. COTTERELL, MARY, Bewdley : Died c. 1840.

1133. COTTERELL, SAMUEL, Bewdley : Died c. 1820.

1133A. COTTERELL, BENJAMIN, London : c. 1680. (" Bennett " Book.) Touch, 382 L.T.P., which he had leave to strike on 14 Dec. 1682.

1133B. COTTINGHAM, THOMAS, Bradford : Insolvent in 1737. Pewterer and Brazier.

1134. COTTON, HENRY, Lynn : 1592/3, F.

1135. COTTON, JOHN, Lynn : 1627/8, F. Apprenticed to Robert Gibson.

1136. COTTON, JONATHAN, SENR., London : 22 Mar. 1704, Y.; 24 April 1711, L.; 1716, S.; 1728, f.R.W.; 1734, U.W.; 1736, M. Touch, 624 L.T.P., which he had leave to strike on 20 April 1705. In 1740 he was on the South End, East Side, of London Bridge.

1137. COTTON, JONATHAN, JUNR., London : 11 Dec. 1735, Y.; 16 Dec. 1736, L.; 1747, S.; 1750, f.R.W.; 1757, U.W.; 1759, M. Touch, 866 L.T.P., dated 1705, but struck in 1736, when he was given leave to strike it. The date in this Touch, 1705, which at first sight is misleading, refers back to the date of the foundation of the business by his father the last named and which same date is found in his Touch.

 LONDON

1139. COTTON, JONATHAN, London : 23 Aug. 1750, L. Probably a partner in Jonathan & Thomas Cotton.

1140. COTTON, JONATHAN & THOMAS, London : c. 1750.

1141. COTTON, THOMAS, London: 20 Dec. 1716, Y.
1142. COTTON, THOMAS, London: 15 Mar. 1749, Y. and L.; 1760, f.S.; 1766, f.R.W.; 1777, U.W.; 1778. M. Probably a partner in Jonathan & Thomas Cotton. Was given leave to strike his Touch on 15 Mar. 1749.

COUCH, see COOCH.

1143. COULSON, WILLIAM, London: Mentioned in 1647 in the records of the Skinners' Company.
1144. COULTER, ALEXANDER, Edinburgh: Mentioned in 1723 and died c. 1732.

1145. COULTER, WILLIAM, Edinburgh: 1751, F.
1146. COULTHARD, ALEXANDER, Edinburgh: 1708, F. Touch, 110. E.T.P.

1147. COULTON, CHARLES, London: 11 Oct. 1711, Y.
1148. COULTON, ROBERT, SENR. (? COWTON), York: Apprenticed to John Bogg for seven years in 1642. Son of Richard and father of Robert Junr. 18 Dec. 1654, F. Searcher in 1669, 1670 and 1676. One of the City Chamberlains in 1672/3, and the last mention found of him is in 1683/4.
1149. COULTON, ROBERT, JUNR., York: Apprenticed to his father, Robert Senr., for seven years from 1677. 1683/4, F. Was one of the City Chamberlains 1691/2.
1150. COULTON, THOMAS, Bristol: 29 Mar. 1634, F. Apprenticed to John ——— ?
1151. COUP (? COX), HUMPHREY, Bristol: Mentioned in 1560.
1152. COUPER, JOHN, London: Was a Freeman in 1457.
1153. COUPER, WILLIAM, London: Was an apprentice with John Warde in 1457.
1154. COUPPER, JAMES, (Scotch): c. 1725. Two flagons bearing his mark and date 1724 are in Whittinghame Kirk.

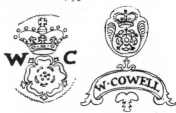

1155. COURIE, JOHN, Edinburgh: Was in 1690 an apprentice with Robert Edgar.
1156. CO(UR)(W)SEY, JOHN, London: 28 Nov. 1667, L. Touch, 49 L.T.P., restruck c. 1670 after the great fire of 1666. Touch, 430 L.T.P. is a later Touch of his, and which he was given leave to strike in 1686/7.

1157. COUSINS, CLEMENT, Bristol and Wells: S. of Robert. Apprenticed to John Lovell and Hannah his wife, 1 July 1713. Is given in the Bristol Poll Book of 1721 as of St. Michael's, and in that of 1739 as of Christchurch, Bristol. Mentioned in 1742.
1157A. COUTES, JOHN, Bristol: Son of Abraham C. Apprenticed to James Cadell and his wife Bridgett, 19 Nov. 1617.
1158. COUTIE, WILLIAM, Edinburgh: 1619, F.
1159. COUTRIE, THOMAS, Edinburgh: 1764, F.
1160. COVENTRY, JAMES, Glasgow: Was in 1794 an apprentice with Robert Graham and James Wardropp.
1161. COVENTRY, SHELTON, Glasgow: Mentioned in 1794.
1162. COVERHAM, WILLIAM, York: 1412, F., by patrimony.
1163. COWAN, THOMAS, Edinburgh: 1598, F.
1164. COWDEROY, RICHARD, London: 1730, died. He was an apprentice with James Spackman and was buried on 29 Dec. 1730 at St. Dionis Backchurch.
1165. COWDEROY, THOMAS, London: 20 June 1689, Y. Touch, 473 L.T.P., which he had leave to strike on 3 Dec. 1691.

1166. COWDWELL, JOHN, London: Was a collector for the Livery in 1598. 1606, R.W.; 1612 and 1617, U.W.; 1620, M.
1167. COWELL, W———, (?) Preston: c. 1740. A Thomas Cowell was a tinman and Brazier in Preston in 1793.

1168. Cowes, Henry, London: Was a Master in 1612. 1614, L.; 1626, R.W.; 1636, U.W.; 1640 and 1645, M. He paid on entering the Livery in 1614 a "fine" of £10 and a silver bowl weighing 14 oz. 3 dwt., with the Arms engraved thereon. In 1639 he was at the South End, East Side of London Bridge.

1169. Cowes, Thomas, London: In 1583 was appointed one of a committee to fix selling prices. In 1596 was fined and imprisoned for making false wares. 1601, R.W.; 1605, U.W.

1170. Cowke, William (? Cooke), York: 1557, F.

1171. Cowley, John (see also Crowley), London: 16 June 1724, Y. and L.; 1730, S.; 1736, f.R.W. Was given leave to strike his Touch in 1728 (? No. 5520).

1172. Cowley, John, London: 17 Dec. 1713, Y.

1173. Cowley, John, London: 23 Mar. 1748, Y.

1174. Cowley, Raffe, London: Is mentioned as being proceeded against by a fellow-member in 1589.

1175. Cowley, William, London: 12 Aug. 1669, L.; 1674, f.S.; 1690, R.W.; 1693, U.W.; 1695, M.

1176. Cowley, William, London: 11 Dec. 1690, Y.; 15 Aug. 1709, L.; 1713, S.; 1725, f.R.W.; 1732, U.W.; 1734, M. Of St. Botolph's, Bishopgate. Married in April 1694 at All Hallows. Marriage Licence granted by the Bishop of London.

1177. Cowling, William, London: 13 Oct. 1737, Y. Touch, 892 L.T.P., struck by leave on 19 June 1740.

1178. Cowlt, Robert, Bristol: S. of Robert. Apprenticed to Thomas Munk, 14 Jan. 1649.

1179. Cowper, James, Edinburgh: 1704, F. Touch, 106 E.T.P.

1180. Cowper, Thomas, London: 10 Aug. 1721, Y.

1181. Cowper, William, London: 14 June 1750, Y.
Cowsey, see Coursey.
Cowton, see Coulton.

1182. Cowyer, Nicholas (? Bowyer), London: Mentioned in 1597. 1607, W.

1183. Cox, Charles (see also Cocks), London: 17 Dec. 1724, Y.

1184. Cox, Humphrey, Bristol: Mentioned in 1567.

1185. Cox, John, London: 20 Oct. 1679, L. Touch, 262 L.T.P., struck c. 1676.

1186. Cox, Ralph, London: Is mentioned as being ordered to use for his mark the initials of his name with the date 1656 and "a knot about it." The knot was a mark of disgrace which he incurred at this date for making faulty wares (see also R. Goudge).

1187. Cox, Richard, London: 9 Oct. 1712, Y. Touch, 763 L.T.P., struck by leave on 19 Mar 1723.

1188. Cox, Richard, London: 18 June 1713, Y.

1189. Cox, Stephen, Bristol: 4 July 1735, F. Apprenticed to Edward Gregory. Is mentioned in the Bristol Poll Books for 1739 and 1754 as of St. Thomas's Bristol. Died c. 1754.

1190. Cox, William, London: 16 Dec. 1708, Y. Touch, 668 L.T.P., struck c. 1710.

1191. Cox, William, London: 18 Mar. 1756, Y.

1191A. Cox, William, Newcastle-on-Tyne: Mentioned in 1793.

1192. Cox, Mrs. ——, London: c. 1800. She was succeeded by Watts & Harton.
Cozens, see Cousins.

1193. Cra——, Stephen, London: 1690. On a plate, Smith Institute Museum, Stirling.

1194. CRAFTE, HENRY, Ludlow : 4 Aug. 1637, F.
1195. CRAIGSONE, ROBERT, Edinburgh : In 1656 was an apprentice with William Abernethie.
1196. CRANE, JOHN, Bristol : 5 Aug. 1712, F. Mentioned in the 1721 Poll Book as of Redcliff, Bristol. Married Alice England.
1197. CRANE, JOHN CARRUTHERS, Bewdley : c. 1800-1838. He died in 1845, having retired in 1838. He sold all his moulds, etc., to James Yates, Birmingham, whose successors, Messrs. Gaskell & Chambers, London and Birmingham, courteously permitted the writer to see them, also an old inventory.

His mark appears with various sets of Hall marks as shown in the proper places.

1198. CRANFIELD, ROBERT, Cork : Mentioned in 1790.
1199. CRANLEY, CHARLES, London : 6 Oct. 1692, Y. Touch, 508 L.T.P., struck c. 1694.

1200. CRANSTONE, JAMES, Edinburgh : Mentioned in the *Edinburgh Burgh Records* in 1559.
1201. CRASKE, STEPHEN, London : Had his clothing " attached " by the Company in 1577.
1202. CRASTON, O——, of ? : c. 1720.

1203. CRAWFORD, CHARLES, Edinburgh : 1784, F. A white-ironsmith whose shop was at 1 South Bridge in 1793.
1204. CRAWFURTH, THOMAS, York : 1578, F.
1205. CRAWLEY, ——, of ? : Late eighteenth century.

CRAWLEY

1206. CREAKE, JAMES, London : 3 Aug. 1738, Y.

1207. CREEDE, CUTHBERT, Salisbury : Mentioned as Bondman in a marriage licence in 1633.
1208. CRELLIN, PHILIP, SENR., London : 20 Mar. 1788, Y.; 1802, L.; 1805, f.S.; 1812, R.W.; 1818, U.W.; 1820, M. Died 4 Dec. 1838.
1209. CRELLIN, PHILIP, London : 20 Oct. 1824, Y.
1210. CREMER, WILLIAM, Lynn : 1674/5, F.
1211. CRICHTON, GEORGE, Edinburgh : Was a Freeman in 1673.
1212. CRICHTOUNE, DAVID (*see* also CHRICHTOUNE), Edinburgh : Was an apprentice with Robert Weir in 1654.
1213. CRICHTOUNE, JAMES, Edinburgh : Was in 1633 an apprentice with Thomas Weir.
1214. CRICHTOUNE, JOHN, Edinburgh : Mentioned in 1687.
1215. CRIEF, RICHARD, Dublin : 1639, F.
1216. CRIPPS, JAMES, London : 7 Aug. 1735, Y.
1217. CRIPPS, MARK, London : 10 Dec. 1727, Y.; 14 Oct. 1736, L.; 1748, S.; 1751, R.W.; 1760, U.W.; 1762, M. 1776, Died. Touch, 786 L.T.P., which he had leave to strike on 12 Oct. 1727.

1217A. CRISP, ELLIS, London : c. 1680. (" Bennett " Book.)
1218. CROFT, JOHN, York : 1435, F.
1219. CROFT, JOHN, York : 1464/5, F., by patrimony. CROIX, DE ST., *see* DE ST. CROIX.
1220. CROOK, RICHARD, London : 22 June 1710. Y.
1221. CROOKE, ROBERT, London : 12 Oct. 1738, Y. Probably Touch, 907 L.T.P. was his, the crook being used to signify his name. Struck c. 1742.

1222. CROOK(ES), WILLIAM, London : Touch, 351 L.T.P., which he had leave to strike in 1680/1. No mention of his name is in the Y. or L. Lists, but is in the " Bennett " Book from 1680-86.

1223. CROOP, WILLIAM, London : 10 Oct. 1706, Y.
1224. CROP, JOHN, Dublin : Mentioned in 1683.

1224A. CROPP, JOHN, London : c. 1680. ("Bennett" Book.) Had leave in 1677/8 to strike Touch, 305 L.T.P.

1225. CROPP, WILLIAM, London : 28 Nov. 1667, L. In 1672 he was admonished for false wares.

1226. CROPPER, MARTIN, Ludlow : Pewterer and Brazier. c. 1555-1580.

1227. CROPWELL, ROBERT, London : Was a warden of the Yeomanry in 1562.

1228. CROSBY, DANIEL, Dublin : 1730-1784. In the latter year he was Warden of the Guild of Smiths.

1229. CROSE, JOHN, London : Received a loan from the Company under the terms of a certain Mr. Lotton's will in 1586.

1230. CROSTHWAITE, EDWARD, York : 1540/1, F. Father of the next named. Mentioned in 1576.

1231. CROSTHWAITE, RICHARD, York : 1576, F., by patrimony. Son of Edward, above. He is mentioned again in 1607/8.
See also CROSTWAYT.

1232. CROSS, ABRAHAM, London : 10 Oct. 1695, Y. Touch, 705 L.T.P., which he obtained leave to strike on 4 Aptil 1717.

1233. CROSS, WILLIAM, London : 1659, f.S. ; 1668, f.R.W.

1234. CROSS, WILLIAM, London : 6 Aug. 1668, L.

1235. CROSS, RICHARD, London : One of a body of soldiers raised by the Company in 1553 to assist in the defence of London Bridge against Sir Thomas Wyatt.

1235A. CROSS, ROBERT, Exeter : In the *London Gazette* it is recorded that his partnership with John Ferris, in John Ferris & Co., was dissolved on 4 April 1795.

1236. CROSS, THOMAS, London : Mentioned in 1494.

1237. CROS(S)FIELD, ROBERT, London : 11 Dec. 1701, Y. Touch, 646 L.T.P., struck and dated 1707.

CROSSWELL, *see* CROPWELL.

1238. CROSTWAYT, RICHARD (*see* also CROSTHWAITE), London : 1523 and 1530, R.W. ; 1536, U.W.; 1541, 1542 and 1550, M.

1239. CROSTWAYT, NICHOLAS, London : 1551, R.W.; 1557 and 1559, U.W.

1240. CROUDLEY, JAMES, Bristol : S. of James. Apprenticed to Robert Bush and his wife Ann, 12 Feb. 1783. Premium £10.

1241. CROW(E)(S), WILLIAM (? DROKE), London : 1512 and 1519, U.W.

1242. CROWDE, WILLIAM (? GOLLDE), London : 1454, U.W. ; 1463, 1473 and 1474, M.

1243. CROWLEY, ABRAHAM, Penrith : c. 1720-1760.

ABRAHAM CROWLEY

1244. CROWSON, JOHN, London : 1586, R.W.

1245. CROZIER, JAMES, London : 16 June 1825, Y.

1246. CRUKE, WILLIAM, York : 1431/2, F.

1246A. CUBIT, THOMAS, London : Of 13 High Street, St. Giles. Dissolution of his partnership with William Duncan is recorded in the *London Gazette*, 20 July 1827.

CUDELL, *see* CADELL.

1247. CUFFE, THOMAS, Bristol : 3 Feb. 1671, F. Apprenticed to Thomas Lloyd.

1248. CULLIMORE, EDWARD, Bristol : 10 Jan. 1680, F. by patrimony. S. of Thos. Mentioned 1690.

1249. CULLOCK, WILLIAM, Timsbury, Somerset : S. of Thomas. Apprenticed to Edward Hackrigge and Ann his wife for seven years from 6 Oct. 1604.

1250. CUM(M)ING, RICHARD, of ? : c. 1780.

1250A. CUM(M)ING, ROBERT, Plymouth Dock : Was dead in 1787.

1251. CUNNINGHAME, WILLIAM, Edinburgh : 1741, F.

1252. CUNSTABLE, ——, London : Appointed in 1570 Grand Captain of twenty soldiers provided by the Company.

1253. CURD, THOMAS, London : 19 Mar. 1729, Y. ; 28 Nov. 1746, L. ; 1756. S.

1254. CURERS, JAMES, London : Was in 1597 a Warden of the Yeomanry.

1255. CURNOM, ROBERT (? TURNOUR), London : 1493, R.W. ; 1498, U.W.

1256. CURNS, ROBERT, London : 1486, R.W.; 1491, U.W.

1257. CURRANCE, DAVID, Dundee : Was a Journeyman to Robert Auchinleck in 1746.

1258. CURRANS, DAVID, Dundee : In 1764 was a Freeman white-ironsmith.

CURTES, *see* CURTIS.

1259. CURTI(E)S, BENJAMIN, London : 13 Jan. 1697, Y.
1260. CURTI(E)S, JAMES, Bristol : c. 1770-1793. Was in a partnership of which the *London Gazette* records the dissolution on 30 July 1793, with Robert Bush and Preston Edgar, trading as Robert Bush & Co. (*cf.* Edgar, Curtis & Co.).

1261. CURTI(E)S, JOHN, London : Received an official allowance from the Company as the marker of lids for stone pots. He was the Company's Beadle in 1555.
1262. CURTI(E)S, HABAKUK, London : In 1598 was appointed a collector from the Yeomanry.
1262A. CURTI(E)S, HENRY, London : c. 1680. (" Bennett " Book.)
1263. CURTI(E)S, PETER (? PIERS), London : 1508, R.W.; 1514 and 1522, U.W.; 1525, M.
1264. CURTI(E)S, THOMAS, London : 1559, Y. Apprenticed to Sir Thomas Curtis and was licenced to open shop in 1559/60.
1265. CURTI(E)S, SIR THOMAS, London : 1524, R.W.; 1538, 1539, 1545 and 1546, M. Sheriff of London, 1546. Lord Mayor, 1557. Alderman 1552. He died in 1559.

1266. CURTI(E)S, WILLIAM, London : 1558, R.W.; 1562, U.W.; 1566, 1569, 1573, 1576, 1577, 1579, 1583 and 1586, M. Used a Touch of a rose and crown with sunbeams.
1266A. CURTI(E)S & CO., Bristol : c. 1800 (*cf.* Edgar, Curtis & Co.).

1267. CUSNONS, JOHN, Bristol : 1453, M.
1268. CUSS, JOHN, Bristol : 1455, M.
1269. CUTHBERT, DAVID, St. Andrews : 1787, F. White-ironsmith.
1270. CUTHBERT, JAMES, Perth : 1747, F. Pewterer, founder and watch-maker.
1271. CUTHBERT, JOHNE, St. Andrews : 1759, F. White-ironsmith.
1272. CUTHBERTSON, JOHN, Edinburgh : 1712, F. 1730 Died. Touch, 115 E.T.P.

1273. CUTLER, JOHN, London : In 1551 was in a dispute with Robert Weble, and in 1556 was fined for false wares.
1274. CUTLOVE, THOMAS, London : Touch, 276 L.T.P. which he had leave to strike in 1676/7. He died in 1680. (" Bennett " Book.)

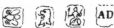

D

1274A. DACE, JOHN, London : c. 1680. (" Bennett " Book.)
1275. DAC(K)OMBE, AQUILA, London : 17 June 1742, Y.; 28 Nov. 1746, L. Touch, 913 L.T.P., struck c. 1744. He was struck out of the Company in 1773 and his fine returned. Was given leave to strike his Touch on 20 Dec. 1744. He was Gazetted as insolvent on 21 Mar. 1761.

1276. DAC(K)OMBE, AQUILA, London : 20 Oct. 1768, Y.; 17 Dec. 1801, L.; 1804, f.S.; 1810, f.R.W.; 1817, f.U.W.; 1818, M. 1819 died.

1277. DAC(K)OMBE, AQUILA RICHARD, London : 9 June 1836, Y. and L.
1278. DAC(K)OMBE, DANIEL, London : 15 June 1820, Y. and L.; 1831, f.S.; 1842, f.R.W. Died 31 July 1842.
1279. DADLEY, EDWARD, London : 23 Mar. 1775, Y.; 30 June 1783, L.; 1788, f.S.; 1798 and 1799, R.W.; 1803, U.W.; 1804, M. 1817, Beadle. 12 July 1829, died. Partner in Pitt & Dadley. He was at 61 Shoe Lane in 1817.
1280. DADLEY, ELIZABETH, London : 7 May 1829, Y. Died 1838.
1281. DADLEY, MARY, London : 15 June 1815, Y. 13 Jan. 1878, died.
1282. DADLEY, WILLIAM, London : 19 Mar. 1818, Y. and L.; 1825, f.S.; 1836, R.W.; 1838, U.W. 1839, Clerk. Died 21 Sept. 1881. (*see* also PITT & DADLEY.)
1283. DAFFEY, ——, Bristol : Mentioned in the Poll Book for 1739 as of St. Nicholas', Bristol.

1284.   DAFFORN, JOSEPH, of ?: c. 1770.

1284A. DAINLER, RALPH, London: c. 1680. ("Bennett" Book.)

1285.   DAKEN, ROBERT, London: 4 April 1698, Y. Touch, 555 L.T.P., which he had leave to strike on 22 May 1699.

1286.   DAKING, JOSEPH, London: Pewterer of St. Mary Abchurch. Was married on 8 Sept. 1681 at St. Saviour's, Southwark, to Annie Ginnot.

1287.   DALE, RICHARD, London: 3 Mar. 1709, Y. Touch, 667 L.T.P., struck c. 1710 (cf. Touch of William Meadows, No. 704).

1288.   DALLAS, JAMES, ? Inverness: On a plate at Ardclagh, dated 1783.

1289.   DALLAS, LACHLAN, Probably of Inverness: c. 1700.

1290.   DALRYMPLE, DAVID, Edinburgh: Was an apprentice with Thomas Inglis in 1691.

1291.   DALTON, WILLIAM, York: Was apprenticed to Leonard Terry in 1728 for seven years. Son of John.

1292.   DALY, JOHN, Dublin: 1635, F.

1293.   DALZELL, ROBERT, Perth: 1653, F. A brazier.

1295.   DANIEL, THOMAS, London: 16 Dec. 1723, Y.

1296.   DANIELL, ALEXANDER, London: 19 Mar. 1812, Y.; 1817, L.; 1818, f.S.; 1829, R.W.; 1832, U.W.; 1834, M. 18 June 1853, died, age 62.

1297.   DANIELL, GEORGE, London: 23 June 1803, Y.; 19 June 1806, L.; 1811, f.S.; 1821, R.W.; 1826, U.W.; 1828, M. 24 Mar. 1837, died, age 68.

1298.   DANIELL, GEORGE, JUNR., London: 13 June 1822, Y. and L.; 1834, f.S.; 1845, R.W.; 1848, U.W.; 1849, M. 31 July 1856, died, age 55.

1299.   DANIELL, WILLIAM, London: 16 Oct. 1828, Y. and L. 27 Oct. 1836, died.

1300.   DARBY, JOHN, Dublin: Mentioned in 1694.

1301.   DARLING, THOMAS, London: 18 June 1741, L.; 1752, S.; 1758, R.W. See Darling & Meakin's Touch.

1302.   DARLING & MEAKIN, London: Touch, 843 L.T.P., which they had leave to strike on 10 Aug. 1732. Partners: Thomas Darling, 1741, L.; and Nathaniel Meakin, 1741, L.

1303.   DARNELL, THOMAS, London: 18 June 1741, Y. This is probably a mis-spelling in the records for Darling who took Livery on precisely the same day.

1304.   DAVESON, WILLIAM, London: 28 Nov. 1667, L.

1305.   DAVIDSON, THOMAS, London: 15 Oct. 1807, Y. and L.; 1813, f.S.; 1824, R.W.; 1829, U.W.; 1831, M. 26 April 1840, died, age 71.

1306.   DAVIDSON, WILLIAM, Edinburgh: Apprenticed with John Abernethie in 1682.

1307.   DAVIDSONE, WILLIAM, Edinburgh: 1693, F. Touch, 90 E.T.P.

1308.   DAVIS, EDMUND (? EDWARD), Bristol: 23 Dec. 1676, F. Bristol Burgess Book Q 16. He was apprenticed to Lewis Roberts. Mentioned in 1694.

1309.   DAVIS, FRANCIS, Bristol: Mentioned in the Bristol Poll Book of 1784 as of Temple, Bristol.

1310.   DAVIS, JAMES, Bristol: Mentioned in the Poll Book for 1734 as of Castle Precincts, Bristol.

1311.   DAVIS, JAMES, Bristol: 19 April 1681, F. Dead in 1686. Married Rachel Hollwey.

1312. DAVIS, JOCEYLIN, London : S. of Richard. Apprenticed to Erasmus Dole, Bristol, 1 Mar. 1670.

1313. DAVIS, JOHN, London : 22 Mar. 1687, Y.

1314. DAVIS, JOHN, London : 13 Oct. 1715, Y.; 18 June 1747, L.; 1758, f.S. Touch, 795 L.T.P., which he had leave to strike on 9 Aug. 1722.

1315. DAVIS, JOHN, Bristol : S. of Edward and Ionise, to whom he was apprenticed, 1 Mar. 1694.

1316. DAVIS, JOSEPH, London : 23 Mar. 1720, Y.

1317. DAVIS, RICHARD, London : 11 Aug. 1664, L.; 1668, f.S.; 1678, f.R.W.

1318. DAVIS, THOMAS, London : 20 Mar. 1788, Y.

1319. DAVIS, THOMAS, Bristol : Mentioned, 27 Nov. 1783.

1320. DAVIS, WILLIAM, London : 13 Oct. 1748, Y.

1321. DAVIS, WILLIAM, Bristol : 19 May 1792, F. S. of Thomas. Apprenticed to Robert Bush, 27 Nov. 1783. Mentioned in the Poll Book for 1812 as of Horsefair, St. James, Bristol.

1322. DAVIS, WILLIAM, Bristol : 1 Oct. 1812, F. Son of Wm. Apprenticed to Thomas Hale and Martha, 10 May 1798. Mentioned in the Poll Book for 1812 as of Nicholas St., Bristol.

1323. DAVISON, GEORGE, Dublin : Of Wood Quay. Mentioned in 1700. He died in 1728.

1324. DAVISON, WILL, Dublin : Died 1738.

1325. DAW(E), RICHARD, Exeter : c. 1780.

1326. DAW(E), ROBERT, Exeter : c. 1680. A slab in the nave of St. Lawrence's Church, Exeter, records the death on 27 May 1671 of Deborah, his first wife, also of Elizabeth his second wife, who died 10 Aug. 1684. On 2 Feb. 1711, a letter was received from him by the London Pewterers' Company.

1327. DAW, WILLIAM, London : c. 1736. His name is in the Yeomanry lists about this time but no actual date is given.

1328. DAWES, ———, London : In 1606 was ordered to alter his Touch and put the date upon it for making faulty wares. He was in partnership with Dudley & Keersey and Mr. Welch calls attention to the fact that this is probably the earliest instance of trade partnership.

1329. DAWES, RICHARD, London : Mentioned in 1646. 1652, f.R.W.; 1660, f.U.W.; 1662, f.M.

1330. DAWKINS, POLLISARGUS, London : 1612, f.S.; 1619, f.R.W.; 1628, U.W.

1331. DAWSON, ALLYN, London : In Dispute with Thomas Hassyll in 1554.

1332. DAWSON, JAMES, Glasgow : 1785, F. Described as a brass founder.

1333. DAWSON, JOSEPH, Edinburgh : Apprenticed to Robert Findlay, 1720.

1334. DAY, JOHN, London : 1540, R.W.; 1546 and 1549, U.W.; 1555, 1560 and 1565, M. Died in 1565.

1335. DAY, THOMAS, London : 17 June 1703, Y.

1336. DEACON, THOMAS, London : 19 Oct. 1780, Y.

1337. DEACON, THOMAS, London : Touch, 272 L.T.P., which he had leave to strike in 1677. There is no record of any maker of this name in Y. or L. Lists (cf. Touch, 364, Gardiner), but his name is in the "Bennett" Book from 1679-85.

1338. DEACON, WILLIAM, London : 20 Mar. 1755, Y.

1339. DEACONSON, THOMAS, Bristol : Was a Master in 1571 when he had an apprentice Johannis Tomson, bound to him.

1340. DEALE, GEORGE, London : 24 Mar. 1711, Y.

1341. DEANE, JOHN, London : 14 Dec. 1775, Y.

1342. DEANE, JOHN, London : In 1586 he received a loan from the Company under the terms of a certain Mr. White's gift. Was Steward at a Lord Mayoral dinner.

1343. DEANE, ROBERT, London : 16 June 1692, Y. Touch, 582 L.T.P., which he had leave to strike on 2 Mar. 1700.

1344. DEANE, WILLIAM, London : 16 Dec. 1731, Y. Touch, 864 L.T.P., which he had leave to strike on 10 June 1736. In 1737 he was in partnership with Robert Peircy.

1345. DE ARLICHESEYE, ARNOLD, London : In 1351 was one of a deputation chosen from the Company to give evidence before the Lord Mayor.

DEAVOR, see BEAVOR.

DECONSON, see DEACONSON.

1346. DEELEY, WILLIAM, London: 14 Aug. 1726, Y.
1347. DE GRESCHIRCHE, WILLIAM, London:
1348. DE HILTONE, JOHN, London:
In 1351 were members of a deputation chosen from the Company to give evidence before the Lord Mayor.
1349. DE JERSEY, WILLIAM, London: c. 1732, Y.; 21 Mar. 1744, L.; 1755, f.S.; 1760, f.R.W.; 1772, U.W.; 1773, M. 1785, died. Touch, 970 L.T.P., struck c. 1756. Was given leave to strike a Touch on 21 Mar. 1744, and another on 19 June 1755.

1350. DE LASAC, LEWIS, London: 17 June 1696, Y.
1351. DE LUDGATE, NICHOLAS, London: In 1349 was chosen to take care of the Articles of the Pewterers' Company and in 1351 one of a deputation to give evidence before the Mayor.
1352. DELYSHEY, ANTHONY, Hertford: Action was taken against him in 1582.
1353. DENIS, JOHN, York: 1466/7, F., by patrimony.
1354. DENT, CHRISTOPHER. York: 1559/60, F., and is mentioned up to 1606.
1355. DENT, MATTHEW, York: 1578, F., and is mentioned again in 1616.
1356. DENT, MICHAEL, York: 1541/2, F.
1357. DEONISE, PHILLIPE, London: Was heavily fined in 1572 for false weights.
1358. DERMONT, GEORGE, Edinburgh: 1717, F.
1359. DERE, WILLIAM, London: Was on the Livery in 1457.
1360. DE ST. CROIX, JOHN, London: 11 Dec. 1729, Y. Touch, 833 L.T.P., which he had leave to strike on 18 June 1730.

1361. DE UPTONE, WILLIAM, London: In 1351 was one of deputation chosen from the Company to give evidence before the Mayor.
1362. DEUXALL, RICHARD, Ludlow: Pewterer and Brazier. Son of Robert, to whom he was apprenticed, 1 May 1700, F.
1363. DEUXALL, ROBERT, Ludlow: Pewterer and Brazier, 20 June 1693, F.
1364. DEUXALL, THOMAS, Ludlow: Pewterer and Brazier. 31 May 1662, F.
1365. DEUXELL, HENRY (? DUXELL), London: Was dismissed from the Livery in 1603. 1589, L., and is mentioned as a workmaster in 1612.
1366. DEUXELL, RICHARD, London: In 1600 was fined for warning Wigan Champen of a forthcoming search. He was chosen an assessor in 1602. 1614, L.; 1616, S.; 1626, f.R.W.; and on 30 April 1629 was dismissed.
1367. DEVAND, JOANES, of ?: His mark, similar to that of Jonas Durand, bears date 1689.

1368. DEVEY, JOHN, London: 20 Oct. 1768, Y.
1369. DEVON, JOHN, London: 18 Dec. 1777, Y.
1370. DEWAR, DAVID, Perth: 1771, F. White-iron-smith. He was granted liberty to trade in 1770, before his freedom was finally accomplished.
1371. DEWE, ROBERT, London: 1452, Y.
1372. DEWELL, JOSEPH, London: 19 Dec. 1734, Y.
1373. DEY, PETER, Lynn: 1477/8, F. Apprenticed to Robert Dey.
1374. DEY, ROBERT, Lynn: Mentioned in 1477/8.
1375. DICK, JAMES, Edinburgh: Apprenticed with William Ballantyne in 1763.
1376. DICKINS, JOHN, London: Buried in 1636.
1377. DICKINSON, CHARLES, Cork: 1773-1817.
1378. DICKINSON, PAULL——, London: Mentioned in 1622.
1379. DICKINSON, ROBERT, London: 24 June 1762, Y.
1380. DICKINSON, THOMAS, London: 28 Nov. 1667, L.
1381. DICKINSON, WILLIAM, London: In 1584 he served as a soldier for the Company.
1381A. DIGBY, JOHN, London: c. 1680. ("Bennett" Book.)
1382. DIGGES, WILLIAM, London: 19 Feb. 1699, Y. Touch, 569 L.T.P., which he had leave to strike on 22 Feb. 1699.

1383. DIGGINS, JOHN, Bristol: 5 May 1634, F. Apprenticed to Thomas Hobson.

1384. DIKSON, JOHN, Dundee: 1791, F. White-iron-smith.

1385. DILSTER, GEORGE, Perth: 1608, F.
DIMOCKE, see DYMOCKE.

1386. DISTON, ANTHONY, London: 11 Aug. 1698, Y.

1387. DISTON, GILES, London: 28 Nov. 1667, L.; 1671, f.S.; 1685, f.R.W.

1388. DITCH, WILLIAM, London: 12 Aug. 1669, L.; 1675, S.; 1680, R.W.

1389. DIXON, HENRY, London: 18 Mar. 1790, Y.

1390. DIXON, JOHN, London: 27 Sept. 1688, Y.

1391. DIXON, JOHN, London: 20 Mar. 1739, Y.

1392. DIXON, WILLIAM, London: Fined in 1612 for making goods below standard.

1393. DIXON, WILLIAM, London: 20 Dec. 1705, Y. In 1719 he was allowed to take one apprentice more than usual.

1394. DIXON & SON, Sheffield: This Firm *never* made pewter wares, only Britannia Metal. This ghost and nightmare of the embryo-collector was finally laid in *The Connoisseur* for March 1918, p. 156, and in a letter to the writer of 7 Feb. 1912 they say " Replying to your letter we beg to say that we never were makers of Pewter-ware. Our Britannia-metal was of course an immense advance on Pewter and B.M. as you know is very often *erroneously* described as Pewter."

1395. DOBBYNS, JOHN, London: Fined in 1552 for faulty wares.

1396. DOBIE, ROBERT, Edinburgh: An apprentice with John Fraser in 1772.

1397. DOBNEY, JOHN, London: 11 Oct. 1744, Y.

1398. DOBSON, RICHARD, London: 19 June 1746, Y.

1399. DOCKRON, WILLIAM, Dublin: 1576, F.

1399A. DOCKWRA, JNO., London: c. 1680. (" Bennett " Book.)

1400. DOD——, ———, London: In 1665 was succeeded by Gabriel Redhead.

1400A. DODD, EDWARD, London: Touch, 188 L.T.P., which he had leave to strike in 1670/1.

1401. DODSON, THOMAS, London: 14 Dec. 1769, Y. Touch, 1026 L.T.P., struck c. 1773.

1402. DODSON, WILLIAM, Coulton, Lancaster: S. of John. Apprenticed to John Knowles, Bristol, and Margaret his wife, for eight years from 24 Mar. 1640.

1403. DOFFELDE, MIGHELL, London: Had faulty wares seized at St. Albans in 1553.

1404. DOGGOWE, JOHN, London: 1451, Y.

1405. DOILEY, JOHN, London: 17 June 1708, Y.

1406. DOKE, ROWLAND, Bristol: S. of Thomas. Apprenticed to Thomas Munk and Julian his wife, 18 April 1655.

1407. DOLBEARE, JOHN, Ashburton: c. 1631. Mentioned in a lawsuit, 7 Chas. 1 (1631/2).

1408. DOLBEARE, JOHN, Ashburton: Was dead in 1761 when his brother Bernard voted on some land at a Parliamentary Election as his heir. His " Hall Mark " appears with the Touch of Benjamin Parham. One John Dolbeare was buried at Ashburton, 1 April 1735.

1409. DOLE, ERASMUS, SENR., Bristol: 20 Sept. 1660, F. S. of Thomas. Apprenticed to William Millard and Jane his wife for seven years from 1 Nov. 1652. Dead in 1682.

1410. DOLE, ERASMUS, JUNR., Bristol: Mentioned from 1679 to 1697.

1411. DOLE, JOHN, Bristol: 9 Aug. 1699, F. Apprenticed to Erasmus Dole. Dead in 1731.

1412. DOLLY, FRANCIS, London: 13 Oct. 1698, Y.

1413. DONALDSON, ANGUS, Edinburgh: In 1787 was an apprentice with John Harvie.

1414. DONALDSONE, DAVID, Perth: In 1712 was an essay master.

1415. DONNE, JAMES (see also DUNNE), London: 9 Oct. 1701, Y.

1415A. DONNE, JAMES, London: Touch, 422 L.T.P., which he had leave to strike in 1685/6.

1416. DONNE, JOHN, London: 19 June 1694, L.; 1700, S.; 1716, R.W.; 1723, U.W.; 1727, M., and died. Touch, 488 L.T.P., struck c. 1692. His rose and crown mark bears the date 1692 which was probably the date of his taking freedom.

1417. DONNE, JOSEPH, London: 2 Mar. 1727, Y.; 21 Mar. 1727, L.; 1736, S.; 1740, f.R.W. Touches, 804 and 807 L.T.P., which he had leave to strike on 20 June 1728.

1418. DONNE, WILLIAM, London: 17 June 1722, Y.
1419. DONNING, JOHN (? DUNNING), London: 1623, Y.
DONNYNG, see DUNNING.
1420. DONTON, JOHN (? DOUNTON or DOWNTON), London: In 1457 was apprenticed to Thomas Donton.
1421. DONTON, THOMAS, London: 1457, mentioned. 1471, U.W.; 1478 and 1481, R.W.
1422. DOOLITTLE, RICHARD, London: Mentioned in 1635.
1422A. DORMAN, JOHN, London: 16 Mar. 1815, Y.; 24 Aug. 1815, L.; 1820, f.S.; 12 Jan. 1832, died.
1423. DORMAN, JOHN, London: 23 Aug. 1838, Y.
1424. DOTTOWE, JOHN, London: 1460, R.W.
1425. DOUGALL, ROBERT, Edinburgh: In 1723 was an apprentice with Robert Findlay.
1426. DOUGLAS, JAMES, Perth: 1757 (or 1765), F. Founder.
1427. DOUGLAS, JAMES, Perth: 1796, F. White-iron-smith.
DOUNTON, see DONTON.
1428. DOVE, JOHN, London: In 1677 he had some buttons seized as being foreign made goods. 6 Mar. 1684, L.; 1696, f.S.; 1703, R.W.; 1713, U.W.; 1713, died. Touch, 295 L.T.P. struck c. 1678.

1429. DOWELL, JEREMIAH, London: 15 Mar. 1721, Y.
1430. DOWELL, WILLIAM, Bristol: Mentioned in 1672.
1431. DOWLAND, THOMAS, Bristol: S. of John. Apprenticed to John Meredith, 21 Oct. 1760. Premium £15.
1432. DOWNE, THOMAS, London: Was a journeyman in 1584.
1433. DOWNES, JAMES, Trelechgrames, Mon.: Son of Alexr. Apprenticed to William Pascall, Bristol, and his wife Marie, 13 Jan. 1646.
DOWNTON, see DONTON.
1434. DOYLE, PATRICK, London: 17 Oct. 1771, Y.
1435. DOYLE & CO., Dublin: 1798, mentioned.
1436. DRABBLE, WILLIAM, London: 16 Dec. 1819, Y.
1437. DRAPER, JAMES, London: Was free in 1582. In 1596 was a member of the Court of Assistants. 1598, W.
1438. DRAPER, JOHN, London: 9 Oct. 1712, Y.
1439. DRAPER, JOHN, Dublin: 1638, F.
1440. DRAPER, JOHN, Bristol: 12 Jan. 1680, F. Apprenticed to Richard Clifford.
1441. DRAYTON, SYMKYN, London: 1466, R.W.
1442. DRAYTON, SYMOND, London: 1457, was of the Livery.
1443. DRAYTON, MRS., London: In 1457 she subscribed towards a set of feast vessels.
1444. DREW, EDWARD, London: 17 Oct. 1728, Y. Touch, 836 L.T.P., which he obtained leave to strike, 20 Mar. 1728/9.

1445. DREW, JOHN, London: 15 Dec. 1720, Y.
1446. DREW, WILLIAM, Glasgow: 1794, F. White-ironsmith.

1447. DRINKWATER, RICHARD, London: 19 Mar. 1712, Y. Touch, 682 L.T.P., struck c. 1713. Was allowed to join in partnership with Greenhill Lindsay on 18 June 1713.

1448. DRINKWATER, TIMOTHY, London : 10 Aug. 1676, L.

1449. DROKE, WILLIAM, London : 1528. M.

1449A. DRONING, JNO., London : c. 1680. ("Bennett" Book.)

1450. DROPWELL, ROBERT, London : 1570, R.W.

1451. DRUMMOND, GEORGE, Edinburgh : 1748, a Master.

1452. DRUMMOND, JOHN, Edinburgh : In 1641 was an apprentice with James Monteith.

1453. DRURY, DRU, London : 21 Mar. 1705, Y.

1454. DRURY, JOHN, London : 1655, S.; 1665, R.W.; 1668. f.U.W.; 1673, M.

1455. DUCKMANTON, JOHN, London : 24 Aug. 1690, Y.

1456. DUDLEY, ———, London : 1605. *See* note under Dawes.

1456A. DUELL, SAMUEL, London : c. 1680. ("Bennett" Book.)

1457. DUFFEILD, JAMES, Lynn : 1685/6, F. Apprenticed to Thomas Lawrence.

1458. DUFFIELD, PETER, London : 1654, S.; 1664, R.W.; 1669, U.W.; 1672 and 1688, M.

1459. DUFFIELD, PETER, London : 12 Aug. 1697, Y.; 9 Mar. 1697, L.

1460. DUFFILDE, THOMAS, London : Granted permission to leave London for 14 days in 1556.

1461. DUNBAR, CHARLES, Aberdeen : 1734, F.

1462. DUNBAR, THOMAS, Aberdeen : 1724 was an apprentice with William Johnston.

1463. DUNCAN, ALLAN, Glasgow : 1777, F. White-ironsmith and coppersmith.

1463A. DUNCAN, WILLIAM, London : Of 13 High Street, St. Giles. His partnership with Thomas Cubit was dissolved, 20 July 1827.

1464. DUNCH, MARY ANN, London : 16 June 1724, Y.

1465. DUNCOMB(E), JOHN (? DUNCUMB), Birmingham : In 1706 was refused admission by redemption, to the London Company.

1466. DUNCOMB(E), SAMUEL, Birmingham : c. 1740-1775 or 1780.

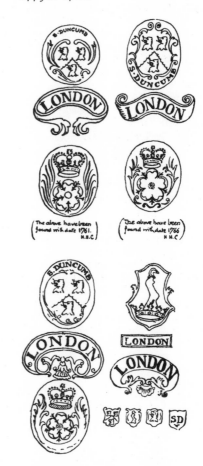

(The above have been found with date 1761. H.B.C.)

(The above have been found with date 1766 H.H.C.)

NOTE.—One feels one cannot let these two makers pass without special reference, for specimens bearing their marks turn up quite as often as, if not more so than those of *all other makers put together.*

From this one can but deduce one of two things ; either they had the most enormous pewtering business the world has ever known or there are a very great number of spurious pieces in existence.

Collectors of experience eschew anything bearing any of this series of marks unless there is some outstanding merit of design or excellence which makes an individual piece desirable.

The quality of the metal, workmanship, etc., is as a rule quite good, some indeed very fine, but they are of far too frequent occurrence to permit of their becoming rare or even uncommon for very many years to come. Out of a pile of ninety-seven plates which the writer saw at a dealer's some years ago, no less than eighty-three were

Duncombs and every one of the eighty-three was of fine metal, well wrought.

The marks themselves fall under two distinct designs made up from the Armorial bearings of the Duncombes, Earls of Feversham. The first embodies the Crest of the family—Out of a ducal coronet or., a horse's hind leg sa. shoe arg. The second displays the Arms of Duncombe—Per chevron gu and arg., three talbot's heads erased, counterchanged.

The *Crest* mark I have seen in conjunction with the names or Hall Marks of the following:

John Duncomb, Samuel Duncomb, James Yates, Yates & Birch, Yates, Birch & Spooner, Villers & Wilkes, and with the initials J.I.

The *Arms* mark, in many forms, is found in conjunction with:

John Duncomb, Samuel Duncomb, J.I., and with griffins' heads substituted for talbots, with Birch & Villers and William Greenbanck.

The series of Hall Marks of several of the above makers reproduce one or other of these devices, as also do those of T. & W. Willshire, Bristol (*q.v.*).

Though much time has been spent in the hope of throwing some light on these mysteries by friends and myself, I regret that no solution has been found. Perhaps the wider publicity which it is hoped this note may achieve may bring the long sought for information.

DUNCON, *see* CHARLES CLARKE.

1467. DUNHAM, THOMAS, London: Was freeman in 1457.
1468. DUNN, JOHN, London: 16 Dec. 1736, Y.
1468A. DUNN, THOMAS, London: c. 1680. ("Bennett" Book.)
1469. DUNNE, RICHARD (*see* also DONNE), London: 1 May 1691, L.; 1696, S. Had leave to strike Touch 292 in 1676/7.

1470. DUNNING, THOMAS, SENR., London: 1590, L. In 1600 was one of a deputation from the Company to the Queen. In 1602 he was a collector for the yeomanry. 1604, 1605, 1610 and 1617, M.
1471. DUNNING, THOMAS, JUNR., London: 1617, W.
1472. DUNNING, THOMAS, London: 1623, Y.
1473. DUNTON, THOMAS, London: In 1457 was apprenticed to Piers Warbylton.
1474. DUPE, ———, London: In 1616 was fined for absence.
1475. DURAND, JONAS, London: 6 Oct. 1692, Y.; 20 June 1695, L.; 1702, S.; 1718, R.W.; 1726, U.W. Touch, 557 L.T.P., which he had leave to strike on 21 June 1694, and to be partner with his uncle, Mr. Taudin. He was refused

permission to add to his Touch the words " Nephew of Taudin " with whom he entered into partnership on 21 June 1694.

1476. DURAND, JONAS, London: 12 Oct. 1732, Y.; 28 Nov. 1746, L.; 1757, S.; 1763, R.W. He had leave to strike his Touch on 12 Oct. 1732. On 2 Mar. 1775 he was gazetted a bankrupt.
1477. DURIE, ———, Inverurie, Aberdeenshire: His name appears on Scottish snuff-mulls. Late eighteenth century.

1478. DUTTON, WILLIAM, Brislington, Somerset: S. of William. Apprenticed to Erasmus Dole, Bristol, 7 Aug. 1675.
DUXELL, *see* DEUXELL.
1479. DYER, JOHN, London: 12 Aug. 1680, L.; 1687, S.; 1693, f.R.W.; 1700, f.U.W.; 1703, M. 1720-1734, Clerk. Touch, 432 L.T.P., which he had leave to strike in 1686/7.

1480. DYER, LAWRENCE, London: Was fined in 1653 for making false wares and for making goods in a metal called Silvorum, also for selling wares without his mark. 1657, S.; 1668, f.R.W.; 1669, U.W.; 1675, M. Touch, 135 L.T.P., struck c. 1670, after the great fire.

1481. DYER, LAWRENCE, London: 6 Aug. 1668, L. (? 1698, L.); 1711, S.; 1726 and 1728, R.W.
1482. DYER, LAWRENCE, London: 10 Aug. 1704, Y. Touch, 691 L.T.P. He had leave to strike his Touch on 19 Mar. 1712.

1483. DYER, LAWRENCE, London: 9 Aug. 1694, Y.
1484. DYER, RICHARD, London: 22 June 1699, Y. Touch, 558 L.T.P., which he had leave to strike on 15 July 1699.

1485. DYER, WILLIAM, London: 28 Nov. 1667, L.; 1669, f.S.; 1682, R.W. At the sign of the Rooke and Trumpet near St. Dunstan's Court, Fleet Street.
1486. DYER, WILLIAM, Bristol and Northwick, Glocs.: 12 Jan. 1680, F. S. of Thomas. Apprenticed to Richard Clifford and Sara his wife. Turned over on 24 Dec. 1677 to William Barron, his master being dead. Dead in 1698.
1487. DYKKS, JOHN, Lynn: 1570/1, F.
1488. DYMOCKE, WILLIAM, London: 18 June 1696, Y. Touch, 531 L.T.P., which he had leave to strike on 18 June 1696.

1489. DYMMES, JOHN, London: In 1457 was an apprentice with Symond Drayton.

E

EAGAN, see EGAN.
1490. EAMES, RICHARD, London: 9 Aug. 1694, Y.; 9 Mar. 1697, L. The birth of his daughter was registered at St. Dionis, Backchurch, on 4 Jan. 1699. He was dead in 1716, when on 27 Sept. his widow was granted leave to join Thomas Hoare in partnership.
1491. EARLE, EDWARD, Bristol and Newport, Mon.: 9 Feb. 1722, F. Apprenticed to Richard Browne, Bristol, and Marie his wife, 9 Feb. 1705.
1492. EARLE, ISAAC, Corston, Wilts.: S. of John. Apprenticed to Wm. Barron, Bristol, and Sarah his wife, 26 May 1685.
1493. EARLE, JOHN, Corston, Wilts.: S. of John. Apprenticed to Wm. Barron, Bristol, and Sarah his wife, 2 Mar. 1686.
1494. EASTBURNE, WILLIAM, York: Was apprenticed in 1655 for seven years to George Peckitt. 1661/2, F. Searcher in 1676 and 1677.
1495. EASTHAM, JOHN, London: 15 Dec. 1748, Y.
1496. EASTLAND, BLACKWELL RICHARD, London: 13 Oct. 1748, Y.
1497. EASTWELL, ABRAHAM, London: 1591, M.
1498. EASTWICK, ADRIAN, London: 18 June 1730, Y. Son of Francis.
1499. EASTWICK, FRANCIS, London: 9 Aug. 1694, Y.
1500. EASTWICK, HENRY SACHEVAROL, London: 9 Oct. 1740, Y.
1501. EASTWICK, ISAAC, London: 10 June 1736, Y.
1501A. EBBS, WILLIAM, Dublin: In 1805 was at 30 Pride Street.
1502. EBRALL, JOHN, London: 19 Dec. 1706, Y.
1503. EDDON, WILLIAM, London: 20 Mar. 1689, Y.; 9 Mar. 1697, L.; 1704, S.; 1721, R.W.; 1729, U.W.; 1732 and 1737, M. Touch, 470 L.T.P., which he had leave to strike on 21 Feb. 1690.

1505. EDGAR, JAMES, Edinburgh: 1709, F. Touch, 111 E.T.P.

1506. EDGAR, PRESTON, Bristol: 31 Oct. 1776, F. S. of John. Apprenticed to James Powell and Mary his wife, 24 Aug. 1769. He was a partner with Robert Bush and James Curtis in the firm of Robert Bush & Co. The *London Gazette* records the dissolution on 30 July 1793. In the Poll Books for 1781 and 1812 he is mentioned as of St. Michael's and of Temple Street, Bristol respectively. His name appears in the 1792 Bristol Directory as of Park, Bristol. Mentioned in 1796 with his wife Rebecca.
1507. EDGAR, PRESTON, JUNR., Bristol: 21 Oct. 1806, F. S. of Preston Edgar, Senr. and Rebecca, to whom he was apprenticed, 24 Dec. 1795. Mentioned in the Poll Book for 1812 as of Temple Street, Bristol.
1508. EDGAR, CURTIS & CO., Bristol: Mentioned in Matthew's First Bristol Directory (1793/4) and in that of 1801 as Pewterers, Worm-makers and Coppersmiths of Temple Street (*cf.* Curtis & Co.).

1509. EDGAR & CO., Bristol : ⎫
1510. EDGAR & SON, Bristol : ⎬
1511. EDGAR, P. & SON, Bristol : ⎭

Pewterers, Worm-makers and Coppersmiths, Edgar & Son being mentioned in the 1840 Directory and P. Edgar and Son in those of 1845 and 1852.

Their marks of *Neptune & Dolphin* are based on the old statue of Neptune which was at the time near the Temple Church, now moved to Victoria Street.

The oval mark appears with date 1814 on the pewter at Dr. White's Hospital, Bristol.

1512. EDGAR, ROBERT, Edinburgh : 1684, F. Touch, 85 E.T.P.

1513. EDGAR, ROBERT, Edinburgh : In 1708 was an apprentice with Alexander Brown.
1514. EDGAR, THOMAS, Edinburgh : 1654, F. Touch, 54 E.T.P.

1515. EDGELL, SIMON, London : 13 Oct. 1709, Y.
1516. EDWARDS, HENRY BARTON, Bristol : S. of John Barton Edwards. Apprenticed to Thos. Wiltshire and Ann, 4 Feb. 1788. Premium £10.
1517. EDWARDS, J——, London : Of Wilderness Row, c. 1800.

1518. EDWARDS, JOHN, London : 14 Aug. 1718, Y. Touch, 742 L.T.P., which he had leave to strike on 15 Mar. 1721.

1519. EDWARDS, JOHN, London : 21 June 1739, Y. Touch, 963 L.T.P. Was given leave to strike his Touch in 1753.

1520. EDWARDS, JOHN, London : In 1457 was an apprentice with Piers Pynton.
1521. EDWARDS, PHILIP, Bristol : S. of Richard. Apprenticed to Thomas Gwinnell and Alice his wife, 20 July 1612.
1522. EDWARDS, RICHARD, Bristol : 27 Sept. 1587, F. Apprenticed to John Addis. Of Redcliff Street. Mentioned in Richard Rogers' Will proved in 1588 (Great Orphan Book of Wills) and again in 1612.
1523. EDWARDS, THOMAS, Bristol : Mentioned in 1635.
1524. EDWARDS, WILLIAM, Stapleton, Glocs. : Mentioned as dead in 1647. S. of Nicholas. Apprenticed to Thomas Hobson, Bristol, 12 Aug. 1643.
1525. EDWARDS, WILLIAM, London : 17 Mar. 1697, Y.
1526. EELLS, LEVY, London : 11 Oct. 1744, Y.
1527. EELLS, WILLIAM, London : 17 June 1752, Y.
1528. EGAN, ANDREW, London : 22 June 1769, Y. ; 25 Sept. 1783, L.
1529. EGERMOND, JOHN, London : In 1457 was apprenticed with Robert Chamberleyn.
1530. EID(D)Y, JAMES, Edinburgh : 1600, F.
1531. ELDERTON, JOHN, London : 14 Feb. 1693, Y. ; 18 June 1696, L. ; 1703, f.S. ; 1720, f.R.W. ; 1728, U.W. ; 1731, M. Touch, 507 L.T.P., which he had leave to strike on 21 June 1694, and to be partner with widow Benton. His "Hall-marks" appear with the Touch of Jo. Stile.

1532. ELDERTON, SAVAGE, London : 19 June 1740, Y.
1533. ELICE, WILLIAM, London : In 1457 was an apprentice with Stephen Tod. 1481, R.W. ; 1487 and 1490, U.W.
1534. ELINE, JOHN (? ELME or ELMYS), London : Was fined in 1451.
1535. ELINOR, CHRISTOPHER, London : 19 June 1755, Y.

1536. ELISE, ROBERT, London : In 1494 he presented a form to the Hall and in 1505 gave a spoon on admission to the Livery.

1537. ELLIOT, BARTHOLOMEW, London : 12 Oct. 1738, Y.; 28 Nov. 1746, L. Touch, 891 L.T.P., which he had leave to strike on 12 Oct. 1738.

1538. ELLIOTT, CHARLES (*see* also ELYOT), London : 12 Oct. 1704, Y.

1539. ELLIOTT, THOMAS, London : In 1565 was chosen Rentor. 1587 and 88, S. 1602 was chosen Assessor; 1603, U.W.; 1604, M. In 1604 he was dismissed from the clothing and the mastership.

1540. ELLIOTT, WILLIAM, London : 13 Mar. 1823, Y. and L.

1541. ELLIS, EDWARD, London : 10 Oct. 1700, Y.

1542. ELLIS, EDWARD, London : 24 June 1762, Y.

1543. ELLIS, JOB, Bristol : 12 June 1818, F. Apprenticed to Preston Edgar, Junr.

1544. ELLIS, JOHN, Bristol and Gloucester : 15 July 1639, F. S. of John. Apprenticed to Edward Lovering, Bristol, 15 Sept. 1631.

1545. ELLIS, JOHN, London : 17 Oct. 1751, Y.; 20 June 1754, L.; 1763, f.S.; 1770, R.W. Of Islington.

1546. ELLIS, JOHN, London : 20 June 1754. Y. Old Fish Street. Used his father, Samuel's, Touch by consent of the Company, 19 Oct. 1758. On 25 July 1761 was Gazetted as insolvent.

1547. ELLIS, SAMUEL, London : 28 Sept. 1721, Y.; 1725, L.; 1730, S.; 1737, R.W.; 1747, U.W.; 1748, M. 1773, died. Touch, 746 L.T.P., which he had leave to strike on 10 Nov. 1721. He was succeeded by Thomas Swanson, (*q.v.*).

1548. ELLIS, SAMUEL, JUNR., London : 20 June 1754, L.; 1763, f.S.; 1771, f.R.W.; 1783, f.U.W.; 1786, f.M.

1549. ELLIS, WILLIAM, London : 17 Dec. 1702, Y. Touch, 606 L.T.P., which he had leave to strike

on 11 Feb. 1702. Of Bishop's Court, Old Baily. Insolvent in 1729.

(The device, so badly struck that it is impossible to copy it, is a (?)man's bust H.H.C)

1550. ELLIS, WILLIAM, London : 23 June 1726, Y. Touch, 778 L.T.P., struck c. 1728.

1551. ELLISON, THOMAS, York : 1781, F., by patrimony. Son of Robert Ellison, butcher.

1552. ELLISON, WILLIAM, Silkstone, Yorks.; S. of Michael. Apprenticed to John Burrowes, Bristol, for seven years from 30 Aug. 1601.

1553. ELLWOOD, WILLIAM, London : 14 Dec. 1693, Y.; 9 Mar. 1697, L.; 1704, f.S.; 1722, R.W.; 1730, U.W.; 1733, M. Touch, 540 L.T.P., which he had leave to strike on 23 Mar. 1696.

1554. ELLWOOD, WILLIAM, London : 8 Aug. 1723, Y.; 15 Mar. 1749, L.; 1766, f.S.; 1775, f.R.W. Was ordered, when leave was given on 17 Dec. 1741 to strike his Touch, to make it "not too much like his mother's" (*see* last).

1555. ELMSLIE & SIMPSON, London : c. 1869. Succeeded to Comptons' business and preceded the present firm of Brown & Englefield.

1556. ELPHINSTONE, ROBERT, Aberdeen : In 1721 was apprenticed with Hugh Ross.

1557. ELTON, JOHN, London : 17 June 1725, Y.

1558. ELWICK, HENRY, London : 11 Mar. 1707, Y. Touch, No. 775 L.T.P., which he had leave to strike on 19 Mar. 1723.

1559. ELWOOD, JAMES (*see* also ELLWOOD), Dublin : Mentioned as starting in 1777 and was Master of the Guild of Smiths in 1790.

1560. ELYOT, THOMAS, London : 1557, S.; 1567, R.W.; 1572 and 1577, U.W.; 1579, M. Died in 1579.

1561. EMBRIS, EDM., ? Bristol : c. 1720.

1562. EMBRY, WILLIAM, London : 10 Aug. 1727, Y.
1563. EMERSON & Co., Bristol : In partnership with Joseph Blinman (*q.v.*), c. 1845. Succeeded by Peter Llewellin.
1564. EMERTON, THOMAS, London : 22 Dec. 1715, Y. ; 1722, L. ; 1728, S. ; 1736, R.W.
1565. EMERY, BERYN, Bristol : Apprenticed to Edward Gregory and Anne his wife, 15 May 1705.
1566. EMES, JOHN, London : 10 Aug. 1676, L. ; 1683, S. ; 1687. R.W. ; 1696, U.W. ; 1700, M. 1700, died. Touch, 244 L.T.P., which he had leave to strike in 1674/5.

1567. EMES, JOHN, London : 11 Nov. 1700, Y. Touch, 578 L.T.P., which he had leave to strike on 11 Nov. 1700.

1568. EMMENSTOW, WILLIAM (HUMMERSTONE ?), London : 1582, S. ; 1591, R.W.
1569. EMPSON, HARRY, London : Served as a soldier for the Company in 1554.
1570. EMPSON, THOMAS, London : Was journeyman to Robert Wilkinson in 1560.
1571. EMPSON, WILLIAM, York : 1613/4, F., by patrimony.
1572. END, JOHN JACOB, London : 16 Mar. 1815, Y.
1573. END, RICHARD, London : 20 Mar. 1777, Y.
1574. END, RICHARD, JUNR., London : 21 Aug. 1828, Y. and L. ; 1839, f.S. Died 29 Sept. 1841.
1575. END, WILLIAM, Limerick : Died 1805.
1576. ENGLEFIELD, WILLIAM JAMES, London : Was an apprentice in 1867 (with John Jarvis Mullens). 21 Mar. 1875, Y. and L. ; 1890. f.S. ; 1907, R.W. ; 1908, U.W. ; 1909, M. Touch, 1091 L.T.P. Was for fifty years the only member of the Company actually engaged in the Industry. Proprietor of the firm of Brown & Englefield, 1 Little James Street, Gray's Inn Road. Mr. Englefield's business is of very ancient foundation and traces its descent as follows :

Thomas Scattergood, 1700, Y. Succeeded by Edward Meriefield, 1716, Y. Succeeded by John Townsend, 1748, Y.-1766, then Townsend & Reynolds, 1766-1777, then

Townsend & Giffin, 1777-1801, then
Townsend & Compton, 1801-1811, then
Thomas & Townsend Compton, 1811-1817, then
Townsend Compton, 1817-1834, then
Townsend & Henry Compton, 1834-c. 1869, then
Elmslie & Simpson, c. 1869-1885, then
Brown & Englefield, 1885-present day.
(The above notes were corroborated by Mr. W. J. Englefield in the years immediately preceding his death.—H.H.C.)

1576A. ENGLEFIELD, RALPH, London : 1921, Y. and L. Son of W. J. Englefield. Continues, with his mother, the business of Brown & Englefield.
1577. ENGLEY, ARTHUR, London : Touch, No. 672 L.T.P., struck c. 1711. No mention of a maker appears under this name in the records but Arthur Ingles who obtained his Freedom in 1710, Y., is probably a misspelling of Arthur Engley, for to anyone familiar with the looseness in such matters in all old records, a lapse to this extent would be in no way surprising.

1577A. ENGRAM, JOHN, Norwich : 1653, F.
1578. ENOS, THOMAS, Dublin : 1612. F.
1579. ERSKINE, ALEXANDER, Edinburgh : Mentioned as a Master in 1766.
1580. ESTERBY, RICHARD, London : Was a Freeman in 1457, when he was a covenantman with Piers Warbylton.
ESTWICKE, *see* EASTWICK.
1581. ETHELL, RICHARD, London : Was a Freeman in 1584. 1590, L. ; and in 1592 is mentioned as being fined for absence from a funeral.
1581A. EVANS, BENJAMIN, London : c. 1680. (" Bennett " Book.)
1582. EVANS, CHARLES, London : 16 Oct. 1760, Y.
1583. EVANS, CHARLES, London : 16 June 1737, Y.
1584. EVANS, ELLIS, London : 11 Dec. 1690, Y.
1585. EVANS, EVAN, Bristol : Apprenticed to Allen Bright and Ann his wife, 30 May 1759.

1586. EVANS, HUMPHREY, Exeter: c. 1730-80.

1587. EVANS, JAMES, London: 17 Oct. 1816, Y. and L.; 1823, f.S. Struck out by order and fine returned 13 Oct. 1836.
1588. EVANS, JOHN, London: 23 Mar. 1720, Y.
1588A. EVANS, JOHN, Exeter: 1790.
1589. EVANS, RICHARD, London: 18 May 1756, Y.
1590. EVANS, SAMUEL, Gloucester: S. of John. Apprenticed to Thomas Baily, Bristol, for eight years from 3 Mar. 1687.
1591. EVATT, THOMAS, London: 19 Mar 1795, Y.; 12 Oct. 1797, L.
1592. EVE, ADAM, London: 16 Mar. 1769, Y.
1593. EVE, JOSEPH, London: 17 June 1725, Y.
1594. EVENWOD, JOHN, York: 1483, F.
1595. EVERARD, GEORGE, London: 8 Oct. 1696, Y. Touch, 532 L.T.P., which he had leave to strike on 4 Dec. 1696.

1596. EVERETT, HENRY, London: 17 Dec. 1719, Y.
1597. EVERETT, JAMES, London: 11 Oct. 1711, Y. Touch, 694 L.T.P., which he had leave to strike on 29 Oct. 1714.

1598. EVERETT, ——, London: 1664, S.
1599. EWEN, JOHN, London: 10 Oct. 1700, Y. Touch, 585 L.T.P., which he had leave to strike on 2

May 1701. His name is spelt wrongly in records it is Yewen on his Touch (*q.v.*). He was charged in 1700 with neglecting his duties as a Whiffler on Lord Mayor's day.

1600. EWER, ROBERT, Rochester: 1607.
1601. EWING, WALTER, Glasgow: In 1790 was an apprentice with Robert Graham and James Wardrop.
1602. EWSTERS, RICHARD, London: 10 Oct. 1717, Y.
1603. EWSTERS, THOMAS, London: 16 Oct. 1746, Y.; 21 June 1753, L.; 1761, f.S.; 1769, f.R.W. 1779, dead.
1603A. EXALL, BENJAMIN, London: c. 1680. ("Bennett" Book.)
1604. EXALL, CHRISTOPHER, London: 10 Oct. 1700, Y.
1605. EXCELL, JAMES, London: 22 Jan. 1718, Y. Touch, 751 L.T.P., which he obtained leave to strike on 21 June 1722.

1606. EXCESTRE, ANDREW, Lynn: 1462/3, F. Apprenticed to John Adam.
1607. EYLES, BARTHOLOMEW, London: In 1457 was apprenticed with William Crowde.
1608. EYNON, SHADRACH, Florence, Pembrokeshire: Apprenticed to Allen Bright, Bristol, and Ann his wife, 9 Dec. 1754.
1609. EYRE, BEATRICE, London: In 1476 subscribed towards a set of feast vessels.
1610. EYRE, WILLIAM, London: 1452 and 1453, R.W.; 1457, U.W.; 1460, 1464, 1468, 1471 and 1475, M.

F

1611. FABING, THOMAS, Edinburgh: In 1787 was an apprentice with John Hardie.
1611A. FACCER, SAMUEL, London: Died 1680. ("Bennett" Book.) Touch, 243 L.T.P., which he had leave to strike in 1674/5.

1612. FAIRBAIRN, THOMAS, Edinburgh: In 1789 was an apprentice with John Hardie.

1612A. FAIRBROTHER, JOHN, Wigan: Will proved at Chester 1693.
1613. FAIRBROTHER, E——, (?) Lancaster or Knutsford: 1723-c. 1750. Touch bears the former date, *cf.* Boulton, Wigan.

1613A. FAIRBROTHER, RALPH, Lancaster : Mentioned as a Pewterer and Brazier in 1724, when he was a bankrupt.

1613B. FAIRHALL, JOSHUA, London : c. 1684. ("Bennett" Book.) Touch, 405 L.T.P., which he had leave to strike in 1684.

1614. FAIRLAY, JOHN, Glasgow : In 1785 was an apprentice with Robert Graham and James Wardrop.

1615. FALCONER, WILLIAM, Glasgow : 1784, F. White-ironsmith.

1616. FALSHAW, JOHN, York : Was apprenticed in 1734, for seven years, to Leonard Terry. Son of Christopher Falshaw.

1617. FAREWEDDER, WILLIAM, York : 1546/7, F. City Chamberlain, 1554, and last mention found of him is in 1561.

1618. FARLEY, JOHN, London : 17 Dec. 1727, Y.

1619. FARNAN, JOHN, London : 15 Mar. 1764, Y.

1620. FARMER, EDWARD, London : 23 Mar. 1786, Y.

1621. FARMER, GEORGE, London : 9 Aug. 1688, Y.

1622. FARMER, HENRY WILLIAM, London : 17 Oct. 1811, Y.

1623. FARMER, JOHN, London : 23 Mar. 1687, Y.

1624. FARMER, JOHN, London : 11 Jan. 1719, Y.; 20 May 1736, L.

1625. FARMER, RICHARD, London : 19 Mar. 1729, Y.

1626. FARMER, THOMAS, London : 4 Oct. 1688, Y.

1627. FARMER, WILLIAM, London : 14 Mar. 1765, Y. Touch, 1014 L.T.P., which he was given leave to strike, 22 Oct. 1767.

1627A. FARMER, WILLIAM, London : Was given leave to strike his Touch in 1744. Touch, 914 L.T.P., struck in 1744.

1628. FARMER, WILLIAM, JUNR., London : 15 Oct. 1795, Y.; 10 Oct. 1799, L.; 1801, f.S. 23 Jan. 1843, died, age 71. On 10 Dec. 1818 his name was struck out by order and his fine returned.

1628A. FARMER, WILLIAM & Co., London : Partners, William Farmer, 1795, Y.; and Henry William Farmer, 1811, Y. Their business was at Clerkenwell Green and the partnership was dissolved on 12 Aug. 1815, William continuing the business.

1629. FARRELL, JOHN, York : Was apprenticed in 1749 for seven years to John Harrison.

1630. FARROW, JOHN, Aller, Somerset : Apprenticed to Stephen Cox, Bristol, and Susannah his wife, 24 April 1758. Premium £10.

1631. FARSHALL, RICHARD, London : 15 Dec. 1692, Y.

1632. FARTHING(E), ROGER, London : 1563, S.; 1573, R.W.

1633. FASETT, ROBERT, York : 1446/7, F.

1634. FASSON, BENJAMIN, London : 31 Aug. 1797, Y. and L.; 10 Oct. 1799, f.S.; 1806, f.R.W.; 1814, U.W.; 1815, M.; 1829, Beadle. Died 3 Jan. 1848, age 74.

1635. FASSON, JOHN, London : 16 Dec. 1725, Y. Touch, 826 L.T.P., which he obtained leave to strike on 23 Sept. 1731.

1636. FASSON, JOHN, London : 25 Feb. 1745, Y. and L. In 1792 his business was at 48 Bishopsgate Within.

1637. FASSON, JOHN, London : 25 Oct. 1753, Y. and L.; 1762, S. Died July 1769. Touch, 964 L.T.P., which he obtained leave to strike in 1753 and his mother consented to his using her Touch.

1638. FASSON, THOMAS, London : 20 Mar. 1783, Y. and L.; 1788. f.S.; 1798, f.R.W.; 1802, U.W.; 1803, M. Died 14 Feb. 1844, age 82. Touch, 1048 L.T.P., struck c. 1783. In 1792 his business was at 48 Bishopsgate Within.

1639. FASSON, WILLIAM, London: 16 Mar. 1758, Y. and L.; 1766, S.; 1776, R.W.; 1785, U.W.; 1787, M. Died 10 June 1800. Touch, 977 L.T.P., which he obtained leave to strike on 16 Mar. 1758. His business was at 320 High Holborn in 1792.

1640. FASSON & SONS, London: c. 1784-c. 1810. Appears with Hall marks of S. Ellis. Probably they succeeded to the Ellis & Swanson business.

1640A. FAULKNER, THOMAS, London: c. 1680. ("Bennett" Book.) Touch, 321 L.T.P., which he had leave to strike, 1678/9.

1641. FAWCETT, JAMES, London: 15 Mar. 1749, Y.
1642. FAWLER, DANIEL, London: 24 June 1698, Y.
1643. FAWSET, GILBERT, York: 1663/4, F.
1644. FAYRBARN, RICHARD, York: Mentioned in 1557. FAYRWETHER, see FAREWEDDER.
1645. FEBBARD, RICHARD, London: 11 Dec. 1690, Y.
1646. FEBBERT, WILLIAM, London: c. 1720.
1647. FEILD, HENRY (see also FIELD), London: 22 Mar. 1693, Y. Touch, 528 L.T.P., which he had leave to strike on 2 May 1696.

1648. FEILDAR, HENRY, London: 14 Dec. 1704, Y. Touch, 673 L.T.P., struck c. 1711 (Fieldar in Records).

FELDE, see FFELDE.

1649. FELL, GEORGE JOHN JONATHAN, London: 18 Mar. 1796, Y.
1649A. FELTON, I——, of ?: c. 1700.

1650. FENN, GEORGE, London: 1577, S.; 1588, f.R.W.
1651. FERGUSON, ALEXANDER, Edinburgh: 1660, F. Dead in 1688. Apprenticed in 1645. Touch, (?) 55 E.T.P.

1652. FERGUSON, ALEXANDER, Edinburgh: 1678, F. Touch, (?) 77 E.T.P.

1653. FERGUSON, EDMUND, Perth: Was in 1773 an apprentice with David Bisset.
1654. FERGUSON, JOHN, Edinburgh: 1678, F. Touch, 82 E.T.P.

1655. FERGUSON, ROBERT, Perth: 1801, F. Brassfounder.
1656. FERGUSONE, THOMAS, Edinburgh: In 1657 was an apprentice with Alexander Ferguson.
1657. FERNER, JOHN, London: 1595, U.W.
1658. FERRIER, WILLIAM, London: 20 June 1776, Y.
1659. FERRIS, JOHN & CO., Exeter: c. 1780-1795. John Ferris and Robert Cross. Dissolution of

the partnership is recorded in the *London Gazette* 4 April 1795.

1659A. FERRIS, JOHN, Exeter: Partner in Ferris & Co.
1660. FESTAM, THOMAS, Dublin: 1479, F.
1661. FATHERS, FRANCIS, London: 14 Dec. 1815, Y. Died 27 Mar. 1865.
1662. FEWTRELL, EDWARD, London: Fined in 1605 for bad wares.
1663. FFELDE, RICHARD, London: Sold some moulds to the Company in 1451, and was "of the Livery" in 1457.
1664. FFELDE, RICHARD, London: Was a covenant servant in 1457 to Thomas Dounton.
1665. FFROST, JOHN, London: In 1459 he took duty for thirty days as watch at the Tower. Was Beadle in 1462.
1666. FIDDES, JAMES, London: 17 Oct. 1754, Y. Touch, 1003 L.T.P., which he obtained leave to strike in 1754.

1667. FIELD, DANIEL SPENCER, London : ⎫ 21 Oct. 1784, (*see also* FEILD)   ⎬ Y. ? same.
1668. FIELD, DANIEL SPENCER, London : ⎭ 20 Mar. 1806 L.; 1810, f.S.; 1823, R.W.; 1828, U.W.; 1830, M.
1669. FIELD, EDWARD SPENCER, London: 13 Dec. 1750, Y.; 20 June 1771, L.
1670. FIELD, EDWARD SPENCER, London: 22 Mar, 1787, Y.
1671. FIELD, HENRY, London: 11 Jan. 1719, Y.
1672. FIELD, PETER, London: 19 June 1794, Y. Died 1847.
1673. FIELD, ROBERT SPENCER, London: 29 Aug. 1782, Y.
FIELDAR, *see* FEILDAR.
1674. FIELDING, CHARLES ISRAEL, London: 20 Aug. 1778, Y.
1675. FILKINS, THOMAS, Woollarfin, Mon.: S. of Thomas. Apprenticed to Richard Browne, Bristol, and Marie his wife, 4 July 1699.
1675A. FINCH, JOHN, London: c.1680. ("Bennett" Book.)
1675B. FINCH, RALPH, Wigan: Is mentioned as a pewterer in the administration of the goods of William Finch, Wigan, on 17 Aug. 1789.
1676. FINDLAY, ALEXANDER, Edinburgh: Mentioned in 1678 and 1694. ? Touch, 55 E.T.P. (*q.v.*), under Alexander Ferguson.

1677. FINDLAY, ROBERT, Edinburgh: 1717, F. Mentioned as a Master in 1709 and again in 1730. ? Touch, 104 E.T.P.

 ⎫ ? same. ⎭

1678. FINDLAY, ROBERT, Edinburgh: Was apprenticed with John Andersone in 1694.
1679. FISH, EDWARD, Edinburgh: Mentioned as dead in 1677 when he is mentioned as being succeeded by his widow Mrs. Sicely Moore, who had married again.
1680. FISHER, FRANK, Bristol: 14 May 1748, F. Apprenticed to Gregory Ash, 12 May 1741. Premium £45.
1681. FISHER, JOHN, York: 1604/5, F., by patrimony. Son of Thomas Fisher, below. Mentioned in 1616.
1682. FISHER, PAUL, London: 13 Dec. 1798, Y.; 24 Mar. 1803, L.; 1806, f.S. Died 1 Oct. 1837, age 68. Struck out by order and fine returned 16 Dec. 1819. Touch, 1071 L.T.P., struck c. 1800.

1683. FISHER, SIMON, London: In 1659 he was cautioned for making bad wares.
1684. FISHER, RICHARD, London : In 1457 was an apprentice with Robert Chamberleyn.
1685. FISHER, SAMUEL, London: 11 Oct. 1744, Y.
1686. FISHER, THOMAS, London: Mentioned in 1557 as being at variance with a Brother-member.
1687. FISHER, THOMAS, York: Mentioned in 1604/5. Father of John, above.
1688. FISHER, WILLIAM, London: 19 Dec. 1771, Y.
1688A. FISHWICK, ROBERT, Manchester: Partner in 1791, in Barton & Fishwick.
1689. FITZ PATRICK, JOHN, Dublin: Mentioned in 1768.
1690. FITZRERE, PATRICK, Dublin: 1559, F.
1691. FLANAGAN, JAMES, Dublin: 1730, Mentioned.
1692. FLEMING, FRANCIS, London: 1832, Y. Died 1838.
1693. FLEMING, WILLIAM, Glasgow: Mentioned as a coppersmith in 1775.
1694. FLEMING, WILLIAM, Edinburgh: 1717. F.

1695. FLETCHER, HANNAH, London : 7 Sept. 1714, Y.

1696. FLETCHER, JAMES, London : 23 Mar. 1775, Y.

1697. FLETCHER, RICHARD, London : 11 Aug. 1681, L.; 1685, f.S.; 1694, R.W.; 1701, U.W. Touch, 312 L.T.P., which he had leave to strike in 1678/9.

1698. FLOOD, JOHN, London : 1537, W. (This name appears as " Stood " in Welch.)

1699. FLOOD, WALTER, Dublin : 1630, F.

1700. FLOWER, RICHARD, York : 1529/30, F.

1701. FLOWREE, JAMES (? FLOWRY), Bristol : 12 April 1699, F. Apprenticed to Anthony Bullock and Esther his wife, 13 April 1683. S. of John. Mentioned in the Poll Book for 1721 as of Castle Precincts, Bristol.

1702. FLOYDE, JOHN, London : 15 Dec. 1748, Y.; 1769, L.; 1775, f.S.; 1787, R.W.; 1795, f.U.W.; 1796, f.M. Partner in Pitt & Floyd under which name see his Touch, No. 1018 L.T.P. They were given leave to strike their Touch, 22 June 1769.

1703. FLY & THOMPSON, London : Touch, 874 L.T.P., which leave was given to strike on 16 June 1737. The partners were Tim Fly (below) and William Thompson, 1738, L.

1703A. FLY, MARTHA, London : Widow of William Fly, c. 1685.

1704. FLY, TIMOTHY, London : 22 Mar. 1710, Y.; 30 July 1713, L.; 1718, f.S.; 1728, f.R.W.;

1737, U.W.; 1739, M. Touch, 675 L.T.P., struck c. 1712. Probably a partner in Fly & Thompson, above.

1705. FLY, WILLIAM, London : 1 May 1691, L. Touch 328 L.T.P., which he had leave to strike in 1679/80.

1706. FODRYNGEY, JOHN, London : In 1457 was an apprentice with John Goodale.

1707. FOLYOT, FFRAUNCES, London : Summoned in 1555 for unseemly behaviour, but forgiven.

1708. FONTAIN, JAMES, London : 26 Oct. 1752, Y.; 22 June 1786, L.; 1791, f.S.; 1800, f.R.W. Touch, 961 L.T.P., which he obtained leave to strike on 14 Dec. 1752. His name is spelled with a terminal " e " in his Touch but without it in the records.

1709. FOONES, HUMPHREY, London : In 1637 received compensation from the Company for having no tin allotted to him.

1710. FOORD, ROGER, Dublin : *Sought* his Freedom in 1692.

1711. FORBES, DANIEL, Edinburgh : Of Canongate incorporation. Mentioned in 1715 as a Master.

1712. FORBES, JOHN, Edinburgh: Of Canongate. Mentioned as being a Master in 1707.

1713. FORBES, JOHNE, Aberdeen: Was an apprentice with George Ross in 1672.

1713A. FORD & ALLMOND, Manchester: John Ford and John Allmond commenced this partnership in 1791.

1714. FORD, ABRAHAM, London: 28 July 1719, Y.; 28 July 1719, L.; 1733, R.W. Touch, 717 L.T.P., which he had leave to strike on 28 July 1719. *Cf.* J. Blenman, who was later allowed to use this man's Touch.

1715. FORD, ALEXANDER, Bristol: 8 Feb. 1677, F. Apprenticed to Richard Clifford. Mentioned in the Poll Book for 1721 as of St. Thomas's, Bristol.

1715A. FORD, ANN & SON, Manchester: Advertised in the Manchester *Mercury*, 24 Nov. 1801. Widow and son of John Ford.

1716. FORD, FRANCIS, Bristol and Beachley in the parish of Tiddenham, Glocs.: 10 Dec. 1642, F. S. of Lawrence. Apprenticed to Thos. Gwinnell, Bristol, and Marie his wife for eight years from 31 Sept. 1634.

1716A. FORD, GEORGE, of Wigan. Will proved at Chester in 1704.

1717. FORD, GILBERT, Bristol: Mentioned in 1674.

(From an imperfectly struck Touch. H.H.C.)

1717A. FORD, GILBERT, of Wigan. Will proved at Chester in 1706.

1717B. FORD, JAMES, of Scholes in Wigan. Will proved at Chester in 1693.

1718. FORD, JOHN, London: 7 July 1701, L.; 1723, U.W. Died 1723.

1718A. FORD, JOHN, Manchester: Died in 1798. Mentioned in the Manchester *Mercury* on 16 Feb. 1790. Partner in Ford & Allmond.

1718B. FORD, ROBERT, of Wigan. Letters of Administration at Chester, in 1739.

1719. FORD, ROGER, Dublin: Retired in 1752. In Cook Street.

1721. FORD, THOMAS, York: Apprenticed on 26 Mar. 1731 for seven years to Richard Chambers. Son of Wm. Ford.

1722. FORD, WILLIAM, Dublin: Died 1731.

1723. FORDE, THOMAS, Whitehaven. Letters of Administration at Chester, in 1708.

1724. FOREST, ALEXANDER, Glasgow: 1792, F. Coppersmith.

1724A. FORMAN, JOHN, Norwich: 1568/9, F.

1725. FORMAN, SIMON, London: 1608, Y., by redemption.

1726. FORREST, THOMAS, Dundee: 1693, F.

FORSTER, *see* FOSTER.

1727. FORTUNE, DAVID, Edinburgh: In 1776 was apprenticed with Robert Brown.

1728. FOSTER, BENJAMIN, London: 20 June 1706, Y. Touch, 639 L.T.P., struck c. 1707.

1729. FOSTER, BENJAMIN, London: 16 Aug. 1730, Y. Touch, 847 L.T.P., which he had leave to strike on 18 Mar. 1730/31.

1730. FOSTER, BONIFACE, London: 1563, S.; 1574, W.

1731. FOSTER, EDWARD, London: 20 Mar. 1734, Y.

1732. FOSTER, GEORGE, London: 17 Oct. 1754, Y.

1733. FOSTER, JOHN, London: 9 Oct. 1735, Y. Touch,
897 L.T.P., struck c. 1741. Was given leave
to strike his Touch in 1741.

1734. FOSTER, JOHN, London: 22 Oct. 1789, Y.; 13
Dec. 1810, L.; 1817, f.S.; 1828, f.R.W.;
1831, U.W.; 1833, M. Died 3 Jan. 1837.
1735. FOSTER, JOSEPH, London: 24 Feb. 1757, Y.
Touch, 1047 L.T.P., struck c. 1783. His
business was at 236 Leather Lane.

1736. FOSTER & CO., London: 1840. Successors to
Joseph Foster.
1736A. FOSTER, RICHARD, Norwich: 1566/7, F.
1736B. FOSTER, RICHARD, Norwich: 1624, F.
1737. FOSTER, ROBERT, London: Was a journeyman
to Richard Lawton in 1457.
1738. FOSTER, THOMAS, London: 11 Oct. 1742, Y.
1738A. FOSTER, WILLIAM, London: C. 1680. ("Bennett" Book.) Touch, 386 L.T.P., which he
had leave to strike on 27 June 1683.

1739. FOSTER, WILLIAM, London: 23 June 1709, Y.
1740. FOTHERGILL, M. & SONS, Bristol: Mentioned in
Matthew's first Bristol Directory (1793-4) as
of Redcliff Street. This partnership, between
Mark, William and Arabella Fothergill, was
dissolved on 17 Aug. 1805.

1741. FOTHERGILL, HENRY, Bristol: Mentioned in
Matthews Bristol Directories for 1840 and
1845 as of Redcliff Street.
1742. FOTHERGILL, MARK, Bristol: S. of Wm. Best
Fothergill. Apprenticed to Benjamin Collier,
Flax Bourton, Somerset, and Elizabeth his wife,
27 Dec. 1745.

1743. FOTHERGILL, WILLIAM BEST, Bristol: Mentioned
in 1745.
1744. FOULL, THOMAS, London: 1505, L.; 1533,
R.W.; 1541, U.W.
1745. FOUNTAIN, THOMAS, London: Of St. Margaret's,
Westminster, pewterer. His daughter married
Andrew Cole, pewterer on 25 Sept. 1662.
Touch, 36 L.T.P., is probably his, the device
is a fountain, with T.F. Died in 1685. ("Bennett" Book.)

1746. FOWL, RICHARD, London: Was an apprentice
with Richard Ffelde in 1457.
1747. FOWLER, JOHN, London: 21 June 1744, Y.
1748. FOWLER, JOHN, York: 1656/7, F.
1749. FOWLER, SAMUEL, London: 22 June 1769, Y.
1750. FOWST, THOMAS, London: Was a Master in 1532.
1751. FOX, EDWARD, London: 1617, S.; 1627, f.R.W.;
1637, f.U.W.
1752. FOX, THOMAS, London: 20 June 1689, Y.
1752A. FOX, WILLIAM, London: c. 1680. ("Bennett"
Book.)
1753. FOXON, WILLIAM, London: 19 Mar. 1723, Y.
Touch, 846 L.T.P., which he had leave to strike
on 23 Mar. 1731.

1754. FOY, PHILIP, (?) Exeter: c. 1725.

1754A. FRANCE, J——, Manchester: In 1783 was a
pewterer and brazier at 10 Deansgate.
1755. FRANCIS, JOHN, London: Was an apprentice with
Boniface Foster in 1578.
1755A. FRANCIS, JOHN, London: c. 1680. ("Bennett"
Book.)
1756. FRANCIS, HUMPHRIE, Abingdon: Mentioned in
1568.
1757. FRANK, JOHN, London: In 1457 he was an apprentice with John Gugge, Senr.
1758. FRANKLIN, THOMAS, Bristol: Mentioned in the
Poll Book for 1754 as of St. James's, Bristol.
1759. FRANKLYN, JEREMIAH, London: 19 Mar. 1729, Y.
1760. FRANKLYN, RICHARD, London: 19 Dec. 1689, Y.;
27 Jan. 1707, L.; 1712, S.; 1730, R.W.

1761. FRANKLYN, THOMAS, Bristol: 27 Mar. 1754, F. S. of Edward. Apprenticed to Philip Brooke and Mary his wife, 6 Aug. 1737. Premium £2.

1762. FRASER, JOHN, Edinburgh: A white-ironsmith with his shop in West Bow in 1774.

1763. FRASER, SIMON, Edinburgh: 1741, F.

1764. FRASER, WILLIAM, Edinburgh: In 1773 his shop was in Luckenbooths, in 1780 in Shakespeare Square and in 1793 at No. 3 St. Andrew's St.

1765. FRAZER, SIMPSON, Edinburgh: Mentioned in 1733.

1766. FREEMAN, HENRY, London: 12 Aug. 1669, L.; 1676, S.

1767. FREEMAN, JAMES, Dublin: Died in 1772.

1768. FREEMAN, THOMAS, London: 21 June 1694, Y.

1769. FREEMAN, THOMAS, London: Received charity from the Company in 1583 as a poor brother.

1770. FREEMAN, WILLIAM, London: 20 June 1728, Y. Partner in Cooke & Freeman. He had leave to strike his Touch (823 L.T.P.) on 5 July 1728. (See No. 1100.)

1771. FREER, ANTHONY, York: 1536/7, F.

1772. FREMLYN, WILLIAM, London: Mentioned in 1552.

1773. FRENCH, MRS., London: Mentioned in 1668.

1774. FRENCH, ABEL, Padstow, Cornwall: S. of John. Apprenticed to John Batcheler, Bristol, and Honor his wife, 12 Dec. 1693.

1774A. FRENCH, ALEXANDER, London: Dead in 1684. ("Bennett" Book.)

1775. FRENCH, JOHN, London: Touch, 456 L.T.P., which he had leave to strike on 12 Jan. 1687. He is mentioned in 1690 as a maker of Spoons. On 20 Mar. 1711 Major Hulls made complaint against him for striking "London" and his own Touch on the new pewter of several country pewterers and he was summoned to appear before the Master and Wardens. In 1661 a John French, pewterer, was married at St. Sepulchre's to Elizabeth Perkins. Another mark which has been attributed to him appears in the next chapter under "I-B. No. 5436."

1776. FRENCH, JOHN, Bristol: 8 Feb. 1784, F. Apprenticed to Charles Tully, 1 May 1776. Mentioned in the Poll Book for 1784 as of Christchurch.

1777. FREND, NICHOLAS, Dublin: 1620, F.

1778. FREND, ROBERT, London: In trouble with the Company in 1625.

1779. FRETHRENE, JOHN, London: Fined in 1602/3 for misdemeanour and for using a Touch while still a journeyman and for not presenting his Touch.

1780. FREZELL, WILLIAM, York: 1666/7, F., by patrimony.

1781. FRIEND, EDWARD, Dublin: 1636, F.

1782. FRIPP, EDWARD (? FREPP), Bristol and Phillips-Norton, Somerset: 22 Nov. 1701, F. S. of Richard. Apprenticed to Thomas Cave, Bristol, and Martha, 4 Aug. 1694. Mentioned in the Poll Book for 1721 as of Temple and in that for 1734 as of St. Peter's, Bristol.

1782A. FRITH, HENRY, London: c. 1680. ("Bennett" Book.) Touch, 242 L.T.P., which he had leave to strike in 1674/5.

1783. FRITH, JOHN MAJOR, London: 16 Oct. 1760, Y.

1784. FRITH, JOHN, London: Supplied a new Touch plate in 1703. Is mentioned in the "Bennett" Book from 1679.

1785. FRITH, THOMAS, London: 22 June 1693, Y. Touch, 601 L.T.P., which he had leave to strike on 1 Oct. 1702.

1786. FRITH, WILLIAM, London: 15 Aug. 1700, Y.

1787. FROOME, WILLIAM, London: 20 Mar. 1760, Y. Touch, 987 L.T.P., which he obtained permission to strike on 17 June 1760.

1788. FROST, JOHN (see also FFROST), London: 20 Mar. 1777, Y.

1789. FRY, ARTHUR, London: In 1638 was one of a deputation to the Lord Treasurer at Fulham.

1790. FRYERS, JOHN, Clonmel: Mentioned on his token (q.v.) in 1668.

1791. FRYERS, SIR JOHN, BART., London: 16 Mar. 1692, Y.; 18 June 1696, L.; 1703, f.S.; 1710 and 1715, M. City Alderman, 1709. Was created a Baronet. Touch, 498 L.T.P., which he had leave to strike on 30 Mar. 1693. His "Hall Marks" appear with the Touch of Henry Sewdley.

1792. FRYERS, WALTER, Bristol and Arlingham, Glocs.: 26 Mar. 1655, F. S. of Thomas. Apprenticed to Richard Clifford, Bristol, and Sarah his wife, 14 Feb. 1648.

1793. FULLER, ANDREW, London : 1602, L.

1794. FULLER, RICHARD, Wells, Somerset: Son of Nicholas. Apprenticed to Roger Willoughby, Bristol, 31 July 1657.

1795. FUL(L)HAM, ANDREW, London : In 1608 he went to law with a brother-member on the advice of the Company. 1614, R.W.; 1622, f.U.W. His widow married John Paltock in 1624.

1796. FUL(L)HAM, JOHN, London : 1613, S.; 1622, R.W.; 1633, U.W.; 1637, M. Buried at St. Michael's, Cornhill, 10 Jan. 1651.

1797. FULSHURST, ABRAHAM, London : 20 June 1689, Y.

1798. FUNGE, WILLIAM, London : 12 Mar. 1701, Y.

1799. FURNYVALL, JOHN, Bristol : Mentioned in the will of John Shipward (proved 14 Dec. 1473) as of Nicholas Street.

G

1800. GABRIEL, EDWARD, Bristol : 13 April 1801, F. S. of Edward. Apprenticed to Robert Bush and Ann his wife, 16 Mar. 1778. Premium £10.

1801. GALBRAITH, JAMES (see also GILBRAITH), Glasgow; 1785, F. White-ironsmith.

1802. GALBRAITH, ROBERT, Glasgow : c. 1840.

1803. GALE, JAMES, Bristol and Wellow, Somerset : S. of William. Apprenticed to Wm. Lansdown, Bristol, 23 Feb. 1758. Turned over, 14 Oct. 1761 to Henry Burgum.

1804. GALL, RICHARDE, London : Clerk to the Company in 1576.

1805. GALPINE, JOSEPH, Bristol and Candlemarsh, Dorset : S. of Joseph. Apprenticed to Ann, widow of Edward Gregory, 22 July 1736. Premium £30.

1806. GAMBLE, NICHOLAS, London : 22 Mar. 1687, Y. GAPE, see GAYE.

1807. GARD(I)NER, ALLEN, London : In 1554 had to forfeit some faulty wares. 1555, S.; 1566, R.W.; 1570 and 1576, U.W.; 1578, M.

1808. GARD(I)NER, JOHN, Edinburgh : 1764, F. Touch 143 E.T.P. Had several other marks (q.v.).

In 1773 his shop was in Netherbow, and in 1793 in Head of Fountain's Close.

1809. GARD(I)NER, JOSHUA, Bristol : In the Poll Book for 1774 he is given as in St. Augustine's and in those for 1781 and 1784 of St. Leonard's, Bristol.

1809A. GARD(I)NER, RICHARD, London : c. 1680. ("Bennett" Book.) Touch, 177 L.T.P., which he had leave to strike in 1670/1.

1810. GARD(I)NER, THOMAS, London : He was of the Livery in 1457.

1811. GARD(I)NER, THOMAS, Armagh : Mentioned in 1783.

1812. GARD(I)NER, THOMAS, London : Touch, No. 364 L.T.P., which he had leave to strike on 30 June 1682. (Cf. Touch of Thomas Deacon.) There is no record of any maker of this name about this time in Y. or L. Lists, but his name appears in the "Bennett" Book from 1680-86.

1813.   GARIOCH, PATRICK, London : 19 Oct. 1735. Touch, 880 L.T.P., which he had leave to strike on 13 Oct. 1737.

1814.   GARLE, CHRISTOPHER, London : 16 Dec. 1714, Y.
1815.   GARMENTIN, WILLIAM, Edinburgh : Touch, 26 E.T.P. 1613, F.

1816.   GARSTANG, WILLIAM, York : 1527/8, F.
1817.   GARTAN, JOSEPH, Dublin : 1659, F. Died in 1665.
1818.   GARTH, CUTHBERT, York : 1557, F.
1819.   GARTON, STEPHEN, London : Mentioned in 1556.
1820.   GARTWELL, ABRAHAM, London : 1595, M.
1821.   GASKELL & CHAMBERS, London and Birmingham : Mid nineteenth-early twentieth centuries. (*See* note under John Carruthers Crane.)
1822.   GASKER, PERCIVAL, London : 1572, S.; 1581, R.W.; 1589 and 1591, U.W.; 1593 and 1597, M.
1823.   GASKER, ROBERT, London : Was granted one of the Company's pensions in 1595.
1823A.   GASS, JAMES, London : c. 1680. ("Bennett" Book.)
1824.   GAULS, ———, Exeter : c. 1810.

1825.   GAVIN, JOHN, Glasgow : Was an apprentice with Robert Graham and James Wardrop in 1787.
1826.   GAVOKEFORD, ROGER, London : 1601, U.W.
1827.   GAYE, JOHN, of ? : His Touch is dated 1666.

1828.   GAYE, MICHAEL (? MILES), London : Of St. Sepulchre's, Newgate Street, and St. Michael's, Cornhill. The birth of his son was registered at St. Helen's, Bishopsgate, 18 Sept. 1658.
1829.   GAYE, THOMAS, London : Mentioned in 1584.
1829A.   GAYLARD, PETER, Dorchester, Dorset : c. 1621.
1830.   GEARY, THOMAS, Cork : Mentioned in 1740.
1831.   GEE, GEORGE, Dublin : Mentioned in 1745 and 1763. In 1745 with William Litchfield, he purchased the pewterer's tools and stock which belonged to Litchfield's father. In the *Dublin Directory* for 1766, he was in Back Lane.
1832.   GEFFERS, ——— (*see* also JEFFERS), Cork : Is thus referred to in Welch's *History of the Pewterers' Co.* : "At the same Court (20 June 1688/9) one Geffers, a free Pewterer of Cork, who had fled thence from danger of his life through persecution, prayed for leave to work and to be relieved. The Court awarded him 20s. in relief."
1833.   GENNYNS, CHRISTOPHER, London : In 1576 was in trouble with the Company.
1834.   GEOGHEGAN, JOHN, Dublin : Is mentioned in *The Dublin Intelligence* as follows : "John Geoghegan, pewterer, Pill Lane, Dublin, sells dishes and plates of the newest fashion, tea kettles, Chafing dishes, tea and coffee pots, warming pans, fish pans, kettle pots, saucepans, candlesticks, round and square brewing pans, &c." 27 Nov. 1714.
1835.   GEPP, MATTHEW, London : 22 Mar. 1715, Y.
1836.   GERAGHTY, JOHN, Dublin : In 1816 worked at 41 Back Lane and from 1820-30 at 57 Back Lane. No mention is found of him later.

1836A.   GERARDIN, FRANCIS, London : In 1817 was at 21 Poland Street.
1837.   GERARDIN & WATSON, London : Early nineteenth century.

1838.   GERY, JOHN, London : 1559, R.W.; 1563, U.W.; 1657, 1570 and 1574, M.
1839.   GIBBINGS, J—— G——, Cork : In the middle of nineteenth century was at North Main Street.
1840.   GIBBON, EDWARD, Bristol and Kinny, Glam. : S. of Pollidore. Apprenticed to Thomas Williams, Bristol, and Christian his wife for seven years from 18 Mar. 1635.

1841. GIBBON, FRANCIS, London : 19 Aug. 1669, L.
1842. GIBBS, ———, London : 1719, Y.
1843. GIBBS, HENRY, London : 9 Oct. 1729, Y.
1844. GIBBS, JAMES, London : 18 Mar. 1741, Y. Touch, 917 L.T.P. Was given leave to strike his Touch in 1745.

1845. GIBBS, JOHN, London : 17 June 1756, Y.
1845A. GIBBS, LAWRENCE, London : c. 1680. (" Bennett " Book.)
1846. GIBBS, THOMAS, London : 19 Aug. 1669, L. Written in pencil in the records.
1847. GIBBS, WILLIAM, London : 21 June 1804, Y. Touch, 1077 L.T.P., struck c. 1804.

1848. GIBSON, EDWARD, Edinburgh : 1719, F. Touch, 122 E.T.P.

1849. GIBSON, EDWARD, Edinburgh : 1754, mentioned.
1850. GIBSON, ELIZABETH, London : A widow. 16 Dec. 1762, Y. Had leave to strike her Touch in 1762.
1851. GIBSON, HENRY, Bristol : 21 Jan. 1559, F. Apprenticed to William (?) Fllary. Mentioned later in 1579.
1852. GIBSON, JAMES, Bristol and Melbury, Dorset : Mentioned with his wife Edith in 1626 and again alone in 1640. Dead in 1655.
1853. GIBSON, JOHN, Bristol and Melbury, Dorset : S. of James. Apprenticed to Peter Lodge, Bristol, 20 June 1655.
1854. GIBSON, RICHARD, Bristol : Mentioned with his wife Marie in 1621 and 1627.
1855. GIBSON, ROBERT, London : 1668.
1855A. GIBSON, ROBERT, Lynn : Mentioned in 1627/8.
1856. GIBSON, THOMAS, Dublin : 1626, F.
1856A. GIBSON & SMITH, London : In 1801 were at 131 Minories.
1857. GIBSONE, JOHN, Edinburgh : In 1673 was an apprentice with William Harvie.
1858. GIDDINGS, JOSEPH, ? West-Country : c. 1710. I have come across this man's Hall Marks in

connection with the spread eagle mark of T. Bennett.

1858A. GIDDY, EDWARD, Truro : 1796. Advertised his moulds for sale on 3 April in this year.
1859. GIFFIN, JONATHAN, London : 8 Aug. 1723, Y.
1860. GIFFIN, THOMAS, London : 23 Mar. 1726, L.; 1734, f.S.; 1740, f.R.W.; 1751, U.W.; 1753 and 1757, M. Touch, 681 L.T.P., which he was granted leave to strike in 1713. His mark is found in conjunction with that of John Townsend (*q.v.*).

1861. GIFFIN, THOMAS, London : 13 Dec. 1759, Y.; 10 Mar. 1760, L.; 1768, f.S.; 1777, f.R.W. and f.U.W. Touch, 1006 L.T.P. Had leave to strike his touch in 1764. In 1776 his business was at 135 Fenchurch Street.

1862. GILBERT, EDWARD, London : 1633, f.S.; 1654, R.W.; 1660, U.W.; 1662, M.
1863. GILBERT, JOHNE, Dundee : 1649, F.
1864. GILBERT, PATRICK, Dundee : 1649, mentioned.
1865. GILBERT, PATRICK, Dundee : 1652, F.
1866. GILBRAITH, JAMES (*see also* GALBRAITH), Glasgow : 1785, F. White-ironsmith.
1867. GILES, WILLIAM, London : 15 Dec. 1737, Y.; 1741, L.; 1753, f.S.; 1760, f.R.W.; 1768, U.W.; 1769, M. Dead in 1771.
1868. GILL, EDWARD, Bristol : 4 Mar. 1641, F. S. of Wm. Apprenticed to Abraham Yeo(re) and Johanna for eight years from 19 Nov. 1632, and

turned over on 18 Feb. 1634 to Peter Lodge and Marjorie his wife.

1869. GILL, ROBERT, York : 1456/7, F.

1870. GILLAM, EVERARD, London : 22 Oct. 1702, Y. Touch, 637 L.T.P., struck c. 1706.

1871. GILLAM, JONAS, London : 16 Dec. 1708, Y.

1872. GILLAM, WILLIAM, London : 11 Aug. 1698, Y. Touch, 550 L.T.P., which he had leave to strike on 29 Aug. 1698.

1873. GILLATE, GEORGE MASON, London : 17 Dec. 1807, Y.

1874. GILLES, JOHN, Edinburgh : 1800, Mentioned as a white-ironsmith when his shop was at 24 George Street.

1875. GILLES, ALEXANDER, Edinburgh : In 1644 was an apprentice with Thomas Weir.

1876. GILLIGAN, ROGER, London : 13 Oct. 1709, Y.

1877. GILLMAN, HENRY, Cork : Mentioned in 1734.

1878. GILLMAN, JOSEPH, Bristol : 2 Oct. 1812, F. Apprenticed to Robert Bush, Junr., 30 Aug. 1796. Mentioned in the Poll Book for 1812 as of Thomas Street, Bristol.

1879. GILLMORE, JOHN, Bristol and Marlborough : 30 Oct. 1689, F. Apprenticed to James Davis, Bristol, 26 April 1681. Turned over in 1686 to John Axford.

1880. GISBURNE,[1] JAMES, London : Touch, 640 L.T.P., struck c. 1707. No mention of him occurs in the records. This Touch is evidently the same as that of John Gisburne, which follows with the name altered, for the " O " of JOHN is plainly visible under the " A " of JAMES.

1881. GISBURNE, JOHN, London : 10 Dec. 1696, Y. Touch, 536 L.T.P., which he had leave to strike on 16 Dec. 1696.

1882. GISBURNE, JOHN, London : 17 Mar. 1691, Y.

1883. GISBURNE, ROBERT, London : 28 Nov. 1667, L. ; 1670, S. ; 1683, R.W. ; 1689, U.W. ; 1691, M.

1884. GLASS, WILLIAM, London : 20 June 1754, Y.

1884A. GLAZEBROOK, JAMES, London : c. 1680. (" Bennett " Book.) A country Member. Touch, 270 L.T.P., which he had leave to strike in 1676/7.

1885. GLEDSTANE, GEORGE, Edinburgh : 1610, F. Touches, 20 and 21 E.T.P.

1886. GLEDSTANE, GEORGE, Edinburgh : 1634, F.

1887. GLEDSTANIS, GEORGE, Aberdeen : 1656, F.

1888. GLEDSTED, GEORGE, Dundee : 1655, F.

1889. GLENDINNING, WILLIAM, Edinburgh : In 1726 was apprenticed to Robert Veitch.

1890. GLENTON, THOMAS, London : In Tower Street. In 1566 some stone pots were seized from him for having Flemish-made pewter lids.

1891. GLOVER, EDWARD, London : Was one of the Yeomanry Wardens in 1611. 1612, S. ; 1620, f.R.W.

1892. GLOVER, HENRY, London : 1612, S. ; 1620, R.W.

1893. GLOVER, JOHN, Edinburgh : Mentioned as a Master in 1779. ? Touch, 136 E.T.P.

1894. GLOVER, RICHARD, London : Mentioned as a Master in 1585. 1589, L. ; 1599, R.W. ; 1606 and 1611, M.

[1] One of the Gisburnes was pewterer to the Royal Hospital, Chelsea, and was succeeded by John Carpenter (*Chelsea Journal*, c. folio 115).

1895. GLOVER, ROBERT, London : In 1611 was sent to prison for "secretly packing away tin."

1896. GLOVER, ROGER, London : Mentioned as free in 1599. 1605, R.W.; 1611, U.W.; 1615, M.

1897. GLOVER, THOMAS, London : 15 Dec. 1814, Y.

1898. GLOVER, THOMAS, London : In 1601 was an apprentice with George Smith.

1899. GLOVER, WILLIAM, London : Was a Freeman in 1560.

1900. GLYNN, WILLIAM, London : 17 Mar. 1691, Y.

1901. GOATER, THOMAS, London : 19 Mar. 1729, Y.; 12 Dec. 1758, L.

1901A. GOBBLE, NICHOLAS, London : c. 1680. ("Bennett" Book.) Touch, 374 L.T.P., which he had leave to strike on 1 Mar. 1682.

1902. GOD, JOHN, London : Was a spoonmaker in 1567. 1590, L.

1902A. GODDARD, WM., London : c. 1680. ("Bennett" Book.)

1903. GODDESMAN, JOHN, London : In 1457 was an apprentice with Robert Chamberleyn.

1904. GODE, THOMAS, London : Subscribed to a set of feast vessels in 1457.

1905. GODELUK, THOMAS, London : 1468, R.W.

1906. GODFREY, JOSEPH HENRY, London : 18 June 1807, Y. Touch, 1081 L.T.P., struck c. 1810.

1907. GODFREY, STEPHEN, London : 14 Oct. 1679, L.

1908. GODFREY, WILLIAM, London : 10 Mar. 1796, Y.

1909. GO(E)ING, RICHARD, Bristol : 7 Feb. 1715, F. Mentioned in the Poll Book for 1734 as of St. Stephens, Bristol. In an advertisement of 1742 he was described as of The Block Inn (his House) on the Quay, (see Plate V., page 21), and as having been there for 25 years and using the Lamb and Flag mark with his name upon his wares. He had an advertisement in *The Bristol Oracle and Miscellany* in 1742, is mentioned in *The Oracle and County Advertiser* 1744. His will dated 1764 is in Bristol Probate Office and in *Felix Farley's Bristol Journal* for 16 Feb. 1766 appeared a long sale notice

of his estate which appears to have been one of some importance, situate on the summit of St. Michael's Hill, Bristol.

1910. GOLD, RICHARD, London : 13 Oct. 1737, Y.

1911. GOLDIE, JAMES, Edinburgh : Mentioned as a Master in 1642.

1912. GOLDIE, JOSEPH, Edinburgh : 1633, F. Touch, 40 E.T.P.

1913. GOLLDE, WILLIAM (? CROWDE), London: 1470, M.

1914. GOOD, ROBERT, London : 13 Oct. 1709, Y.

1915. GOOD, WILLIAM, JUNR., Bristol : 3 Aug. 1641, F. S. of William, Senr. Apprenticed to John Knowles and Margaret his wife for ten years from 18 Dec. 1626.

1916. GOOD, WILLIAM, SENR., Bristol : Mentioned in 1626.

1917. GOODALE, JOHN, London : 1454, R.W.; 1457, M.

1918. GOODE, GEORGE, Barnstaple. Mentioned in 1651.

1919. GOODISON, RICHARD, Dublin : Mentioned in 1771 and died in 1788.

1920. GOODLACK, THOMAS, London : An apprentice with John Parys in 1457.

1921. GOODLUCK, ROBERT, London : 19 Dec. 1771. Y.

1922. GOODLUCK, WILLIAM RICHARD, London : 19 June 1823, Y.

1922A. GOODMAN, EDWARD, London : Touch, 157 L.T.P., which he had leave to strike in 1669/70.

1923. GOODMAN, HARRY, London : 22 June 1693, Y. Touch, 510 L.T.P., struck c. 1694.

1924. GOODMAN, PHILIP, London : 1587 and 1588, S.; 1596, R.W.; 1601, f.U.W.
1925. GOODWIN, RICHARD, London : 20 Mar. 1783, Y.
1926. GOODWIN, THOMAS, London : 21 Aug. 1707, Y. Touch, 671 L.T.P., struck c. 1710.

1927. GOODWYN, JOHN, London : Was a searcher for the Company in 1612 and in 1614 was fined for selling porringers at less than trade prices.
GOODYEAR, see GUDEYERE.
1928. GOOSE, THOMAS, London : 18 Oct. 1770, Y.
1929. GORDON, ALEXANDER, Edinburgh : In 1719 an apprentice with William Herrin.
1930. GORWOOD, JOSEPH (? GORWOD or GOROOD), York : 1684, mentioned as Free.
1931. GORWOOD, JOSEPH, York : Apprenticed on 24 July 1741 for seven years to John Harrison. 1748/9, F. Searcher, 1758. Son of Benjamin Gorwood, Pattrington.
1932. GORWOOD, JOSEPH, York : 1780, F., by patrimony.
1933. GOSEWELL, ALAN, Bristol : Mentioned in 1651.
1935. GOSLIN, THOMAS, London : 14 Dec. 1721, Y.
1936. GOSLING, THOMAS, London : 23 Mar. 1720, Y. Touch, 794 L.T.P., which he had leave to strike on 17 June 1725.

1937. GOSNELL, WILLIAM, London : In 1659 was fined for non-attendance at the King's restoration.
1937A. GOSTLINGE, ALLIN, Bristol : Supplied an oil vat for 2s. to St. Ewen's Church in 1552.
1938. GOUDGE, R——, London : In 1656 was ordered as a mark of disgrace to strike for his Touch the initial letters of his name R.G. with a knot about it and 1656. (See also Ralph Cox.)
1939. GOUGH, WILLIAM, Bristol : Apprenticed to James Reid and Mary, 7 Aug. 1754. Premium £20.

1940. GOULD, WILLIAM, London : 9 Oct. 1712, Y.
1941. GOURLAY, DAVID, Edinburgh : 1794, F.

1942. GOWET, ROBERT, Edinburgh : 1621, F.
GRACE, see GROCE.
1943. GRAHAM & WARDROP, Glasgow : c. 1776-1806. Partners, Robert Graham and James Wardrop. Both were admitted to freedom in 1776 as coppersmiths and white-ironsmiths, but much pewter ware made by them has come down to our time.

1944. GRAHAM, ANDREW, Glasgow : 1798, F. Brass-founder.
1945. GRAHAM, BASILL, London : 10 Aug. 1699, Y. Touch, 560 L.T.P., which he had leave to strike on 28 Aug. 1699.

1946. GRAHAM, JOHN, Edinburgh : In 1709 was an apprentice with David Symmers.
1947. GRAHAM, JOHN, London : 14 Dec. 1758, Y.
1948. GRAHAM, ROBERT, Glasgow : 1776, F. Partner in Graham & Wardrop (q.v.).
1949. GRAHAME, ALEXANDER, Edinburgh : 1654, F. Touch, 60 E.T.P.

1950. GRAHAME, HENRY, Perth : 1712 was appointed as "officer" to the Perth Incorporation of Hammermen.

1951. GRA(I)NGE, JOHN, London : 10 Oct. 1799, Y. and L.; 1801, f.S.; 1808, f.R.W.; 1815, U.W.; 1816, M. Died in 1816.

1952. GRAINGER, WILLIAM, London : Searcher in 1612. 1620, S.; 1628, R.W.; 1638, U.W.

1953. GRAME, THOMAS, of ? : c. 1710.

1954. GRANT, EDWARD, London : 15 Dec. 1698, Y.; 19 May 1715, L.; 1722, S.; 1731, R.W.; 1740, U.W.; 1741, M. Probably a partner in Spackman & Grant, whose Touch, No. 662 (*q.v.*) L.T.P., was struck c. 1708.

1955. GRANT, JOSEPH, London : 15 Oct. 1801, Y. Died 2 Mar. 1844, age 65.

1956. GRAUNT, JOHN, London : In 1625 was an apprentice to Zachary Bayley. 1659, S.; 1669, f.R.W.; 1672, f.U.W.

1957. GRAUNT, JOHN, London : 6 Aug. 1668, L. A pewterer of this name about 67 years of age was married on 15 Jan. 1669 at St. Botolphs, Aldersgate to Alice Warner.

1958. GRAVES, ALEXANDER, London : 12 Mar. 1752, Y.

1959. GRAVES, FRANCIS, London : A workmaster in 1611. 1621, S.; 1629, R.W.

1961. GRAVES, ROBERT, London : Mentioned in 1556.

1962. GRAY, JAMES (*see also* GREY) Dundee : 1648, F.

1963. GRAY, JOHN, Dundee : 1625, F.

1964. GRAY, JOHN, Edinburgh : 1741, F.

1965. GRAY, JOHN, Perth : In 1712 is mentioned as being an Essay-Master.

1966. GRAY, JOHN, London : 15 Dec. 1757, Y.

1967. GRAY, MARTEIN, Dundee : Mentioned in a list of Members in 1587.

1968. GRAY, NINIAN, Perth : 1726, F. Deacon several times between 1724 and 1736 of the Perth Incorporation of Hammermen. Bailie c. 1738.

1969. GRAY, PATRICK, Dundee : 1599, F.

1969A. GRAY, RICHARD, London : c. 1680. ("Bennett" Book.) Touch, 396 L.T.P., which he had leave to strike on 18 Feb. 1683.

1970. GRAY, ROGER, Bristol : S. of Robert. Apprenticed to William Hobson and Mary his wife, 1 Oct. 1644.

1971. GRAY, THOMAS, London : 20 June 1782, Y.

1972. GRAY, WILLIAM, Perth : 1796, F. White-iron-smith.

1973. GRAY & KING, London : Touch, 711 L.T.P., which they had leave to strike on 19 Mar. 1718. Partners, John Grey, 1712, Y. (whose name is probably spelled wrongly in the records), and James King, 1716, Y.

1974. GRAYE, WILLIAM, London : 1558, Y. A spoon-maker in Fridaye Street.

1975. GREATRAKES, JAMES, Cork : Mentioned in 1780.

1976. GREATRIX, JOHN, Cork : Mentioned in 1773 and 1780.

1977. GREAVES, JOHN (*see also* GRAVES), London : 1607, Beadle. Died in 1633.

1978. GREAVES, JOHN, London : 11 Oct. 1733, Y.

1978A. GREEN, GEORGE, Liverpool : In 1793 was a pewterer at 63 Moorfields.

1978B. GREEN(E), HENRY, Chester : Late of Denbigh. Took over the stock and shop of John Thomas, Chester, on 13 Sept. 1774.

1979. GREEN(E), JACOB, London : Mentioned in 1666.

1980. GREEN(E), JAMES, London : 19 June 1746, Y.; 23 Aug. 1750, L.; 1760, S.; 1766, f.R.W.; U.W., first part of 1778. Died in 1784. Partner in Burford & Green (*q.v.*). Touch, No. 929 L.T.P. Was given leave to strike his Touch on 13 Oct. 1748. *See* No. 698.

1981. GREEN(E), JAMES, Wigan : Mentioned in 1655.

1982. GREEN(E), JOHN, London : 14 Aug. 1718, Y.

1983. GREEN(E), JOHN, London : Was a Freeman in 1457 when he was working as a Covenant man to Thomas Dounton.

1984. GREEN(E), JOHN GRAY, London : 21 Mar. 1793, Y. Touch, 1068 L.T.P., struck c. 1799.

1985. GREEN(E), JOSEPH, London : 24 Mar. 1803, Y.

1986. GREEN(E), NATHANIEL, London : 21 June 1722, Y.

1986A. GREEN(E), ROBERT, Liverpool : Mentioned in 1768 and 1793.

1987. GREEN(E), THOMAS, London : Chosen as a soldier to serve for the Company in 1544.

1988. GREEN(E), WILLIAM, London : 19 Mar. 1684, L. Touch, 313 L.T.P., which he had leave to strike in 1678/9.

1989. GREEN(E), WILLIAM, London : Mentioned in 1629.

1990. GREEN(E), WILLIAM, London : 20 Oct. 1774, Y.

1991. GREEN(E), WILLIAM SANDYS, London : Apprenticed on 16 Jan. 1718 to Mary, widow of Wm. Sandys. 17 Mar. 1725, Y.; 16 June 1737, L. Touch, 827 L.T.P., which he had leave to strike on 19 June 1729.

1992. GREENBANCK, WILLIAM, of ? : c. 1670-1725.

1993. GREENER, THOMAS, London : 20 Mar. 1700, Y. Touch, 602 L.T.P., which he had leave to strike on 30 July 1702. Summoned in 1702 for selling bad wares.

1994. GRE(E)NFELL, GEORGE, London : 16 June 1757, Y.; 15 Mar. 1759, L.; 1770, f.S.; 1778, f.R.W. 1784, dead. Touch, 976 L.T.P.

Was given leave to strike his Touch in 1757. *Cf.* Nos. 4678 and 5387.

1995. GREENING, RICHARD, London : 17 June 1756, Y. A partner in Clark & Greening. Touch, 1007 L.T.P. (*q.v.*). Had leave to strike their Touch 14 Mar. 1765.

GREENSTEAD, *see* GRIMSTED.

1996. GREENWOOD, JOHN, London : 5 Aug. 1731, Y.

1996A. GREENWOOD, JOHN, London : c. 1680. (" Bennett " Book.) Touch, 187 L.T.P., which he had leave to strike in 1670/1.

1997. GREENWOOD, THOMAS, London : 15 Mar. 1759, Y. Touch, 997 L.T.P. Was given leave to strike his Touch in 1762.

1998. GREGG(E), JOHN (*see also* GRIGG), London : 1451 M.

1999. GREGG(E), ROBERT, London : 20 Aug. 1678, L.; 1683, S. Touch, 215 L.T.P., which he had leave to strike in 1672/3. Of St. Andrew's, Holborn, married Elizabeth Grantham at Mortlake, Surrey, on 9 April 1674.

2000. GREGG(E), THOMAS, London : 1654, S.; 1664, f.R.W.; 1669, f.U.W.; 1671, 1674 and 1677, M. Sheriff of the City in 1674. Left a legacy to the poor of the Company.

2001. GREGORY, EDWARD, Bristol: Mentioned in 1694 with his wife Anne. He was dead in 1696.

2002. GREGORY, EDWARD, Bristol: 5 May 1705, F. Apprenticed to Erasmus Dole and turned over to Thomas Cade. Dead in 1733 but his wife carried on the business. Mentioned in the Poll Book for 1721 as of Castle precincts, Bristol.

2003. GREGORY, GEORGE, London: 19 June 1740, Y.
2004. GREGORY, GEORGE, Edinburgh: 1784, F.
2005. GREGORY, JOHN, Bristol and Pucklechurch, Glocs.: S. of Edward. Apprenticed to John Jones, Bristol, and Alice his wife, 23 July 1687.
2006. GRENDON, DANIEL, London: 18 Mar. 1735, Y. Touch, 871 L.T.P., which he had leave to strike on 14 Oct. 1736.

2007. GRENE, JOHN, ? Lincolnshire: 10 Feb. 1505, left eight marks to Alson *Gryne* his daughter. (Lincoln Wills.)

GRESCHIRCHE, *see* DE GRESCHIRCHE.

2008. GREY, ALEXANDER (*see* also GRAY), Edinburgh: In 1807 was an apprentice to Adam Anderson.
2009. GREY, JOHN, Edinburgh: In 1730 was an apprentice to Robert Findlay.
2010. GREY, JOHN, London: 18 Dec. 1712, Y. He was a partner in Gray & King (*q.v.*), and his name should be spelled Gray in the records.
2011. GREY, RICHARD, London: 10 Oct. 1706, Y.
2012. GRIER, JAMES, London: 9 Aug. 1694, Y.
2013. GRIER, JOHN, Edinburgh: 1701, F. Touch, 102 E.T.P.

2014. GRIEVE, ANDRO, Dundee: 1611, F.

2015. GRIFFIN, ELIZABETH, London: 19 Oct. 1749, Y.
2016. GRIFFIN, JOHN, Bristol and Tidenham, Glocs.: S. of William. Apprenticed to Wm. James, Bristol, and Anne his wife, 6 Sept. 1676.
2017. GRIFFIN, RICHARD, London: Received a gift from the Company when his house was burned in 1629.
2018. GRIFFIN, THOMAS, London: Was married 27 Dec. 1647 at St. Peter's, Cornhill.
2019. GRIFFIN, THOMAS, London: 22 Sept. 1836, Y.
2020. GRIFFITH, EVAN, Bristol: 26 Dec. 1651, F. S. of John. Apprenticed to Peter Lodge and Marjorie for eight years from 18 Jan. 1635.
2021. GRIFFITH, JOHN, Bristol: 18 June 1747, F. S. of William. Apprenticed to Thomas Lanyon and Ann his wife, 30 Sept. 1737. Premium £50. In the *Bristol Oracle* of 8 Dec. 1744, he advertised his wares and gives his address as in Thomas Street, opposite the White Lion Inn. Dead in 1755.

2022. GRIFFITH, RICHARD, Cork: Mentioned in 1762.
2023. GRIGG, JOHN (*see* also GREGG), London: 13 Dec. 1722, Y.
2024. GRIGG, SAMUEL, London: 19 Dec. 1734, Y. Touch, 879 L.T.P., which he had leave to strike on 22 Sept. 1737. His name is spelled Gregg in the record.

2025. GRIMES & SON, London: In 1817 were pewter pot makers at 3 Osborn Street.

2026. GRIMSHAW, JAMES, London: 12 Aug. 1714, Y.
2027. GRIMSTED, JOHN, London: Touch, 324 L.T.P., which he had leave to strike in 1678/9. No mention of his name appears at this date in the Y. or L. Lists. Possibly he was father of the next named. In the "Bennett" Book he is given as dead in 1685.

2028. GRIMSTEED, JOHN, London: 11 Dec. 1701, Y.

2029. GROCE, THOMAS (? GRACE), London: 16 June 1737, Y. Touch, 876 L.T.P., which he had leave to strike on 16 June 1737.

2030. GROOME, RANDELL, London: Mentioned in 1614. 1615, S.; 1624, R.W. Died in 1624.
2031. GROOME, WILLIAM, London: 11 Oct. 1798, Y. Touch, 1076 L.T.P., struck c. 1803.

2032. GROVE(s), EDMUND, London: 21 June 1753, Y.; 18 Mar. 1773, L. Touch, 992 L.T.P. Was given leave to strike his Touch on 18 Dec. 1760. Partner in Munden & Grove (*q.v.*).
2033. GROVE(s), EDWARD, London: Touch, 294 L.T.P. which he had leave to strike in 1678. No mention is found of his name in the Y. or L. Lists, but he is mentioned in the "Bennett" Book from 1679-86.

2034. GROVE(s), THOMAS, London: Was a covenant man to Thomas Dounton in 1457.
2035. GROVE(s), THOMAS OF, London: 1452, Y., and in 1457 was of the Livery.
2036. GROVE(s), WILLIAM, London: 18 Mar. 1779, Y.
2037. GROVE(s), I. & SON, c. 1800-1840.   } ? same.

2038. GRUNDALL, WILLIAM, York: 1581/2, F.
2039. GRUNWIN, GABRIEL, London: 13 April 1693, L. Touch, No. 401 L.T.P., which he had leave to strike on 15 April 1684. His "Hall Marks" are found with Touch of Wood & Mitchell.

2040. GRUNWIN, RICHARD, London: 17 Dec. 1713, Y.; 17 June 1714, L.; 1700, f.S. (*sic*); 1729, R.W. Touch, 677 L.T.P., struck c. 1713.

His date of fining for the office of Steward is given in the records as 1700, but which is evidently wrong, probably should be 1720. A man could *not* serve the office of steward before being free or before election to the Livery.

2041. GUDEYERE, THOMAS, York: 1535/6, F. City Chamberlain, 1545/6, last mention found of him is in 1554/5.
2042. GUGGE, JOHN, SENR., London: Was a Master in 1457.
2043. GUGGE, JOHN, JUNR., London: Was of the Livery in 1457.
2044. GULD, JOHN, Edinburgh: 1677, F. Touch, 81 E.T.P.

2045. GULLAND, JOHNE, St. Andrews: In 1672 was an apprentice to Robert Scott the elder.
2046. GUNNING, JAMES, Eyrecourt (Ireland): Mentioned in 1782.
2047. GUNTHORP, JONATHAN, London: 14 Dec. 1699, Y.
2048. GURNELL, JOHN, London: 17 Mar. 1768, Y. Touch, 1023 L.T.P., struck c. 1771.

GUSS, *see* CUSS.
GUY, EARL OF WARWICK, *see* THOMAS WIGLEY.
2049. GUY, JOHN, London: 16 June 1692, Y.
2050. GUY, JOHN, Bristol: 11 Aug. 1713, F. Apprenticed to John Dole.
2051. GUY, SAMUEL, London: 19 Mar. 1729, Y. Touch, 845 L.T.P., which he had leave to strike in 1730.

2051A. GWAVAS, CHARLES, Penzance: Gazetted a bankrupt on 29 Aug. 1772.
2052. GWILLAM, RICHARD, Ratchup, Salop: S. of Thomas. Apprenticed to Robert Bush, Bristol, and Susannah his wife, 1 Feb. 1798.

2053. GWILT, HOWELL, London: 17 Mar. 1697, Y.; 15 Aug. 1709, L. Touch, No. 623 L.T.P., which he had leave to strike on 23 Mar. 1704. A hole is struck right through the mark obliterating the Christian name and device.

(A hole has been punched right through this touch to enable the touchplate to hang on a nail. H.H.C.)

2054. GWINNELL, THOMAS, Bristol: 14 July 1610, F. Apprenticed to James Cadell. Died c. 1638.

2055. GWYN, BACON, London: 15 Aug. 1709, L.

2056. GYBON, JOHN, London: In 1457 was an apprentice to John Goodale.

GYLES, see GILES.

2057. GYLMYN, JOHN, London: In 1457 was an apprentice to Robert Haache.

2058. GYNGER, JOHN, London: Was of the Livery in 1457.

2059. GYUES, THOMAS, London: Was covenant-man to Robert Chamberleyn in 1457.

H

2060. HAACHE, ROBERT, London: Was a member of the Livery in 1457.

2060A. HABBEN, JOHN, London: In 1817 was in Brick Lane.

2061. HACKERIGGE, EDWARD, Bristol: 10 Nov. 1593, F. Apprenticed to John Burrowes. Died c. 1620.

2062. HACKERIGGE, THOMAS, Gloucester: Apprenticed to Edward Hacherigge, Bristol, and Agnes his wife for nine years from 8 Oct. 1600.

2063. HADLEY, ISAAC, London: 24 Sept. 1668, L.; 1671, f.S.

2064. HAGGER, STEPHEN KENT, London: 12 Dec. 1754, Y. Touch, 1017 L.T.P., struck c. 1768. (Cf. Touch of John Langford, the use of which he was granted 23 June 1768, Langford being dead.)

2065. HAGSON, JOHN (? MAGSON or ANAYSON), London: 1502, R.W.; 1508 and 1513, U.W.

2066. HAGSON, RICHARD, London: 1478, R.W.; 1482, U.W.

2066A. HAILE, GEORGE, London: c. 1680. ("Bennett" Book.)

2067. HAILE, WILLIAM, Bristol: Mentioned in 1561 and 1569.

2067A. HAILES, CHAS., Derry: His daughter Christian was baptised at Derry Cathedral, 23 June 1678.

2068. HAIR, WILLIAM, London: 19 Dec. 1695, Y.

2070. HALE & SONS (see also HAYLE), Bristol: Mentioned in Matthews's Bristol Directory of 1852 and 1870 as of Narrow Wine Street.

2071. HALE, GEORGE (? HARE). London: Touch, 245 L.T.P., struck c. 1675, which he had leave to strike in 1674/5.

2072. HALE, RICHARD & THOMAS, Bristol: Mentioned in Matthews's first Bristol Directory (1793-4) as of The Back, Bristol, and also in 1805. They were succeeded by Edgar & Son.

2073. HALE, STEVEN, London: The Birth of his sons was registered at St. Peter's, Cornhill: One on 22 Aug. 1578 and another son, Nicholas, on 18 Sept. 1579.

2074. HALE, THOMAS, Bristol: See Richard & Thomas Hale, above. S. of William. Apprenticed to Robert Bush and Ann his wife, 12 Dec. 1771. Premium £150. Mentioned in 1798.

2075. HALFORD, SIMON, London: 15 Dec. 1726, Y. Touch, 830 L.T.P., which he had leave to strike on 8 Oct. 1730.

2076. HALL(s), CHRISTOPHER (*see* also HULL), London :
23 Mar. 1704, Y.

2077. HALL(s), HENRY, London : 13 Oct. 1698, Y.

2078. HALL(s), JAMES, London : 14 Dec. 1699, Y.

2079. HALL(s), JOHN, London : In 1457 was a journeyman to John Kendale.

2080. HALL(s), JOHN, York : 1492/3, F.

2081. HALL(s), JOHN, Newent : Apprenticed to Nathaniel Spicer, Bristol, 13 Oct. 1710.

2082. HALL(s), LEONARD, York : 1597/8, F., by patrimony.

2083. HALL(s), RALPH DE, York : 1442/3, F.

2084. HALL(s), RICHARD, London : Free in 1457 ;
1469, R.W.

2085. HALL(s), ROBERT, London : Was free in 1639.

2086. HALL(s), ROBERT, London : 12 Dec. 1793, Y.

2087. HALL(s), SAMUEL, London : 11 Oct. 1742, Y.

2088. HALL(s), SAMUEL, of ? : c. 1810. Although the
word London appears in this mark, Samuel
Hall was of Exeter and retired from the partnership of Hall & Scott (No. 2089) in 1/1767,
Scott continuing the business, and probably
the marks.

2089. HALL(s) & SCOTT, of ? : Appears in conjunction
with the last named.

2090. HALL(s), THOMAS, London : In 1622 was granted
the use of Mr. Sheppard's Touch.

2091. HALL(s), THOMAS, London : 21 Aug. 1711, Y.

2092. HALL(s), WILLIAM, London : Touch, 338 L.T.P.
which he had leave to strike in 1679/80. No
mention of his name is found in Y. or L. Lists,
but he appears in the " Bennett " Book from
1680-86.

2093. HALL(s), WILLIAM, London : 22 Mar. 1687, Y.
Touch, 447 L.T.P., which he had leave to strike
on 21 Mar. 1688.

2094. HALL(s), WILLIAM, London : Touch, 128 L.T.P.
re-struck after the fire c. 1670. A William Hall
of St. Stephen's, Coleman Street, pewterer,
married Anne Lowe on 20 Feb. 1668 at St.
Bartholomew-the-less.

2094A. HALLIFAX, CHARLES, London : c. 1680. (" Bennett " Book.)

2095. HALLIFAX, FRANCIS, London : 19 Mar. 1690, Y.

2096. HALLY, PATRICK, Perth : 1737, F. Pewterer and
Coppersmith. He was Deacon of the Perth
Hammermen, 1744-1747.

2097. HAMBERGER, JOHN, London : 18 Dec. 1794, Y. ;
14 Oct. 1819, L. A partner in Carpenter &
Hamberger (*q.v.*). Touch, 1066 L.T.P.

HAMERTON, *see* HAMMERTON.

2098. HAMILTON, ALEXANDER, London : 15 June 1721,
Y. ; 20 May 1736, L. ; 1745, S. Touch, 839
L.T.P., which he had leave to strike on 20 June
1728. Of Lombard Street. A partner in
Buckby & Hamilton (*q.v.*).

2099. HAMILTON, WILL, Dublin : 1759-1796.

2100. HAMILTONE, ANDREW, Perth : Was Essay-Master
in 1712.

2101. HAMILTONE, ROBERT, Dundee : 1652, F. ; 1668,
Deacon.

2102. HAMILTONE, S——, Edinburgh : In 1650 was
an apprentice to Thomas Inglis.

2103. HAMILTONE, WILLIAM, Edinburgh : 1613, F.
Touch, 28 E.T.P.

2104. HAMILTONE, WILLIAM, Dundee : 1680, F.

2104A. HAMLIN, JNO., London : c. 1680. ("Bennett" Book.) Of Eastcheap. Touch, 329 L.T.P., which he had leave to strike in 1679/80.

2105. HAMMERTON, HENRY, London : 20 Mar. 1706, Y.; 21 June 1716, L.; 1724, S.; 1733, R.W. Died Nov. 1741. Touch, 642 L.T.P., struck and dated 1707.

2106. HAMMERTON, HENRY, London : 13 Oct. 1748, Y.

2107. HAMMERTON, RICHARD, London : 13 June 1751, Y.

2108. HAMMON, HENRY, York : Was apprenticed to his father, John Hammon, on 19 April 1647 for seven years. 1655, F. Searcher 1666, and is mentioned again in 1668.

2109. HAMMON, JEREMY, York : 1651/2, F., by patrimony. Son of Thomas.

2110. HAMMON, JOHN, York : Was a Freeman in 1647. Father of Henry.

2111. HAMMON, THOMAS, York : Was a Freeman in 1644/5 and mentioned again in 1652/3.

2112. HAMMOND, GEORGE, London : 22 June 1693, Y.; 23 Sept. 1703, L.; 1709, S. Touch, 515 L.T.P., struck c. 1695.

2113. HAMON, SAMUEL, London : Apprenticed to John Chylde, c. 1605. Was a Freeman in 1614.

2114. HAMOND, JOHN, London : Was a covenant-man to William Sexteyn in 1480.

2114A. HAMPHIE, ALEXANDER, Dublin : 1719.

2115. HANCOCK, SAMUEL, London : 15 Aug. 1689, L.; 1704, R.W.; 1714, U.W.; 1718, f.M. ? Touch, 375 L.T.P., which he had leave to strike on 22 Mar. 1682. Complaint was lodged before the Court in 1690/1 of his striking his name in full upon his wares in addition to his Touch.

2116. HAND(s), JAMES (see also HANNS), London : 19 June 1718, Y.

2117. HAND(s), RICHARD, London : 20 Mar. 1717, Y. Touch, 834 L.T.P., which he had leave to strike on 20 Mar. 1728

2117A. HAND(s), ROBERT, London : c. 1681. ("Bennett" Book.) Touch, 381 L.T.P., which he had leave to strike on 1 Mar. 1682.

2118. HANDY, JOHN, London : 17 Oct. 1754, Y.

2119. HANDY, THOMAS, London : 21 Oct. 1784, Y. Died in 1845.

2120. HANDY, WILLIAM, London : 20 June 1728, Y.; 28 Nov. 1746, L. 1773, died. Touch, 884 L.T.P., which he had leave to strike on 23 Mar. 1737/8.

2122. HANDY, WILLIAM, London : 1746, Y.

2123. HANDY, WILLIAM, London : 20 Oct. 1755, Y.

2124. HANKINSON, JOHN, London : 10 Aug. 1693, Y. Touch, 525 L.T.P., which he had leave to strike on 13 Jan. 1697.

2125. HANNS, EDWARD (? HANDS), London : 23 Mar. 1704, Y. Touch, 628 L.T.P., which he had leave to strike on 7 Jan. 1705. (*Cf.* Richard Hands.)

2126. HANNS, RICHARD, London : 21 Mar. 1737, Y.
2127. HANSON, WILLIAM, Walsall : Was buried at St. Matthew's Church, Walsall, in 1614.
2128. HARB(R)IDGE, WILLIAM, London : 9 June 1774, Y.
2129. HARCHALL, WILLIAM (? MARSHALL), London : 1490 and 1494, R.W.; 1497, U.W.; 1500, 1501, 1506, 1507 and 1512, M. Welch has it Marshall but the records give it Harchall.
2130. HARDEMAN, WILLIAM (*see* also HARDMAN), London : Was a Master in 1612.
2131. HARDIE, JOHN, Edinburgh : 1784, Freeman white-ironsmith. In 1780 had a shop at West Bow.
2132. HARDIE, WILLIAM, St. Andrews : 1689, F.
2133. HARDING, JONATHAN, London : 10 Aug. 1693, Y.
2134. HARDING, JONATHAN, London : 21 Mar. 1722, Y.
2135. HARDING, ROBERT, London : 24 Sept. 1668, L ; 1672, f.S.
2136. HARDMAN, JOHN, of Wigan. Will proved at Chester, in 1743 : c. 1690-1730. His mark, or marks to be correct, appear in conjunction with the name T. LETHERBARROW (*q.v.*).

2136A. HARDY, JNO., London : c. 1680. ("Bennett" Book.)
2137. HARE, JOHN (*see* also HALE), London : Apprenticed to John Jackson in 1558 and dismissed the same year.
2138. HARENDON, ———, London : 1664, S.
2139. HARFORD, HENRY, London : 18 June 1696, L. Touch, 395 L.T.P., which he had leave to strike on 25 Jan. 1683. This Touch is struck so badly as to make any hope of deciphering it accurately

extremely remote. Buried at St. Peter's, Cornhill, 8 May 1715.

2140. HARFORD, HENRY, London : 13 Oct. 1715, Y.
2141. HARFORD, WILLIAM, Bedminster, Bristol : S. of William. Apprenticed to John Jones, Bristol, for seven years from 19 Nov. 1700.
2142. HARKAY, ROBERT, York : 1576, F., by patrimony.
2143. HARNESS, ROBERT, York : 1496/7, F.
2144. HARPER, EDWARD, London : Was fined in 1570 for appearing at the Guildhall without his Livery Gown. 1572, S. In 1591 was beadle and appointed keeper of the Company's Bowling Alley.
2145. HARPER, JOHN, London : 11 Aug. 1709, Y.
2146. HARRABEN, WILL, Dublin : Mentioned in 1712.
2147. HARRIS, DANIEL, Cork : 1708, F.; and is mentioned again in 1729.
2148. HARRIS, JABEZ, London : 21 June 1694, Y.; 23 Sept. 1703, L.; 1732, S.; 1734, R.W. Touch, No. 538 L.T.P., which he had leave to strike on 17 June 1697.

2149. HARRIS, JOHN, London : 23 June 1709, Y. Touch, 660 L.T.P., struck c. 1709.

2150. HARRIS, JOHN, Barnstaple : Of Well Street. c. 1651.
2151. HARRIS, JOSEPH, Gloucester : S. of Joseph. Apprenticed to Thomas Hale, Bristol, and Martha his wife, 3 Nov. 1796.
2152. HARRIS, RICHARD, London : 23 June 1763, Y.
2153. HARRIS, ROBERT, Bristol : S. of John. Apprenticed to Thomas Willshire and Ann his wife, 18 April 1792.
2154. HARRIS, THOMAS, Bristol : S. of Francis. Apprenticed to Avice, widow of Thomas Baily, 24 Nov. 1709.

2155. HARRIS, WILLIAM, London: 18 Dec. 1746, Y. Touch, 966 L.T.P. Had leave to strike his Touch, 21 Jan. 1754.

2156. HARRIS, WILLIAM, Barnstaple: 1608-24. Buried at Barnstaple, 3 Dec. 1625.

2157. HARRIS, WILLIAM, Tidenham, Glocs.: Son of John. Apprenticed to Wm. Purdy, Bristol, and Juliana his wife for seven years from 10 Jan. 1638.

2158. HARRIS, ———, ? ? ?: Avoid this mark as you would the plague. It appears on hundreds of reproductions.

2159. HARRISON, GEORGE (*see* also HARYSON), York: Apprenticed on 25 Dec. 1714 for seven years to his father John.

2160. HARRISON, JOHN, SENR., York: Apprenticed in 1651 to John Bradley. Father of John, Junr. 1659/60, F. Searcher in 1669, 1673, 1679, 1682, 1684 and 1688.

2161. HARRISON, JOHN, JUNR., York: Apprenticed to his father, John, for seven years on 7 May 1677. Father of George. 25 Nov. 1693, F. Searcher in 1695, 1696, 1700 and 1708. Probably the Touch illustrated was his.

2162. HARRISON, JOHN, York: Mentioned in 1712/13. 22 Feb. 1724/5, F. City Chamberlain, 1745/6, and was searcher in several years.

2163. HARRISON, JOHN, York: 1719, F.; and was searcher several times.

2164. HARRISON, RUFUS, (? York): c. 1750.

2165. HARRISON, THOMAS, London: 1474, R.W.; 1476, U.W.; 1483, M.

2166. HARRISON, WILLIAM, London: 1557, Y.

2167. HARRSION, WILLIAM, London: In 1592 married Mary Nicholls by special licence. He is referred to as a pewterer of St. Sepulchre's.

2168. HARRISON, WILLIAM, London: 15 Dec. 1748, Y. Touch, 931 L.T.P. Was given leave to strike his Touch, 23 Mar. 1748. The strange looking surname is caused by the mark being badly struck.

2168A. HARROP, THOMAS, Chester: Opened his shop in Lower Bridge Street on 16 Sept. 1766.

2169. HARRYS, JOHN, London: Was free in 1457.

2170. HARRYSON, RICHARD, London: In 1553 served in a band of soldiers raised by the Company. He was evidently a spoonmaker for in 1562/3 he paid a fine to Stephen Calie at the rate of "every week two dozen spoons with latten knobs until the said money be paid."

2171. HART, SAMUEL, Tickenham, Somerset: S. of George. Apprenticed to Henry Burgum, Bristol, and Betty his wife for seven years from 7 Dec. 1769.

2172. HART, THOMAS, Bristol: S. of Edward. Apprenticed to John Stevens and Elizabeth his wife, 25 Feb. 1681.

2173. HART, THOMAS, Malmesbury, Wilts.: S. of Jacob. Apprenticed to Francis Kenton, Bristol, 11 Aug. 1687.

2174. HART, WILLIAM, York: 1624/5, F.

2175. HARTLAND, JOHN, London: 6 Feb. 1823, Y.

2176. HARTLIF, WILLIAM, London: Was a Freeman in 1560.

2177. HARTON & SONS, London: c. 1860-1890. Succeeded Watts & Harton, c. 1860, and closed the business which was in High Holborn in 1890 when the manager and most of their connexion was taken over by Brown & Englefield.

2178. HARTON, SAMUEL, London: 18 Aug. 1836, Y.

2179. HARTSHORNE, MICHAEL, London : 10 Aug. 1676, L.; 1681, S.; 1693. R.W.

2180. HARTWELL, GABRIEL (*see* also GARTWELL), London : Married at St. Clement Danes, 21 April 1673. Touch, 217 L.T.P., which he had leave to strike in 1672/3. He is mentioned in the "Bennett" Book from 1679-86.

2181. HARTWELL, HENRY, London : Of St. Clement Danes. Married 16 June 1666. Touch, 98 L.T.P., struck c. 1663.

2182. HARTWELL, JOHN, London : 12 Aug. 1736, Y. Touch, 925 L.T.P. Was given leave to strike his Touch on 15 Oct. 1747.

2183. HARTWELL, PETER, London : 4 Oct. 1688, Y.

2183A. HARTWELL, PETER, London : 1679-86. ("Bennett" Book.)

2184. HARTWELL, WILLIAM, London : In 1562 used as his mark the Crown and Hammer. Died in 1566.

2185. HARVEY, EDMUND, of ? : c. 1700-1750.

2186. HARVEY, E——, of ? : c. 1670.

2187. HARVEY, WILLIAM, Dublin : c. 1712.

2188. HARVIE, JAMES, Edinburgh : 1654, F. Touch, 57 E.T.P.

2189. HARVIE, JOHN, Edinburgh : 1643, F. Touch, 45 E.T.P.

2190. HARVIE, JOHN, Edinburgh : 1787, mentioned as a master.

2191. HARVIE, WILLIAM, Edinburgh : 1672, F. Touch, 72 E.T.P.

2192. HARVIE, WILLIAM, Edinburgh : 1706, F. Touch, 109 E.T.P.

2193. HARVIE, WILLIAM, Edinburgh : In 1646 was apprenticed to John Harvie.

2194. HARVIE, WILLIAM, Perth : 1688, F. Apprenticed to John Harvie, Edinburgh.

2195. HARVYE, JOHN, London : 1555, S.

2195A. HARWELL, GEOFFREY, Norwich : 1422/3, F.

2196. HARWELL, ROBERT, Co. Worcs. : S. of Richard. Apprenticed to James Cadell, Bristol, and Bridgette his wife for nine years from 17 Jan. 1613.

2197. HARYSON, WILLIAM, London : 1557, Y., by redemption.

2198. HASELL, BAPTIST (*see* also HASSELL), London : Mentioned in 1582. In 1592 he was commissioned to carry an important letter to Sir Francis Godolphin at The Stannaries, in Cornwall.

2199. HASKINS, JOHN, Bristol : S. of Robert. Apprenticed to Thomas Munks and Julian his wife for seven years from 21 April 1656.

2200. HASLAM, WILLIAM, London : 19 Dec. 1734, Y.

2201. HASSELL, JAMES, London : 21 June 1792, Y.

2202. HASSELL, THOMAS, London : Mentioned in 1552, 1554, S.; 1565, R.W. Died in 1566.

2203. HASSELL, MRS., London : Widow of Thomas. In 1569 she used the Rose and Crown as her Touch.

2204. HASSELBOURNE, JACOB, London : 1 May 1691, L.; 1697, f.S.; 1708, R.W.; 1718, U.W.; 1722, M.

2205. HASTINGS, JAMES, London : Was free in 1614.

2206. HATCH, HENRY, London : Touch, 302 L.T.P., which he had leave to strike in 1678. No mention of his name appears in the Y. or L. Lists. In the "Bennett" Book he is given as dead in 1681.

2207. HATFIELD, WILLIAM, London : Searcher in 1611, 1627, S. 1633, Beadle.

2208. HATHAWAY, JAMES, London : 10 Oct. 1734, Y.

2209. HATHAWAY, JAMES, London : 17 Oct. 1754, Y.

2210. HATHAWAY, JOHN, London : 29 Oct. 1725, Y. Touch, 790 L.T.P., which he had leave to strike on 28 July 1726.

2211. HAUTE, JOHN, Priorfelt, Worcs. : S. of John. Apprenticed to James Cadell, Bristol, and Johanna for seven years from 3 Feb. 1620.

2212. HAVELAND, MILES, London : 11 Aug. 1664, L. ; 1668, S.

2213. HAVERING, JOHN, London : 14 Dec. 1699, Y.

2214. HAWARD, THOMAS (see also HOWARD), London : 1651, f.S. ; 1658, R.W. ; 1664, U.W. ; 1666, M. Touch, 5 L.T.P., restruck c. 1670 after the great fire in 1666. (See W. Matthews' Touch.)

2215. HAWARD, THOMAS, JUNR., London : 28 Nov. 1667, L. ; 1671, f.S.

2216. HAWCLIF(E), SIMON, London : 1568, S.

2217. HAWKE(S), THOMAS, London : 1568, S. Was fined in 1569 for striking Thomas Mott, a fellow-member. 1579, R.W. ; 1588, U.W.

2218. HAWKE(S), EDWARD, London : 28 Nov. 1667, L. ; 1669, f.S.

2219. HAWKESFORD, ROGER, London : Mentioned in 1574. Was fined in 1599 for making free an apprentice two years before his indentures expired.

2220. HAWKINS, JOHN, London : 21 Oct. 1738, Y.

2221. HAWKINS, PATRICK, St. Ives, Cornwall : S. of John. Apprenticed to John Batcheler, Bristol, and Honor his wife, 26 June 1688, "Father to find apparel."

2222. HAWKINS, RICHARD, London : 23 Mar. 1727, Y.

2223. HAWKINS, THOMAS, London : 17 Mar. 1742, Y.

2224. HAWKINS, THOMAS, London : 21 Oct. 1756, Y. Touch, 975 L.T.P., which he was granted leave to strike on 20 Oct. 1757.

2225. HAWKINS, WALTER, London : In 1599 was an apprentice with William Walker.

2226. HAWKINS, STEPHEN (? HAWKYNE), London : 1536 R.W. ; 1543, U.W.

2227. HAWKYN, GEORGE, London : 1568/9, Clerk to the Company.

2228. HAWS, JOHN, London : 20 Oct. 1791, Y.

2229. HAY, DAVID, Perth : In 1776 was an apprentice with Patrick Bissett.

2230. HAY, THOMAS, Dundee : 1611, F.

2231. HAYDON, WALTER, London : In 1457 was an apprentice with John Coldham.

2232. HAYES, HUGH, London : 17 June 1697, Y.

2233. HAYES, THOMAS, London : 19 June 1746, Y.

2234. HAYLE, WILLIAM (see also HALE), Bristol : Was the master to whom Tinobus Cadell was bound apprentice on 8 July 1569.

2235. HAYNES, JOHN, London : 6 Sept. 1688, Y.

2236. HAYNES, WILLIAM, London : 1556, R.W. ; 1560, U.W.

2237. HAYTER, GEORGE, Bristol : His name appears in the Bristol Directories of 1870 and 1877 as of 140 and 141 Temple Street. He succeeded Henry Payne.

2238. HAYTON, JOHN, London : 18 Aug. 1743, Y. ; 15 Dec. 1748, L. Touch, 918 L.T.P. (Cf. Touch of George Beeston.) Was given leave to strike his Touch on 22 Aug. 1745.

2238A. HAYTON, PAUL, London : c. 1680. ("Bennett" Book.) Touch, 271 L.T.P., which he had leave to strike in 1676/7.

2239.   HAYWARD, WILLIAM, York : 1391/2, F.
2239A. HAYWARDE, THOMAS, Norwich : 1558/9, F.
2240.   HEAD, JOHN, London : In 1601 he transferred to the Cutlers Company.
2241.   HEALEY, WILLIAM, London : 26 Oct. 1752, Y. Touch, 960 L.T.P., struck c. 1753.

2242.   HEANEY, JOHN, Dublin : Mentioned in 1767 and 1798. In the former year he was Warden of the Guild of Smiths. In 1775 he moved " to where the Robinsons and Richard Palmer (braziers) lived," and purchased the moulds, &c., of the late John Wilkinson. In 1785 he was at 17 Upper Ormond Quay.

2243.   HEARMAN, WILLIAM, London : 19 Mar. 1801, Y.
2244.   HEATH, EDWARD (see also HETHE), London : 1641, f.S.; 1653, f.R.W.; 1656, U.W.; 1660, f.M.
2245.   HEATH, EDWARD, London : 1552, f.S.
2246.   HEATH, JOHN, London : Partner of Anthony Longsay, Lambeth Marsh, in 1662.
2247.   HEATH, JOHN, London : 21 June 1694, Y. Touch, 519 L.T.P., which he had leave to strike on 18 June 1695.

2248.   HEATH, JOHN, London : In 1603 was elected to serve on a Committee formed to devise means of redressing various grievances. 1612, f.S.; 1618, R.W.

2249.   HEATH, JOHN, London : 24 Mar. 1711, Y. Touch, 744 L.T.P., which he had leave to strike on 6 Feb. 1721.

2250.   HEATH, JOHN, Kingston, Somerset : Apprenticed to John Jones, Bristol, and Alice his wife, 21 Mar. 1705.
2251.   HEATH, RICHARD, London : Mentioned in 1672. 10 Aug. 1676, L.; 1682, S.; 1694, U.W.; 1699, M. Touch, 192 L.T.P., which he had leave to strike in 1670/1.

2252.   HEATH, SAMUEL, London : 15 Dec. 1715,
2253.   HEATH, THOMAS, London : 18 Mar. 1714, Y.
2254.   HEATH, THOMAS, London : 23 June 1709, Y.
2255.   HEATH, THOMAS, Warwick : 1666, mentioned on his token (q.v.).
2255A. HEATH, WILLIAM, London : c. 1680. ("Bennett" Book.)
2256.   HEATLEY, ALEXANDER, London : 20 Mar. 1700, Y.
2256A. HEATON, WILLIAM, London : Touch, 342 L.T.P. which he had leave to strike in 1686/7. Also Touch, 335 L.T.P.

2257.   HEDE, JOHN, London : In 1457 was a journeyman with John Kendale.
2258.   HEDGES, GEORGE, Gloucester : S. of Edward. Apprenticed to Robert Bush, Bristol, 2 Aug. 1792. Premium £5.
2259.   HEDGES, THOMAS, London : S. of Thomas. Apprenticed to Thomas Wiltshire, Bristol, and Ann his wife, 14 May 1792.
        HELLINGWORTH, see KILLINGWORTH.
2260.   HELME, ROBERT, York : In 1489/90 was an apprentice.
2261.   HEMMING, HENRY, Glasgow : 1792, F. White-ironsmith.
2262.   HENDERSON, GEORGE, Dundee : In 1718 was a journeyman to Thomas Forrest.
2263.   HENDERSON, WILLIAM, Perth : 1775, F. White-ironsmith.
2264.   HENDRIE, WILLIAM, Edinburgh : In 1691 was an apprentice with William Harvie.
2265.   HENLEY, WILLIAM, London : 19 Dec. 1723, Y.

2266. HENNING, THOMAS, London: 22 June 1693, Y.

2267. HENNYNGHAM, JOHN, London: Was free in 1498.

2268. HENSON, THOMAS, London: 1614, S.

2269. HENTY, JOHN, Lewes, Sussex: c. 1650-60. Mentioned on his token as a pewterer. (*See* end of Chap. IV.)

2270. HERDRIG, THOMAS, Edinburgh: Mentioned in 1761.

2271. HERE, JOHN, London: Was fined in 1487 for working with a man who was not a freeman.

2272. HERIOT, JAMES, Edinburgh: In 1667 was an apprentice with Alexander Fergusone.

2273. HERNE, DAVID, London: 21 Oct. 1756, Y.; 17 Dec. 1767, L.; 1774, f.S.; 1780, f.R.W.; 1792, f.U.W.; 1793, f.M. Of Carleton, Wilts.

2274. HERNIE, JAMES, Edinburgh: 1651, F. Touch, 50 E.T.P.

2275. HERON, ROBERT, York: 1585/6, F.

2276. HERRIN(G), JAMES, Edinburgh: In 1667 was a Master. Touch, 69 E.T.P.

2277. HERRIN(G), JAMES, Edinburgh: 1692, F. Touch, 91 E.T.P.

2278. HERRIN(G), JOHN, Edinburgh: 1693, F.

2279. HERRIN(G), JOHN, Edinburgh: 1688, F. Touch, 89 E.T.P.

2280. HERRIN(G), WILLIAM, Edinburgh: 1693, F. Died c. 1740. Touch, 93 E.T.P.

2281A. HERWERD, THOMAS, Norwich: 1536/7, F.

2282. HESKETH, HENRY, London: 15 Dec. 1698, Y.

2283. HESLOPP, RICHARD, London: 20 Mar. 1700, Y. Touch, 641 L.T.P., struck c. 1707.

2284. HETHE, ROBERT, London: Mentioned in 1553.

2285. HEW, JOHN, London: In 1494 he provided the funds for the glazing of a window at the Hall.

2285A. HEWETT, JOSEPH, London: c. 1680. ("Bennett" Book.)

2286. HEWETT, ROBERT, Maidstone: In 1566 was appointed with two others to abolish hawkers in Sussex and Kent.

2287. HEWITT, HENRY, Salisbury: In 1633 his name appears as a pewterer of St. Thomas', Salisbury.

2288. HEWITT, JOHN, London: 10 Oct. 1723, Y.

2289. HEWISH, SAMUEL (? HUISH), Bristol: Mentioned in the Poll Book for 1774 as of St. Michael's, Bristol.

2290. HEYDON, SAMUEL, London: 16 June 1715, Y.

2291. HEYFORD, WILLIAM, London: 20 Mar. 1698, Y. Touch, 556 L.T.P., which he had leave to strike on 17 June 1699.

2292. HEYGIE, JAMES, Stirling: Mentioned in 1610.

2292A. HEYRICK, DAVID, London: c. 1680. ("Bennett" Book.) Touch, 269 L.T.P., which he had leave to strike in 1675/6.

HEYTON, *see* HAYTON.

2293. HEYTWAITE, MICHAEL, London: 1552, R.W.; 1553, U.W. Died in 1557. Was searcher in 1555.

2294. HEYWOOD, HENRY, Bristol: 2 Jan. 1647, F. S. of Wm. Apprenticed to Thomas Hobson and Elizabeth his wife, 21 April 1634.

2295. HEYWOOD, ROBERT, Barnstaple: c. 1605-1623. Buried 14 Jan. 1623 at Barnstaple.

2296. HIATT, JAMES (*see* also HYATT), Whitchurch, Somerset: S. of William. Apprenticed to Robert Bush, Bristol, and Ann his wife, 6 May 1778.

2297. HICKES, DANIEL, London: 19 June 1690, Y.

2298. HICKES, PETER, London: 29 Oct. 1706, Y.

2299. HICKEY, BENJAMIN, Bristol: S. of Benjamin. Apprenticed to Wm. Calder and Jane his wife, 29 June 1749. Premium £20. Turned over to James Reid on 5 Feb. 1752.

2300. HICKINGBOTTOM, FRANCIS, London: 22 Mar. 1693, Y.

2301. HICKLING, THOMAS, London: 14 Jan. 1685, L.; 1691, S.; 1698, R.W. Touch, 281 L.T.P.

2302. HICKLING, THOMAS, London: 20 Mar. 1717, Y. Touch, 740 L.T.P., which he obtained leave to strike in 1720.

2303. HICKS, (HIX?) JOHN, London: Mentioned in 1555.

2304. HICKS, THOMAS, London: 19 Aug. 1676, L.; 1680, f.S.; 1694, f.U.W.; 1698, M. Touch, 173 L.T.P., which he had leave to strike in 1669/70.

2305. HICKS, WILLIAM, Bristol: S. of Thomas. Apprenticed to Thomas Hobson and Elizabeth his wife for eight years from 27 Oct. 1620.

2306. HIDE, BENJAMIN, London: 13 Aug. 1741, Y.

2307. HIERTON, OBEDIAH, Bristol: S. of Richard. Apprenticed to Thomas Pascall and Joane his wife, 4 May 1682.

2308. HIGDON, JOSEPH, London: In 1683 is mentioned as a spoonmaker. Touch, 284 L.T.P., which he had leave to strike in 1676/7.

2309. HIGGINS, GEORGE, Bristol: S. of Thomas. Apprenticed to Robert Bush, Junr., 30 Aug. 1796.

2310. HIGGINS, JOHN, Bratton, Somerset: S. of Thomas. Apprenticed to Thomas Lodge, 26 April 1677.

2311. HIGHMORE, WILLIAM, London: 18 Mar. 1741, Y.; 19 Aug. 1742, L. Touch, 894 L.T.P. Had leave to strike his Touch, 18 Mar. 1741.

2312. HIGLEY, SAMUEL, London: 19 Oct. 1775, Y. Touch, 1033 L.T.P., struck c. 1776.

2313. HILL(s), EDWARD (see also HYLL and HULL), Bristol and Wedmore, Somerset: 30 Dec. 1644, F. S. of John. Apprenticed to James Gibson, 3 Feb. 1626. Dead before 1654.

2314. HILL(s), GABRIEL, London: Was a Freeman in 1565, working for Hugh Collier.

2315. HILL(s), HUGH, London: 1622, f.R.W.; 1625, U.W.

2316. HILL(s), JAMES, London: His name appears in the records, c. 1730, but without a date.

2317. HILL(s), JOHN, London: In 1457 was an apprentice to Richard Lawton.

2318. HILL(s), ROBERT, London: 19 Mar. 1724, Y.

2319. HILL(s), ROGER, London: 24 Mar. 1791, Y. Probably a partner in Wood & Hill. Touch, 1067 L.T.P., struck c. 1698.

2320. HILL(s), THOMAS, London: 8 Oct. 1696, Y.

2321. HILL(s), THOMAS, London: 19 Mar. 1795, Y.

2322. HILL(s), THOMAS, Dublin: Died in 1741.

2323. HILL(s), WILLIAM, London: 1521, R.W.

2324. HILL(s), WILLIAM, Bristol and Chepstow, Mon.: 2 Oct. 1661, F. S. of Matthew. Apprenticed to Humphrey Beale, Bristol, and Margaret his wife, 30 Nov. 1653.

2325. HILL(s), WILLIAM, London: 1613, f.S.; 1622, f.R.W.; 1633, U.W.; 1636 and 1641, M.

2326. HILL(s), WILLIAM, London: 1668 (sic.), L.; 1660, S.; 1668, f.R.W.; 1672, U.W.; 1677, f.M. The date of his joining the livery is given in the records as 1668 or two years before he served as steward, which is impossible. It is probably meant for 1658.

2327. HILL(s), WILLIAM, Dublin: Mentioned in 1808, 1829 and 1833.

See also WOOD & HILL.

2328. HILLTON, JARVIS, London: In 1541 was fined for usurping another man's standing at Gravesend Fair. Was searcher to the Company in 1555.

HILTONE, see DE HILTONE.

2329. HINCHAM, A., of ?: c. 1720-1750. (Cf. Touches of Watts & Collyer.)

2330. HINDE, JOHN, London: 19 Mar. 1767, Y.; 20 June 1776, L.; 1781, S.; 1790 and 1791, R.W.; 1795, U.W.; 1796, M. Died 26 May 1798. Of 78 Leman Street, Goodman Fields. Touch, 1024 L.T.P., struck c. 1772.

2331. HINDE, JOHN, London: 21 Aug. 1800, Y. and L.; 1821, f.S. Died 2 Oct. 1841, age 62. In Whitechapel High Street, in partnership with his widowed mother. Partnership dissolved 18 June 1803.

2331A. HINDE, SARAH, London: Most probably was the widow of John Hinde, 1767, Y. In 1801 she was at 134 Whitechapel.

2332. HINDES, JOHN, London: 18 Dec. 1760, Y.

2333. HINMAN, BENJAMIN, London: 22 Mar. 1715, Y.

HISLOPP, see HESLOPP.

2334. HITCHCOCK, EVAN, London: 17 June 1708, Y.

2335. HITCHCOCK, JOHN, London: 21 Aug. 1690, Y.

2336. HITCHINS, JOHN (see also HUTCHENS), London: 15 Mar. 1743, Y.; 12 Dec. 1758, L.; 1768, f.S.; 1777, f.R.W.; 1786, U.W.; 1788, f.M.

2337. HITCHINS, WILLIAM, London: 9 Aug. 1705, Y. Touch, 663 L.T.P., struck and dated 1709.

2338. HITCHINS, WILLIAM, London: 15 Mar. 1732, Y. and L. His name is spelt Hitchins in the Yeomanry List and Hutchins in the Livery List.

2339. HITCHINS, WILLIAM, London: 15 Mar. 1759, Y. Touch, 984 L.T.P., which he was granted leave to strike on 20 Mar. 1760, but it is dated 1709, evidently relating back to the foundation of the firm (see William Hitchins, above).

2340. HITCHMAN, JAMES, London: 11 Dec. 1701, Y.; 21 June 1716, L.; 13 Dec. 1733, R.W.

Touch, 593 L.T.P., which he had leave to strike on 11 Dec. 1701.

2341. HITCHMAN, ROBERT, London: 16 June 1737, Y.; 11 Aug. 1737, L.; 1749, S.; 1752, R.W.; 1761, U.W. Touch, 877 L.T.P., which he had leave to strike on 11 Aug. 1737. In 1743 was at St. Margaret's Hill, Southwark.

2342. HOARE, RICHARD, London: In 1672 was accused of using false metal and is mentioned in the "Bennett" Book from 1679/86.

2343. HOARE, THOMAS, London: 22 Mar. 1715, Y.; 10 April 1718, L.; 1726, S. Was given leave to strike a Touch on 21 June 1715, but it is not on the Touchplate. He was given leave on 27 Sept. 1716 to be partner with Mrs. Eames, widow of Richard Eames.

2344. HOBSON, MILES, Bristol: Mentioned in 1609, and in 1584 in St. Ewen's Vestry Minutes.

2345. HOBSON, THOMAS, SENR., Bristol: 12 Dec. 1609, F. Apprenticed to Miles Hobson. Was appointed by the London Pewterers' Company in 1614 to act as their deputy to export pewter, but not tin, from Bristol. Mentioned in 1643.

2346. HOBSON, THOMAS, JUNR., Bristol: 17 May 1647, F. Apprenticed to Thomas Hobson, Senr.

2347. HOBSON, WILLIAM, Bristol: 14 Jan. 1576, F. Apprenticed to John Burrowes. Mentioned in 1592.

2348. HOBSON, WILLIAM, Bristol: Mentioned with his wife Marie from 1602-1644.

2349. HOCKLEY, RICHARD, London: 13 Oct. 1715, Y.

2350. HOCKLEY, RICHARD, London: 6 July 1715, Y.

2351. HODGE(s), JOHN, Dublin: Mentioned in 1804, 1808 and 1833.

2351A. HODGE(s), JOHN, London: Died 1680. ("Bennett" Book.)

2352. HODGE(s), JOSEPH, London: 22 June 1693, Y.

2353. HODGE(s), JOSEPH, London: 19 Dec. 1667, L.

2354. HODGE(s), JOSEPH, London: 14 Aug. 1718, Y.

2355. HODGE(s), ROBERT PEIRCY, London: 22 Oct. 1772, Y.; 20 June 1782, L.; 1787, S.; 1796, R.W.; 1801, U.W.; 1802, M. Touch, 1025 L.T.P., struck c. 1773. *Inter alia*, he made Pewter Toys, and his address in 1793 was 58 Whitecross Street. (*Cf.* Robert Peircy.) *See* his Trade Card.

2356. HODGE(s), SAMPSON, Tiverton: c. 1707.

TIVERTON

2357. HODGE(s), THOMAS, Tiverton: c. 1720-1750.

TIVERTON

2358. HODGE(s), THOMAS BATTS, London: 13 Dec. 1810, Y. Died 17 Dec. 1852.

2359. HODGE(A)RT, WILLIAM, Edinburgh: In 1690 was an apprentice to Thomas Inglis. ? 2360.

2360. HODGE(A)RT, WILLIAM, Dublin: Mentioned 27 July 1719 in the Irish House of Commons *Journal* as one of four petitioners to have certain abuses rectified. ? same as above.

2360A. HODGKINS, EDWARD, London: Died 1681. ("Bennett" Book.)

2361. HODGKIN, THOMAS, ? West-Country: c. 1750-1770.

LONDON

2362. HODGKIS, ARTHUR, London: Was free in 1620 when a complaint was made of his burnishing sad-ware. 1635, S.

2363. HODGSON, JOHN, York: 1664/5, F., by patrimony.

2363A. HODGSON, THOMAS, London: c. 1680. ("Bennett" Book.)

2364. HODLER, THOMAS, York: 1403/4, F.

2365. HOGG, JOHNE, Glasgow: 1794, F. White-ironsmith.

2366. HOGG, JOHN, Paisley: 1794 F.

2367. HOGG, WILLIAM, Newcastle: c. 1760-1795. Succeeded to Robert Sadler (*q.v.*).

2368. HOKES, JOSEPH, Bristol: S. of Jacob. Apprenticed to Christopher Clement and Charity his wife, 10 Feb. 1723.

2368A. HOLDEN, RICHARD, Liverpool: Advertised his business for sale in the *General Evening Post*, 14 June 1760.

2369. HOLDEN, THOMAS, London: In 1555 was twice concerned with falsely made goods.

2370. HOLDER, CHRISTOPHER, Bristol and Long Ashton, Somerset: 14 Oct. 1706, F. S. of Jacob. Apprenticed to Erasmus Dole and Sara his wife, 5 May 1697. Mentioned in the Poll Books for 1721, 1734 and 1739 as of St. James's, Bristol.

2371. HOLDSWORTH, JOHN, London: 23 Feb. 1826, Y. *Cf.* Holsworth, below, probably same man.

2372. HOLFORD, THOMAS, London: 1587, Y.

2372A. HOLLAND, FRANCIS, London: Partner in Holland & Turner, c. 1800.

2372B. HOLLAND, THOMAS F., London: In 1817 was at 34 Chandos Street.

2372C. HOLLAND & TURNER, London: Partnership dissolved, 2 Jan. 1810.—*London Gazette.*

2373. HOLLAND, THOMAS, Lynn: 1645/6, F. Mentioned later in 1666/7.

2374. HOLLENBRIGGE, RICHARD, Bristol : 22 June 1592, F. Apprenticed to William Hobson. Mentioned in 1616.

2375. HOLLEY, JOHN, London : 12 July 1689, Y.; 28 Sept. 1699, L.; 1706, S. Touch, 461 L.T.P., which he had leave to strike on 20 July 1689. He married on 8 Feb. 1689 at St. Giles in the Fields, Ellen, daughter of Robert Crosfeild. He was of St. Andrew's Holborn.

2376. HOLLFORD, STEPHEN, London : 11 Aug. 1664, L.; 1668, S.

2377. HOLLISTER, SAMUEL, Bristol : S. of Samuel. Apprenticed to John Jones and Alice his wife, 9 Mar. 1696.

2378. HOLLINSHEAD, WILLIAM, London : 22 Mar. 1687, Y.

2379. HOLLOWAY, RICHARD, London : 10 Oct. 1745, Y.

2380. HOLLY, see HOLLEY.

2381. HOLMAN, ARY, London : 21 June 1764, Y. and L.; 1770, f.S.; 1778, f.R.W.; 1789, U.W.; 1790 and 1791, M. Dead in 1804.

2382. HOLMAN, EDWARD, London : 21 Mar. 1688, Y. Touch, 454 L.T.P., which he had leave to strike on 26 April 1689.

2382A. HOLME, CHRISTOPHER, Norwich : 1629, F.

2383. HOLMES, GEORGE, London : 17 June 1742, Y.; 28 Nov. 1746, L. Touch, 908 L.T.P. Had leave to strike his Touch, 22 Sept. 1743. His Trade Card (q.v.) gives his address as Drury Lane.

2384. HOLMES, JOHN, London : 23 Oct. 1755, Y.

2385. HOLMES, JOSHUA, London : 15 Mar. 1759, Y.

2386. HOLMES, MARY ELIZABETH, London : 17 Oct. 1751, Y.

2387. HOLMES, THOMAS, London : 23 Mar. 1709, Y.

2388. HOLSTOCK, JOHN, London : Fined for unseemly words to a brother-pewterer in 1563.

2389. HOLSTOCK, LAWRANS, London : Served in a band of trained soldiers raised by the Company in 1553.

2390. HOLSTON, ABRAHAM & CO., Bristol : Advertised on 26 Aug. 1775 and 2 Mar. 1776 in Bonner & Middleton's *Journal* as pewterers, braziers and brassfounders.

2391. HOL(D)SWORTH, JOHN, London : 23 Mar. 1826, L. *See* Holdsworth, above, probably the same man.

2392. HOLTON, ANTONINO, Bristol : Apprenticed to Edward Gregory, 9 Oct. 1707.

2393. HOME, JOHN, London : Of Snowhill, 14 Dec. 1749, Y.; 21 Jan. 1754, L.; 1763, S.; 1771, R.W. Touch, 965 L.T.P. In 1754 he was allowed " Mr. Warden Smith's Touch by consent," but on 19 June 1755 he was " ordered a new Touch as Smith still uses the old one." Struck c. 1754. (*Cf.* Nathaniel Barber, by whom he was succeeded. *See* note pp. 52 and 53.

2394. HONE, JOHN, London : 12 Oct. 1732, Y.

2395. HONE, JOSEPH, Bristol : S. of John. Apprenticed to Ann, widow of Allen Bright, 5 Mar. 1764.

2396. HONE, WILLIAM, London : 27 Sept. 1688, Y.; 30 July 1713, L.

2397. HOOLE, JAMES, Sheffield : 1682.

2398. HOOLE, SAMUEL, of ? : c. 1730.

2399. HOOPER, JOHN, London : 20 June 1765, Y.

2400. HOOPER, THOMAS, London : 24 June 1784, Y.

2401. HOOTON, WILLIAM, London : Mentioned in 1556.

2402. HOPE, ROBERT, London : 11 Oct. 1744, Y.
2403. HOPKINS, JOSEPH, London : 19 Dec. 1667, L.; 1671, f.S.
2404. HOPKINS, JOSEPH, London : c. 1700. Possibly a late mark of the last named.

2405. HOPKINS, THOMAS, London : 20 Mar. 1700, Y. Touch, 584 L.T.P., which he had leave to strike on 21 April 1701.

2406. HOPKINS, WILLIAM, London : In 1806 had a shop at Greek Street, Soho. A member of the firm Chamberlain & Hopkins, who in 1779 were at the same address.
2407. HOPPEY, GEORGE, London : 18 Dec. 1777. Y.
2408. HOPTON, SAMUEL, Eastington, Glocs. : S. of Wm. Apprenticed to Edward Gregory and Anne his wife, Bristol, 2 Nov. 1694. Turned over, 6 June 1696, to John Peters.
2409. HOPTON, SAMUEL, Ross, Herefs. : Mentioned in 1727 and 1736.
2410. HORNEBY, JOHN, York : 1535/6, F.
2410A. HORROD, R——, London : Touch, 28 L.T.P.

2411. HORROD, THOMAS, London : 22 June 1693, Y. Touch, 622 L.T.P., which he had leave to strike on 23 Dec. 1704.

2412. HORTE, RICHARD, Marshfield, Glocs. : S. of John. Apprenticed to James Cadell, Bristol, and Bridget his wife for eight years from 3 Sept. 1610. Turned over, 16 Mar. 1613, to Edward Hackerigge.

2413. HORTON, WILLIAM, London : 17 Mar. 1725, Y. Touch, 812 L.T.P., which he had leave to strike 20 June 1728.

2414. HOSKINS, JOHN, London : 9 Oct. 1735, Y.
2415. HOSKINS, THOMAS, London : 15 Dec. 1763, Y.
2416. HOSKYN, HENRY, Launceston : c. 1680-1730.

2417. HOSKYN, JOHN, TRURO : c. 1750.

2418. HOULDSWORTH, THOMAS, York : Son of John, Father of Thomas, Junr. Was apprenticed on 25 Mar. 1653 for seven years to Thomas Busfield. 1659/60, F. Searcher in 1665, 1668, 1670, 1674, 1678, 1681, 1686 and 1692.
2419. HOULDSWORTH, THOMAS, JUNR., York : Son of Thomas, Senr., to whom he was apprenticed for seven years on 16 Mar. 1680, 1692/3, F. Searcher in 1700.
2420. HOULT, JOHN, Bristol : 6 Sept. 1675, F. Apprenticed to William James.
2421. HOUSE, GEORGE, Bristol : S. of James. Apprenticed to Thomas Hale and Martha his wife, 28 July 1792.
2422. How, JOHN, London : 17 Oct 1762, Y.
2423. How, JOSIAH, London : 18 June 1713, Y.
2424. How, THOMAS, London : 16 Dec. 1714, Y.
2425. HOWARD, WILLIAM, London : 1680, f.S.; 1693, f.R.W.; 1700, U.W.; 1702, M. Touch, 204 L.T.P., which he had leave to strike in 1672.

2426. HOWARD, WILLIAM, ? London : Late seventeenth century. Drury Lane.

W·HOWARD

2427. HOWARD, WILLIAM, London : 13 Mar. 1745, Y.; 22 Oct. 1767, L.; 1773, S.; 1779, R.W. 1785, dead. Of St. Dunstan's in the West. Was gazetted a bankrupt on 8 July 1758. Touch, 920 L.T.P., which he obtained leave to strike on 19 June 1746.

2428. HOWART, ANDRO, Edinburgh : Mentioned in 1607.
2429. HOWE, JOHN, London : 9 Aug. 1711, Y. Had leave to strike a Touch on 21 Mar. 1716, but it is not on the Touchplate.
2430. HOWELL, GEORGE, Bristol : S. of Wm. Apprenticed to Preston Edgar and Rebecca his wife, 14 May 1792.
2431. HOWELL, PHUS (? PHILIP), Peterson, Mon. : S. of Roger. Apprenticed to John Pascall, Bristol, and Lucretia his wife, 23 May 1646.
2432. HOWELL, RALPH, London : 1623, f.U.W.
2432A. HOWELL, WILLIAM, Mangotsfield : S. of Wm. Apprenticed to Robert Bush, Junr., 20 Oct. 1796.
2432B. HOWELL, WILLIAM, London : Given leave to be partner with his father, 21 Mar. 1715
2433. HUBBARD, HENRY, London : 23 Mar. 1731, Y.; 15 Mar. 1732, L. Struck out and fine returned, 19 Mar. 1740.
2434. HUBBARD, ROBERT, London : 19 Mar. 1690, Y.; 12 May 1713, L.; 1717, S.; 1728, f.R.W.
2435. HUBERT, ISAAC, London : 20 Mar. 1755, Y.
2436. HUCHEN, WILLIAM (see also HUTCHEN), London : 1522, R.W.
HUCKS, see HUX.
2437. HUDSON, FRANCIS, York : 1756/7, F.

2438. HUDSON, GEORGE, London : Sent to prison for falsely mixing his metal in 1555.
2439. HUDSON, JOHN, London : Was free in 1494.
2440. HUDSON, JOHN, London : 22 Mar. 1770, Y.; 23 Aug. 1804, L.; 1808, f.S.; 1818, R.W.; 1822, U.W.; 1824, M. Died 17 Feb. 1829. Touch, 1021 L.T.P., which he obtained leave to strike on 20 June 1771. In 1793 and 1801 he was at 41 Fetter Lane.

SUPER FINE HARD METAL

2441. HUDSON, JOHN, JUNR., London : 15 Oct. 1801, Y.
2442. HUDSON, RICHARD, London : Was granted alms by the Company in 1555.
2443. HUDSON, RICHARD, Scarborough : c. 1770.
2444. HUDSON, THOMAS, York : 1604/5, F.
2445. HUDSON, WILLIAM, London : 9 Oct. 1729, Y.
2446. HUES, WILLIAM, London : Married at the Hall in 1572.
2446A. HUGHES, ———, Chester : In *Adams's Weekly Courant*, Chester, his shop and goods, copper, brass and pewter, were advertised on 27 Feb. 1750.
2447. HUGHES, JAMES, London : 17 Dec. 1691, Y. Touch, 493 L.T.P., which he had leave to strike on 15 Dec. 1692.

2448. HUISH, SAMUEL, Bristol : 4 Oct. 1776, F., by patrimony. Mentioned in the Poll Book for 1781 as of St. James's, Bristol.
2449. HULBERT, JOHN, Perth : In 1728 was an apprentice to Ninian Gray.
2450. HULL(s), JOHN (see also HALL and HULSE), London : 20 June 1776, Y.
2451. HULL(s), JOHN, London : Fined for false metal in 1450.
2452. HULL(s), JOHN, London : 28 Aug. 1685, L.; 1691, f.S.; 1697, f.R.W.; 1705, U.W.; 1709, M. Touch, 256 L.T.P., struck c. 1676.

2453. HULL(s), JOHN, London: 21 Aug. 1823, Y. and L.; 1838, f.S. Died 5 Feb. 1845, age 42.

2454. HULL(s), JOHN, London: 15 Mar. 1792, L.; 1795, f.S.; 1803, f.R.W.; 1809, U.W.; 1810 M. Died 10 Mar. 1833, age 80.

2455. HULL(s), JOHN, JUNR., London: 20 June 1799, Y.; 20 Aug. 1807, L.; 1812, f.S.; 1822, R.W.; 1827, U.W.; 1829, M. Died 13 May 1859, age 81.

2456. HULL(s), RALPH, London: 1668, f.S.; 1671, R.W.; 1677, U.W.; 1682, M. Touches, 46 and 208 L.T.P. He had leave to strike the later one in 1671/2.

2457. HULL(s), SAMUEL, London: 22 June 1693, Y.

2458. HULL(s), THOMAS, London: 3 Feb. 1825, Y. and L.; 1836, f.S.; 1847, f.R.W.; 1849, U.W.; 1850, M.

2459. HULL(s), THOMAS, London: 1629, f.S.; 1639, R.W.; 1645, U.W.; 1650, M.

2460. HULL(s), WILLIAM, London: 26 Sept. 1717, Y.; 21 Aug. 1718, L.; 1726, f.S.; 1734, f.R.W.; 1743, U.W.; 1744, M. He was dead in 1768. Touch, 712 L.T.P. He had leave to open shop on 10 April 1718.

2461. HULSE, CHARLES, London: 9 Oct. 1690, Y. Touch, 466 L.T.P., which he had leave to strike on 17 Nov. 1690 (Walter Sturt's Touch) (q.v.).

2462. HULSON, WILLIAM, London: His shop was on Tower Hill in 1524.

2463. HUMBER, BARTHOLOMEW, London: Fined for breach of rules in 1617.

2464. HUME, GEORGE, London: 20 Mar. 1700, Y. Touch, 598 L.T.P., which he had leave to strike on 1 May 1702. (Cf. No. 4326.)

2465. HUME, ROBERT, London: 18 Mar. 1790, Y.

HUMMERSTONE, see EMMERSTOW.

2466. HUNT, JAMES, London: 21 Mar. 1699, Y.

2467. HUNT, JOHN, London: 19 June 1701, Y.

2468. HUNT, SAMUEL, London: 23 June 1743, Y.

2469. HUNT, THOMAS, London: Touch, 194 L.T.P., which he had leave to strike in 1670/1.

2469A. HUNT, THOMAS, Newcastle: Purchased George Lowes' stock in 1765.

2470. HUNTER, ALEXANDER, Edinburgh: 1682, F. Touch, 84 E.T.P. ? same as 2471.

2471. HUNTER, ALEXANDER, Edinburgh: Mentioned as a Master in 1683. ? same as 2470.

2472. HUNTER, WILLIAM, Edinburgh: 1741, F.

2473. HUNTER, WILLIAM, Edinburgh: 1749, F. Touch, 140 E.T.P. In 1773 he had his shop in West Bow Foot. His Hall Mark is sometimes found in conjunction with W. Scott's Touch.

2474. HUNTON, NICHOLAS, London: 28 Nov. 1667, L.; 1670, S. Touches, 13 (?) and 143 L.T.P., struck c. 1663 and 1670 respectively. The small mark has been found in connexion with date 1661.

2475. HUNTON, WILLIAM, London: Touch, 376 L.T.P. which he had leave to strike on 29 Mar. 1683. Mentioned in the "Bennett" Book.

2476. HURDMAN, WILLIAM, London: 1611, R.W.; 1620, U.W.; 1622, 1624 and 1625, M.

2477. HURLOND, ROBERT, London: Was free in 1476 when he subscribed towards a set of feast vessels.

2478. HURST, WILLIAM, London: Touch, 278 L.T.P., which he had leave to strike in 1677 but no mention of him is in the Y. or L. Lists. He died in 1685. ("Bennett" Book.)

2479. HUSBAND, WILLIAM, London: 19 Mar. 1712, Y.

2480. HUSSEY, THOMAS, London: 10 Aug. 1727, Y.

2481. HUST, RICHARD, London: 17 Mar. 1774, Y.; 21 Mar. 1805, L.; 1809, f.S.; 1820, f.R.W.; 1824, U.W.; 1826, M. Died in 1835.

2482. HUSTWAITE, THOMAS (? HUSTWAYTE), London: 1505, L.; 1515, R.W.; 1521 and 1523, U.W. He gave a spoon to the Company on being admitted to the Livery.

2483. HUSTWAITE, RICHARD, London: Died in 1592.

2484. HUSTWAITE, WILLIAM, London: Fined for absence in 1532. 1538, R.W.; 1539 and 1545 U.W.; 1548, 1549 and 1559, M.

2485. HUSTWILL, ROBERT, London: 1571, S.

2486. HUTCHENS, JAMES (?HUTCHINS), London: 21 Mar. 1744, Y.

2487. HUTCHINS, WILLIAM, London: 15 Mar. 1732, Y. and L. Spelt Hitchins in Yeomanry list and Hutchins in Livery list.

2488. HUTCHINS, W——, Tavistock: c. 1680-1730.

W. HVTCHINS

2489. HUTCHINSON, JOHN (? HUTCHIESON), Edinburgh: 1794, F.

2490. HUTCHINSON, KATH, York: A freewoman in 1684.

2491. HUTCHINSON, WILLIAM, York: Father of William, Junr. Was apprenticed on 1 July 1663 for seven years to James Williamson. 20 Feb. 1672 F. Searcher in 1675, 1680, 1682, 1689, 1693, 1697, 1698 and 1699. City Chamberlain in 1698/9.

2492. HUTCHINSON, WILLIAM, JUNR., York: Son of William, Senr. Was apprenticed on 1 May 1698 for seven years to his father. 29 Jan. 1710, F. Searcher in 1712, 1713, 1717, 1718, 1719, 1724, 1731, 1738, 1747, 1749 and 1750.

2493. HUTTON, THOMAS, Edinburgh: In 1678 was an apprentice to Alexander Finlay.

2494. HUTTON, THOMAS, Canterbury: See his Token, which bears the date 1669.

2495. HUTTON, WILLIAM, Bristol and Caldecott, Mon.; 3 Oct. 1739, F. S. of Wm. Apprenticed to Edward Gregory and Anne his wife, 8 July 1730. Premium £30. Died in 1768. Mentioned in the Poll Book of 1739 as of St. Thomas's and in that of 1754 as of St. James's, Bristol. Partner in the firm of Ash & Hutton (q.v.).

2496. HUX, ELIZABETH GRAY, London: 13 Oct. 1763, Y.

2497. HUX, THOMAS, London: 10 Oct. 1723, Y.; 24 June 1739, L. Touch, 754 L.T.P., which he had leave to strike on 10 Oct. 1723.

2498. HUX, WILLIAM, London: 24 June 1700, Y.; 21 June 1722, L.; 1728, S. He was accused of using poor metal in 1703/4. Touch, 574 L.T.P., which he had leave to strike on 24 June 1700.

2499. HUX, WILLIAM, London: 17 Oct. 1751, Y.

2500. HUX, WILLIAM, London: 21 Oct. 1784, Y.

2501. HUXLEY, CHARLES EARLE, London: 21 Aug. 1823, Y. and L.

2502. HYATT, HUMPHREY, London: 11 Aug. 1681, L. Touch, 241 L.T.P., which he had leave to strike in 1674/5.

2502A. HYATT, JOHN, London: c. 1680. ("Bennett" Book.)

2503. HYLL, JOHN (see also HILL), London: Paid a fine in 1583 for having been away in the country for twelve years and was in this year received a brother again, so he must have been a freeman in 1571.

2504. HYLL, WALTER, London: 1583, S.; 1592, R.W.; 1596 and 1598, U.W.; 1601, M. Was imprisoned at Westminster for a cause not stated.

2505. HYLL, WILLIAM, London: 1585, S.; 1594, R.W.; 1599 and 1602, U.W.; 1612, mentioned.

2506. HYLTON, JAMES (see also HILTON), London: In 1457 was an apprentice to William Eyer.

2507. HYLTON, WILLIAM, London : In 1457 was an apprentice to Richard Lawton.

2508. HYLTON, ———, Cambridge : A Country member in 1475.

2509. HYLYNGWORTH, CLEMENT, London : 1537, R.W.; 1544 and 1550, U.W.; 1553, M.

2510. HYNDE, JOHN, London : In 1457 was an apprentice to John Lambard.

2511. HYNDESON, ADAM, London : In 1457 was an apprentice to Symond Drayton.

2512. HYNEFORD, JOHN, London : Was free in 1494.

2513. HYNDSON, JOHN, London : 1489, R.W.; 1493 and 1499, U.W.

2514. HYXSON, THOMAS, London : 1586. Was an apprentice to Christopher Strange and was whipped in the Hall for disobedience.

I

2515. IANSON, JOHN, of ? : c. 1730.

2516. IDLE, GEORGE, York : 1617/8, F.

2517. IEMPSON, SOLOMON (? TOMPSON), London : 8 Oct. 1696, Y. Touch, 541 L.T.P., which he had leave to strike on 15 Oct. 1696.

2517A. ILES, EDWARD, London : c. 1680. ("Bennett" Book.)

2518. ILES, JOHN, London : 14 Dec. 1704, Y.; 17 Aug. 1709, L. ; 1713, f.S., f.R.W., f.U.W. and f.M.

2519. ILES, JOHN, London : 19 Mar. 1723, Y.

2520. ILES, NATHANIEL, London : 17 Dec. 1702, Y.; 24 July 1719, L.

2521. ILES, RICHARD, London : 1697, f.S.; 1710, f.R.W., f.U.W. and f.M.

2522. ILES, ROBERT, London : 17 Mar. 1691, Y.; 12 May 1713, L.; 1717, S.; 1728, f.R.W.; 1735, f.U.W. Touch, 520 L.T.P., which he had leave to strike on 19 Mar. 1695.

2523. INGLEBIE, JOHN, York : 1566, F.

2524. INGLES, ARTHUR, London : 10 Aug. 1710, Y. Touch, 672 L.T.P., struck c. 1711 (q.v.), under Arthur Engley.

2525. INGLES, JONATHAN, London : Was fined for false wares in 1673. 1678, f.S.; 1693, f.R.W.; 1702, f.U.W. Touches, 19 L.T.P. (dated

1671) and 170 (dated 1670), which latter he had leave to strike in 1669/70.

2526. INGLES, SAMUEL, London : Of St. Andrew's, Holborn. Was married in 1667 at Gray's Inn Chapel. Touch, 199 L.T.P., which he had leave to strike in 1671/2.

2527. INGLES, THOMAS, London : 25 Mar. 1706/7 Y.

2528. INGLIS, ———, Southampton : Was excused from serving as U.W. in the London Company in 1698 owing to his having been elected Mayor of Southampton.

2529. INGLIS, ARCHIBALD, Edinburgh : 1732, F. Died c. 1777. Touch, 130 E.T.P. In 1773 his shop was in Kennedy's Close.

2530. INGLIS, GEORGE, Edinburgh : In 1656 was an apprentice to Thomas Inglis.

2531. INGLIS, GEORGE, Edinburgh : In 1792 was an apprentice to James Wright.

2532. INGLIS, ROBERT, Edinburgh : 1663, F. Touch, 65 E.T.P.

2533. INGLIS, ROBERT, Edinburgh : In 1710 was an apprentice to Thomas Inglis.

2534. INGLIS, THOMAS, Edinburgh : 1616, F. Touches, 27, 29 and 30 E.T.P.

2535. INGLIS, THOMAS, Edinburgh : 1647, F. Died c. 1668. Touches 47 and 48 E.T.P.

2536. INGLIS, THOMAS, Edinburgh : 1686, F. Touch, 87 E.T.P.

2537. INGLIS, THOMAS, Edinburgh : 1719, F. Died c. 1732. Touch, 123 E.T.P.

2538. INGOLE, DANIEL, London : 19 Dec. 1667, L.; 1669, f.S.; 1681, R.W.; 1688, U.W.; 1689, f.M. Touch, 52 L.T.P. He probably succeeded John Silk (No. 4286), whose "Hall Marks" and device he used. Left a legacy to the Company. Died 16 July 1691, aged 58. Memorial in West Ham Church.

2539. INGRAM, ROGER, Cork : Died in 1648.
2540. INGRAM, ——, Bewdley : c. 1770.
2541. INNALLS, WILLIAM (? IRMOLLS), Bristol and Keynsham, Somerset : 9 Mar. 1768, F. Apprenticed to Robert Bush and Elizabeth, 30 June 1759. Mentioned in the Poll Book for 1774 as of St. Michael's, Bristol.
2542. INON(E), JAMES, Bristol : 20 Feb. 1689, F., by patrimony. S. of Wm.
2543. INON(E), WILLIAM, Bristol and Chepstow : 21 April 1665, F. S. of John. Apprenticed to Richard Clifford, Bristol, and Sarah, 29 Oct 1656. Mentioned in 1674.
2544. IRELAND, ANN, London : 11 Dec. 1690, Y.
2545. IRMOLLS, WILLIAM (? INNALLS), Bristol : Mentioned in the Poll Book for 1781 as of St. James's, Bristol.
2546. IRVING, HENRY, London : 13 Dec. 1750, Y. Touch, 952 L.T.P., which he had leave to strike in 1750.

2547. IRVING, JAMES, Edinburgh : In 1642 was an apprentice to James Goldie.
2548. ISAAC, ROGER, London : Was free in 1560.
2549. ISADE, ROGER, London : 1569, S.
} ? same.
2550. ITHELL, WILLIAM, Bristol : 20 July 1719, F. S. of Wm. Apprenticed to Erasmus Dole and Sarah his wife, 10 Dec. 1691.
2551. IVES, RICHARD, London : 20 Dec. 1688, Y.

J

2552. JACKMAN, NICHOLAS, London : 8 July 1699, Y.; 15 Aug. 1709, L.; 1715, S.; 1725, f.R.W.; 1733, U.W.; 1735, M. Touch, 612 L.T.P., which he had leave to strike on 23 April 1703.

2553. JACKSON, HENRY (? JACSON, JAXON or JAKSON), London : (Westminster). 8 Aug. 1723, Y. Touch, 760 L.T.P., which he had leave to strike on 10 Oct. 1723. (Cf. Touch of Roger Moser.) Bankrupt on 24 May 1743.

2554. JACKSON, HENRY, London : 20 Oct. 1757, Y.
2555. JACKSON, HESTOR, London : 23 June 1763, Y.
2556. JACKSON, JOHN, London : 19 June 1735, Y.
2557. JACKSON, JOHN, London : 1566, S.; 1576, R.W.; 1584 and 1587, U.W.; 1589, M. Was fined

in 1571 for not accepting office as Master of the Yeomanry.

2557A. JACKSON, JOHN, London: 1684, L. ("Bennett" Book.) Touch, 282 L.T.P., which he had leave to strike in 1676/7.

2558. JACKSON, JOHN, London: 26 Sept. 1689, Y.; 1695, S.; 1704, f.R.W.; 1712, U.W.; 1716, f.M. This mark was not struck upon the Touch Plate.

2559. JACKSON, JOHN, London: 20 June 1728, Y.; 17 June 1731, L. This name and date have been put in the Livery List by a later hand. On 17 June 1731 he was given leave to strike the same Touch as his father had.

2560. JACKSON, JOHN, London: 17 June 1731, Y. Insolvent in 1743. (Son of John Jackson is pencilled in in the Records.) Touch, 855 L.T.P., which he had leave to strike on 20 Mar. 1734.

2561. JACKSON, MICHAEL, London: 15 Dec. 1757, Y.
2562. JACKSON, ROBERT, London: 23 Mar. 1780, Y.; 28 June 1781, L.; 1786, S.; 1795, R.W.; 1800, U.W.; 1801, M. Touch, 1051 L.T.P., struck c. 1785.

2563. JACKSON, SAMUEL, Dublin: Mentioned in 1669.
2564. JACKSON, SAMUEL, London: 1668, f.S.; 1673, R.W.; 1678, U.W.; 1684, 1687, 1690, 1700 and 1714, M.
2565. JACKSON, SAMUEL, London: Touch, 479 L.T.P., which he had leave to strike on 1 Jan. 1691.

White Cooke was apprenticed to him on 19 June 1712.

2566. JACKSON, STARTUPP, London: 1635, Y. Free by redemption.
2567. JACKSON, THOMAS, London: In 1640 he had trouble with the Company. 1647, S.; 1653, f.R.W.; 1658, U.W.; 1660, M.
2568. JACKSON, THOMAS, London: 1477, R.W.; 1485 and 1488, U.W.; 1492 and 1493, M.
2569. JACKSON, THOMAS, London: 20 June 1717, Y. This mark may be his.

2570. JACKSON, WILLIAM, London: 1505, L.; 1512, R.W. Gave a spoon on election to the Livery.
2571. JACKSON, WILLIAM, London: 13 Aug. 1668, L.; 1672, f.S.
2572. JACOB(s), JOHN, London: 1648 and 1649, S.; 1655, R.W.; 1661, U.W.; 1663, M.
2572A. JACOB(s), RICHARD, London: c. 1680. ("Bennett" Book.) Touch, 166 L.T.P., which he had leave to strike in 1669/70.

2573. JACOMB, JOSIAH, London: 12 Aug. 1669, L.; 1675, S.
2574. JACOMB, ROBERT, London: Touch, 236 L.T.P., which he had leave to strike in 1674/5. He is mentioned in the "Bennett" Book from 1679-86.

2575. JACOME, JOHN, London: Was a man of some position in the Company in 1639.
JACSON, JAKSON, see JACKSON.
2576. JAMES, ANTHONY, London: 28 Aug. 1685, L.; 1693, f.S.; 1701, f.R.W.; 1708, U.W.;

1713, M. Touch, 391 L.T.P., which he had leave to strike on 9 Nov. 1683.

2577. JAMES, HENRY, Bristol: S. of Henry. Apprenticed to William Barron and Rebecca his wife, 23 May 1676.
2578. JAMES, DANIEL, London: 17 Dec. 1691, Y.
2579. JAMES, J—— W——, Bristol: Of 81 Temple Street. Partner, c. 1846, with John and Joseph Blinman (*q.v.*).
2580. JAMES, JOHN, Dublin: Mentioned in 1772.
2581. JAMES, JOHN, York: 1477/8, F.
2582. JAMES, LEWIS, London: Touch, 184 L.T.P., which he had leave to strike in 1670/1.

2583. JAMES, PATTON, London: 21 June 1744, Y.
2584. JAMES, RICHARD, London: 13 Oct. 1709, Y.
2585. JAMES, RICHARD, Yarmouth: 1471, F. His trade is queried as pewterer.
2586. JAMES, THOMAS, London: 6 Oct. 1726, Y. Touch, 777 L.T.P., which he had leave to strike on 16 Feb. 1726.

2587. JAMES, THOMAS, Elmore, Glocs.: S. of Wm. Apprenticed to Thomas Williams, Bristol, and Mary his wife, 26 Nov. 1736. Premium £50.
2588. JAMES, WILLIAM, London: 20 June 1689, Y.
2589. JAMES, WILLIAM, Dublin: Died in 1783.
2590. JAMES, WILLIAM, Bristol and Trullicke Grange, Mon.: 18 Sept. 1660, F., S. of William. Apprenticed to Wm. Pascall, Bristol, 6 Aug. 1650. Mentioned in 1686.
2591. JAMES, WILLIAM, London: 14 Dec. 1749, Y.; 13 June 1751, L.; 1761, f.S.; 1766, f.R.W.; 1780, f.U.W.; 1781, f.M. 1782, died.
2592. JAMES, WILLIAM, of ?: c. 1750.

2593. JAMESON, JAMES, London: In 1680/1 was an apprentice, who, his sight not being fit for sadware, was permitted to serve a spoon-maker.
2594. JAMIESON, GEORGE, Perth: 1787, F. Founder.
2595. JAN, THOMAS, London: 1520, R.W.; 1529 and 1533, U.W.; 1535, M.
2596. JANE, GREGORIE, Exeter: Was a searcher for false wares in 1562.
2597. JACQUES, JOHN, London: 17 Dec. 1724, Y.
2598. JARDEIN, NICHOLAS, London: 1572, L. Married the widow of Robert Hustwaite.
    A heavy fine was imposed on him in 1573 for packing pewter without its being viewed. He refused to pay the fine and left the Livery.
2599. JARRET, JOHN (? TARRETT), London: 1638, f.S.; 1649, R.W.; 1653, U.W.; 1656, M.
2600. JARRET, JOHN, Newland, Glam.: In the Bristol Poll Book for 1781 he is mentioned as a Country voter of Claverwall, Newland, Glamorgan.
2601. JARRET, JOHN, Bristol and Clarewell, Glocs.: 30 Sept. 1754, F. S. of Philip. Apprenticed to Stephen Cox and Susannah his wife, 9 Sept. 1747.
2602. JARRET, WILLIAM, London: 22 June 1738, Y.
JAXON, *see* JACKSON.
JEFFERIES, *see* JEFFERYS.
2603. JEFFERS, GEORGE (*cf.* GEFFERS), Dublin: Mentioned in 1726. Died 1731.
2604. JEFFERYS, BENJAMIN (? JEFFERIES), London: 17 June 1731, Y.
2605. JEFFERYS, GEORGE, London: 20 Mar. 1689, Y.
2606. JEFFERYS, JOSEPH, London: 20 Oct. 1757, Y. Touch, 986 L.T.P., which he had leave to strike in 1760.

2607. JEFFERYS, SAMUEL, London: 13 June 1734, Y.; 24 June 1739, L. Of Middle Row, Holborn. Touch, 856 L.T.P., which he had leave to strike on 19 June 1735.

2608. JEFFIN, THOMAS, London: 23 Mar. 1709, Y.

2609. JENGLEY, JOHN, London: Served in a body of trained soldiers raised by the Company in 1553.

2610. JENKINS, DANIEL, London: Died in 1647.

2611. JENKINS, EDWARD, London: 17 Oct. 1805, Y. Died 22 Dec. 1850.

2612. JENNER, ANTHONY, London: 17 Oct. 1754, Y. Touch, 1015 L.T.P., which he obtained leave to strike on 17 Dec. 1767.

2613. JENNER, THOMAS, Bristol: 28 Mar. 1668, F. Apprenticed to Thomas Lodge.

2614. JENNINGS, JACOB, Barton Regis, Glocs.: S. of Thomas. Apprenticed to Wm. Hobson, Bristol, and Marie his wife, 21 Feb. 1602.

2615. JENNINGS, THEODORE, London: 8 Oct. 1713, Y.; 17 June 1731, L.; 1741, S.; 1747, f.R.W. Touch, 680 L.T.P., which he had leave to strike on 8 Oct. 1713.

2616. JENNINGS, THEODORE, London: 24 Mar. 1757, Y.

2617. JENNINS, THOMAS, Walsall: Buried 23 Mar. 1615 at St. Matthew's Church, Walsall.

2618. JENYNS, CHRISTOPHER, London: Was in trouble with the Company in 1576.

2619. JEROME, WILLIAM, London: 21 June 1759, Y.

JERSEY, see DE JERSEY.

2620. JEYES, JOHN, London: 15 Dec. 1763, Y.

2621. JEYES, JOHN, London: 15 Dec. 1791, Y.

2622. JEYES, JOSEPH, London: 24 Mar. 1791, Y.

2623. JOBSON, MATTHEW, York: 1634/5, F. Searcher in 1666.

2624. JODRELL, RAFFE, London: 1593, Y. and L. Probably not a working pewterer. He was granted Robert Nixon's place on the Livery.

JOHNESTONE, see JOHNSTON.

2625. JOHNSON, ALEXANDER (see also JOHNSTON), Dublin: Mentioned in 1688 and 1695.

2626. JOHNSON, AMOS, London: Mentioned in 1636.

2627. JOHNSON, CHARLES, London: Searcher to the Company in 1698.

2628. JOHNSON, GABRIEL, London: 15 Dec. 1785, Y.

2629. JOHNSON, HERMAN, London: Was free in 1581.

2630. JOHNSON, JOHN, London: 1666 and 1667, S.; 1670, f.R.W.

2631. JOHNSON, JOHN, London: 22 Mar. 1715, Y.

2632. JOHNSON, JOHN, London: In 1584 was apprenticed to Andrew Bowyar.

2633. JOHNSON, LUKE, London: 17 Dec. 1713, Y. Touch, 749 L.T.P. (dated 1723), which he had leave to strike on 10 Oct. 1723.

2633A. JOHNSON, NICHOLAS, London: c. 1680. ("Bennett" Book.) Touch, 332 L.T.P., which he had leave to strike in 1679/80.

2634. JOHNSON, RICHARD, London: 9 Aug. 1688, Y. The mark here illustrated may belong to this man, but it was never struck on the Touchplates.

2635. JOHNSON, RICHARD, Ludlow: Mentioned as a Master in 1730.

2636. JOHNSON, ROBERT, YORK: 1478/9, F.

2637. JOHNSON, SAMUEL, Dublin: Mentioned in 1711.

2638. JOHNSON, THOMAS, London: 13 Dec. 1722, Y.

2639. JOHNSON, THOMAS, London: Fined in 1616 for taking an apprentice without leave.

2640. JOHNSON, THOMAS, London: In 1567 was a Freeman.

2641. JOHNSON, THOMAS, London: In 1457 was an apprentice to John Mylys.

2642. JOHNSON, WILLIAM, London: 21 Jan. 1698, Y.

2643. JOHNSON, WILLIAM, London: Touch, 361 L.T.P., which he had leave to strike on 16 Mar. 1681. Is mentioned in the "Bennett" Book from 1680-86.

2644. JOHNSON, MRS., London: In 1666 was accused of mixing false metal for spoons.

2645. JOHNSON, ——, London : c. 1700. ? Wm. Johnson, 1698, Y. *Cf.* Barlow & Smith.

2646. JOHN(E)STON, JAMES, Dublin : Mentioned in 1698 and 1719, in which latter year he was one of a deputation from the pewterers to the Irish House of Commons.

2647. JOHN(E)STON, JOHN, Glasgow : 1659, F.

2648. JOHN(E)STON, R——, Edinburgh : In 1646 was an apprentice to William Sibbald.

2649. JOHN(E)STON, THOMAS, Dublin : Mentioned in 1724.

2650. JOHN(E)STON, WILLIAM, Aberdeen : 1723, F. Deacon 1741/2.

2651. JOLLY, JOHN, Edinburgh : 1714, F. Touch, 117 E.T.P.

2652. JONES, CHARLES, London : 22 June 1786, Y. Touch, 1062 L.T.P., struck c. 1795.

2653. JONES, CHRISTOPHER, London : 11 Aug. 1709, Y.

2654. JONES, CLAYTON, London : 16 Oct. 1746, Y.

2655. JONES, EDWARD, Bromyard, Herefs. : Apprenticed to Stephen Cox, Bristol, and Susannah his wife, 3 July 1758.

2655A. JONES, HENRY, London : c. 1680. (" Bennett " Book.) Touch, 253 L.T.P., which he had leave to strike in 1675/6.

2656. JONES, JAMES, London : In 1605 he had some porringers seized for being below the standard. He is mentioned again in 1609 as brother of Nicholas, who was at variance with him. 1628, S.

2657. JONES, JOHN, London : 13 Oct. 1763, Y.

2658. JONES, JOHN, London : 17 Oct. 1833, Y. Died 15 June 1845.

2659. JONES, JOHN, Bristol : 6 July 1671, F. Appren-to Erasmus Dole. Mentioned in 1712.

2660. JONES, JOHN, Bristol : S. of John. Apprenticed to Jacob Davis and Rachel his wife, 5 Sept. 1684.

2661. JONES, JOHN, SENR., London : 24 June 1700, Y.; 8 Aug. 1717, L.; 1725, S.; 1735, R.W.; 1744, U.W.; 1745, M. Touch, 553 L.T.P., which he had leave to strike on 24 June 1700. The same device " as John Jones " was granted to Wm. Glover Annison. (*See* No. 95.)

2662. JONES, JOHN, JUNR., London : 11 Dec. 1707, Y.; 18 Mar. 1735, L.; 1745, S.; 1750, R.W.; 1756, U.W.; 1758 and 1766, M. Dead in 1783. Touch, 822 L.T.P., which he had leave to strike on 11 Dec. 1729. Gave £600 in consols in 1780 in trust for poor Members and their widows.

2663. JONES, JOHN, London : 12 Oct. 1727, Y.; 23 Aug. 1750, L. His Touch does not appear on the Touchplate, but embodies the same device as that of the last named.

2664. JONES, JONATHAN, Chippenham, Wilts. : S. of John. Apprenticed to Erasmus Dole and Sarah his wife, Bristol, 26 Oct. 1680.

2665. JONES, JOSEPH, London : 23 Mar. 1748, Y.

2666. JONES, MARY, London : 11 Jan. 1719, Y.

2667. JONES, NICHOLAS, London : Fined in 1608 for approbrious words against his brother James.

2668. JONES, OWEN, London : Mentioned in 1641, 1647 and 1649, S.

2669. JONES, PHILIP, London: 11 Oct. 1733, Y.
2670. JONES, PHUS (? PHILIP), St. Michael's, Lanterna, Mon.: S. of Roger. Apprenticed to Bernard Benson, Bristol, and Marie for eight years from 12 June 1632.
2671. JONES, RICHARD, London: 17 Oct. 1728, Y.
2672. JONES, ROBERT, London: 28 Nov. 1667, L.; 1669, f.S.
2673. JONES, SAMUEL, London: 22 Mar. 1687, Y.
2674. JONES, SETH, London: 17 Dec. 1719, Y. Touch, 714 L.T.P., which he had leave to strike in 1719.

2675. JONES, THOMAS, London: 1632, f.S.
2676. JONES, THOMAS, London: 20 Mar. 1755, Y. Touch, 990 L.T.P., which he had permission to strike on 16 Oct. 1760.

2677. JONES, WILLIAM, London: 1666 and 1667, S.; 1671, R.W.; 1676, U.W.
2678. JONES, WILLIAM, London: In 1557 was in trouble with a brother member.
2679. JONES, WILLIAM, Bristol: S. of Richard. Apprenticed to Thomas Gwinnell, Bristol, and Marie, 4 Sept. 1627.
2680. JORDAN, JAMES, London: 18 June 1691, Y.
2681. JORDAN, JAMES, London: Pewterer and Church-warden. Was buried at St. Helen's, Bishopgate, 6 Dec. 1655.
2682. JORDAN, JOHN, London: 15 June 1727, Y. Touch, 828 L.T.P. He struck his Touch on 15 June 1732, being the same as Mr. John Stiles (*q.v.*), who, having left off consented thereto.

LONDON

2683. JORDAN, SAMUEL, Gloucester: S. of John. Apprenticed to Humphrey Beale, Bristol, and Margaret his wife, 12 Aug. 1652.
2684. JORDAN, THOMAS, London: 14 Dec. 1732, Y.
2685. JOSELYN, WILLIAM, London: 19 Dec. 1734, Y. and L.

2686. JOSEPH, HENRY, London: 24 Mar. 1736, Y.; 23 June 1743, L.; 1754, f.S.; 1760, f.R.W.; 1770, U.W.; 1771, M. Touch, 906 L.T.P., which he had leave to strike, 19 June 1740. Of New Street, St. Bride's, London. His Touch has been found in conjunction with that of Francis Piggott (*q.v.*). Partner in Henry & Richard Joseph.

2687. JOSEPH, HENRY & RICHARD, London: Touch, 1054 L.T.P., struck c. 1787. Partners, Henry (above) and Richard (below). Business at 9 New Street, Shoe Lane. They used the same address mark as Henry Joseph.

2688. JOSEPH, RICHARD, London: 23 June 1785, Y. and L.; 1790, f.S.; 1799, f.R.W.; 1804, U.W.; 1805 and 1806, M. Touch, 1054 L.T.P., struck c. 1687, *see* above. His moulds were sold in New Street, Shoe Lane, in 1815, as old brass for breaking up.
2689. JOSEPH, SARAH, London: 17 Aug. 1780, Y.
2690. JOYCE, JOHN, Bristol: Mentioned 1620.
2690A. JOYCE, JOHN, London: c. 1680. ("Bennett" Book.) Touch, 393 L.T.P., which he had leave to strike on 11 Jan. 1683.

2691. JUDSON, FARSHALL, London: 20 Mar. 1755, Y.
2692. JUPE, ELIZABETH, London: 20 Dec. 1781, Y.
2693. JUPE, JOHN, London: 9 Oct. 1735, Y. and L.; 1744, S.; 1750, R.W.; 1759, U.W.; 1761, M. Was elected Beadle, 17 Oct. 1765 and died in 1781. Touch, 878 L.T.P., which he had leave to strike, 11 Aug. 1737. His shop

was "The Pewter Dish," in Queen Street, Cheapside. *See* his Trade card.

2694. JUPE, ROBERT, London: 12 Aug. 1697, Y.; 30 July 1713, L.; 1718, S.; 1728, f.R.W.; 1735, U.W.; 1737, M. Died in 1737. Touch, 621 L.T.P., which he had leave to strike on 14 Dec. 1704.

2695. JUPE, ROBERT, London: 17 Oct. 1776, Y. Touch, 1040 L.T.P., struck c. 1780. (*Cf.* Touch of Robert Barnett.)

2696. JURY, GEORGE, London: His name appears in the Records, c. 1735, but is not dated.

K

2697. KAYFORD, FRANCIS, London: c. 1725. His name appears in the Records about this period, but no date appears.

2697A. KEBLE, THOMAS, London: c. 1680. (" Bennett" Book.)

2698. KEBORNE, WILLIAM (*see* also KEYBOURN), Cork: Mentioned in 1758.

2699. KEENE, NATHANIEL, Hawkfield, Lancs.: S. of Richard. Apprenticed to John Benson, Bristol, and Matilda his wife, 19 Dec. 1617. Dead in 1641.

2700. KEENE, NATHANIEL, Bristol: 28 Jan. 1621, F. Married Bridgette, daughter of Thomas Bushe.

2701. KEERSEY, ———, London: 1605. *See* note under Dawes.

2702. KELEFET, JOHN, London: In 1457 was an apprentice to William Randolf.

2703. KELK, JAMES, London: Son of Nicholas Kelk, with whom he was in partnership. 1677, S.; 1685, U.W.; 1687, M. Died in 1688. He was displaced from the office of Master in 1687 by order of King James II, but was Master again in 1688 until his death.

2704. KELK, NICHOLAS, London: Was a Freeman before 1641. 1659, f.R.W.; 1663, U.W.; 1665, 1681 and 1686, M. He died in 1687

and was buried at St. Michael's, Cornhill. In 1641 he was allowed an extra apprentice to replace one serving in the army. Touch, No. 4 L.T.P., restruck c. 1670 after the great fire of London.

2704A. KELK, THOMAS, London: Touch, 319 L.T.P., which he had leave to strike in 1678/9.

2705. KELLOWE, ROBERT, Edinburgh: 1715, F. Touch 118 E.T.P.

2706. KELLY, JOHN, Edinburgh : 1773, his shop was in West Bow.

2707. KELLY, JOHN, Edinburgh : 1794, F.

2708. KELSALL, ARNOLD, London : 9 Oct. 1740, Y.

2709. KELSEY, ELLIS, London : At one time apprentice and servant to Mr. Cacher, he was with others dismissed the Company for ever in 1555.

2710. KEMP, JOHN, Perth : In 1762 was an apprentice to David Young.

2711. KEMPE, THOMAS, London : In 1572 was fined being in possession of a false beam.

2711A. KEMPSTER, JNO., London : c. 1680. ("Bennett" Book.)

KENDALE, see RENDALE.

2712. KEN(D)RICK, JOHN, London : 23 Mar. 1737, Y. ; 24 June 1739, L. ; 1751, f.S. ; 1754, R.W. ; Touch, 885 L.T.P., which he had leave to strike on 23 Mar. 1737. His shop was near Cherry-Garden Stairs, Rotherhithe. (*See* illustration of his Trade Card.)

2712A. KEN(D)RICK, WILLIAM, London : c. 1680. ("Bennett" Book.) Touch, 291 L.T.P., which he had leave to strike in 1676/7.

2713. KENT, EDWARD, London : 26 Sept. 1680, Y. ; 1684, L. Touch, 385 L.T.P., which he had leave to strike on 21 June 1683.

2714. KENT, JOHN, London : 9 Oct. 1718, Y. ; 22 June 1749, L. ; 1759, f.S. Touch, 736 L.T.P., struck c. 1723.

2715. KENT, ROBERT, London : 16 Oct. 1794, Y.

2716. KENT, STEPHEN, London : 19 June 1766, Y.

2717. KENT, WILLIAM, London : Was free before 1611. 1623, S.

2718. KENTISH, SIMON, London : 12 Oct. 1693, Y.

2719. KENTON, FRANCIS, Bristol : 12 July 1687, F., S. of William. Apprenticed to Nicholas Lott, 23 April 1680. Turned over 26 Mar. 1683 to Thomas Baily and Avice his wife.

2720. KENTON, JOHN, London : 1684, L. ; 1694, S. ; 1702, R.W. ; 1711, U.W. ; 1717, f.M. Touches, 250 L.T.P., struck c. 1677, and 490 L.T.P., struck c. 1692.

2721. KERKEBY, WILLIAM, Canterbury : In 1475 is mentioned as a country member.

2722. KERR, GEORGE, Edinburgh : In 1774 was white-ironsmith with a shop in Nether Bow.

2723. KERR, GEORGE, Edinburgh : 1784, F.

2724. KERR, NORMAN, Glasgow : 1797, F. Coppersmith.

2725. KERSLAKE, ———, Crediton : c. 1720.

KERSLAKE
CREDITON

2726. KEUX, PETER LE, London : 18 Mar. 1779, Y. Touch, 1061 L.T.P., struck c. 1794.

2727. KEY, JOSHUA, London : His son Joshua was born 21 June 1656 and registered at St. Helen's, Bishopgate.

2728. KEYBOURN, GEORGE (*see* also KEBORNE), Dublin : 1817, F.

2729. KEYMER, JOHN, Llandewy, Pembroke : S. of John. Apprenticed to John Batcheler, Bristol, and Honor his wife, 3 Mar. 1700.

2730. KEYTE, HASTINGS, London : 10 Dec. 1730, Y.

2730A. KIDD, JAMES, Liverpool : In 1768 he is mentioned as a brazier and tinman, assigning his goods to his creditors ; in the same year John Parson has taken his old shop and in April 1769 Kidd appears as a Pewterer in Walter Street.

2731. KILBOURNE, PETER, London : Used the Crown and Hammer for his Touch Mark until 1565, when he was awarded the cost of a new Touch.

2732. KILPATRICK, ALEXANDER, Edinburgh: Mentioned as being a Master in 1810.

2733. KIMBERLEY, FRANCIS, London: Mentioned in 1609 and in 1628 was fined for taking away a customer from a fellow-member.

2734. KIMPTON, NATHANIEL, London: 16 Dec. 1697, Y.

2735. KING, ABRAHAM, London: 19 Aug. 1669, L.; 1674, f.S.; 1686, R.W.; 1691, U.W.; 1693, M.

2736. KING, ANTHONY, Dublin: Mentioned in 1745 and again in 1763 as of Cook Street, when he was Warden of the Dublin Guild of Smiths. He was subsequently knighted and was an Alderman and Coroner. His mark is found in conjunction with that of John Heaney.

2737. KING, CHARLES, Cork: Mentioned in 1830.

2738. KING, DENIS, Dublin: 1618, F.

2739. KING, HASTINGS, London: His name is in the Yeomanry Lists at Pewterers' Hall, c. 1731, but no date is given.

2740. KING, HUMPHREY, London: Was a Master in 1584.

2741. KING, JAMES, London: 21 June 1716, Y. Partner in Gray & King (q.v.). Touch, 711 L.T.P., which they had leave to strike on 19 Mar. 1718.

(This mark is not struck on the touchplate see Gray & King) H.H.C.

2742. KING, JOHN, Dublin: 1632, F.

2743. KING, JOHN, London: 27 Aug. 1694, L.

2744. KING, JOHN, London: 16 Oct. 1783, Y.

2745. KING, JOHN, London: 24 Mar. 1757, Y. Touch, 995 L.T.P., which he obtained leave to strike on 17 Dec. 1761.

2746. KING, JOSEPH, London: 1 May 1691, L.; 1709, R.W. (Cf. Nos. 4263, 5626 and 5650.)

Touch, 379 L.T.P., which he had leave to strike on 22 Mar. 1682.

2747. KING, RICHARD, London: Served as a soldier in 1552 against Sir Thomas Wyatt. Received alms from the Company in 1563 as a poor brother. 1580, S.

2748. KING, RICHARD, London: 14 Dec. 1704, Y.

2749. KING, RICHARD, London: 17 June 1714, Y.; 8 Aug. 1723, L.; 1729, S.; 1736. f.R.W.; 1745, U.W.; 1746, M. Touch, 723 L.T.P., struck c. 1722. Shop was known as "The Ostrich" against White Hart Court, in Gracechurch Street. See illustration of his Trade Card.

2750. KING, RICHARD, JUNR., London: 12 Dec. 1745, Y.; 18 Dec. 1746, L.; 1758, f.S.; 1762, f.R.W.; 1776, f.U.W.; 1777, f.M. Died in 1798. On 12 Dec. 1745 was granted leave to strike a Touch the same as his father's.

LONDON

2751. KING, ROBERT, London : 24 June 1698, Y.; 21 June 1711, L.; 1717, f.S. Touch, 648 L.T.P., struck c. 1707.

2752. KING, THOMAS, London : 11 Aug. 1681, L.; 1687, S. Touch, 259 L.T.P., struck c. 1676.

2753. KING, THOMAS, London : 17 Dec. 1719, Y.
2754. KING, WILLIAM, London : 20 June 1706, Y.
2755. KING, WILLIAM, London : 15 June 1732, Y.
2756. KING, WILLIAM HARRISON, London : 22 June 1786, Y. Touch, 1057 L.T.P., struck c. 1700, dated 1786.

2757. KINGSBURGH, ROBERT (? KINNIBURGH), Edinburgh : In 1794 was an apprentice with William Hunter.
2758. KINGSMILL, DANIEL, Bristol and London : 10 Aug. 1713, F. Son of William. Apprenticed to Theophilus Newton, Bristol, 1 Aug. 1700. In the Poll Book for 1721 he is given as of St. Ewin's, Bristol, in that of 1734 as of St. James's, and in that of 1739 as of Temple, Bristol.
2759. KINLOCH, JOHN, Edinburgh : From 1780-c. 1823 his shop was in West Bow. He is mentioned in 1781 as a master white-ironsmith.
2760. KINLOCK, JAMES, Edinburgh : In 1774 was a white-ironsmith with his shop in West Bow.
2761. KINNEAR, ANDREW, Edinburgh : 1750, F. In 1773 his shop was on the north side of Lawn market, in 1780 in Kennedy's Close, and in 1793 at head of Wardrop's Court. Touch, 141 E.T.P.

2762. KINNEAR, THOMAS, Dundee : Mentioned in 1716 as servitor to Thomas Forrest.
2763. KINNIBOROUGH, ———, Perth : 1607, F.
2764. KINNI(E)BURGH, JAMES (KINNIBRUGH), Glasgow : 1785, F. Was at 435 Gallowgate in 1805 as pewterer, copper and tinsmith.
2765. KINNI(E)BURGH, ROBERT, Edinburgh : 1794, F. In 1800 and 1805 his shop was on the east side of West Bow. Cf. Mark of William Hunter. Was in business in 1831.

2766. KINNI(E)BURGH & SON, Edinburgh : 1823. Successors to Robert Kinniburgh. Their shop was at 112 West Bow.

KINNIBURGH
&SON
1826

2767. KINNI(E)BURGH, SHERRIF, Edinburgh : 1803, F.
2768. KINNI(E)BURGH & SCOTT, Edinburgh : Robert Kinniburgh and William Scott, c. 1800.

2769. KIRBY, THOMAS, London : 13 Dec. 1722, Y. Touch, 806 L.T.P., which he had leave to strike on 7 Aug. 1729.

2770. KIRBY, WILLIAM, Bristol : 16 June 1579, F. Apprenticed to Henry Gibson.
2771. KIRKE, THOMAS, London : 8 Aug. 1728, Y. Touch, 773 L.T.P., which he had leave to strike on 8 Aug. 1728.

2772. KIRKE, WILLIAM, London : Was Beadle in 1503.

2773. KIRTON, JOHN, London: 28 Sept. 1699, Y. Touch, 597 L.T.P., which he had leave to strike on 2 June 1702.

 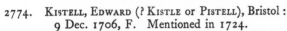

2774. KISTELL, EDWARD (? KISTLE or PISTELL), Bristol: 9 Dec. 1706, F. Mentioned in 1724.

2775. KITCHEN, THOMAS, Lawrence Weston, Glocs.: S. of Thomas. Apprenticed to George Benson, Bristol, 24 Sept. 1605.

2776. KNIGHT, ALEXANDER, Dublin: Mentioned in 1696.

2777. KNIGHT, FRANCIS, London: 1 Sept. 1685, L.; 1692, S. Touch, 345 L.T.P., struck c. 1680.

2778. KNIGHT, JAMES, London: 12 Oct. 1704, Y.

2779. KNIGHT, JAMES, London: Of Chancery, married 21 Feb. 1676. Touch, 261 L.T.P., struck c. 1676. Died 1685. ("Bennett" Book.)

2780. KNIGHT, JOHN, London: 4 Aug. 1715, Y.

2781. KNIGHT, RICHARD, London: 6 Aug. 1730, Y.

2782. KNIGHT, ROBERT, London: 22 Mar. 1770, Y. Touch, 1053 L.T.P., struck c. 1786.

2783. KNIGHT, ROBERT BENJAMIN, London: 13 Oct. 1808, Y.

2784. KNIGHT, SAMUEL, London: 14 Oct. 1703, Y. Touch, 689 L.T.P., which he was granted leave to strike, 9 Oct. 1712.

2785. KNIPE, STEPHEN, London: 14 Aug. 1718, Y.

KNOLLES, see KNOWLES.

2786. KNOWLES, JOHN, Bristol: 30 May 1625, F. S. of Richard. Apprenticed to Thomas Hobson for seven years from 12 Mar. 1613. Mentioned in old deeds in 1647 and 1651, and with his wife Marie in 1657.

2787. KNOWLES, RICHARD, Ashburton, Devon: Mentioned in 1613.

2788. KNOWLES, THOMAS, SENR., Ashburton, Devon: Mentioned in 1631.

2789. KNOWLES, THOMAS, JUNR., Bristol and Ashburton, Devon: 14 May 1647, F. Son of Thomas K. Senr. Apprenticed to John Knowles, Bristol, and Margaret his wife, 11 Nov. 1631.

2790. KNOWLES, TOBIAS (CAPT.), London: 4 Aug. 1664, L.; 1664, f.S., f.R.W., f.U.W. and f.M.

2791. KYCHYNE, THOMAS, London: Was Warden of the Yeomanry in 1549.

2792. KYKESBY, HARRY, London: In 1457 was a journeyman to Thomas Dounton.

KYLYNGWORTH, see HYLYNGWORTH.

KYMBLEY, see KIMBERLEY.

2793. KYNTHORP, JOHN, London: In 1457 was an apprentice to Thomas Grove.

2794. KYRKE, RICHARD, London: Was free in 1457.

L

2795. LACKFORD, JOHN, London: 4 Aug. 1664, L.; 1668, f.S. Of St. Botolph's, Aldgate. Was married on 22 Nov. 1670 at St. Mary's, Savoy.

2796. LAFFAR, JOHN, London: 20 Mar. 1706, Y.; 11 June 1714, L.; 1720, S. Touch, 684 L.T.P., which he was given leave to strike on 21 June 1711.

2797. LAIDLAW, ALEXANDER, Edinburgh: 1783, F. White-ironsmith. In 1774 his shop was at West Bow, 1786 in Luckenbooths, and in 1800 in Blackfriars Wynd.

2798. LAIDLAW, JOHN, Edinburgh: 1780, F. White-ironsmith, with his shop in Bridge Street.

2799. LAIGHT, WILLIAM (? LAYTE), Bristol and Tewkesbury: 8 July 1686, F. S. of Joseph. Apprenticed to William Barron, Bristol, 13 Mar. 1678.

2800. LAING, JAMES, Glasgow: 1783, F. Copper and White-ironsmith.

2801. LAING, JOHN, Edinburgh: In 1667 was an apprentice to Samuel Mabie.

2802. LAKE, RICHARD, London: 6 Oct. 1692, Y.

2803. LAKFORD, WILLIAM, York: 1480/1, F.

2804. LAMB(E), CATHERINE, London: 23 Mar. 1737, Y.

2805. LAMB(E), JAMES, Dublin: Mentioned in 1737.

2806. LAMB(E), JOHN, London: In 1457 was apprenticed to Piers Bisshop.

2806A. LAMB(E), JOHN, London: c. 1680. ("Bennett" Book.)

2807. LAMB(E), JOSEPH, MAJOR, London: 24 Mar. 1708, Y.; 17 Dec. 1724, L.; 1731, S.; 1738, R.W.

2808. LAMB(E), PENELOPE, London: 10 Oct. 1734, Y.

2809. LAMB(E), THOMAS, London: Died in 1452.

2810. LAMBARD, JOHN, London: Was of the Livery in 1457.

2811. LAMBERT, JOHN, London: 11 Oct. 1739, Y.

2812. LAMKYN, WILLIAM, London: Searcher in 1555.

2813. LANCASHIRE, ROBERT, Bristol and Critherington, Somerset: 25 Mar. 1651, F. S. of Jacob.

Apprenticed to William Lansdown, Bristol, 12 Feb. 1750. Appears in the *Bristol Journal*, 2 May 1772, in a list of prisoners for debt.

2814. LANCASTER, ALEXANDER, London: 9 Aug. 1711, Y. Touch, 750 L.T.P., struck c. 1725.

2815. LANDER, WALTER (? LAUDER), Edinburgh: In 1701 was an apprentice to David Symmer.

2816. LANDER, WILLIAM (*see* also LAUDER), Perth: 1597, F.

2817. LA(U)NDES, ROGER, York: 1597/8. F. City Chamberlain, 1605/6.

2818. LANDRY, JAMES, Bristol: 30 Mar. 1807, F. S. of John. Apprenticed to Preston Edgar and Rebecca his wife, 24 July 1794. Mentioned in the Poll Book for 1812 as of Rosemary Street, Bristol.

2819. LANDRY, JOHN, Bristol: Mentioned in the Poll Book for 1812 as of Rosemary Street, Bristol.

2820. LANDRY, JOHN, Bristol: Dead in 1794.

2820A. LANE, E——, London: Touch, 198 L.T.P., which he had leave to strike in 1671/2.

2821. LANE, JOHN, London: Served in 1543 in a body of soldiers raised from the Company.

2822. LANE, PHILIP (? LEANE), Bristol: Mentioned 1616-27.

2823. LANGFORD, JOHN, London: 18 June 1719, Y.; 26 Feb. 1734, L.; 1742, S.; 1746, f.R.W.; 1755, U.W.; 1757, M. and died. Touch, 713 L.T.P., which he had leave to strike on 24 Mar. 1719 (*cf.* Touch of Stephen Kent Hagger).

2824. LANGFORD, JOHN, London: 19 Oct. 1780, Y. *See* his Trade Card, which gives his address as "At the Riseing Sun, within Bishops-gate."

2825. LANGFORD, PERCIVAL, Bristol: S. of Robert. Apprenticed to Robert Belton and Jane his wife, 24 Oct. 1677. Discharged Feb. 1678.
2826. LANGFORD, THOMAS, London: 17 Oct. 1751, Y. Touch, 969 L.T.P., struck c. 1755.

2827. LANGFORD, WILLIAM, London: 16 Sept. 1679, L.
2828. LANGLEY, ADAM, London: 28 Nov. 1667, L.; 1669, f.S.; 1680, R.W. ? Touch, 91 L.T.P., restruck c. 1670, after the great fire.

2829. LANGLEY, JOHN, London: 22 Mar. 1693, Y.
2830. LANGLEY, JOHN, London: 21 Mar. 1716, Y. Touch, 727 L.T.P., which he had leave to strike on 6 Oct. 1720.

2831. LANGLEY, JOHN, London: 16 Oct. 1788, Y.
2832. LANGSHAWE, HENRY, London: In 1575 was ordered to alter his Touch for making false wares.
2833. LANGSTAY, THOMAS, York: 1591/2, F.

2834. LANGTON, JOHN, London: 14 Oct. 1731, Y. Touch, 865 L.T.P., which he was given leave to strike on 12 Aug. 1736.

2835. LANGTOSTE, NICHOLAS, London: 1517, R.W.; 1524, U.W.
2836. LANGTOSTE, ROBERT, London: 1499 and 1505, R.W.; 1509, U.W.; 1519 and 1520, M.
2837. LANGTOSTE, THOMAS, London: 1472, R.W.
2838. LANGTOT, THOMAS, London: Was of the Livery in 1457. 1468, U.W.; 1478, M.
2839. LANGWORTHY, LAWRANCE, Exeter: Touch dated 1719.

2840. LANSDOWN, NICHOLAS, Bristol and Sherbourn, Dorset: 1 Aug. 1727, F. S. of Thomas. Apprenticed to Roger Perkins, 4 April 1709. Mentioned in the Bristol Poll Books for the years 1734 and 1739 as a country voter.
2841. LANSDOWN, WILLIAM, Bristol: c. 1740. He died c. 1761, when an apprentice of his was turned over to Henry Burgum.

2842. LANYON, FRANCIS, Bristol: 26 June 1747, F., by patrimony. S. of Thomas. Mentioned in the Poll Book for 1754 as of St. Nicholas, Bristol.
2843. LANYON, THOMAS, Bristol and Coventry: 9 April 1715, F. Apprenticed to John Batcheler, Bristol, 2 Feb. 1707. Mentioned in the Poll Books for 1721 and 1739 as of St. Nicholas, Bristol. Last mention of him is in 1755.

2844. LANYON, THOMAS, Coventry: Mentioned in 1774.
2845. LARGE, WILLIAM, London: 1455, R.W.; 1459, 1463, 1469, 1472 and 1477, U.W.
2846. LARGE, THOMAS, London: In 1457 was an apprentice to William Large.
2847. LARKIN, FRANCIS, London: 8 Sept. 1685, L.
LASAC, *see* DE LASAC.
2848. LATHER, JAMES, Dublin: Mentioned in 1691.
2849. LATOMES, GEORGE, London: 23 Mar. 1737, Y.
2850. LAUDER, JAMES (*see* also LANDER), Bristol: 9 Mar. 1768, F. S. of Michael. Apprenticed to John Griffith, 20 Oct. 1750. Premium £10. Turned over to Allen Bright, 3 Dec. 1755. Mentioned in the Poll Book for 1774 as of St. Thomas's, Bristol.
LAUGHER, ———, ?: *See* Russell & Laugher.
2851. LAUGHTON, JOHN, London: Touches, 297 (which he had leave to strike in 1677/8) and 480 L.T.P., struck c. 1692. He is mentioned in the "Bennett" Book from 1679-86.

LAUNDRY, *see* LANDRY.
LAUNTOT, *see* LANGTOT.
2852. LAVYND, WILLIAM, London: Was an apprentice to Thomas Turnour in 1457.
2853. LAW, JAMES, Glasgow: Mentioned in 1784 as a coppersmith.
2854. LAW, JAMES, Glasgow: Mentioned in 1800 as a white-ironsmith.
2855. LAW, JOHN, Edinburgh: 1660, F. ? Touch, 61 E.T.P.

2856. LAW, JOHN, London: 15 Mar. 1759, Y.
2857. LAW, SAMUEL, London: 23 June 1768, Y. Touch, 1020 L.T.P., which he obtained leave to strike on 20 Dec. 1771.

2858. LAWE, GEORGE, London: In 1553 he served as a soldier in a body raised from the Company.
2859. LAWLER, WILLIAM, Cork: Mentioned in 1717.
2860. LAWLOR, JOHN, Carlow: Died in 1770.

2861. LAWRANCE, EDWARD (? LAWRENCE), London: 18 June 1713, Y. Touch, 741 L.T.P. Leave was given to him in 1713 to strike his Touch and be partners with his father.

2862. LAWRANCE, JOHN, London: 18 Mar. 1724, Y.; 15 Dec. 1726, L.; 1732, S.; 1739, f.R.W.; 1749, U.W.
2863. LAWRANCE, JOHN, London: 1 May 1691, L.; 1698, S.; 1710, R.W.; 1719, U.W.; 1723, M. Touch, 426 L.T.P., struck c. 1686.

2864. LAWRANCE, STEPHEN, London: 20 Nov. 1667, L.; 1671, f.S.; 1684, R.W.; 1686, f.U.W.; 1689, f.M. Touches, 123 L.T.P., restruck c. 1670 after the great fire, and 357 L.T.P., struck c. 1681 with his name in full.

2865. LAWRANCE, STEPHEN, London: 14 Oct. 1708, Y. Of Drury Lane. This Touch appears in conjunction with that of Nicholas Okeford.

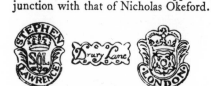

2866. LAWRANCE, THOMAS, London: Was free in 1457.
2867. LAWRENCE, ANTHONY (? LAURENS and LOWERANCE), York: 1559/60, F., and is later mentioned in 1593/4 and 1598/9. Father of Thomas.
2868. LAWRENCE, CHRISTOPHER, York: 1554/5, F. City Chamberlain, 1585/6. Father of Edmund.

2869. LAWRENCE, EDMUND, York: Son of Christopher. 1585/6, F., by patrimony.

2870. LAWRENCE, EDWARD, York: Mentioned in 1632/3.

2871. LAWRENCE, THOMAS, York: Son of Anthony. 1593/4, F., by patrimony.

2871A. LAWRENCE, THOMAS, Lynn: 1666/7, F. Apprenticed to Thomas Holland.

2872. LAWSON, DANIEL, London: 15 Mar. 1749, Y. Touches, 938 and 942 (repeated) L.T.P., which he obtained leave to strike in 1749. Of St. John, Wapping. Gazetted insolvent on 17 May 1755.

2873. LAWSON, JOHN, London: 17 Dec. 1713, Y. Touch, 688.B., L.T.P., which he had leave to strike on 18 Mar. 1713/14.

2874. LAWSTON, JOHN, London: Was an apprentice in 1457 to William Crowde.

2875. LAWTON, RICHARD, London: 1453, U.W. 1457, expelled.

2876. LAY, HENRY, London: 13 Aug. 1724, Y.

2877. LAYBURN, THOMAS, York: 1422, F. Father of the next named.

2878. LAYBURN, THOMAS, York: 1447/8, F., by patrimony. Son of the above.

2879. LAYCOCK, JOHN, London: 18 Dec. 1755, Y.

2880. LAYKOT, RICHARD, London: In 1457 was an apprentice to Thomas Dounton.
LAYNON, see LANYON.
LAYTE, see LAIGHT.

2881. LAYTON, WILLIAM, London: 19 Mar. 1729, Y.

2882. LEA, FRANCIS, London: 11 Aug. 1664, L.; 1668, f.S. Touches, 18, 39 and 40 L.T.P., all restruck c. 1670, after the great fire. His several marks may have been allowed to him as being a toy-maker for the faulty making of which he was fined in 1668/9.

2883. LEACH, JOHN, Bristol: 21 Mar. 1712, F. Apprenticed to John Jones. Mentioned in the Poll

Book for 1721 as of Christchurch, Bristol. He was recorded a bankrupt on 22 Sept. 1719.

2884. LEACH, JONATHAN, London: 12 Oct. 1732, Y.

2885. LEACH, JONATHAN, London: 7 Mar. 1742, Y.; 16 June 1748, L. Of St. Dunstan's in the East. He was gazetted as insolvent on 6 May 1755. Struck off and fine returned 19 Oct. 1769. Touch, 922 L.T.P., which he obtained leave to strike, having Mr. Tidmarsh's consent to quarter the same, on 20 Nov. 1746.

2886. LEACH, THOMAS, London: 1 May, 1691, L. Touch, 304 L.T.P., struck c. 1678.

2887. LEACH, THOMAS, London: 20 May 1736, L.; 1747, S. Touch, 725 L.T.P., which he had leave to strike on 8 Aug. 1721. Left a legacy to the Company.

2888. LEACH, THOMAS, London: 19 Dec. 1734, Y.

2889. LEACH, WILLIAM, London: 18 Oct. 1770, Y.

2890. LEADBETTER, EDMUND, London: 22 June 1699, Y.

2891. LEADBETTER, JOHN, London: 13 Oct. 1763, Y.

2892. LEAK, WILLIAM, London: 17 June 1703, Y.
LEANE, see LANE.

2892A. LEAPIDGE, ANNE, London: 20 June 1728, Y. Took up her freedom with her brother Edward (q.v.), but Anne only struck a Touch, and subsequently married Samuel Smith. See Touch, 808 L.T.P., under Smith & Leapidge.

2893. LEAPIDGE, EDWARD, London: 19 Feb. 1699, Y.; 2 Oct. 1702, L.; 1709, S.; 1724, R.W.

Touch, 568 L.T.P., which he had leave to strike on 19 Feb. 1699.

2894. LEAPIDGE, EDWARD, London : 20 June 1728, Y. Partner with Samuel Smith, 1727, Y., in Smith & Leapidge (*q.v.*).

2895. LEAPIDGE, JOHN, London : 23 Mar. 1737, Y. and L.; 1749, S.; 1753, R.W.; 1762, U.W.; 1763, M.

2896. LEAPIDGE, THOMAS, London : 17 Dec. 1691, Y.; 18 June 1696, L. Touch, 492 L.T.P., struck c. 1693.

LEATH, *see* LEACH.
LEATHERBARROW, *see* LETHERBARROW.

2897. LECHEFORD, JOHN, London : In 1457 was journeyman to John Pecok and in 1476 was a subscriber to a set of Feast-vessels.

2898. LEE, ABRAHAM, Bristol : 4 June 1705, F. Apprenticed to Thomas Baily. Mentioned in the Poll Books for 1721, 1734 and 1739 as of St. James's, Bristol.

2899. LEE, BENJAMIN, ? of Bristol : ? date.

2900. LEE, EDWARD, London : 20 June 1689, Y.

2901. LEE, JOHN, London : 19 Aug. 1669, L. Pensioned in 1685.

2902. LEE, SAMUEL, Barnstaple : c. 1720. He was buried at Barnstaple.

2903. LEE, THOMAS CHARLES, London : 22 Sept. 1785, Y.

2904. LEE, WILLIAM, Waterford, Ireland : S. of John. Apprenticed to Thomas Baily, Bristol, and Avice his wife, 19 Oct. 1691.

2905. LEACHMAN, JOHN, Glasgow : 1797, F. Whiteironsmith.

2906. LEESON, JOHN, London : 1663, f.S.; 1670, f.R.W.; 1675, U.W.; 1680, M. ? Touch, 15 L.T.P., restruck c. 1670, after the great fire.

2907. LEESON, JOHN, London : 15 Aug. 1689, L. Touch, 237 L.T.P., which he had leave to strike in 1674/5.

2908. LEESON, ROBERT, London : 1626, S.; 1635, R.W.; 1643, U.W.; 1648, M.

2909. LEETON, ROBERT, London : 18 June 1691, Y.

2910. LEFRENCH, ARTHUR, Perth : c. 1590.

2911. LEFRENCH, JAMES, Perth : 1603, F.

2912. LEGGAT(T), JAMES, London : 14 Aug. 1755, Y. and L.

2913. LEGGAT(T), RICHARD, London : 1746, Y.; 28 Nov. 1746, L.

2914. LEGGAT(T), RICHARD, London : 21 June 1722, Y. Touch, 771 L.T.P., struck c. 1727.

2915. LEID, GEORGE, Edinburgh : In 1667 was an apprentice to James Herrin.

2916. LEIGH, JAMES, Dublin : 1655, F.

LE KEUX, *see* KEUX.

2917. LENNIS, ROBERT, London: In 1630 was found with faulty metal.

2918. LESLEY, THOMAS, Bristol: In the Poll Book for 1754 is given as of Temple, Bristol.

2919. LESTER, ALLEN, Bristol: 30 Sept. 1637, F. Apprenticed to Thomas Gwinnell.

2919A. LESTER, GEORGE, Dorchester, Dorset: 1744.

2919B. LESTER, GEORGE, of ?: c. 1690-1700.

2920. LESTER, THOMAS, Cork: Mentioned in 1763 and 1775.

2921. LESTRAUNGE, STEPHEN, London: In 1349 was chosen an overseer of the Articles.

2922. LETHAM, JOHN, Edinburgh: 1718, F. Died 1756. Touch, 120 E.T.P.

2923. LETHARD, JAMES, London: 10 Oct. 1745, Y. Touch, 932 L.T.P., which he obtained leave to strike in 1746.

2923A. LE(A)THERBARROW, EDWARD, Liverpool: In 1757 was at the "Dish," near St. George's Square.

2924. LE(A)THERBARROW, JAMES, ? Liverpool: c. 1710.

2925. LE(A)THERBARROW, THOMAS, ? Liverpool: c. 1690-1730. See I. Hardman.

2925A. LE(A)THERBARROW, THOMAS, Wigan: Will proved at Chester in 1767.

2926. LEUETT, SAMUEL, of ?: c. 1720.

2927. LEWIS, DAVID, Bristol and Petersen, sup. Elz., Glam.: 3 July 1655, F. S. of William. Apprenticed to William Millard, Bristol, and Jane his wife, 15 June 1647.

2928. LEWIS, GEORGE, London: 19 Dec. 1706, Y.

2929. LEWIS, JOHN, London: 17 Dec. 1761, Y. Partner in John Brown, John Lewis & Joseph Brown. See Touch, 1002 L.T.P., under No. 631, which they had leave to strike, 15 Mar. 1764.

2929A. LEWIS, SQUIRE, Ripon: Mentioned in 1793.

2930. LEWIS, THOMAS, Llaneller, Mon.: S. of David. Apprenticed to William Pascall, Bristol, and Mary his wife, 25 Nov. 1642.

2930A. LEWIS, WILLIAM, London: c. 1680. ("Bennett" Book.)

2931. Ley, JOHN, Barnstaple: 1705-1733. Buried at Barnstaple, 30 June 1733.

2932. LICKORISH, JOSEPH, London: 17 June 1697, Y.

2933. LIDDEL, ARCHIBALD, Edinburgh: In 1784 was an apprentice to William Hunter.

2933A. LIFE, WILLIAM, London: c. 1700. See his Trade Card. Of 87 Golden Lane, Old Street.

2934. LIFFLEY, THOMAS (? LISSLEY), Bristol: 30 Oct. 1739, F. Mentioned in 1741. Married Margaret Pennington. Mentioned in the Poll Book for 1739 as of St. Stephen's, Bristol.

2935. LIGGINS, ROBERT, London: 9 Aug. 1733. Y.

2936. LINCOLN(E), THOMAS, London: 19 Mar. 1718, Y. Touch, 716 L.T.P., which he had leave to strike on 24 Mar. 1719.

2937. LINCOLN(E), THOMAS, London: 18 Dec. 1740, Y. Obtained leave to strike his Touch on 19 Mar. 1746, but probably used his father's, as his is not on the Touchplates.

2938. LINDSEY, GREENHILL, London: 17 June 1708, Y. Touch, 674 L.T.P., struck c. 1711. Was allowed to join Richard Drinkwater in partnership on 18 June 1713.

2939. LINDZIE, PATRICK, Glasgow : 1781, F. White-ironsmith.

2940. LINK, HENRY, Bristol : On 10 Nov. 1777 he advertised in Bee & Sketchley's *Weekly Advertiser* as a "Pewterer, Brazier and Brass-founder, next door to the Three Kings, in St. Thomas Street, Bristol."

2941. LINNUM, JOHN, London : 13 Jan. 1701, Y. LIPSLEY or LISSLEY, *see* LIFFLEY.

2942. LITCHFIELD, FRANCIS, London : 12 Aug. 1697, Y. Touch, 571 L.T.P., which he had leave to strike on 24 May 1700.

2943. LITCHFIELD, JOSHUA, Dublin : Of Back Lane. Died in 1745.

2944. LITCHFIELD, VINCENT, London : 9 Aug. 1716, Y.

2945. LITCHFIELD, WILLIAM, Dublin : Mentioned as succeeding in 1745 with George Gee, to the business of Joshua Litchfield, whose stock they purchased.

2946. LITSTER, JOHN, Darlington : On 10 Nov. 1770 a decree was made for the Administration of his estate (*London Gazette*).

2947. LITTLE, ANN, London : 14 Mar. 1765, Y.

2948. LITTLE, HENRY, London : 13 June 1734, Y.; 9 Aug. 1739, L.; 1751, S.; 1755, R.W. Touch, 875 L.T.P., which he had leave to strike on 16 June 1737.

2949. LITTLEFARE, THOMAS, London : 21 June 1705, Y.

2950. LIVINGSTONE, JOHN, Edinburgh : In 1770 was an apprentice to John Brown.

2951. LLEWELLIN, JOHN, Bristol : Was a partner with his brother Peter and J. W. James in 1846 at Castle Green, Bristol.

2952. LLEWELLIN, PETER, Bristol : In 1840-45 was a pewterer, brass cock founder, clock and copper manufacturer. In 1851 he had moved to Castle Street, where he was in partnership with his brother John, and J. W. James. He succeeded to the business of Emerson & Co.

2953. LOADER, CHARLES WILLIAM, London : Of New Street, Fetter Lane. 24 June 1784, Y.; 16 Oct. 1788, L.; 1794, f.S. Was struck off by order, 22 Mar. 1798. Touch, 1050 L.T.P., struck c. 1784.

2954. LOADER, JERE(MIAH), London : c. 1671. Touch, 156 L.T.P., struck c. 1671, but no mention of this name appears in the Y. or L. lists, but is mentioned in the "Bennett" Book from 1679-86.

2955. LOBB, WILLIAM, London : Was sent to prison in 1612 for using false alloy.

2956. LOCK, ROBERT, London : Had leave to strike his Touch in 1677/8. Mentioned in the "Bennett" Book from 1679-86. 20 Feb. 1692, L. His business was in Newgate Street and he was accused in 1689 of advertising by card. Touch, 303 L.T.P., struck c. 1678.

2956A. LOCK, THOMAS, London : c. 1680. ("Bennett" Book.) Touch, 411 L.T.P., which he had leave to strike in 1684/5.

2957. LOCK, WILLIAM, Wily, Wilts. : Apprenticed to Christopher Clements, Bristol, 3 Feb. 1707.

2958. LOCKHART, JAMES, Perth : In 1752 was an apprentice to David Young.

2959. LOCKHART, JOHN, Edinburgh : 1784, F. White-ironsmith. His shop was in West Bow in 1786.

2960. LOCKWOOD, EDWARD, London : 20 Oct. 1768, Y.; 24 June 1779, L.; 1785, S.; 1793, R.W.;

1797, U.W.; 1798, M. Dead in 1819. Touch, 1055 L.T.P., struck c. 1785.

2961. LOCKWOOD, GEORGE, York : Presented a mould to the York Pewterers' Company in 1616.

2962. LODER, HARRY, London : Mentioned in 1457.

2963. LODGE, PETER, Bristol and Nesherkellet, Lancs. : 6 Oct. 1630, F. Apprenticed to George Benson, Bristol, 10 Nov. 1609. Mentioned, with his wife Marjorie, up to 1677.

2964. LODGE, THOMAS, Bristol : 30 April 1659, F. S. of Peter, to whom he was apprenticed, 4 Mar. 1655.

2965. LOE, GILBERT, Dublin : Mentioned in 1668 and 1678.

2966. LOFTAS, JAMES, SENR. (? LOFTUS), York : Was apprenticed on 16 May 1661 for seven years to Matthew Jobson. 1670/71, F. Searcher in 1673, 1680, 1685, 1688, 1689, 1694, 1697, 1701 and 1702. Father of Richard Loftus, Junr.

2967. LOFTAS, JAMES, JUNR., York : Apprenticed on 22 Aug. 1707 to Richard Loftus, Senr. for seven years.

2968. LOFTAS, JANE, York : Was Free in 1684.

2969. LOFTAS, RALPH, York : Was Free in 1684.

2970. LOFTAS, RALPH, York : Apprenticed for eight years on 11 Nov. 1680 to James Loftus. 1696/7 F. Mentioned in 1707 and 1714.

2971. LOFTUS, RICHARD, SENR., York : Was free in 1684. Mentioned in 1707-8.

2972. LOFTUS, RICHARD, JUNR., York : Apprenticed on 1 May 1701 for seven years to his father, James Senr. 1706, F. Searcher in 1708.

2973. LOGAN, JOHN, Glasgow : 1792, F. Coppersmith.

2974. LONDON, CHARLES, Bristol : 22 Oct. 1679 F. Apprenticed to Lawrence Wyke. Mentioned in 1714.

2975. LONG, SEFTON, London : 1680, f.S.

2976. LONG, SEFTON, London : 1692, f.S.

2977. LONG, WILLIAM, London : 2 Oct. 1702, L.; 1707, S.

2977A. LONG, WILLIAM, London : Touch, 400 L.T.P., which he had leave to strike on 4 April 1684. 1684, L. (" Bennett " Book.)

2978. LONGE, JOHN, Bristol : 13 June 1670, F. Apprenticed to William James.

2979. LONGSAY, ANTHONY, London : Had ware seized at Lambeth Marsh in 1622. He was a partner with John Heath at Bedlam.

2980. LORYMER, FREDERICK, Bristol : 12 June 1818, F. Apprenticed to William Davis.

2980A. LORYMER, J. W., Bristol : In 1833 was in Thomas Street.

2981. LOTH, THOMAS, London : In 1457 was an apprentice to John Kendale.

2982. LOTON, EDWARD, London : In 1568 his tools were sold to pay a debt to John Sherwyn.

2983. LOTON, WILLIAM, London : 1558, S.; 1564, R.W.; 1567 and 1571, U.W.; 1575, f.M.

2984. LOTT, NICHOLAS, Bristol : 15 Sept. 1679, F. Apprenticed to John Jones. He relinquished the trade of a pewterer in 1683 and became a merchant.

2985. LOTT, WILLIAM, Bristol and Pensford, Somerset : S. of Nathaniel. Apprenticed to John Jones, Bristol, 20 Oct. 1671.

2986. LOTTE, THOMAS, London : In 1459 did thirty days duty as Watch at the Tower of London.

LOUGHTON, see LOTON.

2987. LOUND, JOHN, Edinburgh : In 1643 was an apprentice to Robert Thompson.

2988. LOVELL, DANIEL, Bristol : 8 Dec. 1685, F. S. of Edward. Apprenticed to William Inon and Marie his wife, 28 Aug. 1674.

2989. LOVELL, JOHN, Wells : 19 Nov. 1700, F. S. of Elie. Apprenticed to John Jones, Bristol, and Alice his wife, 17 Nov. 1693. Mentioned in the Bristol Poll Book for 1734 as a country voter.

2990. LOVELL, JOHN, JUNR., Bristol : 17 Aug. 1725, F. S. of John L. Senr., to whom and his mother Hanna he was apprenticed, 25 June 1717. Mentioned in the Poll Book for 1734 as of St. Thomas's, Bristol. He died c. 1742 and notices of the sale of his effects appear in the *Bristol Oracle* of 24 July 1742 and 21 July 1744.

2991. LOVELL, JOHN, Bristol : 26 June 1747, F. S. of John, to whom, with Betty, his mother, he was apprenticed, 1 April 1740.

2992. LOVELL, ROBERT, Bristol : 18 Nov. 1752, F. Apprenticed to his father John.

2993. LOVELY, JOHN, London : 19 Dec. 1734, Y.

2994. LOVERING(E), EDWARD, Bristol and Charlton-in-Hanbury, Glocs. : 28 June 1631, F. S. of Thomas. Apprenticed to Edward Hackrigge, Bristol, and Agnes his wife, 9 Mar. 1615. Turned over, Oct. 1620, to Thomas Gwinnell. Dead in 1652.

2995. LOVERING(E), EDWARD, Bristol and Sodbury, Glocs. : 9 Dec. 1654, F. S. of Thomas. Apprenticed to Edward Lovering, Bristol, and Alice his wife, 10 Nov. 1646.

2996. LOVERING(E), JOHN, Bristol : 7 May 1655, F. S. of Edward, to whom and his mother Alice he was apprenticed, 15 Aug. 1648. Died in 1679.

2997. LOVERING(E), JOHN, Bristol and Charlton, Glocs. : 21 Mar. 1682, F. S. of Thomas. Apprenticed to John Lovering, Bristol, 13 Nov. 1675, and turned over, 6 Feb. 1679, to Nicholas Lott and Elizabeth his wife. Mentioned in a Ch. Ch. Indenture, 24 April 1684.

2998. LOVERING(E), ROGER, Bristol and Charlton, Glocs : S. of Thomas. Apprenticed to Edward Lovering and Alice his wife for eight years from 3 July 1639.

2999. LOWE, ———, Glasgow : c. 1840-1870. This mark appears inside lid of a pear-shaped measure.

3000. LOWE, JOHN, London : Served in 1543 in a body of soldiers raised from the Company's members.

3001. LOWES, GEORGE, Newcastle : In the *Newcastle Courant* for 30 July 1774, appeared the following :

> " On Sunday morning died here Mr. George Lowes, formerly a pewterer in this place who had retired from business some years ago. He sold his stock to Thomas Hunt in 1765."

3002. LOWRIE, ROBERT, Edinburgh : In 1724 was an apprentice to James Cowper.

3003. LOWRIE, THOMAS, Edinburgh : 1675, F.

3004. LOXTON, RICHARD, Worcester : Mentioned in 1654.

3005. LUCAS, FRANCIS, York : Was free in 1684.

3006. LUCAS, FRANCIS, York : Apprenticed on 18 July 1697 for seven years to Janne Waid (a woman).

1704/5, F. Searcher in 1710 and 1711. Mentioned in 1732/3.

3007. LUCAS, JOHN, London : 19 Mar. 1746, Y.

3008. LUCAS, JOHN, London : 18 Aug. 1836, Y. and L. Struck out on his own petition and his fine returned on 21 Jan. 1847. Died 29 Aug. 1849, age 63.

3009. LUCAS, ROBERT, London : 1651, S.; 1659, R.W.; 1664, U.W.; 1667, M. Touch, No. 1 L.T.P., restruck c. 1670 after the great fire.

3010. LUCAS, SAMUEL, London : 20 Mar. 1734, Y.

3011. LUCAS, STEPHEN, London : 17 June 1756, Y.

3012. LUCAS, STEPHEN, London : 11 Oct. 1804, Y. and L.; 1809, f.S.; 1819, R.W.; 1823, U.W.; 1825. M. Died 5 Aug. 1844.

3013. LUCAS, WILLIAM, London : 24 June 1779, Y.

3014. LUDDINGTON, PAUL, London : 16 Dec. 1736, Y. LUDGATE, *see* DE LUDGATE.

3015. LUGG, JOHN, Ludlow : Pewterer and Brazier. 30 Aug. 1701, F.

3016. LUPTON, ROBERT, London : 23 Mar. 1775, Y. Touch, 1042 L.T.P., struck c. 1781.

3017. LUSSUM, HENRY, London : 18 Dec. 1760, Y.

3018. LUTON, THOMAS, London : 16 Dec. 1742, Y.

3018A. LYDIAT, SAMUEL, London : c. 1680. (" Bennett " Book.)

3019. LYFORD, NATHANIEL, London : 16 Dec. 1725, Y.

3020. LYMELL, RICHARD, Bristol : 8 June 1648, F. Apprenticed to Thomas Hobson and Elizabeth his wife, 17 Jan. 1626.

3021. LYNDSAY, ALEXANDER, Edinburgh : 1648, F.

3022. LYNDSAY, JOHN, Glasgow : 1706, F. Founder.

3023. LYNNE, WILLIAM OF, London : 1475, Y.

3024. LYNSEY, WILLIAM, London : Appointed in 1598 a collector for the Livery.

3025. LYON, GEORGE, Glasgow : 1785, F. White-ironsmith.

3026. LYON, JOHN, Glasgow : 1794, F. White-iron-smith.

3027. LYON, WILLIAM, Cork : Mentioned in 1747.

3027A. LYTH, WILLIAM, York : Partner with John Watson, Junr. Partnership dissolved 5 Sept. 1801, *vide London Gazette.*

M

3028. MABBERLEY, STEPHEN, London : In (16)76 he issued a token on which his address is given as Broad Street. Touch, 209 L.T.P., which he had leave to strike in 1671/2. *See* list of tokens at end of Chap. IV. Mentioned in " Bennett " Book, 1679-84.

3029. MABBOTT, WILLIAM, London : His birth was registered at St. Peter's, Cornhill. He is mentioned in 1659, and he died in 1680. (" Bennett " Book.)

3030. MABB(E)s, SAMUEL, London : 28 Aug. 1685, L.; 1685, f.S. Touch, 288 L.T.P., struck c. 1678.

3031. MABIE, SAMUEL, Edinburgh : Was a freeman in 1663.

3032. MABOR, RICHARD, London : 20 June 1706, Y.

3033. MACALLASTED, JOHN, Glasgow : 1777, F. White-ironsmith.

3034. MACDONNEL, JOHN, Limerick : Mentioned in 1820.

3035. MACGROWTHER, JOHN, Perth : Fined in 1532 for absence.

3036. MACHAN, ANDREW, Glasgow : 1787, F. Brass-founder.

3037. MAC——, A——, of ? : c. 1790 (? A. Machan).

3038. MACHGEY, THOMAS, London : 1539, R.W.

3039. MACKAIL, JOHN, Canongate, Edinburgh : 1707, was a master at this date.

3040. MACKEDOWNIE, WILLIAM, Edinburgh : In 1679 was an apprentice to John Watson.

3041. MACKENE, JOHN, Glasgow : 1793, F. Brass-founder.

3042. MACKENZIE, WILLIAM, London : 19 June 1794, Y.

3043. MACKIE, DAVID, Perth : 1801, F. Copper and white-ironsmith.

3044. MACKRIFFE, THOMAS, Hackfold, Lancs. : S. of Richard. Apprenticed to George Benson, Bristol, and Frances his wife, 12 Aug. 1618.

3045. MACNIVEN, MALCOM, Perth : In 1734 was an apprentice to Patrick Campbell.

3046. MACPHERSON, JOHN, Edinburgh : In 1719 he was an apprentice to John Letham.

3047. ? MACUGNAGA, RATELL, ? : Of Cornhill, London. Compare this mark with those of the Spackman family. It appears on a Tazza bought in Paris by Mrs. Carvick-Webster.

3049. MADDER, WILLIAM, London : 19 Oct. 1775, Y.

3050. MADDOX, RICHARD, London : Fined for approbrious words to Richard Staple in 1591.

3051. MADDOX, THOMAS, London : 15 June 1727, Y.

3051A. MADGWICK, GILES, London : c. 1680. (" Bennett " Book.) Touch, 371 L.T.P., which he had leave to strike on 8 Mar. 1681.

3052. MADLEY, STEPHEN, Landogar, Mon. : 20 June 1747, F. S. of John. Apprenticed to Thos. Page, Bristol, and Mary his wife, 1 June 1738. Premium £10.

3053. MAISTER, NICHOLAS, Lynn : 1471/2, F.

3054. MAITLAND, JAMES, ? Edinburgh : c. 1750. His mark appears on a flagon in Kilbernie Kirk.

3055. MAITLAND, JOHN, Edinburgh : In 1708 was an apprentice to John Weir.

3056. MAJOR(S), JOHN, London : 1638, S.; 1650, R.W.; 1654, U.W.; 1657, M.

3057. MAJOR(S), JOHN, London : c. 1700. This mark appears on some pewter formerly at St. John's College, Cambs., bearing also the crest of the Beauforts, founders of the College.

3058. MAJOR(s), THOMAS, London : 6 Oct. 1726, Y.

3058A. MAKEPEACE, THOMAS, London : c. 1680. ("Bennett" Book.)

3059. MAKYNS, WALTER, London : Previous to 1533 he must have been free as he was working for Thomas Fowst before then. 1559, R.W.

3060. MALLOM, LAWRENCE, York : 1504/5, F. City Chamberlain in 1527/8.

3061. MALLOM, THOMAS, York : 1527/8, F.

3062. MALLOM, WILLIAM, York : 1493/4, F.

3063. MALPAS, THOMAS, London and Feversham : Mentioned in 1494 and 1498.

3064. MALTON, JOHN, London : Was alleged to have infringed the Touch of Warden Allen in 1565.

3064A. MANISON, THOMAS, Birmingham : Given in the 1805 Directory as a pewter spoon maker of Snowhill.

3065. MANLEY, WILLIAM, London : 14 Oct. 1813, Y.

3066. MANN, JAMES, London : 17 Oct. 1793, Y.

3067. MANN, JOHN, London : 28 Nov. 1667, L.; 1669, f.S.; 1680, f.R.W.; 1684 and 1688, U.W.

3067A. MANNOCKE, JOHN, Norwich : 1575/6, F.

3067B. MANNOCKE, WILLIAM, Norwich : 1521/2, F.

3068. MANNYNGE, RICHARD, London : In 1555 was fined for failing to keep a contract to deliver certain goods. 1574, S. His wife was buried in 1571/2.

3069. MANSELL, RICHARD, London : 22 June 1769, Y.

3070. MANWARING, PHILEMON, London : 16 Oct. 1766, Y.

3070A. MARCH, EDWARD, Manchester : In 1788 was in Old Bridge Street. Pewterer and Brazier.

3071. MARCH, RICHARD, London : In 1635 was censured for bad workmanship.

3072. MARCHALL, WALTER, London : Was covenant man to John Whitehed in 1457.

3073. MARKHAM, RICHARD, London : 1702, L.

3074. MARKHAM, VALENTIN, London : Clerk to the Company in 1640, and presented them with a Bible in 1648 to replace the stolen one.

3075. MARKLAND, JOHN, London : 22 Mar. 1770.

3076. MARLER, THOMAS, London : Was free in 1457.

3077. MARROTT, HARRIS, London : 22 June 1710, Y.

3078. MARSEY, WILLIAM, London : 25 Oct. 1753, Y.

3078A. MARSH, JOHN, London : c. 1680. ("Bennett" Book.) Touch, 363 L.T.P., which he had leave to strike on 10 July 1682.

3079. MARSH, RALPH, London : 1650, f.S.; 1657, R.W.; 1662, U.W.; 1665, M. He died of plague the day following his election as Master.

3080. MARSH, RALPH, London : 28 Nov. 1669, L.; 1671, S.

3081. MARSH, THOMAS, Sebarrington, Notts.: S. of William. Apprenticed to George Benson, Bristol, for nine years from 25 Aug. 1601.

3082. MARSHALL, GEORGE, Hull : Was a pewterer who in 1598 signed the ordinances of the Guild of Smiths, in which the pewterers were incorporated.

3083. MARSHALL, HENRY, York : 1411, F.

3084. MARSHALL, JAMES, Perth : 1801, F. White-ironsmith.

3085. MARSHALL, JOHN, Perth : In 1747 was an apprentice to Patrick Halley.

3086. MARSHALL, ROBERT, London : In 1603 he married Anne, daughter of Thomas Steventon, pewterer, late of St. John's, Walbrook, at St. John's.

3086A. MARSHALL, THOMAS, Newcastle-on-Tyne : Bankruptcy is recorded on 25 April 1761.

3087. MARSHALL, THOMAS, London : 13 Dec. 1722, Y.

3088. MARSHALL, THOMAS, London : Touch, 406 L.T.P., which he had leave to strike in 1684/5. No mention of the name appears about this time in the Y. or L. Lists, but he is mentioned in the "Bennett" Book, 1684-1686.

3089. MARSHALL, WILLIAM, Maidstone : In 1566 was chosen to safeguard the Company's rights in Sussex and Kent.

MARSHAM, see MASHAM.

3090. MARSON, RICI, Walsall : His daughters Jone and Elizabeth were baptized at St. Matthew's Ch., Walsall, on 26 June 1592 and 24 Aug. 1595 respectively.

3091. MARSTON, NATHANIEL, London : 22 June 1671, Y.

3091A. MARSTON, SAMUEL, London : c. 1680. ("Bennett" Book.)

3092. MARTEN, ROBERT, London : 1655, S.; 1666, R.W.; 1669, f.U.W.; 1674, M. Died in 1674. Touch, 7 L.T.P., restruck c. 1670, after the great fire.

3093. MARTIN, JOHN, London : 19 June 1766, Y.

3093A. MARTIN, THOMAS, London : c. 1680. ("Bennett" Book.)

3094. MARTIN, WILLIAM, London : 15 Dec. 1726, Y. Touch, 799 L.T.P., which he had leave to strike on 14 Feb. 1726/7.

3094A. MARTIN, WILLIAM, London : c. 1680. (" Bennett " Book.)

3095. MARTYN, HARRY, London : In trouble with a fellow-member, Thomas Hassell, in 1552.

3096. MARTYN, JOHN, London : Was of the Livery in 1457.

3097. MARTYN, JOHN, York : 1473/4, F.

3098. MARYOT, THOMAS, London : Mentioned in 1476 as subscribing towards the cost of a set of Feast vessels.

3099. MARYNER, ROBERT, London : Mentioned in 1556.

3100. MARYNOR, EWARD, London : Was dead in 1601.

3101. MASHAM, HUGH, London : 18 April 1709, L. ; 1713, S.

3102. MASHERODER, ROGER, York : 1547/8, F., by patrimony, and is mentioned again in 1579.

3103. MASON, DANIEL, London : Fined in 1673 for false wares. Touch, 214 L.T.P., which he had leave to strike in 1672/3. Died 1681. (" Bennett " Book.)

3104. MASON, GUILBART, London : Mentioned in 1585

3105. MASON, JOHN, London : 1695, S. ; 1704, f.R.W.; 1713, U.W.

3106. MASON, JOHN, London : 11 Oct. 1722, Y.

3107. MASON, RICHARD, London : 19 Dec. 1667, L. ; 1669, f.S. ; 1679, R.W.

3108. MASON, RICHARD, London : Son of Thomas. 1573, Y.

3108A. MASON, RICHARD, Bristol : Mentioned in 1555 in St. Ewen's Accounts.

3109. MASON, SAMUEL, London : 16 June 1720, Y.

3110. MASON, SAMUEL, Dublin : Mentioned in 1798.

3111. MASON, SAMUEL, London : Of St. Mary's, Whitechapel. Married on 12 May 1665 to Elizabeth Champneys at Trinity Church, Minories. His name appears in the " Bennett " Book from 1679-85.

3112. MASON, THOMAS, London : Father of Richard. He was a poor member in 1554, to whom the Company granted alms. Dead in 1573.

3113. MASON, THOMAS, Bristol and Monmouth : 21 Jan. 1679, F. S. of Thomas. Apprenticed to Lewis Roberts and Ann his wife, 10 Jan. 1672.

3114. MASON, WILLIAM, London : 12 Aug. 1714, Y.

3115. MASSAM, ROBERT, London : 9 Oct. 1735, Y. ; 19 June 1740, L. Touch, 867 L.T.P., which he had leave to strike on 12 Aug. 1736.

3116. MASSIE, GEORGE, Perth : 1608, F. Potter.

3117. MASTEAD, RICHARD, London : Touch, 134 L.T.P., restruck c. 1670, after the great fire.

3118. MASTIN, GEORGE, London : 20 June 1749, Y.

3119. MASTIN, WILLIAM, London : 16 June 1748, Y.

3120. MATHERS, JAMES, London : In 1587 was Journeyman to Lawrence Wright, and in 1593 was fined for casting buttons of false metal.

3121. MATTERSON, THOMAS, York : 1684, F.

3122. MATTERSON, THOMAS, York : He was apprenticed for seven years on 14 May 1700 to Richard Williamson. 14 April 1712, F.

3123. MATTHEW(s), ABRAHAM, London : 6 April 1721, Y.

3124. MATTHEW(s), EDWARD, London : 18 June 1691, Y. ; 20 June 1695, L. ; 1701, S. ; 1717, f.R.W. ; 1724, U.W. ; 1728, M. Touch, 472 L.T.P., which he had leave to strike on 3 Dec. 1691.

3125. MATTHEW(s), F. H. & SON, LTD., London : Incorporated with Gaskell and Chambers, London and Birmingham. Nineteenth century.

3126. MATTHEW(s), GEFFREY, London : Was a master in 1559 when he had an apprentice. He is again mentioned in 1560 and 1561, in which latter year he was an overseer.

3127. MATTHEW(s), JAMES, London : 13 Dec. 1722, Y. ; 20 May 1736, L. ; 1746, S. ; 1747, f.R.W. Touch, 780 L.T.P., which he had leave to strike on 18 Mar. 1724.

3128. MATTHEW(s), JAMES, ? Bristol : c. 1740.

 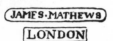

3129. MATTHEW(s), JOHN, London : Was in trouble with the Company in 1549. 1556, S.; 1569, U.W.
3130. MATTHEW(s), JOHN, London : 11 Oct. 1695, Y.
3131. MATTHEW(s), JOHN, Perth : 1724, a coppersmith.
3132. MATTHEW(s), NATHANIEL, Exeter : Opposite the Mint in Fore Street. c. 1850.

Nathl. Matthew

MAKER

Opposite the Mint

Fore Street EXON

3133. MATTHEW(s), PETER, London : 1624, f.S.; 1632, R.W.
3134. MATTHEW(s), PHILEMON, London : 12 Aug. 1736, Y.
3135. MATTHEW(s), PHILIP, London : 23 June 1743, L. Touch, 869 L.T.P., which he obtained leave to strike in 1736. } Same.

3136. MATTHEW(s), RICHARD, Bristol and Swansea : 14 May 1734, F. S. of Thos. Apprenticed to Thomas Cave, Bristol, 1 Feb. 1724. Premium £30. Mentioned in the Bristol Poll Books for 1739 and 1774 as a country voter.
3137. MATTHEW(s), ROBERT, London : 12 Oct. 1721, Y. Touch, 783 L.T.P., which he had leave to strike on 15 June 1727.

3138. MATTHEW(s), THOMAS, London : 20 Mar. 1711, Y. Touch, 702 L.T.P., struck c. 1716.

3139. MATTHEW(s), THOMAS, JUNR., London : 24 Mar. 1736, Y. Touch, 898 L.T.P., which he obtained leave to strike in 1741.

3140. MATTHEW(s), WILLIAM, London : 1676, S.; 1685, f.R.W.; 1686, U.W.; 1689, M. Died in 1689. Touch, 203 L.T.P., which he had leave to strike in 1674.

3141. MATTHEW(s), WILLIAM, London : 13 Oct. 1698, Y.; 28 Sept. 1699, L. Touch, 551 L.T.P., which he had leave to strike on 2 Mar. 1698/9.

3142. MATTHEW(s), WILLIAM, London : 8 Oct. 1721, Y.; 12 Oct. 1732, L.; 1741, S.
3143. MATHOS, HUGH, Bristol : 18 June 1572, F. Apprenticed to John Northall.
3144. MATTINSON, PETER, London : 15 Mar. 1743, Y.
3145. MATTOCK, ROBERT CLAYTON, Wells : Son of George. Apprenticed to Allen Bright, Bristol, and Ann his wife, 1 Aug. 1751. Premium £50.
3145A. MAUDSLEY, WILLIAM, Nantwich : Insolvent in 1737.
3146. MAUNDRILL, RICHARD, London : 3 Aug. 1693, L. A patentee of hollow pewter buttons with John Williams.
3146A. MAW, GEORGE, London : In 1817 was a Pewterer and Brazier at 48 Whitecross Street.
3147. MAW, JOHN HORNBY, London : 13 June 1822, Y. and L.; 1835, f.S.; 1847, f.R.W. Touch, 1087 L.T.P.

3148. Mawman, John, Cork: Mentioned in 1710. 1711, Warden; and 1716, Master of the Cork Goldsmith's Guild.

3149. Maxey, Charles Puckle, London: 14 June 1750, Y.; 17 June 1752, L. Touch, 950 L.T.P. On 14 June 1750 he was permitted to strike a Touch of a "Pelican in her nest," which on 13 Dec. 1750 was changed to a "Pelican on Globe." Never clothed in his Livery gown. He was allowed the use of the Pelican and Globe Touch instead of the late James King's (Welch, ii. 194). *Cf.* Gray & King, 1973, also 2741.

3150. Maxted, Henry, London: 16 Dec. 1731, Y. Touch, 861 L.T.P., struck c. 1735.

3151. Maxton, James, Perth: In 1761 was an apprentice to James Richardson.

3152. Maxwell, Matthew, Glasgow: 1785, F. White-ironsmith.

3153. Maxwell, Stephen, Glasgow: In 1781 is mentioned as Copper and White-ironsmith of Maxwell's Street, and in 1784 as a Pewterer. In 1787 he was on the south side of Argyle St. His Christian name is spelled Steven in a list of members of the Trades House.

3154. Maxwell, Stephen & Co., Glasgow: c. 1800.

3155. Mayes, George, Bristol and Doynton, Glocs.: 1 Oct. 1812, F. S. of George. Apprenticed to Robert Bush, Junr., Bristol, 14 Jan. 1796.

Mentioned in the Poll Book for 1812 as of Avon Buildings, Bristol. Was alive in 1833.

3156. Mayman, Thomas, York: Was free in 1616.

3157. Maynard, Josiah, London: 19 Mar. 1772, Y.

3158. Maynard, Thomas, London: 19 Mar. 1767, Y.

3159. Mayo, Daniel, London: 23 June 1709, Y.

3160. Mayors, Anthony, London: 1667, R.W.; 1668, U.W. ? Touch, 3 L.T.P., restruck c. 1670 after the great fire.

3161. McBeth, Adam, Edinburgh: In 1724 was an apprentice to John Clarkson.

3162. M'Call, John, Edinburgh: Mentioned in 1672.

3163. McCabe, Owen, Dublin: Died in 1769.

3164. McCulla, James, Dublin: Mentioned in 1719 and 1729. Was one of four petitioners to the Irish House of Commons, the former year, for the redress of certain abuses in the trade.

3165. McDaniel, Michael, Limerick: Mentioned in 1779.

3166. M'Clane, Robert, Edinburgh: In 1646 was an apprentice to James Monteith.

3167. M'Clean, Andrew, Edinburgh: 1660, F. ? Touch, 62 E.T.P.

3168. McNally, Ann, Dublin: Mentioned in 1788.

3169. M'Dougall, Hugh, Glasgow: 1798, F. White-ironsmith.

3170. Meacock, George, Bristol: 17 Sept. 1616, F. Married Mary Watkins.

3171. Meacock, Richard, Westchester (? Wistaston), Co. Chester: Mentioned in 1617.

3172. Meacock, William, Westchester (? Wistaston), Co. Chester: S. of Richard. Apprenticed to George Meacock, 2 Mar. 1617.

3173. Mead, Thomas, London: 23 Mar. 1720, Y.

3174. Meadows, William, London: 17 June 1714, Y. Touch, 704 L.T.P., which he was given leave to strike in 1716.

3175. Meakin, Nathaniel, London: 6 Oct. 1726, Y.; 18 June 1741, L.; 1753, S.; 1759, R.W.; 1767, U.W.; 1768, M. Dead in 1770. Touch, 843 L.T.P. Partner in Thomas Darling & N. Meakin, *q.v.*

3176. MEAKIN, NATHANIEL, London : 18 June 1741, Y.
3177. MEAKIN, NATHANIEL, JUNR., 17 Dec. 1761, Y.
and L.; 1768, S. Was appointed Porter on
20 Mar. 1783. Touch, No. 1000, which he
obtained leave to strike on 16 Dec. 1762, and
which see under No. 1302.

3178. MEARCER, ROBERT, London : 23 Mar. 1709. Y.
3179. MEARES, JOHN, London : 1657, S. Mentioned
in 1688.
3180. MEARS, JOHN, London : 11 Oct. 1750, Y.
3181. MEARS, RALF, London : 1631, f.S.; 1643, R.W.
3182. MEARS, THOMAS, London : Resigned the post of
Beadle in 1608.
3183. MEARS, WILLIAM, London : 1571, S.; 1582,
R.W.; 1592, U.W.; 1598, M. Committed
to the Fleet Prison in 1592 for an offence, the
nature of which is not recorded.
3184. MEARSE, JOHN, London : 1565, mentioned.
3185. MEASE, MATTHEW, ? Bristol : c. 1770. This
mark appears on pieces in conjunction with that
of Bush & Perkins, Bristol.

3186. MECHI——, ——, London : Nineteenth century. 4 Leadenhall Street.

3187. MEDCALF, STEVEN, London : 1587, Y.
3188. MEDDOM(s), RICHARD, London : Touch, 212
L.T.P., which he had leave to strike in 1672/3.
No mention of him appears in the Y. or L.
Lists, but he appears in the " Bennett " Book
from 1679-86.

3189. MEGGAL, ALEXANDER, Edinburgh : In 1663 was
an apprentice to John Harvie.
3190. MEGGOTT, GEORGE, London : 1637, S.; 1647,
R.W.; 1651, U.W.; 1655, M.

3191. MEGYLL, JOHN, London : In 1457 was an apprentice to Thomas Smyth.
3192. MELCH(IO)R, JOHN, Norwich : 1689, F. This
mark appears on a plate in the Castle Museum,
Norwich. The Melchiors were pewterers in
St. John's, Madder-market, and St. Stephen's,
Norwich.

3193. MELLAWES, ——, London : In 1570 was appointed grand captain of twenty soldiers provided by the Company.
MELLETT, see MILLETT.
3194. MENZIES, ALEXANDER, Edinburgh : 1675, F.
3195. MENZIES, ROBERT, Perth : 1781, F. Coppersmith.
3196. MERCHANT, ALEXANDER, Edinburgh : In 1755
was an apprentice to William Hunter.
3197. MERCHANT, JOHN, ? Edinburgh : Eighteenth century.
3198. MEREDITH, JOHN, Bristol and English Bicknor,
Glocs.: 15 Feb. 1756, F. S. of James. Apprenticed to Allen Bright, Bristol, 1 Sept. 1747.
Premium £40. Turned over, 30 Jan. 1752, to
Stephen Cox and his wife Susannah. In the
Poll Book for 1774 he is given as of St. Stephen's,
Bristol, and in those of 1781 and 1784 as a
pewterer (country voter) of Fountain's Court,
Shoe Lane, London. He was gazetted as
Insolvent on 1 April 1777.
3199. MERIEFIELD, EDWARD, London : 9 Aug. 1716,
Y. Touch, 770 L.T.P., which he had leave to
strike on 8 Oct. 1724. He was succeeded by
John Townsend.

3200. MERIEFIELD, ROBERT, London : 21 June 1705, Y.
3201. MERLOWE, THOMAS, London : 1452, Y.
3202. MERRIOTT, JOHN, London : 8 Aug. 1717, Y.
3203. MERRIT, JONATHAN, London : 13 Oct. 1743, Y.
3204. MERRIWEATHER, JOHN, London : 22 Jan. 1718,
Y. Touch, 720 L.T.P., which he had leave
to strike on 19 Mar. 1718/9.

3205. MERRIWEATHER, JOHN CORNELIUS, London : 17 Mar. 1747, Y. Touch, 936 L.T.P., which he obtained leave to strike on 19 Oct. 1749. He was allowed the same device as his late master, John Wyat (q.v.), No. 5314.

3206. MERRY, LAWRENCE, Dublin : c. 1845/65. Partner in Lawrence & Richard Merry.
3207. MERRY, LAWRENCE & RICHARD, Dublin : c. 1850.

3208. MERRY, MARTIN, Dublin : Mentioned in 1824.

3209. MERRY, RICHARD, Dublin : c. 1845/65. Partner in Lawrence & Richard Merry.
3210. MERRY, RICHARD, London : Mentioned in 1621.
3211. METCALF, GEORGE, York : 1598/9, F. Mentioned later in 1616.
3212. METCALF, WILLIAM, York : Apprenticed for seven years on 26 Oct. 1692 to James Secker.
3213. M'EWEN, JAMES, Perth : Apprentice in 1798 to John Clerk.
3213A. MICHETT (? MITCHELL), THOMAS, Norwich : 1466/7, F.
3214. MIDDLETON, CHARLES, London : 19 Mar. 1690, Y. Touch, 524 L.T.P., which he had leave to strike on 28 Mar. 1695.

3215. MIDDLETON, LEONARD, London : 14 Dec. 1749, Y.; 17 June 1752, L.
3216. MIDDLETON, THOMAS, London : Touch, 226 L.T.P., which he had leave to strike in 1673/4. No mention of the owner's name appears in the Y. or L. Lists, but it is in the "Bennett" Book from 1679-86.

3216A. MILBURN, RICHARD, Newcastle : Gazetted as insolvent on 20 June 1769.

3217. MILES, SAMUEL, London : 21 Jan. 1726, Y. Touch, 776 L.T.P., struck 20 Jan. 1728, when he had leave to strike Touch of John Blenman, deceased.

3218. MILES, WILLIAM, London : 22 Mar. 1715, Y. Touch, 706 L.T.P., which he was given leave to strike on 18 Mar. 1716.

3219. MILLAR, ROBERT, Dundee : 1773, F. White-ironsmith.
3220. MILLARD, WILLIAM (? MILLER), Bristol : 11 Oct. 1645, F. Mentioned in 1664.
3221. MILLER, CHARLES, Glasgow : 1785, F. Coppersmith.
3222. MILLER, GEORGE, London : In 1597 was in trouble with a fellow-member, Humfry Baker.
3223. MILLER, JOHN, London : Mentioned. Probably a clerical error for George, see last entry.
3224. MILLER, ROBERT, Glasgow : 1777, F. Coppersmith.
3225. MILLER, SAMUEL, Edinburgh : 1672. F.
3226. MILLETT, CAPT. RICHARD, London : 1652, S.; 1657, f.R.W.; 1660, R.W.; 1665, f.U.W. Did not serve as Upper Warden on account of the Plague being in his house.
3227. MILLIN, WILLIAM, London : 21 Mar. 1776, Y.; 22 June 1786, L.; 1792, f.S. Touch, 1044 L.T.P., struck c. 1782 (cf. Touch, 989 under T.S.). Business at Saffron Hill.

3228. MILLIS, NICHOLAS (? WILLIS), London : 1529, R.W.
3228A. MILLS, EDMUND (? MYLLS), Exeter : Retired in 1789.
3229. MILLS, NATHANIEL (MYLLS), London : 6 Aug. 1668, L. and f.R.W.; 1672, f.U.W.
3230. MILLS, WILLIAM (? MYLLS), London : 1556, S.; 1557, R.W.; 1561, U.W.; 1564, 1568 and 1571, M.
3231. MILLWARD, WILLIAM, London : 11 Oct. 1711, Y.

3231A. MILMAN, JNO., London : c. 1680. ("Bennett" Book.)

3232. MILTON, WHELER, London : 1650, S.
3233. M'ILVEEAR, ? ——, Glasgow : 1652, F. White-ironsmith.
3234. M'INDOE, JOHN, Glasgow : 1789, F. White-ironsmith.
3235. MISTER, EDWARD ATKINS, London : 21 Aug. 1823, Y. and L.; 1836, f.S. Died 15 Sept. 1846.
3236. MISTER, RICHARD, London : 17 June 1802, Y.; 20 June 1805, L.; 1810, f.S.; 1820, R.W.; 1825, U.W.; 1827, M. Died 20 Oct. 1839, age 65. Of 86 Bermondsey Street. Touch, 1085 L.T.P. John Moody (q.v.) was at the same address.

3237. MISTER, WILLIAM, London : 24 Aug. 1820, Y. Of 232 Kent Street, Borough.
3238. MITCHELL, ANDREW, Edinburgh : In 1695 was an apprentice to David Symmers.
3238A. MITCHELL, BENNET, St. Austell (Cornwall) : Mentioned in 1793.
3239. MITCHELL, DAVID, Edinburgh : In 1718 was an apprentice to Robert Reid.
3240. MITCHELL, HUGH, Edinburgh : 1741, F.
3241. MITCHELL, HUMPHREY, London : Mentioned in 1614.
3242. MITCHELL, JAMES, Penzance : At a Court, 5 Oct. 1681/2, he was refused the Freedom of the London Company as a country member, though he had served a seven years' apprenticeship to a pewterer in Penzance.
3243. MITCHELL, JOHN, London : 1619, S.
3243A. MITCHELL, JOHN, London : c. 1680. ("Bennett" Book.)
3244. MITCHELL, JOHN, London : It is recorded that in 1742 he struck his Touch. 21 Mar. 1744, L.; 1755, S. 1758, dead. He was apprenticed to Thomas Cartwright. Touch, 893 L.T.P. (See Wood & Mitchell.)
3245. MITCHELL, PAUL, London : 10 Aug. 1721, Y.; 5 July 1728, L.; 1739, S. Touch, 766 L.T.P., which he had leave to strike in 1723.

3246. MITCHELL, THOMAS, Edinburgh : 1704, F. Touch, 107 E.T.P.

3247. MITCHELL, WILLIAM, Edinburgh : 1717, F.
3248. M'KELL, MATTHEW, Edinburgh : In 1716 was an apprentice to John Jolly.
3249. M'KENDRICK, ANDREW, Glasgow : 1788, F.
3250. M'KENDRICK, JOSEPH, Glasgow : In 1776 was an apprentice to Matthew Connel.
3251. M'KENZIE, JOHN, Aberdeen : In 1682 was an apprentice to George Row.
3252. M'NAB, ALEXANDER, Edinburgh : In 1793 was a white-ironsmith with his shop in Potter-row.
3253. M'NEILL, HENRY, Glasgow : 1784, F. Copper-smith.
3254. MOGG, CHRISTOPHER, London : 16 Dec. 1708, Y.
3255. MOIR, ALEXANDER, Edinburgh : 1675, F. ? Touch, 76 E.T.P.

3256. MOIR, ROBERT, Edinburgh : 1664, F.
3257. MOIRSON, WILLIAM, Edinburgh : In 1687 was an apprentice to William Harvie.
3258. MOKLAY, JOHN, Edinburgh : 1693, F.
3259. MOLENS, ROBERT, London : Fined in 1614 for allowing his apprentice to buy from another apprentice.
MOLESWORTH, see MOULESWORTH.
3260. MOLLINS, ROBERT (see also MOULINS), London : 1658, S.; 1668, f.R.W.; 1670, U.W.; 1676 and 1689, M.
3261. MOLLYNARS, RAWFFE, London : Served in 1553 as a soldier.
3262. MOLTON, JOHN, London : 19 Dec. 1667, L.; 1669, f.S.; 1678, f.R.W.; 1683, f.U.W.; 1688, f.M. A member of the Company but a weaver by trade.
3263. MOMFORD, EDWARD (see also MUMFORD), London: 19 June 1712, Y.
3264. MOMFORD, JOHN, London : 1630, S.; 1641, R.W.
3265. MONCRIEFF, MUNGO, Perth : In 1733 was an apprentice to Ninian Gray.
3266. M'ONEE, ANDREW, Edinburgh : In 1656 was an apprentice to James Harvie.
3267. MONK, GEORGE, London : 23 Mar. 1731, Y.

3268. MONK, JOSEPH, London: 20 Oct. 1757, Y. Touches, 1022 and 1030 L.T.P., struck c. 1771.

3269. MONKHOUSE, EVERARD, London: 16 June 1715, Y.
3270. MONROE, JAMES, Dublin: Mentioned in 1728.
3271. MONTEITH, JAMES, Edinburgh: 1634, F. Touch, 41 E.T.P.

3272. MONTEITH, JAMES, Edinburgh: 1643, F. Touch, 44 E.T.P.

3273. MONTEITH, JAMES, Edinburgh: 1778, F.
3274. MON(T)GOMBERYE, JOHN, Bristol: 22 Nov. 1610, F. Married Mary Baker.
3275. MOODY, JOHN BOUCHER, London: 20 June 1816, Y. Entered first in the Records as John Moody, but altered by order of the Court on 24 April 1845, Boucher being added. His address is the same as Richard Mister (q.v.).

3276. MOOK, RICHARD, York: 1767, F., by patrimony. Son of Thomas Mook, tailor.
3277. MOOR, SAMUEL, London: 22 Mar. 1704, Y.
3278. MOORE, BRYAN, London: 17 Dec. 1691, Y.
3278A. MOORE, HENRY, Derby: Apprentice to Edward Leapidge, 20 Dec. 1711.
3278B. MOORE, HENRY, Derby: Father of the last named.
3279. MOORE, JOHN, London: 10 Oct. 1700, Y.
3280. MOORE, SAMUEL, Bristol: 4 April 1671, F., by redemption.
3281. MOORE, MRS. SICELY, London: 1679, Y.
3282. MORE, BENJAMIN, London: 11 Mar. 1707, Y.
3283. MORESLEY, RICHARD, London: In 1457 was an apprentice to John Kendale.
3284. MORGAN, CHARLES, Bristol and Bedminster: 3 Oct. 1812, F. S. of John. Apprenticed to Robert Bush, Bristol, 8 Dec. 1791. Is mentioned in the Poll Book for 1812 as of Pipe Lane, Temple, Bristol.

3285. MORGAN, DAVID, Bristol: 11 Sept. 1671, F. Apprenticed to Lewis Roberts.
3286. MORGAN, GEORGE, Bristol: 19 June 1790, F. Apprenticed to Richard Hale, 15 May 1782.
3287. MORGAN, HENRY, Caerlion, Mon.: S. of Robert. Apprenticed to William Barron, Bristol, and Jocose his wife, 2 Aug. 1682.
3288. MORGAN, JOHN, Bristol: S. of William. Apprenticed to Allen Bright and Ann his wife, 11 Feb. 1761. Premium £10.
3289. MORGAN, JOSEPH, Bristol: 30 April 1807, F. S. of John. Apprenticed to Robert Bush, Junr., 14 Jan. 1796.

3290. MORGAN, PHILIP, Monmouth: Apprenticed to Thomas Hobson, Bristol, and Elizabeth his wife, 11 July 1618.
3291. MORGAN, REECE, Glamorgan: S. of George. Apprenticed to Peter Lodge, Bristol, for twelve years from 22 May 1654. Premium £20.
3292. MORGAN, WILLIAM, London: 1614. Was fined for false wares.
3293. MORGAN & GASKELL, ? Birmingham or London: c. 1840.

MORGAN & GASKELL

3294. MORING, RANDALL, London: 23 Mar. 1780, Y.; 24 Mar. 1803, L.; 1806, f.S.; 1814 and 1815, R.W.; 1819, U.W.; 1821, M.
3294A. MORING, RICHARD, London: In 1817 was at 16 Clerkenwell Green.
3295. MORRIS, HENRY, London: 20 June 1749, Y.
3296. MORRIS, THOMAS, London: Of St. Sepulchre's, was married at St. Helen's, Bishopgate, on 5 Nov. 1656.
3297. MORRISON, JOHN, Belfast: 1661, F.
3298. MORS, WILLIAM, London: Touch, 308 L.T.P., which he had leave to strike in c. 1678. His name does not appear in the Y. or L. Lists. Mentioned in the "Bennett" Book from 1679-86.

3299. MORSE, HENRY, London: Touch, 265 L.T.P., which he had leave to strike in 1676. His name is not in the Y. or L. Lists, but is in the "Bennett" Book, 1679-86.

3300. MORSE, ROBERT, London : Touch, 283 L.T.P., which he had leave to strike in 1676, but his name is not in the Records.

3301. MORSE, ROBERT, London : 18 June 1702, Y.; 15 Aug. 1709, L. Touch, 643 L.T.P., struck c. 1707.

3302. MORTIMER, J—— H——, Exeter : c. 1760-1800.

3303. MORTON, ALEXANDER, Glasgow : 1789, F. White-ironsmith.
3304. MORTON, ALEXANDER, Glasgow : 1791, F. White-ironsmith.
3305. MORTON, WILLIAM, London : 18 June 1795, Y. Died 1 Oct. 1850.
3306. MORYS, RICHARD, London : In 1457 was an Apprentice to John Parys.
3307. MOSER, ROGER, London : 19 June 1806, Y. and L. Touch, 1078 L.T.P., struck c. 1806. (Cf. Jackson.)

3307A. MOSS, PETER, Newcastle : Insolvent in 1725.
3308. MOTT, THOMAS, London : Mentioned in 1569.
3308A. MOULESWORTH, PETER, London : c. 1683. ("Bennett" Book.) Touch, 398 L.T.P., which he had leave to strike on 18 Mar. 1683.

3309. MOULINS, ROBERT (see also MOLLINS), London : 4 Oct. 1688, Y.; 18 June 1696, L.; 1704, S.
3310. MOUNTEYN, ROBERDE, London : In 1457 was covenant man to Nicholas Walker, and is mentioned again in 1465.
3311. MOUNTFORD, BENJAMIN, London : 18 June 1691, Y.
3312. MOURGUE, FULERAND, London : 20 June 1799, Y. and L.; 1800, f.S.; 1807 and 1808, R.W.
3313. MOURTON, PETER, West-Country : c. 1675.

3314. MOWER, GEORGE, Bristol and Gloucester : 19 Sept. 1687, F. S. of John. Apprenticed to Robert Belton and Jane his wife, 27 April 1680.

3315. MOXON, SAMUEL, London : 17 Oct. 1771, Y.; 20 June 1776, L.; 1782, S.; 1794, R.W.; 1798, U.W.; 1799, M. Dead in 1822.
3316. MOY, RICHARD, London : In 1457 was covenant man to Thomas Dounton, and in 1462 was dismissed for robbery.
3317. MOYES, J——, Edinburgh : In 1872 his shop was in West Bow. He was the last pewterer to practise the trade in Edinburgh.

3318. M'QUEEN, MRS., Edinburgh : 1774, was a white-ironsmith with shop in Nether Bow.
3319. MUCKLAWN, WILLIAM (? MUCKLEVAYNE), Bristol and Wellow, Somerset : 9 Aug. 1727, F. S. of John. Apprenticed to John Lovell and Hanna his wife, 26 July 1716. Given in the Poll Books for 1734 and 1739 as of Temple, Bristol.
3320. MUDGE, WALTER, London : 21 June 1764, Y.; 22 June 1769, L.; 1775, f.S.; 1781, f.R.W.; 1792, U.W.; 1793, M.
3321. MUIR, JOHN, Glasgow : 1777, F. Copper and white-ironsmith.

3322. MUIRHEAD, ALEXANDER, Edinburgh : A master in 1677.
3323. MULCASTER, JOHN, London : 20 Dec. 1792, Y.
MULLENDER, see MOLLYNARS.
3324. MULLENS, JOHN, London : 17 June 1802, Y.; 26 Sept. 1805, L.; 1811, f.S. Dead in 1819.
3325. MULLENS, JOHN JARVIS, London : 18 Aug. 1831, Y. and L. 26 Feb. 1872, died. Of Leather Lane, Holborn.
3326. MULLINS, ROBERT, London : Fined in 1625 for false wares. 1626, S.; 1634, R.W.; 1642, U.W.; 1647, M.
3327. MULLYNS, WILLIAM, London : In 1555 he received alms from the Company as a poor brother.
3327A. MUMFORD, JOSEPH, London : Touch, 421 L.T.P. which he had leave to strike in 1685/6.

3328. MUNCKE, THOMAS, Bristol and Chipping-Sodbury : 30 Nov. 1626, F. S. of Richard. Apprenticed to Philip Lane and Anne his wife, 12 Oct. 1616. Mentioned up to 1656.
3329. MUNDAY, THOMAS, London : 21 Mar. 1754, Y.; 22 June 1758, L.; 1767, S. Gazetted a Bankrupt, 22 Mar. 1774. Touch, 978 L.T.P., which he obtained leave to strike on 13 April 1758.

3330. MUNDAY, THOMAS, London : 14 Oct. 1790, Y.
3330A. MUNDEN & GROVE, London : 1760-1773. Touch, 992 L.T.P. (See next entry.)

3331. MUNDEN, WILLIAM (? MUNDER), London : 15 June 1757, Y.; 11 Oct. 1764, L.; 1771, S. Dead in 1773. Partner in Munden & Grove.

Touch, 992 L.T.P. They were given leave to strike their Touch on 18 Dec. 1760.
3332. MUNNS, NATHANIEL, London : 19 Dec. 1667, L.; 1669, f.S.; 1678, f.R.W.
3332A. MUNNS, THOMAS, London : c. 1680. ("Bennett" Book.)
3333. MUNROE, ANDREW, Edinburgh: 1677, F. Touch, 80 E.T.P.

3334. MUNSTER, IRON CO., Cork : c. 1833 - c. 1905. (Cf. Austen & Son.)

3335. MURRAY, PATRICK, Perth : Apprenticed in 1738 to Patrick Campbell.
3336. MURRAY, WILLIAM, London : 20 Mar. 1734, Y. Summoned in 1739 to " take the Cothing," but for his misbehaviour to the Court was refused. Touch, 857 L.T.P., which he had leave to strike on 7 Aug. 1735.

MYLLS, see MILLS.
3337. MYLYS, JOHN, London : Was free in 1457.
3338. M'VAIN, DUGALD, Glasgow : 1791, F. Pewterer and White-ironsmith.
3339. M'VEAN, DOUGALD, Glasgow : Mentioned in 1793 as a copper and white-ironsmith. ⎱? same.
3340. M'VICAR, JAMES, Glasgow : 1798, F. White-ironsmith.
3341. M'WHANNEL, WILLIAM, Glasgow : In 1797 was an apprentice to William Coats.

N

3342. NANSON, JOHN, Canongate, Edinburgh : 1733, F. White-ironsmith.
3343. NAPIER, ARCHIBALD, Edinburgh : 1666, F. Touch, 68 E.T.P.

3345. NAPIER, JOHN, Edinburgh : 1700, F. Touch, 99 E.T.P.

3346. NAPTON, HENRY, London : Issued a halfpenny token in 1670 whereon his address appears as

Bishopsgate Street. His son was born and registered at St. Helen's, Bishopsgate, on 12 April 1672. Touch, 159 L.T.P., which he had leave to strike in 1670. His name does not appear in the existing Y. and L. Lists. *See* list of tokens at end of Chap. IV. Mentioned in the "Bennett" Book as dead in 1684.

3347. NASH, EDWARD, London : 19 Dec. 1717, Y.; 5 July 1728, L.; 1738, S. Touch, 755 L.T.P., which he had leave to strike on 15 Dec. 1720.

3348. NASH, GERARD, Wells : 27 Mar. 1754, F. S. of William. Apprenticed to Allen Bright, Bristol, 20 Oct. 1746. Premium £30.
3349. NASH, JOHN, London : 14 Dec. 1749, Y.
3350. NASH, JOHN, London : Mentioned in 1591.
3350A. NASH, ——, London : Mentioned in 1647 in the records of the Skinners' Company.
3351. NASH, THOMAS, London : 7 Aug. 1729, Y.
3352. NASSHE, THOMAS, London : 1485, R.W.
3353. NEATON, JOHN, London : 16 Dec. 1714, Y. Touch, 699 L.T.P., which he was given leave to strike in 1715.

3354. NEAVE, ROBERT, London : 22 June, 1693 Y.
3355. NEEDHAM, THOMAS, London : In 1656 he was fined for using bad metal. 1665, f.S.
3356. NEELSON, CHRISTOPHER, London : Served in 1543 in a body of soldiers raised from the Company.
3357. NEGERBY, ARNOLD, London : In 1457 was an apprentice to Morys Panton.
3358. NEIL, THOMAS, Edinburgh : In 1793 was in business as a white-ironsmith at South Frederick Street.
3359. NEILL, ADAM, Edinburgh : Mentioned in 1634.

3360. NELHAM, THOMAS, London : 18 June 1795, Y.
3361. NELHAM, WILLIAM, London : 16 Mar. 1815, Y.
3362. NEST, ROBERT, Bewdley : c. 1820-50. A spoon-maker.
3363. NE(I)THERWOOD, CHARLES, London : 20 Dec. 1716, Y.
3364. NE(I)THERWOOD, JOHN, London : In 1622 he was granted the use of Mr. Sheppard's Touch.
3365. NETTLEFOLD, WILLIAM, London : 24 Mar. 1785, Y. Touch, 1072 L.T.P., struck c. 1800. Of 6 St. Catherine's, Tower Hill, in 1817.

3366. NETTLEFOLD, WILLIAM, JUNR., London : 16 Dec. 1819, Y.
3367. NEVILL, JOSEPH, London : 24 June 1762, Y.
3368. NEWCHIRCH, EVERARD, London : Was a subscriber in 1476 to a set of feast vessels.
3369. NEWELL, SAMUEL, London : 20 June 1689, Y. Touch, 516 L.T.P., struck c. 1695.

3370. NEWES, RAPHE, London : Was brought before the Company for debt in 1562.
3371. NEWES, ROBERT, London : Was free in 1561, and in 1575 was sent to Ipswich on business for the Company. 1578, S.
3372. NEWHAM, JOHN (*see* also NEWMAN), London : 14 Dec. 1699, Y.; 23 Sept. 1703, L.; 1710, S.; 1725, R.W.; 1731, U.W. Touch, 581 L.T.P., which he had leave to strike on 14 Jan. 1700.

3373. NEWHAM, WILLIAM, London : 24 Mar. 1708, Y.; 1727, S. Touch, 685 L.T.P., which he was given leave to strike on 31 Mar. 1712.

3374. NEWHAM, WILLIAM, London : 18 Mar. 1730, Y. and L.; 1740, S.; 1745, R.W. His shop was at New Street, near Shoe Lane.

3375. NEWLAND, CHARLES, London : 14 Dec. 1758, Y.

3376. NEWMAN, ——, London : Buried in 1604.

3377. NEWMAN, MICHAEL, London : 1629, S.; 1640, R.W.; 1646, U.W.; 1652, M.

3378. NEWMAN, MICHAEL, JUNR., London : 1653, S.; 1662, R.W.; 1667, U.W.; 1670, M.

3378A. NEWMAN, RALPH, London : Died 1684. (" Bennett " Book.)

3379. NEWMAN, RICHARD, London : 17 Dec. 1747, Y.; 13 Dec. 1753, L.; 1781, Beadle. Died in 1789. Of Basinghall Street. Touch, 926 L.T.P., which he obtained leave to strike in 1747.

3380. NEWMAN, THOMAS, London : 1660, f.S.

3381. NEWMAN, THOMAS, London : 23 June 1768, Y.

3382. NEWNAM, ——, London : 1642, S.

3382A. NEWSON, THOMAS, London : c. 1680. (" Bennett " Book.)

3383. NEWTH, ELIJAH, London : 11 Oct. 1722, Y.

3384. NEWTON, BRIAN, Hereford : Mentioned in 1641.

3385. NEWTON, HUGH, London : Was free in 1591. 1604, R.W.; 1610, U.W.; 1616 and 1621, M.

3386. NEWTON, THEOPHILUS, Bristol : 31 July 1700, F. S. of Theophilus. Apprenticed to John Jones and Anne his wife, 22 April 1680. Mentioned in 1713.

3387. NEWTON, THOMAS, London : 9 Oct. 1735, Y.

3388. NICHOLAS, PHILIP, Killgrooke, Mon. : S. of William. Apprenticed to Roger Perkins, Bristol, 15 Sept. 1670.

3389. NICHOLL(s), HENRY (? NICOLL), London : 10 Dec. 1696, Y.

3390. NICHOLL(s), HENRY, Ludlow : Pewterer and Brazier. 26 June 1659, F.

3391. NICHOLL(s), J. & Co., London : Incorporated with Gaskell & Chambers, London and Birmingham. Nineteenth century.

3392. NICHOLL(s), J——, London : Touch, 87 L.T.P., restruck c. 1670, after the great fire.

3392A. NICHOLL(s), JAMES, London : Touch, 424 L.T.P., which he had leave to strike in 1685/6. Mr. Stone complained against his striking another Touch, which is here illustrated. His name is in the " Bennett " Book in 1686.

3393. NICHOLL(s), RICHARD, Walsall : Buried at the Parish Church, Walsall, 13 Mar. 1627.

3394. NICHOLL(s), THOMAS, London : Was elected temporary Warden of the Yeomanry in 1556. 1566, S.

3395. NICHOLL(s), THOMAS, London : 20 June 1765, Y.; 22 June 1786, L.

3396. NICHOLL(s), WILLIAM, London : Touch, 417 L.T.P., which he had leave to strike in 1685/6. His name is not in the existing Y. or L. Lists but it appears in the " Bennett " Book in 1685 and 1686.

3397. NICHOLSON, A——, of ? : c. 1730. Used same device as R. Nicholson, London, probably his son.

3398. NICHOLSON, JAMES, London : 10 Dec. 1730, Y. and L. The King's pewterer who worked out a table of various alloys and weights. Was given leave to strike his Touch on 10 Dec. 1730, but it is not on Touchplates.

3399. NICHOLSON, ROBERT, York : 1563/4, F., by patrimony. Mentioned later in 1607/8. Son of Roger.

3400. NICHOLSON, ROBERT, London : 19 Mar. 1690, Y.; 14 June 1692, L.; 1699, S.; 1714, R.W.;

1722, U.W.; 1725, M. Touch, 462 L.T.P., which he had leave to strike in 1686/7.

3401. NICHOLSON, ROGER, York: Father of Robert. 1536, F., by patrimony. City Chamberlain in 1546/7, and is mentioned later in 1563/4.

3402. NICHOLSON, WILLIAM, London: 23 Mar. 1720, Y. Touch, 728 L.T.P., which he had leave to strike on 3 Sept. 1721.

3403. NISBET, SAMUEL, London: 18 Mar. 1730, Y.
3404. NIXON, ROBERT, London: 1589, S.
3405. NODES, JOHN, London: 21 Oct. 1756, Y.; 15 Oct. 1778, L.; 1784, f.S.; 1793, f.R.W.; 1797, f.U.W.; 1798, f.M.
3406. NOGAY, THOMAS, London: Was fined in 1561 for using bad metal. 1562, S.; 1567, f.R.W.; 1568, 1575 and 1579, U.W.; 1580, M.
3407. NORFOCK, LAWRENCE, London: Had some salts confiscated in 1552 for being of poor metal.
3408. NORFOLK, JOSEPH, London: 15 Mar. 1764, Y. and L.; 1769, f.S.
3409. NORFOLK, RICHARD, London: 24 Mar. 1736, Y.; 25 Feb. 1745, L.; 1755. S.; 1761, R.W.; 1775, U.W.; 1776, M. Died in 1783. Touch, 902 L.T.P., which he had leave to strike on 9 Oct. 1741. Of St. Margaret's Hill, Southwark.

3410. NORFOLK, THOMAS, London: In 1517 he was fined for making bad wares.
3410A. NORFOLK, WILLIAM, Norfolk: Alias Whistyll, 1462/3, F.
3410B. NORFOLK, WILLIAM, JUNR., Norfolk: Son of the last named. 1494/5, F.
3410C. NORGET, RICHARD, Norwich: 1670.

3411. NORGROVE, JOHN, London: 21 June 1722, Y. Touch, 762 L.T.P., struck c. 1726. (*Cf.* Touch of Robert Pole.)

3412. NORKETT, SAMUEL, Bristol: Mentioned with his wife Martha in 1606.
3413. NORMAND, HENRY London: Was in trouble in 1556 over a private quarrel with William Abdye.
3414. NORRIS, WILLIAM, London: 20 June 1771, Y.
3415. NORTH, GEORGE, London: 22 June 1693, Y.; 23 Sept. 1703, L.; 1711, f.S. Touch, 539 L.T.P., which he had leave to strike on 19 June 1697.

3416. NORTH, JOHN, Dublin: Mentioned in 1824.
3417. NORTHALL, JOHN, Bristol: Mentioned in a will proved in 1572 as of Wine Street.
3418. NORTHALL, ROLAND, Bristol: 20 May 1563, F. S. of John.
3419. NORTHCOTE, HENRY JAMES, London: 16 June 1808, Y. and L.; 1814, f.S. Died 30 Dec. 1859. He was struck off by order and his Livery fine returned on 15 Oct. 1829.
3420. NORTON, JOHN, London: In 1558 was covenant servant to Raphe Mollyners. 1573, S.; 1581, was appointed a receiver of fines. 1583, R.W.
3421. NORTON, ROGER, Ludlow: Pewterer and Brazier. 20 Nov. 1660, F.
3422. NORWOOD WILLIAM, London: 14 Dec. 1727, Y. Touch, 815 L.T.P., which he had leave to strike on 14 Dec. 1727.

3423. NOWELL, SIMON, London: 14 Oct. 1731, Y.
3424. NUTT, JACOB, London: 20 Mar. 1689, Y.
3425. NYCOLL, THOMAS, London: In 1457 was an apprentice to John Parys.
3426. NYXON, ROBERT, London: In 1583 was appointed one of a Committee to fix selling prices of wares.

3427. OAK(E)LE, JOHN, London: In 1457 was an apprentice to John Coldham.

OFTHWAITE, *see* HUSTWAITE.

3428. OKEFORD, MICHAEL (? OAKFORD), London: 11 Aug. 1696, Y.

3429. OKEFORD, NICHOLAS, London: 21 Mar. 1699, Y. Touch, 596 L.T.P., which he had leave to strike on 2 April 1702. I have seen this touch in conjunction with that of S. Lawrence's (1708, Y.) secondary and Hall Marks. His Rose and Crown Mark on a plate at Chelveston Church, Higham Ferrers, bears the date 1702 at foot.

3430. OLIPHANT, ANDREW, Perth: In 1782 was an apprentice to Patrick Bisset.

3431. OLIPHANT, GEORGE, London: 13 Dec. 1798, Y.

3432. OLIPHANT, GEORGE, London: 18 Oct. 1826, Y.

3433. OLIVER, JOHN, London: 22 Mar. 1687, Y. Touch, 478 L.T.P., which he had leave to strike on 4 Feb. 1689. Of St. Giles, Cripplegate. Was married on 2 Jan. 1692.

3434. OLIVER, ROBERT, London: 20 June 1706, Y.

3435. OLIVER, WILLIAM, London: 20 June 1689, Y.

3436. OLYFFE, WILLIAM, London: In 1483 had his goods seized for arrears of quarterage.

3437. O'NEALE, RICHARD, London: 18 June 1719, Y.; 1722, L.; 1728, S.; 1735, f.R.W.

ONION, *see* INON(E).

3438. ONLY, WILLIAM, London: Touch, 248 L.T.P., which he had leave to strike in 1674/5. No mention of him in the Y. or L. Lists, but his name is in the "Bennett" Book from 1679-84.

3439. ONTON, JOHN, London: 1513 and 1514, M. This name is Onton in the Records, but it is given as Burton in Welch's list of Officers of the Company.

3439A. ONWEN, THOMAS, Beverley: Insolvent in 1720.

3440. ORDESALE, WILLIAM DE, York; 1347/8, F.

3441. ORDOWE, JOHN, York: 1437/8, F.

3441A. ORFORD, S——, ? London: c. 1825.

3442. ORME, ROBERT, London: 20 April 1663, L., f.S., and f.R.W. Mentioned in the "Bennett" Book, 1679-86.

3443. ORMISTON, JOHN, Edinburgh: In 1649 was an apprentice to James Monteith.

3444. ORMISTON, JOHN, Dublin: Mentioned in 1769 and 1796, and is referred to on 11 Nov. 1769 in *Faulkner's Dublin Journal* as a maker of "Pewter dishes cast from brass moulds, turned in an oval engine, also numbered Army Buttons."

3444A. ORMROD, OLIVER, Manchester: The dissolution of his partnership with George Stirrup is recorded in the *London Gazette* for 31 Dec. 1793.

3444B. ORMROD & STIRRUP, Manchester: In 1790 acquired the business of Thomas Radford, Market Street Lane. Their partnership was dissolved in 1793, Ormrod carrying on the business.

3445. OROXTHALL, ROLAND, Bristol: 20 May 1563, F. Son of John.

3446. ORTON, JOSEPH, London: 21 June 1694, Y.

3447. OSBARN, HARRY, London: In 1457 was journeyman to Stephen Auncell.

3448. OSBORN(E), ——, London: In 1698 was a brazier, selling (and perhaps making) pewter wares.

3448A. OSBORN(E), CHARLES, London: c. 1683. ("Bennett" Book.) Touch, 413 L.T.P., which he had leave to strike in 1683/4.

3449. OSBORN(E), JOHN, London : 11 Dec. 1701, Y.;
19 May 1715, L. Touch, 687 L.T.P., which
he was given leave to strike on 30 Sept. 1712.

3450. OSBORN(E), JOHN, London : 18 Mar. 1713, Y.
Touch, 721 L.T.P., struck c. 1721.

3451. OSBORN(E), JOHN, London : 24 Mar. 1785, Y.

3452. OSBORN(E), ROBERT, London : Pewterer of St.
Botolph, Bishopgate. His daughter Elizabeth
was married at St. Leonard's, Shoreditch, in
1595 when he was of St. Andrew's, olborn.
3453. OSBORN(E), SAMUEL, London : 22 June 1693, Y.
3454. OSBORN(E), SAMUEL, London : 16 Sept. 1679, L.
His name appears in the " Bennett " Book in
1685 and 1686.
3455. OSBORN(E), THOMAS, London : 17 Dec. 1719, Y.
3455A. OSBORN(E), THOMAS, London : Died in 1685.
(" Bennett " Book.)

3456. OSBORN(E), THOMAS, London : 11 Dec. 1729, Y.
3457. OSBORN(E), WILLIAM, London : 11 Oct. 1733, Y.
3457A. OSGOOD, EDWARD, London : Mentioned in the
" Bennett " Book, 1679-86.
3458. OSGOOD, JOSEPH, Bristol : 2 May 1807, F. S. of
John. Apprenticed to Preston Edgar and
Rebecca his wife, 31 Dec. 1796. In the Poll
Book for 1812 he is given as of Temple Backs,
Bristol.
3459. OSMODERLEY, WILLIAM, York : 1496/7, F.
3460. O(Y)STLER, THOMAS, York : 1536/7, F., and is
mentioned in 1561/2.
3461. OSWALD, WILLIAM, Edinburgh : In 1695 was an
apprentice to David Penman.
3462. OTWAY, THOMAS, London : 11 Oct. 1733, Y.
3463. OTWAY, THOMAS, London : 22 June 1786, Y.
3464. OTWEY, LEONARD, London : In 1457 was an
apprentice to William Crowde.
3465. OUDLEY, ROBERT, London : 17 June 1708, Y.;
6 July 1725, L. Touch, 665 L.T.P., struck
c. 1709.

3466. OUTLAW(E), THOMAS, London : 1504, R.W.
OUTON, see ONTON.
3467. OVEREND, GEORGE, Dublin : Died in 1733.
3468. OVERY, THOMAS, London : c. 1450.
3469. AP OWEN, EDWARD, Ludlow : Was made Master
in 1578.
3470. OXDIN, WILLIAM, London : 22 Mar. 1687, Y.
3471. OXFORD, JACOB, Bath : S. of Isaac. Apprenticed
to Allen Bright, Bristol, and Ann his wife, 14
April 1755. Premium £40.
3472. OXFORD, JOHN, Bath : S. of John. Apprenticed
to John Leach, Bristol, 16 Sept. 1714.

P

3473. PACKER, DANIEL, Bristol : 2 Dec. 1670, F.
Apprenticed to Wm. Pascall.
3474. PADDICOMBE, JOHN, Crediton : S. of William.
Apprenticed to Robert Bush of Bristol, and Ann
his wife, 5 Feb. 1784.
3475. PADDON, THOMAS, London : 28 Sept. 1699, L;

1705, S. Touch, 433 L.T.P., which he had
leave to strike in 1686/7.

3476. PAGE, JOHN, London : 7 Feb. 1692, Y.; 9 Mar.
1697, L. Touch, 494 L.T.P., which he had
leave to strike on 7 Feb. 1692.

3477. PAGE, SAMUEL, Bristol : In the Poll Book for 1754
he is given as of Castle Precincts, Bristol.

3478. PAGE, THOMAS, Bristol: 10 Oct. 1737, F. S. of Thomas. Apprenticed to Thomas Lanyon and Anne his wife, 24 Jan. 1729. Premium £31 10s. In the Poll Book for 1739 he is given as of St. Stephen's, Bristol.

3479. PAGE, THOMAS, London: 1456 and 1459, R.W.; 1462, 1466 and 1470, U.W.
3480. PAGE, WILLIAM, London: 15 Dec. 1748, Y. PAGITER, see PARGITER.
3481. PAILLY, JOHN, York: 1466/7, F.
3482. PAINE, ——, London: 1661, f.S.
3483. PAINE, EDWARD, London: 21 June 1716, Y.
3484. PAINE, JAMES, Bristol: 30 Sept. 1659, F. S. of John. Apprenticed to Humphrey Beale and Margaret his wife, 10 May 1651. Turned over to Edward Lovering. Mentioned in 1679.
3485. PAINTER, JOHN, London: 19 June 1718, Y.
3486. PAIP, ANDREW, Aberdeen: In 1689 was an apprentice to George Ross.
3487. PALMER, EBENEZER, London: 19 Mar. 1818, Y. and L.; 1826, f.S.
3488. PALMER, JOHN, London: 11 Mar. 1702, Y. Touch, 693 L.T.P., which he was given leave to strike on 17 June 1714.

3489. PALMER, JOHN, London: 7 Oct. 1725, Y.
3490. PALMER, JOHN, London: 14 Dec. 1749, Y.
3491. PALMER, JOHN, London: 17 Mar. 1763, Y.
3492. PALMER, JOHN, London: Was fined in 1533 for absence without leave.
3492A. PALMER, JOHN, Whitchurch: Of Market Street. He was a brazier, but probably made pewterwares too. (Cf. Hughes, Chester.)
3493. PALMER, RICHARD, Dublin: Apprenticed to John Robinson and is mentioned in 1759 and 1773.
3494. PALMER, RICHARD, London: 19 Dec. 1771, Y.
3495. PALMER, RICHARD, London: 13 Oct. 1803, L.; 1807, f.S.; 1816, and 1817, R.W.; 1820, U.W.; 1822, M. Died 24 Jan. 1830.

3496. PALMER, ROGER, London: 1634, f.R.W.; 1642, f.U.W.
3497. PALMER, ROGER, London: Was free in 1560.
3498. PALMER, THOMAS, London: 18 Mar. 1756, Y.
3498A. PALMER, THOMAS, London: Touch, 459 L.T.P., which he had leave to strike on 20 June 1689.

3499. PALMER, WILLIAM, London: 18 Mar. 1730, Y.
3500. PALMER, WILLIAM, London: 13 Oct. 1743, Y. Touch, 911 L.T.P., which he obtained leave to strike on 21 June 1744.

3501. PALTOCK, JOHN, London: 1625, Y.; 1627, S. Married the widow of Andrew Fulham.
3502. PANTON, MORYS, London: Was a Livery man in 1457.
3503. PANTON, SAMUEL, Dublin: Mentioned in 1727.
3504. PAPE, ROBERT, Edinburgh: In 1687 was apprenticed to Alexander Manzies.
3505. PARADICE, FRA(NCIS), London: Touch, 306 L.T.P., which he had leave to strike in 1677/8. His name does not appear in the Y. or L. Lists but is in the "Bennett" Book, 1679-86 as a country Member.

3506. PARADICE, WILLIAM, Bristol and Shownstonin, Wilts.: 4 Mar. 1656, F. S. of William. Apprenticed to Roger Willoughby, 12 Feb. 1649.
3506A. PARGITER, WILLIAM, London: c. 1680. ("Bennett" Book.)
3507. PARHAM, BENJAMIN, Plymouth Dock: c. 1725.

3508. PARHAM, BENJAMIN, Ashburton: Successor to John Dolbeare. c. 1770.
3509. PARISH, JOHN (? PARIS), London: Mentioned in 1466.
3510. PARK, THOMAS, London: 13 Oct. 1743, Y.
3511. PARKE, PETER, London: 1662, f.R.W.; 1666, U.W.; 1669, M.

3512. PARKE, RICHARD, London : In 1574 was journey-man to John God, spoonmaker.

3513. PARKER, DANIEL, London : 1686, Y. and L.; 1694, S.; 1702, f.R.W.; 1710, U.W.; 1714, f.M. Touch, 441 L.T.P., which he had leave to strike in 1685/6.

3514. PARKER, DANIEL, Bristol : Mentioned in 1690.
3515. PARKER, JOHN, Limerick : Mentioned in 1768.
3516. PARKER, JOSEPH, London : 1679, S. Touch, 180 L.T.P., which he had leave to strike in 1670/1

3517. PARKER, ROBERT, Walsall : Buried at Walsall Parish Church, 12 Dec. 1577.
3518. PARKER, THOMAS, London : 19 Dec. 1695, Y. Touch, 579 L.T.P., which he had leave to strike on 2 Dec. 1700.

3518A. PARKER, THOMAS, London : Touch, 576 L.T.P., which he had leave to strike on 18 July 1700.

3519. PARKER, WILLIAM, London : 15 June 1809, Y. and L.
3520. PARKER, WILLIAM, York : 1420/1, F.
3521. PARKER, WILLIAM THOMAS, London : 18 Mar. 1802, Y.
3522. PARKES, FFRAUNCIS, London : Mentioned in 1589.
3522A. PARKINSON, JOHN, London : Touch, 384 L.T.P., which he had leave to strike on 4 April 1683.

PARKYNS, see PERKINS.

3522B. PARN, ROBERT, London : Died 1685. (" Bennett " Book.)

3523. PARNALL & SONS, Bristol : Founded in 1820 as H. G. Parnall, it was changed to Parnall & Sons c. 1860, and in 1883 was converted into a Limited Company, and c. 1903 the shares were acquired by W. & T. Avery. Parnalls were not actual makers but factors of pewter-wares. Of Narrow Wine Street.

3524. PARR, NORTON, Cork : Mentioned in 1742 and died in 1773.

3525. PARR, ROBERT, London : 17 June 1703, Y.; 19 June 1740, L.; 1752, f.S.; 1758, f.R.W.; 1767, U.W.; and died.
3526. PARR, ROBERT, London : Touch, 352 L.T.P., struck c. 1681, but his name does not appear in the Records. The device in this Touch is explained by a note in *Berrow's Worcester Journal* of 29 Jan. 1767, when in speaking of the death of the wife of the last named it says :

" Died, Mrs. Parr, aged 74, wife of Mr. Parr, an eminent pewterer in Greek Street, and a lineal descendant of the famous old Parr who lived to the age of 152 years and upwards and died in the reign of King Charles II."

Old Thomas Parr was born in 1483 and died on the 13 Nov. 1635. He was buried in West-minster Abbey, and there is a mural tablet giving fuller details, erected to his memory in Great Wolaston Chapel, a chapel-of-ease to Alderbury Church, Salop.

3527. PARRETT, THOMAS, London : In 1602 was chosen a collector from the Livery. 1609, R.W.
3528. PARRETT, WILLIAM, London : Mentioned in 1591. He resigned the Livery through Poverty in 1615.

3528A. PARSON, JOHN, Liverpool: Apprenticed to Robert Green. In 1768 he took the shop of James Kidd.

3529. PARSON, ROBERT, London: In 1457 was covenant man to John Gugge, the elder.

3529A. PARSONS, FRANCIS, London: c. 1680. (" Bennett " Book.)

3530. PARTRIDGE, RICHARD, London: 16 June 1715, Y. Touch, 700 L.T.P., struck c. 1716. Of Foster Lane. Bankrupt in 1724.

3531. PARUYS, THOMAS, London: Is mentioned in 1451 as having sold some moulds to the Company.

3532. PARYS, JOHN, London: 1457, R.W.; 1461, U.W.; 1467, 1476, 1480 and 1484, M. Of Fleet Street.

3533. PASCALL, JOHN, Churchill, Somerset: Son of Thomas. Apprenticed to William Pascall, Bristol, and Jane his wife for seven years from 12 Feb. 1634. He is mentioned with his wife Lucretia in 1646.

3534. PASCALL, THOMAS, SENR., Bristol: 24 Oct. 1661, F. S. of William and Mary, to whom he was apprenticed for seven years from 16 Nov. 1652. He is mentioned in 1682.

3535. PASCALL, THOMAS, JUNR., Bristol: S. of Thomas and Jane, to whom he was apprenticed, 4 May 1682.

3536. PASCALL, WILLIAM, SENR., Bristol and Wrington, Somerset: 19 Oct. 1632, F. S. of Thomas. Apprenticed to Abraham Yeo(re), Bristol, and Johanna his wife, 20 July 1622. Mentioned in 1652.

3537. PASCALL, WILLIAM, JUNR., Bristol: S. of Thomas and Joan, to whom he was apprenticed, 4 Mar. 1679. Brother of Thomas P., Junr.

3538. PASKIN, GEORGE, London: 18 June 1730, Y.

3539. PASKIN, JEREMIAH, London: 26 Oct. 1752, Y.

3540. PASKIN, ROBERT, London: 24 Mar. 1757, Y.

3541. PASKIN, WILLIAM, London: 19 Dec. 1695, Y.

3542. PASKIN, WILLIAM, London: 8 Oct. 1724, Y. Beadle in 1744, and was permitted to surrender his freedom and be disfranchised from the Company. He was readmitted a Freeman, 1750.

3543. PASSHE, THOMAS, London: 1495, U.W. Welch gives it Nasshe, but it is Passhe in the Livery List.

3544. PATASON(E), JAMES, Edinburgh: In 1693 was an apprentice to David Penman.

3545. PATASON(E), ROBERT, Stirling: 1607, mentioned.

3546. PATASON(E), THOMAS, Edinburgh: In 1694 was an apprentice to Alexander Findlay.

3547. PATASON(E), WALTER, Edinburgh: 1710, F. Touch, 113 E.T.P.

3548. PATIENCE, ROBERT, London: 23 Mar. 1737, Y.

3549. PATIENCE, ROBERT, London: 1 Aug. 1734, Y.; 15 Dec. 1743, L.; 1754, f.S.; 1760, f.R.W.; 1771, U.W.; 1772, M. Died in 1777. Touch, 883 L.T.P., which he had leave to strike on 23 Mar. 1737. (Cf. Touches of William Barnes and Thomas Wheeler.) In 1743 he was in Fleet Street.

3550. PATRICK, WILLIAM, London: 10 Aug. 1699, Y.

3551. PATTERN, JOHNE, Edinburgh: In 1603 was an apprentice to James Sibbett.

3552. PATTERSON, THOMAS, Edinburgh: In 1686 was an apprentice to John Ramsay.

3553. PATTERSON, WALTER, Edinburgh: Was a master in 1711.

3554. PATTERSONE, CHARLES, Edinburgh: In 1679 was an apprentice to Alexander Constein.

3555. PATTISON, ABRAHAM (? BATTISON), York: Mentioned in 1712/3.

3556. PATTISON, JOHN, York: Mentioned in 1754/5.

3557. PATTISON, JOHN, York: 1758, F.

3558. PATTISON, PETER, Dublin: Died in 1715.

3559. PATTI(N)SON, SIMON, London: 24 Mar. 1715, Y.; 26 Feb. 1733, L. Touch, 767 L.T.P., which he had leave to strike 19 Mar. 1723.

3560. PAUL, PETER, London: 20 Oct. 1791, Y.

3561. PAULING, HENRY, London: 1660, Y. First used as his Touch the Anchor and Rose.

3561A. PAWLE, CHRISTOPHER, Barnstaple: Died in 1786.

3562.   PAWSON, RICHARD, London : 12 Mar. 1752, Y. Touch, 962 L.T.P., which he obtained leave to strike on 22 Mar. 1753.

3563.   PAXTON, JAMES, London : 13 Oct. 1698, Y. Touch, 636 L.T.P., struck c. 1706.

3564.   PAXTON, JOHN, London : 20 Mar. 1717, Y. Touch, 769 L.T.P., which he had leave to strike on 16 June 1724.

3565.   PAXTON, RICHARD, London : 3 Aug. 1738, Y.
3566.   PAXTON, WILLIAM, London : 10 Aug. 1676, L.; 1681, S.; 1692, f.R.W.; 1694, f.U.W.; 1696, M. Touch, 168 L.T.P., which he had leave to strike in 1669/70.

3567.   PAYABLE, JOHN, York : 1441/2, F.
3567A.   PAYN(E), EDWARD, Norwich : 1492/3, F.
3567B.   PAYN(E), PETER, Norwich : 1461/2, F.
3568.   PAYN(E), HENRY, Bristol : Of 133 Temple Street in 1860. He succeeded to the business of Preston Edgar & Sons, to whom he had been foreman. He carried it on until c. 1880, when he in his turn was succeeded by his foreman, F. E. Vowles.
3569.   PAYN(E), JOHN, London : 16 Dec. 1725, Y. Touch, 789 L.T.P., struck c. 1728.

3569A.   PAYNELL, JNO., London : c. 1680. (" Bennett " Book.) Touch, 290 L.T.P., which he had leave to strike in 1676/7.

3570.   PEA, FRANCIS, Dublin : Mentioned in 1798 and 1808. In 1805 he was at 100 Thomas Street.
3571.   PEACOCK, JOHN (see also PECOCK), London : 20 June 1706, Y.
3572.   PEACOCK, SAMUEL, London : 15 Dec. 1763, Y.; 20 June 1771, L.; 1778, f.S.; 1785, R.W.
3573.   PEACOCK, THOMAS, London : 24 Oct. 1782, Y.; 11 Dec. 1783, L.; 1790, f.S. Was struck off and fine returned on 19 Mar. 1807, by order.
3574.   PEAKE, GEORGE, London : 18 Oct. 1759, Y.
3575.   PEAKE, RICHARD, London : 11 Oct. 1750, Y. Touch, 953 L.T.P., which he obtained leave to strike on 13 June 1751.

3576.   PEARCE, DANIEL, Bristol : 6 July 1812, F. S. of Daniel. Apprenticed to Robert Bush, 8 May 1794. In the Poll Book for 1812 he is given as of Burton Hill, Bristol.
3577.   PEARCE, JAMES, Bristol : 23 Oct. 1806, Y.
3578.   PEARCE, THOMAS, Bristol : S. of Thomas. Apprenticed to Robert Bush and Ann his wife, 11 Mar. 1778.
3579.   PEAT, WILLIAM, London : In 1596 was appointed a collector of Levies from the Yeomanry.
3580.   PECK(E), DANIEL, London : 6 Oct. 1720, Y.
3581.   PECK(E), THOMAS, London : Mentioned in 1704, and in the " Bennett " Book from 1679-86.
3582.   PECK(E), WILLIAM HENRY, London : Of Fetter Lane, Holborn. 16 June 1831, Y. Retired c. 1870.
3583.   PECK(E), NICHOLAS, London : 1548, R.W.
3584.   PECK(E), WILLIAM, London : In 1487 was fined for insolent behaviour.
3585.   PECKHAM, RICHARD, London : 19 Mar. 1761, Y.
3586.   PECKITT, GEORGE, York: 1640/1 F. Mentioned in 1655.
3587.   PECO(C)K, JOHN (see also PEACOCK), London : Was free in 1457.
3588.   PECO(C)K, THOMAS, London : 1506, R.W.; 1511 and 1518, U.W.
3589.   PECO(C)K, WILLIAM, London : 1492, 1498 and 1503, R.W.; 1504 and 1505, U.W.; 1510 and 1511, M.
3590.   PEDDER, HENRY, London : 23 Mar. 1748, Y.

3591. PEDDER, JOSEPH, London: Of St. George's, Southwark. Was married to Dorothy Warren on 10 Sept. 1684 at Christchurch, Surrey.

3592. PEDDER, JOSEPH, London: 14 Dec. 1727, Y. Touch, 821 L.T.P., which he had leave to strike on 19 Mar. 1729.

3593. PEDDIE, ANDREW, Edinburgh: 1766, F.

3594. PEEK, WILLIAM HENRY, London: 16 June 1831, L.; 1841, f.S.; 1851, R.W.; 1853, U.W.; 1854, M. In business in Fetter Lane, Holborn. Retired c. 1870.

3595. PEIRCE, JAMES HENRY, London: 21 June 1798, Y.; 23 Oct. 1806, L.; 1813, f.S.; 1825, R.W. Died 9 May 1840, aged 64.

3596. PEIRCY, ROBERT (see also PIERCY), London: Of Whitecross Street (see his Trade Card). 21 June 1722, Y.; 22 June 1749, L.; 1760, S. Touch, 858 L.T.P., which he had leave to strike on 9 Oct. 1735. In 1737 he was in partnership with William Dean.

3597. PEISLEY, GEORGE, London: 23 June 1718, Y.; 14 July 1719, L. Of St. Thomas Apostles Parish. Touch, 709 L.T.P., which he had leave to strike on 23 June 1718. A quaker. He was insolvent in 1729.

3598. PEISLEY, THOMAS, London: 12 Oct. 1693, Y. Touches, 635 L.T.P., struck c. 1706, and 670 L.T.P., struck c. 1710. In 1710 he was granted special permission to strike another Touch (No. 670) although he had already a small one with two letters only (No. 635).

3599. PEISLEY, THOMAS, London: 12 Oct. 1732, Y. PEKE, see PECKE.

3600. PELHAM, JOHN, London: 13 Dec. 1698, Y.

3601. PELL, JOSEPH, Lynn: 1654/5, F. Apprenticed to Thomas Holland.

3602. PELLETT, JOSEPH HUMBER, London: 3 July 1817, Y.

3603. PELLETT, JOSEPH RICHTER, London: 16 Oct. 1788, Y. and L. Struck out by order and fine returned 21 Aug. 1794. His business in 1792 was at Bethnal Green.

3604. PELLITORY, MATTHEW (? PELLITER), London: Apprenticed to Roger Hawkesford, 1599, Y. Was fined in 1606 for making bad wares and ordered to alter his touch for a punishment. He died in 1609. } ? Same

3605. PELLYTORYE, MORYCE, London: Apprenticed to Roger Hawkesford. 1583, Y., by redemption. In 1592 he was poverty stricken.

PENDER, see RENDER.

3606. PENMAN, DAVID, Edinburgh: 1693, F. Died c. 1715. Touch, 95 E.T.P.

3606A. PENN, HUMPHRY, London: Died 1685. ("Bennett" Book.) Touch, 279 L.T.P., which he had leave to strike in 1676/7.

3607. PENNINGTON, JOHN, Tavistock: c. 1680-1729. The following reference is in a lease dated 8 Jan. 1729:

"Premises late in the occupation of John Pennington of the said Borough of Tavistock in the County of Devon, Pewterer."

3608. PENNINGTON, WILLIAM, Bristol: 7 April 1676, F. Apprenticed to John Lovering.

3608A. PENROSE, RICHARD, Penzance: Gazetted Bankrupt, 26 May 1772.

3609. PENY, THOMAS, York: 1431/2, F.

PEPOND, see PYPOND.

3609A. PEPPER, JNO., London: c. 1680. ("Bennett" Book.) Touch, 317 L.T.P., which he had leave to strike in 1678/9.

3610. PEPPERCORN, THOMAS, London : 20 June 1728, Y.
3611. PERCHARD, HELLIER (*or* HELLARY), London : His Christian name is spelt in various ways on different pieces—Hellary, Hellier, Hillier. 11 Aug. 1709, Y. ; 7 June 1714, L. ; 1719, S. ; 1728, f.R.W. ; 1738, U.W. ; 1740, M. Touch, 661 L.T.P., struck c. 1709 and dated.

3612. PERCHARD, SAMUEL, London : 18 Aug. 1743, Y. ; 17 June 1752, L.
3613. PERKINS, ARTHUR, London : 19 Dec. 1734, Y.
3613A. PERKINS, FRANCIS, London : c. 1680. (" Bennett " Book.) Touch, 340 L.T.P., which he had leave to strike in 1679/80.

3614. PERKINS, GEORGE, Bristol : S. of Roger. Apprenticed to Roger Perkins, Junr., and Marie his wife, 21 Mar. 1700.
3615. PERKINS, JOHN, London : 18 June 1713, Y.
3616. PERKINS, PHILIP, St. Ives : S. of John. Apprenticed to William Snellgrove, Bristol, and Ann his wife, 14 May 1675.
3617. PERKINS, RICHARD, Bristol : S. of Richard. Apprenticed to Robert Bush and Elizabeth his wife, 31 Jan. 1764. Premium £40. Mentioned in the Poll Book for 1774 as of Castle Precincts, Bristol. Partner in Bush & Perkins.

3618. PERKINS, WILLIAM, ? Bristol : c. 1750.

See also BUSH & PERKINS.

3619. PERKYNS, RICHARD (*see* also PARKYNS), London : Fined in 1574 for occupying the standing of Henry Barret's widow at a Fair in Essex. 1587, R.W. ; 1593, U.W. In 1598 he died and left a legacy to the Company.
3620. PERKYNS, RICHARD, London : Was buried on 12 Mar. 1585 at Christ Church, Newgate Street.
3621. PERKINS, ROGER, SENR., Bristol : 7 Mar. 1667, F. Apprenticed to Thomas Pascall. Mentioned in 1700.
3622. PERKINS, ROGER, JUNR., Bristol and Kilgarick, Mon. : 26 Feb. 1679, F. S. of George. Apprenticed to Roger Perkins and Jane his wife, 27 Nov. 1672. Mentioned in 1727.
3623. PERRIS, HENRY (? PERRIN), London : 1662, S. 1668, R.W. ; 1673, U.W. ; 1678, M.
3624. PERRY, JAMES, London : 19 Mar. 1772, Y.
3625. PERRY, JOHN, London : 25 Nov. 1743, Y. ; 19 June 1755, L. ; 1764, S. ; 1773, R.W. Touch 909 L.T.P., which he obtained leave to strike, 15 Mar. 1743.

3626. PERRY, JOHN, London : 20 June 1765, Y. Touch 1009 L.T.P., which he obtained leave to strike on 20 June 1765. Was at 35 Moor Lane in 1801.

? Same.

3627. PERRY, JOHN, London : 23 Aug. 1804, L. ; 1808, f.S. ; 1817, f.R.W. Died in 1818.
3628. PERRY, JOHN, Longhope, Glocs.: S. of Humphrey. Apprenticed to Samuel Norkett, Bristol, and Martha his wife for seven years from 11 July 1606.
3629. PERRY, RICHARD, London : 16 June 1757, Y.
3630. PERRY, WILLIAM, Bristol : 1 Oct. 1812, F. S. of Thomas. Apprenticed to Thomas Hale and Martha his wife, 28 July 1794. Mentioned in the Poll Book for 1812 as of Philadelphia Street, St. Peter's, Bristol.
3631. PERSON, ROBERT, London : 1452, Y.
3632. PERVIS, JOHN, Edinburgh : In 1647 was an apprentice to John Abernethie.

3633. PETERS, ISAAC, London : 17 Mar. 1725, Y.

3634. PETERS, JACOB, Bristol : S. of John. Apprenticed to his father and mother, Sarah, 15 Aug. 1716.

3635. PETERS, JOHN, Bristol : 27 June 1691, F. Apprenticed to Thomas Salmon. Dead in 1719, when his widow Sarah was carrying on the business.

3636. PETERS, MATTHEW, Bristol and Blakeney, Glocs. : 27 April 1689, F. S. of Edward. Apprenticed to Erasmus Dole, Bristol, and Sara his wife, 31 May 1681. Turned over on 5 July 1682 to Thomas Salmon and Damaris his wife.

3637. PETT, HENRY, London : 16 Oct. 1783, Y.

3638. PETTIT, JOHN, London : Touch, 415 L.T.P., struck c. 1685. This name is not in the Y. or L. Lists, but is in the " Bennett " Book, and on 14 Dec. 1713 his widow, Sarah Pettitt, presented an apprentice. John Pettitt is there mentioned as " late citizen and Pewterer of London, but an inhabitant of Cambridge."

3639. PETTIVER, JOHN, London : Was summoned for bad work in 1680, and is mentioned in the " Bennett " Book, 1680-86. Touch, 349 L.T.P., which he had leave to strike in 1680/1.

3640. PETTIVER, SAMUEL, London : 10 Oct. 1695, Y. Touch, 616 L.T.P., which he had leave to strike on 1 Aug. 1704/5.

3641. PETTIVER, WILLIAM, London : Apprenticed to Oliver Roberts, was free in 1655. 1668, f.S. ; 1674, R.W. ; 1679, U.W. Died in 1680. (" Bennett " Book.) Touch, 322 L.T.P., which he had leave to strike in 1678/9.

3642. PHELAN, PHILIP, Kilkenny : Mentioned in 1755 and 1767.

3643. PHELPS, THOMAS, Bristol : S. of Thomas. Apprenticed to Richard Lymmell, 8 June 1648.

3644. PHILLIPS, DANIEL, Edinburgh : In 1711 was apprenticed to James Edgar.

3645. PHILLIPS, JAMES, London : 1632, f.S. ; 1642, R.W. ; 1647, U.W. ; 1651, M. Was a City Alderman in 1651, and Sheriff in 1653/4.

3645A. PHILLIPS, JOHN, London : c. 1680. (" Bennett " Book.)

3646. PHILLIPS, JOHN, London : 25 Mar. 1784, Y. In 1793 was a " Flatter and Planisher " at 13 King Street, Seven Dials.

3647. PHILLIPS, JOHN, London : 24 Aug. 1815, L. ; 1821, f.S. In 1817 was at 61 Whitecross Street.

3648. PHILLIPS, RICHARD, London : Served in 1543 in a body of soldiers raised from the Company.

3649. PHILLIPS, THOMAS, London : In 1622 he used " The Touch of the Lyon."

3650. PHILLIPS, THOMAS, London : 15 June 1727, Y. Touch, 784 L.T.P., struck c. 1728.

3651. PHILLIPS, THOMAS, London : 15 Oct. 1795, Y. ; 11 Dec. 1800, L. ; 1803, f.S. ; 1809 and 1810, R.W. ; 1816, U.W. ; 1817, M. Died 29 Nov. 1849, age 80. Touch, 1073 L.T.P., struck c. 1800. Of West Smithfield.

3652. PHILLIPS, THOMAS, JUNR., London : 13 Oct. 1832, Y. and L. ; 1841, f.S. Died 9 Aug. 1851, aged 40.

3653. PHILLIPS, WILLIAM, London : 13 Aug. 1719, Y. Touch, 841 L.T.P., which he had leave to strike on 18 Mar. 1730.

3654. PHILLIPS, WILLIAM, London : 21 June 1744, Y. Touch, 949 L.T.P., which he obtained leave to strike on 13 Dec. 1750.

3655. PHILLIPS, WILLIAM, London : 20 Mar. 1750, Y. ; 21 Aug. 1783, L. ; 1789, f.S. Touch, 1028 L.T.P., struck c. 1774. In 1793 was at 31 Watling Street.

3656. PHILLIPS, WILLIAM, London : 18 Oct. 1787, Y. In 1801 was at 16 Lamb Street, Spitalfields.
3657. PHILLIPS, WILLIAM, London : 1 May 1823, Y. and L. ; 1835, f.S. Died 24 July 1841, aged 40.
3658. PHILLIPS, WILLIAM AUGUSTUS, London : 19 Oct. 1815, Y. ; 18 June 1818, L. ; 1826, f.S. Died 28 April 1844, age 52.
3659. PHIPPS, JOSEPH, London : 21 June 1722, Y.
3660. PHIPPS, ROBERT, London : 22 June 1738, Y.
3661. PHIPPS, WILLIAM, London : 12 Oct. 1693, Y.
3662. PHIPPS, WILLIAM, London : 15 Mar. 1743, Y. Touch, 945 L.T.P., which he obtained leave to strike in 1750.

3663. PHYLLYPES, HOWELL, London : Was a pensioner of the Company's in 1591.
3664. PHYPPYS, WILLIAM, London : Mentioned in 1538.
3665. PICKARD, JOSEPH, London : 17 Dec. 1691, Y. ? Touch, 500 L.T.P., struck and dated 1693.

3666. PICKERING, DANIEL, London : 19 Dec. 1723, Y. Touch, 811 L.T.P., which he had leave to strike on 10 Jan. 1727.

3667. PICKERING, JOHN, London : 14 Dec. 1727, Y.
3668. PICKERING, LYDIA, London : 11 Oct. 1750, Y.

3669. PICKERYN, JOHN, Lynn : 1627/8, F.
3670. PICKEVER, BENJAMIN, Dublin : Died in 1773.
3671. PICKEVER, WILLIAM, Dublin : Died in 1778.
3672. PICKFAT, THOMAS, London : Touch, 350 L.T.P., which he had leave to strike in 1680. His name is not in the Y. or L. Lists, but is in the " Bennett " Book from 1680-86.

3673. PIDDEL, JOSEPH, London : 18 Mar. 1685, L. Touch, 407 L.T.P., which he had leave to strike in 1684/5.

3674. PIDGION, JOHN, London : 23 Mar. 1780, Y. ; 23 June 1785, L.
3675. PIERCE, FRANCIS (? PEIRCE), London : 25 Mar. 1784, Y.
3676. PIERCE, TRISTRAM, London : 15 Jan. 1702, Y. Touch, 607 L.T.P., which he had leave to strike on 19 Feb. 1702.

3677. PIERCY, THOMAS (see also PEIRCY), Dublin : Died in 1749.
3678. PIERIE, WILLIAM, London : 25 Sept. 1783, Y.
3679. PIERSON, JOSEPH, Bristol : 29 June 1747, F., by patrimony. S. of Joseph.
3680. PIERSON, THOMAS, York : 1462/3, F.
3681. PIGGENITT, BERTRAND, Dublin : 1685, F. A French refugee.
3682. PIGGOTT, FRANCIS, London : 24 Mar. 1736, Y. Touch, 886 L.T.P., which he had leave to strike on 22 June 1738. Appears in conjunction with Henry Joseph's Touch.

3683. PIGGOTT, FRANCIS, London: 18 June 1741, Y. and L.; 1753, f.S.; 1760, f.R.W.; 1769, U.W.; 1770, M. Died 1784. His Trade Card (*q.v.*) gives his address as "The Golden Dish, Paternoster Row, next Cheapside."

3684. PIGGOTT, JOHN, London: 10 June 1736, Y.; 3 Aug. 1738, L.; 1751, S. Touch, 868 L.T.P., which he had leave to strike on 12 Aug, 1736. (*Cf.* Touch of Sherwin.)

3685. PIGGOTT, THOMAS, London: 15 Dec. 1698, Y.; 16 Dec. 1725, L. Touch, 800 L.T.P., which he had leave to strike on 6 Dec. 1725. (*Cf.* Touch of . . . Sherwin.)

3686. PIGHT, HENRY, London: 20 Aug. 1678. L.
3687. PIGHT, JOHN, London: 23 Mar. 1693, Y.
3688. PILKINGTON, JOHN, London: 16 Dec. 1714, Y.
3689. PILKINGTON, ROBERT, London: 22 Mar. 1704, Y.; 19 April 1709, L. Touch, 625 L.T.P., which he had leave to strike on 18 May 1705.

3690. PINKARTOWN, JAMES, Edinburgh: In 1693 was an apprentice to Robert Edgar.
3691. PINNOCK, JOSEPH, London: 13 Oct. 1698, Y.
3692. PISTELL, BENJAMIN (? PISTOLL, *see* also KISTELL), London: 17 June 1703, Y.
3693. PITCHER, JOHN, London: 21 Mar. 1744, Y.
3694. PITT(s), & DADLEY, London: Touch, 1043 L.T.P., struck c. 1781. Partners probably R. Pitt, 1780, W.; and E. Dadley, 1799, W.

3695. PITT(s) & FLOYD, London: Touch, 1018 L.T.P., struck c. 1769, which they obtained leave to strike on 22 June 1769. Partners, R. Pitt, 1747, Y.; 1780, W.; and J. Floyd, 1748, Y.; 1787, W.

3696. PITT(s), JOHN, London: 21 Oct. 1779, Y.
3697. PITT(s), RICHARD, London: 18 June 1747, Y.; 22 June 1749, L.; 1759, S.; 1766, R.W.; 1780, U.W.; 1781, M. Touch, 924 L.T.P. Obtained leave to strike his Touch in 1747. His shop in 1792 was at 61 Shoe Lane.

3698. PITT(s), THOMAS, London: 19 Mar, 1778, Y.
3699. PIXLEY, JOSEPH, London: 20 June 1706, Y.
3699A. PIZZEY, HENRY, London: In 1817 was at 14 New Inn Yard, Shoreditch.
3699B. PIZZEY, ROBERT, London: In 1817 was at 11 Church Street, Shoreditch.
3700. PLATT, THOMAS, London: 1619, S.
3701. PLIVEY, WILLIAM, London: 17 Mar. 1697, Y. Touch, 548 L.T.P., which he had leave to strike on 29 May 1698.

3702. PLOMER, THOMAS, London: In 1457 was apprenticed to Thomas Launtot.
3703. PLUMBER, DANIEL, London: 23 Mar. 1720, Y.
3704. PLUMER, JOHN, York: On 30 Sept. 1721 he was apprenticed for seven years to Leonard Terry. 1732, F. Son of Antony.
3705. PLUMER, RICHARD, Ludlow: Pewterer and Brazier. 14 Nov. 1668, F.
3706. PLUMER, RICHARD, Ludlow: Pewterer and Brazier. Apprenticed to Richard P., 17 April 1693, F. Dead in 1717.
3707. PLUMER, RICHARD, Ludlow: S. of the last named, to whom he was apprenticed. 22 April 1717, F.
3708. PLUMER, RICHARD, Ludlow: S. of the last named, to whom he was apprenticed. 20 Mar. 1749, F.

3709. PLUMMER, JOHN, York: Free in 1684.
3710. PLUMMER, JOHN, London: 20 Mar. 1717, Y.
3711. PLUMMER, ROBERT, London: 20 Mar. 1689, Y.
3711A. PODSHORE, JOHN, London: c. 1680. ("Bennett" Book.)
3712. POLE, ROBERT, London: 19 Dec. 1717, Y. Touch, 738 L.T.P., which he had leave to strike on 13 Aug. 1719. (Cf. Touches of Norgrove & Spateman.)

3713. POLLARD, JAMES, Glasgow: 1785, F. Coppersmith.
3714. POLLARD, JOHN, York: Was free in 1684.
3715. POLLARD, JOHN, York: On 23 April 1709 he was apprenticed for eight years to John White. 17 May 1717, F. Mentioned again in 1739/40. Son of Elizabeth.
       POLTOCK, see PALTOCK.
3716. PONDER, SYMOND, London: In 1549 he was a Warden of the Yeomanry. 1555, R.W. A searcher to the Company.
3717. PONTON, ARCHIBALD, Edinburgh: In 1780 he was an apprentice to William Fraser.
3718. PONTON, JOHN, London: 16 Dec. 1708, Y.
3719. PONTY, JAMES, Dublin: Mentioned in 1732.
3720. POOL(E), JOHN, London: 18 June 1747, Y.
3721. POOL(E), RICHARD, London: 15 Oct. 1747, Y.; 15 Dec. 1748, L. Touch, 930 L.T.P., which he obtained leave to strike on 15 Dec. 1748.

3722. POOL(E), ROBERT, Dublin: Mentioned in 1740.
3723. POOL(E), ROWLAND, London: 20 Mar. 1717, Y. Touch, 782 L.T.P., which he had leave to strike on 17 Dec. 1724.

3724. POOLER, THOMAS, London: Worked as a spoon-maker with John Backhouse.
3725. POPE, JOHN, London: 21 June 1688, Y.
3726. PORT, RICHARD, London: 9 May 1723, Y.
3727. PORTER, JOHN, London: 17 Dec. 1691, Y.

3728. PORTER, LUKE, London: 21 June 1722, Y.
3729. PORTER, LUKE, London: Was evidently a free-man of the Company in 1679/80, when he made complaint against certain irregular actions of the Beadle, William Bowden. Touch, 327 L.T.P., which he had leave to strike in 1679. He is mentioned in the "Bennett" Book from 1680-84.

3730. PORTER, THOMAS, London: In 1683 was ordered to use for his Touch the device of the "Angel and Glister Serreng" (or Clyster Syringe). Touch, 394 L.T.P., which he struck on 20 Dec. 1683.

3731. PORTEOUS, ROBERT, London: 16 Oct. 1760, Y.; 20 June 1765, L.; 1771, f.S.; 1778, R.W.; 1790, U.W. Touch, 999 L.T.P. (R. & T. Porteous), which he obtained leave to strike in 1762.

3732. PORTEOUS, ROBERT & THOMAS, London: Touch, 999 L.T.P., struck c. 1762. Of Gracechurch Street. Successors to Richard King, hence the ostrich.

3733. PORTEOUS, THOMAS, London: 17 Oct. 1762, Y.; 20 June 1765, L.; 1772, f.S.; 1779, f.R.W. Dead in 1786. Touch, 999 L.T.P., struck c. 1762 (see above).
3734. POSKITT, WILLIAM, York: On 9 April 1679 was apprenticed for seven years to James Secker. 1690/1, F.

3735. POSTILTHWAYTE, RICHARD, York: 1465/6, F.
3736. POSTILTHWAYTE, THOMAS, York: 1459/60, F.
3737. POTTEN, WILLIAM, London: 11 Dec. 1729, Y.
3738. POTTER, GEORGE, London: 17 Mar. 1814, Y. and L.; 1819, f.S.; 1831, R.W. Died 27 Dec. 1865, aged 74.
3739. POTTER, THOMAS, London: 30 June 1783, Y.
3740. POTTERILL, GEORGE, London: 13 Oct. 1715, Y.
3741. POTTS, ISAAC, London: 10 Oct. 1723, Y.
3742. POTTS, JOHN, Dublin: Mentioned in 1753 and 1775.
3743. POWELL, JAMES, Caerleon, Monmouth: S. of James. Apprenticed to William Watkins, Bristol, 6 Mar. 1728. Premium £10. Mentioned in the Bristol Poll Book for 1739 as a country voter of Caerleon.
3744. POWELL, JAMES, Bristol: In the Poll Books for 1754 and 1774 he is given as of St. Thomas's, and in that of 1781 as of St. James's, Bristol.
3745. POWELL, JOHN, London: Was a Warden of the Yeomanry in 1548, and in 1553 he served as a soldier for the Company.
3746. POWELL, JOHN, London: In 1584 he served as a soldier for the Company.
3747. POWELL, RALPH, London: In 1605 he was fined for giving warning to another pewterer of an impending search for bad wares. 1612, R.W.; 1621, U.W.
3748. POWELL, ROBERT, Cork: Mentioned in 1728 and died in 1769.

3749. POWELL, ROBERT, JUNR., Cork: Mentioned in 1787.
3750. POWELL, THOMAS, London: 6 Mar. 1684, L.; 1689, S.; 1697, f.R.W.; 1704, f.U.W.; 1706 and 1707, M. Touch, 350A L.T.P., which he had leave to strike in 1680/1.

3751. POWELL, WILLIAM, London: 17 June 1824, Y. Died 13 Aug. 1860.
3752. POWELL, WILLIAM, Lidney, Glocs.; S. of Henry. Apprenticed to James Cadell, Bristol, and Bridgette his wife, 16 Feb. 1600.

3753. POWER, NICHOLAS, London: 14 Oct. 1824, Y. Died 1843.
3754. POYER, THOMAS, Lamphy, Pembroke: S. of John. Apprenticed to William Millard, Bristol, and Jane his wife, 10 July 1646.
3755. POYNTON, TOUNDROW, York: On 1 Oct. 1712 he was apprenticed for seven years to Richard Chambers. 21 May 1735, F. S. of John.

3756. POYNTON, TOUNDROW, York: Was free in 1684.
3757. PRATT, ALFRED, London: 23 June 1763, Y.
3758. PRATT, BENJAMIN, London: 6 Aug. 1730, Y.
3759. PRATT, CRANMER, London: 17 Dec. 1761, Y.
3760. PRATT, HENRY, London: Touch, 238 L.T.P., which he had leave to strike in 1675/6. His name is not in the existing Y. or L. Lists, but appears in the "Bennett" Book, 1679-86.

3761. PRATT, JAMES, London: 15 Nov. 1724, Y.
3761A. PRATT, JOHN, London: c. 1680. ("Bennett" Book.)
3762. PRATT, JOSEPH, London: 1 May 1691, L.; 1696, f.S.; 1706, R.W.; 1716, U.W.; 1720, M. Touch, 201 L.T.P., which he had leave to strike in 1671/2.

3763. PRATT, JOSEPH, London: 13 Oct. 1709, Y. S. of Joseph. Touch 753 L.T.P., which he had leave to strike on 15 June 1721.

3764. PRATT, THOMAS, London: 17 Sept. 1714, Y.
3765. PRENTICE, ROBERT, Edinburgh: 1781, F.
3766. PRENTICE, ROBERT, London: Fined in 1570.
3767. PRENTYS, WILLIAM, York: 1373/4, F.

3767A. PRESTON, WILLIAM, Liverpool: In 1767 was at Redcross Street.
3768. PRICE, BENJAMIN, London: 24 June 1784, Y.
3769. PRICE, JACOB, Gloucester: Dead in 1691.
3770. PRICE, JAMES, London: 24 June 1784, Y.
3771. PRICE, JOHN, London: 19 June 1755, Y.; 19 Oct. 1769, L.; 1776, S.; 1781, R.W.
3772. PRICE, JOHN, Thornbury, Glocs.: S. of Thomas. Apprenticed to Abraham Yeo(re), Bristol, for seven years from 5 April 1620.
3772A. PRICE, RICHARD, Gloucester: Mentioned in Marriage Licence in 1642.
3773. PRICE, THOMAS, Dublin: Mentioned in 1768. Died in 1807.
3774. PRICE, THOMAS, Pembroke: S. of William. Apprenticed to William James, Bristol, and Ann his wife, 7 July 1675.
3775. PRICHARD, POLIDORE, London: 1628, S.; 1638, R.W.; 1644, U.W.; 1649, M.
3776. PRIDDEN, WILLIAM, London: 16 Oct. 1807, Y.; 20 Aug. 1818, L.; 1827, f.S.; 1838, R.W.; 1840, U.W.; 1841, M. Died 14 June 1848, aged 76.
3777. PRIDDLE, SAMUEL, London: 19 Aug. 1773, Y.; 11 Oct. 1798, L.; 1800, f.S. Touch, 1039 L.T.P., struck c. 1777.

3778. PRIER, RICHARD, London: Had false salts seized in 1552 and died in 1559.
3779. PRIER, MRS., London: Mentioned in 1562.
PRIESLEY, see PEISLEY.
3780. PRIEST, PETER, London: 28 Nov 1667, L.
3781. PRINCE, JOHN, London: 17 Mar. 1697. Y. Touch, 583 L.T.P., which he had leave to strike on 18 April 1701.

3782. PRIOR, WILLIAM, London: Mentioned in 1568.
3783. PROBERT, WILLIAM, London: 21 Mar. 1688, Y.
3784. PROCTOR, FRANCIS, London: 1631, f.S.
3785. PROCTOR, JOHN, London: 26 Oct. 1752, Y.
3786. PROCTOR, ROBERT, Dundee: 1729, F. Copper and White-ironsmith.
3787. PROSSER, PETER, Cork: Mentioned in 1755.

3788. PROWDE, WILLIAM, London: Sold some moulds to the Company in 1451.
3789. PRUDEN, JAMES, London: 13 Dec. 1750, Y.
PRYER, see PRIER.
3789A. PUDDEPHAT, JOSEPH, London: c. 1680. ("Bennett" Book.)
3790. PUGH, ROWLAND, London: 22 Mar. 1763, Y.
3791. PULESTON, JAMES, London: 26 Oct. 1752, Y. Touch, 983 L.T.P., which he obtained leave to strike on 18 Oct. 1759.

3792. PULLER, SAMUEL, London: 18 June 1702, Y.; 15 Aug. 1709, L.; 1714, S.
3793. PURCELL, BALTAZAR, Dublin: 1640, F.
3794. PURCELL, LAURENCE, Dublin: c. 1800. Of Back Lane. Mentioned in 1833.

3795. PURDY, WILLIAM, Bristol: April 1635, F. Apprenticed to Abraham Yeo(re), Bristol, and Joan his wife, 12 Mar. 1627.
3796. PURLE, RICHARD, London: 24 Oct. 1822, Y.
3796A. PUSEY, EDWARD, London: c. 1680. ("Bennett" Book.) Touch, 314 L.T.P., which he had leave to strike in 1678/9.

3797. PYCKWELL, JOHN, Bristol: 20 Oct. 1567, F. Apprenticed to Humphrey Cox.
3798. PYCROFT, WALTER, London: 1624, f.S.
3799. PYE, ROGER, London: 13 Oct. 1737, Y. Touch, 882 L.T.P., which he had leave to strike on 23 Mar. 1737/8.

3800. PYNTON, PIERS, London: 1452, Y. He was a Liveryman in 1457.
3801. PYPOND, JOHN (? PEPOND), London: 1461 and 1464, R.W.
3802. PYTSEY, JOHN, London: Before 1457 he was apprenticed to Mr. Coldham, but in this year he was covenant man to Thomas Marler.

Q

3802A. QUICK, EDWARD, London: Touch, 451 L.T.P., which he had leave to strike on 23 Mar. 1687.

3803. QUICK, EDWARD, London: 6 Dec. 1714, Y.; 18 June 1730, L.; 1739, S.; 1744, R.W.; 1754, U.W.; 1756, M.

3804. QUICK, EDWARD, London: 6 Dec. 1708, Y. Touch, 657 L.T.P., struck c. 1708.

3805. QUICK, EDWARD, London: 18 Mar. 1735, Y.; 11 Oct. 1744, L.; 1754, f.S.; 1760, f.R.W.;

1772, U.W.; 1773, Died. Touch, 900 L.T.P., which he had leave to strike on 9 Oct. 1741.

3806. QUICK, HUGH, London: 3 April 1685, L.; 1697, f.R.W.; 1704, U.W.; 1708, M. Touch, 230 L.T.P., which he had leave to strike in 1674/5, dated (16)74.

3807. QUICK, JOHN, London: 12 Oct. 1699, Y. Touch, 591 L.T.P., which he had leave to strike on 14 Nov. 1701.

3808. QUISSENBOROUGH, SAMUEL, London: 20 Mar. 1672, Y. Touch, 213 L.T.P., which he had leave to strike in 1675. His name appears in the "Bennett" Book, 1679-86.

R

3809. RABSON, THOMAS, London: 15 June 1732, Y.

3810. RACK, CHARLES, London: 1 May 1691, L. Touch, 355 L.T.P., which he had leave to strike on 25 Aug. 1681.

3811. RACTLYF, HARRY, London: In 1556 he was allowed to leave London for Yorkshire on the understanding that he never worked there as a pewterer. Had faulty goods seized in 1558 at Stourbridge Fair. In 1563 he was receiving charity from the Company as a poor brother.

3811A. RADCLIFF, THOMAS, London: c. 1680. ("Bennett" Book.) Touch, 210 L.T.P., which he had leave to strike in 1671/2.

3811B. RADCLYFFE, WILLIAM, Doncaster: Gazetted a Bankrupt, 25 Jan. 1757.

3811C. RADFORD, THOMAS, Manchester: 1769-1781, was at Market Street Lane.

3812. RADYSH, JOHN, London: In 1518 was fined for disobedience.

3813. RAE, ADAM, Edinburgh: In 1691 was an apprentice to Alexander Findlay.

3814. RAINBOW, WILLIAM, London: 15 Oct. 1743, Y.

3815. RAIT, JAMES, Edinburgh: 1718, F. Touch, 121 E.T.P.

3816. RALPHS, HENRY, London: 25 June 1778, Y.

3817. RAMAGE, ADAM, Edinburgh: In 1805 he was apprenticed to James Wright.

RAMAGE EDIN[R]

3818. RAMAGE, JAMES, Edinburgh: In 1793 had his shop in Bristow Street.

3819. RAMSAY, JAMES, Edinburgh: In 1682 was apprenticed to James Abernethie.

3820. RAMSAY, JAMES, Perth: 1776, F. Coppersmith.

3821. RAMSAY, JOHN, Edinburgh: 1659, F. Touch, 63 E.T.P.

3822. RAMSAY, JOHN, Edinburgh: In 1683 was an apprentice to Alexander Findlay.

3823. RAMSAY, JOHN, Edinburgh: In 1812 was an apprentice to Adam Anderson.

3824. RAMSAY, JOHN, Perth: Mentioned in 1714.

3825. RAMSAY, RICHARD, London: Mentioned in 1457.

3826. RAMSDON, JOHN, London: 17 Dec. 1795, Y.

3827. RANCE, ROBERT, London: 20 June 1771, Y.

3828. RANDALL, ?———, London: Touch, 333 L.T.P., struck c. 1679. This is evidently a Christian name, the surname being obliterated.

3829. RANDALL, CHARLES, London: 22 June 1699, Y. Touch, 572 L.T.P., which he had leave to strike on 17 June 1700.

3830. RANDALL, EDWARD, London: 14 July 1692, L.; 1698, f.S.; 1711, R.W.

3831. RANDALL, EDWARD, London: 24 Mar. 1715, Y. Touch, 696 L.T.P., which he had leave to strike in 1715.

3832. RANDALL, JOHN, London: 8 Aug. 1723, Y. Touch, 747 L.T.P., which he had leave to strike on 8 Aug. 1723.

3833. RANDALL, LEWIS, London: In 1585 was chosen to serve in a body of soldiers raised from the Company, but paid another pewterer to serve for him. 1609 and 1613, M. Left a legacy to the Company in 1616 of £50 Consols for poor members.

3834. RANDALL, RICHARD, London: In 1584 he was fined at Bartholomew Fair and in 1607 is mentioned again.

3835. RANDALL, ROBERT, London: 13 Oct. 1748, Y. Touch, 955 L.T.P., which he obtained leave to strike on 17 Oct. 1751.

3836. RANDALL, THOMAS, Lynn: 1646/7, F.

3837. RANDESFELD, JOHN, London: 1477, Y.

3838. RANDOLF, WILLIAM, London: Was free in 1457.

3839. RAPER, CHRISTOPHER, London: 10 Aug. 1676, L.; 1680, S.; 1687 and 1688, R.W. (he was displaced in the latter year); 1692, U.W.; 1694, M. Touch, 140 L.T.P., struck c. 1670.

3840. RAUSON, WILLIAM, York: 1440/1, F. In 1451/2 his name again appears in the list of freemen, with this note:

"Reconciliatus est ad libertatem dictæ civitatis sub condicione. . . ., etc."

3841. RAVENELL, WILLIAM, Bristol and Ross, Herefs.: 31 Jan. 1781, F. S. of William. Apprenticed to Robert Bush and Ann his wife, 3 July 1771. Mentioned in the Poll Books for 1781 and 1784 as of Temple, Bristol.

3842. RAVENHILL, THOMAS, Bristol and Ross, Herefs.: 6 Sept. 1780, F. Apprenticed to Robert Bush. Mentioned in the Poll Book for 1781 as of Castle Precincts, and in that for 1812 as of Temple Street, Bristol.

3843. RAVENHILL, THOMAS, Bewdley: Mentioned in the Bristol Poll Book for 1784 as a country voter.

3843A. RAVES, WILLIAM, London: Touch, 559 L.T.P., which he had leave to strike on 31 July 1699.

3844. RAWLINS, SAM, London: Mentioned in 1620.

3845. RAWLINS, WILLIAM, London: 1652, S.; 1661, R.W.; 1665, U.W.; 1668, M.
3846. RAWLINSON, JOHN, London: Touch, 249 L.T.P., which he had leave to strike in 1674/5.

3847. RAWSON, JAMES, London: 17 Mar. 1774, Y.
3848. RAYMOND, BENJAMIN, London: 15 Mar. 1749, Y.
3849. RAYMOND, CHRISTOPHER, Thornbury, Glocs.: S. of George. Apprenticed to Edward Gregory, Bristol, and Anne his wife, 18 Oct. 1718.
3850. RAYMOND, JAMES, London: 15 Mar. 1749, Y.
3851. RAYMOND, JOHN, London: 17 Dec. 1691, Y.
3852. RAYMOND, THOMAS, London: 17 June 1756, Y.
3853. RAYNE, ELIZABETH, London: 16 June 1724, Y.
3854. RAYNE, JOSEPH, London: 14 Dec. 1693, Y.
RAYNOLDE, see REYNOLDE.
3855. RAYSBEKE, THOMAS, York: 1504/5, F.
3856. READ(E), ELIZABETH, London: Had an apprentice, Lucy Sellars, bound to her for seven years on 13 April 1713/4.
3857. READ(E), ISAAC, London: 23 June 1743, Y. Touch, 940 L.T.P., which he obtained leave to strike on 15 Mar. 1749.

3858. READ(E), JOHN, London: In 1596 he was committed to ward for various offences and dismissed the Company for ever. He was, however, forgiven and re-admitted at the next Court.
3859. READ(E), JOHN, Bristol: 12 Nov. 1669, F. Apprenticed to Richard Baker.
3860. READ(E), JOSEPH, London: 2 Mar. 1727, Y.
3861. READ(E), ROBERT, Bristol: Mentioned 1649-59.
3862. READ(E), SAMUEL, London: 29 Nov. 1688, Y.
3863. READ(E), SIMON, London: In 1654 his daughter Deborah was christened at St. Peter's, Cornhill. 1660, f.S.
3864. READ(E), THOMAS, London: 25 Oct. 1753, Y.
3865. READ(E), WILLIAM, London: In a token he issued in 1666 he describes himself as of Milton, near Gravesend. See list of tokens at end of Chap. iv.
3866. READING, ROGER (see also RIDDING), London: Touch, 175 L.T.P., which he had leave to strike in 1669/70. His name does not appear in the Y. or L. Lists, but is in the "Bennett" Book, 1679-86.

3867. READING, THEOPHILUS, London: Touch, No. 263, struck c. 1676. In 1687/8 he was permitted to strike another Touch in place of No. 263. ? No. 6. If this is so it is obviously out of place.

READMAN, see REDMAN.
3868. REAVELY, A——, of ?: c. 1725.

3869. REBATE, JOHNE, Edinburgh: 1588, F. ? Touches, 1 and 2 E.T.P.

3870. REDBURN, JOHN, York: 1495/6, F.
3871. REDDETH, JAMES, Edinburgh: Mentioned as a master in 1603.
REDDING, see READING.
3872. REDFEARN, THOMAS, London: 16 Dec. 1756, Y.
3873. REDHEAD, ANTHONY London: 19 Mar. 1684, L.; 1691, f.S.; 1695, R.W. Used the sign of a swan. Touch, 264 L.T.P., which he had leave to strike in 1675/6.

3874. REDHEAD, GABRIEL, London: Was successor to Mr. Dod. 1667, L.; 1671, f.S.; 1689, R.W.
3875. REDNAP, PETER, London: 17 Dec. 1713, Y.; 16 June 1720, L. Touch, 678 L.T.P., struck

c. 1713. His mark appears with the Hall Marks of Benjamin Withers.

3876. REDMAN, JAMES, London : Was free in 1598, and in 1600 he applied for the post of Beadle or Clerk.

3877. REDMAN, WILLIAM, London : Was free in 1554. 1569, R.W. ; 1574, U.W.

3878. REDSHAW, JOHN, London : Touch, 219 L.T.P., struck c. 1675. His name is not in the Records.

3879. REDSHAW, MARY, London : 9 Aug. 1733, Y. She used the same device as her father, John Redshaw, with the date of her freedom (1733) added, and this mark appears on the pewter which was formerly in use at Staple Inn and bears the inscribed date 1751. Made free by patrimony.

3880. REDWORTH, JOHN, Dublin : 1635, F.

3881. REECH, CHARLES, London : 8 Nov. 1723, Y.

3882. REEVE, ISAAC, London : 20 June 1754, Y. Touch, 972 L.T.P., which he obtained leave to strike in 1755.

3883. REEVE, JOHN, London : 19 Mar. 1818, L.

3884. REEVE, JOHN, London : 18 Mar. 1819, Y.

3885. REEVE, JOSEPH, London : 23 Mar. 1786, Y. ; 18 June 1807, L. ; 1812, f.S.

3886. REEVE, JOSEPH BOULTON, London : 15 Mar. 1810, Y. Died 14 Feb. 1856, age 67.

3887. REEVE, WILLIAM, London : 14 Dec. 1815, Y. and L. ; 1822, f.S. ; 1833, R.W. Died 1834.

3888. REEVES, JOHN, London : 17 June 1714, Y.

3889. REID, H——, Glasgow : ? c. 1850.

3890. REID, H—— & J——, Glasgow : ? c. 1800.

3891. REID, JAMES, Perth : Apprentice in 1739 to Patrick Campbell.

3892. REID, JAMES, Bristol and Keigg, N.B. : 16 Dec. 1751, F. S. of Archibald. Apprenticed to William Calder, Bristol, 30 April 1744. Gazetted as Insolvent on 24 Mar. 1761.

3893. REID, ROBERT, Edinburgh : 1718, F. Touch, 119 E.T.P.

3894. REID, W——, Glasgow : Mentioned in 1800.

3895. REID & SONS, Glasgow : c. 1830.

3896. RELFE, EDWARD, London : Touch, 202 L.T.P., which he had leave to strike in 1671/2. His name is not in the existing Y. or L. Lists, but is in the " Bennett " Book from 1679-86.

3897. RENDALE, JOHN, London : 1451, U.W. ; 1454, 1459 and 1462, M.

3898. RENDER, CHARLES, London : 22 June 1699, Y. Touch, 570 L.T.P., which he had leave to strike on 6 May 1700.

3899. RENNIE, JAMES, Glasgow : 1789, F. White-ironsmith.

3899A. RENSHAW, HENRY, Liverpool : 1757-1763 was in Dale Street.

3900. REN(T)STON, JOHN, London : 1527 and 1532, R.W.

3901. RENTON, JOHN, London : 11 Aug. 1687, L.
REO, *see* ROE.

3902. REWCASTLE, MORGAN, London : 22 Mar. 1687,Y.

3903. REYMERS, JAMES, London : 17 June 1703, Y.

3904. REYNOLD(s), ANTHONY (? RAYNOLDE), Dublin : 1623, F.

3905. REYNOLD(s), EDMUND, Lynn : 1697/8, F.

3905A. REYNOLD(s), EDWARD, London : c. 1680. ("Bennett" Book.)

3906. REYNOLD(s), HENRY, Kilkenny : Retired in 1746.

3907. REYNOLD(s), JOHN, Dublin : 1616, F.

3908. REYNOLD(s), JOHN, Dublin : 1639, F.

3908A. REYNOLD(s), JOHN, London : Touch, 530 L.T.P., which he had leave to strike on 27 Mar. 1696.

3909. REYNOLD(s), PETER, Cork : S. of George. Apprenticed to Thomas Hobson, Bristol, and Elizabeth his wife, 13 April 1632.

3910. REYNOLD(s), ROBERT, London : 12 Oct. 1704, Y. Touch, 618 L.T.P., which he had leave to strike on 13 Nov. 1704.

3911. REYNOLD(s), ROBERT, London : 18 June 1761, Y.; 19 Mar. 1767, L.; 1775, f.S.; 1782, f.R.W.; 1793, f.U.W.; 1794, f.M. Partner in Townsend & Reynolds. Touch, 1012 L.T.P. He was granted John Townsend's Touch on 19 Mar. 1767.

3912. REYNOLD(s), THOMAS, Dublin : Mentioned in 1545 and 1551.

3913. REYNOLD(s), THOMAS, London : 20 Dec. 1716,Y.

3914. REYNOLD(s), THOMAS, London : Mentioned in 1640. 19 Aug. 1669, L.; 1673, f.S.
See also TEMPLE & REYNOLDS.

3915. REYNOLDSON, JOHN, London : 22 June 1693, Y.

3916. RHODES, THOMAS, London : 18 June 1730, L.; 1740, S.; 1746, R.W. Touch, 734 L.T.P., which he had leave to strike on 15 June 1721.

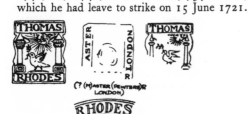

3917. RICE, JOSEPH, London : 19 June 1719, Y.

3918. RICE, MATTHEW, London : 4 June 1719, Y. He had leave to strike his Touch on 4 June 1719, but it is not on the Touchplates.

3919. RICE, RICHARD, Dublin : 1595, F.

3920. RICH, CHARLES, Bristol : 30 April 1807, F. S. of Samuel. Apprenticed to Robert Bush and Ann his wife, 11 Sept. 1784. In the Poll Book for 1812 is given as of St. Thomas's, Bristol.

3921. RICH, DANIEL, Bristol : 15 June 1818, F. S. of Robert. Apprenticed to Robert Bush, Junr., 7 April 1796. Premium £10.

3922. RICH, GEORGE, Bristol : 5 Oct. 1812, F. S. of Robert. Apprenticed to Preston Edgar and Rebecca his wife, 24 July 1794. In the Poll Book for 1812 is given as of Pithay, Christ Church Parish, Bristol.

3923. RICH, ROBERT, Bristol : 6 Sept. 1780, F. Apprenticed to James Powell. Dead in 1794. In the Poll Book for 1781 is given as of St. Michael's, Bristol.

3924. RICH, WILLIAM, Bristol : Described in the 1840 Directory as a "Pewterer, plumber, beerengine and Britannia-metal manufacturer of 40 Redcliff Street."

3925. RICHARDS, RICHARD, London : 15 Dec. 1709, Y.

3926. RICHARDS, TIMOTHY, London : 21 Mar. 1699, Y. Touch, 647 L.T.P., struck c. 1707.

3927. RICHARDS, WILLIAM, London : 23 June 1768, Y.

3927A. RICHARDS, WILLIAM, London : c. 1680. ("Bennett" Book.) Touch, 193 L.T.P., which he had leave to strike in 1670/1.

3928. RICHARDSON, CHARLES, London : Was free in 1668, and is in the "Bennett" Book from 1679-84.

3929. RICHARDSON, EDMUND, York : 1539/40, F. City Chamberlain in 1545/6; Mayor in 1574/5.

3930. RICHARDSON, GEORGE, York : 1664/5, F., by patrimony.

3931. RICHARDSON, HUMFREY, York : Free in 1616.

3932. RICHARDSON, HUMFREY, York: Mentioned in 1630/1, when he was free, and 1668/9. Father of William.

3933. RICHARDSON, JAMES, Perth: 1756. Mentioned as Coppersmith, Founder, Pewterer and Box Master.

3934. RICHARDSON, JOHN, London: 22 Sept. 1709, Y.

3934A. RICHARDSON, ROBERT, York: Free by patrimony, 1657/8.

3935. RICHARDSON, WILLIAM, London: In 1457 was an apprentice with Stephen Auncell.

3936. RICHARDSON, WILLIAM, Perth: In 1771 was a pewterer and coppersmith.

3937. RICHARDSON, WILLIAM, Perth: In 1761 was an apprentice to David Young. } ? Same.

3938. RICHMOND, WILLIAM, London: Mentioned in 1494.

3939. RICROFT, WALTER, London: Mentioned in 1614. In 1622 he was ordered instead of giving on his Touch three ears of corn to give one only with (the) letters (of his name).

3940. RIDDING, JOSEPH (see also READING), London: 12 Mar. 1701, Y.; 18 July 1727, L.; 1735, S.

3941. RIDDING, THOMAS, London: 28 Aug. 1685, L.; 1690, f.S.; 1697, R.W. Touch, 233 L.T.P., which he had leave to strike in 1674/5.

3942. RIDDING, THOMAS, London: 22 June 1699, Y.

3943. RIDDOCK, JOHN, Edinburgh: 1780. White-ironsmith. Shop in West Bow Head.

3944. RIDEING, WILLIAM, York: On 1 July 1662 was apprenticed for nine years to Robart Cowton. 1671/2, F.

3945. RIDEING, WILLIAM, York: 1704/5, F.

3945A. RIDER, NATHANIEL, London: c. 1680. ("Bennett" Book.) Touch, 331 L.T.P., which he had leave to strike in 1679/80.

3946. RIDGE, GABRIEL, London: 11 Aug. 1698, Y.

3947. RIDGLEY, WILLIAM, London: 17 Mar. 1691, Y.; 28 Sept. 1699, L.; 1723, f.R.W.; 5 Aug. 1731, U.W. William Buckley's Touch has been wrongly ascribed to this man in other works.

3948. RIGHTON, SAMUEL, London: 14 Dec. 1732, Y.; 11 Aug. 1737, L. Touch, 851 L.T.P., which he had leave to strike on 19 Dec. 1734. He was made a bankrupt, 17 Feb. 1743.

3949. RIGSBY, PETER, London: Servant to Edward Reo (or Roe) in 1557.

3950. ROAFF(E), GEORGE, London: In 1583 was a Warden of the Yeomanry. 1600, U.W.

3951. ROAFF(E), JASPER, London: In 1602 was chosen a collector from the Yeomanry.

3952. ROANE, CAPT. GEORGE, Dublin: Advertised in the Dublin Gazette of 29 May 1711 as of the Pewterer's and Brazier's Shop in Charles Street.

3952A. ROBERTS, ABRAHAM, London: Touch, 619 L.T.P., which he had leave to strike on 17 Nov. 1704.

3953. ROBERTS, EDWARD, London: Touch, 425 L.T.P., struck c. 1686. No mention of his name is in the existing records.

3954. ROBERTS, EDWARD, Pucklechurch, Mon.; S. of John. Apprenticed to Edward Gregory, Bristol, and Anne, 3 June 1724.

3955. ROBERTS, GEORGE, London: 21 Mar. 1722, Y.

3956. ROBERTS, GEORGE, London: 15 Oct. 1801, Y.

3957. ROBERTS, JEREMIAH, Bristol: S. of Lewis and Emery, to whom he was apprenticed for seven years from 28 April 1685.

3958. ROBERTS, JOHN, London: In 1574 was an apprentice to John Russell, and is mentioned again in 1614.

3959. ROBERTS, JOHN, London: In 1457 was an apprentice to Thomas Dounton, and is mentioned in 1486.

3960. ROBERTS, LEWIS (LUDOVIC), Bristol and Treleckgrames, Mon.: 6 Nov. 1662, F. S. of Lewis. Apprenticed to William Pascall and Marie his wife, 13 Jan. 1646. Edmund Davis was apprenticed to him c. 1670. Mentioned in 1685.

3961. ROBERTS, OLIVER, London: Was free in 1605. 1627, R.W.; 1637, U.W.; 1644, M.

3962. ROBERTS, PHILIP, London: 22 June 1738, Y.; 17 June 1742, L.; 1753, S. Touch, 888 L.T.P., which he had leave to strike on 22 June 1738.

3963. ROBERTS, RICHARD, London: 21 June 1733, Y.

3964. ROBERTS, THOMAS, London: 4 Oct. 1688, Y. Touch, 443 L.T.P., which he had leave to strike on 4 Oct. 1688.

3965. ROBERTS, THOMAS, London: 22 Mar. 1693, Y.
3966. ROBERTS, THOMAS, London: 21 Mar. 1727, Y.
3967. ROBERTS, WILLIAM, London: 1618, S.
3968. ROBERTS, WILLIAM, London: 21 Mar. 1727, Y.
3969. ROBERTS, WILLIAM, London: 17 Oct. 1762, Y.
3970. ROBERTSON, ROBERT, Perth: In 1779 was an apprentice to James Ramsay.
3971. ROBERTSON, ROBERT, Dundee: In 1780 was a Freeman white-ironsmith.
3972. ROBERTSON, ROBERT, Stirling: In 1599 was a pewterer and Deacon in this year.
ROBESON, see ROBSON.
3973. ROBINS, JAMES, London: 17 June 1714, Y.; 21 Aug. 1718, L.; 1725, S.
3974. ROBINS, JOHN, London: Free in 1611. 1614, S.; 1623, R.W.; 1635, U.W.; 1638, M. Died in 1647. Left a house in Barbican to the Company.
3974A. ROBINS, JOHN & SON, Birmingham: In the 1805 Directory are given as Pewter spoon, pressed hinge, etc., manufacturers at Vauxhall Street.
3975. ROBINS, JOSEPH, London: 1819, Y.
3976. ROBINS, LUKE, London: 18 June 1761, Y.

3977. ROBINS, OBEDIENCE, London: In 1680 was admonished for faulty wares. She is mentioned in the "Bennett" Book from 1679-86. Touch, 260 L.T.P., which she had leave to strike in 1675/6.

3978. ROBINS, OBEDIENCE, London: 15 Mar. 1743, Y.
3979. ROBINS, ROBERT, London: 30 Sept. 1712, Y.
3980. ROBINS, THOMAS, London: 9 Oct. 1740, Y.
3981. ROBINSON, ABSOLUM, London: 9 Oct. 1735, Y.
3982. ROBINSON, BRITANUS, York: 1614/5, F.
3983. ROBINSON, CHRISTOPHER, Dublin: 1759, died.

3984. ROBINSON, GEORGE, London: 16 Oct. 1783, Y.; 20 Mar, 1788, L.; 1794, f.S.; 1802, f.R.W.; 1807, U.W.; 1808, M. Died 7 Sept. 1834.
3985. ROBINSON, GEORGE, London: 18 Mar. 1819, Y.
3986. ROBINSON, JAMES, London: 17 Oct. 1776, Y.
3987. ROBINSON, JOHN, Dublin: Died in 1758.
3988. ROBINSON, JOHN HENRY, London: 16 Dec. 1802, Y.
3988A. ROBINSON, JOHN, London: Touch, 183 L.T.P., which he had leave to strike in 1670/1.

3989. ROBINSON, JOSEPH, London: 17 Oct. 1754, Y.
3990. ROBINSON, LEONARD, London: Married 28 Nov. 1666 at St. Mary's, Reading, to Margaret Atkins.
3991. ROBINSON, RICHARD, York: 1448/9, F.
3992. ROBINSON, THOMAS, York: 1442/3, F.
3993. ROBINSON, WILLIAM, Newcastle: Died in 1652.
3994. ROBINSON, WILLIAM, Dublin: Pewterer and Brazier. Opened shop in Castle Street in 1740.
3995. ROBSON, JOHN, London: Fined in 1553 and in 1559 was chosen amongst others to carry out a proclamation of the Lord Mayor.
3996. ROBSON, RICHARD, London: 1598, Y. Was an apprentice to James Redman.
3997. ROBYNET, JOHN, London: In 1457 was an apprentice to Piers Pynton.
3998. ROBYNSON, JOHN, London: In 1457 was an apprentice to Robert Haache.
3999. RODEN, JOHN, London: 2 April 1696, Y.

4000. RODES, NICHOLAS, London: In 1561 was dismissed for making false wares in the sight of strangers but was received back in the same year on payment of fines. In 1578 he was in arrears with his quarterage which was forgiven him.

4001. RODWELL, HENRY, York: Apprenticed 15 June 1665 for seven years to Thomas Busfield. 1671/2, F. Searcher, 1683 and 1693.

4002. RODWELL, HENRY, York: 1702/3, F.

4003. RODWELL, THOMAS, York: Was Free in 1684.

4004. RODWELL, THOMAS, York: On 1 Aug. 1697 was apprenticed for seven years to James Loftus. 8 Aug. 1704, F. Searcher in 1707, 1711, 1715, 1716, 1720, 1721, 1724, 1729 and 1730. Father of Thomas, Junr. and William.

4005. RODWELL, THOMAS, JUNR., York: On 6 Jan. 1726 was apprenticed for seven years to his father Thomas (see above). 1732/3, F., by patrimony.

4006. RODWELL, WILLIAM, York: On 13 June 1679 was apprenticed for seven years to Henry Rodwell. 1683/4, F.

4007. RODWELL, WILLIAM, York: 1733/4, F., by patrimony.

4008. ROE, EDWARD, London: 1560, R.W.; 1564, U.W.; 1582 and 1588, M.

4009. ROE, JOHN, Dublin: Mentioned in 1759.

4010. ROE, THOMAS, London: 22 June 1749, Y.

4011. ROGERS, HENRY, Skewis (Cornwall): Hanged in 1735 for the murder of two Sheriff's Officers and three others. Mr. Port, Worthing, has an old engraving commemorating the fact.

4012. ROGERS, JOHN, London: Clerk in 1614.

4013. ROGERS, JOHN, London: 14 Oct. 1703, Y.

4014. ROGERS, JOHN, Cork: Died in 1762.

4015. ROGERS, JOHN, London: 19 Dec. 1717, Y. Touch, 793 L.T.P., which he had leave to strike on 17 Mar. 1725.

4016. ROGERS, JOHN SMITH, Cork: Mentioned in 1764 and 1779.

4017. ROGERS, JOSEPH, Bristol and Malmesbury: 1 Feb. 1697, F. S. of John. Apprenticed to Roger Perkins, Junr., and Marie his wife, 26 Jan. 1696.

4018. ROGERS, PHILIP, London: 3 June 1708, Y. Touch, 653 L.T.P., struck c. 1708.

4019. ROGERS, THOMAS, Perth: Mentioned in 1619.

4020. ROGERS, THOMAS, Cork: Mentioned in 1774.

4021. ROGERS, WILLIAM, Cork: Mentioned in 1758 and died in 1781.

4022. ROGERS, WILLIAM, York: 1603/4, F., by patrimony, and is mentioned later in 1631/2.

ROLF, see RELFE.

4023. ROLLS, ANTHONY, London: 6 Aug. 1668, L. (sic.); 1659, S.; 1668, R.W. The dates are given thus in the Records, probably 1658, L. is intended.

4024. ROLLS, THOMAS, London: 19 Mar. 1690, Y.

4025. ROLLS, THOMAS, London: 18 Mar. 1713, Y.

4026. ROLT, JOHN, London: 11 Oct. 1716, Y. Touch, 710 L.T.P., which he had leave to strike on 23 June 1718.

4027. ROOKE, GEORGE, London: Touch, 152 L.T.P.; struck (or restruck after the great fire) c. 1670, His name does not appear in the existing Record.

4028. ROOKE, RICHARD, London: 25 Aug. 1748, Y. and L.; 1759, S.; 1765, R.W.; 1776, U.W.; 1777, M.

———. ROOKER, JOSEPH, London: Joseph Brooker's Touch has hitherto been transcribed as "Rooker" in other works.

4030. ROSE, EDMUND COLLISON, London: 15 June 1826, Y.

4031. ROSE, EDWARD, London: 17 Mar. 1691, Y.

4032. ROSE, ROBERT, London: Received charity in 1563 as a poor brother.

4033. ROSH, JOHN, Wells: Mentioned in 1655.

4034. ROSOELL, CHRISTOPHER (? RUSSELL), Southton, Somerset: S. of Christopher. Apprenticed to Richard Burrns, Bristol, and Francis his wife for eight years from 23 June 1608.

4035. ROSS, EDWARD, London: 13 Oct. 1803, Y.

4036. Ross, Francis, Aberdeen : In 1669 was apprenticed to George Ross.

4037. Ross, George, Aberdeen : 1664, F. 1672, Deacon.

4038. Ross, Hugh, Aberdeen : 1713, F.

4039. Ross, John, ? Tain : In 1748 he made Communion tokens for Tain Kirk.

4040. Ross, William, Aberdeen : In 1695 was apprenticed to George Ross.

4041. Rossell, Thomas, London : In 1603 was chosen a collector for the Yeomanry.

4042. Rothwell, John, London : 8 April 1756, Y.

4043. Rothwell, John, London : Touch, 195 L.T.P., which he had leave to strike in 1670/1. No mention in the Y. or L. Lists, but his name is in the " Bennett " Book as dying in 1681.

Rowden, *see* Roysdon.

4044. Rowe, Francis, London : 17 Dec. 1691, Y.

4045. Rowe, William, London : 1507, R.W.

4046. Rowell, William, London : 4 Aug. 1726, Y. Touch, 816 L.T.P., which he had leave to strike on 14 Dec. 1727.

4047. Rowland, ―― (? Rowlandson), London : In 1556 he subscribed towards a gift to Sir Thomas Curtis, Knight, Lord Mayor.

4048. Rowland, Richard, York : 1590, F., by patrimony. Mentioned in 1627/8. Father of William.

4049. Rowland, William, York : 1627/8, F., by patrimony. City Chamberlain in 1645/6. Son of Richard.

4050. Rowlandson, Stephen, London : 1550, R.W.; 1556, U.W.; 1563, M.

4051. Rowles, Thomas, London : 15 Mar. 1732, L.

4051A. Rowley, Sarah, Birmingham : In 1793 was a pewter spoon-maker on Snow Hill.

4052. Rowyn, Richard, London : In 1457 was an apprentice to John Kendale.

4053. Roysdon, John, London : 1519, R.W.; 1526 and 1532, U.W.

4053A. Royce, Charles, London : c. 1685. (" Bennett " Book.) Touch, 423 L.T.P., which he had leave to strike in 1685/6.

4054. Royden, Elizabeth (? Boyden), of ? : c. 1720. *Cf.* Richard Boyden.

  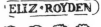

4055. Royse, Lawrence, London : 11 Oct. 1742, Y.

4056. Royston, ――, London : 1620, f.R.W.

4057. Royston, Ambrose, London : Mentioned in 1582. 1597, R.W.; 1609, U.W.

4058. Royston, John, London : 1545, R.W.; 1551 and 1555, U.W.; 1558 and 1562, M.

4059. Rudd, Anthony, London : 1629, S.

4060. Ruddock, George, Bristol : 23 Oct. 1742, F. S. of Andrew. Apprenticed to Thomas Lanyon and Anne his wife, 30 Dec. 1734. Premium £40.

4061. Rudduck, Philip, London : 9 Oct. 1690, Y. Touch, 495 L.T.P., dated 1690, struck c. 1693. In 1691 he was working as a journeyman to Mr. Taudin.

4062. Rudsby, Andrew, London : 18 Dec. 1712, Y. Touch, 823 L.T.P., which he had leave to strike on 5 July 1728. His mark has been found in conjunction with that of Edward Nash.

4063. Rudsby, Andrew, London : 14 July 1692, L. Touch, 330 L.T.P., which he had leave to strike in 1679/80.

4064. Rudsby, John, London : 18 Dec. 1712, Y.

4065. Ruffin, Thomas, London : 8 Feb. 1790, Y.; 14 Oct. 1790, L.; 1795, f.S.; 1802 and 1803, R.W.; 1808, U.W.; 1812, f.M. 1819, died.

4066. Ruge, Richard, London : 1593, R.W.

4066A. Rumball, John, London : c. 1679-86. (" Bennett " Book.)

4067. Rumball, Robert, London : 17 Dec. 1691, Y.

4068. Rumbold, John, London : 13 Dec. 1694, Y.

4069. Runciman, John, Edinburgh : In 1807 was an apprentice to John Kelly.

4070. Rundall, John (? Runder), York : Mentioned as free in 1617/8.

4071. RUNNINGTON, WILLIAM, London : Married on 27 May 1667 at Trinity Church, Minories.

4072. RUSSELL, FRANCIS, Limerick : Mentioned in 1766.

4073. RUSSELL, FRANCIS, London : A freeman in 1559.

4074. RUSSELL, JOHN, Limerick : Died in 1747.

4074A. RUSSELL, JOHN, London : c. 1680. ("Bennett" Book.) Touch, 275 L.T.P., which he had leave to strike in 1676/7.

4075. RUSSELL, THOMAS, St. Andrews: 1771, F. White-ironsmith.

4076. RUSSELL, THOMAS, London : 1611, S.

4077. RUSSELL & LAUGHER, London : c. 1760.

4077B. RUSSELL & BIGGAR, Manchester : Mentioned in 1799 and 1800 as Braziers and Pewterers, of Apple Market.

4078. RUTHERFORD, WILLIAM, Edinburgh : In 1772 was an apprentice to William Fraser.

4079. RUTLAND, ROBERT, London : 18 Dec. 1806, Y.

4079A. RUTLIDGE, JNO., London : c. 1680. ("Bennett" Book.)

4080. RYCHARDSON, DAVY, London : In 1591 he received alms from the Company.

4081. RYCHE, GEORGE, York : 1567, F., by patrimony.

4082. RYCHE, WILLIAM, York : 1420/1, F. RYCROFT, see RICROFT.

4083. RYDGE, WILLIAM, London : Mentioned in 1612.

4083A. RYLEY, NATHANIEL, London : c. 1680. ("Bennett" Book.)

4084. RYMILL, THOMAS, London : 17 Dec. 1691, Y.

4085. RYSBY, THOMAS, London : In 1476 subscribed towards a set of feast vessels.

S

SADGWICK, see SEDGWICK.

4086. SADILBOWE, RALPH, Lynn : 1445/6, F.

4086A. SADLER, GEORGE, Newcastle : In Newcastle Directory, 1778.

4087. SADLER, ROBERT, York : On 25 July 1684 was apprenticed to Janne Waid for seven years. 1690/1, F. Mentioned in 1692.

4088. SADLER, ROBERT, Newcastle : 1730-1780. Was in the 1778 Directory. Was succeeded by Wm. Hogg.

SAINT CROIX, see DE ST. CROIX.

4088A. SALKELD, HENRY, Newcastle : 1741.

4089. SALL, GEORGE, Dublin : Mentioned in 1775 as father of John.

4090. SALL, JOHN, Dublin : Pewterer and Brazier. Purchased the business of William Burroughs in 1771. S. of George.

4091. SALMON, FERDINANDO, London : 21 Mar. 1699, Y.

4092. SALMON, JOHN, Bristol : S. of Thomas and Marie to whom he was apprenticed, 29 Oct. 1713.

4093. SALMON, RICHARD, Colerne, Wilts. : S. of Thomas to whom he was apprenticed, 9 April 1686.

4094. SALMON, THOMAS, London : 7 Mar. 1742, Y.

4095. SALMON, THOMAS, Bristol : 27 Nov. 1674, F. Apprenticed to Erasmus Dole. Mentioned in 1713.

4096. SALTFORD, THOMAS, London : In 1457 was an apprentice to John Turnour.

4097. SAMPSON, PATRICK, St. Andrews : 1720, F.

4098. SAMSON, PATRICK, Dundee : 1727, F.

4099. SANDERS, SIMON, Langtree, nr. Bideford : c. 1700. A spoonmaker.

4100. SANDERS & SON, London : Founded in 1781. Now incorporated with Gaskell & Chambers.

4101. SA(U)NDERSON, HUGH, Edinburgh : In 1805 was an apprentice to John Kelly.

4102. SA(U)NDERSON, JOHN, York: Was free in 1684.
4103. SA(U)NDERSON, JOHN, York: On 1 Aug. 1697 was apprenticed for seven years to John Harrison. 1703/4, F.
4103A. SANDFORD, JOSEPH, London: c. 1680. ("Bennett" Book.) Touch, 234 L.T.P., which he had leave to strike in 1674/5.

4104. SANDIE, ROBERT, Edinburgh: In 1657 was an apprentice to John Sandie.
4105. SANDIE, JOHN, Edinburgh: A master in 1657.
4106. SANDRYNGHAM, JOHN, Lynn: 1478/9, F., apprenticed to John Adam.
4106A. SANDRYNGHAM, JOHN, Norwich: 1487/8, F.
4106B. SANDRYNGHAM, WILLIAM, Norwich: 1532/3, F.
4107. SANDS, ——, London: In 1689 was ordered to remove his place of abode from his Touch.
4108. SANDS, JOHN, Bristol: Mentioned with Alice his wife in 1688.
4109. SANDWICH, WILLIAM, York: On 2 Aug. 1725 was apprenticed for seven years to Richard Chambers. Son of Ralph Sandwich.
4109A. SANDYS, MARY, London: (Widow of William Sandys, 1681, Y.) In 1718 she took as an apprentice William Sandys Green.
4110. SANDYS, WILLIAM, London: 23 Sept. 1703, L. See his Trade Card, where his address is given as at the corner of Newport Street, St. Martin's Lane. Touch, 491 L.T.P., struck c. 1692.

4110A. SANDYS, WILLIAM, London: 1681, Y. ("Bennett" Book.) Touch, 350B L.T.P., which he had leave to strike in 1680/1.

4111. SANKEY, HUMPHREY, London: 10 Aug. 1710, Y.
4112. SANSBRY, JOHN, London: 15 Mar. 1810, Y. and L.
4113. SARES, RICHARD, London: Free in 1560.
4113A. SARGENT, JOHN, Manchester: In 1794 was at 11 Deansgate.

4114. SARNE, RICHARD, London: 20 June 1745, Y.
4115. SARPLES, GEORGE, London: Mentioned in 1567.
4116. SAUNDERS, THOMAS, London: Touch, 404 L.T.P., which he had leave to strike in 1684. His name is in the "Bennett" Book, 1684/6.

4117. SAUNDERS, EDWARD, Bristol: S. of John. Apprenticed to Edward Hackrigge and Agnes his wife for seven years from 12 Feb. 1610.
4118. SAUNDERS, JOHN, London: Touch, 239 L.T.P., which he had leave to strike in 1674/5. His name is not in the existing Y. or L. Lists, but is in the "Bennett" Book, 1678-86.

4119. SAUNDERS, RICHARD, London: Mentioned in 1588.
4120. SAUNDERSON, JOHN, London: Fined in 1557 for going to work in the country.
4122. SAVAGE, JOHN (see also SAVIDGE), London: 20 Mar. 1711, Y.; 19 June 1714, L.; 1721, S.; 1729, R.W.; 1739, U.W.; 1741, M.
4123. SAVAGE, JOHN, London: 19 June 1746, Y.; 25 Aug. 1748, L.; 1758, S.
4124. SAVAGE, JOHN, London and Leicester. 14 Dec. 1699, Y. Touch, 620 L.T.P., which he had leave to strike on 6 Dec. 1704.

| LONDON

4124A. SAVAGE, JOHN, London: c. 1680. ("Bennett" Book.)
4125. SAVAGE, SILVESTER, Dublin: Mentioned in 1788 and 1827. In 1798 he was at 41 Back Lane and in 1805 at 45 Back Lane. From 1819-27 he was at 105 Thomas Street.

S·SAVAGE
············
BACK·LANE

4126. SAVELL, JACOB, London: 23 Mar. 1748, Y.
4127. SAVELL, MATTHEW, London: 23 Mar. 1715, Y.

4128.   SAVIDG(E), J——, London : Touch, 369 L.T.P., which he had leave to strike on 28 Nov. 1681.

4128A. SAVORY, JAMES, London : In 1817 was at 4 Church Street, Shoreditch.

4129.   SAWER, JOHN, York : 1578, F., by patrimony.

4130.   SAWER, THOMAS, York : 1603/4, F., by patrimony.

4131.   SAWGE, JOHN, London : Contributed towards a set of feast vessels in 1476.

4131A. SAYERS, ROBERT, London : Died 1684. ("Bennett" Book.)

4132.   SAYSE, HENRY, London : Of St. Giles, Cripplegate. Was married in 1619.

4133.   SCARLET, ANTHONY, Ludlow : Pewterer and Brazier. 5 June 1771, F.

4134.   SCARLET, SAMUEL, London : 20 Dec. 1744, Y.; 14 Mar. 1765, L.; 1771. f.S.

4135.   SCATCHARD, ROBERT, London : 16 Dec. 1756, Y.; 20 Aug. 1761, L. Dead in 1766. Touch, 980 L.T.P., struck c. 1758.

4136.   SCATTERGOOD, JOHN, London : 3 Aug. 1732, Y. Touch, 859 L.T.P., which he had leave to strike on 26 Nov. 1735.

4137.   SCATTERGOOD, JOHN, London : 21 June 1716, Y. S. of Thomas.

4138.   SCATTERGOOD, THOMAS, London : 15 Aug. 1700, Y.; 15 Aug. 1709, L.; 1714, S.; 1733, R.W. Touch, 610 L.T.P., which he had leave to strike on 2 April 1703. He was succeeded by Edward Meriefield.

4139.   SCATTERGOOD, THOMAS, London : 16 Dec. 1736, Y.; 21 Mar. 1744, L.; 1754, f.S.; 1760, R.W.; 1773, U.W.; 1774 and 1775, M. Touch, 873 L.T.P., which he had leave to strike

on 24 Mar. 1736. *See* his Trade Card, where his address is given as "The Blackamoor's Head," near the South Sea House in Bishopsgate Street. Left £600 to the Company in **trust** to be paid to poor members.

4140.   SCHALKE, ROBARD, London : Sold some moulds to the Company in 1451.

4142.   SCHETTELLWORTHE, RYCHARD, London : Buried in 1518.

4143.   SCHIPWAYSSHE, ERNALD, London : Chosen in 1349 to uphold the Articles of the Company.

4144.   SCHLEICHER, JOHN HENRY, London : 17 June 1802, Y.

4144A. SCHOLEFIELD & CO., Birmingham : Pewterers, Prospect Row. In 1805 Directory.

4145.   SCOT, ROBERT, St. Andrews : 1651, F.

4146.   SCOTT, ALEXANDER, St. Andrews : 1713, F.

4147.   SCOTT, BENJAMIN, London : 1656, f.S.

4147A. SCOTT, ELIZABETH, Exeter : In 1793 was in North Street.

4148.   SCOTT, GEORGE, London : Touch, 348 L.T.P., which he had leave to strike in 1680/1. His name is not in the Y. or L. Lists, but appears in the "Bennett" Book, 1680-86.

4149.   SCOTT, JAMES, London : 16 Dec. 1708, Y.

4150.   SCOTT, JAMES, Glasgow : 1788, F. Copper and white-ironsmith.

4151.   SCOTT, JOHN, Edinburgh : 1629, F.

4152.   SCOTT, JOHN, Edinburgh : In 1757 as an apprentice, he was transferred to Adam Anderson.

4153.   SCOTT, JOHN, Stirling : 1605, F.

4154.   SCOTT, JOSEPH, London : 12 Feb. 1827, Y. and L.; 1837, f.S. Died Oct. 1844.

4155.   SCOTT, RICHARD, London : 1562, R.W.

4156.   SCOTT, SAMUEL, London : 11 Oct. 1705, Y.

4156A. SCOTT, SAMUEL, London : c. 1680. ("Bennett" Book.)

4157.   SCOTT, THOMAS, St. Andrews : 1691, F.

4158.   SCOTT, WILLIAM, Edinburgh : Mentioned in 1779. ? Touch, 135 E.T.P. In 1773 he had his shop in West Bow.

4159. Scott, William, Edinburgh: 1634, F. Touch, 38 E.T.P.

4160. Scott, William, Edinburgh: 1779, F. In 1793 and 1805 his shop was in North Side of Grassmarket. He seems to have been in partnership with William Hunter and Robert Kinniburgh at different times.

4161. Scott, William, Edinburgh: 1794, F. S. of the last named.

See also Kinniburgh & Scott.

4162. Scupholm, Thomas, Hull: Was one of two pewterers who signed the Ordinances of the Guild of Smiths in 1598. The pewterers were members of the Guild.

4163. Seabright, Charles, London: 28 Aug. 1685, L.

4164. Seabright, White, London: 11 Mar. 1707, Y.

4165. Seabroke, Robert, London: 20 June 1776, Y.; 21 Aug. 1794, L.

4166. Seabrook, John, London: 19 Mar. 1812, Y. and L.; 14 Oct. 1819, f.S.; 1830, R.W.; 1834, U.W.; 1836, M. 15 Dec. 1839, died.

4167. Seager, James, Dublin: Mentioned in 1706.

4168. Seagood, Francis (*see also* Seegood), Lynn: 1656/7, F. Mentioned again in 1667/8.

4169. Seagood, Henry, Lynn: 1667/8, F. Apprenticed to his father, Francis.

4170. Seaman, Timothy, London: 11 Oct. 1764, Y.

4170A. Seare, Robert, London: Touch, 165 L.T.P., which he had leave to strike in 1669/70.

4171. Seare, William, London: 11 Oct. 1705, Y.

4172. Searle, James, Bristol: 2 May 1807, F. S. of James. Apprenticed to Preston Edgar and Rebecca his wife, 9 May 1792. In the Poll Book for 1812 is given as of Elbroad, S.S. Philip and Jacob, Bristol.

4173. Seaton, Samuel, London: Mentioned in 1689. Appears in the "Bennett" Book, 1683-6. Touch, 387 L.T.P., which he had leave to strike on 28 June 1683.

4174. Seawell, Edward, London: 18 Mar. 1779, Y.; 22 June 1797, L. Touch, 1064 L.T.P., struck c. 1797.

4175. Seckar, James, York: On 2 June 1663 he was apprenticed for seven years to Richard Wroghan. 1669/70, F., by patrimony. Searcher in 1677, 1678, 1683, 1686, 1690, 1691, 1695, 1698, 1703, 1704 and 1705.

4176. Seddon, Charles, London: 19 Aug. 1669, L.; 1673, f.S.

4177. Seddon, John, Warfield, Berks.: S. of John. Apprenticed to William Watkins, Bristol, and Mary his wife, 24 Dec. 1740. Premium £20.

4179. Sedgwick (? Sidgwick), John, ? York: c. 1730.

4180. Seears, Roger, London: 1651, S.

4180A. Seegood, Francis (*see also* Seagood), Norwich: 1645, F.

4181. Seeling, John, London: 1656, R.W.; 1662, f.U.W.; 1665, M. He died of plague in the latter year.

4182. Selborne, John, Wotton-under-Edge, Glocs.: S. of William. Apprenticed to Peter Lodge, Bristol, 16 Nov. 1630.

4183. Selby, Richard, London: Fined in 1551 for making false wares.

4184. Selby, Robert, London: 25 Sept. 1712, Y.

4185. Sele, Richard, Abchurch: Entered in 1485 as a country member.

4186. Sellers, Lucy, London: Apprenticed in 1713 to Elizabeth, widow of Samuel Read.

4187.   SELLMAN, THOMAS, London : 1612, Y. Son of William.

4188.   SELLMAN, WILLIAM, London : Mentioned in 1612.

4189.   SELLON, JOHN, London : 19 June 1740, Y. Touch, 935 L.T.P., which he obtained leave to strike in 1749.

4190.   SELMON, RICHARD (Probably same as Richard Salmon), West Country : c. 1690.

4191.   SENNENT, GEORGE, Edinburgh : In 1693 was an apprentice to William Harvie.

4192.   SETON, JOHN, Edinburgh : An Apprentice in 1704 to James Cowper.

4193.   SEWDLEY, HENRY, London : 20 June 1706, Y.; 12 May 1713, L.; 1718, S.; 1728, R.W.; 1736, U.W.; 1738, M. Touch, 658 L.T.P., struck c. 1709. His Touch is found in conjunction with the " Hall-Marks " of Sir John Fryer.

(H: SEWDLEY)

4194.   SEXTEYN, WILLIAM, London : In 1457 was a freeman (covenant man) with William Crowde. 1476, R.W.; 1479, U.W ; 1482, 1485, 1490, 1491, 1496, 1502 and 1503, M.

4195.   SEXTON, HUGH, Truro : S. of Henry. Apprenticed to John Knowles, Bristol, and Marie his wife, 25 April 1648.

4196.   SEYKE, ROBERDE, London : Was free in 1457.

4197.   SEYMOUR, GEORGE, Cork : Mentioned in 1754. 18 Feb. 1783, F. Master of the Cork Guild of

Goldsmiths in 1787. Mentioned later in 1795.

4198.   SEYMOUR, HENRY, Cork : Of Paul Street. Mentioned in 1793 and 1817.

4199.   SEYMOUR, JOHN, Cork : Mentioned in 1779.

4200.   SEYMOUR, NICHOLAS, Cork : Mentioned in 1739. Died in 1763.

4201.   SEYMOUR, NICHOLAS GEORGE, Cork : S. of George. Mentioned in 1799 and 1817.

4202.   SEYMOUR, WILLIAM, Cork : Mentioned in 1817.

4203.   SEYMOUR, W. & SON, Cork : Early nineteenth century.

4204.   SHABOE, THOMAS, London : 21 Oct. 1773, Y.

4205.   SHABROLES, MARK HENRY, London : Was refused permission in 1692, being a foreigner, to work after 24 Aug.

4206.   SHA(C)KLE, JOHN, London : Touch, 416 L.T.P., struck and dated 1685, but his name does not appear in the existing Records.

4207.   SHA(C)KLE, THOMAS, London : 16 Aug. 1680, L.; 1686, S.; 1693, f.R.W.; 1700, f.U.W.; 1703, f.M. Touch, 287 L.T.P., struck c. 1677.

4208.   SHA(C)KLE, THOMAS, JUNR., London : 19 June 1701, Y. and L.

4209.   SHARP, DURHAM, London : 20 June 1754, Y.

4210.   SHARP, JOHN, London : 16 June 1692, Y.

4211.   SHARP, JOHN, Salisbury : Apprenticed to Hugh Newton in 1591.

4212.   SHARP, THOMAS, London : Served in 1584 as a soldier in place of Robert Nixon.

4213. SHARROCK, EDMUND, London : 15 Dec. 1737, Y.; 23 Sept. 1742, L. Touch, 881 L.T.P., which he had leave to strike on 15 Dec. 1737.

4214. SHARWOOD, JAMES, London : 23 Mar. 1748, Y.; 22 June 1769, L., 1776, S. Spelt Sherwood in Y. List.

4215. SHATH, THOMAS, London : 1680, f.S.

4216. SHAW, JOHN, Newcastle : c. 1760. Is mentioned in the Directory for 1778.

4217. SHAW, GEORGE, Edinburgh : Apprenticed in 1679 to John Harvie.

4218. SHAW, JACOB, Walsall : c. 1580, in which year his son was baptised at St. Matthew's Church there.

4219. SHAW, JAMES, London : In 1680 was a spoon-maker.

4220. SHAW, JAMES, London : 22 Mar. 1693, Y.

4221. SHAW, JAMES, London : 23 Aug. 1785, Y.; 20 Oct. 1796, L.; 1799, f.S.

4222. SHAW, JOHN, London : A master in 1584.

4223. SHAW, JOHN, London : 27 May 1726, Y. Touch, 779 L.T.P., which he had leave to strike on 27 Mar. 1726.

4224. SHAW, JOHN, London : 21 Mar. 1776, Y. In 1793 was at 23 King Street, Borough.

4224A. SHAW, JOHN & WILLIAM, London : In 1817 were at 3 Snow's Fields, Bermondsey.

4225. SHAW, THOMAS, Bristol : Mentioned in 1634.

4226. SHAYLER, WILLIAM, London : 13 June 1734, Y. Touch, 849 L.T.P., which he had leave to strike on 10 Oct. 1734.

4227. SHEARMAN, FRANCIS, Dublin: Mentioned in 1772.

4228. SHEFF(I)ELD, THOMAS, London : In 1603 was chosen with others to look after the due carrying out of the Company's ordinances.

4229. SHELTON, ELLIS, London : Mentioned in 1614.

4230. SHENE, JOHN, Dublin : Mentioned in 1768 and 1796.

4232. SHEPHARD, ANDREW (?SHEPHERD), London : 16 Mar. 1692, Y.

4233. SHEPHARD, NICHOLAS, Barnstaple : His mark appears in conjunction with the " Hall-Mark " and " Best Bismuth " marks of Richard Going. Mentioned in 1747. Succeeded in Jan. 1792 by Thomas Copner.

4234. SHEPHARD, DAVID, Cork : Mentioned in 1810.

4235. SHEPPARD, ANDREW, London : 9 Aug. 1694, Y.

4236. SHEPPARD, JOHN, Bristol : Mentioned with his wife Elizabeth in 1681.

4237. SHEPPARD, ROBERT, London : In 1584 he was chosen to serve in a body of soldiers, raised from the Company. 1602, R.W.; 1607 and 1613, U.W.; 1619, M. His daughter was married to Lawrence Spike on 16 Feb. 1620.

4238. SHEPPARD, ROBERT, London : Of St. Mildred's, Bread Street. Was married on 20 Sept. 1625 to Jane Osborn at St. Faith's.

4238A. SHEPPARD, SAMUEL, London : c. 1684. (" Bennett " Book.) Touch, 419 L.T.P., which he had leave to strike in 1685/6.

4239. SHEPPARD, THOMAS, London : 11 Oct. 1705, Y. Touch, 654 L.T.P., struck c. 1708.

4240. SHEPPARD, ——, London : Was a spoonmaker in 1566.

4241. SHERCLIFFE, HECTOR, Dublin : Mentioned in 1786. His widow, Sarah, was at 5 Back Lane in 1805.

4241A. SHERLOCK, SIMON, Dublin : Mentioned in " Dublin Directory," 1766.

4242. SHERMAN, HENRY HARCOURT, London : 6 Oct. 1720, Y.

SHERMAR, see SHURMAR.

4243. SHERSTONE, THOMAS, London : 14 Dec. 1693, Y.

4244. SHERWIN, DANIEL (*see* also SHERWYN), London : 16 Dec. 1714, Y.

4245. SHERWIN, JOSEPH, Ashbourne : Issued a halfpenny token (*q.v.*) in 1666.

4246. SHERWIN, JOSEPH, London : 15 Dec. 1726, Y. Touch, 809 L.T.P., which he had leave to strike on 21 Mar. 1727. (*Cf.* Piggott.)

4247. SHERWIN, STEPHEN, London : 13 Oct. 1709, Y.

4248. SHERWOOD, HENRY (? SHARWOOD), London : Struck his Touch 18 Mar. 1741. So it is stated in the Records, but it is not on the Touchplates.

4249. SHERWOOD, JOHN, Lynn : 1667/8, F. Apprenticed to Francis Seagood.

4250. SHERWOOD, JOSEPH, London : 19 Mar. 1767, Y.

4251. SHERWOOD, WILLIAM, SENR., London : 12 Dec. 1700, Y.

4252. SHERWOOD, WILLIAM, JUNR., London : 23 Mar. 1731, Y.

4253. SHERWOOD, WILLIAM HENRY, London : 22 Sept. 1774, Y.

4254. SHERWYN, JOHN (*see* also SHERWIN), London : 1528, R.W. ; 1535 and 1540, U.W. ; 1547, M.

4255. SHERWYN, JOHN, London : Mentioned in 1567, 1572, R.W. ; 1578, U.W.

4256. SHIEL, WILLIAM, Edinburgh : In 1713 was an apprentice to Robert Findlay.

4257. SHIELS, ROBERT, Perth : In 1751 was an apprentice to Patrick Campbell.

4258. SHIELS, WILLIAM, Perth : 1726, F. 1729/30, Box-Master. Died 1737.

4259. SHIRLEY, JAMES, Dublin : Mentioned in 1818 and 1840.

4260. SHIRWYN, ROBERT, York : 1459/60, F.

4261. SHOREY, BARTHOLOMEW, London : 10 Aug. 1721, Y. ; 14 April 1724, L. ; 1729, S. ; 1736, f.R.W. ; 1746, U.W. ; 1747 and 1749, M.

4262. SHOREY, COL. JOHN, London : 14 July 1692, L. ; 1698, S. ; 1712, R.W. ; 1720, U.W. Of

Cateaton Street. Touch, 390 L.T.P., which he had leave to strike on 22 Oct. 1683.

4263. SHOREY, JOHN, JUNR., London : 17 June 1708, Y. ; 22 June 1708, L. ; 1711, S. ; 1725, f.R.W. (*Cf.* Nos. 2746, 5626 and 5650.)

4264. SHOREY, JOHN, London : 22 June 1738, Y.

4265. SHORT, JOHN, London : 11 Oct. 1694, Y.

4266. SHORTGRAVE, NATHANIEL, London : Touch, 452 L.T.P., which he had leave to strike on 16 Mar. 1687. His name is not in the existing Y. or L. Lists.

4267. SHOSWELL, JAMES, London : 16 Dec. 1736, Y.

4268. SHOWARD, ROBERT, Bristol : Mentioned in 1642.

4269. SHRYVE, THOMAS, Dublin : 1591, F.

4270. SHURMER, RICHARD, London : 18 Mar. 1685, L. ; 1693, S. (Spelt Shermer in the Records.) Touch, 346 L.T.P., struck c. 1680.

4271. SHYGAN, NICHOLAS, Dublin : 1640, F.
4272. SIAR, WILLIAM, London : 1625, f.S. ; 1633, R.W. ; 1641, U.W.
4273. SIBBALD, ALEXANDER, Edinburgh : 1605, F. Touches, 22 and 23 E.T.P.

4274. SIBBALD, JAMES, Edinburgh : 1588, F.
4275. SIBBALD, JAMES, Edinburgh : 1631, F. Touch, 33 E.T.P.

4276. SIBBALD, JAMES, Edinburgh : 1798, a master at this date.
4277. SIBBALD, JOHN, Edinburgh : A master in 1798.
4278. SIBBALD, WALTER, Edinburgh : In 1598 was an apprentice to John Weir.
4279. SIBBALD, WILLIAM, Edinburgh : A master in 1646.
4280. SIBBET, ANDREW, Edinburgh : Died in 1605.
4281. SIBBET, JAMES, Edinburgh : 1600, F. Touches, 5 and 6 E.T.P.

4282. SIBLEY, HENRY, London : Touch, 372 L.T.P., which he had leave to strike on 4 Dec. 1682. His name is not in the Y. or L. Lists, but is in the " Bennett " Book, 1681-84.

4283. SIBTHORP, JOSEPH, London : 29 Sept. 1699, Y.
4284. SIDEY, EDWARD, London : 17 Dec. 1772, Y. Touch, 1027 L.T.P., struck c. 1773.

SIDGWICK, *see* SEDGWICK.

4285. SILK, JOHN, London : 1640, f.S. ; 1652, R.W. ; 1655, U.W. ; 1658, M. Touch, 2 L.T.P., restruck c. 1670 after the great fire. The registration of the birth of his son John is recorded at St. Peter's, Cornhill. Of Leadenhall Street.

4286. SILK, JOHN, London : 22 June 1693, Y. ; 19 June 1694, L. ; 1700, S. Touch, 499 L.T.P., which he had leave to strike on 22 June 1693.

4287. SILK, VINCENT, London : Touch, 71 L.T.P., restruck c. 1670 after the great fire. His name is not in the existing Records.

4288. SILVER, DAVID, London : 20 Dec. 1744, Y.
4289. SILVESTER, WILLIAM, London : 19 Mar. 1746, Y.
4290. SIMKIN, JAMES, London : 1659, S.
4290A. SIMMS, THOMAS, London : Touch, 337 L.T.P., which he had leave to strike in 1679/80. c. 1680. (" Bennett " Book.)

4290B. SIMONS, RICHARD, Taunton : Mentioned in 1549 as of East Street.
4290C. SIMONS, THOMAS, Taunton : Mentioned in 1549 as of High Street. By his will dated 1572 he gave half his moulds and tools to his son Henry.
4291. SIMPKIN, JAMES, Dublin : 1639, F.
4292. SIMPSON, GEORGE, Dublin : Mentioned in 1757 and 1796.
4293. SIMPSON, GEORGE, Perth : In 1794 was an apprentice to Robert Menzies.
4294. SIMPSON, JOHN, London : 18 Dec. 1760, Y.
4295. SIMPSON, JOHN, London : 19 Dec. 1771, Y.
4296. SIMPSON, ROBERT, Edinburgh : 1631, F. Touch, 39 E.T.P.

4297. SIMPSON, THOMAS, Edinburgh : In 1721 was an apprentice with John Weir. 1728, F. Touch, 126 E.T.P. In 1773 his shop was at the head of Halkerston's Wynd, and in 1780 at Head of Bridge Street.

See also ELMSLIE & SIMPSON.

4298. SINGLETON, HUGH, York : Apprenticed to Robert Gill. 1482, F.

4299. SINGLETON, LEONARD, London : Mentioned in 1597. 1608, R.W.; 1615 and 1619, U.W.

4300. SISSON, ——, Dublin : Mentioned in 1754.

4301. SIVEDALL, HENRY, London : 8 July 1699, Y.

4302. SKENFIELD, JOHN, Llandogan, Glam. : S. of John. Apprenticed to Robert Bush, Bristol, 8 Dec. 1791.

4303. SKEPPER, ROBERT, London : 16 Mar. 1692, Y.

4304. SKIN(N), JOHN, London : Mentioned in 1672. 1679, S. Fined in 1683 for omitting to impress his Touch on his wares. His daughter Martha married William Cowley, Junr. Touch, 176 L.T.P., which he had leave to strike in 1669/70.

4305. SKIN(N), THOMAS, London : Touch, 223 L.T.P., which he had leave to strike in 1673/4.

4306. SKINNER, PATRICK (? SKYNNER), Perth : In 1738 was an apprentice to Patrick Halley.

4307. SKINNER, RICHARD, London : 22 June 1738, Y. Probably this is an error in the Records and should be Robert, the owner of the following mark. The date would be in order.

4308. SKINNER, ROBERT, London : Touch, 889 L.T.P., which he had leave to strike on 3 Aug. 1738. No mention of *Robert* Skinner in Y. or L. Lists. *See* note under last entry.

} ? Same.

4309. SKINNER, ROBERT, Dundee : 1746, F. A copper-smith, but was apprenticed to a pewterer.

4310. SKINNER, ROBERT, Dundee : 1747, F. White-ironsmith.

4310A. SKINNER, ROBERT, Exeter : Mentioned in 1689.

4311. SKINNER, WILLIAM, London : In 1457 was covenant man to Thomas Dounton.

4312. SKOLLS, ROBERT, London : In 1531 he was in trouble with the Company for leaving London without leave.

4313. SLACKE, JOHN, London : In 1552 was in trouble over some faulty salts.

4314. SLACKE, WILLIAM, London : Mentioned in 1553.

4315. SLACKE, MRS., London : Mentioned in 1565.

4316. SLADE, CHARLES, Dublin : Died in 1754. Father of William.

4317. SLADE, WILLIAM, Dublin : Son of Charles, to whose business he succeeded in 1754.

4318. SLAUGHTER, NATHANIEL HALL, London : 28 June 1781, Y.

4319. SLAUGHTER, RICHARD, London : 14 Feb. 1711, Y.; 15 Mar. 1732, L.; 1742, S.; 1746, f.R.W.

4320. SLOCUM, ARTHUR, Barnstaple : S. of John. Apprenticed to Thomas Hobson, Bristol, and Elizabeth his wife for seven years from 13 Jan. 1630.

4320A. SLOUGH, JOHN, London : Touch, 231 L.T.P., which he had leave to strike in 1674/5.

4321. SLOW, JOSEPH, London : 11 Mar. 1702, Y. Touch, 614 L.T.P., which he had leave to strike on 20 June 1703.

4322. SLOW, WILLIAM, London : 21 Mar. 1716, Y.

4323. SMACKERGILL, THOMAS, London : In 1569 was covenant man to John Hobstock. Mentioned as a master in 1594.

4324. SMACKERGILL, WILLIAM, London : 1610, R.W.

4325. SMALLEY, JOHN, London : 17 Dec. 1691, Y.; 1703, L.

4326. SMALLEY, SAMUEL, London : Mentioned in 1694; 20 June 1695, L.; 1701, S. Touch, 469 L.T.P., which he had leave to strike on 7 Jan. 1690.

4327. SMALLWODE, WILLIAM, London: 1462, R.W.; 1458 (*sic*) and 1465, U.W.; 1469, 1477, 1481 and 1486, M. (The date 1458 above is as the Records give it, but is evidently an error. —H.H.C.)

4328. SMALMAN, ARTHUR, London: 18 June 1713 Y. Touch, 726 L.T.P., struck c. 1722.

4329. SMALPIECE, RICHARD, London: Touch, 397 L.T.P., which he had leave to strike on 18 Feb. 1683. His name is in the "Bennett" Book from 1683-6.

4330. SMALPIECE, WILLIAM, London: 22 June 1710, Y.
4331. SMART, JOHN, London: 16 Dec. 1768, Y.
4332. SMART, ROBERT, Holt, Wilts.: S. of Daniel. Apprenticed to Lewis Roberts, Bristol, and Anne his wife, 8 April 1676.
4333. SMELLIE, WILLIAM, Glasgow: 1791, F. Coppersmith.
4334. SMITE, GEORGE, London: 1672, f.S., f.R.W., f.U.W. and f.M.
4335. SMITH(E), —— (*see* also SMYTH), Walsall: c. 1590. A dishmaker. (? Pewterer.)
4336. SMITH(E), ALEXANDER, Dundee: 1739, F. Pewterer, cutler and watchmaker.
4337. SMITH(E), ANN, London: 16 Dec. 1762, Y. Obtained leave to strike her Touch in 1762, but it is not on the Touchplates.
4337A. SMITH(E), ANN, London: In 1817 was at 131 Minories, Tower Hill.
4338. SMITH(E), ANTHONY, London: 15 Dec. 1698, Y. 2 Oct. 1702, L. Touch, 575 L.T.P., which he had leave to strike on 10 July 1700.

4339. SMITH(E), BENJAMIN, London: 16 Dec. 1714, Y.
4340. SMITH(E), BENJAMIN, London: 10 Dec. 1730, Y.
4341. SMITH(E), CARRINGTON JOHN, London: 17 Dec. 1801, Y.

4342. SMITH(E), CHARLES, London: 12 Oct. 1765, Y.; 20 June 1776, L.; 1780, S.; 1789, R.W.; 1797, f.M. Touch, 1011 L.T.P., which he obtained leave to strike in 1766.

4342A. SMITH(E), CHARLES, Derry: Buried at Derry Cathedral, 1 Sept. 1663.
4343. SMITH(E), CHRISTOPHER, London: 18 Mar. 1730, Y.
4344. SMITH(E), DANIEL, London: Mentioned in 1621.
4345. SMITH(E), DANIEL, London: 16 Dec. 1731, Y.
4345A. SMITH(E), EDWARD, London: Touches, 467 and 468 L.T.P., which he had leave to strike on 17 Nov. 1690.

4345B. SMITH(E), EDWARD, London: In 1817 was at 15 Charles Street, Westminster.
4346. SMITH(E), EMMATT, York: Free in 1683. A woman.
4347. SMITH(E), G——, London: c. 1681. Touch, 353 L.T.P. No mention of a G. Smith appears in the records about this time. (*Cf.* Touch of John Barlow & Johnson.)

4348. SMITH(E), GEORGE, London: Was free in 1601. Chosen a collector from the Livery in 1602.
4349. SMITH(E), GEORGE, York: Apprenticed for seven years to Emmatt Smith on 23 April 1683.
4350. SMITH(E), GEORGE, London: 1623, U.W. (Welch has it John Smith, but it is George in the Livery list.)
4351. SMITH(E), GEORGE, London: 19 June 1712, Y. Touch, 676 L.T.P., which he was given leave to strike on 27 Mar. 1714.

4352.   SMITH(E), GEORGE, London : 17 Mar. 1768, Y. ;
18 June 1772, L.; 1779, f.S.; 1786, R.W.;
1794, U.W.; 1795, M.

4353.   SMITH(E), HENRY, London : 18 Aug. 1724, Y.
Touch, 787 L.T.P., which he had leave to strike
on 23 Mar. 1726.

4353A.   SMITH(E), HUMPHRY, London : c. 1680. (" Bennett " Book) where in 1680 he is described as
" Coppersmith, Ireland."

4354.   SMITH(E), ISAAC, London : 17 Dec. 1795, Y. and
L.; 1798, f.S.; 1805, f.R.W.; 1812, U.W.;
1813, M. Died 1 Feb. 1856, aged 81. On
4 Oct. 1855 he gave £500 to the Company for
poor members and widows of Pewterers.

4355.   SMITH(E), JAMES, London : 15 June 1732, Y.
Touch, 840 L.T.P., which he had leave to strike
on 21 June 1733.

4356.   SMITH(E), JAMES, Edinburgh : 1794, F.
4357.   SMITH(E), JAMES EDWARD, London : 13 Dec.
1764, Y. Formerly of Sea-Cole Lane and later
of Minories. Gazetted as insolvent on 25 June
1774.

4358.   SMITH(E), JOHN, York : 1451/2, F.
4359.   SMITH(E), JOHN, London : 1456, f.S.
4360.   SMITH(E), JOHN, London : Touch, 252 L.T.P.,
which he had leave to strike in 1675/6. His
name is not in the Y. or L. Lists at this time, but
is in the " Bennett " Book, 1679-84.

4361.   SMITH(E), JOHN, London : 13 Aug. 1702, Y.;
15 Aug. 1709, L. Touch, 613 L.T.P., which
he had leave to strike on 30 April 1703.

4361A.   SMITH(E), JOHN, London : c. 1685. (" Bennett "
Book.)

4362.   SMITH(E), JOHN, London : 21 June 1716, Y.
4363.   SMITH(E), JOHN, London : 13 Aug. 1724, Y.
Touch, 788 L.T.P., which he had leave to strike
on 23 Mar. 1726.

4364.   SMITH(E), JOHN, Edinburgh : c. 1730.

4365.   SMITH(E), JOHN, London : 17 Oct. 1765, Y.
4366.   SMITH(E), JOHN, London : 18 Oct. 1770, Y.
4367.   SMITH(E), JOHN, Perth : In 1712 was essay-
master.
4368.   SMITH(E), JOHN, Coventry : Issued a token in
1651. *See* list of tokens at end of Chap. IV.
4369.   SMITH(E), JOHN, Aberdeen : 1765, F. 1780-82,
Deacon.
4370.   SMITH(E), JOHN, Bristol : 30 Sept. 1811, F.
Apprenticed to Robert Bush.
4371.   SMITH(E), JOSEPH, London : 19 Mar. 1695, Y.;
28 Sept. 1699, L.; 1706, S. Touch, 522
L.T.P., which he had leave to strike on 19 Mar.
1695.

4371A.   SMITH(E), LANCELOT, Cork : In 1805
was at South Main Street.
4372.   SMITH(E), LAWRENCE, Cork : Mentioned in 1810.   } ? Same.

4373.   SMITH(E), MAURICE, London : 22 Mar. 1770, Y.
4374.   SMITH(E), RICHARD, London : 6 Mar. 1684, L. ;
1688, S.; 1696, R.W.; 1702, U.W.; 1705,
M. Touch, 301 L.T.P., struck c. 1677 and
dated.

4375.   SMITH(E), RICHARD, London : 21 June 1733, Y.
Mentioned in 1760. Touch, 860 L.T.P.,

which he had leave to strike on 11 Dec. 1735.

4376. SMITH(E), ROBERT, York : On 6 April 1661 was apprenticed for seven years to Henry Hammon. 1667/8, F. Searcher, 1672, and is mentioned later in 1688/9.

4377. SMITH(E), ROBERT WALLER, London : 4 Feb. 1830, Y. and L.; 1840, f.S. Died 23 Dec. 1842, age 34.

4378. SMITH(E), ROWLAND, London : 10 Oct. 1734, Y. Touch, 948 L.T.P., struck c. 1750.

4379. SMITH(E), SAMUEL, London : 17 Oct. 1728, Y. S. of Jno. Smith. Touch, 796 L.T.P., which he had leave to strike on 21 Mar. 1727/8.

4380. SMITH(E), SAMUEL, London : 10 Aug. 1727, Y.; 20 June 1728, L.; 1737, S.; 1741, R.W.; 1753, U.W. He was gazetted a Bankrupt on 9 Aug. 1755, and again on 21 Nov. 1761. He was apprenticed to Leapidge, and a partner in Smith & Leapidge. Touch, 808 L.T.P., struck c. 1728. His partner was Anne Leapidge 1728, Y., whom he subsequently married. Of Snowhill. *See* also notes under John Home and Nathaniel Barber.

4381. SMITH(E), STEPHEN, London : Was fined for absence in 1615.

4382. SMITH(E), THOMAS, London : Mentioned in 1611. 1616, R.W.; 1629, U.W.; 1631 and 1632, M.

4383. SMITH(E), THOMAS, London : 1654, L.

4384. SMITH(E), THOMAS, London : 12 Aug. 1669, L.

4385. SMITH(E), THOMAS, London : 19 Mar. 1684, L.; 1689, S.; 1696, f.R.W.; 1703, f.U.W. Touches, 258 and 258b L.T.P., struck and dated 1675, and 428, which he had leave to

strike in 1686/7, but which is dated 1675 back to his other Touches, this being most probably the year he obtained his freedom.

 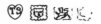

4385A. SMITH(E), THOMAS, London : 1686, L. ("Bennett" Book.) Touch, 362 L.T.P., which he had leave to strike on 10 July 1682.

4386. SMITH(E), THOMAS, London : Touch, 436 L.T.P., struck c. 1687. No owner of this Touch is found in the Y. or L. Lists.

4386A. SMITH(E), THOMAS, London : Touch, 388 L.T.P., struck c. 1683.

4387. SMITH(E), THOMAS, London : 21 Mar. 1705, Y. Touch, 632 L.T.P., which he had leave to strike on 15 April 1706.

4388. SMITH(E), THOMAS, London : 13 Oct. 1709, Y.

4389. SMITH(E), THOMAS, London : 23 Mar. 1731, Y.

4390. SMITH(E), THOMAS, London : 15 Mar. 1732, Y.

4391. SMITH(E), THOMAS, London : 12 June 1739, Y. Touch, 989 L.T.P., which he obtained leave to strike in 1760.

4392. SMITH(E), THOMAS, London : 23 Oct. 1755, Y. Touch, 1005 L.T.P., which he obtained leave to strike on 21 June 1764.

4393. SMITH(E), THOMAS, London : 8 Oct. 1761, Y. Touch, 1016 L.T.P., which he obtained leave to strike on 17 Mar. 1768.

4394. SMITH(E), THOMAS, London : 20 June 1771, Y.
4395. SMITH(E), THOMAS, Edinburgh : 1780, F. His shop in 1780 was in Potter Row and in 1793 in Blair Street.
4396. SMITH(E), WILLIAM, London : Touch, 167 L.T.P., which he had leave to strike in 1669/70. No mention of him in the Y. or L. Lists, but his name is in the " Bennett " Book, 1678-86.

4397. SMITH(E), WILLIAM, York : In 1481/2 was apprenticed to Robert Johnson.
4398. SMITH(E), WILLIAM, London : 18 June 1691, Y. Mentioned as a poor brother in 1706. Touch, 497 L.T.P., which he had leave to strike on 28 Mar. 1693.

4399. SMITH(E), WILLIAM, Edinburgh : 1712, F.
4400. SMITH(E), WILLIAM, London : 15 Mar. 1732, Y. Touch, 829 L.T.P., which he had leave to strike on 15 Mar. 1732.

4401. SMITH(E), WILLIAM, London : 15 Dec. 1796, Y.; 12 Dec. 1799, L. ; 1802, f.S. Died Feb. 1849.
4402. SMITH(E), WILLIAM, ? York or Leeds : c. 1730. (Cf. Touch of Christopher Clifton.)

4403. SMITH(E), WILLIAM, Bristol : 15 June 1818, F. Apprenticed to Robert Bush.
4403A. SMITH(E) & GIBSON, London : In 1793 were at 131 Minories. (Cf. Ann Smith.)
4404. SMITH(E) & LEAPIDGE, London : Touch, 808 L.T.P., struck c. 1728. Partners, Samuel Smith, 1728, L. ; and Anne Leapidge, 1728, Y.

4405. SMYTH(E), ANTHONY, London : Mentioned in 1558 and 1572, in which latter year his wife died. 1576, f.R.W.
4406. SMYTH(E), GEORGE, London : 1660, f.S. ; 1669, f.R.W.; 1672, f.U.W.
4407. SMYTH(E), JAMES, Perth : 1633, F.
4408. SMYTH(E), JOHN, London : In 1552 was apprenticed to Geffery Mathewe. He is mentioned later in 1558.
4408A. SMYTH(E), JOHN, Norwich : 1599, F.
4409. SMYTH(E), NICHOLAS, London : 1538, U.W.
4410. SMYTH(E), ROBERT, London : In 1457 was journeyman to Morys Panton.
4411. SMYTH(E), THOMAS, London : Was of the Livery in 1457. 1460, R.W.
4412. SMYTH(E), WILLIAM, London : Apprenticed to Hugh Newton. 1598, Y. He was dismissed from the Livery in 1603.
4412A. SMYTH(E), WILLIAM, Norwich : 1633, F.
4413. SMYTHER, GEORGE, London : Mentioned in 1612.
4414. SNAPE, WILLIAM, London : 13 Dec. 1764, Y. Touch, 1013 L.T.P., which he obtained leave to strike in 1767.

4415. SNAYLAM, JOHN, London: In 1457 was an apprentice to Walter Warde, and in 1477 contributed towards a set of feast vessels.

4416. SNAWEDON, THOMAS DE, York: 1395, F.

4417. SNELL, LAMBARD, London: 1475, Y.

4417A. SNELL, WILLIAM, Bristol: In Poll Books of 1722 is given as of The Temple.

4418. SNELLGROVE, WILLIAM, Bristol and Cansion (? Corsham), Wilts.: 20 Sept. 1660, F. Apprenticed to William Pascall, Bristol, and Marie his wife, 12 Jan. 1647. Mentioned in 1675.

4419. SNODGRASS, JAMES, Glasgow: 1794, F. White-ironsmith.

4420. SNOSSWELL, JAMES, London: 16 Dec. 1736, Y.

4421. SNOW, ELIAS, London: 18 Mar. 1724, Y.

4422. SNOW, SAMUEL, London: 1665, f.S.; 1670, f.R.W.; 1676, f.U.W.; 1681, M. He died in the latter year.

4423. SNOXELL, EDWARD, London: 20 June 1706, Y.

4424. SNOXELL, JOHN, London: Pewterer of St. Sepulchre's. Married Mary Andrews, Edgborough, Co. Bucks., on 28 Aug. 1685. Touch, 251 L.T.P., which he had leave to strike in 1675/6. His name is not in the existing Y. or L. Lists, but is in the "Bennett" Book, 1679-86 as a country pewterer.

4425. SNOXELL, RICHARD, London: 13 Oct. 1709, Y.

4426. SNUGGS, RICHARD, London: 10 Mar. 1842, Y.

4427. SOMERS, ROBERT, London: In 1554 was servant to John Day. In 1559 he was fined for buying false metal, and in 1561 he was dismissed for a whole host of offences. He was forgiven in the same year on payment of a fine.

4428. SOMERTON, WILLIAM, London: 18 Mar. 1730, Y.

4429. SOMERVELL, JAMES, Edinburgh: 1616, F.

4430. SOMERVELL, ROBERT, Edinburgh: A master in 1632.

4431. SOUTAR, THOMAS, Dundee: 1782, F. White-ironsmith.

4432. SOUTH, JOHN, London: Mentioned in 1494.

4433. SOUTHEY, WILLIAM, London: 17 Oct. 1811, Y. Died 1836.

4434. SOUTHWELL, CHARLES, London: 18 Mar. 1713, Y.

4435. SPACKMAN & GRANT, London: Touch, 662 L.T.P., struck c. 1709. (James Spackman, 1704, Y.; 1715, L.; and Edward Grant, 1698, Y.; 1715, L.)

4436. SPACKMAN & LITTLE, London: The marks of Joseph Spackman and Henry Little appear, c. 1760, on one specimen.

4437. SPACKMAN, JAMES, London: 22 June 1704, Y.; 9 May 1715, L.; 1722, S.; 1732, R.W.; 1741, U.W.; 1742, M. Died 1758.

4438. SPACKMAN, JAMES, London: 16 Aug. 1781, Y. and L.; 1786, S.; 1797, R.W. Struck out and fine returned by order, 24 Sept. 1801. (Cf. Macugnaga.)

4439. SPACKMAN, JOHN, London: 8 Aug. 1723, Y.

4440. SPACKMAN, JOSEPH, London: 19 Oct. 1749, Y.; 21 June 1753, L.; 1761, f.S. Touch, 982 L.T.P. Of Cornhill and Fenchurch Street. Had moved from Fenchurch Street to Cornhill in 1764. He was, on 25 Oct. 1753, granted leave to strike his uncle's, (James Spackman), Touch, which he did until 1758, when his uncle died.

4441. SPACKMAN, JOSEPH, JUNR., London: 21 Oct. 1784, Y. and L.

4442. SPACKMAN, JOSEPH & JAMES, London: Touch, 1045 L.T.P., struck c. 1782.

4443. SPACKMAN, JOSEPH & Co., London: Touch, 1052 L.T.P., struck c. 1785.

4443A. SPACKMAN & MOURGUE, London: In 1801 were at 9 Union Buildings, Leather Lane. Partners, Fulerand Mourgue and Mary Spackman.

4444. SPACKMAN, MARY, London: 21 Mar. 1799, Y. SPADEMAN, see SPATEMAN.

4444A. SPARKE, SAMUEL, Norwich: 1708, Y.

4445. SPARLING, JOSEPH, London: 12 Aug. 1714, Y.

4446. SPARROW, FRANCIS, London: 23 Feb. 1746, L. Excused S. Died in 1760.

4447. SPATEMAN, JOHN, London: 19 June 1755, Y.

4448. SPATEMAN, SAMUEL, London: 24 Mar. 1719, Y.; 3 Aug. 1738, L.; 1750, S.; 1754, f.R.W.; 15 Mar. 1759, Beadle. Resigned office of Beadle 17 Oct. 1765. Died 1768. Touch, 825 L.T.P., which he had leave to strike on 20 Mar. 1728.

4449. SPELLER, JOSEPH, London: 15 Oct. 1818, Y.

4450. SPENCE, STEPHEN, York: 1616/7, F.

4451. SPENCER, GABRIELL, London: Worked for Robert Hustwaite, but was licensed to open shop for himself in 1567.

4452. SPENCER, JOHN, Axbridge, Somerset: S. of William. Apprenticed to Thomas Gwinnell, Bristol, and Marie his wife, 2 Mar. 1628.

4453. SPENCER, THOMAS, London: 13 Aug. 1702, Y. Touch, 600 L.T.P., which he had leave to strike on 15 Aug. 1702. (Cf. L.S. under Initialled Touches.)

4454. SPERYNG, RICHARD, London: In 1457 was an apprentice to Thomas Page.

4455. SPICER, JOHN, London: 14 Dec. 1699, Y. Touch, 631 L.T.P., which he had leave to strike on 21 Mar. 1705.

4456. SPICER, NATHANIEL, Bristol and Newent, Glocs.: 12 Oct. 1710, F. S. of John. Apprenticed to Thomas Baily, Bristol, and Avice his wife, 20 Nov. 1680.

4457. SPICER, RICHARD, London: 18 Mar. 1735, Y.

4458. SPILSBURY, JAMES, London: 16 Dec. 1773, Y.

4459. SPINKS, JOHN, London: 19 Oct. 1815, Y.

4460. SPINKS, THOMAS, London: 17 Oct. 1793, Y. Died in 1834.

4461. SPOONER, RICHARD, London: 24 Mar. 1719, Y.; 20 Jan. 1726, L.; 1733, S.; 1738, f.R.W.; 1748, U.W.; 1749, f.M. Died 1761. Touch, 764 L.T.P., which he had leave to strike on 19 Dec. 1723.

4462. SPRING, PENTLEBURY, London: 8 Aug. 1717, Y. Touch, 724 L.T.P., which he had leave to strike on 19 June 1718.

4463. SPRING, THOMAS, London: 22 June 1710, Y.; 27 May 1714, L.; 1720, S.; 1742, Beadle. 1743, died.

4464. SPRING, THOMAS, London : Touch, 523 L.T.P., which he had leave to strike on 14 Mar. 1694. No mention of his name in the Y. or L. Lists about this date.

4465. SPRING, THOMAS, London : 21 Oct. 1756, Y.
4466. SQUIRES, BENJAMIN, London : 19 Oct. 1815, Y. Died 1841.
4467. SQUIRES, NICHOLAS, London : 20 Dec. 1716, Y.
4468. SQUYER, ROBERT, London : In 1457 was an apprentice to John Goodale.
4469. STABLEY, NICHOLAS, York : Was free in 1683/4.
4470. STACEY, EDWARD, London : 4 Aug. 1715, Y.
4471. STAFFORD, GEORGE, London : 18 June 1730, Y.; 19 June 1740, L.; 1753, f.S. Touch, 820 L.T.P. On 18 June 1730 he had leave to strike the same Touch as Joseph Donne, to whom he had been apprentice, Donne being present and consenting. Of St. Martin's Lane.

4472. STAGG, THOMAS, York : 1516, F.
4473. STALKER, JAMES, Edinburgh : A master in 1601.
4474. STANBROW, JOHN, London : 21 June 1694, Y.
4475. STANBROW, SAMUEL, London : 20 Mar. 1728, Y.
4476. STANLEY, FRANCIS, London : 19 Mar. 1690, Y.
4477. STANLEY, FRANCIS, London : 21 June 1722, Y. and L.
4478. STANLEY, I——, of ? : c. 1760.
4479. STANSBY, JOHN, London : Mentioned in 1608.
4480. STANTON, JAMES, London : 19 Oct. 1815, Y.; 19 Oct. 1826, L. Died 3 Nov. 1835. Of Shoe Lane and Little Britain. Touch, 1089 L.T.P., struck c. 1819.

4481. STANTON, LUCY, London : 20 May 1847, Y.
4482. STANTON, ROBERT, London : 21 Oct. 1773, Y.
4483. STANTON, ROBERT, London : 13 Dec. 1810, Y.; 15 Oct. 1818, L.; 1829, f.S.; 1839, f.R.W. Died 16 Jan. 1842. Of 37 Blackman Street.

His mark has been found with that of H. & R. Joseph. Touch, 1082 L.T.P.

4484. STANTON, WILLIAM, London : 22 Feb. 1810, Y.
4485. STAPLEHIRST, HENRY, London : In 1457 was an apprentice to Thomas Grove, and in 1477 he contributed towards a set of feast vessels.
4486. STAPLES, HENRY, London : 20 Mar. 1817, Y. and L.; 1823, f.S. Died 27 Oct. 1856, aged 64.
4487. STAPLES, RICHARD, London : In 1590 fined for boasting of his wares. 1618, U.W.; 1623, M.
4488. STAPLES, WILLIAM, London : 20 Mar. 1698, Y.
4489. STARKEY, BENJAMIN, London : 21 June 1753, Y.
4490. STARKEY, JAMES, London : 17 June 1708, Y.
4491. STARKEY, JAMES, London : 16 June 1748, Y. and L. Bankrupt, struck off by order and fine returned, 18 June 1767.
4491A. STARR, THOMAS, London : In 1817 was at 5 Albemarle Street, Clerkenwell.
4492. STARTON, ——, London : In 1622 he used the mark of a star.
4493. STASY, JOHN, York : 1451/2, F.
4494. STATHAM, ROBERT, London : 14 Aug. 1690, Y.
4495. STAVELEY, THOMAS, York : In 1641/2, was a City Chamberlain.
4496. STEALE, MARTIN, Edinburgh : 1784, F.
4497. STEEL(E), JOHN, Edinburgh : 1794, F.
4498. STEEL(E), PETER, London : 22 June 1797, Y.
4499. STEEL(E), THOMAS, Glasgow : 1797, F. Brass-founder.
4499A. STEEL(E), WILLIAM, London : In 1817 was at 9 North Street, City Road.
4500. STEEVENS, JAMES, London : 13 Dec. 1753, Y. Touch, 968 L.T.P., which he obtained leave to strike in 1754.

4501. STENT, JOHN, London : 29 Mar. 1709, Y.
4502. STEPHENS, JOHN, Exeter : In 1562 was an overseer of false wares.
4503. STEVENS, ANTHONY (? STEPHENS; See also STEEVENS) London : 1734, Y.
4504. STEVENS, ELIZABETH (? STEPHENS), London : Spinster. 22 Sept. 1724, Y. Bankrupt 9 Nov. 1742.

4505. STEVENS, JAMES, (? STEPHENS), London : 13 Dec. 1753, Y.; 9 June 1774, L.; 1781, f.S.

4506. STEVENS, JOHN, (? STEPHENS), London : 19 Dec. 1771, Y.

4507. STEVENS, JOHN, (? STEPHENS), London : 18 Mar. 1724, Y.

4508. STEVENS, JOHN, (? STEPHENS), London : 10 Dec. 1756, Y.

4509. STEVENS, JOHN (? STEPHENS), London : 15 Mar. 1821, Y. Died 17 Oct. 1853, age 80.

4510. STEVENS, JOHN (? STEPHENS), Bristol and Beachley, Glocs. : 20 Oct. 1654, F. Apprenticed to John Knowles, Bristol, and Marie his wife, 28 Sept. 1646. Mentioned in 1694.

4511. STEVENS, JONATHAN (? STEPHENS), London : 21 Mar. 1744, Y. Touch, 915 L.T.P., which he obtained leave to strike in 1745.

4512. STEVENS, PHILIP (? STEPHENS), London : 20 Jan. 1709, Y.; 21 June 1716, L. Touch, 664 L.T.P., struck c. 1709.

4513. STEVENS, THOMAS (? STEPHENS), London : 21 June 1716, Y.; 12 Oct. 1732, L. Touch, 757 L.T.P., which he had leave to strike on 23 Mar. 1720.

4514. STEVENS, THOMAS (? STEPHENS), Bristol and Tidenham, Glocs. : 23 May 1642, F. S. of William. Apprenticed to John Knowles, Bristol, and Margaret his wife, 14 July 1634.

4515. STEVENS, WILLIAM (? STEPHENS), London : 17 June 1697, Y. Touch, 552 L.T.P., struck c. 1700.

4516. STEVENS, WILLIAM (? STEPHENS), London : Licensed to open shop in 1576.

4517. STEVENS, WILLIAM (? STEPHENS), London : 17 Aug. 1729, Y. and L.; 1710, S. (sic? 1740).

Touch, 817 L.T.P., which he had leave to strike on 7 Aug. 1729.

4518. STEVENS, WILLIAM (? STEPHENS), Bristol : S. of Alexander. Apprenticed to Jane, widow of Robert Belton, 4 July 1699.

4519. STEVENSON, HENRY, York : 1509/10, F. He is mentioned again in 1539/40 as father of the next named.

4520. STEVENSON, HENRY, York : Son of the above. 1539/40, F., by patrimony.

4521. STEVENSON, ROBERT, Edinburgh : 1794, F.

4522. STEVENTON, RICHARD, London : Fined in 1595 for selling unmarked goods. 1603, R.W.; 1608 and 1614, U.W.

4523. STEVENTON, THOMAS, London : Fined in 1591 for selling unmarked wares. Was a Master at that time. His daughter married Robert Marshall.

4524. STEWARD, JOHN, London : 1590, R.W.; 1595, U.W.; 1600, 1603 and 1608, M.

4525. STEWARD, JOHN, London : 1634, S.; 1652, f.R.W.; 1658, f.U.W.; 1660, f.M.

4526. STEWARD, JOHN, London : 1641, S.; 1653, f.R.W.

4527. STEWARD, MOSES, London : 25 Sept, 1712, Y.

4528. STEWARD, ROWLAND, London : 12 June 1694, L.

4529. STEWARD, ROWLAND, London : 23 Mar. 1720, Y.

4530. STEWARD, THOMAS, London : 13 Dec. 1694, Y.

4531. STEWARD, TOBY (or TOBIAS), London : 1616, f.R.W.; 1626, U.W.; 1630, M.

4532. STEWART, ALEXANDER, Edinburgh : Mentioned in 1770.

4533. STEWART, JOHN, Aberdeen : In 1731 was an apprentice to William Johnston.

4534. STEWART, THOMAS, Edinburgh : 1781, F.

4535. STEWART, THOMAS, Edinburgh : A master in 1788.

4536. STEWART, THOMAS, Edinburgh : In 1722 was an apprentice to William Fraser.

4537. STEYLL, LAUNCELOT, York : 1536/7, F.

4538. STEYNFORD, THOMAS, London : In 1457 was an apprentice to William Crowde.

4539. STIFF, WILLIAM, Bristol : 13 Mar. 1761, F. Apprenticed to Gregory Ash.

4540. STILE(S), HENRY, London : 27 Sept. 1688, Y.

4541. STILE(S), HENRY, London : 19 June 1760, Y.

4542. STILE(S), JOHN, London : 18 June 1696, L.; 1703, f.S.; 1719, R.W.; 1727, U.W.; 1730, M. Touch, 453 L.T.P., which he had leave to strike on 9 April 1689. His mark has been found in conjunction with John Elderton's "Hall Marks."

4543. STIRZEKEN, THOMAS, London : 23 June 1726, Y.

4543A. STIRRUP, GEORGE, Manchester : His partnership with Oliver Ormrod is recorded in the *London Gazette* for 31 Dec. 1793 as being dissolved.

STOAKES, *see* STOKES.

4544. STO(C)KTON, WALTER, London : Was accused of using Mr. Allen's Touch in 1565.

4545. STODE, JOHN, London : 1527, U.W.; 1530, M.

4546. STOKES, JOSEPH, Bristol : 11 Feb. 1730, F. Apprenticed to Christopher Clement. In the Poll Books for 1734 and 1739 he is given as of Temple, Bristol.

4547. STOKESLAY, WILLIAM, York : 1419/20, F.

4548. STONE, EDWARD, London : 19 Dec. 1695, Y.

4549. STONE, EDWARD, Dublin : Died in 1702.

4549A. STONE, HOWARD, London : Touch, 547 L.T.P., which he had leave to strike on 30 April 1698.

4550. STONE, ISAAC, Dublin : Mentioned in 1736.

4551. STONE, JOHN, Belfast : Went from Belfast to Newry in 1768.

4552. STONE, THOMAS, London : 28 Nov. 1667, L.; 1671, f.S.; 1685, R.W.; 1687, U.W.; and was displaced by order of King James. In 1690 he was U.W. again and 1692, M.

4553. STONELEY, WILLIAM, London : 19 June 1766, Y.

4554. STONES, CHRISTOPHER, York : 1579, F. Mentioned later in 1607/8.

STOOD, *see* STODE.

4555. STOOK, JOHN, York : Mentioned in 1616 as a searcher.

4556. STOOKES, EDWARD, Bristol : 31 Jan. 1562, F. Apprenticed to Alan Gosewell.

4557. STOTT, JOHN, York : 1612/3, F. Mentioned in 1616 in a list of members.

4558. STOUT, ALEXANDER, London : 13 Dec. 1733, Y. Touch, 872 L.T.P., which he had leave to strike on 24 Mar. 1736.

4558A. STOUT, RICHARD, Norwich : 1579/80, F.

4558B. STOWE, JNO., London : c. 1680. ("Bennett" Book.)

4559. STOWELL, JOHN, London : In 1457 was an apprentice to Thomas Dounton.

4560. STRACHAN, JOHN, Perth : Mentioned in 1714.

4561. STRADLEY, ROBERT, London : Mentioned in 1457.

4562. STRANGE, CHRISTOPHER, London : Was a master in 1578.

4563. STRANGE, JOHN, London : Covenant servant to Raphe Mollyners in 1558.

4564. STRATTON, ALEXANDER, Cannongate, Edinburgh : in 1709 was an apprentice to John Forbes.

4565. STRAY(E), RALPH, London : In 1570 was of the Livery. 1578, R.W.; 1582, U.W.; 1587, 1590 and 1594, M. Died of Plague in 1602. In 1570 he was fined for appearing at the Lord Mayor's feast without his Livery Gown. Left a legacy to the Company in 1602.

4566. STREET, ROBERT, London : 7 Mar. 1742, Y.

4567. STREET, THOMAS, London : 11 Oct. 1750, Y.

4568. STRIBBLEHILL, JOHN, London : 13 Dec. 1722, Y.

4569. STRIBBLEHILL, JOHN, London : Touch, 300 L.T.P., which he had leave to strike in 1678. No mention of his name appears in the Y. or L. Lists, but it is in the "Bennett" Book, 1679-86.

4570. STRIBBLEHILL, THOMAS, London : 13 May 1693, L.

4571. STRIBBLEHILL, THOMAS, London : 10 Aug. 1704, Y. Touch, 772 L.T.P., which he had leave to strike on 17 Dec. 1724.

4572. STRIBBLEHILL, THOMAS, London : 17 June 1742, Y. Was granted leave to strike his Touch on 20 June 1745, but it is not on the Touchplates.

4573. STRICKLAND, JOHN, London: 16 Dec. 1703, Y. Touch, 703 L.T.P., which he had leave to strike on 11 Oct. 1716.

4574. STRINGFELLOW, WILLIAM, London: 17 June 1756, Y.

4575. STRONG, FRANCIS, London: 13 Dec. 1759, Y.

4576. STUCKE, WILLIAM, South Petherton, Somerset: S. of Roger. Apprenticed to Thomas Hobson, Bristol, and Elizabeth his wife for eight years from 25 Jan. 1616.

4577. STUKELEY, THOMAS, London: 1559, Y. Was not a pewterer by trade, but married a grand-daughter of Alderman Curtis.

4578. STURT, WALTER, London: 21 Aug. 1679, L. Touch, 221 L.T.P., which he had leave to strike in 1672/3.

4579. STURTON, ——— (? STRUTON), London: c. 1730, Y. His name is in the Records about this time without date.

4580. STURTON, ANTHONY (? STRUTON), London: Touch, 599 L.T.P., which he had leave to strike on 18 June 1702. His name is not in the existing Records.

4580A. STURROP, ROBERT (? RICHARD), London: c. 1683. ("Bennett" Book.) Touch, 389 L.T.P., which he had leave to strike on 1 Oct. 1683.

4581. STUYTE, WILLIAM, York: 1473/4, F.

4582. STYAN, HENRY, London: 19 Dec. 1723, Y.

4583. SULLIVAN, THOMAS, Waterford: Mentioned in 1820.

4584. SULLOCK, RICHARD, SENR., Bristol: 1 Mar. 1697, F. S. of Richard. Apprenticed to Erasmus Dole and Joan his wife, 15 July 1674. Mentioned in 1709.

4585. SULLOCK, RICHARD, JUNR., Bristol: 4 Aug. 1718, F. S. of Richard, Senr., and Judith, to whom he was apprenticed, 11 June 1709. Mentioned in the Poll Book for 1721 as of Castle Precincts, and in that for 1734 as of St. Leonard's, Bristol.

4586. SUMMERS, JOHN, London: 1697, Y. Touch, 543 L.T.P., which he had leave to strike on 9 Mar. 1697.

4587. SUMMERS, JOHN, London: 22 Mar. 1715, Y.; 13 June 1734, L.; 1743, S.; 1747, R.W.; 1756, U.W. Died in 1756.

4587A. SUTHERLAND, JOHN, Liverpool: In 1805 he appears as a pewterer, brazier, coppersmith, brassfounder, iron and tin-plate worker.

SURNDALL, see SWINDELL.

4588. SUTHFOLKE, WILLIAM, London: 1474, Beadle.

4589. SUTTON, WILLIAM, Cork: Mentioned in 1697.

4589A. SWAINE, LAWRENCE, London: c. 1680. ("Bennett" Book.)

4590. SWAN, DAVID, Dundee: In 1755 was an apprentice to John Thompson.

4591. SWAN, HUGH, London: Mentioned in 1451 and 1457, in which latter year he was of the Livery.

4592. SWANBOROUGH, THOMAS, London: 18 June 1741, Y.

4593. SWANSON, THOMAS, London: 13 Dec. 1753, Y.; 15 Mar. 1764, L.; 1769, f.S.; 1777, R.W. Dead in 1783. Touches, 991b L.T.P., which he obtained leave to strike in 1760, and 1008 L.T.P., when in 1765 he obtained leave to strike Mr. Samuel Ellis's Touch. He succeeded to the business of Samuel Ellis as is shown by a label on some of his plates. On 10 June 1783 he gave to the Company Consols by which £30 is distributed annually between six poor widows of pewterers.

4593A. SWAYNE, MARSHALL, Barnstaple: Mayor in 1747.

4594. SWEATMAN, JOHN, London: 19 June 1766, Y.

4595. SWEATMAN, JOHN, London: 14 June 1827, Y. Died in 1846.
4596. SWEATMAN, JOHN, London: 23 June 1803, Y.
4597. SWEATMAN, NICHOLAS, London: 24 June 1698, Y. Touch, 561 L.T.P., which he had leave to strike on 13 July 1699.

4598. SWEATMAN, SAMUEL, London: c. 1730, Y. His name is in the Yeomanry lists about this time, but no date is given.

4599. SWEATMAN, SAMUEL, London: 17 Oct. 1728, Y. Touch, 901 L.T.P., which he had leave to strike in 1741.

} Same.

4600. SWEETING, CHARLES, London: 1658, f.R.W.; 1663, f.U.W.; 1666, f.M. Buried 1 June 1680 at St. Dionis, Backchurch.
4601. SWEETING, CHARLES, London: 18 Mar. 1685, L.; 1685, f.S.; 1690, f.R.W., f.U.W., and f.M.
4602. SWEETING, CHARLES, London: 27 Sept. 1688, Y.; 8 Aug. 1717, L.
4603. SWEETING, CHARLES, London: 20 Dec. 1716, Y. S. of Charles.
4604. SWEETING, HENRY, London: 1622, S.; 1631, R.W.; 1640, U.W.; 1646, M. Held the Key of the Seal in 1647.
4605. SWEETING, CAPT. JOHN, London: 1653, R.W.; 1659, U.W.; 1661, M.
4606. SWEETING, JOHN, London: 27 Jan. 1707, Y.
4607. SWENERTON, JOHN, London: Accused of using Mr. Allen's Touch in 1565.
4608. SWIFT, CORNELIUS, London: 18 Oct. 1770, Y.; 20 Jan. 1796, L.; 1798, f.S.; 1805, f.R.W.; 1813, U.W.; 1814, M. Touch, 1036 L.T.P., struck c. 1778.

4609. SWIFT, WILLIAM CORNELIUS, London: 16 Mar. 1809, Y.; 21 Aug. 1817, L.; 1824, f.S. Struck out by order and fine returned on 14 June 1827. Died in 1832. Touch, 1088 L.T.P.

4610. SWINDELL, THOMAS, London: 21 June 1705, Y. Touch, 802 L.T.P., which he had leave to strike on 10 Aug. 1727.

4611. SWINGLAND, JOSHUA, London: 26 Sept. 1723, Y.
4612. SWINNERTON, RICHARD, London: Granted a pension by the Company in 1625.
4613. SWINTON, THOMAS, London: 18 Mar. 1713, Y.
4614. SWYNBANKE, ROBERT, York: 1573/4, F. 1588/9, City Chamberlain.
4615. SYDE, JAMES, Edinburgh: 1693, F.
4616. SYDE, JOHN, Edinburgh: 1660, F. ? Touch, 59 E.T.P.

4617. SYDE, JOHN, Edinburgh: 1680, F. Touch, 83 E.T.P.

4618. SYDENHAM, THEODORE, London: In 1747 he was in partnership with Nicholson, then refused his Freedom and finally was prosecuted for trading as a pewterer, not having served an apprenticeship.
4619. SYKES, ANTHONY, London: A master in 1612.
4620. SYMMER, DAVID, Edinburgh: 1692, F. Touch, 92 E.T.P.

4621. SYMMER, DAVID, Edinburgh: In 1684 was an apprentice to Alexander Hunter.
4622. SYMONDS, DAVID, Edinburgh: Mentioned in 1704.
4623. SYMONDS, WILLIAM, London: In 1457 was an apprentice to Thomas Turnour.
SYMONS, see SIMONS.
4624. SYMONTOUN, ARCHIBALD, Edinburgh: In 1724 was an apprentice to James Edgar.
4625. SYMONTOUN, JAMES, Edinburgh: 1696, F. Touch, 97 E.T.P.

4626. SYMONTOUN, JAMES, Edinburgh: In 1715 was an apprentice to James Edgar.

4627. Symson, James, York : 1534, F. 1541/2, City Chamberlain.

4628. Symson, John, York : 1493/4, F.

4629. Symson, John, London : Warden of Yeomanry in 1495.

4630. Symson, Ralph, York : 1509/10, City Chamberlain. Mentioned in 1547/8.

4631. Symson, William, York : 1637/8, F.

4632. Syward, John, London : In 1349 was chosen as an overseer of the Company's ordinances.

4633. Syward, Roger, London : Of All Hallow's, Bread Street. His will dated 1 Nov. 1348, was proved in the Court of Husting on 20 July 1349.

T

4634. Tabor, Richard, London : 20 June 1706, Y.

4635. Tail, Cornelious, Edinburgh : A master in 1630.

4636. Tait, Adam, Edinburgh : 1747, F. Touch, 138 E.T.P.

4637. Tait, John, Edinburgh : 1700, F. Touch, 100 E.T.P.

4638. Tait, John, Edinburgh : 1742, F.

4639. Tait, William, Edinburgh : 1729, F.

4640. Talbut, Elisha, London : 16 June 1748, Y.

4641. Talbut, Elisha, London : 17 Oct. 1776, Y.

4642. Tallent, William, London : In 1597 was of the Livery, but being poor and unable to pay the dues he returned his Livery hood.

4643. Tamplin, Thomas, Cork : Mentioned in 1759 and died in 1769.

4644. Tanfeld, John, York : 1463/4, F.

4645. Tanner, Benjamin, Bristol : 7 Dec. 1709, F. Apprenticed to Thomas Cave.

4646. Tanner, William, London : 18 June 1702, Y.

4647. Tarlton, Robert, London : 1717, Clerk. Died 1720. The birth of his son was registered at St. Dionis, Backchurch, 7 June 1676.

Tarrett, see Jarrett.

4648. Tate, Matthew, Cork : Mentioned in 1729.

4649. Taudin, Daniel, London : In 1688 was permitted to work for five months *only*. A Protestant refugee from France.

4650. Taudin, James, London : 21 Jan. 1657, Y. and L. In 1667/8 complaint was made against him of using two Touches. 1663, f.S. ; 1670, f.R.W. ; 1675, f.U.W. ; 1669, f.M. Touch, 16 L.T.P., restruck after the great fire c. 1670,

He probably died in 1680. Father of James Taudin below.

4651. Taudin, James, London : 9 Sept. 1680, L. ; 1685, f.S. ; 1700, R.W. Touch, 344 L.T.P., struck c. 1680. In partnership with his father.

4652. Taverner, James, London : In 1566 was ordered to forfeit his Touch for making bad wares and strike a new one with ff. therein.

4653. Tayleour, Cornelious, Edinburgh : 1610, F. Touches, 18 and 19 E.T.P.

4654. Taylor, Abraham, London : 1651, S. Mentioned in the " Bennett " Book until 1684.

4655. Taylor, Anthony, London : In 1595 was committed to Ward for false wares. In 1614 he is mentioned as a master.

4656. Taylor, Ebenezer, London : 16 Dec. 1819, Y. ; 7 Feb. 1822, L. ; 1823, f.S. ; 1844, R.W. ; 1846, U.W. ; 1847, M. Died 21 Oct. 1851, age 73.

4657. Taylor, Edward, London : Was dead in 1574.

4658. Taylor, George, London : 21 Mar. 1722, Y. Touches, 745 and 758 L.T.P. (both alike), which he had leave to strike on 21 Mar. 1722.

4659. TAYLOR, GEORGE, London : 13 Dec. 1764, Y.; 21 June 1770, L.; 1777, S.; 1783, R.W.; 1805, U.W.; and died.

4660. TAYLOR, GEORGE, London : 23 June 1791, Y.

4661. TAYLOR, HENRY, Bristol : 24 July 1700, F. Apprenticed to William Barron. In 1701 he left off the trade and went to sea.

4662. TAYLOR, JAMES, London : Mentioned in 1666 as using his mother's Touch.

4663. TAYLOR, JOHN, London : 16 Oct. 1783, Y.

4664. TAYLOR, JOHN, London : In 1557 he was received back into the Company after working in the Country.

4666. TAYLOR, JOHN, Bristol : Mentioned in 1617.

4667. TAYLOR, JOSEPH, Perth : 1706, F.

4668. TAYLOR, RICHARD, London : 1509, R.W.; 1515 and 1520, U.W.; 1524, and 1529, M.

4669. TAYLOR, RICHARD, London : Of St. Giles, Cripplegate, pewterer. Married at St. Martin's in the Fields, 20 June 1667, and is mentioned in the " Bennett " Book from 1679-86.

4670. TAYLOR, ROBERT, London : 1535, R.W.; 1542 and 1547, U.W.; 1551, M.

4671. TAYLOR, ROGER, Ludlow : Mentioned as a master in 1600.

4672. TAYLOR, SAMUEL, London : 23 Mar. 1731, Y.; 20 Mar. 1734, L.; 1743, S.; 1748, R.W. Touch, 850 L.T.P., which he had leave to strike on 19 Dec. 1734.

4673. TAYLOR, THOMAS, London : 11 Aug. 1681, L.; 1685, S.; 1693, f.R.W.; 1700, f.U.W.; 1704 and 1716, M. Touch, 178 L.T.P., which he had leave to strike in 1670/1. He was admonished in 1688 for adding his address to his Touch, and of which addition an illustration is given here.

4674. TAYLOR, THOMAS, London : 16 June 1737, Y.

4675. TAYLOR, TIMOTHY, London : 22 Mar. 1760, Y. Obtained leave to strike his Touch in 1760, but it is not on the Touchplates.

4676. TAYLOR, W——, London : In 1611 was apprentice to Nicholas Kelk.

4677. TAYLOR, WILLIAM, London : 20 June 1728, Y.

4677A. TAYLOR, WILLIAM, London : c. 1680. (" Bennett " Book.)

4678. TAYLOR, WILLIAM, Exeter and Bristol : 14 Sept. 1780, F. Married Elizabeth Davis. In 1793 he was in Goldsmith Street. In the Bristol Poll Books for 1781 and 1784 he is given as a country voter. Cf. 1994 and 5387.

4680. TAYLOR, WILLIAM, Bristol and Keinbell, Wilts. : S. of William. Apprenticed to William Barron, Bristol, and Sarah his wife 14 Aug. 1691.

4681. TAYLOR, WILLIAM GARDNER, London : 15 June 1819, Y.; 19 Aug. 1819, L.; 1829, f.S.; 1839, R.W.; 1842, U.W. and M. Died 6 Dec. 1869.

4682. TAYNTON, BENJAMIN, Bristol : 24 July 1805, F. S. of Walter. Apprenticed to Robert Bush and Susannah his wife, 19 June 1799.

4683. TAYNTON, JAMES BADY, Bristol : S. of Nathaniel. Apprenticed to Robert Bush, 8 Dec. 1791.

4684. TAYNTON, JOHN, Bristol : S. of Thomas. Apprenticed to Thomas Lanyon and Ann his wife, 20 Jan. 1745.

4685. TAYNTON, NATHANIEL, Bristol : 3 Oct. 1770, F. S. of Thomas. Apprenticed to Allen Bright and Ann his wife, 9 Nov. 1761. Premium £10. In the Poll Book for 1774 he is given as of Castle Precincts, in that for 1781 as of S.S. Philip and Jacob, and in that for 1784 as of St. Mary-le-Port, all of Bristol. Mentioned in 1791

4686. TAYNTON, THOMAS, SENR., Bristol and Gloucester : 20 July 1727, F. S. of John. Apprenticed to Sarah, widow of John Peters, Bristol, 10 Feb. 1719. In the Poll Book for 1734 he is given as of St. Nicholas, in those for 1739 and 1754 as of St. James's, and in that of 1774 as of St. Thomas's, all of Bristol. Died c. 1745

4687. TAYNTON, THOMAS, JUNR., Bristol : 28 Mar. 1754, F., by patrimony. S. of Thomas. Apprenticed to William Hutton and Elizabeth his wife, 6 April 1747.

4688. TAYNTON, THOMAS, Bristol : 24 July 1805, F. S. of Walter.

4689. TAYNTON, THOMAS, Bristol: S. of Thomas. Apprenticed to Thomas Hale and Martha his wife, 28 July 1794.

4690. TAYNTON, WALTER, Bristol and Ashburton: 9 Mar. 1768, F. S. of Thomas. Apprenticed to Allen Bright and Ann his wife, 23 Sept. 1761. In the Bristol Poll Book for 1774 he is given as a country voter of Ashburton, in that for 1781 as of St. Peter's, Bristol, and in that for 1784 as of S.S. Philip and Jacob, Bristol.

4691. TEALE, JOHN, London: 14 Jan. 1685, L.; 1690, S. Of Charing Cross. Touch, 255 L.T.P., struck c. 1676.

4692. TEMPLE & REYNOLDS, London: First half of nineteenth century. Of Prince's Street.

4693. TEMPLEMAN, THOMAS, London: 1677, S.; 1692, f.R.W.; 1695, U.W.; 1697, M. Touch, 122 L.T.P., restruck c. 1670 after the great fire of London. In 1686 his address was "At The Sun, near Norfolk Street, in the Strand." His Touch is found on pieces bearing Queen Anne's Royal cypher.

4694. TENNENT, GEORGE, Edinburgh: 1706, F. Touch, 108 E.T.P.

4695. TERRALL, FRANCIS, London: 25 Sept. 1712, Y.

4696. TERRY, LEONARD (see also TIRRY), York: Was Free in 1684.

4697. TERRY, LEONARD, York: On 1 May 1692 was apprenticed for seven years to Robert Sadler,

1698/9, F. Searcher in 1705, 1710, 1714, 1718, 1719, 1722, 1727 and 1734.

4698. TERRY, NICHOLAS, York: 1390/1, F.

4699. TEYATON, BENJAMIN, Bristol: Mentioned in the Poll Book for 1812 as of Elbroad, S.S. Philip and Jacob, Bristol.

4700. TEYATON, THOMAS, Bristol: Mentioned in the Poll Book for 1812 as of Elbroad, S.S. Philip and Jacob, Bristol.

4701. THEARSBY, THOMAS (? THURSBY), York: On 6 Feb. 1717 was apprenticed for eight years to Richard Chambers. 1729/30, F., by patrimony. Was a searcher in 1734. Son of Emanuel.

4702. THEARSBY (? THURSBY), THOMAS, York: Free in 1684.

4703. THEOBALD, JOHN, London: 19 Dec. 1723, Y.

4704. THEOBALD, WILLIAM, London: 15 Mar. 1764, Y.

4705. THEOBALD, WILLIAM, London: 15 Dec. 1791, Y.

4706. THEPLER, SYMOND, London: In 1457 was apprentice to John Kendale.

4707. THICKNESS, SAMUEL, London: 24 Mar. 1736, Y.

4708. THOMAS, ARTHUR, Bristol and Barrow, Somerset: 18 Aug. 1699, F. S. of John. Apprenticed to Erasmus Dole, Bristol, and Sarah his wife, 19 Jan. 1677.

4709. THOMAS, JOHN, London: 4 April 1698, Y. Touch, 545 L.T.P., which he had leave to strike on 4 April 1698.

4710. THOMAS, JOHN, Maidstone: Appointed in 1566 to look after the Company's interests in Kent and Sussex.

4710A. THOMAS, JOHN, Chester: Near the Cross. His stock and shop were bought on 13 Sept. 1774 by Henry Green late of Denbigh.

4711. THOMAS, JOSIAH, London: 10 Aug. 1717, Y.

4712. THOMAS, PHILIP, London: 16 Dec. 1731, Y.

4713. THOMAS, RICHARD, Yatton, Somerset: S. of John. Apprenticed to Edward Gregory, Bristol, and Anne his wife, 26 Feb. 1722.

4714. THOMAS, SAMUEL, Bristol: Mentioned in the Poll Book for 1781 as of St. James's, Bristol.

4715. THOMAS, WALTER, London: 10 Feb. 1756, Y. and L.

4716. THOMAS, WILLIAM, London : 13 Dec. 1722, Y.
4716A. THOMAS, WILLIAM, Wales : His son was buried at Haverford West, 14 Sept. 1602.
4717. THOMINGS, SAMUEL, London : 16 Oct. 1760, Y.
4717A. THOM(P)SON, BENEDICTUS, London : c. 1680. ("Bennett" Book.) Touch, 222 L.T.P., which he had leave to strike in 1672/3.

4718. THOM(P)SON(E), GILBERT (see also TOMSON), Edinburgh : 1668, F.
4719. THOM(P)SON(E), JOHN, Dundee : 1753, F. White-ironsmith.
4720. THOM(P)SON(E), JOHN, Dundee : 1746, apprentice. Journeyman to Robert Auchinleck.
4721. THOM(P)SON(E), JOHN, Perth : 1706, F.
4721A. THOM(P)SON(E), JOHN, London : In 1801 was at 388 Oxford Street.
4722. THOM(P)SON(E), LEONARD, York : Free in 1588/9.
4723. THOM(P)SON(E), MICHELL, London : Of St. Mary Axe. Fined in 1568 for using opprobrious words to a brother pewterer.
4724. THOM(P)SON(E), PAUL, London : 21 Mar. 1733, Y.
4725. THOM(P)SON(E), RICHARD, London : In 1558 was an apprentice to Clement Killingworth.
4726. THOM(P)SON(E), ROBERT, Edinburgh: Mentioned in 1643. Died c. 1663. Touches, 36 and 37 E.T.P.

4727. THOM(P)SON(E), THOMAS, London : 19 June 1755, Y. Touch, 1004 L.T.P., which he obtained leave to strike in 1764.

4728. THOM(P)SON(E), WILLIAM, London : 3 Aug. 1738, L. Partner in Fly & Thompson (q.v.). (Touch, 874 L.T.P.)
4729. THOM(P)SON(E), WILLIAM, York : 1496/7. F.
4730. THORBURN, GEORGE, Edinburgh : In 1682 was an apprentice to Alexander Menzies.
4731. THORNDELL, RICHARD, London : 17 June 1752, Y.
4731A. THORNE, CHRISTOPHER, London : c. 1680. ("Bennett" Book.) Touch, 247 L.T.P., which he had leave to strike in 1674/5.

4732. THORNE, THOMAS, Lynn : 1456/7, F.
4733. THORNEBOURNE, THOMAS, Perth : 1665.
4734. THOROGOOD, NICHOLAS, London : 1634, S.
4735. THURGOOD, JOHN, London : 1497, R.W.; 1503 and 1515, U.W.; 1524 and 1529, M.
4736. THURLOAD, ROBARD (?HURLOND), London : 1483, Y. Had his goods seized in payment of his entrance fee.
4737. THURSTON, THOMAS, London : 12 Oct. 1738, Y.
4738. TIBBING, WILLIAM (? TIPPING), London : Touch 334 L.T.P. which he was given leave to strike in 1679. He is mentioned in the "Bennett" Book as dying in 1681.

4739. TIDMARSH, ANN, London : 20 June 1728, Y. Daughter of Thomas T. Touch, 803 L.T.P., which she had leave to strike on 20 June 1728.

4740. TIDMARSH, JAMES, London : 19 June 1701, Y. Touch, 615 L.T.P., which he had leave to strike on 31 Mar. 1704.

4741. TIDMARSH, JAMES, London : 19 Dec. 1734, Y.; 11 Oct. 1750, L. Touch, 852 L.T.P., which he had leave to strike in 1734.

4742. TIDMARSH, JOHN, London : 18 June 1713, Y.; 16 Mar. 1726, L.; 1734, f.S.; 1739, R.W.; 1750, U.W.; 1752, M. Son of Thomas. Touch, 697 L.T.P., which he was given leave to strike on 13 Oct. 1715.

4743. TIDMARSH, RICHARD, London : 16 Dec. 1714, Y.

4744. Tidmarsh, Thomas, London : 1 May 1691, L. ; 1707, R.W.; 1717, U.W.; 1721, M. ? Touch, 296 L.T.P., struck c. 1677.

4745. Tidmarsh, Thomas, London : 23 June 1709, Y.
4746. Tierman, Richard, York : 1642/3, F.
4747. Till, John, London : Served in 1585 in place of Thomas Gaye as a soldier for the Company.
4747A. Tillott, Robert, London : c. 1680. (" Bennett " Book.) Touch, 286 L.T.P., which he had leave to strike in 1676/7.

4748. Tillyard, Thomas, London : 24 June 1698, Y. ; 2 Oct. 1702, L. ; 1711, f.S. Touch, 549 L.T.P., which he had leave to strike on 27 June 1698.

4749. Timmins, John, Bewdley : A spoonmaker in Dog Lane. Died c. 1840.
4749A. Tine, William, Wakefield : Bankrupt in 1728.
4750. Tinsley, Thomas, London : 19 Dec. 1695, Y.
Tipping, see Tibbing.
4751. Tipson, Richard, Bristol : Mentioned in 1645.
4752. Tirry, Robert (see also Terry), York : 1632/3, F.
4753. Tirry, Thomas, York : 1615/6, F. Mentioned later in 1656/7.
4754. Tisoe, James, London : 14 Oct. 1688, Y. Of St. Margaret's, Westminster. Touch, 449 L.T.P., which he had leave to strike on 1 April 1689.

4755. Tisoe, James, London : 9 Aug. 1733, Y. ; 19 Mar. 1746, L. ; 1758, f.S. ; 1764, R.W. Dead in 1771. Touch, 854 L.T.P., which he had leave to strike on 20 Mar. 1734.

4756. Tisoe, James, London : 13 Dec. 1764, Y.
4757. Tisoe, John, London : 9 Aug. 1733, Y.; 21 Mar. 1744, L. ; 1755, f.S. ; 1761, f.R.W.; 1774, U.W.
4759. Toby, John, Bristol : S. of John. Apprenticed to William Barron and Sarah his wife, 8 Feb. 1703.
4760. Toller, John, York : 1480/1, F.
4761. Tollerton, Peter, London : In 1566 was an apprentice to Edward Reo.
4762. Tolley, Edward, London : 20 June 1805, Y.
4763. Tomkin, Benjamin, London : 12 Dec. 1691, Y.
4764. Tomkin, James, London : 12 Aug. 1708, Y.
4765. Tomkyns, Roger, Ludlow : Mentioned in 1603.
4766. Tomlin, Daniel, London : 11 Dec. 1735, Y.
4767. Tomlin, William, London : 14 Mar. 1765, Y.
Tomlinson, see Tonkison.
4768. Tompson, Harry (see also Thompson), London : In 1554 was in trouble with the Company.
4769. Tompson, Richard, London : 1576, S.
4769A. Tompson, William, Norwich : 1594/5, F.
4770. Toms, Edward, London : 21 June 1744, Y. ; 13 June 1751, L. ; 1761, f.S. ; 1768, R.W. ; 1781, U.W. ; 1783, M. Touch, 912 L.T.P., which he was given leave to strike in 1744. In 1792 his business was at 77 Tower Street.

4771. Tomson, Bagnitilous, Grayesdale, Lancs. : S. of George. Apprenticed to John Benson, Bristol, and Matilda his wife for eight years from 17 June 1611.
4772. Tomson, John, Bristol : 3 April 1572, F., having been apprenticed to Thomas Deaconson and turned over later to John Burrowes.
4773. Tomson, John, Bristol : S. of Martin. Apprenticed to Edward Cullimore and Marie his wife, 4 Dec. 1690.
4774. Tonkin, Matthew, London : 15 Mar. 1749, Y. and L. Of Cannon Street. Touch, 941 L.T.P., which he was given leave to strike in 1749.

4775. TONKINSON, R——, of ?: c. 1730. (? Tomlinson.)

4776. TOPLIFFE, RICHARD, York: Free in 1684.
4777. TOPLIFFE, RICHARD, York: In 24 June 1716
was apprenticed for eight years to John White.
1724/5, F. Son of William.
4778. TOPP, JOSEPH, Bristol: His wife was buried
at St. James's Church, Bristol, on 28 Nov.
1705.
4779. TORBUCK, PETER, London: 21 June 1739, Y.
4780. TORDOFT, WILLIAM, York: 1499, F.
4781. TOUGH, CHARLES, London: 28 Nov. 1667, L.;
1669, f.S.; 1680, f.R.W.
4782. TOUGH, CHARLES, London: 15 Aug. 1689, L.;
1705, f.R.W. Touch, 442 L.T.P., which he
had leave to strike in 1687/8.

4783. TOUK, WILLIAM, York: 1469/70, F.
4784. TOULMIN(GE), GEORGE, London: 16 Mar. 1797,
Y.; 20 June 1805, L. Struck out by order
and fine returned, 15 June 1820.
4785. TOVEY, WILLIAM, London: 13 Dec. 1787, Y.
and L.; 1793, f.S.; 1801, R.W.; 1805,
U.W.
4786. TOWERS, JOHN GREEN, London: 14 Dec. 1809,
Y. and L.; 1815, f.S. Struck out by order and
fine returned, 14 Mar. 1839. Died 16 June
1849, age 70.
4787. TOWERS, ROBERT, London: 21 Mar. 1771, Y.;
14 Dec. 1786, L.; 1793, f.S.; 1800, R.W.;
1806, U.W.; 1807, M.
4788. TOWERS, WILLIAM, London: 22 Mar, 1781,
Y.
4789. TOWGOOD, GEORGE, Cork: Mentioned in 1764
and 1787, and died in 1797.
4790. TOWGOOD, JOHN, Llanmaes, Glam.: S. of William.
Apprenticed to William Barron, Bristol, and
Sarah his wife, 19 Oct. 1691.
4791. TOWNS, WILLIAM GARDNER, London: 15 Dec.
1808, Y. Died 23 April 1859, age 73.
4792. TOWN(S)END, BENJAMIN, London: 21 June
1744, Y. Touch, 967 L.T.P., which he
obtained leave to strike on 20 June 1754.
(Cf. Bagshaw.)

4793. TOWN(S)END, EDWARD, London: 18 Mar. 1730,
Y.
4794. TOWN(S)END, GEORGE HERBERT, London: 16
June 1808, Y.; 15 Mar. 1810, L.
4795. TOWN(S)END, JOHN, London: 16 June 1748, Y.;
21 Jan. 1754, L.; 1762, S.; 1769, R.W.;
1782, U.W.; 1784, M. Died in 1801.
Touch, 928 L.T.P., which he was given leave
to strike on 16 June 1748. He was apprenticed
to Samuel Jefferys in Middle Row, Holborn,
Commenced his business at 47 Prescott Street,
Goodman's Fields. Succeeded to the business
founded by Thomas Scattergood, carried on by
Edward Merriefield, whose Touch of a daisy
in a hand he struck with his own (q.v.). For
further details of his many partnerships see note
under W. J. Englefield. In 1792 his business
was at 125 Fenchurch Street.

4796. TOWN(S)END, JOHN, London: 15 Oct. 1778, Y.
4797. TOWN(S)END, J. & REYNOLDS, R., London: Touch
1012 L.T.P.. struck c. 1766. The Partners,
John Townsend, 1748, Y.; and R. Reynolds,
1761, Y. Of Fenchurch Street. Leave to
strike this Touch was granted on 19 Mar. 1767.

4798. TOWN(S)END, MARY, London: 20 Oct. 1774, Y.

4798A. Town(s)end, Richard, London: c. 1680. (" Bennett " Book.)

4799. Town(s)end, William, London: 12 Oct. 1699, Y. Touch, 644 L.T.P., struck c. 1707.

4800. Town(s)end & Compton, London: 1801-1811. Of Prescott Street, Goodman's Fields, and later of Booth Street, Spittalfields.

4801. Town(s)end & Giffin, London: 1777-1801. In 1793 were of 135 Fenchurch Street.

4802. Trahern, Edward, London: 28 Aug. 1685, L.; 1685, S.; 1700, R.W.; 1707, U.W.; 1712, and 1718, M. ? Touch, 336 L.T.P., device, " 3 Herons," struck c. 1680.

4803. Trapp, John, London: 20 June 1695, Y. Touch, 731 L.T.P., which he had leave to strike on 22 Aug. 1720.

4804. Travers, Henry, London: 16 June 1720, Y.
4805. Treasure, John, London: 22 June 1758, Y.

4806. Tredaway, William, London: 22 June 1710, Y. Treherne, see Trahern.
4807. Tregelles, I——, Falmouth: c. 1725.

4808. Trekill, Richard, London: In 1457 was journeyman to Thomas Dounton.
4809. Trekill, William, London: In 1457 was journeyman to Stephen Tod.
4810. Trenchfield, William, London: 24 Sept. 1696, Y.
4811. Trew, James, London: Touch, 227 L.T.P., which he had leave to strike in 1673/4. No mention of his name is in the existing Y. or L. Lists, but he is given in the " Bennett " Book as dead in 1681.

4812. Trewallon, Charles, London: 23 Mar. 1731, Y.
4812A. Trewallon, William, London: Died in 1681. (" Bennett " Book.)
4813. Trewella, Charles, London: 14 Oct. 1689, Y.
4814. Triggs, John, Cork: Mentioned in 1763.
4815. Tristram, Robert, London: 16 June 1757, Y.
4816. Trix, Edward, Cork: Mentioned in 1748.
4817. Trotter, William, London: Appointed one of several in 1591 to uphold the Company's rights.
4818. Trotman, Thomas, Bristol: 27 Aug. 1658, F. S. of John. Apprenticed to John Knowles and Marie his wife, 21 Aug. 1650.
4819. Trout, John, London: 19 Dec. 1689, Y. Touch, 464 L.T.P., which he had leave to strike on 20 Mar. 1689.

4820. Trucknell, William, Wedmore, Somerset: S. of John. Apprenticed to Richard Gibson, Bristol, and Marie his wife, 31 Oct. 1627.

4821. TUBB, JOHN, of ? : c. 1690.

4822. TUCK, THOMAS, Bristol and Sth. Cerney, Glocs. : 5 June 1794, F. S. of John. Apprenticed to Robert Bush and Ann his wife, 2 June 1784.

4823. TUCKER, ISAAC, London : 1585, Y. ; 1590, L.

4824. TUCKER, JOHN, London : In 1570 was fined for not marking his wares.

4825. TUDMAN, HUMPHREY, Walsall : Buried at St. Matthews Church, Walsall, 2 Aug. 1647.

4826. TUDMAN, SAMUEL, Evesham : Mentioned in 1691.

4827. TUGLEY, JOHN, London : Received alms from the Company in 1563 as a poor brother.

4828. TULK, JAMES, Bristol : 27 June 1747, F. In the Poll Book for 1754 he is given as of St. Nicholas, Bristol. Married Sarah Green.

4829. TULLY, CHARLES, Bristol : 5 Oct. 1776, F. In the Poll Books for 1774 and 1781 he is given as of Castle Precincts, Bristol. Married Mary Lewis.

TUMBERVILLE, *see* TURBERVILLE (it is spelt both ways in the Records).

4829A. TUNKS, JOHN, Gloucester : Mentioned in 1583.

4830. TUNWELL, RICHARD, London : 11 Oct. 1804, Y. Died 1853, age 79.

4831. TURBERVILLE, DAUBENY, London : 14 Oct. 1703, Y. ; 1 Sept. 1714, L. ; 1728, f.R.W. Touch, 626 L.T.P., which he had leave to strike on 21 June 1705.

4832. TURNER, ANDREW, Aberdeen : In 1685 was an apprentice to George Ross.

4833. TURNER, BENJAMIN, London : 20 June 1765, Y.

4834. TURNER, EDWARD, Bristol : S. of John. Apprenticed to Thomas Willshire and Ann his wife, 31 Dec. 1785.

4835. TURNER, NICHOLAS, London : 1561, R.W. Mentioned in 1584.

4836. TURNER, NICHOLAS, London : 1606, U.W.
} ? Same.

4837. TURNER, PETER, London : In 1552 received alms from the Company as a poor brother.

4838. TURNER, PETER, of ? : c. 1730-1760.

4839. TURNER, ROBERT, Glasgow : In 1792 was an apprentice to Robert Graham and James Wardrop.

4840. TURNER, SAMUEL, London : 14 Oct. 1790, Y. Partner in Holland & Turner. Partnership dissolved 2 Jan. 1810, Turner continuing the business.

4841. TURNER, STEPHEN, London : 19 June 1694, L.

4842. TURNER, THOMAS, London : 1452, Y. Expelled in 1457.

4843. TURNER, WILLIAM, London : 2 Oct. 1702, Y. Touch, 627 L.T.P., which he had leave to strike on 22 Aug. 1705.

4844. TURNER, WILLIAM ROBERT, London : 14 Dec. 1815, Y. and L. ; 1822, f.S. Struck out by order and fine returned, 19 Mar. 1846.

4845. TWEEDISON, JOHN, Edinburgh : In 1716 was apprenticed to Robert Kellowe.

4846. TWIDDELL, NICHOLAS, London : 18 Mar. 1741, Y.

4846A. TWIST, JOHN, London : c. 1680. ("Bennett" Book.)

4847. TWIST, JOHN, London : A master in 1611.

4847A. TWITNY, ROBERT, Norwich : 1663, F.

4848. TYLER, SAMUEL, Bristol : 30 April 1690, F. Apprenticed to James Lovering and turned over to William Barron. In the Poll Book for 1721 he is given as of St. John's, Bristol.

4849. TYLSH, NICHOLAS, Dublin : 1581, F.

4850. TYMME, ROBERT, London : A master in 1558.

4851. TYNDALE, JOHN, York : 1495/6, F.

4852. TYRMAN, RICHARD, York : 1627/8, F.

TYSOE, *see* TISOE.

U

4853.　Ubl(e)y, Edward, London : 20 Feb. 1716, Y. ; 21 Mar. 1727, L.　Touch, 759 L.T.P., which he had leave to strike on 15 Mar. 1721.

4854.　Ubl(e)y, John, London : 13 Dec. 1722, Y.
4855.　Ubl(e)y, John, London : 21 Feb. 1748, Y.　Of Minories.　Was gazetted a bankrupt on 24 May 1755.　Touch, 944 L.T.P., which he obtained leave to strike on 11 Oct. 1750.

4856.　Ubl(e)y, Thomas, London : 15 Oct. 1741, Y. ; 1751, L.　Obtained his freedom by patrimony.　Son of Richard.　Touch, 896 L.T.P., which he obtained leave to strike on 15 Oct. 1741.

4857.　Underwood, George, London : 19 June 1712,

Y.　Touch, 686 L.T.P., which he obtained leave to strike on 14 Aug. 1712.

4858.　Underwood, Jonathan, London : 15 Dec. 1698, Y.
4859.　Underwood, Matthew, London : 17 June 1752, Y.　Touch, 958 L.T.P., which he obtained leave to strike on 17 June 1752.　Of St. Mary, Aldermary.　He was gazetted a bankrupt on 29 Sept. 1761.

Uptone, see De Uptone.
Urswycke, see Beswick.
4860.　Usher, Thomas, ? Banbury : Touch dated 1739.　Thomas Usher, Banbury, Brazier, was in a debtors' prison in 1743.

Ustwaite, see Hustwaite.
4861.　Utle, William, ? Banbury : In 1457 was apprentice to Thomas Page.

V

4862.　Vallet, Richard (? Vallatt), Cork : Mentioned in 1637.
4863.　Vaughan, John, London : 25 Oct. 1753, Y. ; 23 June 1768, L. ; 1774, f.S. ; 1780, R.W. ; 1791, U.W. ; 1792, M.　Died 1807.　Touch, 985 L.T.P., which he obtained leave to strike in 1760.

On stem of a spoon.

4864.　Vaughan, Thomas, Brecknock : S. of Thomas.　Apprenticed to Thomas Bailey, Bristol, and Avice his wife, 22 June 1695.
4865.　Vaughan, Walter, London : In 1591 was fined for absence without leave, and in 1603 was chosen to serve on a committee elected to redress certain grievances.
4866.　Vaughan, William, London : 18 Mar. 1773, Y.
4867.　Ven(n)ables, William, London : 17 Dec. 1772, Y.
4868.　Veitch, Robert, Edinburgh : 1725, F.　Touch, 125 E.T.P.

4869. VERDON, THOMAS, London : 17 June 1732, Y.

4870. VERNON, RICHARD, London : 1650, S.

4871. VERNON, SAMUEL, London : Touch, 232 L.T.P., which he had leave to strike in 1674/5.

4872. VERTSON, PATRICK, Edinburgh : In 1716 was an apprentice to Robert Findlay.

4873. VEYSEY, JOHN, London : Sold some moulds to the Company in 1451 and was a master in 1457.

4873A. VIBART, GEORGE, London : c. 1680. (" Bennett" Book.) Touch, 273 L.T.P., which he had leave to strike in 1676/7.

4874. VICKERS, I—— (or ? L.), Bewdley : c. 1830.

4875. VILE, THOMAS, London : 12 Aug. 1669, L.; 1675, S.

4876. VILLERS & WILKES, Birmingham : In 1805 Directory they are given as wholesale braziers, pewterers and dealers in metal at Moor Street.

4876A. VILLERS, WILLIAM, Birmingham : In 1793 was a pewterer, brazier and dealer in metals in Moor Street.

See also BIRCH & VILLERS.

VILSONE, *see* WILSONE.

4876B. VINCENT, AMBROSE, Blandford, Dorset : Signed an inventory in 1690.

4877. VINCENT, JOHN, London : 28 Aug. 1685, L.

4878. VINCENT, JOHN, London : 1475, R.W.; 1483. U.W.

4879. VINCENT, PETER, London : Served in 1584 in a body of soldiers raised from the Company, in place of Nicholas Collier.

4880. VINE, WILLIAM, Bristol : 5 Aug. 1700, F. Married Hannah Web.

4881. VIRGIN, GEORGE, London : 25 Oct. 1817, Y.

4882. VIVEASH, SIMEON, London : 17 June 1756, Y.

4883. VOKINS, B——, London : Touch, 182 L.T.P., struck c. 1672. No mention of his name is in the existing Records.

4884. VOOGHT, JAMES, London : 17 Mar. 1774, Y.

4885. VOWLES, FRANK EDWARD, Bristol : Succeeded George Hayter and was the last genuine pewterer of Bristol. His business was at 30 Temple Street from 1887-1902.

4886. VOWLES, JOHN, Abbotsleigh, Somerset : S. of Samuel. Apprenticed to Robert Bush, Bristol, and Susannah his wife, 12 Dec. 1799.

W

4887. WADDEL, ALEXANDER, Cannongate, Edinburgh, 1720, F.

4888. WADDEL, ALEXANDER, Edinburgh : 1714, F. In 1721 he committed the great offence of " Packing and peiling with unfreemen." Touch 116 E.T.P.

4889. WADDEL, WALTER, Edinburgh : Mentioned in 1719.

4890. WACE, WILLIAM, London : In 1457 was an apprentice to John Veysy.

4891. WADDOCE, THOMAS, London : 1549, R.W.; 1554, U.W.; 1565, M.

4892. WADDYNGTON, ROBERT, London : Had foreign pewter seized from him in 1543.

4893. WADE, JOHN, London : 19 Mar. 1829, Y.

4894. WADE, WILLIAM, London : 20 Oct. 1785, Y.

4895. WADELOW, HUGH, London : False wares were seized from him in 1554. He is mentioned again 1561.

4896. WADSWORTH, WILLIAM, London : 19 Oct. 1780, Y. Touch, 1060 L.T.P., struck c. 1693.

4897. WAID, JANNE, York : Free in 1684, and is mentioned up to 1699. (A woman.)

4898. WAID, PHILIP, York : On 24 June 1656 was apprenticed to John Hammon for seven years. 1666/7, F., by patrimony.

4899. WAIDSON, GEORGE, London : 11 Aug. 1709, Y.

4900. WAIGHT, RICHARD (? WAITE), London : A master in 1555.

4901. WAIGHT, THOMAS (? WAITE), London : 11 Mar. 1702, Y.

4902. WAIGHT, THOMAS (? WAITE), London : A spoon-maker in 1683. Touch, 325 L.T.P., which he had leave to strike in 1678/9.

4903. WAITE, JOHN (? WAIGHT) London : 15 Aug., 1706 Y. Touch, 688 L.T.P., which he was granted leave to strike on 16 May, 1712.

4903A. WAITE, JOHN (? WAIGHT), London : c. 1680. ("Bennett" Book.) Touch, 224 L.T.P., which he had leave to strike in 1673/4.

4904. WAKEFIELD, JOHN, London : 16 Mar. 1809, Y. and L.; 1815, f.S.; 1826, R.W. Died 1828.

4905. WAKEFIELD, RICHARD, London : 15 Dec. 1720, Y.

4905A. WALBANK, MILES, London : c. 1680. ("Bennett" Book.)

4906. WALDBY, DIONYSIUS, London : 25 Mar. 1759, Y.

4907. WALKER, ALEXANDER, Edinburgh : 1676, F. Touch, 74 E.T.P.

4907A. WALKER, BENJAMIN, London : c. 1680. ("Bennett" Book.)

4907B. WALKER, EDWARD, London : c. 1682. ("Bennett" Book.) Touch, 380 L.T.P., which he had leave to strike on 29 Mar. 1683.

4908. WALKER, JAMES, London : 20 June 1745, Y.

4909. WALKER, JAMES, Edinburgh : 1643, F.

4910. WALKER, JAMES, Edinburgh : 1681, F. Had been apprenticed to Samuel Walker.

4911. WALKER, JOHN, London : 1615, L.; 1617, S.

4912. WALKER, JOHN, London : 8 Oct. 1713, Y. Touch, 695 L.T.P., which he obtained leave to strike on 24 Mar. 1714.

4913. WALKER, JOHN, London : 23 Mar. 1748, Y. Touch, 957 L.T.P., struck c. 1752.

4914. WALKER, JOHN, York : 1567, F.

4915. WALKER, JOHN, Woolverston, Lancs. : Apprenticed to George Benson, Bristol, for eight years from 28 July 1619.

4916. WALKER, NICHOLAS, London : Was of the Livery in 1457. 1465, R.W.; 1473, U.W.

4917. WALKER, PATRICK, Edinburgh : 1607, F. Touch, 24 E.T.P.

4918. WALKER, PATRICK, Edinburgh : 1631, F.

4919. WALKER, RALPH, London : 1607, f.S. Resigned the Livery through poverty in 1614/5.

4920. WALKER, RICHARD, York : 1591/2, F. Searcher in 1616.

4921. WALKER, ROBERT, Edinburgh : Was dead in 1688. ? Touch, 78 E.T.P.

4922. WALKER, SAMUEL, Edinburgh : 1660, F. Touch, 64 E.T.P.

4923. WALKER, THOMAS, York : 1636/7, F., by patrimony.

4924. WALKER, WILLIAM, London : 11 Oct. 1739, Y.

4925. WALKER, WILLIAM, London : A master in 1600.

4926. WALKER, WILLIAM, London : 13 Dec. 1787, Y.; 24 Sept. 1818, L.; 1828, f.S.; 22 Sept. 1849, died. Of 15 Brown's Lane, Spitalfields. His name has been struck out in the Records. Touch, 1079. In 1817 he was at 15 Brown's Lane, Spitalfields.

4927. WALKER, WILLIAM, Bristol: 14 April 1694, F. S. of William. Apprenticed to John Stevens and Elizabeth his wife, 7 April 1687.

4928. WALKER, WILLIAM GEORGE, London: 10 Dec. 1829, Y. and L. Died 23 Nov. 1839.

4928A. WALKER, WILLIAM & Co., London: In 1793 were at Brooks' Wharf.

4929. WALL, CHRISTOPHER, London: 23 Mar. 1704, Y.

4930. WALLACE, JOSEPH, Edinburgh: In 1639 was an apprentice to James Monteith.

4931. WALLACE, PATRICK, Perth: In 1796 was an apprentice to Robert Menzies.

4932. WALLDEN, THOMAS, London: 22 June 1797, Y.

4933. WALLENGER, RICHARD (? WARGNYER, *q.v.*), London: Was of the Livery in 1560.

4934. WALLER, ROBERT, London: 21 Oct. 1779, Y. Touch, 1046 L.T.P., struck c. 1782. Of 234 Borough in 1786.

4934A. WALLEY, ALLEN, London: c. 1680. ("Bennett" Book.)

4935. WALLIS, ARTHUR, Bristol: 31 Mar. 1685, F. Apprenticed to Erasmus Dole. The Poll Book for 1721 gives him as of Castle Precincts, Bristol.

4937. WALLIS, ROBERT, London: 14 Dec. 1738, Y.

4937A. WALMSLEY, EDWARD, London: Touch, 445 L.T.P., which he had leave to strike on 4 Oct. 1688.

4938. WALMSLEY, JOHN, Gainsborough: 17 Dec. 1702. Touch, 679 L.T.P., struck c. 1712/3. On 13 Aug. 1712/3 John Walmsley, Gainsborough, asked permission to strike for his Touch "The Lion rampant with a crown over his head." On 29 Oct. it was ordered "that he may strike the h(e)art and Crown, but *not* the word LONDON." This is an authoritative instance of a Touch being granted to a country member, and is the more interesting in that we have his Touch before us.

4939. WALMSLEY, SIMON, London: 21 June 1716, Y.

4940. WALSH, PIERS, Dublin: Mentioned in 1685.

4941. WALSH, WALTER, London: 1483, R.W.; 1486 and 1487. U.W.

WALTAM, *see* WALTHAM.

4942. WALTER, JOHN, London: A master in 1603.

4943. WALTER, ROBERT, Edinburgh: In 1666 was an apprentice to John Law.

4944. WALTER, THOMAS, Huntingdon: Mentioned in 1621.

4945. WALTHAM, THOMAS, London: 1669, f.R.W., f.U.W. and f.M.

4945A. WALTON, RICHARD, London: c. 1680. ("Bennett" Book.) Touch, 246 L.T.P., which he had leave to strike in 1674/5.

4946. WALY, WALTER, London: In 1457 was an apprentice to John Turnour.

4947. WANDSWORTH, THOMAS, London: Mentioned in 1573. 1575, S.; 1585, R.W. Dismissed from the Livery in 1577.

4948. WAPLE, THOMAS, London: 20 Mar. 1698, Y.

4949. WARBYLTON, PIERS, London: Was of the Livery in 1457.

4950. WARD(E), JAMES, London: 22 June 1693, Y.

4951. WARD(E), JAMES, London: 20 Mar. 1711, Y.

4952. WARD(E), JOHN, London: Was a master in 1457.

4953. WARD(E), JOHN, York: 1420/1, F.

4954. WARD(E), JOHN, Lynn: 1570/1, F.

4955. WARD(E), RICHARD, London: Married W. Hartwell's widow and used his Touch, c. 1567.

4956. WARD(E), ROGER, York: 1479/80, F.

4957. WARD(E), MRS. WATKIN, London: Free in 1457.

4958. WARDMAN, BALDWIN, London: 23 June 1743, Y.

4959. WARDROP, J. & H., Glasgow: c. 1800-1840.

J. & H. WARDROP

J. & H. WARDROP

4960. WARDROP, JAMES, Glasgow: c. 1776. Partner in J. & H. Wardrop, and in Graham & Wardrop (*q.v.*).

4961. WAREING, JOHN, London: 20 Mar. 1698, Y.

4962. WAREING, SAMUEL, London: 12 Aug. 1714, Y.

4962A. WARFORD, ANTHONY, London: Touch, 544 L.T.P., which he had leave to strike on 26 Mar. 1698.

4963. WARGNYER, RICHARD, London: 1561, S.

4964. WARHAM, ELIZABETH, London: 1799, Y. Died 1840.

4965. WARHAM, PETER, London : 21 June 1759, Y.
4965A. WARI—R, CHARLES, of ? —— : c. 1690.

4966. WARKMAN, RICHARD, London : 17 Mar. 1697, Y.; 1 Sept. 1710, L.; 1716, S.; 1727, R.W. Touch, 546 L.T.P., which he had leave to strike on 4 April 1698.

4967. WARKMAN, WILLIAM, London : 17 Dec. 1713, Y. Touch, 719 L.T.P., which he had leave to strike in 1720.

4967A. WARNE, JAMES & THOMAS, London : Of Blackfriars Road. Their partnership was notified on 4 Feb. 1829 in *London Gazette*.

4968. WARNE, JOHN, London : Founded in 1796. Of Blackfriars Road. Now incorporated in Gaskell & Chambers.

4969. WARNER, JOHN, London : In 1457 was an apprentice to Thomas Dounton.

4969A. WARREN, JOHN, London : Touch, 566 L.T.P., which he had leave to strike on 14 Dec. 1699.

4970. WARREN, LAWRENCE, London : Touch, 207 L.T.P., which he had leave to strike in 1671/2. Of St. George's, Southwark. Married on 23 Aug. 1680 to Dorothy Bullevant. He is mentioned in the "Bennett" Book, 1679-84.

4971. WARREN, ROBERT, Lynn : 1610/1, F.
WARRENER, *see* WARGNYER.
WARWICK, *see* WIGLEY.

4972. WARYING, JOHN, London : Mentioned in 1555 as using for his Mark—a Maltese Cross with a dot in each angle, possibly as drawn here.

4973. WARYSON, SIR PETER, London : 1555, Y.

4974. WASS, ROBERT, London : 14 Aug. 1712, Y. Touch, 748 L.T.P., which he had leave to strike on 26 Sept. 1723.

4975. WASTELL, CLEMENT, London : In 1655 was refused the use of a second Touch.
WATERER, *see* WATTERER.

4976. WATERMAN, HENRY, London : 22 June 1693, Y.

4977. WATERS, JOHN, Bristol and Pontipool, Mon. : 3 Dec. 1755, F. S. of John. Apprenticed to John Griffith, Bristol, 31 Oct. 1748. Mentioned in the Poll Book for 1774 as of St. Mary-le-Port, Bristol.

4977A. WATERS, WILLIAM, London : 1684, L. ("Bennett" Book.) Touch, 289 L.T.P., which he had leave to strike in 1676/7.

4978. WATERSON, THOMAS, London : Mentioned in 1576.

4979. WATKINS, JOHN, Caerleon, Mon. : S. of Charles. Apprenticed to Richard Brown, Bristol, and Marie his wife, 1 Feb. 1704.

4980. WATKINS, WILLIAM, Bristol and Trellech, Mon. : 12 Aug. 1668, F. S. of David. Apprenticed to William Pascall, Bristol.

4981. WATKINS, WILLIAM, Bristol and Brecon : 1728, F. S. of William. Apprenticed to Honor, widow of John Bacheler, 24 May 1721. Mentioned in the Poll Books for 1734 and 1739 as of St. Nicholas, Bristol.

4982. WATMOUTH, WILLIAM, London : 22 June 1704, Y.

4983. WATSON, DAVID, Belfast : Mentioned in 1760 and 1779. Retired 1793.

4984. WATSON, EDWARD, Newcastle : 18 June 1656/7, Y.

4985. WATSON, GEORGE, London : 17 Mar. 1697, Y.

4986. WATSON, JOHN, Edinburgh : 1671, F. Touch, 71 E.T.P.

4986A. WATSON, JOHN, JUNR., York : The dissolution of his partnership with William Lyth is announced in the *London Gazette* for 5 Sept. 1801.

4987. WATSON, JOSEPH, London : 8 Oct. 1713, Y. Touch, 732 L.T.P., which he had leave to strike on 22 Aug. 1720.

4988. WATT, WILLIAM, London : 30 June 1783, Y.

4989. WATTERER, THOMAS, London : 17 June 1686, L.; 1693, S.; 1701, R.W.; 1709, U.W. Touch, 370 L.T.P., which he had leave to strike on 21 Mar. 1681.

4990. WATTS, JAMES, London : 19 Oct. 1749, Y.

4991. WATTS, JOHN, London : 19 Oct. 1725, Y.; 24 Mar. 1736, L.; 1748, S.; 1750, f.R.W.; 1758, U.W.; 1760, M. Of Tokenhouse Yard. Touch, 801 L.T.P., which he had leave to strike on 29 Oct. 1725.

4992. WATTS, JOHN, London : 14 Dec. 1749, Y.; 13 June 1751, L.; 1761, f.S.; 1766, f.R.W.; 1779, U.W.; 1780, M. His business in 1792 was at 19 Aldgate High Street. *See* his Trade-Card.

4993. WATTS, THOMAS, London : 20 Dec. 1744, Y.

4994. WATTS, WILLIAM, London : In 1475 was searcher for the Company for false wares.

4995. WATTS, ——, London : Partner in Watts & Harton, whose business after the dissolution of partnership he continued alone at Shoe Lane, and afterwards with his brother-in-law at Euston Road.

4996. WATTS & HARTON, London : c. 1810-1860.

4997. WAUGH, THOMAS, of ? : c. 1695.

4997A. WAUGH, THOMAS, Durham : 1750.

4998. WAYLETT, WILLIAM, London : 12 Mar. 1701, Y. Touch, 609 L.T.P., which he had leave to strike on 11 Mar. 1702.

4999. WEAVER, SAMUEL, London : 17 Dec. 1691, Y.

5000. WEAVER, WILLIAM, London : 15 Oct. 1801, Y. and L.; 1803, f.S. His name has been struck out.

5001. WEB, WILLIAM, Walsall : c. 1600.

5002. WEBB, ARTHUR, Felton, Glocs. : S. of Daniel. Apprenticed to John Cam, Bristol, and Mary his wife, 17 Mar. 1738. Premium £10.

5003. WEBB, CHRISTOPHER, London : 1669, f.R.W., f.U.W. and f.M.

5003A. WEBB, GEORGE, Dublin : 1641, F.

5004. WEBB, ISAAC, London : 11 Oct. 1705, Y.

5005. WEBB, JOSEPH, London : 18 June 1691, Y.; 7 June 1695, L.; 1701, S.; 1715, R.W.; 1723, f.U.W.; 1726, M.

5006. WEBB, PETER, Bristol : S. of Thomas. Apprenticed to Thomas Gwinnell and Marie his wife for eight years from 8 Nov. 1637.

5007. WEBB, RICHARD, London : 14 July 1692, L.; 1699, S. Touch, 458 L.T.P., which he had leave to strike in 1686/7.

5008. WEBB, ROBERT, London : Mentioned in 1551.
5009. WEBB, ROBERT, Blaisdon, Glocs.: S. of John. Apprenticed to James Cadell, Bristol, and Bridget his wife for seven years from 18 Nov. 1605.
5010. WEBB, THOMAS, London : 12 Aug. 1714, Y. Touch, 701 L.T.P., which he was given leave to strike on 6 Mar. 1716.

5011. WEBB, WILLIAM, Walsall : c. 1600-1647.
5012. WEBB, WILLIAM, London : Fined in 1574. Mentioned in 1600 as coming to blows with a fellow-member.
5013. WEBB, WILLIAM, London : 17 Oct. 1751, Y.
5014. WEBB, WILLIAM, Walsall : c. 1600-1640.
5015. WEBBER, ALEXANDER, Barnstaple : S. of John W., Junr. Born 1685, died 1739. In partnership with his father until 1735, and afterward carried on the business alone.

 BARNESTAPLE

5016. WEBBER, JOHN, Barnstaple : Born c. 1629, buried 1700. *See* list of Tokens at end of Chap. IV.

BARNESTAPLE

5017. WEBBER, JOHN, JUNR., Barnstaple : c. 1680-1735. Buried 7 Aug. 1735. Baptised 21 Feb. 1653.

5018. WEBBER, RICHARD, Barnstaple : Issued a token in 1667. *See* List at end of Chap. IV.
5019. WEBBER, WILLIAM, Charkhampton, Somerset : S. of Joseph. Apprenticed to Robert Bush, Bristol, and Ann his wife, 6 Nov. 1782.

5020. WEBSTER, R———, of ? : c. 1800. This name has been found on a slipper-shaped snuff box.

5021. WEDDERELL, JOHN, York : 1549/50, F.
5022. WEDDERELL, ROBERT, York : 1541/2, F. 1555, City Chamberlain.
WEETWOOD, *see* WETWOOD.
5023. WEIR, ALEXANDER, Edinburgh : A master in 1677.
5024. WEIR, ALEXANDER, Edinburgh : 1693, F. Died 1714.
5025. WEIR, ANDREW, Edinburgh : A master in 1585.
5026. WEIR, CORNELIUS, Edinburgh : 1595, F.
5027. WEIR, HERBERT, Edinburgh : 1595, F.
5028. WEIR, JAMES, Edinburgh : A master in 1571.
5029. WEIR, JOHN, Edinburgh : Mentioned in 1560.
5030. WEIR, JOHN, Edinburgh : A master in 1584. Touches, 3 and 4 E.T.P.

5031. WEIR, JOHN, Edinburgh : 1594, F.
5032. WEIR, JOHN, Edinburgh : 1701, F. Touch, 101 E.T.P.

5033. WEIR, JOHN, Edinburgh : In 1596 was an apprentice to John Weir.
5034. WEIR, LAWRENCE, Edinburgh : A master in 1572.
5035. WEIR, RICHARD, Edinburgh : 1597, F. Touches, 14 and 15 E.T.P.

5036. WEIR, ROBERT, Edinburgh : 1596, F.
5037. WEIR, ROBERT, Edinburgh : 1646, F. Died 1668. Touch, 46 E.T.P.

5038. WEIR, SAMUEL, Edinburgh : A master in 1590.
5039. WEIR, THOMAS, Edinburgh : 1596, F. Touch, 13 E.T.P.

5040. WEIR, THOMAS, Edinburgh : 1597, F.
5041. WEIR, THOMAS, Edinburgh : 1631, F.
5042. WEIR WILLIAM, Edinburgh : In 1614 was an apprentice to Thomas Weir.

WELBEY, *see* WILBEY.

5043. WELFORD, JAMES, London: 21 Mar. 1727, Y. and L.; 1736, S.; 1740, R.W.; 1752, U.W.; 1754, M. Dead in 1773.

5044. WELLES, PIERS, London: Died c. 1452.

5045. WELLFORD, JOHN, London: 19 June 1760, Y.; 10 Mar. 1760, L. (*sic.* obviously one is an error in the Records); 1768, f.S.; 1777, f.R.W.; 1787, U.W.; 1788, M.

5046. WELLS, EDMUND, London: 19 Mar. 1772, Y.

5047. WELLS, JAMES, London: 20 Mar. 1777, Y.

5048. WELLS, RICHARD, York: 1603/4, F.; 1631/2, M.

5049. WELLS, SAMUEL, Gloucester: S. of Edward. Apprenticed to Henry Taylor, Bristol, 24 July 1700. Turned over, 4 Mar. 1701, to John Peters.

5050. WELLWOOD, R., Dunfermline: On a quaich in the National Museum of Antiquities, Edinburgh. Probably it is the name of an owner and not a maker.

5050A. WELTON, SAMUEL, Coventry: Bankruptcy recorded in the *London Gazette* on 4 Nov. 1755.

5051. WENCELOW, JOHN (*see* also WYNSLEY), London: Mentioned in 1532.

5051A. WENTWORTH, MOSES, London: c. 1680. ("Bennett" Book.)

5051B. WEOLY, ROBERT, London: Dead in 1681. ("Bennett" Book.)

5051C. WERKINSON, JOHN, London: c. 1682. ("Bennett" Book.)

5052. WES(T)COTT, HENRY, London: 1640, S.; 1653, f.R.W.

5053. WES(T)COTT, JOHN, London: Touch, 171 L.T.P., which he had leave to strike in 1669/70. No mention of him is in the existing Y. or L. Lists, but he appears in the "Bennett" Book, 1679-86.

5054. WES(T)COTT, THOMAS, London: 19 Mar. 1761.

5055. WES(T)COTT, WILLIAM, London: 1652, S.; 1668, f.R.W., f.U.W. and f.M.

5056. WES(T)COTT, WILSON, London: 12 Mar. 1752, Y.

5057. WEST, JAMES, York: 1659/60, F. 1688/9, mentioned. Father of John.

5058. WEST, JOHN, York: 1688/9, F., by patrimony. S. of James.

5059. WEST, JOHN, London: 9 Oct. 1729, Y.

5060. WEST, MOSES, London: Touch, 285 L.T.P., which he had leave to strike in 1676/7. His name is not in the existing Y. or L. Lists, but appears in the "Bennett" Book, 1679-86, as a country pewterer.

5061. WEST, ROBERT, London: Mentioned in 1551. A notorious offender against the Company's regulations. In 1556 he was sent to prison for making false wares, was dismissed the Company in that year, but later was ordered to use a Touch of " ff," but he would not.

5062. WESTBERE, JOHN, Stapleton, Glocs.: S. of Thomas. Apprenticed to Roger Willoughby, Bristol, and Sarah his wife, 9 May 1653.

5063. WESTELL, WILLIAM, Llandeggar, Mon.: S. of Daniel. Apprenticed to Robert Bush, Bristol, and Ann his wife, 5 Feb. 1784.

5064. WESTERBY, JOHN, London: In 1457 was journeyman to John Pepond.

5065. WESTLAND, GEORGE, Aberdeen: In 1741 was an apprentice to William Johnston.

5066. WESTON, THOMAS DE, York: 1349, F.

5067. WESTON, THOMAS, Dublin: Son of Bethe. Apprenticed to John Dole, Bristol, 7 Nov. 1719.

5068. WESTWODE, NICHOLAS, London: Dead in 1450.

5069. WESTWOOD, JOSEPH, London: 20 Dec. 1706, Y. and L.

5070. WE(E)TWOOD, HUMPHREY, London: Mentioned from 1580-1610. He was imprisoned for making false wares and ordered to bring in his Touch, and in its place to strike a double ff.

5071. WE(E)TWOOD, KATHARINE, London: Daughter of Humphrey. 1633, Y., by patrimony.

5072. WESTWYK, ROBERT, York: 1435/6, F.

5073. WETTE(? R), WILLIAM, London: Touch, 78 L.T.P., restruck c. 1668. (*Cf.* No. 6091.)

5074. WHARRAM, RALPH, London: 16 Dec. 1756, Y. Touch, 996 L.T.P., which he obtained leave to strike on 14 Oct. 1762.

5075. WHARTON, ARTHUR, York: Free in 1684.
5076. WHARTON, ARTHUR, York: On 13 Jan. 1726 was apprenticed for seven years to Leonard Terry. 1739/40, F. Searcher, 1752 and 1758. S. of John.

5077. WHEELER, GEORGE, London: 15 June 1732, Y.
5078. WHEELER, JAMES, Bewdley: c. 1820-1850. A spoonmaker of Dog Lane.
5079. WHEELER, THOMAS, London: 11 Aug. 1692, Y. Touch, 692 L.T.P., which he was given leave to strike on 20 July 1713. (Cf. Touches of W. Barnes and Robert Patience.)

5080. WHEELER, WILLIAM, London: 7 Aug. 1701, Y.
5081. WHEELER, WILLIAM, London: 20 June 1728, Y.
5082. WHEELERITE, FRANCIS, Dublin: Mentioned in 1683 and 1686.
5083. WHEELY, ROBERT, London: A spoonmaker in 1666.
5084. WHELEMAN, WILLIAM, London: Died in 1495.
5085. WHIBBY, WILLIAM, Brislington, Somerset: Nov. 1616, F. S. of Thomas. Apprenticed to Richard Burrns, Bristol, for nine years from 7 Feb. 1605. Turned over to Thomas Hobson, Bristol.
5086. WHITAKER, BENJAMIN, London: 17 Dec. 1691, Y.; 4 June 1695, L.; 1712, S. Touch, 485 L.T.P., which he had leave to strike on 17 Mar. 1691. Spelt Whiteacre in the Yeomanry List.

5086A. WHITAKER, JOHN, of ?: c. 1690.

WHITBE, see WHYTBE.

5086B. WHITE, ALEXSANDER (sic.), Derry: His daughter was baptised at Derry Cathedral 16 May 1673.
5087. WHITE, BENJAMIN, York: On 3 Feb. 1726 was apprenticed for seven years to John White. 1739/40, F. Son of Benjamin.
5088. WHITE, EDWARD, Bristol: S. of John. Apprenticed to Thomas Muncke, Bristol, and Julian his wife, 2 June 1646.
5088A. WHITE, DANIELL, London: c. 1684. ("Bennett" Book.) Touch, 403 L.T.P., which he had leave to strike in 1684.

5089. WHITE, FAITHFUL, Bristol and Llanvyhanpill, Mon.: 27 Feb. 1682, F. S. of George. Apprenticed to William James, Bristol, and Ann his wife, 25 May 1671.
5090. WHITE, JOHN, York: Free in 1684.
5091. WHITE, JOHN, York: On 15 July 1691 was apprenticed for seven years to James Loftus. 1697/8, F. Searcher in 1703, 1704, 1707, 1710, 1715, 1720, 1725, 1732 and 1738.
5091A. WHITE, JOHN, London: c. 1680. ("Bennett" Book.)
5092. WHITE, JOHN, London: 19 June 1755, Y. Touch, 971 L.T.P., which he obtained leave to strike in 1755.

5093. WHITE, JOHN, Dublin: 1468, F.
5094. WHITE, JOSEPH, London: 1658, S.
5095. WHITE, JOSEPH, London: 17 Dec. 1747, Y. Touch, 927 L.T.P., which he obtained leave to strike on 17 Dec. 1747.

5096. WHITE, PHILIP, London: 20 Aug. 1778, Y. Touch, 1056 L.T.P., struck c. 1789.

5097. WHITE, RICHARD, London: 20 Oct. 1695, L.; 1702, S.; 1717, R.W.; 1725, U.W.; 1729,

M. 1744, Beadle. Died 1750. Acted as Clerk in 1717 during the illness of Robert Tarlton. Of St. Gabriel's, Fenchurch St. He married Susanna Stone on 24 April 1693 at St. Margaret's. Touch, 448 L.T.P., which he had leave to strike on 21 Mar. 1688.

5098. WHITE, RICHARD, Dublin : 1480, F., and is mentioned in 1477 and 1487.

5099. WHITE, SAMUEL, London : 18 June 1696, Y. Partner in White & Bernard. *See* No. 5109.

5100. WHITE, SAMUEL, London : 11 Dec. 1729, Y.

5101. WHITE, WILLIAM, Rotherham : 1608, Y., by patrimony. A country member.

5102. WHITE, WILLIAM, York : 1472/3, F.

5103. WHITE, WILLIAM, London : 28 Nov. 1667, L. ; 1669, f.S. ; 1683, f.R.W.

5104. WHITE, WILLIAM, London : 18 June 1702, Y.

5105. WHITE, WILLIAM, London : 16 Dec. 1714, Y.

5106. WHITE, WILLIAM, London : 23 June 1743, L.

5107. WHITE, WILLIAM, London : 22 Aug. 1751, Y. ; 22 Aug. 1765, L. ; 1772, S. Dead in 1783. Of Golden Lane, Barbican. Touch, 954 L.T.P., which he obtained leave to strike in 1751

5108. WHITE, ——, London : 1640, S. No Christian name is given in the Records.

5109. WHITE & BERNARD, London: Touch, 743 L.T.P., which leave was given to strike on 17 Feb. 1721/2. Partners, Samuel White and Onesipherous Bernard, 1722, Y.

5110. WHITEAR, WILLIAM, London : 22 June 1749, Y.
WHITEBED, *see* WITHEBED.

5111. WHITEBREAD, JAMES, London : 18 Mar. 1735, Y.

5112. WHITEHEDE, BERNARD, York : An apprentice in 1489/90.

5113. WHITEHEDE, JOHN, London : 1463 and 1470, R.W. ; 1475, U.W.

5114. WHITEHEDE, JOSEPH, London : 15 Mar. 1721, Y.

5115. WHITEHEDE, WILLIAM, York : 1444/5, F.

5116. WHITEHILL, ANTHONY, York : Was free in 1697/8. Mentioned in 1720/1.

5117. WHITEMAN, BENJAMIN (*see* also WIGHTMAN), London : 16 June 1692, Y.

5117A. WHITEMAN, WILLIAM, London : Subscribed towards a set of feast vessels in 1476.

5118. WHITFELD, CHRIS, of ? : c. 1740.

5118A. WHITFIELD & SCOFIELD, Birmingham : In 1793 were spoonmakers (? Pewter) in Digbeth.

5119. WHITING, THOMAS, London : 19 June 1701, Y.

5120. WHITTINGTON, ROBERT, London : 24 Mar. 1757, Y.

5121. WHITTLE, FRANCIS, London : 13 Oct. 1715, Y. ; 15 Dec. 1726, L. ; 1731, S. ; 1738, f.R.W. Touch, 715 L.T.P., which he had leave to strike on 24 Mar. 1719. In 1722 some plates of his were confiscated, he having stamped them "Superfine Hard Metal."

5122. WHITTLE, WILLIAM, London : 19 June 1760, Y.

5123. WHITTORNE, JOHN, London: 19 June 1701, Y.

5124. WHYTBE, THOMAS, London : 1551, S.

5125. WHYT(E), DAVID, Edinburgh : In 1721 was an apprentice to John Cuthbertsone.

5126. WHYT(E), GEORGE, Edinburgh : 1676, F. Touch, 79 E.T.P.

5127. WHYT(E), GEORGE, Edinburgh : In 1688 was apprentice to George Whyt(e).

5128. WHYT(E), JAMES, Edinburgh : In 1694 was an apprentice to Samuel Walker.

5129. WHYT(E), JOHN, Dublin: 1619, F. Buried at Derry Cathedral, 13 Feb. 1659.

5130. WHYT(E), ROBERT, Edinburgh: 1805, F. No. 40 Cowgate Head. *See* his Token.

5131. WHYTSONE, ALEXANDER, Edinburgh: In 1646 was an apprentice to Robert Weir.

5132. WHYTYNG, JOHN, London: In 1457 was covenant man to Piers Pynton.

5133. WIDDOWES, JOHN, London: Touch, 191 L.T.P., which he had leave to strike in 1670/1. His name is not in the existing Y. and L. Lists, but is in the "Bennett" Book, 1679-86.

5134. WIDLAKE, JAMES, Bristol and Charhompton, Somerset: 6 Sept. 1780, F. S. of George. Apprenticed to Robert Bush and his wife Ann, 2 May 1772. In the Poll Book for 1784 is given as of St. Thomas's, Bristol.

5135. WIGGIN, ABRAHAM, London: 11 Dec. 1707, Y. Touch, 651 L.T.P., struck c. 1708.

5136. WIGGIN, HENRY, London: 1 May 1690, L. Touch, 373 L.T.P., which he had leave to strike on 1 Mar. 1682.

5137. WIGGIN, JOHN, London: 22 June 1738, Y.

5138. WIGGINTON, THOMAS, London: 18 June 1730, Y.

5139. WIGHTMAN, WILLIAM (*see* also WHITEMAN), London: 22 June 1758, Y. Touch, 993 L.T.P., which he obtained leave to strike on

19 Mar. 1761. His name is spelt Whiteman in the Records.

5140. WIGLEY, JOHN, London: 7 Jan. 1713, Y.

5141. WIGLEY, THOMAS, London: 21 Mar. 1699, Y. Touch, 630 L.T.P., which he had leave to strike on 6 Mar. 1705.

5142. WIKE, MATHEW (*see* also WYKES), Bristol: 14 Aug. 1638, F. S. of Francis. Apprenticed to Thomas Gwinnell and Marie his wife, 20 July 1630.

5143. WIKELIN, WILLIAM, London: 19 Oct. 1758, Y.

5144. WIKES, MATTHEW, Cork: Died in 1642.

5145. WILBEY, WILLIAM (*see* also WYLBY), London: 1467, R.W.; 1471, 1474 and 1484, U.W.; 1487, 1494 and 1498, M.

5146. WILCOCKE, JOHN, Thornbury, Glocs.: S. of Richard. Apprenticed to John Burrowes, Bristol, and Rachel his wife, 13 Dec. 1602.

5147. WILDASH, GEORGE, London: 24 Aug. 1820, Y.

5148. WILDIN, JOHN, London: 23 Aug. 1832, Y.

5149. WILDMAN, RICHARD, London: 20 Mar. 1728, Y. Touch, 831 L.T.P., which he had leave to strike on 10 Dec. 1730.

5150. WILKES, RICHARD, London: 14 Oct. 1708, Y. Touch, 655 L.T.P., struck c. 1708.

5151. WILKES, ROBERT, Doynton, Glocs.: S. of Robert. Apprenticed to John Jones, Bristol, 17 Mar. 1675.

5152. WILKIE, WILLIAM, Edinburgh: 1784, F.

5153. WILKINSON, GEORGE, London: 16 Dec. 1742, Y.

5154. WILKINSON, JOHN, Dublin: Mentioned in 1764. Died in 1775.
5155. WILKINSON, MICHAEL, York: On 20 May 1666 was apprenticed for seven years to John Harrison. 1667/8, F.
5156. WILKINSON, OLIVER, Dublin: Died in 1762.
5157. WILKINSON, RICHARD, London: Free in 1579.
5158. WILKINSON, ROBERT, London: Was free in 1561.
5159. WILKINSON, ROBERT, York: 1464/5, F.
WILKS, see WILKES.
5160. WILLE, NICHOLAS, London: 1534, U.W.
5161. WILLETT, EDWARD, London: Touches, 409 and 412 L.T.P., which he had leave to strike in 1684/5. His name is not in the existing Y. or L. Lists.

5162. WILLETT, RICHARD, London: 1666, f.U.W.
5163. WILLEY, MARY, London: Touch, 988 L.T.P., which she obtained leave to strike on 25 Sept. 1760, but one does not find her name in the membership lists.

5164. WILLIAMS, ——, Falmouth: c. 1720.

5165. WILLIAMS, A——, Bideford: c. 1730.

5166. WILLIAMS, ANDREW, Bristol: Mentioned in 1672.
5167. WILLIAMS, ANTHONY, London: Free in 1610.
5168. WILLIAMS, ANTHONY, London: Born 23 Aug. 1618.
5169. WILLIAMS, DANIEL ANTHONY, London: In 1616 was journeyman to Mr. Child. An early instance of a double Christian name.
5170. WILLIAMS, EDWARD, London: 17 Mar. 1697, Y.
5171. WILLIAMS, GEORGE, London: 16 Dec. 1731, Y.

5172. WILLIAMS, JAMES, Bristol: 6 June 1774, F. Apprenticed to Thomas Lanyon. In the Poll Books for 1774, 1781 and 1784 is given as of St. Mary-le-Port, and in that for 1812 as of 38 Redcliff Street, all of Bristol.
5173. WILLIAMS, JAMES, Bristol: 7 Oct. 1812, F. Apprenticed to Thomas Willshire.
5174. WILLIAMS, JOHN, London: 14 Oct. 1697, Y.
5174A. WILLIAMS, JOHN, London: c. 1680. (" Bennett " Book.) Touch, 299 L.T.P., which he had leave to strike in 1677/8. Was a patentee of hollow pewter buttons with Richard Maundrill.

5175. WILLIAMS, JOHN, London: 13 Aug. 1719, Y.
5176. WILLIAMS, JOHN, London: 16 June 1724, Y. Touch, 819 L.T.P., which he had leave to strike on 6 Aug. 1730. Son of John.

5177. WILLIAMS, JOHN, London: 19 Mar. 1724, Y. Son of Thomas.
5178. WILLIAMS, JOHN, London: 19 Mar. 1729, Y. Touch, 903 L.T.P., which he had leave to strike on 9 Oct. 1741.

5179. WILLIAMS, OWEN, Bristol and Swansea: 2 Sep. 1647, F. S. of John. Apprenticed 4 April 1640 to John Knowles, Bristol, and Margaret his wife.
5180. WILLIAMS, ROBERT, London: 20 June 1689, Y. Of St. John Baptist, City. Married on 11 April 1693 at St. Mary Magdalene, Elizabeth, daughter of John Blunt, pewterer. Touch, 482 L.T.P., which he had leave to strike on 16 June 1692.

5181. WILLIAMS, ROGER, Cork: Mentioned in 1755.
5182. WILLIAMS, ROGER, Bristol: S. of Roger. Apprenticed to Daniel Lovell and Anne his wife, 2 June 1692.

5183. WILLIAMS, THOMAS, London : 20 Mar. 1698, Y.
5183A. WILLIAMS, THOMAS, London : Pensioned in 1685. (" Bennett " Book.)
5184. WILLIAMS, THOMAS, London : 15 Oct. 1741, Y.
5185. WILLIAMS, THOMAS, Bristol : Mentioned with Christian his wife in 1635.
5186. WILLIAMS, THOMAS, Bristol : Mentioned with his wife Mary in 1736.
5187. WILLIAMS, WILLIAM, Hillgurrieck, Mon. : S. of John. Apprenticed to Roger Perkins, Bristol, and Marie his wife, 19 Sept. 1684.
5188. WILLIAMSON, CHARLES, Birr : Died in 1715.
5189. WILLIAMSON, JAMES, Dublin : Died in 1694.
5190. WILLIAMSON, JAMES, York : On 1 April 1647 was apprenticed for seven years to George Clarke. 1657/8, F. Searcher in 1666, 1668 and 1675. Mentioned in 1677. Son of Thomas. Father of Richard.
5191. WILLIAMSON, JAMES, York : 1682/3, F.
5192. WILLIAMSON, JAMES, Dundee : 1715, F. Copper and white-ironsmith.
5193. WILLIAMSON, PATRICK, Dundee : 1715, F. Copper and white-ironsmith.
5194. WILLIAMSON, RICHARD, York : On 7 May 1677 was apprenticed for seven years to his father, James. 1684, F. Searcher in 1690, 1691 and 1698. Mentioned in 1700.
5195. WILLIAMSON, RICHARD, London : 1553, S. Fined in 1552.
5196. WILLIS, NICHOLAS, Barton Regis, Glocs. : S. of Nicholas. Apprenticed to Arthur Wallis, Bristol, and Sarah his wife, 12 Jan. 1703.
5197. WILLISON, THOMAS WELLS, London : 18 June 1795, Y.
5197A. WILLOT, EDWARD, London : c. 1684. (" Bennett " Book.)
5198. WILLOUGHBY, CHRIS, Bristol : 19 July 1669, F. Apprenticed to Roger Willoughby.
5199. WILLOUGHBY, ROGER, Bristol and Warminster : 15 Oct. 1646, F. S. of Thomas. Apprenticed to Bernard Benson and Marie his wife for eight years from 18 May 1634. Mentioned in an old Deed dated 1678 relating to premises in Brislington.
5200. WILLOUGHBY, ROGER, Bristol : 21 Jan. 1680, F. Son of Roger and Sarah, to whom he was apprenticed, 16 Feb. 1670. Died c. 1687.

5201. WILLS, WILLIAM, London : 21 Mar. 1733, Y.
5201A. WILLSHIRE & LINK, c. 1770.

5202. WILLSHIRE, THOMAS, Bristol : Was a brass founder in Thomas Street in 1793. Mentioned in 1785 with Ann his wife.

5203. WILLSHIRE, T. & W., Bristol : c. 1800.

5204. WILMORE, SAMUEL, London : 22 June 1758, Y.
5205. WILSHERE, THOMAS, London : Mentioned in 1553, 1559 and 1568.
5206. WILSON(E), ALEXANDER, Aberdeen : Mentioned in 1633.
5207. WILSON(E), ALEXANDER, Aberdeen : 1656, F.
5208. WILSON, C—— W——, of ? : c. 1730.

5209. WILSON, DANIEL, London : 19 Mar. 1690, Y. Touch, 481 L.T.P., struck c. 1692.

5210. WILSON, EDWARD, York : Free in 1684. Father of the next mentioned.
5211. WILSON(E), EDWARD, York : On 14 Feb. 1707/8 was apprenticed for seven years to Leonard Terry. 1715, F. City Chamberlain, 1721/2. Son of the last named.
5213. WILSON(E), GEORGE, Lurgan : Mentioned in 1773.
5214. WILSON(E), HENRY, London : 19 Oct. 1749, Y.
5215. WILSON(E), JAMES, Perth : 1605, F.
5216. WILSON(E), JAMES, Edinburgh : 1588, F.
5217. WILSON(S), JOHN, Edinburgh : In 1693 was an apprentice to William Harvie.
5218. WILSON(E), JOHN, London : 1496, R.W.; 1502, U.W.
5219. WILSON(E), JOHN, Edinburgh : 1732, F. Touch, 129 E.T.P.

5220. WILSON(s), JOHN, Glasgow : 1778, mentioned as a brassfounder.

5221. WILSON(E), JOSEPH, Lurgan : Mentioned in 1760-1773.

5222. WILSON(E), NATHANIEL, Bristol : 19 Feb. 1753, F. S. of Vincent. Apprenticed to James Powell and Mary his wife, 7 Nov. 1745. In the Poll Book for 1754 he is given as of St. Thomas's, Bristol.

5223. WILSON(E), PATRE, Aberdeen : Mentioned in 1581.

5223A. WILSON(E), RALPH, Chester : Will proved at Chester in 1697. This mark appears with those of James Banck(e)s of Wigan (No. 228), who probably succeeded him and continued to use this touch along with his own.

5224. WILSON(E), THOMAS, Perth : 1695, F.

5225. WILSON(E), THOMAS, Perth : 1641, F.

5226. WILSON(E), THOMAS, Glasgow : In 1791 was an apprentice to Robert Graham and James Wardrop.

5227. WILSON(E), THOMAS, London : 19 Mar. 1801, Y.

5228. WILSON(E), WILLIAM, London : 16 Mar. 1758, Y.

5229. WIN, JAMES, London : Pewterer of St. Giles', Cripplegate. Married at St. Helen's, Bishopgate in 1652, Mary Randall of All Hallows in the Wall.

5230. WINCHCOMBE, THOMAS, London : 18 June 1691, Y.; 9 Mar. 1697, L. Touch, 509 L.T.P., which he had leave to strike on 11 Oct. 1694.

WINGARD, see WINGOD.

5231. WINGOD, CASSIA, London : 21 Mar. 1771, Y.

5232. WINGOD, JOHN, London : 16 June 1748, Y.; 16 Dec. 1756, L.; 1766, S. Was gazetted a bankrupt on 7 Nov. 1767. Died in 1784. Of Jewin Street in 1776. Touch, 934 L.T.P., which he obtained leave to strike on 22 June 1749.

5233. WINGOD, JOSEPH, London : 14 Dec. 1721, Y.; 1739, L.; 1757, R.W.; 1766, U.W.; 1767, M. Of Tower Wharf in 1776. Touch, 774

L.T.P., which he had leave to strike on 10 Oct. 1723. Spelt Wingard in Y. List and Wingod in L. List.

5234. WINGOD, JOSEPH, London : 26 Sept. 1811, Y.

5234A. WINKWORTH, MOSES, London : Touch, 218 L.T.P., which he had leave to strike in 1672/3.

5234B. WINSHIP, THOMAS, Newcastle : Was gazetted a bankrupt on 11 Sept. 1781.

5235. WINTER, GEORGE, London : 12 Mar. 1701, Y. Touch, 608 L.T.P., which he had leave to strike on 11 Mar. 1702.

5236. WINTLE, CHARLES, London : 20 Oct. 1785, Y.

5237. WISE, JAMES, Glasgow : In 1791 was an apprentice to Graham & Wardrop.

5238. WISEMAN, ROBERT, JUNR., London : 15 Oct. 1747, Y.

5239. WITHEBED, RICHARD, London : 1678, f.S. Touch, 162 L.T.P., which he had leave to strike in 1669/70.

5240. WITHERS, BENJAMIN (see also WITTER), London : 11 Jan. 1719, Y.; 18 June 1730, L. Touch, 729 L.T.P., which he had leave to strike on 27 April 1720. His " Hall Marks " appear in conjunction with the Touch of Peter Redknap.

5241. WITHERS, SAMUEL, Bridgewater, Somerset : S. of Thomas. Apprenticed to George Benson, Bristol, for nine years from 18 July 1615.

5242. WITHERS, WILLIAM, London : 28 Nov. 1667, L.; 1669, f.S. Touch, 53 L.T.P., restruck c. 1670 after the great fire, dated (16)55.

5243. WITHERS, WILLIAM, London : 20 Feb. 1692, L. Touch, 438 L.T.P., which he had leave to strike in 1686/7.

5244. WITTE, LUDEWIG, London : 19 Oct. 1815, Y. & L.; 1821, f.S.

5245. WITTER, SAMUEL (? WITHER), London : 10 Aug. 1676, L.; 1682, S. Touch, 196 L.T.P., which he had leave to strike in 1670/1.

5246. WITTER, ELINOR, London : 15 Sept. 1712, Y. Daughter of Samuel, made free by patrimony.

5247. WITTER, ELIZABETH, London : 18 Dec. 1712, Y.

5247A. WITTER, ELIZABETH, London ; Touch, 475 L.T.P., which she had leave to strike on 17 Dec. 1691.

5248. WITTER, MARY, London : 18 Dec. 1712, Y. Daughter of Samuel, made free by patrimony.

5249. WITTICH, JOHN CHRISTIAN, London : 15 June 1820, Y. and L.; 1830, f.S.; 1841, R.W.; 1843, U.W.; 1844, M. Died 31 Aug. 1854.

5250. WITTORN, THOMAS, Chanksbury, Glocs.: S. of Mathew. Apprenticed to Richard Lymell, Bristol, 12 May 1653.

5251. WOD, S——, Edinburgh : In 1618 was an apprentice to Cornelius Tayleour.

5252. WODE, WILLIAM, London : In 1457 was an apprentice to John Kendale.

5253. WODWOSE, ROBERT (? WOODHOUSE), London : Mentioned in 1494.

WOLSCHERE, see WILCHERE.

5254. WOO, THOMAS, London : In 1457 was an apprentice to John Couper.

5255. WOOD, EDWARD, Ludlow : Pewterer and brazier, 20 June 1704, F.

5256. WOOD, EDWARD, Ludlow : Mentioned as a master in 1752.

5257. WOOD, EDWARD, Ludlow : Apprenticed to his father, the last named. 2 June 1752, F.

5258. WOOD, HENRY, London : 17 Mar. 1768, Y. 14 Dec. 1786, L. Touch, 1019 L.T.P., which he obtained leave to strike in 1769.

5259. WOOD, JAMES, St. Andrews : Mentioned in 1619.

5260. WOOD, JOHN, Edinburgh : In 1680 was an apprentice to John Ramsay.

5261. WOOD, JOHN, DR., London : 1612, and 1618 M. The Company's Parish Priest.

5262. WOOD, JOSEPH, Gloucester : S. of John. Apprenticed to Rowland Collins, Bristol, and Sarah his wife, 16 May 1674.

5263. WOOD, MARK, Perth : 1708, F.

5264. WOOD, ROBERT, London : 1551, S.

5265. WOOD, ROBERT, London : 20 Aug. 1678, L.; 1684, S.; 1691, R.W.; 1697, f.U.W.; 1698, U.W.; 1701, M. Touch, 200 L.T.P., which he had leave to strike in 1671/2.

5266. WOOD, ROBERT, London : 26 Sept. 1700, Y.

5267. WOOD, ROWLAND, Gloucester : S. of William. Apprenticed to John Burrowes, Bristol, and Rachel his wife, 13 Aug. 1600.

5268. WOOD, THOMAS, London : 1570, S.; 1580, R.W.; 1586 and 1590, U.W.; 1592 and 1596, M.

5269. WOOD, THOMAS, JUNR., London : 1591, L. In 1596 he was one of the " Court of Assistants."

5270. WOOD, THOMAS, London : 27 Sept. 1705, Y.

5271. WOOD, THOMAS, London : 20 Dec. 1792, Y.

5272. WOOD, WILLIAM, London : Mentioned in 1564. 1580, S.; 1589, R.W.

5273. WOOD, WILLIAM, London : 15 Dec. 1726, Y.

5274. WOOD, WILLIAM, London : 10 June 1736, Y.; 21 Mar. 1744, L. Partner in Wood & Mitchell (q.v.), No. 5277.

5275. WOOD, WILLIAM, St. Andrews : 1680, F.

5276. WOOD & HILL, London : Touch, 1067 L.T.P., struck c. 1798. Partners were probably Roger Hill, 1791, Y.; and Thomas Wood, 1792, Y.

5277. Wood & Mitchell, London: Touch, 893 L.T.P., which they obtained leave to strike on 12 Aug. 1742. Partners, William Wood, 1744, L.; and John Mitchell, 1744, L. The Hall Marks are those of Gabriel Grunwin.

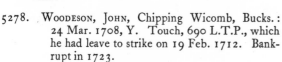

5278. Woodeson, John, Chipping Wicomb, Bucks.: 24 Mar. 1708, Y. Touch, 690 L.T.P., which he had leave to strike on 19 Feb. 1712. Bankrupt in 1723.

5279. Woodford, John, London: 19 Aug. 1669, L.; 1679, f.S.

Woodhouse, see Woddoce.

5280. Woodley, Thomas, London: 13 Oct. 1743, Y.

5281. Woods, John (? Woodward), York: 1607/8, F.

5282. Woods, Samuel, Waterford: Circa 1820-1840.

5283. Woodward, Robert, London: 28 Sept. 1699, L.

5284. Wooldrige, Robert, London: 14 Dec. 1749, Y. Disfranchised 19 Dec. 1771.

5285. Wooldrige, Robert, London: 18 June 1795, Y.

5286. Wormlayton, Joseph, London: 17 Dec. 1691, Y.

5287. Wormlayton, Fulk Humphrey, London: 19 June 1701, Y. Touch, 588 L.T.P., which he had leave to strike on 7 Aug. 1701.

5288. Wratten, Richard, London: 14 Dec. 1749, Y.

5289. Wratten, Robert, London: 9 Oct. 1718, Y.

5290. Wreggett, Richard, York: 1652/3, F.

5291. Wright, Adam, Glasgow: 1786, F. Coppersmith.

5292. Wright, Alexander, Edinburgh: 1732, F. Touch, 131 E.T.P. In 1773 his shop was in West Bow.

Wright, Daniel, see White.

5293. Wright, Edward, Lynn: 1663/4, F. Apprenticed to Thomas Holland.

5294. Wright, Herman, London: 16 Oct. 1766, Y.; 25 Sept. 1785, L.; 1789, S. Struck out by order and fine returned, 23 Mar. 1820. Died 15 May 1831.

5295. Wright, James, Edinburgh: 1780, F. In 1773 his shop was in Bristo Street, in 1786 in Cowgate Head, and in 1800-1805 in West Bow.

5296. Wright, John, London: 19 Dec. 1717, Y.

5297. Wright, John, London: 23 June 1743, L. Touch, 870 L.T.P., struck c. 1736.

5298. Wright, John, London: Fined in 1477 for late working.

5299. Wright, John, York: 1559/60, F.

5300. Wright, Lawrence, London: A master in 1586.

5301. Wright, Nicholas, London: Mentioned in 1630, 1635 and 1638.

5302. Wright, Nicholas, Lynn: 1454/5, apprenticed to John Adam.

5303. Wright, Peter, York: 1633/4, F., by patrimony. Mentioned in 1662/3.

5304. Wright, Richard, York: On 2 April 1711 was apprenticed for seven years to William Hutchinson. Son of Richard.

5305. Wright, Richard, London: 18 Dec. 1712, Y. Touch, 737 L.T.P., struck c. 1723.

5306. WRIGHT, ROBERT, London: Of Bankside. Had false wares seized in 1566.

5307. WRIGHT, THOMAS, London: Touch, 399 L.T.P., which he had leave to strike on 21 Mar. 1683. No mention of him in the Y. and L. Lists, but his death in 1685 is recorded in the "Bennett" Book.

5308. WRIGHT, THOMAS, Walsall: c. 1690.

5309. WRIGHT, THOMAS SMITH, London: 24 Mar. 1803, Y.

5310. WRIGHT, WILLIAM, London: 15 Mar. 1764, Y.; 18 June 1772, L. Touch, 1041 L.T.P. Of Little Minories. He was also a publican.

5311. WRIGHT, WILLIAM, Edinburgh: In 1793 his shop was in Cowgate Head.

5312. WRIGHT, WILLIAM, York: On 11 May 1738 was apprenticed for seven years to William Hutchinson. Son of William, Thirsk.

5313. WROGHAN, RICHARD, York: On 10 June 1645 was apprenticed for eight years to Matthew Jobson. 6 Mar. 1653, F. Searcher in 1667 and 1672. Son of Richard, of Burdsall.

5314. WYATT, JOHN, London: 19 Mar. 1718, Y. Touch, 739 L.T.P. See note under John Merriwether, No. 3205.

5314A. WYATT, JOHN, London: Touch, 439 L.T.P., which he had leave to strike in 1687/8.

5315. WYATT, THOMAS, London: 10 Oct. 1723, Y. Touch, 761 L.T.P., which he had leave to strike in 1723.

5316. WYCHERLEY, THOMAS, London: 1607, S.; 1613, R.W.; 1622 and 1626, U.W.; 1626 and 1627, M.

5317. WYCLYFF, PETER, York: 1541/2, F., by patrimony. Son of the next named.

5318. WYCLYFF, RICHARD, York: 1516, F. Father of the above.

WYDDOWS, see WADDOCE.

5319. WYER, DANIEL, Dublin: Mentioned in 1754.

5320. WYETH, WILLIAM, London: 21 June 1733, Y.

5321. WYKES, LAWRENCE, Bristol: 10 June 1669, F. Apprenticed to William Pascall. Mentioned in 1679.

5322. WYLBY, WILLIAM (see also WILBEY), London: Was of the Livery in 1457.

5323. WYLIE, J——, Glasgow: c. 1840.

5324. WYLLARDBY, THOMAS, York: 1416/7, F.

5325. WYLLIE, JAMES, Glasgow: 1786, F. Copper and white-ironsmith.

5325A. WYLLIE, JOHN, Chester: Formerly journeyman to Mr. Harrop. Set up shop on 13 Dec. 1785 and applied for an apprentice.

5326. WYLLS, CHARLES, London: 1 Aug. 1734, Y.

5327. WYNDE, THOMAS, London: In 1457 was an apprentice to Thomas Smyth. In 1466 he was expelled for disobedience to the Master and Wardens.

5328. WYNDER, JOHN, York: 1505/6, F.

5329. WYNDER, RICHARD, York: 1472/3, F.

5330. WYNN, JACOB, London: 22 Mar. 1687, Y.

5331. WYNN, JOHN, London: 16 Oct. 1746, Y.; 20 June 1754, L.; 1763, S.; 1772, f.R.W. Touch, 923 L.T.P., which he obtained leave to strike on 18 Dec. 1746.

5332. WYNSLAYE, JOHN, London: 1525, R.W.

5332A. WYNTER, JOHN, Norwich: 1491/2, F.

5333. WYNTER, ROGER, York: 1461/2, F.

5334. WYSBECH, JOHN, London: In 1457 was covenant man to Piers Warbylton.

5335. WYSEMAN, JOHN, York: 1559/60, F.

5336. WYSHAM, ANTHONY, London: 1587, Y.

X

X., I.D.S., *see* DE ST. CROIX.

Y

5337. YALDER, MARTIN, London : 17 Dec. 1691, Y.
5337A. YATES, JAMES, London : In 1817 was at 20 Shoreditch.
5338. YATES, JAMES, Birmingham : c. 1800-1840. Now incorporated with Gaskell & Chambers, who have in their possession an old cost book of his in which is a list of the moulds, etc., of John Carruthers Crane, Bewdley, purchased by him in 1838. " James Yates, late Yates & Birch," is found on some pieces.

5339. YATES, JAMES EDWARD, London : 18 Mar. 1802, Y. Died 19 Oct. 1851. From 1807-1833 he was a pewterer, worm-maker and pipe-lead maker at 20 Shoreditch, and in 1817 he was at 20 Bishopsgate Street, Within, Cornhill.
5339A. YATES, JOHN & SONS, Birmingham : Virginian Silver Works. c. 1800.
5340. YATES, JOHN, London : 18 Mar. 1741, Y.
5340A. YATES, JOHN, Birmingham : c. 1835.

5341. YATES, JOHN THOMAS, London : 22 Jan. 1846, Y. Died 1847.
5342. YATES, LAWRENCE, London : 22 June 1738, Y.; 28 Nov. 1746, L.; 1757, S. Died 1774. Touch, 905 L.T.P., which he had leave to strike in 1740.

5343. YATES, LOUISA, London : 1 Feb. 1838, Y.
5344. YATES, RICHARD, London : 19 Mar. 1772, Y.; 4 July 1777, L.; 1783, S. Struck out and fine returned 17 June 1824. Touch, 1031 L.T.P., struck c. 1775. From 1792 to 1807 his

business was at 20 Shoreditch but up to 1785 it was at 198 Shoreditch. *See* his Trade Card.

5345. YATES, RICHARD, JUNR., London : 13 Oct. 1803, Y. From 1814-1817 he is given as a plumber and lead merchant of Pleasant Row, Kingsland Road.
5346. YATES, THOMAS, Birmingham : c. 1780.

5347. YATES & BIRCH, Birmingham : c. 1800. Succeeded by James Yates.

5348. YATES, BIRCH & CO., Birmingham : c. 1800.

5349. YATES, BIRCH & SPOONER, Birmingham : c. 1800.

5350. YATES & GREENWAYS, Birmingham : c. 1870. Successors to James Yates.

5351. YEAMANS, FREDERICK, Bristol: Mentioned in the Poll Book for 1739 as a tinplate (? pewter) worker of Castle Precincts, Bristol.

5352. YEAMANSON, ROBERT, Lynn: 1583/4, F.

5353. YEATES, GEORGE ALLISON, London: 15 Dec. 1763, Y.

YENGLEY, see JENGLEY.

5354. YEO(RE), ABRAHAM, Bristol: Mentioned with Joanna his wife, 1620-1635.

5355. YEW, THOMAS, London: 1520, R.W.

YEWEN, see EWEN.

5356. YOMAN, ROBERT, York: 1485/6, apprenticed to Robert Johnson.

YONGE, see YOUNG.

5357. YORKE, ALICE, London: 22 April 1847, Y.

5358. YORKE, EDWARD, London: 12 Oct. 1732, Y.; 18 Mar. 1735, L.; 1764, S.; 1772, R.W. 1776, Died. In 1776 he was in Snow Hill. *See* his Trade Card. Touch, 848 L.T.P., which he had leave to strike on 13 Dec. 1733.

5359. YORKE, JAMES SAMUEL, London: 17 June 1773, Y.

5360. YOUNG(E), ARCHIBALD, Edinburgh: In 1709 was apprenticed to Robert Findlay.

5361. YOUNG(E), DAVID, Perth: 1750, F. 1760, Deacon. Founder, coppersmith, pewterer and white-ironsmith.

5362. YOUNG(E), DAVID, Perth: 1801, F. Coppersmith.

5363. YOUNG(E), FRANCIS, Dundee: 1637, F.

5363A. YOUNG(E), GEORGE, Norwich: 1622, F.

5364. YOUNG(E), JAMES, Edinburgh: In 1637 was an apprentice to James Monteith.

5365. YOUNG(E), JAMES, Perth: In 1751 was an apprentice to David Young.

5366. YOUNG(E), JAMES, Perth: In 1777 was an apprentice to David Young.

5367. YOUNG(E), JOHN, Edinburgh: In 1697 was an apprentice to James Symontoun.

5368. YOUNG(E), JOHN, Perth: 1772, F. Founder.

5369. YOUNG(E), JOHN, Perth: In 1761 was an apprentice to David Young.

5369A. YOUNG(E), MATTHEW, Norwich: 1637, F.

5370. YOUNG(E), PETER, Newnam, Glocs.: S. of William. Apprenticed to Robert Bush and Ann his wife, 3 Aug. 1768.

5370A. YOUNG(E), PETER, Norwich: 1558/9, F.

5371. YOUNG(E), PHILIP, Bristol: Mentioned in 1680.

5372. YOUNG(E), THOMAS, Perth: In 1771 was an apprentice to David Young.

5373. YOUNG(E), THOMAS, London: 22 Mar. 1693, Y.

5374. YOUNG(E), WILLIAM, Perth: In 1750 was an apprentice to Patrick Halley.

CHAPTER VII

INITIALLED MARKS

ALPHABETICAL LIST OF THOSE MARKS WHICH, WITH THE DEVICE, BEAR THE INITIAL
LETTERS ONLY OF THEIR OWNERS' NAMES

THE marks illustrated, and described as well as may be, in the present chapter are such as to warrant their inclusion in no other.

The want of any known indication of the owners' full names, forbids their appearing in Chapter VI, whereas the initials permit of some sort of alphabetical arrangement, and so removes them from the realm of utter obscurity which pervades Chapter VIII.

The names of *possible* owners for these various touches are given in italics, opposite each one; see "Explanatory Note," p. xiii.

The enumeration in this and the next Chapter is continued from Chapter VI, and the numbers which are missing from the sequence are those which have been transferred to the preceding chapter (through the instrumentality of the BENNETT Book, already referred to) since these notes were first prepared for the printer.

A

5375. A..., ?..., of ?: Appears on sixteenth century slip-top spoons.

5376. A..., ?..., of ?: Is found on sixteenth century hexagonal-knopped and slipped-in-the-stalk spoons.

5377. A..., B..., London: Touch, 43A L.T.P., restruck c. 1670 after the great fire of London.

5378. A..., E..., of ?: c. 1695.

5379. A..., E..., London: Touch, 56 L.T.P., restruck c. 1670 after the great fire.

5380. A..., E... (? *Allanson, Edward*, 1702, L.), London: Touch, 418 L.T.P., struck c. 1685.

345

5381. A . . . , G . . . , London : Touch, 33 L.T.P., restruck c. 1670 after the great fire.

5382. (?) A . . . , H . . . , Edinburgh : Touches, 16 and 17 E.T.P., dated 1600.

——   A . . . , I . . . , London : Touch, 708 L.T.P., *see* Ansell, No. 97.

5384. A . . . , I . . . (? *Angell, John*, 1677, f.R.W.), London : Touch, 120 L.T.P., restruck c. 1670 after the great fire.

5384A. A . . . , I . . . E . . . C . . . , of ? : c. 1700.

5385. A . . . , L . . . , (?) West-Country : c. 1680.

Obverse:-

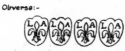

Reverse:-

5386. A . . . , L . . . , West-Country : Appears on a paten from Wells, c. 1700.

5387. A . . . , L . . . , West-Country : Is found on pieces from the West-Country, with dates

ranging from 1763-1812. *Cf.* Nos. 1994 and 4678.

5388. A . . . , R . . . , London : Touch, 84 L.T.P., restruck c. 1670 after the great fire.

5389. A . . . , R . . . , of ? : On a piece in Mr. W. G. M. Townley's collection. (*Cf.* No. 5388.)

5390. A . . . , R . . . , of ? : On a flagon in Stratford St. Mary Church.

5391. A . . . , R . . . , London : Touch, 149 L.T.P., struck c. 1670.

5392. A . . . , R . . . , of ? : Is found on sixteenth century acorn-knopped and slip-top spoons.

5393. A . . . , R . . . , of ? : Is found on sixteenth century acorn-knopped and slip-top spoons.

5394. A . . . , S . . . (? *Attley, Samuel*, 1667, L.), London : Touch, 115 L.T.P., restruck c. 1670 after the great fire.

5395. A . . . , S . . . (? *Attley, Samuel*, 1667, L.), London : Touch, 34 L.T.P., restruck c. 1670 after the great fire.

5396. A . . . , T . . . , of ? : Is found on early sixteenth century slip-top and hexagonal knopped spoons.

5397. A . . . , T . . . , London : Touch, 147 L.T.P., struck—or restruck—c. 1670 after the great fire.

5398. A . . . , T . . . , of ? : Found on apostle knopped and slipped-in-the-stalk spoons of early seventeenth century.

5399. A . . . , T . . . , of ? : Appears on slip-top spoons of early seventeenth century.

5400. A . . . , W . . . (? *Atkinson, William*, 1672. ? *Aylife, William*, 1667, L. ? *Austyn, William*, 1667, L.), London : Touch, 20 L.T.P., restruck c. 1670 after the great fire.

5401. A . . . , W . . . (? *Atkinson, William*, 1672. ? *Aylife, William*, 1667, L. ? *Austyn, William*, 1667, L.), London : Touch, 25 L.T.P., restruck c. 1670 after the great fire.

5402. A . . . , W . . . (? *Atkinson, William*, 1672. ? *Aylife, William*, 1667, L. ? *Austyn, William*, 1667, L.), London : Touch, 43 L.T.P., restruck c. 1670 after the great fire.

5403. A . . . , W . . . (? *Atkinson, Willlam*, 1672. ? *Aylife, William*, 1667, L. ? *Austyn, William*, 1667, L.), London : Touch, 113 L.T.P., restruck c. 1670 after the great fire. The device is the same as in No. 5402, and this touch, being in a lozenge, may be that of the widow of the owner of Touch 43.

—— A . . . , W . . . , London : Touch, 240 L.T.P., *see* William Allen, No. 61.

—— A . . . , W . . . , London : Touch, 377 L.T.P., struck c. 1682. *See* Atwood, No. 143A.

5406. A . . . , W . . . , of ? : Appears on sixteenth century acorn-knopped spoons.

5407. A . . . , W . . . , of ? : Is found on sixteenth century slip-top spoons.

5407A. A . . . , Z . . . , of ? : On a Stuart type flat domed tankard, c. 1690.

B

5408.   B ..., ? ..., of ?: On a Stuart candlestick in Mr. H. C. Moffatt's collection.

5408A.   B ..., ? ..., of ?: c. 1710-1730.

5411.   B ..., A ..., Scotland: c. 1650. Appears on a bowl at Stirling.

5412.   B ..., A ..., of ?: Is found on several types of sixteenth century spoons.

5413.   B ..., A ..., of ?: Is found on several types of sixteenth century spoons.

5414.   B ..., A ..., of ?: Appears on early seventeenth century slip-top spoons.

5415.   B ..., B ..., London: Touch, 35 L.T.P., restruck c. 1670 after the great fire.

5416.   B ..., B ..., London: Touch, 108 L.T.P., restruck c. 1670 after the great fire.

5417.   B ..., C ..., of ?: On a flagon, c. 1700.

5418.   B ..., C ..., ? Bewdley: c. 1760.

5419.   B ..., C ..., of ?: c. 1740. Appears on a flagon in Mr. Walter Churcher's collection.

5420.   B ..., C ..., London: Touch, 315 L.T.P., struck c. 1678.

——   B ..., D ..., London: Touch, 181—See Daniel Barton, No. 280.

——   B ..., D ..., London: Touch, 604 L.T.P., struck c. 1703. See Brocks, No. 586.

5422.   B ..., E ..., of ?: c. 1750.

5423.   B ..., F ... (? Beeslee, Francis, 1693, Y.), London: Touch, 505 L.T.P., struck c. 1694.

5424.   B ..., G ..., Edinburgh: Touch, 32 E.T.P., c. 1630.

5424A.   B ..., G ..., of ?: c. 1690-1700.

5425. B . . . , H . . . , ? Bristol : ? Henry Burgum, Bristol.

5426. B . . . , H . . . , London : Touch, 54 L.T.P., restruck c. 1670 after the great fire. *Cf.* James Brettell, No. 564.

—— B . . . , H . . . , London : Touch, 268 L.T.P., struck c. 1676. *See* No. 546B.

5428. B . . . , H . . . , of ? : Appears on sixteenth century seal-top and slipped-in-the-stalk spoons.

5429. B . . . , H . . . , of ? : Is found on sixteenth century slip-top spoons.

—— B . . . , I . . . , London : Touch, 67 L.T.P.— *See* James Bullevant, No. 683.

5430. B . . . , I . . . , of ? : Appears on a Jacobean candlestick in the collection of Dr. P. Seymour Price.

5431. B . . . , I . . . , of ? : c. 1690.

5432. B . . . , I . . . , of ? : c. 1690.

5433. B . . . , I . . . , of ? : c. 1660. Appears on the Henley-in-Arden pewter dishes. *Cf.* R. G., No. 5633, and William Green, No. 1988.

5434. B . . . , I . . . , of ? : c. 1770.

5435. B . . . , I . . . , of ? : c. 1680-1700.

—— B . . . , I . . . , London : Touch, 190 L.T.P., *see* Jabez Boston, No. 498B.

—— B . . . , I . . . , London : Touch, 323 L.T.P., *see* John Blunt, No. 464.

5435B. B . . . , I . . . , of ? : c. 1670-1690.

5436. B . . . , I . . . , of ? : c. 1690. (*See* 5593A.)

5437. B . . . , I . . . , London : Touch, 562 L.T.P., struck c. 1699.

5438. B . . . , I . . . , of ? : Appears on early fifteenth century horned-headdress knopped spoon.

5439. B . . . , I . . . , of ? : Appears on sixteenth century slip-top spoons.

5440. B . . . , I . . . , of ? : Is found on sixteenth century maiden-head spoons.

5441. B . . . , I . . . , of ? : On a seventeenth century Pied-de-Biche spoon.

5442. B . . . , I . . . , of ? : c. 1750.

5442A. B . . . , I . . . , of ? : Dated 1679.

5443. B . . . , M . . . , of ? : Appears on a sixteenth century stump-end spoon.

5444. B . . . , N . . . , of ? : Is found on sixteenth century slip-top and hexagonal knopped spoons.

5445. B . . . , N . . . , of ? : Is found on sixteenth century slip-top and hexagonal knopped spoons.

5446. B . . . , N . . . , of ? : Appears on sixteenth century slip-top spoons.

5447. B . . . , N . . . , of ? : Is found on sixteenth century hexagonal-knopped spoons.

5448. B . . . , N . . . , of ? : Early nineteenth century.

5449. B . . . , P . . . (? *Brocklesby, Peter,* 1667, L.), London : Touch, 42 L.T.P., restruck c. 1670 after the great fire.

5450. B . . . , P . . . , of ? : Appears on a broad-rimmed dish, c. 1670, in Mr. W. D. Thomson's collection.

5451. B . . . , R . . . , of ? : c. 1680.

5451A. B . . . , R . . . , of ? : c. 1600.

5452. B . . . , R . . . , of ? : c. 1680. Appears on a salt in Capt. N. G. Harries' collection.

—— B . . . , R . . . , London : Touch, 160 L.T.P. *See* Ralph Browne, No. 642A.

5454. B . . . , R . . . , London : Touch, 318 L.T.P., struck c. 1678.

—— B . . . , R . . . , London : Touch, 805 L.T.P. *See* Bowcher, No. 522.

5456. B . . . , R . . . , of ? : Found on sixteenth century acorn-knopped spoons.

5457. B . . . , R . . . , of ? : Appears on sixteenth century slip-top spoons.

—— B . . . , R . . . , London : Touch, 1001 L.T.P. *See* Bowler, No. 529.

5459. B . . . , S . . . , of ? : c. 1665.

5461. B..., S..., of ?: c. 1680.

5462. B..., S..., of ?: c. 1690.

5463. B..., S..., of ?: c. 1690.

5463A. B..., S..., of ?: c. 1660.

—— B..., S..., London: Touch, 527 L.T.P.
See Stephen Bridges, No. 572.

5464. B..., S..., of ?: c. 1690.

5465. B..., T... (or ? I.) (? *Bateman, John*, 1653,
S. ? *Bennett, John*, 1661, f.S.), London:
Touch, 14 L.T.P., restruck c. 1670 after the
great fire. This mark appears with date 1648
on an alms-dish at Mildenhall Church, Suffolk.
(*Cf.* No. 6075.)

5467. B..., T..., of ?: c. 1690.

5468. B..., T..., of ?: c. 1680.

5469. B..., T..., of ?: c. 1720.

5470. B..., T..., London: Touch, 45 L.T.P.,
restruck c. 1670 after the great fire.

—— B..., T..., London: Touch, 86 L.T.P.
See Thomas Batteson, No. 319.

5471. B..., T..., of ?: c. 1680.

5472. B..., T..., of ?: C. 1680-1710.

5473. B..., T..., London: Touch, 82 L.T.P.,
restruck c. 1670 after the great fire. *Cf.* No.
5489.

5474. ? B..., T... A... O..., London: Touch,
471 L.T.P., struck c. 1691.

—— B..., T..., London: Touch, 496 L.T.P.
See Thomas Buttery, No. 758.

5475. B..., T..., of ?: c. 1780.

5476.   B . . . , T . . . (? *Badcock, Thomas*, 1688, Y.), London : Touch, 446 L.T.P., struck c. 1688.

——   B . . . , T . . . , London : Touch, 564 L.T.P., struck c. 1699. *See* Bosworth, No. 499.

5478.   B . . . , T . . . (? *Boyden, Thomas*, 1706, Y. ? *Blackwell, Thomas*, 1706, Y.), London : Touch, 650 L.T.P., struck c. 1708.

5478A.   B . . . , T . . . , of ? : Circa 1675.

5479.   B . . . , W . . . , of ? : Nineteenth century. *Cf.* No. 5409.

5480.   B . . . , W . . . , of ? : On a Stuart tankard in Mr. Lewis Clapperton's collection.

5482.   B . . . , W . . . , of ? : c. 1760.

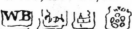

5483.   B . . . , W . . . , of ? : c. 1690. On a dish in Dr. Young's collection.

(Repeated five times on one piece)

5484.   B . . . , W . . . , of ? : c. 1690.

5485.   B . . . , W . . . (? *Blagrave, William*, 1664, L. ? *Bennett, William*, 1662, Y.), London : Touch, 66 L.T.P., restruck c. 1670 after the great fire.

——   B . . . , W . . . , London : Touch, 434 L.T.P., struck c. 1687. *See* Buttery, No. 760A.

5487.   B . . . , W . . . (? *Buckley, William*, 1689, Y. ? *Batteson, William*, 1673), London : Touch, 444 L.T.P., struck c. 1688.

5488.   B . . . , W . . . , of ? : Appears on early eighteenth century rounded-end spoons.

——   B . . . , W . . . , London : Touch, 629 L.T.P., dated (16)75, but struck c. 1706. *Cf.* No. 5473. *See* William Brown, No. 651.

5490.   B . . . , W . . . , Dublin : On a rounded-end spoon in the National Museum, Dublin. (16)98

——   B(rai)ne, William, London : Touch, 356 L.T.P., struck c. 1681. *See* Braine, No. 555A.

C

——   C . . . , A . . . , London : Touch, 705 L.T.P. *See* Abraham Cross, No. 1232.

——   C . . . , A . . . , London : Touch, 457 L.T.P. *See* Alexr. Cleeve, No. 960.

5492.   C . . . , ? . . . , Edinburgh : Touch, 73 E.T.P., dated 1675.

5493.   C . . . , B . . . (? *Cole, Benjamin*, 1668, f.S. ? *Claridge, Benjamin*, 1672, f.R.W.), London : Touch, 95 L.T.P., restruck c. 1670 after the great fire.

—— C..., B..., London: Touch, 339 L.T.P. *See* Benjamin Cooper, No. 1101.

—— C..., B..., London: Touch, 617 L.T.P., struck c. 1704. *See* Casimir, No. 840.

—— C..., B..., London: Touch, 382 L.T.P., struck c. 1683. *See* Cotton, No. 1133A.

—— C..., C..., London: Touch, 206 L.T.P. *See* Christopher Clarke, No. 925A, 1672.

5498. C..., C..., London: Touch, 266 L.T.P., struck c. 1676.

5499. C..., F... (? *Caffee, Francis, q.v.* [*Cf.* Jeremiah Cole, No. 1021, also I.C., No. 5504]), London: Touch, 148 L.T.P., struck c. 1670.

—— C..., F..., London: Touch, 476 L.T.P., struck c. 1691. *See* Cliffe, No. 981.

—— C..., G..., London: Touch, 164 L.T.P. *See* Gilbert Cornhill, No. 1126A.

5502. C..., H... (? *Cock, Humphrey*, 1670, f.R.W.), London: Touch, 60 L.T.P., restruck c. 1670 after the great fire.

5503. C..., I... (? *Chassy, Joseph*, 1650, S. ? *Campion, John*, 1662, L. ? *Clarke, John*, 1667, L.), London: Touch, 32 L.T.P., restruck c. 1670 after the great fire.

—— C..., I..., London: Touch, 305 L.T.P. *See* John Crop, No. 1224A.

5504. C..., I... (? *Chassy, Joseph*, 1650, S. ? *Campion, John*, 1662, L. ? *Clarke, John*, 1667, L. [*Cf.* Jeremiah Cole, No. 1021, also F.C., No. 5499.]), London: Touch, 51 L.T.P., restruck c. 1670 after the great fire.

5505. C..., I... (? *Chassy, Joseph*, 1650, S. ? *Campion, John*, 1662, L. ? *Clarke, John*, 1667, L.), London: Touch, 132 L.T.P., restruck c. 1670 after the great fire.

5506. C..., I... (*Cf.* Nos. 884, 1107 and 5521), London: Touch, 153 L.T.P., struck c. 1671.

—— C..., I..., London: Touch, 172 L.T.P. *See* Joseph Collier, No. 1036.

—— C..., I..., London: Touch, 179 L.T.P. *See* Joseph Collson, No. 1057A.

—— C..., I..., London: Touch, 378 L.T.P., struck c. 1683. *See* John Cooper, No. 1106A.

—— C..., I..., London: Touch, 49 L.T.P. *See* John Coursey, No. 1156.

—— C..., I..., London: Touch, 587 L.T.P. *See* John Carpenter, No. 809.

—— C..., I..., London: Touch, 383 L.T.P., struck c. 1683. *See* Joseph Cabell, No. 765A.

5511. C..., I..., of ?: Appears on a William and Mary candlestick in the possession of Mrs. Black.

—— C..., I..., London: Touch, 512 L.T.P., struck c. 1695. *See* John Coke, No. 1012.

—— C..., I..., London: Touch, 563 L.T.P., struck c. 1700. *See* John Compere, No. 1061.

—— C..., I..., London: Touch, 752 L.T.P. *See* Carr, No. 815.

—— C..., I..., London: Touch, 305 L.T.P. *See* John Cropp, No. 1224A.

—— C..., I..., London: Touch, 537 L.T.P., struck c. 1697. *Cf.* No. 5514. *See* John Carr, No. 814.

5515. C..., I..., of ?: c. 1710.

5516. C..., I..., of ?: Appears on *pied-de-biche* spoons. 1684.

5517.   C . . . , I . . . , of ? : c. 1750.

——   C . . . , L . . . , London : Touch, No. 526 L.T.P., struck c. 1695. *See* Lawrence Child No. 908.

5519.   C . . . , L . . . , of ? : c. 1700.   Appears with mark of W. Banckes, No. 240.

5520.   C . . . , L . . . , London : Touch, 838 L.T.P., struck c. 1733.

5521.   C . . . , M . . . , of ? : c. 1790.   *Cf.* Nos. 884, 994, 1107 and 5506.   Appears with mark No. 5593—I.F.

5522.   C . . . , M . . . , London : Touch, 358 L.T.P., struck c. 1681.

——   C . . . , P . . . , London : Touch, 567.   *See* Peter Carter, No. 830.

5523.   C . . . , R . . . , of ? : On a flagon dated 1685 in S. Tawnton Ch., Devon.

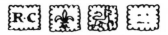

5524.   C . . . , R . . . , of ? : c. 1720.   On inside of a flagon in Mr. Port's collection.

——

5525.   C . . . , R . . . , of ? : c. 1670.   On a dish formerly in Captain Young's collection.

5526.   C . . . , R . . . , of ? : Is found on early eighteenth century rounded-end spoons.

5527.   C . . . , R . . . , of ? : c. 1680.

——   C . . . , R . . . , London : Touch, 907.   *See* Robert Crooks, No. 1221.   (A lamb with Crook.)

5528.   CRA . . . , STEPHEN, of ? : Touch bears date 1690.

——   C . . . & S . . . , *See* " S."

——   C . . . , T . . . , London : Touch, 31 L.T.P.   *See* Thomas Cooper, No. 1111.

——   C . . . , T . . . , London : Touch, 326 L.T.P.   *See* Thomas Cooper, No. 1111A.

5530.   C . . . , T . . . , of ? : c. 1730.   On pieces in Mr. Port's and other collections.

5531.   C . . . , T . . . , of ? : c. 1670.

5531A.   C . . . , T . . . , of ? : Dated 1697.

5532.   C . . . , T . . . , of ? : c. 1800.   (I have come across this mark on pewter buckles.)

5533. C . . . , T . . . , Edinburgh : Touch, 75 E.T.P. c. 1675.

5534. C . . . , T . . . , of ? : Appears on late seventeenth century *pied-de-biche* spoons.

5535. C . . . , W . . . , of ? : c. 1700. (*Cf.* No. 6053.)

5536. C . . . , W . . . (? *Cross, William*, 1659, f.S. ? *Cropp, William*, 1666, L. ? *Cowley, William*,

1669, L.), London : Touch, 24 L.T.P., restruck c. 1670 after the great fire.

5537. C . . . , W . . . (? *Cooper, William*, 1655, f.S. ? *Cross, William*, 1659, f.S. ? *Cropp, William*, 1666, L. ? *Cowley, William*, 1669, L.), London : Touch, 76 L.T.P., restruck c. 1670 after the great fire.

—— C . . . , W . . . , London : Touch, 502 L.T.P., struck c. 1693. *See* William Coleman, No. 1055A.

—— C . . . , W . . . , London : Touch, 842 L.T.P. *See* Charlsley, No. 888.

D

—— D . . . , E . . . , London : Touch, 188 L.T.P. *See* Edward Dodd, No. 1400A.

—— D . . . , E . . . , London : Touch, 836 L.T.P. *See* Drew, No. 1444.

5543. D . . . , H . . . , London : Touch, 360 L.T.P., struck c. 1681.

—— D . . . , I . . . , London : Touch, 795 L.T.P. *See* Davis, No. 1314.

5545. D . . . , I . . . , of ? : c. 1800. This possibly is continental.

—— D . . . , I . . . , London : Touch, 422 L.T.P., struck c. 1685. *See* James Donne, No. 1415.

—— D . . . , I . . . , London : Touch, 432 L.T.P., struck c. 1686. *See* John Dyer, No. 1479.

5548. D . . . , I . . . , of ? : Is found on sixteenth century baluster-knopped spoons.

5548A. D . . . , I . . . , of ? : c. 1670.

5549. D . . . , I . . . , of ? Bristol : c. 1690. (*Cf.* John Dole.)

5550. D . . . , I . . . , of ? : c. 1680-90. *Cf.* Nos. 5923 and 6027.

5551. D . . . , L . . . , London : Touch, 133 L.T.P., restruck c. 1670.

5552. D . . . , P . . . (? *Duffield, Peter,* 1654, S.), London : Touch, 41 L.T.P., restruck c. 1670 after the great fire.

5553. D . . . , R . . . , of ? : I have found this mark with the date 1694.

—— D . . . , R . . . , London : Touch, 292 L.T.P. *See* Richard Dunne, No. 1469.

5554A. D . . . , R . . . , of ? : Appears with Touch 5801, dated 1716.

5554B. D . . . , S . . . , of ? : c. 1500. Appears on a "wedge" baluster in the collection of Mr. Harry Walker.

5555. D . . . , T . . . (? *Dickinson, Thomas,* 1667, L. ? *Drinkwater, Timothy,* 1676, L.), London : Touch, 12 L.T.P., restruck c. 1670 after the great fire.

5556. D . . . , T . . . (? *Dickinson, Thomas,* 1667, L. ? *Drinkwater, Timothy,* 1676, L.), London : Touch, 146 L.T.P., struck (or restruck) c. 1670.

5557. D . . . , W . . . (? *Dyer, William,* 1667, L. ? *Daveson, William,* 1667, L. ? *Ditch, William,* 1669, L.), London : Touch, 81 L.T.P., restruck c. 1670 after the great fire.

5558. D . . . , W . . . (? *Dyer, William,* 1667, L. ? *Daveson, William,* 1667, L. ? *Ditch, William,* 1669, L.), London : Touch, 107 L.T.P., restruck c. 1670 after the great fire.

5559. D . . . , W . . . , London : Touch, 114 L.T.P., restruck c. 1670 after the great fire.

5560. D . . . , W . . . , of ? : Dated 1670.

5561. D . . . , W . . . , of ? : c. 1680.

—— D . . . , W . . . , London : Touch, 864 L.T.P. *See* Dean, No. 1344.

5562. D . . . , W . . . (? *Davison, William, died* 1738), Dublin : c. 1730.

5562A. D . . . , W . . . , of ? : 1668.

E

5563. E ..., B ..., London: Touch, 185 L.T.P., struck c. 1672.

—— E ..., I ..., London: Touch, 244 and 578. *See* John Emes, Senr., and John Emes, Junr., Nos. 1566 and 1567.

—— E ..., I ..., London: Touch, 694 L.T.P. *See* Everett, No. 1597.

—— E ..., I ..., London: Touch, 742 L.T.P. *See* Edwards, No. 1518.

—— E ..., I ..., London: Touch, 751 L.T.P. *See* Excell, No. 1605.

—— E ..., I ... & C ... A ..., London: *See* 5384A.

5567. E ..., N ..., of ?: Tempus Henry VIII.

5568. E ..., T ..., London: Touch, 125 L.T.P., restruck c. 1670 after the great fire.

5569. E ..., T ..., of ?: c. 1680.

5570. E ..., T ..., of ?: c. 1660.

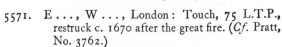

5571. E ..., W ..., London: Touch, 75 L.T.P., restruck c. 1670 after the great fire. (*Cf.* Pratt, No. 3762.)

5572. E ..., W ..., of ?: c. 1690. (*Cf.* Jackman.)

—— E ..., W ..., London: Touch, 470 L.T.P. *See* William Eden, No. 1503.

F

5573. F ..., ? ..., of ?: Is found on late sixteenth and early seventeenth century slip-top spoons.

5574. F ..., A ..., London: Touch, 10 L.T.P., restruck c. 1670 after the great fire.

5575. F ..., A ..., of ?: Appears on slip-top spoons.

5575A. F ..., C ..., of ?: c. 1639–c. 1655.

5576. F ..., C ..., of ?: c. 1690.

5576A. F ..., C ..., of ?: c. 1675.

5577. F ..., D ..., of ?: Is found on sixteenth century acorn-knopped spoons.

5578. F ..., E ..., of ?: Is found on early seventeenth century slip-top spoons.

5579. F . . . , G . . . , of ? : c. 1690.

5581. F . . . , H . . . , of ? : Appears with date 1680.

5582. F . . . , H . . . (? *Freeman, Henry,* 1669, L.),
London : Touch, 124 L.T.P., restruck c. 1670
after the great fire.

—— F . . . , H . . . , London : Touch, 242 L.T.P.
See Henry Frith, No. 1782A.

5584. F . . . , H . . . , of ? : With dates 1672 and 1680.

5584A. F . . . , H . . . , of ? : c. 1650. On a paten at
Shiplake, Oxon.

5585. F . . . , I . . . , of ? : c. 1690.

5586. F . . . , I . . . (? *French, John,* q.v.), London :
Touch, 9 L.T.P., restruck c. 1670 after the
great fire.

5587. F . . . , I . . . (? *French, John,* q.v.), London :
Touch, 30 L.T.P., restruck c. 1670 after the
great fire.

—— F . . . , I . . . , London : Touch, 405 L.T.P.,
struck c. 1684. *See* Joshua Fairhall, No. 1613A.

5589. F . . . , I . . . (? *Foster, John,* 1810, L.), London:
Touch, 1074 L.T.P., struck c. 1801.

5590. F . . . , I . . . , of ? : Is found on sixteenth century
slip-top and hexagonal knopped spoons.

5591. F . . . , I . . . , of ? : c. 1675. This mark appears
on Mr. de Navarro's " Master salt " and on
tankards in Mr. Clapperton's and Dr. Young's
collections.

5592. F . . . , I . . . , of ? : Appears on sixteenth century
slip-top spoons.

5593. F . . . , I . . . , ? Glasgow : Appears with the
mark of Archd. and William Coats, No. 994,
and with No. 5521—M.C.

5593A. F . . . , I . . . , of ? : c. 1690. *Cf.* No. 5436.

5594. F . . . , L . . . , of ? : Is found on early seventeenth
century slip-top spoons.

—— F . . . , R . . . , London : Touch, 312 L.T.P.
See Richard Fletcher, No. 1697.

5597. F . . . , R . . . , of ? : Is found on sixteenth century
monk's-head and lion-sejant knopped spoons.

5597A. F . . . , R . . . , of ? : Appears with the mark of James Bancks, No. 228.

—— F . . . , S . . . , London : Touch, 243 L.T.P. *See* Samuel Faccer, No. 1611A.

—— F . . . , T . . . , London : Touch, 321 L.T.P. *See* Thomas Faulkner, No. 1640A.

5600. F . . . , T . . . , of ? : c. 1685.

—— F . . . , T . . . , London : Touch, 36. *See* Thomas Fountain, No. 1745.

5601. F . . . , T . . . , of ? : c. 1750.

5602. F . . . , W . . . (? *Frith, William*, 1700, Y. ? *Funge, William*, 1701, Y.), London : Touch, 645 L.T.P., struck c. 1707.

—— F . . . , W . . . , London : Touch, 987 L.T.P. *See* Froome, No. 1787.

5604. F . . . , W . . . , of ? : c. 1730.

5605. F . . . , W . . . , of ? : c. 1680.

5606. F . . . , W . . . , London : Touch, 92A L.T.P., restruck c. 1670 after the great fire. (*Cf.* Foxon, No. 1753.)

5607. F . . . , W . . . , of ? : c. 1740.

5608. F . . . , W . . . , of ? : c. 1670.

G

5609. G . . . , ? . . . , of ? : c. 1675.

5609A. G . . . , ? . . . , of ? : c. 1685.

—— G . . . , E . . . & W . . . M . . . , London : Touch, 992 L.T.P. *See* Munden and Grove, Nos. 3330A and 3331.

5610. G . . . , E . . . (& R . . . A . . .), of ? : On a flagon c. 1710 in Stratford St. Mary Church.

5611. G . . . , E . . . , of ? : c. 1730.

5612. G . . . , E . . . , of ? : On an alms bowl in Parracombe Church.

5613. G . . . , E . . . , of ? : Appears on early seventeenth century slip-top spoons.

—— G . . . , E . . . , London : Touch, 157 L.T.P. *See* Edward Goodman, No. 1922A.

5614A. G . . . , E . . . , of ? : Appears on Church flagons with date 1634.

5615. G . . . , F . . . (? *Gibbon, Francis*, 1669, L.), London : Touch, 65 L.T.P., restruck c. 1670 after the great fire.

—— G . . . , G . . . , London : Touch, 401 L.T.P. *See* Gabriel Grunwin, No. 2039.

5616. G . . . , H . . . , of ? : c. 1770.

5617. G . . . , I . . . , of ? : c. 1720.

5618. G . . . , I . . . , of ? : c. 1720.

5619. G . . . , I . . . , of ? : 1680-1720. Has been found in conjunction with W. Greenbanck's " Best Pewter " Touch. *See* No. 1992.

5620. G . . . , I . . . (? *Guy, John*, 1692, Y. ? *Gisburne*, 1691, Y.), London : Touch, 486 L.T.P., struck c. 1692.

—— G . . . , I . . . , London : Touch, 917 L.T.P. *See* James Gibbs, No. 1844.

5621. G . . . , I . . . (? *Green, Jacob, q.v.*), London : Touch, 155 L.T.P., struck c. 1671.

—— G . . . , I . . . , London : Touch, 187 L.T.P. *See* John Greenwood, No. 1996A.

—— G . . . , I . . . , London : Touch, 270 L.T.P. *See* James Glasebrook, No. 1884A.

5625. G . . . , I . . . , of ? : Appears on sixteenth century acorn-knopped and slip-top spoons.

5626. G . . . , I . . . , of ? : c. 1690. (*Cf.* E. H., Nos. 2746, 4263 and 5650.)

5627. G . . . , M . . . , of ? : c. 1680-?.

5628. G . . . , ROBERT, of ? : c. 1680.

5629. G . . . , R . . . , of ? : c. 1690.

5629A. G . . . , R . . . , of ? : c. 1675.

—— G . . . , R . . . , London : Touch, 177 L.T.P. *See* Richard Gardner, No. 1809A.

—— G . . ., R . . ., London : Touch, 396 L.T.P., struck c. 1684. *See* Richard Gray, No. 1969A.

5632. G . . ., R . . ., of ? : c. 1670.

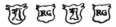

5632A. G . . ., R . . ., of ? : c. 1700.

5633. G . . ., R . . ., of ? : c. 1670. (*Cf.* I.B., No. 5433, and W.G., No. 1988.)

5634. G . . ., T . . . (? *Gibbs, Thomas*, 1669, L. ? *Gregg, Thomas*, 1654, S.), London : Touch, 64 L.T.P., restruck c. 1670 after the great fire.

5635. G . . ., T . . ., London : Touch, 267 L.T.P., struck c. 1676.

5636. G . . ., T . . ., of ? : Appears on sixteenth century slip-top spoons.

5637. G . . ., W . . . (? *Gosnell, William*), London : Touch, 8 L.T.P., restruck c. 1670 after the great fire. *Cf.* S.M., No. 5799.

—— G . . ., W . . ., London : Touch, 313 L.T.P. (*See* Wm. Green, No. 1988, and *Cf.* I.B., No. 5433, and R.G., No. 5633.)

—— G . . ., W . . . M . . . & E . . ., London : Touch, 992 L.T.P. *See* Munden and Grove, Nos. 2032 and 3331.

H

5638. H . . ., ? . . ., of ? : c. 1690-1720.

5639. H . . ., ? . . ., of ? : c. 1750.

5639A. H . . ., ? . . ., of ? : c. 1670.

5640. H . . ., ? . . ., of ? : Is found on sixteenth century slip-top spoons.

5640A. H . . ., A . . ., of ? : c. 1680.

—— H . . ., A . . ., of ? : *See* Hincham, No. 2329.

5641. H . . ., C . . ., London : Touch, 141 L.T.P., restruck c. 1670 after the great fire.

5642. H . . . , C . . . , London : Touch, 144 L.T.P., restruck c. 1670 after the great fire.

—— H . . . , D . . . , London : Touch, 269 L.T.P. *See* David Hayrick, No. 2292A.

5644. H . . . , E . . . (? *Hawkes, Edward*, 1667, L. ? *Heath, Edward*, 1641, f.S.), London : Touch, 61 L.T.P., restruck c. 1670 after the great fire.

—— H . . . , E . . . , London : Touch, 628 L.T.P. *See* Edward Hanns, No. 2125.

—— H . . . , E . . . , of ? : *See* Edmund Harvey, No. 2185.

5645. H . . . , E . . . (? *Hawkes, Edward*, 1667, L. ? *Heath, Edward*, 1641, f.S.), London : Touch. 62 L.T.P., restruck c. 1670 after the great fire.

5646. H . . . , E . . . (? *Hawkes, Edward*, 1667, L. ? *Heath, Edward*, 1641, f.S.), London : Touch, 101 L.T.P., restruck c. 1670 after the great fire.

5647. H . . . , E . . . , London : Touch, 174 L.T.P., struck c. 1672.

—— H . . . , E . . . , London : Touch, 454 L.T.P., struck c. 1689. *See* Edward Holman, No. 2382.

5650. H . . . , E . . . , of ? : c. 1690. (*Cf.* Nos. 2746, 4263 and 5626.)

5651. H . . . , F . . . , of ? : c. 1770.

—— H . . . , G . . . , London : Touch, 217 L.T.P. *See* Gabriel Hartwell, No. 2180.

—— H . . . , H . . . , London : Touch, 98 L.T.P. *See* Henry Hartwell, No. 2181.

—— H . . . , H . . . , London : Touch, 241 L.T.P. *See* Humphrey Hyatt, No. 2502.

—— H . . . , H . . . , London : Touch, 642 L.T.P. *See* Henry Hammerton, No. 2105.

5653. H . . . , I . . . (? *Hopkins, Joseph*, 1667, L. ? *Hodge, Joseph*, 1667, L. ? *Hadley, Isaac*, 1668, L.), London : Touch, 44 L.T.P., restruck c. 1670 after the great fire.

5654. H . . . , I . . . (? *Hopkins, Joseph*, 1667, L. ? *Hodge, Joseph*, 1667, L. ? *Hadley, Isaac*, 1668, L.), London : Touch, 92 L.T.P., restruck c. 1670 after the great fire.

5655. H . . . , I . . . (? *Hopkins, Joseph*, 1667, L. ? *Hodge, Joseph*, 1667, L. ? *Hadley, Isaac*, 1668, L.), London : Touch, 99 L.T.P., restruck c. 1670 after the great fire.

5656. H . . . , I . . . (? *Hopkins, Joseph*, 1667, L. ? *Hodge, Joseph*, 1667, L. ? *Hadley, Isaac*, 1668, L.), London : Touch, 112 L.T.P., restruck c. 1670 after the great fire.

5657. H . . . , I . . . , of ? : 1677. Appears on *pied-de-biche* spoons.

5658. H . . . , I . . . (? *Hopkins, Joseph*, 1667, L. ? *Hodge, Joseph*, 1667, L. ? *Hadley, Isaac*, 1668, L.), London : Touch, 130 L.T.P., restruck c. 1670 after the great fire.

5659.   H ..., I ... (? *Hopkins, Joseph,* 1667, L. ? *Hodge, Joseph,* 1667, L. ? *Hadley, Isaac,* 1668, L.), London : Touch, 136 L.T.P., restruck c. 1670 after the great fire.

5660.   H ..., I .... London : Touch, 186 L.T.P., struck c. 1672.

———   H ..., I ..., London : Touch, 284 L.T.P. *See* Joseph Higdon, No. 2308.
———   H ..., I ..., London : Touch, 329 L.T.P. *See* John Hamlin, No. 2104A.
———   H ..., I ..., London : Touch, 525 L.T.P., struck 1696. *See* John Hankinson, No. 2124.

5664.   H ..., I ..., of? : Is found on sixteenth century slip-top spoons.

5665.   H ..., I ..., of? : Appears on a " Chanticleer " knopped sixteenth century spoon.

5666.   H ..., I ..., of? : On a piece c. 1680.

———   H ..., I ..., London : Touch, 593 L.T.P. *See* Hitchman, No. 2340.

5667.   H ..., I ..., London : Touch, 254 L.T.P., struck c. 1676.

5668.   H ..., I ..., of? : c. 1630.

5669.   H ..., I ..., of? : Is found on sixteenth century slip-top spoons.

———   H ..., I & of? : *See* I. & H., 5708.

5670.   H ..., ? N ... (or R), London : Touch, 89 L.T.P., restruck c. 1670 after the great fire.

———   H ..., P ..., London : Touch, 271 L.T.P. *See* Paul Hayton, No. 2238A (? Heyton).

5672.   H ..., P ..., of? : Appears on sixteenth century baluster-knopped spoons.

5673.   H ..., R ..., of? : c. 1780.   (*Cf.* Mark on Paisley Abbey plate, No. 6046.)

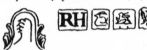

———   H ..., R ..., London : Touch, 46 L.T.P. *See* Ralph Hulls, No. 2456.

5674.   H ..., R ... (? *Harding, Robert,* 1668, L.), London : Touch, 121 L.T.P., restruck c. 1670 after the great fire.

———   H ..., R ..., London : Touch, 192 L.T.P. *See* Richard Heath, No. 2251.
———   H ..., R ..., London : Touch, 381 L.T.P., struck c. 1682. *See* Robert Hands, No. 2117A.

5677.   H ..., R ..., of? : Appears on sixteenth century baluster-knopped spoons.

5678.   H ..., R ..., of? : Appears on early seventeenth century slip-top spoons.

5679.   H ..., R ..., Edinburgh : Touch, 31 E.T.P., c. 1663.

—— H . . . , R . . . , London : Touch, 28, restruck c. 1670 after the great fire. *See* R. Horrod, No. 2410A.

5681. H . . . , S . . . , of ? : c. 1670.

—— H . . . , T . . . , London : Touch, 622 L.T.P., struck c. 1705. *See* Thomas Horrod, No. 2411.

5683. H . . . , T . . . (? *Hull, Thomas,* 1650, M.), London : Touch, 17 L.T.P., restruck c. 1670 after the great fire. (*Cf.* Hux, Nos. 2497 and 2498, also Howard, No. 2426.)

—— H . . . , T . . . , London : Touch, 5 L.T.P. *See* Thomas Howard, No. 2214.

5684. H . . . , T . . . , London : Touch, 85 L.T.P., restruck c. 1670 after the great fire.

5685. H . . . , T . . . , London : Touch, 216 L.T.P., struck c. 1675.

5686. H . . . , T . . . , London : Touch, 277 L.T.P., struck c. 1677.

—— H . . . , T . . . , London : Touch, 281 L.T.P. *See* Hickling, No. 2301.

—— H . . . , T . . . , London : Touch, 740 L.T.P. *See* Hickling, No. 2302.

—— H . . . , T . . . , London : Touch, 173 L.T.P. *See* Thomas Hicks, No. 2304.

5689. H . . . , T . . . , of ? : Is found on sixteenth century slip-top spoons.

5690. H . . . , T . . . , of ? : c. 1680.

5691. H . . . , W . . . , London : Touch, 161 L.T.P., struck c. 1671.

5692. H . . . , W . . . , London : Touch, 359 L.T.P., struck c. 1681.

—— H . . . , W . . . , London : Touch, 812 L.T.P. *See* Horton, No. 2413.

5694. H . . . , W . . . , of ? : c. 1655, with which date it appears at Beeby Church, Leics., and with date 1677 on plates in the Richardson collection.

—— H . . . , W . . . , London : Touches, 335 and 342 L.T.P. *See* William Heaton, No. 2256A.

—— H . . . , W . . . , London : Touch, 663 L.T.P. *See* William Hitchins, No. 2337.

—— H . . . , W . . . , London : Touch, 984 L.T.P. *See* William Hitchins, No. 2339.

—— H . . . , W . . . , London : Touch, 574 L.T.P. *See* William Hux, No. 2498.

I

5695. I . . . , ? . . . , of ? : Is found on sixteenth century slip-top spoons.

5696. I . . . , ? . . . , of ? : Appears on sixteenth century slip-top spoons.

5697. I . . . , ? . . . , of ? : Appears on sixteenth century slip-top spoons.

5698. I . . . , A . . . , of ? : Is found on sixteenth century slip-top spoons.

5699. I . . . , A . . . , of ? : Appears on sixteenth century slip-top spoons.

5700. I . . . , A . . . , of ? : c. 1670.

5701. I . . . , B . . . , of ? : Has been found with date 1621.

—— I . . . , D . . . , London : Touch, 52 L.T.P. *See* Daniel Ingole, No. 2538.

5703. I . . . , D . . . (? *James, Daniel*, 1691, Y.), London : Touch, 521 L.T.P., struck c. 1694.

5704. I . . . , E . . . , London : Touch, 257 L.T.P., struck c. 1675.

—— I . . . , H . . . , London : Touch, 253 L.T.P. *See* Henry Jones, No. 2655A.

5707. I . . . , H . . . , London : Touch, 450 L.T.P., struck c. 1689.

5708. I . . . & H . . . (? *Ingram & H . . .*), ? Bewdley : c. 1780-1820. (*Cf.* Crane, No. 1197.)

5709. I . . . , H . . . , of ? : Appears on sixteenth century slip-top spoons.

5710. I . . . , H . . . , of ? : Is found on sixteenth century spoons.

5711. I . . . , I . . . , London : Touch, 90 L.T.P., restruck c. 1670 after the great fire.

5712. I . . . , I . . . , London : Touch, 103 L.T.P., restruck c. 1670 after the great fire.

5713. I . . . , I . . . , London : Touch, 116 L.T.P., restruck c. 1670.

5714. I . . . , I . . . , of ? : c. 1670.

—— I . . . , I . . . , London : Touch, 282 L.T.P. *See* John Jackson, No. 2557A.

—— I . . . , I . . . , London : Touch, 393 L.T.P., struck c. 1683. *See* John Joyce, No. 2690.

—— I ..., I ..., London : Touch, 553 L.T.P. *See* John Jones, No. 2661.

5716. I ..., I ..., London : Touch, 21 L.T.P., restruck c. 1670 after the great fire.

5717. I ..., I ..., of ?: Is found on sixteenth century slip-top spoons.

5718. I ..., I ..., of ?: Is found on sixteenth century slip-top spoons.

—— I ..., I ..., London : Touch, 170 L.T.P. *See* Jonathan Ingles, No. 2525.

5719. I ..., I ..., of ?: Appears on late seventeenth century slip-top spoons.

5720. I ..., I ..., of ?: Appears on sixteenth century spoons.

5721. I ..., I ..., of ?: Is found on sixteenth century stump-end spoons.

5721A. I ..., I ..., of ?: With date 1672 on a Stuart tankard.

5722. I ..., I ..., of ?: c. 1650.

5722A. I ..., I ..., of ?: With date 1666.

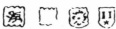

5723. I ..., I ..., of ?: Dated 1709.

5724. I ..., I ..., of ?: c. 1670-1700.

5724A. I ..., I ..., of ?: (16)68.

5725. I ..., J ... (? *Ingram*, *J* ...), ? Bewdley : c. 1780. (*Cf.* Duncomb, Nos. 1465 and 1466.)

5726. I ..., L ..., of ?: Appears on sixteenth century baluster-knopped spoons.

—— I ..., N ..., London : Touch, 332 L.T.P. *See* Nicholas Johnson, No. 2633A.

5728. I ..., N ..., of ?: Appears on sixteenth century spoons.

5729. I ..., P ..., of ?: Is found on sixteenth century slip-top spoons.

5730. I ..., R ... (? *Jones, Robert*, 1667, L.), London: Touch, 27 L.T.P., restruck c. 1670 after the great fire.

5731. I ..., R ..., London: Touch, 102 L.T.P., restruck c. 1670.

—— I ..., R ..., London: Touch, 166 L.T.P. *See* Richard Jacob, No. 2572A.

5732A. I ..., R ..., of?: c. 1760.

—— I ..., R ..., London: Touch, 520 L.T.P., struck c. 1696. *See* Robert Iles, No. 2522.

5734. I ..., R ..., London: Touch, 666 L.T.P., struck c. 1709.

5735. I ..., R ..., of?: c. 1680.

5736. I ..., R ..., of?: Appears on sixteenth century spoons.

5737. I ..., R ..., of?: Is found on early seventeenth century spoons.

5738. I ..., R ..., of?: On sixteenth century slip-top spoons.

5739. I ..., R ... (? *Jones, Robert*, 1667, L.), London. Touch, 88 L.T.P., restruck c. 1670 after the great fire.

5740. I ..., S ..., of?: On a late seventeenth century spoon.

5741. I ..., S ... (? *Jackson, Samuel*, 1668, f.S. ? *Jackson, Startupp*, 1635, Y.), London: Touch, 11 L.T.P., restruck c. 1670 after the great fire.

—— I ..., S ..., London: Touch, 199 L.T.P. *See* Samuel Ingles, No. 2526.

5743. I ..., T ..., of?: c. 1670.

—— I ..., T ..., London: Touch, 680 L.T.P. *See* Jennings, No. 2615.

5745. I ..., W ..., ? Scotland: Appears on Scotch measures, c. 1700.

5746. I ..., W ... (? *Jones, William*, 1666, S. ? *Jackson, William*, 1668, L.), London: Touch, 26 L.T.P., restruck c. 1670 after the great fire.

5747. I ..., W ... (? *Jones, William*, 1666, S. ? *Jackson, William*, 1668, L.), London: Touch, 68 L.T.P., restruck c. 1670.

J

5747A. J . . . , (?) H . . . , of ? : c. 1750.

K

5747B. K . . . , F . . . , of ? : c. 1730. (? Francis Kayford, No. 2697.)

5748. K . . . , G . . . , of ? : Appears on pieces c. 1675.

5749. K . . . , I . . . , of ? : c. 1680.

—— K . . . , I . . . , London : Touch, 379 L.T.P., struck c. 1683. *See* Joseph King, No. 2746.

—— K . . . , I . . . , London : Touch, 250 L.T.P. *See* John Kenton, No. 2720.

—— K . . . , N . . . , London : Touch, 5 L.T.P. *See* Nicholas Kelk, No. 2704.

—— K . . . , T . . . , London : Touch, 806 L.T.P. *See* Kirby, No. 2769.

—— K . . . , W . . . , London : Touch, 291 L.T.P. *See* William Kendrick, No. 2712A.

5753. K . . . , W . . . (? *King, William*, 1706, Y.), London : Touch, 656 L.T.P., struck c. 1708.

L

5754. L . . . , ? . . . , of ? : c. 1710.

5755. L . . . , (? T.) . . . , London : Touch, 55 L.T.P., restruck c. 1670 after the great fire.

5755A. L . . . , A . . . , of ? : c. 1600.

5755B. L . . . , A . . . , of ?.

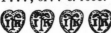

—— L . . . , A . . . , London : Touch, 91 L.T.P. *See* Adam Langley, No. 2828.

5756. L . . . , CHRISTOPHER, of ? : c. 1730.

—— L . . . , E . . . , London : Touch, 198 L.T.P. *See* Lane, No. 2820A.

5757. L . . . , E . . . , of ? : c. 1710.

5758. L . . . , F . . . (? *Larkin, Francis*, 1685, L.), London : Touch, 309 L.T.P., struck c. 1678.

—— L . . . , F . . . , London : Touches, 39 and 40 L.T.P. *See* Francis Lea, No. 2882.

—— L . . . , F . . . , London : Touch, 571 L.T.P., struck c. 1700. *See* Francis Litchfield, No. 2942.

—— L . . . , G . . . , of ? : c. 1675. *See* George Lester, 2919B.

5761. L . . . , I . . . , of ? : c. 1720.

—— L . . . , I . . . , London : Touch, 688B L.T.P. *See* Lawson, No. 2873.

—— L . . . , I . . . , London : Touch, 15 L.T.P. *See* John Leeson, No. 2906.

5762. L . . . , I . . . (? *Lee, John*, 1669, L. ? *Langford, John*, 1664, L.), London : Touch, 23 L.T.P., restruck c. 1670 after the great fire.

—— L . . . , I . . . , London : Touch, 297 L.T.P. *See* John Laughton, No. 2851.

5764. L . . . , I . . . , London : Touch, 211 L.T.P., struck c. 1675.

5764A. L . . . , R . . . , of ? : c. 1750.

—— L . . . , R . . . , London : Touch, 1 L.T.P. *See* Robert Lucas, No. 3009.

—— L . . . , S . . . , London : Touch, 123 L.T.P. *See* Stephen Lawrence, No. 2864.

—— L . . . , T . . . , London : Touch, 411 L.T.P., struck c. 1684. *See* Thomas Locke, No. 2956A.

5766. L . . . , T . . . , of ? : Dated 1619.

5767. L . . . , T . . . , of ? : c. 1680.

5767A. L . . . , T . . . , of ? : c. 1660.

5768. L . . . , W . . . , London : Touch, 105 L.T.P., restruck c. 1670 after the great fire.

M

5769. M . . . , A . . . , of ? : Tempus Hen. VIII. Appears on a baluster with wedge-shaped thumb piece. The mark of King Hen. VIII appears three times and that of the bull's head twice on outside of lid and on the inside is a mark of a woman kneeling to the right of an altar (?), a star with rays and another indecipherable mark.

—— M . . . , A . . . , London : Touch, 3 L.T.P. *See* Anthony Mayors, No. 3160.

5770. M . . . , A . . . , of ? : With date 1679.

—— M . . . , C . . . , London : Touch, 524 L.T.P. *See* Middleton, No. 3214.

5771. M . . . , E . . . , of ? : c. 1730.

—— M . . . , E . . . , London : Touch, 472 L.T.P., struck c. 1691. *See* Edward Matthews, No. 3124.

5773.   M . . . , E . . . (? B . . . or R . . .) (? *Mountford, Benjamin*, 1691, Y.   ? *Moore, Bryan*, 1691, Y.   ? *Moulins, Robert*, 1696, L.), London : Touch, 503 L.T.P., struck c. 1693.

5774.   M . . . , H . . . (? *Masham, Hugh*, 1709, L., London : Touch, 506 L.T.P., struck c. 1694. (*Cf.* No. 3137.)

5775.   M . . . , I . . . , London : Touch, 151 L.T.P., struck c. 1670.

——   M . . . , I . . . , London : Touch, 363 L.T.P., struck c. 1681. *See* John Marsh, No. 3078A.

——   M . . . , I . . . , London : Touch, 421 L.T.P., struck c. 1685. *See* Joseph Mumford, No. 3327A.

5779.   M . . . , I . . . , of ? : c. 1760.

——   M . . . , I . . . , London : Touch, 720 L.T.P. *See* Merriwether, No. 3204.

——   M . . . , I . . . , London : Touch, 936 L.T.P. *See* Merriwether, No. 3205.

5782.   M . . . , I . . . (? *Maynard, Josiah*, 1772, Y. ? *Mann, James*, 1793, Y. ? *Mulcaster, John*, 1792, Y.), London : Touch, 1069 L.T.P., struck c. 1799.

——   M . . . , I . . . , London : Touch, 235 L.T.P. *See* John Millman, No. 3231A.

5784.   M . . . , I . . . , Bideford : c. 1700.

5785.   M . . . , L . . . , Edinburgh : Touches, 7 and 8 E.T.P.   c. 1600.

5786.   M . . . , N . . . (? *Mills, Nathaniel*, 1668, L. ? *Munns, Nathaniel*, 1667, L.), London: Touch, 47 L.T.P., restruck c. 1670 after the great fire. Dated 1640.

5787.   ? M . . . , ? N . . . (? *Marston, Nathaniel*, 1671, Y.), London : Touch, 435 L.T.P., struck c. 1685.

——   M . . . , N . . . T . . . D . . . , London : Touch 843. *See* Darling and Meakin, No. 1302.

——   M . . . , N . . . , London : Touch, 1000. *See* Meakin, No. 3175.

——   M . . . , P . . . , London : Touch, 398 L.T.P., struck c. 1684. *See* Peter Moulesworth, No. 3308A.

——   M . . . , P . . . , London : Touch, 766 L.T.P. *See* Mitchell, No. 3245.

——   M . . . , P . . . , London : Touch, 869 L.T.P. *See* Matthews, No. 3135.

5791.   M . . . , R . . . (? *Moulins, Robert*, 1678, M. ? *Mason, Richard*, 1667, L. ? *Marsh, Ralph*, 1669, L. ? *Marsh, Ralph*, 1650, f.S. ? *Millett, Richard*, 1660, R.W.), London : Touch, 37 L.T.P., restruck c. 1670 after the great fire.

——   M . . . , R . . . , London : Touch, 7 L.T.P. *See* Robert Marten, No. 3092.

5792.　M . . . , R . . . (? *Moulins, Robert,* 1678, M. ? *Millett, Richard,* 1660, R.W. ? *Mason, Richard,* 1667, L. ? *Marsh, Ralph,* 1650, f.S. ? *Marsh, Ralph,* 1669, L.), London : Touch, 94 L.T.P., restruck c. 1670 after the great fire.

——　M . . . , R . . . , London : Touch, 134 L.T.P. *See* Mastead, No. 3117.

——　M . . . , R . . . , London : Touch, 783 L.T.P. *See* Matthews, No. 3137.

5794.　M . . . , R . . . (? *Moring, Randall,* 1794, Y.), London : Touch, 1065 L.T.P., struck c. 1798.

5795.　M . . . , R . . . , of ? : 1826.

5797.　M . . . , S . . . , of ? : c. 1670.

5798.　M . . . , S . . . , of ? : c. 1725.

5799.　M . . . , S . . . (? *Mason, Samuel, q.v.*), London : Touch, 83 L.T.P., restruck c. 1670 after the great fire. (*Cf.* No. 5637.)

5800.　M . . . , T . . . , of ? : 1716.

5801.　M . . . , T . . . , of ? : 1716.

——　M . . . , T . . . , London : Touch, 898 L.T.P. *See* Matthews, No. 3139.

5802.　M . . . , W . . . , London : Touch, 58 L.T.P., restruck c. 1670 after the great fire.　Dated 1666.

5803.　M . . . , W . . . (? *Milton, Wheler,* 1650, S.), London : Touch, 69 L.T.P., restruck c. 1670.

——　M . . . , W . . . , London : Touch, 799 L.T.P. *See* Martin, No. 3094.

——　M . . . , W . . . , London : Touch, 203 L.T.P., struck c. 1672. *See* Matthews, No. 3140.

——　M . . . , W . . . , London : Touch, 551 L.T.P., struck c. 1698. *See* Matthews, No. 3141.

5806.　M . . . , W . . . (? *Morton, William,* 1795, Y. ? *Manley, William,* 1813, Y. ? *Mister, William,* 1820, Y.), London : Touch, 1086 L.T.P., struck c. 1818-1820.

5807.　M . . . , W . . . , ? Dublin :　These initials appear on a stone spoon-mould for casting seal-top spoons in the National Museum, Dublin. c. 1625.

N

5808.　N . . . , A . . . , Edinburgh : 1733.　Touch, 133 E.T.P.

5809.　N . . . , C . . . , of ? : c. 1640.

5810. N . . . , E . . . , London : Touch, 126 L.T.P., restruck c. 1670 after the great fire.

5811. N . . . , E . . . , of ? : Appears on sixteenth century spoons.

—— N . . . , H . . . , London : Touch, 159 L.T.P. *See* Napton, No. 3346.

5812. N . . . , I . . . , of ? : c. 1640, or earlier.

5813. N . . . , I . . . , of ? : c. 1760. (Irish.)

—— N . . . , I . . . , London : Touch, 87 L.T.P. *See* Nichol, No. 3392.

5814. N . . . , I . . . , London : Touch, 311 L.T.P., struck c. 1678.

5815. N . . . , I . . . , of ? : c. 1680.

5815A. N . . . , I . . . , Channel Isles : c. 1740. ? An English maker.

5816. N . . . , R . . . , of ? : Appears on sixteenth century spoons.

5817. N . . . , R . . . , of ? : Appears on sixteenth century spoons.

5818. N . . . , R . . . , of ? : Appears on sixteenth century spoons.

—— N . . . , W . . . , London : Touch, 728 L.T.P., struck c. 1722. *See* William Nicholson, No. 3402.

O

—— O . . . , C . . . , London : Touch, 413 L.T.P., struck c. 1685. *See* Charles Osborne, No. 3448A.

5822. O . . . , I . . . , of ? : Is found on sixteenth century spoons.

5823. O . . . , T . . . , of ? : 1646.

5824. O . . . , T . . . , London : Touch, 137 L.T.P., restruck c. 1670 after the great fire.

P

4825. P . . . , ? . . . , of ? : c. 1690.

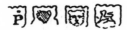

5826. P . . . , ? . . . , of ? : c. 1670.

5827. P . . . , A . . . , of ? : c. 1680.

5828. P . . . , B . . . (? *Pickever, Benjamin,* 1773), Ireland : c. 1773.

—— P . . . , E . . . , London : Touch, 314 L.T.P. (*Cf.* No. 3638). *See* Edward Pusey, No. 3796A.

5829. P . . . , F . . . , London : Touch, 138 L.T.P., restruck c. 1670 after the great fire.

—— P . . . , F . . . , London : Touch, 340 L.T.P. *See* Francis Perkins, No. 3613A.

5832. P . . . , F . . . , of ? : On sixteenth century spoons.

5833. P . . . , H . . . , London : Touch, 29 L.T.P., restruck c. 1670 after the great fire.

—— P . . . , H . . . , London : Touch, 279 L.T.P. *See* Humphrey Penn, No. 3606A.

5835. P . . . , I . . . , of ? : c. 1680.

—— P . . . , I . . . , London : Touch, 500 L.T.P. *See* Pickard, No. 3665.

—— P . . . , I . . . , London : Touch, 201 L.T.P. *See* Pratt, No. 3762.

5836. P . . . , I . . . , of ? : c. 1650.

5837. P . . . , I . . . , London : Touch, No. 100 L.T.P., restruck c. 1670 after the great fire.

—— P . . . , I . . . , London : Touch, 290 L.T.P. *See* John Paynell, No. 3569A.

—— P . . . , I . . . , London : Touch, 317 L.T.P. *See* John Pepper, No. 3609A.

—— P . . . , I . . . , London : Touch, 349 L.T.P. *See* John Pettiver, No. 3639.

—— P . . . , I . . . , London : Touch, 384 L.T.P., struck c. 1683 (*Cf.* No. 5869). *See* John Parkinson, No. 3522A.

5842. P . . . , I . . . (? *Prince, John,* 1697, Y. ? *Pelham, John,* 1698, Y. ? *Pinnock, Joseph,* 1698, Y. ? *Pixley, Joseph,* 1706, Y. ? *Peacock, John,* 1706, Y.), London : Touch, 638 L.T.P., struck c. 1706.

5843. P . . . , I . . . (? *Prince, John,* 1697, Y. ? *Pelham, John,* 1698, Y. ? *Pinnock, Joseph,* 1698, Y. ? *Pixley, Joseph,* 1706, Y. ? *Peacock, John,* 1706, Y. ? *Pratt, John,* 1709, Y. ? *Pratt, Joseph,* 1709, Y.), London : Touch, 659 L.T.P., struck c. 1709.

5844. P . . . , I . . . , of ? : Appears on sixteenth century spoons.

5845. P . . . , I . . . , of ? : c. 1700.

5846. P . . . , P . . . , of ? : 1675.

5847. P . . . , P . . . (? *Parke, Peter,* 1662, f.R.W. ? *Priest, Peter,* 1667), London : Touch, 104 L.T.P., restruck c. 1670 after the great fire. Dated 1668.

5848. P . . . , R . . . , of ? : c. 1660.

5850. P . . . , R . . . , of ? : c. 1700.

5851. P . . . , R . . . , of ? : c. 1680-1710. (*See* No. 3530, Richard Partridge.)

5852. P . . . , R . . . , of ? : c. 1730.

5853. P . . . , R . . . , London : Touch, 158 L.T.P., struck c. 1671.

—— P . . . , R . . . , London : Touch, 858 L.T.P. *See* Peircy, No. 3596.

—— P . . . , R . . . , London : Touch, 882 L.T.P. *See* Pye, No. 3799.

—— P . . . , S . . . , London : Touch, 616 L.T.P., c. 1704. *See* Samuel Pettiver, No. 3640.

5857. P . . . , T . . . , of ? : c. 1700.

5857A. P . . . , T . . . , of ? : c. 1680.

—— P . . . , T . . . , London : Touch, 459 L.T.P., struck c. 1689. (*Cf.* Nos. 5706 and 3488.) *See* Thomas Palmer, No. 3498A.

5859. P . . . , T . . . (? *Powell, Thomas,* 1684, L., London : Touch, 368 L.T.P., struck c. 1682.

—— P . . . , T . . . , London : Touch, 635 L.T.P. *See* Peisley, No. 3598.

—— P . . . , T . . . , London : Touch, 394 L.T.P. *See* Porter, No. 3730.

5860. P . . . , T . . . , of ? : c. 1800.

—— P . . . , T . . . , London : Touch, 576 L.T.P., struck c. 1700. *See* Thos. Parker, No. 3518A.

5862. P . . . , T . . . , of ? : Appears on sixteenth century spoons.

5862A. P . . . , T . . . , of ? : c. 1690.

5863. P . . . , T . . . , of ? : c. 1750.

5864. P . . . , W . . . , London : Touch, 74 L.T.P., restruck c. 1670. Dated 1655.

5865. P . . . , W . . . , London : Touch, 73 L.T.P., restruck after the great fire c. 1670. Dated 1663.

5866. P . . . , W . . . , London : Touch, 111 L.T.P., restruck c. 1670. Dated 1663.

5867. P . . . , W . . . , London : Touch, 139 L.T.P., restruck c. 1670 after the great fire of London.

—— P . . . , W . . . , London : Touch, 322 L.T.P. *See* William Pettiver, No. 3641.

—— P . . ., W . . ., London : Touch, 548 L.T.P., struck c. 1698 (*Cf.* No. 5841). *See* Wm. Plivey, No. 3701.

—— P . . ., W . . ., London : Touch, 911 L.T.P. *See* Palmer, No. 3500.

5871. P . . ., W . . ., of ? : c. 1700-1740.

5872. P . . ., W . . ., of ? : c. 1690.

Q

—— Q . . ., E . . ., London : Touch, 451 L.T.P., struck c. 1689. *See* Edward Quick, No. 3802A.

—— Q . . ., H . . ., London : Touch, 230 L.T.P. *See* Hugh Quick, No. 3806.

—— Q . . ., I . . ., London : Touch, 591 L.T.P. *See* John Quick, No. 3807.

—— Q . . ., S . . ., London : Touch, 213 L.T.P. *See* Samuel Quissenborough, No. 3808.

R

5874. R . . ., A . . . (? *Rolls Anthony*, 1668, L.), London : Touch, 96 L.T.P., dated 1646, restruck c. 1670 after the great fire.

—— R . . ., A . . ., London : Touch, 264 L.T.P. *See* Anthony Redhead, No. 3873.

—— R . . ., A . . ., London : Touch, 330 L.T.P. *See* Andrew Rudsby, No. 4063.

5877. R . . ., C . . . (? *Richardson, Charles, q.v.*), London : Touch, 150 L.T.P., restruck c. 1670 after the great fire. (*Cf.* No. 5878).

5878. R . . ., C . . ., London : Touch, 220 L.T.P., struck c. 1674. (*Cf.* No. 5877.)

—— R . . ., C . . ., London : Touch, 355 L.T.P., struck c. 1681. *See* Charles Rack, No. 3810.

—— R . . ., C . . ., London : Touch, 423 L.T.P., struck c. 1686. *See* Charles Royce, No. 4053A.

5881. R . . ., G . . ., of ? : c. 1730.

5882. R . . ., G . . ., of ? : c. 1690.

5883. R . . ., G . . . (? *Redhead, Gabriel*, 1667, L.), London : Touch, 50 L.T.P., restruck c. 1670 after the great fire. (*Cf.* No. 5884.)

5884. R . . ., G . . ., London : Touch, 109 L.T.P., restruck c. 1670. (*Cf.* No. 5883.)

5885. R . . ., H . . ., of ? : c. 1650.

5886. R . . ., I . . . of ? : This *may* be continental, the type of rose suggests it.

5887. R . . . , I . . . , of ? : c. 1760.

5888. R . . . , I . . . , of ? : c. 1630-50. It has been found with date 1634 on flagon at Glympton Church Oxon.

5889. R . . . , I . . . , of ? : c. 1690.

5890. R . . . , I . . . , London : Touch, 117 L.T.P., restruck c. 1670 after the great fire of London.

5891. R . . . , I . . . (? *Raymond, John*, 1691, Y. ? *Rayne, Joseph*, 1693, Y. ? *Reynoldson, John*, 1693, Y. ? *Rumbold, John*, 1694, Y.), London. Touch, 513 L.T.P., struck c. 1695.

—— R . . . , I . . . , London : Touch, 530 L.T.P., struck c. 1697. *See* John Reynolds, No. 3908A.
—— R . . . , I . . . , London : Touch, 972 L.T.P. *See* Reeve, No. 3882.

5894. R . . . , I . . . , of ? : 1660. Appears on a spoon in the National Museum, Dublin.

5895. R . . . , I . . . , of ? : Is found on sixteenth century spoons.

5896. R . . . , I . . . (? *Reddeth, James*, 1603. ? *Rebate, Johne*, 1588, F.), Edinburgh : Touches, 11 and 12 E.T.P., dated 1600.

—— R . . . , I . . . , London : Touch, 275 L.T.P. *See* John Russell, No. 4074A.

—— R . . . , I . . . , London : Touch, 183 L.T.P. *See* John Robinson, No. 3988A.
—— R . . . , N . . . , London : Touch, 331 L.T.P. *See* Nathaniel Rider, No. 3945A.
—— R . . . , O . . . , London : Touch, 260 L.T.P. *See* Obedience Robins, No. 3977.

5900. R . . . , R . . . , of ? : c. 1720.

5901. R . . . , R . . . , Scotland : sixteenth century.

—— R . . . , R . . . , London : Touch, 618 L.T.P., struck c. 1704. *See* Robert Reynolds, No. 3910.

5903. R . . . , R . . . , of ? : Appears on sixteenth century spoons.

5904. R . . . , R . . . , of ? : Is found on early seventeenth century spoons.

5905. R . . . , T . . . , of ? : c. 1670.

5906. R . . . , T . . . , of ? : c. 1760.

—— R . . . , T . . . , London : Touch, 263 L.T.P. *See* Reading, No. 3867.
—— R . . . , T . . . , London : Touch, 210 L.T.P. *See* Thomas Radcliffe, No. 3811A.
—— R . . . , W . . . , London : Touch, 193 L.T.P. *See* William Richards, No. 3927A.
—— R . . . , W . . . , London : Touch, 559 L.T.P., struck c. 1700. *See* William Raves, No. 3843A.

5910. R . . . , W . . . , of ? : c. 1670.

S

5912. S..., ?..., of?: Appears on sixteenth century spoons.

5913. S..., ?..., of?: Is found on sixteenth century spoons.

5914. S..., A..., Edinburgh: Touch, 34 E.T.P., 1631.

5915. S..., A..., of?: c. 1670.

5916. S..., C..., of?: c. 1660.

5917. S..., C... (? *Sweeting, Charles*, 1658, f.R.W. ? *Seddon, Charles*, 1669, L.), London: Touch, 22 L.T.P., restruck c. 1670 after the great fire. This mark is found chiefly on Church vessels. A fine paten with cabled edge and several chalices are known, all bearing this same touch.

5918. S..., D..., London: Touch, 440 L.T.P., struck c. 1687.

5919. S..., D..., of?: 1725.

—— S..., E..., London: Touch, 467 L.T.P., struck c. 1690. (*Cf.* Nos. 5957 and 5921.) *See* Edward Smith, No. 4345A.

—— S..., E..., London: Touch, 468 L.T.P., struck c. 1690. (*Cf.* No. 5921.) *See* Edward Smith, No. 4345A.

5921. S..., F..., of?: c. 1640-1670.

5922. S..., H... (? *Sivedell, Henry*, 1699, Y. ? *Sankey, Humphrey*, 1710, Y.), London: Touch, 669 L.T.P., struck c. 1710.

—— S..., I..., London: Touch, 703 L.T.P., struck c. 1716. *See* Strickland, No. 4573.

5923. S..., I..., of?: c. 1720. (*Cf.* Nos. 5550, 6027 and 5931.)

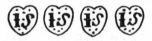

5923A. S..., I..., of?: c. 1720. (*Cf.* Shorey, No. 4263.)

5924. S..., I..., of?: c. 1680.

—— S..., I..., London: Touch, 176 L.T.P. *See* John Skinn, No. 4304.

—— S..., I..., London: Touch, 231 L.T.P. *See* John Slough, No. 4320A.

—— S..., I..., London: Touch, 390 L.T.P., struck c. 1683 and dated. *See* John Shorey, No. 4262.

—— S..., I..., of?: 1687. *See* John Shorey, No. 4262.

5929. S..., I..., of?: c. 1735.

5930. S . . . , I . . . , London : Touch, 420 L.T.P., struck c. 1685 and dated. (*Cf.* No. 4400.)

5931. S . . . , I . . . , London : Touch, 427 L.T.P., struck c. 1685. (*Cf.* Nos. 5923 and 6027.)

5932. S . . . , I . . . (? *Silk, John,* 1694, L. ? *Smalley, John,* 1691, Y.), London : Touch, 489 L.T.P., dated and struck 1692.

——   S . . . , I . . . , of ? : Touch, 614 L.T.P., struck c. 1703 and dated. *See* Joseph Slow, No. 4321.

——   S . . . , I . . . , London : Touch, 631 L.T.P., struck c. 1706 and dated. *See* John Spicer, No. 4455.

——   S . . . , I . . . , London : Touch, 915 L.T.P. *See* Stevens, No. 4511.

5936. S . . . , I . . . , of ? : Is found on sixteenth century spoons.

5937. S . . . , L . . . , London : Dated 1702. (*Cf.* Spencer, No. 4453.)

5938. S . . . , L . . . , of ? : Appears on sixteenth century spoons.

5940. S . . . , R . . . , of ? : c. 1690.

——   S . . . , R . . . , London : Touch, 165 L.T.P. *See* Robert Seare, No. 4170A.

——   S . . . , R . . . , London : Touch, 389 L.T.P., struck c. 1683. *See* Richard Sturrop, No. 4580A.

——   S . . . , R . . . , London : Touch, 764 L.T.P. *See* Spooner, No. 4461. (*Cf.* No. 5925.)

5944. S . . . , S . . . , Ireland : c. 1775.

5945. S . . . , S . . . , ? Ireland : c. 1820.

——   S . . . , S . . . , London : Touch, 419 L.T.P., struck c. 1685. *See* Samuel Sheppard, No. 4238A.

——   S . . . , S . . . , London : Touch, 901 L.T.P. *See* Sweatman, No. 4599.

——   S . . . , T . . . , London : Touch, 337 L.T.P. *See* Thomas Simms, No. 4290A.

——   S . . . , T . . . , London : Touches, 258 and 258B. *See* Thomas Smith, No. 4385.

5949. S . . . , T . . . , of ? : c. 1660. (*Cf.* No. 5950).

Probably same.

5950. S . . . , T . . . (? *Stone, Thomas,* 1667, L. ? *Smith, Thomas,* 1669, L.), London : Touch, 48 L.T.P., restruck c. 1670 after the great fire. (*Cf.* No. 5949.)

5951. S . . . , T . . . , of ? : c. 1675.

5952. S . . . , T . . . , of ? : c. 1675.

5953. S . . . , T . . . (? *Stone, Thomas,* 1667, L. ? *Smith, Thomas,* 1669, L.), London : Touch, 70 L.T.P., restruck c. 1670 after the great fire. (*Cf.* No. 5954.)

5954. S . . . , T . . . (? *Stone, Thomas*, 1667, L. ? *Smith, Thomas*, 1669, L.), London : Touch, 110 L.T.P., restruck c. 1670 after the great fire. (*Cf.* No. 5953.)

—— S . . . , T . . . , London : Touch, 600 L.T.P.— The Arms of Spencer—*See* Spencer, No. 4453.

5955. S . . . , T . . . (? *Stone, Thomas*, 1667, L.), London : Touch, 119 L.T.P., restruck c. 1670 after the great fire.

—— S . . . , T . . . , London : Touch, 362 L.T.P., struck c. 1681. *See* Thomas Smith, No. 4385A.

—— S . . . , T . . . , London : Touch, 388 L.T.P., struck c. 1683. (*Cf.* No. 5920.) *See* Thomas Smith, No. 4386A.

—— S . . . , T . . . , London : Touch, 989 L.T.P. *See* Smith, No. 4391.

5959. S . . . , W . . . , London : Touch, 895 L.T.P., struck c. 1741.

5960. S . . . , W . . . (? *Seare, William*, 1705, Y. ? *Sherwood, William*, 1700, Y. ? *Staples,*

William, 1698, Y.), London : Touch, 634 L.T.P., struck c. 1706.

—— S . . . , W . . . , London : Touch, 849 L.T.P. *See* Shayler, No. 4226.

5961. S . . . , W . . . , of ? : c. 1630-1650.

—— S . . . , W . . . , London : Touch, 221 L.T.P. *See* Walter Sturt, No. 4578.

5963. S . . . , W . . . , of ? : Appears on sixteenth century spoons.

5964. S . . . , W . . . , of ? : c. 1730. (Note the word LONON—not London—in one of the Touches.)

—— S . . . , W . . . , London : Touch, 552 L.T.P. *See* Stevens, No. 4515.

T

5965. T . . . , ? . . . , of ? : c. 1670.

5965A. T . . . , ? . . . , of ? : c. 1690.

5966. T . . . , B . . . , of ? : c. 1700.

—— T . . . , B . . . , London : Touch, 222 L.T.P. *See* Benedictus Thomson, No. 4717A.

5968. T . . . , C . . . , of ? : c. 1680.

—— T . . . , C . . . , London : Touch, 247 L.T.P. *See* Christopher Thorn, No. 4731A.

—— T . . . , E . . . , London : Touch, 336 L.T.P.— Three Herons—*See* Trahern, No. 4802.

5969. T . . . , E . . . , of ? : c. 1690.

5970. T . . . , G . . . , London : Touch, 57 L.T.P., restruck c. 1670 after the great fire.

5971. T . . . , G . . . , of ? : This mark appears on the rim of a 4¼" candle sconce in Mr. Davison's collection. c. 1670.

5972. T . . . , H . . . , London : Touch, 343 L.T.P., struck c. 1680 and dated.

5972A. T . . . , H . . . , of ? : c. 1690.

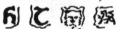

5972B. T . . . , H . . . , of ? : c. 1650-1670.

5973. T . . . , I . . . (? *Taylor, James*, 1666), London : Touch, 129 L.T.P., restruck c. 1670 after the great fire.

—— T . . . , I . . . , London : Touch, 545 L.T.P. *See* John Thomas, No. 4709.

—— T . . . , I . . . , London : Touch, No. 615 L.T.P. *See* Tidmarsh, No. 4740.

—— T . . . , I . . . , London : Touch, 852 L.T.P. *See* Tidmarsh, No. 4741.

5975. T . . . , I . . . , of ? : c. 1660.

5976. T . . . , I . . . , of ? : c. 1750. *Cf.* No. 5988.

5977. T . . . , I . . . , of ? : c. 1670-1700.

5978. T . . . , P . . . , of ? : c. 1670.

5979. T . . . , R . . . , London : Touch, 127 L.T.P., restruck c. 1670 after the great fire.

—— T . . . , R . . . , London : Touch, 286 L.T.P. *See* Robert Tillott, No. 4747A.

5981. T . . . , R . . . , of ? : Appears on sixteenth century spoons.

5982. T . . . , S . . . (? *Turner, Samuel*, 1790, Y.), London : Touch, 1075 L.T.P., struck c. 1802.

5983. T . . . , S . . . , of ? : Is found on sixteenth century spoons.

5984. T . . . , T . . . , of ? : c. 1650.

—— T . . . , T . . . , London : Touch, 296 L.T.P *See* Tidmarsh, No. 4744.

5986. T . . . , V . . . , Edinburgh : Touch, 35 E.T.P., 1631.

5987. T . . . , W . . . , London : Touch, 916 L.T.P., struck c. 1745.

5988. T . . . , W . . . , ? Leeds : c. 1770. (*Cf.* No. 5976.)

V

—— V . . . , G . . . , London : Touch, 273 L.T.P. *See* George Vibart, No. 4873A.

—— V . . . , G . . . , London : Touch, 686. *See* Underwood, No. 4857.

5991. V . . . , Q . . . , Edinburgh : Touches, 9 and 10 E.T.P. Not later than 1600.

5992. V . . . , R . . . (? *Vernon, Richard,* 1650, S.), London : Touch, 93 L.T.P., restruck c. 1670 after the great fire.

5993. V . . . , T . . . (? *Vile, Thomas,* 1669, L.), London : Touch, 80 L.T.P., restruck c. 1670.

5994. V . . . , T . . . (? *Vile, Thomas,* 1669, L.), London : Touch, 106 L.T.P., restruck c. 1670 after the great fire.

5995. V . . . , W . . . , London : Touch, 310 L.T.P., struck c. 1678.

—— V . . . & W . . . , Birmingham : *See* Villers and Wilkes, No. 4876.

W

5996. W . . . , A . . . , London : Touch, 79 L.T.P., restruck c. 1670 after the great fire. (*Cf.* Nos. 5997 and 4374.)

5997. W . . . , A . . . , London : Touch, 154 L.T.P., struck c. 1671. (*Cf.* Nos. 5996 and 4374.)

—— W . . . , A . . . , London : Touch, 544 L.T.P., struck c. 1698. *See* Warford, No. 4962A.

5998. W . . . , A . . . , of ? : c. 1705.

5999. W . . . , C . . . , of ? : c. 1680.

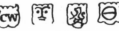

6000. W . . . , C . . . , of ? : Appears on seventeenth century spoons.

—— W . . . , D . . . , London : Touch, 403 L.T.P., struck c. 1684. *See* Daniel White, No. 5088A.

—— W . . . , E . . . , London : Touch, 445 L.T.P., struck c. 1688. *See* Edward Walmsley, No. 4937A.

—— W . . . , E . . . , London : Touch, 475 L.T.P., struck c. 1691. *See* Elizabeth Witter, No. 5247A.

6001. W . . . , I . . . , of ? : c. 1625-1650.

—— W . . . , I . . . , London : Touch, 224 L.T.P. *See* John Waits, No. 4903A.

6002. W . . . , I . . . , of ? : c. 1700-1730.

—— W . . . , I . . . , London : Touch, 299 L.T.P. *See* John Williams, No. 5174A.

—— W . . . , I . . . , London : Touch, 694 L.T.P.— a man walking— *See* Walker, No. 4912.

—— W . . . , I . . . , London : Touch, 439 L.T.P., struck c. 1686. *See* John Wyatt, No. 5314A.

—— W . . . , I . . . , London : *See* John Waite, No. 4903.

—— W . . . , I . . . , London : Touch, 566 L.T.P., struck c. 1699 and dated. *See* John Warren, No. 4969A.

—— W . . . , I . . . , London : Touch, 739 L.T.P. *See* Wyatt, No. 5314.

6010. W . . . , I . . . , London : Touch, 455 L.T.P., struck c. 1689.

—— W . . . , I . . . , London : Touch, 870 L.T.P. *See* No. 5297.

6011. W . . . , J . . . , of ? : c. 1775.

—— W . . . , L . . . , London : Touch, 207 L.T.P. *See* Laurence Warren, No. 4970.

—— W . . . , M . . . , London : Touch, 218 L.T.P. *See* Moses Winkworth, No. 5234A.

6014. W . . . , P . . . , of ? : Appears on sixteenth century spoons.

—— W . . . , R . . . , London : Touch, 162 L.T.P. *See* Richard Withebed, No. 5239.

—— W . . . , R . . . , London : Touch, 246 L.T.P. *See* Richard Walton, No. 4945A.

—— W . . . , R . . . , London : Touch, 482 L.T.P., struck c. 1692. *See* Robert Williams, No. 5180.

6018. W . . . , R . . . , of ? : Appears on sixteenth century spoons.

6018A. W . . . , R . . . , of ? : c. 1675.

—— W . . . , R . . . , London : Touch, 546 L.T.P., struck c. 1699. (*Cf.* No. 5096.) *See* Richard Warkman, No. 4966.

6020. W . . . , S . . . , London : Touch, 189 L.T.P., struck c. 1673.

—— W . . . , S . . . , London : Touch, 196 L.T.P. *See* Samuel Witter, No. 5245.

6022. W . . . , S . . . , of ? : c. 1670.

6023. W . . . , T . . . , London : Touch, 169 L.T.P., struck c. 1672.

—— W . . . , T . . . , London : Touch, 761 L.T.P. *See* Wyat, No. 5315.

6025. W . . . , T . . . , Edinburgh : Touch, 86 E.T.P. c. 1686.

6026. W . . . , T . . . , of ? : c. 1680.

—— W . . . , T . . . , London : Touch, 325 L.T.P. *See* Thomas Waite, No. 4902.

6027. W . . . , W . . . , of ? : c. 1720. (*Cf.* Nos. 5550, 5923 and 5931.)

6028. W . . . , W . . . , of ? : Appears with date 1729 on a flagon in Mr. Port's collection.

—— W . . . , W . . . , London : Touch, 609 L.T.P., struck c. 1703. *See* Wm. Waylett, No. 4998.

6030. W . . . , W . . . (? *Westcott, William*, 1652, S. ? *White, William*, 1667, L.), London : Touch, 72 L.T.P., restruck c. 1670 after the great fire.

6031. W . . . , W . . . , of ? : c. 1700-1730.

—— W . . . , W . . . , London : Touch, 289 L.T.P. *See* William Warters, No. 4977A.

—— W . . . , W . . . , London : Touch, 719 L.T.P. *See* Warkman, No. 4967.

—— W . . . , W . . . , London : Touch, 53 L.T.P. *See* Withers, No. 5242.

—— W . . . , W . . . , London : Touch, 438 L.T.P. *See* Withers, No. 5243.

—— W . . . , W . . . , London : Touch, 78 L.T.P. *See* Wette(r), No. 5073.

6033. W . . . , ? . . . , of ? : Appears with date 1826 on an Imperial Pint sized tappit-hen in Dr. Young's collection.

X

—— X . . . , I . . . D . . . S . . . , London : *See* No. 1360 (de St. Croix).

Y

6033A. Y . . . , D . . . , Perth : With date 1739. This may be one of the Youngs of Perth, but is earlier than any recorded with these initials.

—— Y . . . , L . . . , London : Touch, 905 L.T.P. *See* Yates, No. 5342.

CHAPTER VIII

ILLUSTRATIONS OF THOSE MARKS

WHICH BEAR NEITHER THEIR OWNERS' NAMES NOR INITIALS

OBSCURE TOUCHES

In this the concluding chapter I have gathered together all those marks which one comes across from time to time, which either through their appearing without a maker's name or initials, or through the latter being detrited, can not be included in Chapters VI or VII. The vast majority of these touches are those of provincial makers, and failing all other methods of classifying them they are arranged as well as may be, according to the devices, *e.g.* Lions, Figures, Roses, etc.

6034. "Nobilis est," of ?: c. 1650. On a dish belonging to the North United Free Church, Crieff, Perthshire.

6035. ....?: c. 1740.

6036. (Cle) ... t, Peter, of ?: c. 1660. Appears on a Communion flagon of this period in Major Richardson's collection.

6037. ... ett, Sam ..., of ?: c. 1720.

6038. ..., William, of ?: c. 1780.

6039. ....?: This mark has been found on a piece bearing date 1796.

6040. ....?: c. 1770-1800.

—— ....London : Touch, 319 L.T.P. *See* Thomas Kelk, No. 2704A.

6042. ....?: c. 1780.

6044. ....?: c. 1670.

6045. ..., R...?: c. 1660.

6046. ....? Birmingham or Bewdley: c. 1770.

6046A. ....?: c. 1770-1780.

6047. ....?: c. 1760. (Cf. No. 5639.)

6048. ....?: c. 1670.

6049. ....?: c. 1760-1790. (Cf. No. 5639.)

6051. .... London : Touch, 145 L.T.P., restruck c. 1670 after the great fire. (Cf. No. 5473.)

6052. ....?: c. 1780.

6053. ..., A... of ?: c. 1720. (Cf. No. 5535.)

6055. " LIVE BY HOPE," of ?: c. 1750.

—— WIL ... London : Touch, 386 L.T.P., struck c. 1683. See William Foster, No. 1738A.

—— .... London : Touch, 627 L.T.P., dated 1705. See Wm. Turner, No. 4843.

6058. ..., W ... London : Touch, 77 L.T.P., restruck c. 1670 after the great fire. It bears the date 164–. (Cf. Nos. 55 and 5097.)

6059. W ..., ?..., of ?: Appears on a Stuart flagon, c. 1660.

6060. ....?: c. 1770.

6061. . . . . ?: c. 1770.

LONDON

6062. C (or G) . . . , I . . . , of ?: c. 1720.

6063. . . . , W . . . of ?: On a Stuart Rose water dish in Bristol Museum.

6064. . . . on . . . , of ?: c. 1700.

—— E . . . , London : Touch, 380 L.T.P., struck c. 1683. *See* Edward Walker, No. 4907B.

—— Br . . . ATER FIDE . . . , London : Touch, 619 L.T.P., struck c. 1705. *See* Abraham Roberts, No. 3952A.

—— . . . BRA . . . , London : Touch, 408 L.T.P., struck c. 1685, *See* Richard Brafield, No. 553A.

—— THO . . . 1703, London : Touch, 602 L.T.P., struck and dated 1703. *See* Thomas Greener, No. 1993.

6069. HI . . . , of ?: c. 1680.

6070. FRA . . . . . . NG, of ?: c. 1730.

6071. . . . INHAM, of ?: c. 1730.

6072. . . . ELTON, of ?: c. 1700.

6073. . . . . ?: c. 1760.

—— T . . . , ? . . . , London : Touch, 350A L.T.P *See* Thomas Powell, No. 3750.

6077. . . . . ?: Is found on sixteenth century spoons.

6078. . . . . ?: Appears on sixteenth century spoons.

6079. . . . , ALLAN, Scotland : c. 1740.

6080. . . . . ?: ? Sixteenth century.

6081 . . . . ?: c. 1650.

—— WILLIAM (? SANDYS), London : Touch, 350B L.T.P. *See* 4110A, William Sandys.

6083. . . . . London : Touch, 437 L.T.P., struck c. 1687.

6084. (M)ADAGASC(A)R, of ?: c. 1760.

6085. .... Scotland : c. 1670.

6086. I ..., E ... B ..., of ? : c. 1700.

6087. Cu ... ND ..., of ? : ?

6088. .... Edinburgh : c. 1686. Touch, 88 E.T.P.

6089. .... Edinburgh : c. 1651. Touch, 51 E.T.P.

6091. .... London : Touch, 402 L.T.P., struck c. 1684. (*Cf.* Wetter, No. 5073.)

6092. ... W ..., London : Touch, 118 L.T.P., restruck c. 1670 after the great fire. (*Cf.* Cleeve, No. 960.)

6093. .... ? : c. 1710.

—— ? ... ANTHONY, London : Touch, 575 L.T.P., struck c. 1700. *See* Anthony Smith, No. 4338.
—— ? ... SAMUEL, London : Touch, 469 L.T.P., struck c. 1690. (*Cf.* No. 2464.) *See* Samuel Smalley, No. 4326.

6096. .... ? : c. 1760.

6097. .... ? : Is found on sixteenth century spoons.

6098. .... ? : Sixteenth century. These marks appear on dishes in Mr. de Navarro's and Mr. A. B. Yeates' collections.

6099. .... ? : c. 1790.

6100. ..., L ..., of ? : c. 1670.

6101. ..., (RI)CHARD, of ? : c. 1730.

6104. .... ? : 1621.

6105. .... ? : c. 1720.

6106. .... ? : c. 1820. Appears on a snuff-box in Mr. Walter Churcher's collection.

6107. ....?: c. 1730.

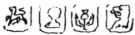

6108. ..., T..., of ?: c. 1735.

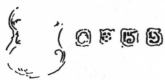

6109. ....?: c. 1680.

6110. ....?: c. 1750.

6111. ....?: c. 1730.

6112. .... Bristol: c. 1760.

6113. ....?: On a Chalice in Mr. de Navarro's collection.

6114. ....?: c. 1730. Appears with Hall Marks of Benjamin Withers, No. 5240.

6115. ....?: c. 1650. On a flagon in Parracombe Church.

6116. FORD, ..., of ?: c. 1680.

6117. ....?: c. 1680.

6118. ....?: c. 1670.

6119. ....?: c. 1760.

6120. ....?: c. 1680.

6121. ....?: Appears on sixteenth century spoons.

6122. ....?: Appears on sixteenth century spoons.

6123. ....?: Appears on sixteenth century spoons.

6124. ....?: Appears on sixteenth century spoons.

6125. ....?: Appears on sixteenth century spoons.

6126. ....?: Appears on seventeenth century spoons.

6127. ....?: Appears on seventeenth century spoons.

6128. ....?: Appears on sixteenth century spoons.

6129. ... R..., of ?: Appears on sixteenth century spoons.

6130. . . . . ? : Appears on fifteenth century spoons.

6131. . . . . ? : Appears on sixteenth century spoons.

6132. . . . . ? : Appears on late seventeenth century spoons.

6133. . . . . ? : c. 1810.

6134. . . . . ? : c. 1720.

6135. . . . . ? : Appears with date 1704.

6136. (?) E . . . . , N . . . . , of ? : Circa 1660. Appears on the larger chalice illustrated at p. 153 of de Navarro's *Causeries on English Pewter*.

6137. . . . , John, London : Circa 1680.

6138. . . . . Bristol : Circa 1690.

6139. . . . , I . . . , ? : c. 1640.

6140. . . . . ? : c. 1695-1730.

6141. . . . , PATRICK, ? Bristol : This is very probably the Touch of Patrick Hawkins (No. 2221) *q.v.* He was apprenticed to John Bacheler and may have adopted the latter's device.

CHAPTER IX

INDEX TO THE DEVICES

IN THE MARKS ILLUSTRATED THROUGHOUT CHAPTERS VI, VII, AND VIII

In order that the reader may derive the greatest possible amount of assistance from it, it seems advisable to re-direct his attention to the remarks made about this Index in the "Explanatory Note" which follows immediately after the preliminary matter at the commencement of this volume, to which one must add here the following further notes :—

a. The numbers which appear after the short description of the various devices have reference, *not* to the number of the touch on the touchplates, *nor* to the pagination, but to the numbers which appear at the extreme left-hand side of the pages in Chaps. VI, VII and VIII ; in other words they are the numbers which *I* have given to each individual pewterer or mark.

b. In compiling this index, my aim has been as far as possible to group the devices under *Main Headings*, with a full use of cross references. This has seemed the only way because, in so many of the smaller touches it is quite impossible to state with absolute certainty what kind of insect, plant, bird or human figure the device was intended to represent. Hence a figure, be it man, woman, fisherman, saint or what not, will be found under " Figure," but if it be sought for under Man, or Woman, it will be found as follows : Man, see " Figure " —Woman, see " Figure," and so on. Flies, Bees, etc., in like manner will appear as such, with direction to the main heading, " Insects." A few moments consideration of these *Main Headings* will save valuable time in reference ; they are as follows :—

> ANIMALS ; ARMORIAL ; BIRDS ; BUILDINGS ; DATES ; DRINKING-VESSELS ; FIGURES (Human, Allegorical, etc.) ; FISH ; FLOWERS ; FRUIT AND VEGETABLES ; INSECTS ; MONSTERS ; PLANTS AND TREES ; REPTILES ; SHIPS ; SUN AND STARS ; and WEAPONS.

c. The Rose and Crown as a complementary mark to the " makers' proper touch " is omitted, as stated in the " Explanatory Note." *But* where it appears as a probable " Proper Touch " it has been included.

The " Hall-Marks," as will have been noted, are indexed separately in Chapter X.

Parts of Dates and Words in Parenthesis ( ), though not actually appearing in the Touches, are implied.

I cannot refrain from again tendering my thanks to my daughter, Gertrude Joan Cotterell, for her painstaking care in writing out the whole of the slips for this Index, and in typing much of the MSS. for Press.

DATES, etc., *continued*—

1614, with W.H. and Castle -	2103
1616, with T.I. and Castle -	2534
1616, with T.I. and Rose -	2534
1620, with A.B. and Castle -	493
1621 - - - - -	5701
1621, with Tree - - -	6104
1631, with A.S. and Castle -	5914
1631, with I.S. and Castle -	4275
1631, with R.T. - - -	4726
1631, with V.T. and Castle -	5986
1633, with R.S. and Castle -	4296
1634, with I.G. and Castle -	1912
1634, with I.M. and Castle -	3271
1634, with W.S. and Castle -	4159
164 ?, with W.– and Pelican -	6058
1640, with I.A. and Castle -	5
1640, with N.M. and Windmill - - - -	5786
1643, with I.B. and Castle -	675
1643, with I.H. and Castle -	2189
1643, with I.M. and Castle -	3272
1646, with T.O. - - -	5823
1646, with A.R. and Roll in a Hand - - - -	5874
1646, with R.W. and Castle -	5037
1648, with T.I. and Hammer	2535
1649, with W.A. and Castle -	10
1651, with I.H. and Castle -	2274
16(? 52), with W.C. and Castle	915
1653, with W.B. and Castle -	496
1654, with W.A. and Castle -	82
1654, with D.B. and Castle -	663
1654, with T.E. and Castle -	1514
1654, with A.F. and Castle -	1651
1654, with I.H. and Castle -	2188
1655, with A.G. and Castle -	1949
1655, with W.P. and Slipped Flower - - - -	5864
1655, with I.S. and Castle -	4616
1655, with W.W. and Cock -	5242
1656, with Grasshopper and R.H. - - - -	2456
1657, with R.I. and Crook Crowned - - - -	5730
1658, with I.L. and Castle -	2855
1659, with A.M. and Castle -	3167
1659, with I.R. and Castle -	3821
1660, with I.R. - - -	5894
1660, with S.W. and Castle -	4922
1662, with N.H. and Talbot passant - - -	2474
1663, with W.P. and Slipped Flower - - - -	5865
1663, with I.A. and Castle -	6
1663, with W.A. and Spoon in Hand - - - -	5402
1663, with I.B. and Elephant	683
1663, with T.C. and Coiled Snake - - - -	1111
1663, with W.C. - - -	5536
1663, with W.D. and Fleur-de-Lys - - - -	5559
1663, with I.F. and Artichoke	5587
1663, with I.H. and Fagot -	5659

DATES, etc., *continued*—

1663, with I.H. and Chessboard - - - -	5655
1663, with I.H. and Crossed spoons - - - -	5670
1663, with I.H. and Crossed Spoon and Key - -	5654
1663, with R.I. and Castle -	2532
1663, with I.L. and Escallop Shell - - - -	5762
1663, with R.M. and Bird (Martin) - - -	3092
1663, with G.R. and double-headed Eagle - -	5883
1663, with I.R. and Cushion -	5890
1663, with T.S. and Rose -	5953
1663, with T.S. and Flaming Star - - - -	5955
1664, with B.B and Star -	5415
1664, with G.C. and Castle -	913
1664, with R.H. and two Naked Figures - -	2410A
1665, with W.I. - - -	5747
1666, with double-headed Eagle	1827
1666, with S.A. and Bear's Head - - - -	5395
1666, with I.I. and Hammer and Crown - -	5713
1666, with W.M. and two Fusils - - - -	5802
1666, with A.N. and Castle -	3343
1666, with W.W. and two Thistles - - -	5073
1667, with I.H. and Castle -	2276
1668, with W.A. and Spoon in Hand - - - -	5403
1668, with B.B. and Flaming Heart - - - -	5416
1668, with L.D. and Flaming Heart - - - -	5551
1668, with W.D. - 5558,	5562A
1668, with H.F. - - -	5582
1668, with I.H. and two Spoons	5656
1668, with I.I. - - -	5724A
1668, with I.I. and Key -	5712
1668, with R.I. and Crossed Key and Sword - -	5731
1668, with W.L. - -	5768
1668, with I.M. and Bust -	5775
1668, with P.P. and Still -	5847
1668, with W.P. and Slipped Flower - - -	5866
1668, with G.R. and double-headed Eagle, displayed -	5884
1668, with T.S. and Rose -	5954
1668, with R.T. and Moose's Head - - - -	5979
1669, with I.A. and Castle -	7
1669, with R.S. and Book -	4170A
1669, with R.W. and Skipping Figure - - - -	5239
1670, with D.B. and Helmet -	280
1670, with W.D. - -	5560
1670, with E.H. and Crossed Spoons - - - -	5646

DATES, etc., *continued*—

1670, with E.H. and Crossed Key and Sword - -	5647
1670, with T.H. and Crown and Sceptres - - -	2304
1670, with I.I. and Clasped Hands - - - -	2525
1670, with T.W. - - -	6023
1671, with I.I. and Clasped Hands - - - -	2525
1671, with S.I. and Bird -	2526
1671, with R.P. and Bird -	5853
1671, with I.W. and Castle -	4986
1671, with Pelican and " ANNO "	55
1672, with C.C. in cypher and Fish - - - -	925A
1672, with E.D. - -	1400A
1672, with W.H. and Castle -	2191
1672, with A.M. and Castle -	3255
1672, with T.R. and Monument - - - -	3811A
1672, with slipped Flower and I.L. - - - -	5764
1673, with Angel -	4305
1673, with M.W. and Spoon in Hand - - -	5234A
1674, with C.R. and Slipped Tulip - - - -	5878
1674, with H.Q. and Cross -	3806
1674, with I.S. and Tree -	4320A
1675, with W.B. and Animal's Head - - - -	651
1675, with –.C. and Castle -	5492
1675, with T.C. and Castle -	5533
1675, with I.E. and Bird -	1566
1675, with I.H. and three Horseshoes - -	2655A
1675, with E.I. and Ram's-head - - - -	5704
1675, with Hare at speed -	2071
1675, with S.F. and Hare at speed - - -	1611A
1675, with T.S. and Pomegranate - - -	4385
1675, with C.T. - -	4731A
1675, with A.W. and Castle -	4907
1675, with R.W. and Barrel	4945A
1675, with Anchor and Crown 2752,	5846
1675, with two Hearts, point to point - - -	4360
1676, with H.B. and Lion's Head erased - -	546B
1676, with C.C. over Crown and Horseshoe - -	5498
1676, with M.C. and Pear -	5522
1676, with A.F. and Castle -	1652
1676, with D.H. and Key -	2292A
1676, with P.H. and Armour	2238A
1676, with I.N. and Fleur-de-Lys - - - -	5814
1676, with A.R. and Mascle -	3873
1676, with I.R. and Castle -	4074A
1676, with O.R. and Hand with Spear - - -	3977

CHAPTER X

INDEX TO THE "HALL-MARKS"

ILLUSTRATED THROUGHOUT CHAPTERS VI, VII AND VIII

Wʜᴇɴ the sets of Hall-Marks contain initials they are arranged according thereto, in alphabetical order. Where no initials appear they are grouped as well as may be, according to their devices, at the end of the chapter.

1. H.P. *2.* Cat sejant. *3.* Buckle.
4. Three Fleurs-de-Lys - 3760
1. I.P. *2.* Lion rampant. *3.*
Leopard's Face. *4.* Port-
cullis - - - - 5845
1 and *3.* I.P. *2.* Rose and Crown.
4. Three Fleurs-de-Lys 989
1. Lion passant. *2.* B. *3.* Leopard's Face crowned. *4.*
I.P. - - - - 3638
1. N.P. *2.* ?. *3.* Lion's Head
erased. *4.* ? - - 3524
1. Leopard's Face. *2.* Lion passant. *3.* ?. *4.* P.P. - 5846
1. R.P. *2.* Britannia. *3.* Lion's
Head, erased. *4.* Golden
Fleece - - - 3748
1. R.P. *2.* Leopard's Face. *3.*
Buckle. *4.* Lion passant to
sinister - - - 5851
1. R.P. *2.* Lion rampant. *3.*
Leopard's Face. *4.* Double-
headed Eagle - - 3617
1. Lion passant. *2.* Leopard's
Face. *3.* Buckle. *4.* R.P.
3694, 3697
1. ?. *2.* Leopard's Face crowned.
3. Cinquefoil. *4.* R.P. - 5852
1. T.P. *2.* Harp. *3.* Britannia.
4. Griffin's Head erased - 3478
1. T.P. *2.* Lion rampant. *3.*
Lion's Head erased. *4.* ? - 3475
1. T.P. *2.* Rose and Crown.
3. Leopard's Face. *4.* Lion
passant - - - 3750
1, 2, 3 and *4.* W.P., with Unicorn 5872
1. W.P. *2.* Angel. *3.* ?. *4.* ? 3653
1. Double-headed Eagle. *2.*
Rose and Crown. *3.* Port-
cullis. *4.* W.P. - 5871

Q

1. E.Q. *2.* Lion passant. *3.*
Wheel. *4.* Buckle - - 3802A

R

1. A.R. *2.* Wheatsheaf. *3.*
Lion rampant - - 4062
1 and *3.* Fleur-de-Lys. *2.* Lion
rampant. *4.* C.R. - 3983
1. E.R. *2.* Buckle. *3.* (?) Animal.
4. ? - - - - 3831
1. Lion passant. *2.* Leopard's
Face crowned. *3.* Buckle.
4. G.R. - - - 5881
1. I.R., Crowned. *2.* F. (Black
letter). *3.* Leopard's Face.
4. Lion passant - - 5887
1. I.R. *2.* Globe. *3.* Leopard's
Face. *4.* Lion passant 5889
1. I.R. *2.* Leopard's Face,
crowned. *3.* Castle. *4.*
Lion passant - - - 4074A
1 and *3.* Dog courant. *2.*
Britannia. *4.* I.R. - 3878 879

1. Lion rampant. *2.* Leopard's
Face. *3.* Bird. *4.* I.R. - 4991
1. Cock. *2.* Leopard's Face.
3. S.R. - - - 3948
1. Lion passant. *2.* Britannia.
3. Cock. *4.* S.R. - 3948
1. T.R. *2.* Thistle in Glory.
3. Globe. *4.* Lion rampant 3942
1. W.R. *2.* Fleur-de-Lys. *3.*
Lion passant. *4.* ⌐. *5.*
Star - - - 3924

S

1. Y.B.
& S *2.* Crest of Pewterers'
Co. *3.* On a Fesse, three
Escallops. *4.* Griffin's Head
erased - - - 5349
1. G.S. *2.* Demi-Eagle. *3.*
Lion's Head erased. *4.*
Golden Fleece - - 4197
1. Acorn. *2.* Buckle. *3.* Eagle's
Head. *4.* G.S. - - 4347
1. Leopard's Face. *2.* Lion's
Head erased. *3.* Lion rampant. *4.* G.S. - - 4347
1, 2, 3 and *4* I.S., in Heart-
shaped Punches - - 5924
1. I.S. *2.* R. (Black letter). *3.*
Leopard's Face crowned.
4. Lion passant - - 2538,
4286
1. I. (Black letter). *2.* S. (Black
letter). *3.* Rose. *4.* (?) Ship 4216
1. Lion passant. *2.* Leopard's
Face. *3.* Wheatsheaf. *4.*
I.S. - - - 4263, 5923A
1. Lion passant. *2.* Cock. *3.*
Leopard's Face crowned.
4. I.S. - - - 4263
1. Lion passant. *2.* Leopard's
Face crowned. *3.* Cock.
4. I.S. - - - 4263
1. Lion passant. *2.* Leopard's
Face crowned. *3.* Buckle.
4. I.S. - - - 4435
1. Lion passant. *2.* Leopard's
Face. *3.* Bird on nowed
Snake. *4.* I.S. - - 4542
1. Per Chevron—?. *2.* Per
Chevron, three Shuttles.
3. Leopard's Face, *4.* I.S. 4262
1. Leopard's Face. *2.* Lion
passant. *3.* Buckle. *4.* I.S. 5615
1. J.S. *2.* ?. *3.* Animal's Head
erased. *4.* Lion rampant - 4179
1. R.S. *2.* Lion rampant. *3.*
Three Fleurs-de-Lys. *4.*
Britannia to sinister - 4483
1. Leopard's Face crowned. *2.*
R. (Black letter). *3.* S.
(Black letter). *4.* Rose 4088
1. Lion passant. *2.* Leopard's
Face crowned. *3.* Rose.
4. R.S. - - - 4374

1. S.S. *2.* Britannia. *3.* Leopard's Face crowned. *4.*
Lion's Head erased 250, 2393, 4379
1. Three Fleurs-de-Lys. *2.*
Lion rampant. *3.* Harp.
4. S.S. - - - 5944
1. Lion passant. *2.* Leopard's
Face. *3.* Fleur-de-Lys.
4. T.S. - - 4386A
1. T.S. *2.* Leopard's Face. *3.*
Lion passant. *4.* ? - 4385
1. Leopard's Face. *2.* Lion
passant. *3.* Rose. *4.* T.S. 5951
1. T.S. *2.* (P) (*sic*). *3.* Leopard's
Face crowned. *4.* Lion
passant - - - 5952
1. T.S. *2.* Crown. *3.* Port-
cullis. *4.* Buckle - 5949
1. W.S. *2.* Britannia. *3.* Golden Fleece. *4.* Lion's Head
erased - - - 4402
1. W.S. *2.* Britannia. *3.* Lion's
Head erased. *4.* Tankard 39, 40
1. W.S. *2.* Britannia. *3.* Rose.
4. Lion rampant - - 4539

T

1. Arms of Pewterers' Co. *2.*
Arms of London City. *3.*
Lion passant. *4.* T. & C. 1064, 4800
1. Lion rampant. *2.* Sword. *3.*
T. & C. - - - 4800
1. C.T. *2.* Lion statant. *3.*
Leopard's Face. *4.* Buckle 5968
1, 2, 3 and *4,* Bell, with G.T. - 5971
1. H (Black Letter). *2.* T (Black
Letter). *3.* Leopard's Face.
4. Lion passant - - 5972A
1. I.T. *2.* Arms of Pewterers'
Co. *3.* Leopard's Face
crowned. *4.* Lion rampant
to sinister - - - 5977
1. I.T. *2.* Leopard's Face. *3.* ?.
4. Lion passant - - 4755
1. I. (Black letter). *2.* T. (Black
letter). *3.* Leopard's Face.
4. Lion rampant - - 4821
1. (?) Crown. *2.* Dog courant.
3. Leopard's Face crowned.
4. I.T. - - - 5976
1. Lamb. *2.* Leopard's Face.
3. Britannia. *4.* I.T. - 4795
1. Leopard's Face crowned. *2.*
Rose. *3.* Buckle. *4.* I.T. 4819
1 and *3.* Buckle. *2* and *4.* L.T. 4697
1. (?) Bird or Angel volant. *2.*
P.T. *3.* Leopard's Face.
4. Lion passant - - 4838
1. T.T. *2.* Lion rampant. *3.*
Buckle. *4.* Leopard's Face 1636
1. T.T. *2.* Water bouget. *3.*
Rose. *4.* Buckle - 4673
1. Golden Fleece. *2.* Lion's
Head erased. *3.* Britannia.
4. W.T. - - - 5988

Arranged alphabetically, as well as may be, according to the FIRST device :

1. Bird. *2*. Lion's Head. *3*. Britannia. *4*. Stag - - 639

1, 2, 3 and *4*. Bird - - - 5086A

1. Britannia. *2*. Lion's Head to sinister. *3*. Leopard's Face crowned - - - - 2695

1 and *3*. Buckle. *2* and *4*. Lion rampant - - - - 6120

1, 3, and *5*. Buckle. *2, 4* and *6*. Unicorn's Head - - 213

1. Castle. *2*. Fleur-de-Lys. *3*. Griffin's Head erased. *4*. Rose - - - - 1992

1, 2, 3 and *4*. Eagle displayed - 5724

1, 2, 3 and *4*. Eagle, double-headed, displayed - - 4190

1. Eagle displayed. *2*. Leopard's Face crowned. *3. ?. 4*. Britannia - - - - 1140

1 and *3*. Eagle displayed. *2* and *4*. Lion rampant - - 5424A

1. Eagle, double-headed, displayed. *2*. Rose. *3*. Swan's Head erased. *4*. Lion passant 2070

1, 2, 3 and *4*. Escallop Shell - 5835

1. Fleur-de-Lys. *2*. Leopard's Face crowned. *3. ?. 4. ?* 4440

1, 2, 3 and *4*. Fleur-de-Lys beneath two five-pointed Stars 6138

1, 2, 3 and *4*. Goat's Head - 835

1. Greyhound statant. *2*. Leopard's Face. *3*. Buckle. *4*. Rose - - - - 6048

1. Griffin's Head erased. *2*. Fleur-de-Lys. *3*. (?) Leopard's Face. *4*. Lion passant 6119

1, 2, 3 and *4*. Leopard's Face - 4811, 5431, 5436, 5468

1. Leopard's Face. *2. ?. 3*. Escallop. *4*. Lion passant 6109

1. Leopard's Face crowned. *2*. Buckle. *3. ?* - - - 4437

1. Leopard's Face. *2*. Thistle. *3*. Lion passant. *4*. Wheel 1469

1. Leopard's Face. *2, 3* and *4*. (?) - - - - 3429

1 and *3*. Leopard's Face. *2* and *4*. Wheel - - - 5562A

1, 2 and *3*. Lion passant in Lozenge - - - - 3392A

1, 2 and *3*. Lion passant in Shield - - - - 5561

1, 2, 3 and *4*. Lion passant 5463, 5468, 5475, 6105

1, 2, 3 and *4*. Lion passant to sinister - - - - 437A

1, 2, 3, 4 and *5*. Lion passant - 6117

1. Lion passant. *2*. Britannia. *3*. Leopard's Face crowned 1648

1 and *3*. Lion passant, over Star. *2* and *4*. Buckle over Star - 2186

1. Lion passant. *2. ?* Bust, or slipped Rose. *3*. Thistle. *4*. Lion's Head erased 6110

1 and *3*. Lion passant. *2* and *4*. Leopard's Face - - 5569

1 and *3*. Lion passant. *2* and *4*. Leopard's Face crowned - 6116

1. Lion passant. *2*. Leopard's Face. *3*. Rose. *4*. T.–. 6108

1, 2, 3 and *4*. Lion rampant 1101, 2592, 3441A, 5200, 5977, 6018A, 6037, 6044

1, 2, 3 and *4*. Lion rampant in Lozenge - - 2522, 4270, 6134

1, 2, 3 and *4*. Lion rampant in Hexagon - - - - 5200

1, 2, 4 and *5*. Lion rampant. *3*. Monogram - - - 6034

1, 2, 3, 4 and *5*. Lion rampant - 6118

1. Lion rampant. *2*. Britannia. *3*. Lion's Head erased. *4*. Three Fleurs-de-Lys - 4480

1. Lion rampant. *2*. Crown. *3. ?. 4. ?* - - - 1704

1. Lion rampant. *2*. Crown. *3*. Britannia to sinister. *4*. Leopard's Face (?) - - 6040

1 and *3*. Lion rampant. *2* and *4*. Rose and Crown - - 989

1. Lion statant. *2. ?. 3*. I. (Black letter). *4. ?* - 6137

1, 2, 3 and *4*. Lion's Head erased 6101

1. Lion's Head erased. *2*. Lion rampant. *3*. Dove with olive branch - - - 5601

1. Plant with three Flowers. *2*. Leopard's Face crowned. *3*. Lion passant. *4. ?* - - 6096

1 and *3*. Rose. *2* and *4*. Lion rampant - - - - 6135

1, 2, 3 and *4*. Rose - - 5378

1, 2, 3 and *4*. Rose and Crown 5835

1, 2, 3 and *4*. (?) Scorpion - 210

1. Stag at speed. *2*. Dog at speed. *3*. Two Dogs at speed. *4*. Huntsman - - - 6107

1 and *3*. Stag regardant. *2* and *4*. Britannia - - - 5387

1, 2, 3 and *4*. Stag's Head in Lozenge - - - - 5748

1. Swan. *2*. Rose. *3*. Lion passant. *4. ?* - 369

1. Thistle. *2*. Rose. *3*. Bust. *4*. Fleur-de-Lys - - 218

1. Thistle. *2*. Rose. *3*. Fleur-de-Lys. *4*. Harp - 6085

1. ?. 2. Britannia. *3*. Lion's Head erased. *4*. (?) - 3682

1. ?. 2. Leopard's Face. *3*. Britannia. *4*. Lion passant 5358

1. ?. 2. Leopard's Face. *3*. Buckle. *4*. Three Stars 4173

1. ?. 2. Lion passant. *3*. Leopard's Face - - - 572

1. ?. 2. Lion's Head erased. *3*. Lion passant. *4*. Tun - 2823

1. ?. 2. Lion's Head erased. *3*. Branch, with kaves - 716

1. ?. 2. Rose. *3*. Black letter? *4*. Black letter? - - 6111

1. ?. 2. ?. 3. Buckle. *4*. Lion passant - - - - 5609

1. ?. 2. ?. 3. Rose. *4*. Fleur-de-Lys - - - - 2098

1. ?. 2. Rose. *3. ?. 4*. Lion passant - - - 5407A

1. ?. 2. Buckle. *3*. Boar's Head. *4*. Fleur-de-Lys - 3867

1. ?. 2. Lion's Head. *3*. (?) Heart. *4. ?* - - - 5638

1. ?. 2. Lion rampant. *3*. (?). *4*. (?) - - - 3618

Indistinguishable - - 6115

BIBLIOGRAPHICAL LIST

OF WORKS DEALING WITH BRITISH PEWTER AND PEWTERERS

BELL, MALCOLM - - - - - - - "Old Pewter," 1905.

COTTERELL, HOWARD H. - - - - - "York Pewterers," 1916.

  „   „   „ - - - - - "Bristol and West Country Pewterers," 1918 (One of the Official Guides issued by the Bristol Museum).

  „   „   „ - - - - - "National Types of Old Pewter," 1925.

  „   „   „ - - - - - "Catalogue of the Loan Collection of Old British Pewter (organised by the writer) at the "Daily Telegraph" International Exhibition of Antiques & Works of Art, at Olympia, 1928.

  „   „   „ AND M. S. D. WESTROPP - "Irish Pewterers," 1917.

GALE, EDWARDS J. - - - - - - "Pewter and the Amateur Collector," 1910.

MARKHAM, C. A. - - - - - - "Pewter Marks and Old Pewter Ware," 1909.

MASSÉ, H. J. L. J. - - - - - - "Pewter Plate" (1st edition), 1904.

  „   „ - - - - - - "Pewter Plate" (2nd edition), 1910.

  „   „ - - - - - - "Catalogue of the First Pewter Exhibition at Clifford's Inn," 1904.

  „   „ - - - - - - "Ditto of the Second Exhibition," 1908.

  „   „ - - - - - - "Chats on Old Pewter," 1911.

  „   „ - - - - - - "The Pewter Collector," 1921.

MOORE, N. HUDSON - - - - - "Old Pewter, Copper and Sheffield Plate," (N.D.).

NAVARRO, ANTONIO F. DE - - - - "Causeries on English Pewter," 1911.

PRICE, F. G. HILTON - - - - - "Old Base-metal Spoons," 1908.

ROWED, C. - - - - - - - "Collecting as a Pastime," 1920.

WELCH, C. - - - - - - - "History of the Worshipful Company of Pewterers of London," 1902.

WOOD, L. INGLEBY - - - - - - "Scottish Pewterware and Pewterers," (N.D.).

Magazine & other articles, though often valuable contributions to knowledge, are easily lost sight of and in this connexion the following will be found very helpful :—

COTTERELL, HOWARD H. - - - - "Rim-types of Old Pewter Plates," in the *Connoisseur* for February 1919.

  „   „   „ - - - - "Pewter Baluster Measures," *Ibid.* August 1919.

  „   „   „ - - - - "Old Pewter or Britannia Metal," *Ibid.* March 1921.

MAY, H. E. - - - - - - "Old Pewter" (Chiefly on Scottish Measures), in *Country Life*, 18th September, 1915.

NAVARRO, A. F. DE - - - - - "Cisterns and Wine Coolers," *Ibid.* 26th April, 1924.

  „   „ - - - - - "The Salt," *Ibid.* 4th July, 1925.

NEATE, RICHARD - - - - - - "English Pewter Candlesticks of the Seventeenth Century," in "The Book of Antiques," 1928.

PORT, CHARLES G. J. - - - - - "Some Uncommon Pieces of Pewter," in the "Connoisseur" for April & December 1917; October 1918; September 1921 & March 1925.

YEATES, ALFRED B. - - - - - "Old English Pewter. A Collector's Notes," in "Old Furniture" for July & August, 1927.

GENERAL INDEX

(*Note.*—This general Index makes no extensive reference to Chapters **VI, VII** and **VIII**, which, being in dictionary order themselves and amplified with exhaustive indices both to devices and to " Hall-Marks," are already sufficiently provided for.

Numbers, when in *thin type* (67), refer to *pages in the text*; when in *heavy black type* (**67**), an *illustration* is indicated; whilst *Roman* figures (xiv) have reference to the *preliminary pages* of the volume.)

NOTES

NOTES

NOTES

NOTES

NOTES

NOTES

NOTES

NOTES